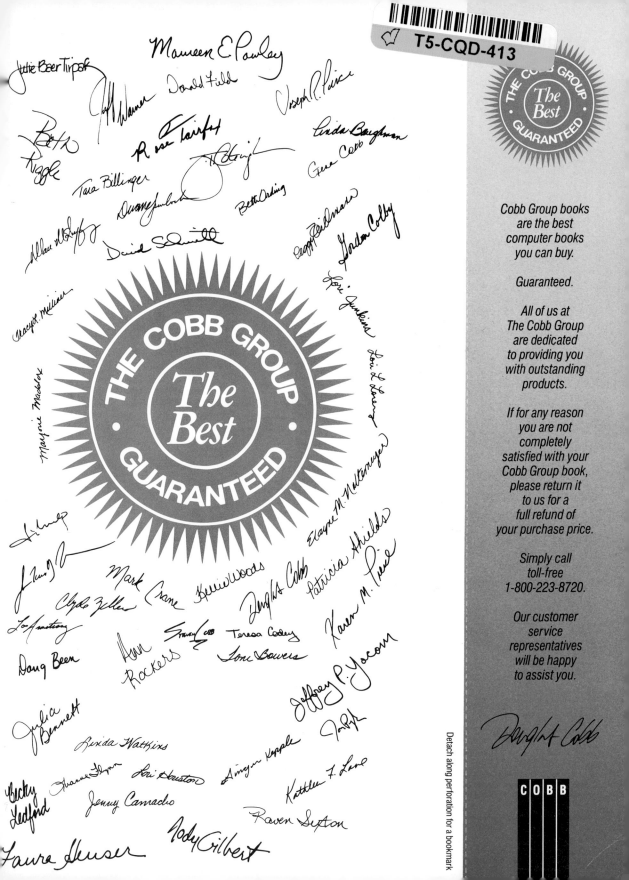

Detach along perforation for a bookmark

COBB

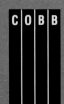

WORKS 2

COMPANION

The Cobb Group supports many business software programs with books, workbooks, and journals:

IBM PC and Compatibles

BRIGHTBILL-ROBERTS HYPERPAD
HyperPAD Companion
Inside HyperPAD

BORLAND PARADOX
Douglas Cobb's Paradox 3 Handbook
Hands-On Paradox 3
Paradox User's Journal

BORLAND QUATTRO
Quattro Companion
For Quattro

BORLAND TURBO C
Inside Turbo C

BORLAND TURBO PASCAL
Inside Turbo Pascal

HEWLETT-PACKARD LASERJET
LaserJet Companion
LaserJet Companion TechNotes:
   •Microsoft Word 5
   •Paradox 3
   •XyWrite III Plus
   •Quattro

LOTUS SYMPHONY
Mastering Symphony
The Hidden Power of Symphony
The Symphony User's Journal

LOTUS 1-2-3
Douglas Cobb's 1-2-3 Handbook
123 User's Journal

MICROSOFT EXCEL
Running Microsoft Excel
The Expert

MICROSOFT WORKS
Works Companion
The Workshop

MICROSOFT WORD
Word for Word

Apple Macintosh

MICROSOFT EXCEL
Excel in Business
Doug Cobb's Tips for Microsoft Excel
Hands-On Microsoft Excel
Microsoft Excel Functions Library
Excellence

MICROSOFT WORD
Word 4 Companion
Word Companion
Inside Word

PROVUE OVERVUE
Understanding OverVUE

For more information, please call toll-free 1-800-223-8720.

WORKS 2
COMPANION

Steven Cobb
Allan McGuffey

With:
Douglas Cobb

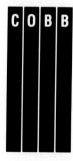

Louisville, Kentucky

WORKS 2 COMPANION

Published by
The Cobb Group, Inc.
9420 Bunsen Parkway
Louisville, Kentucky 40220

Library of Congress Catalog Number: 89-081591
ISBN 0-936767-20-0

Editing	**Production**	**Design**
Toni Frank Bowers	Maureen Pawley	Julie Baer Tirpak
Jody Gilbert	Beth Riggle	
Clyde Zellers		

Throughout this book, the trade names and trademarks of many companies and products have been used, and no such uses are intended to convey endorsement of or other affiliations with this book.

Printed in the United States of America

RRD-C 0 9 8 7 6 5 4 3 2 1

TABLE OF CONTENTS

Dedication

To Buck and Sylvia, for sharing their daughter with me—SSC

To Michael and Dan, for the future—AMcG

To my son David—DFC

Acknowledgments

Lots of people worked exceptionally hard to make this book possible. We'd like to thank them here:

Douglas Cobb, for his help in writing this book and managing the process of producing it. Without him, there wouldn't be a book.

Toni Bowers, Linda Watkins, Jody Gilbert, Clyde Zellers, and Mary Welp for doing such a fine editing job.

Maureen Pawley and Beth Riggle, for working so diligently to produce this book.

Gena Cobb, for her indexing macros and tips.

Tom Cottingham, for discovering the opportunity.

Julie Tirpak, for the layout and design.

Roy Harper, for supplying software and answering questions.

Dave and Jo-Ann Parks at Printer's Type Service, for all their work.

Michelle Cobb, for her support.

Timothy Cobb, for making us smile.

Finally, to the rest of The Cobb Group—Lou Armstrong, Gary Barnhart, Linda Baughman, Lisa Beebe, Doug Been, Julia Bennett, Tara Billinger, Jenny Camacho, Martha Clayton, Teresa Codey, Gordon Colby, Jeff Crane, Mark Crane, Karl Feige, Donald Fields, Luanne Flynn, Laura Heuser, Godwin Ighodaro, Lori Junkins, Ginger Kepple, Tim Landgrave, Kathleen Lane, Becky Ledford, Lori Lorenz, Tracy Milliner, Elayne Noltemeyer, Beth Ording, Patty Parr, Joe Pierce, Karen Pierce, Jonathan Pyles, Ann Rockers, Raven Sexton, Patricia Shields, Gina Sledge, Duane Spurlock, Jeff Warner, Jim Welp, Kellie Woods, Jeff Yocom, and Peggy Zeillmann—thanks for being "The Best."

Preface

A new generation of computer users is emerging. In the past few years, the prices of personal computers have fallen dramatically. The increasing afford-ability of PC technology has brought the benefits of personal computing to many people who could not previously afford it. These new computer users need powerful software that is easy-to-learn, easy-to-use, and affordable. Microsoft Works is that software.

Works is an all-in-one program that offers all the tools most people need—word processing, spreadsheeting (complete with charting), database manage-ment, and data communications—at a price anyone can afford. Works is designed to be easy to learn and use, but powerful enough to handle your toughest computing tasks. Works is no-compromise software at a no-compromise price.

Works offers performance and features that are unprecedented in inexpensive software. The heart of Works is its powerful word processor, which allows you to create professional-looking memos, letters, and reports. Works also includes a full-featured spreadsheet that is completely compatible with the industry standard, Lotus 1-2-3. From the information in your spreadsheets, you can create presentation-quality charts. The Works forms-based database allows you store and manipulate lists of information. Works' communications environment makes it easy to communicate with other computers. Because Works is integrated, you can share information easily between different environments.

Works offers everything you expect of an integrated software package, plus a whole lot more. For example, Works offers a powerful database reporting environment, more types of charts and more ways to enhance those charts than most stand-alone spreadsheet programs, and an amazing number of formatting options. Works also offers a built-in spelling checker, a mail-merge facility, and a powerful macro program.

Works 2 increases Works' original powers significantly. For example, Works 2 now lets you overlap your document windows so you can see simultaneously all the documents you have open. Additionally, Works lets you preview your documents before you print them, print your database forms, create footnotes for your word processor documents, look up synonyms in the Works Thesaurus, create document templates for each environment, and launch other programs directly from Works. Finally, Works 2 includes an alarm clock, calculator, and automatic telephone dialer in each environment.

Clearly, Works is both broad and deep. Although you'll probably be able to learn the basics fairly quickly, it can take months to explore every feature of this powerful program. Mastering Works is a big job.

ABOUT THIS BOOK

We wrote *Works 2 Companion* to help make Works easier to learn and use. No matter what your level of expertise, you'll find a great deal of useful information in this book. If you are new to computing and to Works, you can use this book as a tutorial. If you are an experienced computer user, you can use it as a reference guide. Either way, this book will help you harness the power of Works.

Works 2 Companion is organized functionally, rather than by command name. Consequently, you'll be able to find the answer to any "How to?" question quickly and easily. We think you'll find this approach to be a useful complement to the manuals that come with Works. However, *Works 2 Companion* doesn't skim the surface—it digs down into the program, exploring many of Works' nooks and crannies. *Works 2 Companion* doesn't just tell you what to do; it explains how Works operates.

Works 2 Companion is loosely divided into five sections. Chapter 1, "Works Basics"; Chapter 2, "File Basics"; and Chapter 3, "Printing Basics," offer an overview of Microsoft Works and explain a number of skills that apply to all Works environments, such as how to use menus and dialog boxes, how to save and open files, and how to print your work. If you are new to Works, you'll want to read this section carefully. If you have been using Works for a while, you'll probably want to skim these chapters to familiarize yourself with our terminology and style before moving on.

In Chapters 4 through 7, we explore Works' word processing powers. Chapter 4, "Word Processing Basics," covers the basics: creating word processor documents, entering and editing text, moving the cursor, and printing. Chapter 5, "Editing and Formatting," shows you how to use editing commands and how to format your documents. Chapter 6, "Advanced Word Processing Topics," explores a few advanced concepts, including Works' powerful spelling checker, thesaurus, and footnoting capability.

Chapters 7 through 11 deal with Works' spreadsheet environment. In Chapter 7, "Spreadsheet Basics," we show you how to create, make entries into, and print spreadsheets. In Chapter 8, "Formatting a Spreadsheet," we show you how to use the commands on the Format menu to format a spreadsheet. In Chapter 9, "Cut and Paste Commands," we explore the commands on the Edit menu: Copy, Move, Clear, and so on. In Chapter 10, "Functions," we demonstrate the use of each of Works' 60 spreadsheet functions. In Chapter 11, "Other Spreadsheet Topics," we explain advanced spreadsheet topics, including named ranges, windows, titles, cell protection, and searching.

In Chapters 12, 13, and 14, we examine Works' charting capabilities. Chapter 12, "Chart Basics," shows you how to create, manage, and print charts. Chapter 13, "Chart Types," covers each of Works' chart types in detail. Chapter 14, "Enhancing Charts," shows you how to add titles, legends, data labels, and so forth to your charts.

Chapters 15, 16, and 17 deal with Works' database management powers. In Chapter 15, "Database Fundamentals," we show you how to create and manage database documents. In Chapter 16, "Using a Database," we teach you how to sort, search, and query your databases. In Chapter 17, "Printing and Reporting," we explain the process of printing databases and show you how to use Works' report generator to create and print sophisticated reports.

In Chapter 18, "Communications," we show you how to use Works to communicate with other computers. In that chapter, we explain the process of connecting with a remote computer, sending information to it, and receiving information from it.

Chapter 19, "Sharing Information between Environments," explains all of the ways you can transfer information from one type of Works document to another. In that chapter, you'll learn how to copy information among word processor, spreadsheet, and database documents; how to create mailing labels and form letters; and how to insert charts into word processor documents.

Chapter 20, "Macros," explains Works' powerful macro programming language. In that chapter, we show you how to create, manage, and use macros.

We organized each chapter in this book into sections marked by four levels of headings. The major chapter section names, which we include in the Table of Contents, appear boldfaced in capital letters. Then, we divide each major section into three subsections, the first section marked by a boldface heading, the second section by a regular heading, and the third section by a heading embedded in the first line of text. We hope you'll use this heading structure as a convenient tool for locating the information you need to read.

ABOUT THE COBB GROUP

The Cobb Group is a leading publisher of books and journals about business software for personal computers. Best-selling Cobb Group books include *Douglas Cobb's 1-2-3 Handbook, Mastering Symphony, Excel in Business, Word Companion, LaserJet Companion, HyperPad Companion,* and *Word 4 Companion.* Cobb Group journals include *The Workshop: The Journal for Users of Microsoft Works, The 1-2-3 User's Journal,* and *The Symphony User's Journal* among others.

ABOUT THE AUTHORS

Steven Cobb is a Vice President and senior author at The Cobb Group, Inc. He has authored, co-authored, and contributed to a number of books, including *Mastering Symphony, Douglas Cobb's 1-2-3 Handbook, Paradox Companion, Excel in Business,* and *Understanding OverVUE.* He is the editor-in-chief of *The Symphony User's Journal, The 1-2-3 User's Journal, Excellence,* and *The Expert.* Steve received a B.A. from Vanderbilt University and an M.B.A. from the University of Chicago.

Douglas Cobb, President of the Cobb Group, is the author and co-author of many best-selling computer books, including *Using 1-2-3* and *Mastering Symphony.* He has published and authored or co-authored *Douglas Cobb's 1-2-3 Handbook, Quattro Companion,* and *Hands-on Paradox.*

Allan McGuffey is an author and ex-Ph.D. candidate from the University of Louisville. He has co-authored the *Write Companion* and *Word 4 Companion* for the Cobb Group and *Excel in Business, 2d edition* for Microsoft Press.

THERE'S MORE

In developing the *Works 2 Companion,* we spent months exploring every feature of Works—poking, prodding, and putting the program through its paces. We came up with more material than we could conceivably include in one book. Even as we go to press, we continue to discover new tips, traps, techniques, and shortcuts that we'd like to tell you about.

If you're interested in learning more about Microsoft Works, we urge you to subscribe to The Cobb Group's monthly journal for Works users: *The Workshop.* Each month, this journal explains tips and techniques that will help you become more proficient with Works. Our journal allows us to pass along to you all the exciting new capabilities and techniques we uncover as we continue to use Works. To receive a free issue of *The Workshop,* simply send us the card you'll find at the back of this book.

Works Basics 1

Works combines four distinct environments—word processing, spreadsheet (including charting), database, and communications—into a single software package. (Because each environment is designed for a different type of work, each is unique.) Since all four environments are combined into a single program, however, many skills apply equally to every Works environment.

In this chapter and the two that follow, we'll teach you a number of basic Works skills. In this chapter, we'll talk about the hardware you need to run Works and show you how to use Setup to install Works. Then we'll show you how to start Works, how to choose menus, how to reset dialog box settings, how to use Works' Help and tutorial facilities, and how to exit Works. In Chapters 2 and 3, we'll discuss file management and printing, respectively.

HARDWARE

To use Works, you must have an IBM Personal Computer (PC, XT, AT, or PS/2-series) or any 100% IBM-compatible computer. Your computer must be outfitted with at least 512K of memory and two disk drives. It may have either a monochrome or a color monitor, and almost any available video controller card: non-graphics monochrome, CGA, EGA, VGA, Hercules, and so forth. (However, Works won't be able to display charts or display the screen in Graphics mode on systems with a non-graphics monochrome card.) You must boot your computer with MS or IBM DOS version 2.0 or higher.

Memory

In order to do any meaningful work within Works, your computer must have at least 512K of random access memory (RAM). If possible, it should have 640K— the maximum that current versions of DOS can address. More memory means that you can create larger documents, have more documents open at one time, or both. Works 2 supports the Lotus/Intel/Microsoft Expanded Memory Specification for spreadsheets and databases.

Disk drives

To use Works effectively, your computer should have two disk drives: either two floppy drives or one floppy drive and one hard drive. If you use Works on a dual-floppy machine, you'll need one drive to hold the disk that contains the Works program files and another to hold a disk on which you will store your Works documents. If you have a hard disk, you'll probably store your Works program files and your documents on that drive. However, you'll need the floppy drive to copy the Works program to the hard disk in the first place.

Running Works from a hard disk has two advantages over running it from a floppy disk. First, because your computer can read from and write to a hard disk significantly faster than it can a floppy disk, it takes less time to load Works and to save and open document files. Second, you can store significantly more text on a hard disk than you can on a floppy. To run Works on a dual-floppy machine, you have to use several disks (the Program disk, the Spell and Help disk, the Accessories disk, and so forth). You can run Works from a hard disk without ever touching a floppy disk.

Graphics cards
►WORKS 2◄

►You can use Works on a machine with any kind of display, including monochrome, CGA, EGA, VGA, and so forth, but to view charts and graphs, and to see on the screen exactly what Works will print, you need a graphics card for your computer. During the Works Setup program, which we'll discuss in a few pages, you'll be able to customize Works to suit the specific graphics configuration your computer uses.◄

Printers

If you want to create print-outs of your work, as you almost certainly will, you'll also need a text and/or graphics printer (or plotter). Works supports a large number of printers and plotters, including many of the most popular models as well as some obscure ones. Works allows you to choose within the Setup program the printer that you'll be printing to—a topic we'll cover later in this chapter.

Modems

If you are planning to use Works to communicate with other computers, you'll need a modem—preferably one manufactured by Hayes or one that is Hayes-compatible (that is, a modem that uses the same command set as a Hayes modem). If you have a modem that is not Hayes-compatible, you'll still be able to use it with Works. However, you won't find it as easy.

The mouse

If you want, you can use a mouse with Works. Although Works operates quite well without a mouse, certain tasks (such as moving quickly to remote portions of a document) are easier to do if you have one.

►WORKS 2◄

►Works is designed to operate with a Microsoft mouse—either the serial or bus version. If you have a mouse, you can install it using the software that came with it. The Works Setup program—the subject of the next section of this chapter—will automatically adjust the mouse to perform optimally with Works. Throughout this book, we will show you how to perform tasks both with and without a mouse.◄

Before you begin to use Works, you must use the Setup program on the Setup disk to install Works for your computer. The Setup program allows you to create a working copy of Works, either on a floppy disk or on your hard disk, that is customized for your computer system's hardware (video driver, monitor, printers, and so forth).

THE SETUP PROGRAM

►To create or modify a customized copy of Works on a hard disk, turn on your computer and insert the Works Setup disk in drive A. Type *a:setup* and press [Enter]. When you do this, Works will examine your computer hardware, determining the number and type of disk drives it has, what sort of video driver it has, and so forth. After Works does this, the Setup program will display the screens shown in Figures 1-1 and 1-2. The screen shown in Figure 1-1 introduces the Works Setup program. The screen shown in Figure 1-2 on the next page gives basic instructions for using the Setup program and offers three choices: Create a New Working Copy of Works 2.0, Modify an Existing Working Copy of Works 2.0, and Cancel SETUP.◄

►WORKS 2◄

Figure 1-1

```
            M I C R O S O F T ◆ W O R K S ◆ S E T U P


Welcome to the Microsoft Works 2.0 SETUP program.

When you run SETUP the first time, it creates a customized
copy of Works that you will use whenever you run Works. This
copy is called the "working copy of your Works program disk."

SETUP can either create a new working copy or modify an
existing working copy.

 ■ To continue, press the ENTER (◄┘) key.
 ■ To cancel, use the DOWN (↓) key to move the highlight
   to "Cancel SETUP," and press the ENTER (◄┘) key.




              ┌─────────────────┐
              │ Continue        │
              │ Cancel SETUP    │
              └─────────────────┘
```

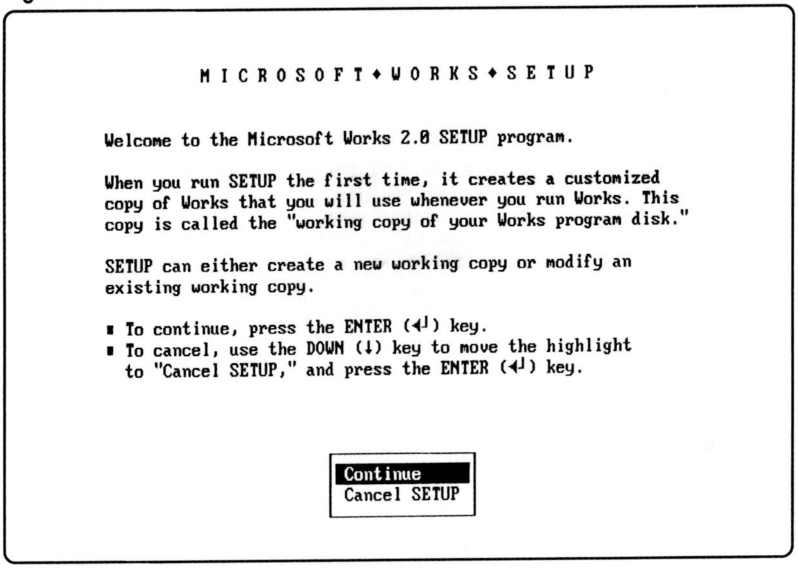

You'll see this screen when you start the Works Setup program.

Figure 1-2

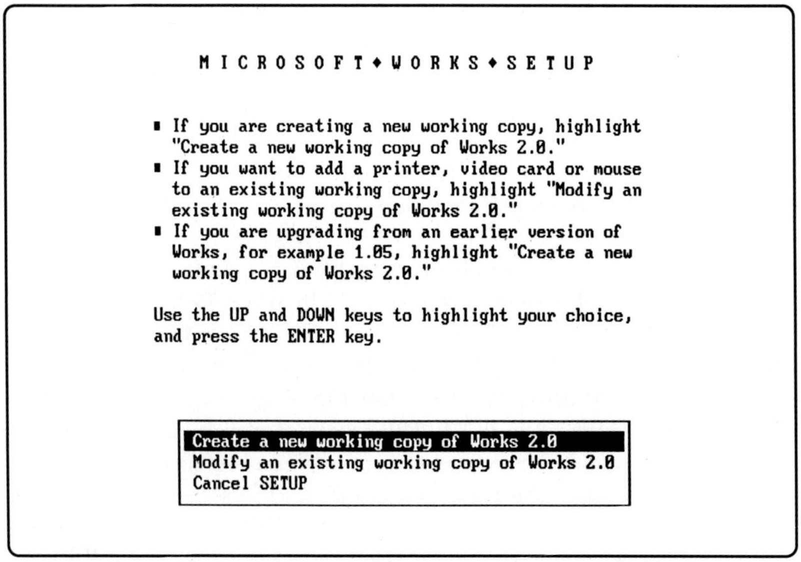

```
            M I C R O S O F T ◆ W O R K S ◆ S E T U P


     ▪ If you are creating a new working copy, highlight
       "Create a new working copy of Works 2.0."
     ▪ If you want to add a printer, video card or mouse
       to an existing working copy, highlight "Modify an
       existing working copy of Works 2.0."
     ▪ If you are upgrading from an earlier version of
       Works, for example 1.05, highlight "Create a new
       working copy of Works 2.0."

     Use the UP and DOWN keys to highlight your choice,
     and press the ENTER key.




      ┌────────────────────────────────────────────┐
      │ Create a new working copy of Works 2.0      │
      │ Modify an existing working copy of Works 2.0 │
      │ Cancel SETUP                                 │
      └────────────────────────────────────────────┘
```

This second Setup screen offers three choices.

To create or modify a customized working copy of Works on floppy disks, begin by booting your computer. After doing this, place the Works Setup disk in drive A, type *a:setup* at the DOS prompt, and press [Enter]. Finally, follow the instructions that the Setup program presents. Just as though you were installing Works on a hard disk, Works will examine your computer hardware, determining the number and type of disk drives, video driver, and so forth.

**Creating a new
Works program disk**

If you are installing Works for the first time, you should choose Create a New Working Copy of Works 2.0 from the menu shown in Figure 1-2. When you choose this option, the Setup program first will list all the disk drives available on your computer system and ask you on which drive you want to create your copy of Works. If your computer has a hard disk, you probably will want to install Works on it. If your computer does not have a hard disk, you'll want to install Works on a floppy disk in drive B.

If you are installing Works on a hard disk, the Setup program will ask you to specify in which subdirectory of that disk you want it to make the working copy of Works. The Setup program will always suggest a subdirectory named \WORKS. To accept this suggestion (a good idea), simply press [Enter]. If you are installing Works on a disk in drive B, you should insert a blank disk into that drive.

Once you specify a drive, the Setup program will prompt you to place the Program disk in drive A and press any key. When you do this, the Setup program will copy the Works program file WORKS.EXE and a special file named COMM.SCD from the Program disk in drive A to the drive/directory you specified.

Next, the Setup program will display a list of several popular video drivers and ask you to specify the one you will use. The card that the Setup program identifies as being in your computer will be highlighted. To select a different card, just press ↓ or ↑ to point to its name (if necessary), and press [Enter].

Selecting a video driver

▶At this point, the Setup program will ask if you prefer to display Works in Text or Graphics mode. If you select Text mode, Works will operate quicker and display any special formatting by coloring and boldfacing the characters you formatted. If you select Graphics mode, Works will operate slower, but whatever formats you apply to the text of a document will appear on the screen just as they will when you print your document. The appearance of the mouse pointer depends on which mode you choose. In Text mode, the mouse pointer looks like a rectangle. In Graphics mode, the mouse pointer looks like an arrowhead.

Selecting Text or Graphics mode ▶WORKS 2◀

If you have a graphics card in your computer, choose the Graphics mode during the Setup program. This mode will allow you to use both Text and Graphics modes in Works. If you want, you can switch between these two options from within Works using the Works Settings... command on the Options menu in all environments.◀

Next, the Setup program will display a screen that allows you to select the best color configuration for your system. Choose the option that matches what you see on your screen.

Next, the Setup program will present a list of popular printers and ask you to select the one you will use to print text. To select your printer, just press ↓, ↑, [Pg Up], or [Pg Dn] to highlight its name, then press [Enter]. (If you don't see your printer in the list, choose the second option, Can't Find My Printer. Setup will tell you how to get support for the printer you have.) After you specify a printer, the Setup program will ask you to indicate to which port that printer will be attached. If you have a parallel printer, it probably is attached to the LPT1 port. If you have a serial printer, it probably is attached to the COM1 port. If you don't know to which port your printer is attached, choose any selection. You can respecify the port at the time you actually print a document.

Selecting a printer

Once you have chosen a printer, the Setup program will prompt you to insert the Supp. Printer 1 disk and then the Supp. Printer 2 and Video disk into the drive from which you started the Setup program. Then, the Setup program will copy from these disks the driver files for the printer you selected and place them on the disk on which you are installing Works.

Installing the Learning Microsoft Works Tutorial

If the disk on which you are installing Works has at least 1 Mb of empty space, the Setup program will ask if you want to copy the Learning Microsoft Works Tutorial to it. This tutorial is an interactive, on-screen learning device that teaches you about Works. If you choose the Yes option, Works will copy the files from the three Learn disks into the directory on which you are installing Works. If you choose No, Works will move on to the next step of the Setup program without copying those files.

If you are installing Works on a hard disk, you won't be able to use the tutorial from within Works unless you copy the Learning Microsoft Works Tutorial files onto that disk. To use the tutorial, you'll have to exit Works.

Selecting the proper Country conventions
►**WORKS 2**◄

►The next step in the Setup procedure is to choose the correct Country conventions. If you choose USA, the default convention, Works will use inches as the default measurement for applicable dialog box options and the dollar ($) symbol for currency formats. You can change the Country convention anytime from within Works.◄

Copying the Program, Spell and Help, Accessories, and Thesaurus files to your hard disk

If you are copying onto any disk other than a 360K floppy disk, the Setup program will begin copying files to the disk on which you are installing Works. First, Setup will copy some sample files and drivers from the Setup disk. Then, it will ask you to replace the Setup disk with the Program disk, the Spell and Help disk, the Accessories disk, and the Thesaurus disk, and will copy those files onto the disk on which you are installing Works.

Completing the process
►**WORKS 2**◄

►Next, the Setup program will ask if it can modify your CONFIG.SYS file. (Setup will also modify your MOUSE.COM file and AUTOEXEC.BAT file to suit Works, if necessary.) These are minor adjustments that allow Works to run smoothly. You should choose Yes.◄

After it has completed these steps, you'll see a screen that reminds you to register your Works software. When you press any key to continue, the Setup program will display the message *SETUP is finished.* on the screen. When you press any key again, the Setup program will return you to DOS. At that point, you should remove the Setup disk from drive A and store it in a safe place.

If you set up Works on a dual-floppy machine and have not copied the files from the Spell and Help, Accessories, or Thesaurus disks to your working copy of Works, you should make a copy of each disk. Similarly, you should make copies of the three Learn disks if you have not copied the tutorial files to your copy of the Works Program disk. When you use Works, you always should use these copies—never the originals.

Exiting from the Setup program prematurely

The Cancel SETUP option at the bottom of most of the menus in the Setup program lets you exit that program without completing it. Whenever you choose this option, Works will display a menu with two options: Cancel SETUP and Continue. If you choose Cancel SETUP, the Setup program will return you to DOS. If you choose Continue, the Setup program will continue where it left off.

Unfortunately, the Setup program doesn't give you a way to return to a previous step of the process of creating a working copy of Works. To change a setting, you must exit from the Setup program and start over. Alternatively, you can complete the Setup program, then restart it and choose the Modify an Existing Working Copy of Works 2.0 option from the second Setup menu.

▶The second option on the second Setup menu, Modify an Existing Working Copy of Works 2.0, lets you modify a working copy of Works that you have created previously. When you choose this option, the Setup program will first ask you to locate the working copy you want to modify. When you respond, the Setup program will display screens that let you change your video driver, printer, and so forth, and let you alter the choices you made when installing Works. To change any of these settings, choose Yes and follow the Setup program instructions.◀

Modifying your Works disk
▶WORKS 2◀

Before you can use Works, you must load it into your computer. The way you load Works depends on whether you have installed it on a hard disk or a floppy disk. If you have set up Works on a floppy disk, you'll want to load it from drive A of your computer. If your computer is off, begin by inserting a DOS disk into drive A and turning the computer on. After a few moments, it will boot and display an A> prompt. If your computer is on but not at an A> prompt, type *a:*, then press [Enter] to return it to that prompt. Once you are at the A> prompt, insert your Works disk (that is, the copy that you made with the Setup program) into drive A, close the door of that drive, type *works*, and press [Enter].

STARTING WORKS

If you set up Works on a hard disk, you should load Works from that disk. When you turn on your computer, it will boot and display a C> prompt. If your computer is on but not at a DOS prompt, return it to a DOS prompt by exiting whatever program you are running at the time. If you see a prompt other than C> at this point, type *c:* and press [Enter] to produce that prompt.

When C is the current drive, you should access the directory that contains your Works program files. In most cases, this will be C:\WORKS. To make C:\WORKS the current directory, type *cd c:\works* and press [Enter]. Now you can load Works simply by typing *works* and pressing [Enter].

Loading Works from a hard disk

Because the four types of Works documents are designed for different sorts of work, the appearance of each screen is different. For example, word processor documents have a ruler at the top; spreadsheet documents consist of a grid of rows and columns; and database documents can be viewed either as grids or through custom-designed forms.

A TOUR OF THE SCREEN

Despite these differences, all Works documents share a number of common structural features: the menu bar, the status line, the message line, and the work area. Figure 1-3 identifies these and other features in a database document.

Figure 1-3

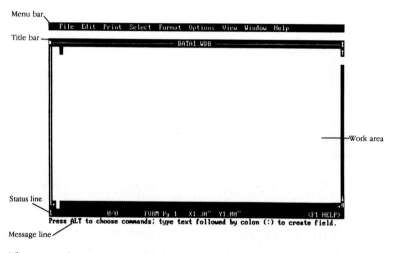

These are the structures that are common to all types of Works documents.

The menu bar

The inverse-video strip at the top of any document is its menu bar. The names of the various menus that are available in that type of document appear on this bar. For example, as you can see in Figure 1-3, database documents have nine menus: File, Edit, Print, Select, Format, Options, View, Window, and Help.

Each of the menus in any document contains a number of commands that allow you to manipulate the information in the current document. To access these commands, you must pull down the menus that contain them. For example, Figure 1-4 shows an Edit menu for a database document. As you can see, this menu contains nine commands: Move, Copy, Clear, Delete Line, Insert Line, Move Record, Copy Record, Delete Record, and Insert Record. We'll explain how to access the menu bar and select commands from menus later in this chapter.

Figure 1-4

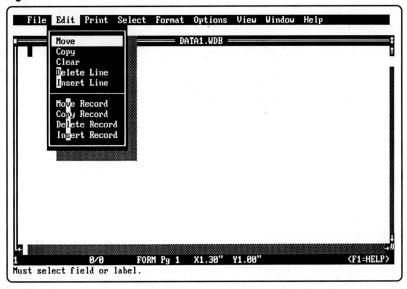

The Edit menu in a database document has nine commands.

The second line from the bottom of the screen in any Works document is the status line. On this inverse-video line, Works displays information about the current document. For example, in spreadsheet documents, Works displays the address of the active cell or range at the left edge of this line. In word processor documents, Works displays the number of the current page and the format characteristics of the currently highlighted text. In database documents, Works displays the record you are viewing, the number of records in the database, and the database viewing mode you are using. In communications documents, Works uses this line to display the amount of time it has been connected to a remote computer. ▶In all environments, to the right of the status line, you'll find the <F1=HELP> hot key, which we'll discuss later in this chapter.◀ We'll further explain the uses of the status line in the sections of this book that deal with each type of Works document.

The line at the bottom of the screen in any Works document is the message line. Works uses this line to display prompts and instructions—primarily, explanations of what particular commands do and what you need to do to complete a command. We'll explain more about the message line later in this chapter when we show you how to issue commands.

The status line

▶WORKS 2◀

The message line

The workspace

The workspace for Microsoft Works is the area below the menu bar and above the status line. This is the area into which the document window opens. We will discuss the document window and its parts starting on page 14 in the section called "Working with Windows."

CREATING DOCUMENTS

When Works has finished loading, your screen will look like the one shown in Figure 1-5. The structure in the upper-left corner of this screen is the File menu. This menu allows you to create a new document, open an existing document, manage your files, run DOS or another program, and so forth.

Figure 1-5

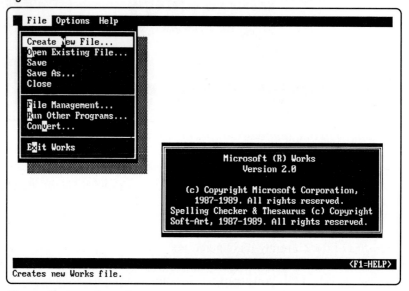

This is the initial Works screen.

To create a new Works document, you must choose the Create New File... command from the File menu, then choose the type of document you want to create from the list in the Create New File dialog box shown in Figure 1-6. The four options in the dialog box—<New Word Processor>, <New Spreadsheet>, <New Database>, and <New Communications>—correspond to the four possible types of Works documents. Each type is designed for a certain type of work. Consequently, the type of work you need to do determines the document you should create. If you need to write a letter or a report, you should create a word processor document; if you need to perform financial analyses, you should create a spreadsheet document; if you need to store lists of information, you should create a database document; if you need to exchange information with other computers, you should create a communications document.

Figure 1-6

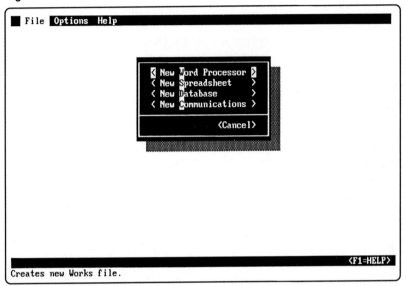

The Create New File dialog box lets you choose the type of document you want to create.

You can choose the type of document you want to create by using the ↓ and ↑ keys to move the highlighted brackets and flashing cursor down and up the list. Each press of the ↓ key selects the next item down the list. If you press the ↓ key while the highlight marks the last item (<New Communications>), Works will highlight the brackets of the <Cancel> button. Each press of the ↑ key selects the previous item. (If you press ↑ while the first item, <New Word Processor>, is activated, however, Works will not move the highlight.)

Selecting a document type

Once you have highlighted the type of document you want to create, you can tell Works to create it by pressing [Enter]. You can also create a document type by typing its highlighted letter in either uppercase or lowercase form. For example, if you type *S* or *s*, Works will create a spreadsheet document; if you type *D* or *d*, Works will create a database document; and so forth. If you have a mouse, simply click on a document type to create that document.

Creating the document

If you choose <New Word Processor>, Works will create a new word processor document, like the one in Figure 1-7; if you choose <New Spreadsheet>, Works will create a new spreadsheet document, like the one in Figure 1-8; if you choose <New Database>, Works will present a new database document (a Form screen) like the one in Figure 1-9; and if you choose <New Communications>, Works will create a new communications document, like the one shown in Figure 1-10 on page 14.

If you choose the <Cancel> button from the Create New File dialog box, Works will close the dialog box without creating a new document. Since you can't do any work unless you are in a document, you should choose this option only if you want to exit Works without opening a document. Later in this chapter, we'll show you how to exit Works after working in it.

Figure 1-7

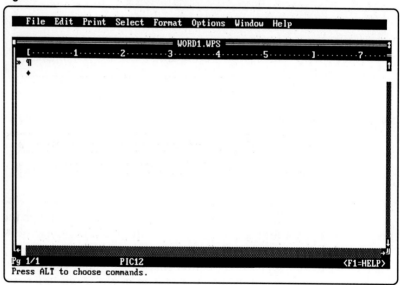

This is a new word processor document.

Figure 1-8

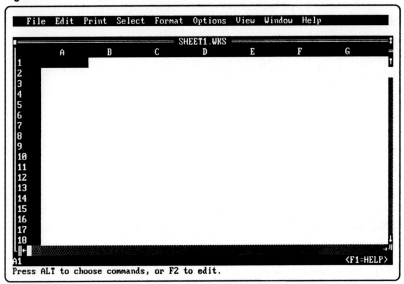

This is a new spreadsheet document.

Figure 1-9

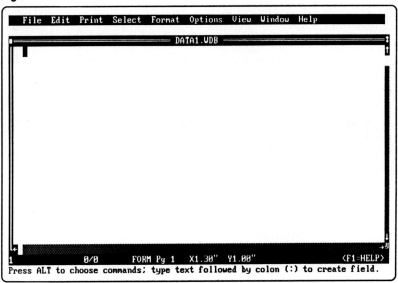

This is a new database document.

Figure 1-10

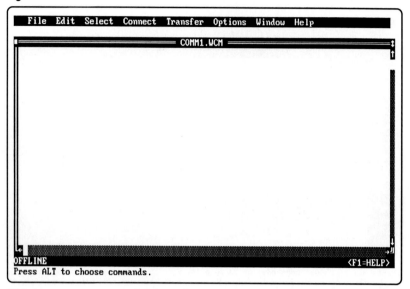

This is a new communications document.

**WORKING WITH
WINDOWS**
▶WORKS 2◀

▶All documents that you create or open in Works appear in windows. A Works window is bounded by the menu bar at the top of the screen and the status line at the bottom. Understanding how to use windows will help you be a more effective Works user. In this section, we will discuss the parts of the window shown in Figure 1-11: the work area, the maximize arrow, the size box, the title bar, the window border, the scroll bars, the split bars, and the close box.◀

The work area

The work area is where you will enter information into your document. Think of the work area as a blank slate that lets you group information into a meaningful unit called a document. As you saw in Figures 1-7 through 1-10, the work area differs in each Works environment.

In a word processor document, the work area lets you arrange lines of text into series of paragraphs. In a spreadsheet document, you can enter text and values into a grid that illustrates expenditures, credits, statistics, and so forth, over a period. In a database document, you can store information in the same grid pattern spreadsheet documents use, or you can build a form in which to display that information. In a communications document, you can type information to transmit to another computer and receive information from other computers. The work area in this environment lets you verify the information you send and receive.

Figure 1-11

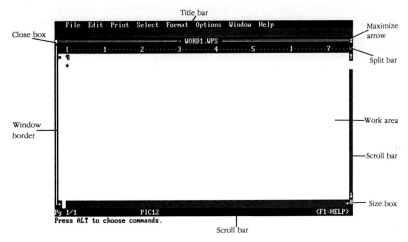

This figure identifies the various parts of a Works window.

►Works includes two icons to let you alter the size of your window with the mouse: the size box and the maximize arrow. You can reduce your window with the size box, then enlarge it with the maximize arrow once you've reduced it. Works also provides two commands on the Window menu, the Size and Maximize commands, that let you size your window from the keyboard.

Sizing the window
►WORKS 2◄

The size box, which is located in the lower-right corner of the window, allows you to change the size of the window. You just point to the size box and hold down the mouse button. As you drag the mouse around the screen, the size and shape of the window will change.

For example, Figure 1-11 shows a default-size window. Figure 1-12 on the following page shows a reduced window. To reduce the first window to the size of the second, click the mouse pointer on the icon at the lower-right corner of the window and drag the corner up and leftward until the window reaches the size you want it to be. When you release the mouse button, the window will remain that size until you resize it or close the document.

In the upper-right corner of the window is the maximize arrow. When you click this icon, a default or sized window will expand to fill the screen. If you click the maximize arrow a second time, the window will return to its previous size. Clicking the maximize arrow repeatedly lets you alternate between the original size and full-screen size.

Figure 1-12

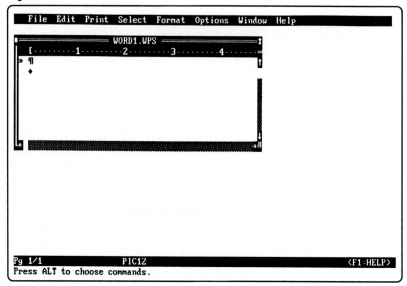

We used the size box to reduce the size of the document in Figure 1-11.

If you want to return the screen in Figure 1-12 to full size, click the maximize arrow in the upper-right corner of the window. The window will fill the screen. To alternate between the two window sizes, click the maximize arrow again. Until you resize the window with the size box or close the document, your window will alternate between these two sizes each time you click the arrow.

If you would rather use the keyboard to size your windows, the Size and Maximize commands on the Window menu allow you to size your document window with the arrow keys. Choose the Size command to reduce or enlarge your window incrementally. When you choose the Size command, a black-lined border will surround the window. When this border appears, you can use any of the arrow keys to size the window. (If you haven't sized your window, you will only be able to use the ← and ↑ keys to reduce its size.) Once your window is smaller than its default size, you can use all four arrow keys to size your window. When you're satisfied with the size of the border, press [Enter] and your regular window border will reappear. If you choose the Size command and change your mind before you press [Enter], you can press [Esc] to cancel the command.

The Maximize command is a toggle switch that lets you perform the same action as the maximize arrow at the right end of the title bar. When you choose the Maximize command on the Window menu, your document will immediately fill the workspace. Since this command is equivalent to the action of the maximize arrow, you can reissue the command to return your window to its previous size. When you choose the command again, you'll notice that a dot appears to the left of the command name, meaning that the command is active. Choosing the command at this point will turn the command off and return your document to its previous size.◄

►Once you have sized your window, the top and the left borders of the document window (the title bar and the window border, respectively) allow you to use the mouse to move the window anywhere you want on the workspace. On the Window menu, Works provides the Move command so you can move the window using the keyboard.

The title bar appears at the top of each window, between the screen's menu bar and the window's work area. The title bar contains the name of the document, complete with the name's extension, so you can keep track of the documents you have open on the screen. Functionally, the title bar lets you reposition the window on the workspace.

To move a window, just point to the title bar and hold down the left mouse button. As you drag the mouse, the window will move. For example, if you want to center the resized document shown in Figure 1-12, simply point to the title bar, then press and hold the left mouse button. When you do, a black-lined border will surround the window, as shown in Figure 1-13. At this point, drag the window to the center of the workspace and release the mouse button. Figure 1-14 shows the repositioned window.

Moving the window
►WORKS 2◄

Figure 1-13

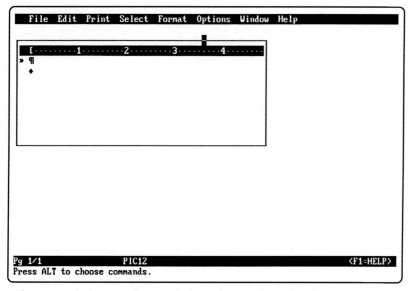

When you click a window's title bar, the window's border changes.

Figure 1-14

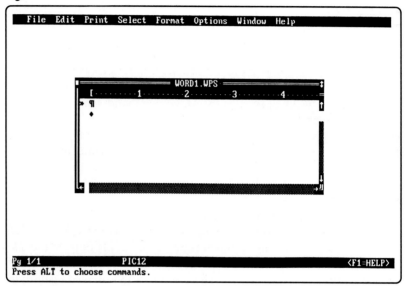

Once you size a window, you can easily move it anywhere on the workspace.

To the left of the window is a vertical bar called the window border. Just like the title bar, the window border also lets you move a window. To do this, point to the border, press and hold the left mouse button, then drag the window to a new position on the screen. For example, in Figure 1-13, when you used the title bar to center the sized window from Figure 1-12, you could have repositioned the window with the window border. The technique is identical: You point to the window border, then press and hold the left mouse button. When the black-lined border appears, drag the window anywhere you want on the workspace.

To use the keyboard to move your window, you can choose the Move command on the Window menu. The Move command allows you to move the active window with the arrow keys. To do this, choose the Move command. When the black-lined border appears, you can use any of the arrow keys to move the window in a specific direction. When you press [Enter], you'll see the window repositioned where you moved it. If you choose the Move command and make a mistake or change your mind before you press [Enter], you can press [Esc] to cancel the command.

There are a few notions to remember about moving windows. If your window is full-screen size, it becomes troublesome to move. In the example shown in Figure 1-15, you can see that two window borders have disappeared from the screen. With those two borders missing, you have no access to the window's features on those borders: the maximize arrow, the size box, and the scroll bars. To save these features, we suggest you size the window before using the window border to move the window.◄

Figure 1-15

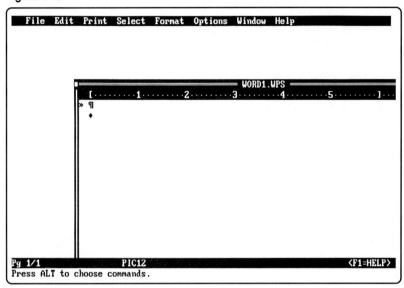

If you don't size your window before you move it, you lose access to part of it.

Scrolling

Works makes it very easy for you to gain access to different areas of your document. You simply use a window's scroll bars to move anywhere in your document from beginning to end. Most of Works' document windows contain scroll bars along both their right and bottom borders. (The Query view of a database document uses only the horizontal scroll bar along the bottom border of the window.)

Scroll bars are devices that allow you to use your mouse to move around in a Works document. The vertical scroll bar (the one at the right edge of the screen) lets you move down and up through the document. The horizontal scroll bar (the one at the bottom of the screen) lets you move right and left across a document. Later, we'll explain how scroll bars work in each type of Works document.

Splitting the window
►WORKS 2◄

►You can use the split bars to divide a window and view different areas of your document at the same time. You'll see a set of split bars to the left of the horizontal scroll bar in spreadsheet documents and in the List view of database documents, and above the vertical scroll bars in word processor, spreadsheet, and the List view of database documents. As you may notice in Figure 1-14, split bars accompany most scroll bars in Works. If you're working in a spreadsheet document, you'll see split bars at the top of the vertical scroll bar and to the left of the horizontal scroll bar. In a word processor document, Works provides split bars only at the top of the vertical scroll bar.

To use the split bars, simply move the mouse pointer to the bars, press and hold the left mouse button, then drag the split bars into the document's work area. At the point where you release the mouse button, the window will divide into two windows. Works gives each window its own set of scroll bars so you can scroll through the document independently of the other window. This ability lets you view two areas of your document at the same time. If you split the original window horizontally, both windows will share the horizontal scroll bar. If you split the original window vertically, both windows will share the vertical scroll bar.◀

If you want to split your screen without using a mouse, you can use the Split command on the Window menu. This command is equivalent to the split bars in the document windows. When you issue the Split command, your document's split bars will appear across the top and along the left side of your workspace. (If your active document has only one set of split bars, then only one set of bars will appear when you issue the Split command. If your document has no split bars, this command will appear dimmed on the Window menu.)

When you see the split bars, you can use the arrow keys to place the bars where you want them, then you can press [Enter] to enter them into your document. If you make a mistake before pressing [Enter], you can cancel the command by pressing [Esc].

Closing the document
▶ WORKS 2 ◀

▶A Works window lets you close your document with a click of the mouse button. On the far left of the title bar is the close box. Clicking the close box is equivalent to choosing the Close command from the File menu. If you attempt to close a document before saving your changes, Works will present a dialog box asking if you want to save the changes.◀

MANAGING MULTIPLE DOCUMENTS

Works allows you to have up to eight document windows open on the Works workspace at one time. Works places each document in a window and arranges these windows in a "stack" on the workspace. Typically, only one document is fully visible on the screen. The other documents are below the top one, largely hidden from view. (Works overlaps these documents. Only their title bars appear unless you resize the windows.)

Overlapping windows
▶ WORKS 2 ◀

▶Each time you create a new document or open an existing one from its file, Works places that document on top of the stack. Consequently, that document will be fully visible, and the remaining documents (including the one that was visible before you created or opened the most recent one) will be largely hidden below it.

For example, suppose you have loaded Works and created a new word processor document named WORD1.WPS. Since this is the only open document, it will be the active one (that is, the one that is fully visible on the screen). After creating this document, suppose you open a spreadsheet document named BUDGET.WKS. When you do this, Works will place that document on top of the stack, overlapping most of WORD1.WPS (now second in the stack). After opening BUDGET.WKS, suppose you create a new spreadsheet document, which Works names SHEET1.WKS. When you do this, Works will place SHEET1.WKS on top of the stack, overlapping BUDGET.WKS (now second in the stack) and WORD1.WPS (now third). Figure 1-16 shows how Works overlaps windows when you first open documents.

Figure 1-16

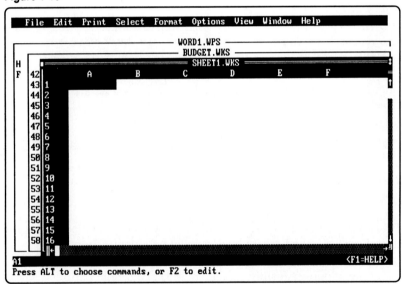

Works overlaps windows when you open more than one document.

Works doesn't require you to accept its default arrangement of your document windows. You can change a window's size at any time. We discussed this capability in the previous section of this chapter.◄

►When you have more than one document open on the screen, you can size and move your windows manually or you can choose the Arrange All command on the Window menu to arrange your documents automatically. The Arrange All command distributes all the windows on your workspace. When you choose this command, you'll be able to see each document in a reduced but complete

Arranging documents
►WORKS 2◄

window. For example, the screen in Figure 1-17 shows three documents after we issued the command. When there is an uneven number of documents open on the workspace, the document active at the time you chose the command receives the largest window. Works reduces the other documents to windows of equal size.

Figure 1-17

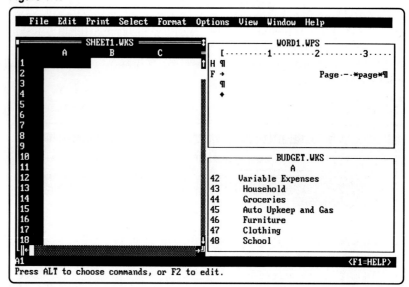

This screen shows three documents after we issued the Arrange All command.

To activate a document after you have arranged your documents on the screen, either click anywhere in the document window or choose the document from the Window menu. When you activate a document, it will have four borders with all of the window's features: title bar, scroll bars, split bars, and so forth.◄

Activating documents
►WORKS 2◄

►Although you can have up to eight documents open at the same time, you can have only one document active at a time. Before you can work with a document, therefore, you must activate it—that is, bring it to the top of the stack.

To activate a document, you can click on any visible part of it. (Usually, you'll be able to see the title bar.) For example, if you want to activate the document BUDGET.WKS in Figure 1-17, simply click anywhere in that document's window. Alternatively, you can activate a document by choosing its name from the bottom of the Window menu. When you pull down the Window menu, you'll see a list of all the documents that are currently open. Their names will appear in the order in which those documents were created or opened.

For example, Figure 1-18 shows what your Window menu would look like if you followed the steps outlined in the previous example. Since we created the document WORD1.WPS before creating or opening any other document, WORD1.WPS appears at the top of the list. Because we opened BUDGET.WKS after creating WORD1.WPS, the name BUDGET.WKS appears second. Since we created SHEET1.WKS after creating WORD1.WPS and opening BUDGET.WKS, its name appears third. You'll notice in Figure 1-16 that the last document we created appears on the screen in its entirety, but its window size is reduced to accommodate the display of the other two documents' title bars.

Figure 1-18

This Window menu displays the open documents in the order that they were opened.

As you can see in Figure 1-18, Works displays a number to the left of each document name at the bottom of the Window menu. These numbers are the key characters of those selections.

To activate a document, simply select its name from the Window menu by clicking on or highlighting its name, or by typing its key character. When you activate a document in any of these ways, Works will bring it to the top of the stack. Consequently, it will appear on the screen and become the active document. Also, the document will retain its dimension until you resize it. If a document in a full-size window is activated, that document will completely obscure any document that is smaller. Once you've activated a document, you can work within it—make and edit entries, issue commands, and so forth.◄

WORKING WITH MENUS

Each Works document has a unique set of menus. However, many of the menus in each type of document have the same names as menus in other types of documents. For example, both word processor and spreadsheet documents have File, Edit, Print, Select, Format, Options, Window, and Help menus. Some menus, such as File, Window, and Help contain the same commands in all types of documents. However, most menus with the same name in different types of documents have at least some commands that are unique.

Although each type of Works document has its own set of menus, you use the same techniques to select commands. Selecting a command from a menu is a three-step process. First, you must access the menu bar. Next, you must pull down the menu that contains the command you want to issue. Finally, you must select that command.

Accessing the menu bar

You can access the menu bar in any Works document simply by pressing the [Alt] key. When you press this key, Works will highlight the first item on the menu bar (always the menu name *File*), boldface one letter in each of the menu names, and display the prompt *Press letter on menu title, or use DIRECTION keys and press ENTER.* on the message line. For example, Figure 1-19 shows how your screen will look when you access the menu bar from a blank spreadsheet document.

Figure 1-19

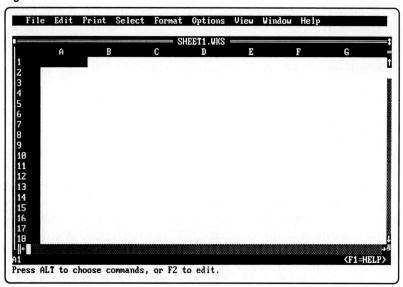

When you activate the menu bar, Works will boldface the key character of each menu name.

Another way to open a menu is by holding down the [Alt] key while typing the key character of the menu. For example, you could pull down the Edit menu by pressing [Alt]e.

Pulling down a menu

After you have accessed the menu bar, you can select and pull down the menu that contains the command you want to issue. There are two ways to do this. First, you can use the → and ← keys to move the highlight to the name of the menu you want to open, then press [Enter], ↓, or ↑ to open that menu. If you press → while the last menu name on the menu bar is highlighted, Works will wrap the highlight back to the first menu name. Similarly, if you press ← while the first menu name is highlighted, Works will move the highlight to the last menu name.

Alternatively, you can move the highlight to a menu name and pull down that menu all in one step simply by typing the key character of the menu name. You can type this letter in either uppercase or lowercase form. For example, to open the Edit menu, you would type *e* or *E*; to open the Print menu, you would type *p* or *P*; and so forth.

►Figure 1-20 shows the result of pulling down the File menu in our blank spreadsheet document. As you can see, this menu contains eight commands: Create New File..., Open Existing File..., Save, Save As..., Close, File Management..., Run Other Programs..., Convert..., and Exit Works. Like many menus, this one is divided into sections. These sections group the commands according to function and make it easier to find a certain command within a menu.◄

►WORKS 2◄

Figure 1-20

This figure shows the Works File menu in a spreadsheet document.

Once you pull down a menu, the key character of the menu names will no longer be highlighted. This indicates that you can no longer access other menus by typing their key characters. Instead, you must use the → and ← keys. If you press → while a menu is open, Works will close that menu and open the one to its right. If you press ← while a menu is open, Works will close that menu and open the one to its left.

Once you have pulled down a menu, you can select a command from it using two methods. First, you can use the ↓ and ↑ keys to move the highlight to the command you want to issue, then press [Enter] to select that command. Each time

Selecting a command from a menu

you press the ↓ key, Works will move the highlight down one command. Each time you press the ↑ key, Works will move the highlight up one command. If you press ↓ while the last command in a menu is highlighted, Works will move the highlight to the first command in that menu. If you press the ↑ key while the highlight is on the first command in a menu, Works will move the highlight to the menu's last command. While Works is highlighting a command on an open menu, it displays on the message line a brief explanation of that command.

Like the menu names on the menu bar, each of the commands within Works' menus has a key character. When you pull down a menu, Works will boldface the key character of each command. As you would expect, you can select any command by typing its key character in either uppercase or lowercase form. For example, you can type either *s* or *S* to select the Save command from the File menu shown in Figure 1-20.

When you type the key character for a command, Works will execute that command immediately; it will not move the highlight to that command and wait for you to press [Enter]. Until you are fairly comfortable with Works menus, therefore, we suggest that you select commands by pointing and pressing [Enter]. That way, it's easier to avoid issuing commands that you didn't intend.

If you want, you can hold down the [Alt] key while typing the key character of the command you want to issue. As we explained earlier, pressing [Alt] and the key character of a menu opens that menu. Consequently, you can hold down the [Alt] key during the entire process of issuing a command, if you want.

In some cases, you may want to close a menu without selecting a command from it. To do this, simply press the [Esc] key instead of issuing a command. When you do this, Works will close the open menu and deactivate the menu bar.

If you use a mouse

If you have installed Works for use with a mouse, you can use it to select commands from menus, either by clicking or dragging. You also can use the keystroke methods described above, of course, either alone or in conjunction with the mouse techniques.

Clicking. One way to use a mouse to issue a command involves clicking to open the menu, then clicking again to issue a command from that menu. To open a menu, simply point to it with the mouse pointer and click the left button on your mouse. When you do this, Works will pull that menu down onto the screen and position the highlight on the first command, just as it does when you highlight the name of the menu and press [Enter] or type the key character of that menu. Once the menu is open, you can select a command simply by pointing to it and clicking the left button again. When you do this, Works will execute the command—just as it would if you had highlighted the command and pressed [Enter] or typed the key character of that command.

If you don't want to select a command from a menu after clicking the menu open, you can press [Esc] or point to an area outside the menu and click the left mouse button. If you press [Esc], or if you click while pointing to the name of the open menu, Works will simply close the menu. If you click while pointing to the name of another menu, Works will close the current menu and open the new one. If you click while pointing to another area of the screen, Works will close the open menu, then do whatever that click instructs it to do.

Dragging.   As an alternative to clicking, you can pull down a menu and select a command from it by dragging. To select a command in this way, begin by pointing to the name of the menu that contains the command you want to issue, pressing the left mouse button, and holding it down. When you do this, Works will pull down the menu to which you are pointing, but will not highlight a command within that menu. To select a command from the open menu, simply drag the mouse pointer to it and release the button. As you drag the pointer, Works will highlight the commands that it touches, one at a time. As the pointer touches each command, Works will display the brief explanation of that command in the message line at the bottom of the screen. When you release the button, Works will issue the highlighted command.

If you don't want to issue a command from a menu after you open it, you must drag the mouse pointer out of the menu before releasing the button. If you drag the mouse pointer out of the open menu, the menu will remain open until you do one of two things: point to the name of another menu or release the button. If you point to the name of another menu while you're holding down the button, Works will close the menu that was open and open the one to which you are pointing. If you release the button while the pointer is outside any menu, Works will simply close the open menu. If you release the mouse button while pointing to the name of the open menu, Works will leave that menu open and highlight the first item on that menu—just as if you had opened the menu by clicking it.

In certain situations, some of the commands on a menu will be inactive. For example, the Delete Page Break command on a spreadsheet document's Print menu will be inactive until you insert a page break into the document. When a command is inactive, Works dims the command name, including its key character. Works does not allow you to issue inactive commands.

Inactive commands

So far, we've shown you how to issue commands, but we haven't shown you the result of issuing them. Of course, different commands do different things. Overall, however, all Works commands can be divided into four functional groups: commands that execute immediately, commands that toggle on and off, commands that require you to perform an action, and commands that require additional information. In this section, we'll explore the characteristics of these four commands.

Types of commands

Commands that execute immediately

When you issue many commands, Works performs an action immediately. For example, when you pull down the Edit menu within a word processor document and select the Delete command, Works erases whatever is selected at the time.

Many commands that execute immediately require you to select the data the command will act upon before you issue the command. For example, you must select the text you want to erase before you issue the Delete command in a word processor document. We'll show you how to select information in various types of documents in the appropriate sections of this book.

Commands that toggle

Some Works commands are actually toggle switches that turn a particular characteristic on and off. For example, the Manual Calculation command on a spreadsheet's Options menu toggles the spreadsheet between automatic and manual recalculation. If you issue a toggle command while the characteristic it controls is off, Works will turn that characteristic on. If you issue the command while the characteristic is on, Works will turn it off. Also, when you issue this command, you'll see a dot to the left of that command. If the characteristic is off, the area to the left of the command will be empty.

Commands that require you to perform an action

Many Works commands require you to perform an action after you select them. When you select one of these commands, Works will display a prompt on the message line that tells you what you need to do to complete the command. In most cases, Works needs you to specify a destination and then press [Enter]. The Copy command in Works' word processor environment is a good example of this sort of command. After you select this command from the Edit menu, Works displays the message *Select new location and press ENTER. Press ESC to cancel.* on the message line. When you point to a destination and press [Enter], Works will complete the command, copying the text to the destination you specified.

Like commands that execute immediately, commands that require you to perform an action require you to select what you want the command to act upon before you issue it. For example, the Copy and Move commands in all Works environments require you to select what you want to copy or move before you issue the commands. Again, we'll show you how to select information in various environments in later sections of this book.

Commands that require additional information

Most of Works' commands require you to supply more information after you issue them. The names of these commands end with an ellipsis—a series of three dots. For example, the Create New File... command on the File menu, the Print... command on the Print menu, and the Works Settings... command on the Options menu are commands of this type.

Whenever you issue a command that requires you to supply more information, Works will display a dialog box—a window that contains choices, spaces for you to enter information, and so forth. For example, you'll see a dialog box like the one shown in Figure 1-21 when you pull down the File menu and select the Open Existing File… command.

Figure 1-21

You'll see a dialog box like this one when you select the Open Existing File… command from the File menu.

The simplest dialog boxes contain only a few choices. For example, the dialog box that Works presents when you issue the Create New File… command only requires you to select one of five buttons: one for each Works environment and <Cancel>. Most dialog boxes contain a variety of choices. For example, the dialog box shown in Figure 1-21 contains a box that you fill in (a text box), two boxes that contain a list of possible choices (list boxes), an option that you can turn on or off (a check box), and two buttons—<OK> and <Cancel>.

Once you issue a command that requires you to supply more information, Works lets you operate in the dialog box until you choose one of the buttons at the bottom of the box. One button (frequently <OK>) instructs Works to invoke the command using the settings (if any) that you specified in the dialog box. Another button (usually <Cancel>) cancels the command.

WORKING WITH DIALOG BOXES

As we have explained, commands whose names end with ellipses present you with a dialog box when you issue them. The information you enter into that box determines the way that Works will carry out the command.

Using a dialog box is a two-step process. First, you must supply the various pieces of information that the dialog box solicits from you. Then, you must choose one of the buttons at the bottom of the box to tell Works what action to take.

The types of elements in a dialog box

Five types of elements can appear in a dialog box: text boxes, check boxes, option boxes, list boxes, and buttons. All dialog boxes contain buttons; many contain other elements as well. For example, the Save As dialog box shown in Figure 1-22 contains a text box, a list box, an option box, two check boxes, and two buttons.

Figure 1-22

This dialog box contains a text box, a list box, an option box, two check boxes, and two buttons.

Each type of element is best suited for soliciting a particular type of information. Text boxes are appropriate when there are more choices than can easily be listed in a list box. Check boxes are appropriate for toggle options—ones that must be either on or off. Option boxes are appropriate when there is a fixed number of mutually exclusive choices. List boxes are appropriate when there is a variable number of non-fixed choices, like names of files. Buttons are used exclusively for telling Works what action to take to resolve the command.

Moving among the elements in a dialog box

When Works first displays any dialog box, it places the cursor in the first element in that box—the element closest to the upper-left corner of that box. In the dialog box shown in Figure 1-22, for example, Works places the highlight in the Save file as text box.

To edit an element in a dialog box, you must move the cursor to that element. Works gives you three ways to do this. First, you can use the [Tab] key and the [Shift][Tab] key combination. Alternatively, you can hold down the [Alt] key and type the key character of that element. If you have a mouse, you can simply click that element.

Using the [Tab] and [Shift][Tab] keys

The [Tab] key and the [Shift][Tab] key combination provide one way to move the cursor among the various elements in a dialog box. When you press the [Tab] key, Works will move the cursor forward to the next element in the dialog box. When you press [Shift][Tab], Works will move the cursor to the previous element in the box.

The effect of moving the cursor to an element in a dialog box depends on what type of element you move it to. When you move the cursor to a text box, Works will highlight the entire contents of the box, if any. If the box is blank, Works simply will place the cursor at the beginning of the box. When you move the cursor into a list box, Works will move the cursor to the item that is currently selected. If no item is selected, Works will place the cursor on the first item in the list but will not select it. When you move the cursor to an option box, Works will place the cursor on the currently selected option. When you move the cursor to a check box, Works will place the cursor in that box but will not change its state. When you move the cursor to a button, Works will position the cursor on that button and highlight the angle brackets that surround it.

Like the names of menus and the commands on them, the names of options and boxes in dialog boxes have key characters. You can use these key characters to move the cursor to the options and boxes in a dialog box. To do this, simply hold down the [Alt] key and type the key character of that element. Of course, you can type that letter in either lowercase or uppercase form.

Using key characters

Text boxes, list boxes, and check boxes.   The key characters for the text boxes, list boxes, and check boxes are within the names of those elements. When you hold down the [Alt] key and type the key character of a text box, Works will move the cursor to that box. If the box contains an entry, Works will highlight that entire entry. If the box is empty, Works will place the cursor at the beginning of the empty box. When you hold down the [Alt] key and type the key character of a list box, Works will move the cursor to that box. If one of the items in that box is already selected, Works will position the cursor on the item. If no item is selected, Works will place the cursor on the first item in the list but will not select it. When you hold down the [Alt] key and type the key character of a check box, Works will move the cursor to that box and toggle it to its opposite state. If the setting is off, Works will turn it on, and vice versa. We'll return to our discussion of selecting key characters later in this chapter.

Option boxes.   Unlike the other elements in a dialog box, option boxes do not have key characters. Instead, each of the items within an option box has its own key character. For example, let's look at the Save As dialog box shown in Figure 1-22. The Works option in the Format option box has the key character *W*, the Text option has the key character *T*, and the Printed Text option has the key character *P*. The key characters of the items in Works' option boxes are usually, but not always, the first letter of those options.

When you hold down the [Alt] key and type the key character of one of the options in an option box, Works will move the cursor to that option and select it.

Since only one of the options can be selected at a time, this action automatically deselects the option that currently is selected if it is different from the one whose key character you typed.

Buttons.   As in many of Works' dialog boxes, the buttons in the dialog box shown in Figure 1-22 do not have key characters. In fact, buttons labeled <OK> and <Cancel> never have key characters. However, some buttons do. When you hold down the [Alt] key and type the key character of a button, Works will not only move the cursor to that button—it will also perform the action that button commands it to perform. We'll discuss this method of choosing buttons later in this chapter.

Although you can hold down the [Alt] key while typing the key character of an element in a dialog box, it is not always necessary. If the cursor is in an option box, in a check box, or on a button, you can move the cursor to another element simply by pressing the key character of that element. If the cursor is in a text box or list box, however, you must hold down the [Alt] key.

Using a mouse

If you have installed Works for use with a mouse, you can use it to move among the elements in a dialog box. You simply point to an area within that element and click the left button on your mouse. Then, Works will move the cursor to the element on which you clicked. If you click on a check box, Works will change the state of that box. If you click on a button, Works will perform the action that button commands it to perform. If you click on an option box or a list box, Works will select the option on which you clicked. If you click on a text box, Works will position the cursor on the letter (if any) on which you clicked.

Using the elements in a dialog box

As you have seen, Works gives you three ways to move to the elements in a dialog box. Once the cursor is on an element, you can change the settings it specifies. In the following paragraphs, we'll explain how to alter the settings in each type of element in a Works dialog box.

Check boxes

Check boxes are toggle elements—they are either on or off. An X in a check box indicates that the setting controlled by that box is on. If the box is empty, the setting it controls is off.

While the cursor is positioned in a check box, you can turn it on or off. One way to do this is with the [Spacebar]. If you press the [Spacebar] while the element is off (indicated by a blank box), Works will turn it on, filling the box with an X. If you press the [Spacebar] while the element is on (indicated by an X within the box), Works will turn it off, removing the X.

Of course, you can use the key character and mouse techniques to change the status of a check box while the cursor is on that element. If you type the key character of the check box on which the cursor is currently positioned, Works will toggle that box to its opposite state and keep the cursor in that box. Works also will change the state of the check box and keep the cursor in place if you point to that box with your mouse and click it.

Option boxes

Works uses option boxes to present a group of mutually exclusive choices. Within any option box, one option is always selected. Consequently, selecting one option automatically deselects another. The cursor will always be on the option that is currently selected.

While the cursor is in an option box, you can select alternative options by using the ↓ and ↑ keys to move the cursor down and up through the options in the box. Alternatively, you can type the key character of the option you want to select (it's not necessary to hold down the [Alt] key), or you can point the mouse to that option and click.

List boxes

Works uses list boxes to present a variable number of non-fixed choices. Like the options in an option box, only one can be selected at a time. However, the items in a list box are not fixed; different items may appear in the box at different times. For example, Works uses list boxes most often to present the names of the files on a disk. The list of file names will grow as you add files to the list, contract as you delete files from the disk, and change completely if you place a new disk in the drive.

Using the cursor-movement keys. Once the cursor is positioned in a list box, you can use a variety of techniques to select items from that list. First, you can use the ↑ and ↓ keys to move the cursor up and down through the list one item at a time. Since Works selects the option on which the cursor is positioned, moving the cursor selects different items in the list. If you press ↑ while the cursor is on the first item in a list or press ↓ while the cursor is on the last item in a list, the cursor will simply remain in place.

When you use the [Tab] key, the [Shift][Tab] combination, or an [Alt] key combination to enter a list box, Works will place the cursor on the first item in the list but will not select it. Pressing ↓ at this point selects the first item in the list— it doesn't select the second item in the list, as you might expect.

In many cases, there will be more items in a list box than Works can display at one time. If so, you can use the ↑ and ↓ keys to scroll through the list, bringing the hidden items into view.

You also can use the [End], [Home], [Pg Up], and [Pg Dn] keys to bring different portions of a list into view. The [End] key brings the last boxful of items into view and selects the final item in the list. The [Home] key brings the first boxful of items into view and selects the first item in the list. The [Pg Dn] key shifts the next boxful of items into view and selects the item that appears at the top of the box. The [Pg Up] key shifts the previous boxful of items into view and selects the item that appears at the bottom of the box.

Works displays a scroll bar at the right edge of every list box. The position of the scroll box (the black square) within this bar indicates the portion of the list you currently are viewing relative to the top and bottom of the list. For example, if you are viewing the top boxful of items in the list, the scroll box will be at the top of the scroll bar.

Works always arranges the items in any list box in alphabetical order. You can move the cursor to any group of entries in a list simply by typing the first letter of those entries. When you type a letter, Works will move the cursor to the first item (the one closest to the top of the list) that begins with the letter specified. If none of the items in the list begins with the letter you type, the cursor will remain where it is.

Using a mouse.   If you have installed Works for use with a mouse, you can use a variety of techniques to select items within a list box. If the item you want to select is visible within the list box, you can select it simply by pointing to it and clicking the left mouse button.

Using the scroll bar.   If the item you want to select is not in view, you must bring it into view before you can select it. To do so within a list box, you can use any of the techniques described above. Alternatively, you can use the mouse to manipulate the scroll bar at the right edge of the list box.

You can use the arrows at the bottom and top of the scroll bar to bring new items into view. Clicking the top arrow scrolls the previous item into the list box; clicking the bottom arrow scrolls the next item into the list box.

You also can bring new items into view by clicking the scroll bar above or below the position of the scroll box. Clicking above the scroll box has the same effect as pressing the [Pg Up] key—it shifts the preceding boxful of records into the list box. Clicking below the scroll box has the same effect as pressing the [Pg Dn] key—it shifts the next boxful of records into the list box.

Dragging the scroll box within the scroll bar is the third way to bring new items into view. To drag the scroll box to a new position within the scroll bar, point to it, hold down the left mouse button, point to a new position in the scroll bar, and release the button. When you release the button, Works will shift the list within the list box. The position of the scroll box within the bar determines what part of the list Works will bring into view. For example, if you drag the scroll box to the top of the scroll bar, you'll see the first boxful of items in the list.

Finally, you can click the mouse on the top or bottom border of the list box to bring new items into view. Generally, this scrolling technique is similar to scrolling with the arrow at the top or bottom of the scroll bar. Clicking the top border scrolls the previous item into the list box; clicking the bottom border scrolls the next item into the list box. However, there is one slight difference. To scroll a new item into view immediately, the item closest to the border you click must be highlighted. If an item in the middle of a list box is highlighted and you try to scroll through the list by clicking on the top or bottom border of the list box, Works first will move the highlight toward the border you are clicking on before it scrolls through the list.

As you have seen, single-clicking an item in a list box moves the highlight to that item. Double-clicking an item (that is, pointing to it and clicking the button two times in quick succession) has the same effect as single-clicking the item, then choosing <OK>.

Works uses text boxes to solicit information that it cannot obtain in any other way. Generally, you specify information in a text box by typing. However, the way you specify information in a text box depends on whether you use a mouse and whether that box already contains an entry.

Text boxes

Using the cursor-movement keys. When you use the [Tab] key, the [Shift][Tab] combination, or a key character to move the cursor to an empty text box, Works will place the cursor at the beginning of that box. If the box already contains an entry, however, Works will automatically highlight that entry when you move the cursor to that box.

Once the cursor is in a text box, you can make an entry, replace an existing entry, or edit an existing entry. If the box is empty, you can make an entry into it simply by typing. If the box contains an entry, you can replace that entry or edit it. If you type while the entire entry is highlighted (as it will be when you first move into the box), Works will replace it with whatever you type.

If you want to edit the entry instead of replacing it, you must remove the highlight from it. To do this, you must press the ←, →, [Home], or [End] keys. If you press the → or [End] keys, Works will remove the highlight from the entry and place the cursor on the space following the final character in that entry. If you press the ← or [Home] keys, Works will remove the highlight from the entry and place the cursor on the first character in the entry.

Removing the highlight from the entry allows you to use the ←, →, [Home], and [End] keys to move the cursor around within the entry. The → key moves the cursor one character to the right; the ← key moves the cursor one character to the left; the [Home] key moves the cursor to the first character in the entry; and the [End] key moves the cursor to the right of the final character in the entry.

If you type one or more characters while nothing is highlighted, Works will insert what you type to the left of the character on which the cursor is positioned. If you press the [Delete] key, Works will delete the character on which the cursor is positioned. If you press the [Backspace] key, Works will delete the character to the left of the cursor. In both cases, Works will pull the characters to the right of the deleted character one space to the left.

If you want to delete a group of adjacent characters, you can highlight them and press either [Delete] or [Backspace]. To highlight a group of characters, move the cursor to one end of the group, hold down the [Shift] key, and press the ➡, ⬅, [Home], or [End] keys. Once you have highlighted a group of characters, you can delete them by pressing either the [Delete] or [Backspace] keys. Alternatively, you can replace the highlighted characters simply by typing the replacement text.

Using a mouse. If you have installed Works for use with a mouse, you can use some alternative techniques to select characters within a text box. When you point to a text box and click the left mouse button, Works will not highlight the entire entry in that box. Instead, Works will position the cursor on the character to which you were pointing when you clicked. If you click to the right of the last character in the box, Works will position the cursor immediately to the right of the entry. If the box is empty, Works will position the cursor at the left edge of the box. Once you have positioned the cursor on a character, you can use the [Delete] key to delete that character, use the [Backspace] key to delete the character to its left, or type to insert characters into the entry.

You also can use your mouse to highlight groups of one or more characters within a text box. To select a group of characters, simply point to one end of the group, hold down the left button on your mouse, drag to the opposite end of the group, and release the button. Once you have selected the characters, you can use the [Delete] or [Backspace] keys to delete them, or type to replace them.

The capacity of a text box. The width of a text box does not limit the number of characters you can type into it. If you type more characters into a text box than the width of that box can accommodate, Works will scroll the existing characters in the box to the left to accommodate the new characters.

Works does not check the entries you make into text boxes until you choose a "positive" button (like <OK> or <Yes>) to complete the command. If the entry in the text box is inappropriate (too long, too short, too big, or too small), Works will display an alert box at that point. When you choose <OK> to clear the alert box, Works will return you to the dialog box and highlight the offending entry.

Buttons

Every Works dialog box contains at least one button. Buttons appear at the bottom of dialog boxes and are enclosed in angle brackets (<>). Buttons are immediate-action elements. When you choose one, Works will perform an action—usually executing or cancelling the command that produced that dialog box.

You can choose buttons in a dialog box in a variety of ways. First, you can use [Tab] or [Shift][Tab] to move the cursor to the button you want to choose, then press [Enter]. When you do this, Works will perform whatever action that button commands it to perform.

The default button. One button in every dialog box is the default button. Unlike the angle brackets for other buttons, Works highlights the angle brackets for the default button. To choose a default button, you don't need to move the cursor to it; you can simply press [Enter] while the cursor is anywhere in the dialog box (except on another button). When you do this, Works will choose the default button, performing whatever action that button instructs it to perform. In dialog boxes that contain an <OK> button, that button is always the default.

Key characters. Although many buttons (including <OK> and <Cancel>—the two most common) do not have key characters, some do. If a button has a key character, you can choose that button by holding down the [Alt] key and typing that letter in either lowercase or uppercase form. (If the cursor is in a check box, in an option box, or on another button, you can type the letter without holding down the [Alt] key.) When you choose a button in this way, Works immediately will perform whatever action that button commands it to perform.

If you have a mouse. If you have a mouse, you can choose buttons simply by pointing to them and clicking. When you do this, Works will perform whatever action that button commands it to perform.

The <Cancel> button. Every Works' dialog box has a <Cancel> button. Since this button never has a key character, you cannot choose it simply by holding down the [Alt] key and typing a letter. You can choose it by moving the cursor to it and pressing [Enter] or by clicking it with your mouse. You also can choose it by pressing [Esc]. When you press this key, Works will cancel the current command and close the dialog box, just as it does when you select the <Cancel> button.

GETTING HELP

Works is fairly easy to use. However, until you have used it for a long time, you probably will have a hard time remembering what each command, function, key, and so forth, does in different contexts among the various environments.

Fortunately, Works provides an on-line Help facility that provides instant information on a variety of topics. You can access Works' Help facility in three ways: by pressing the [Help] key ([F1]), by pressing the <F1=HELP> hot key on the right end of the status line, or by selecting the Help Index command from the Help menu.

Pressing the
[Help] key

When you press the [Help] key, Works will bring up a help screen that provides information about what you were doing when you pressed that key. (If you are using Works on a dual-floppy system, Works will ask you to replace the Works Program disk in drive A with the Works Spell and Help disk.) For example, if you press the [Help] key when you are in the middle of an Open Existing File... command, Works will overlay the current document with a help screen like the one shown in Figure 1-23. As you can see, this window explains the Open Existing File... command.

Figure 1-23

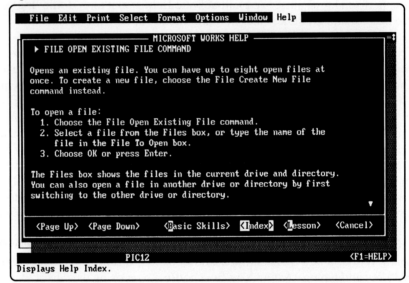

You'll see this help screen when you press the [Help] key during an Open Existing File...command.

Like many of the subjects covered by Works' on-line Help facility, this one includes more information than will fit on a single screen. Pressing the [Pg Dn] key on your keyboard or the <Page Down> button on the screen brings the next screenful of information into view; pressing the [Pg Up] key on your keyboard or the <Page Up> button on the screen redisplays the previous screenful. When there is more information than you currently see on the screen, Works will display a red arrow in a white rectangle at the lower-right corner of the help screen. When you reach the end of the Help topic, Works will display two red squares in a white square in that corner of the help screen. (If you set your color options for monochrome display, the red arrow and squares will not appear. Instead, the white rectangle and square appear with no red shape in them.) In this case, for example, the white rectangle tells you that you are viewing the final windowful of information on the Open Existing File... command.

Like all Help topic screens, the one shown in Figure 1-23 contains six buttons: <Page Up>, <Page Down>, <Basic Skills>, <Index>, <Lesson>, and <Cancel>. These buttons allow you to scroll backward and forward through the topic, select the Basic Skills Help Index, get help on other topics, work through an in-depth lesson on the current topic, and exit from the Help facility, respectively.

▶The <F1=HELP> hot key appears at the right end of the status line in all Works environments. Even though a dialog box is open on the screen, you can use the <F1=HELP> hot key. You can activate Help at any time by moving your mouse pointer to this hot key and pressing the left mouse button.◀

The <F1=HELP> hot key
▶WORKS 2◀

▶The <Basic Skills> button tells Works to display the Help Index. Pressing this button is equivalent to choosing the Help Index command from the Help menu. However, when you press the <Basic Skills> button, the Help Index's Basic Skills Topics list box highlights the name of the help screen you just left.◀

The <Basic Skills> button
▶WORKS 2◀

The <Index> button lets you access other subjects within the Help facility. When you choose the <Index> button, Works will reveal a Help Index screen like the one shown in Figure 1-24 on the following page. The list box within this window contains a listing of all the topics for which help is available—over 170 in all. As you can see, these topics are listed in alphabetical order. If the topic applies only to particular environments, Works places an abbreviation of the names of those environments to the right of that topic. The letters *CM* denote topics that relate to communications documents; *DB* denotes topics that relate to database documents; *SS* denotes topics that relate to spreadsheet documents; and *WP* denotes topics that relate to word processor documents.

The <Index> button

You can choose a topic from this list either by highlighting it, then selecting the <Topic> button or double-clicking the topic. When you choose a topic, Works will display a help screen for that topic.

The <Lesson> button lets you access the Learning Microsoft Works Tutorial program. When you choose the <Lesson> button (or press Shift [F1] on the keyboard), Works will enter its tutorial program, accessing a lesson that works you through the topic that the current help screen covers. For example, if you choose the <Lesson> button while viewing the help screen shown in Figure 1-24, Works will work you through an interactive lesson about the Data Titles... command. As soon as you finish the lesson (or press [Ctrl]q to exit from it), Works will return you to the help screen from which you chose the <Lesson> button. We'll explain more about Works' tutorial program in the next few pages.

The <Lesson> button

Figure 1-24

When you press the <Index> button, you'll see a Help Index screen like this one.

The <Cancel> button

If you choose the <Cancel> button from a help screen, Works will close the help screen, revealing the Works screen exactly as you left it. At this point, you should be able to use the information provided by the help screen to complete the command in which you were engaged when you pressed the [Help] key.

The Using Help and Help Index commands
►WORKS 2◄

►The Using Help and Help Index commands on the Help menu provide other ways to access Works' Help facility. When you pull down the Help menu and issue the Using Help and Help Index commands, Works will display dialog boxes that you can use to access help on any listed topic.◄

USING THE MICROSOFT WORKS TUTORIAL

In addition to its on-line Help facility, Works features an interactive tutorial— Learning Microsoft Works. This tutorial contains a series of lessons, each of which covers a different Works skill. For example, the tutorial features one lesson that teaches you how to create, open, save, and close Works documents; another that teaches you how to format text in a word processor document; another that shows you how to use formulas and functions in a spreadsheet document; and so forth.

Works gives you three ways to enter the tutorial. First, you can choose the <Lesson> button from a help screen. When you do this, Works will access the tutorial and begin a lesson that teaches you about the topic covered by the current help screen. In most cases, the scope of the tutorial lessons is broader than the scope of the Help topics. For example, if you choose the <Lesson> button while viewing a help screen for the Open Existing File... command, Works will run a lesson entitled *Working with Files* that covers all file operations—opening, saving, closing, and so forth.

Second, you can choose the Works Tutorial command from the Help menu of any Works document. When you do this, Works will enter the tutorial and let you choose the lesson you want to run. Before you can choose a lesson, you must first enter your name, then choose one of the six categories listed on the screen: The Works Essentials, Word Processing Spreadsheets & Charts, Databases & Reports, Communications, and Using Tools Together. Afterward, the tutorial will present a listing of the lessons available within that category. To access a lesson, you must choose it from that list.

Third, you can run the tutorial directly from DOS. To do this, simply insert the Learn One Tutorial disk into drive A of your computer, type *learn* at the A> prompt, and press [Enter]. Just as when you access the tutorial by choosing Works tutorial from the Help menu, you'll have to enter your name, then choose the lesson you want to run at this point.

If you are running Works from a floppy disk, you can access the Works tutorial in any of these three ways. Due to space restrictions, however, the disk that contains your copy of Works will not contain the tutorial files. Consequently, Works will ask you to insert the first Learning Microsoft Works disk into drive A when you choose the <Lesson> button from a help screen or when you choose the Works Tutorial command from a Help menu.

If you are running Works from a hard disk, you won't be able to access the tutorial from within Works unless you copied the tutorial files to that disk during the Setup program. However, you can run the Setup program again and modify your Works program to include the tutorial.

Running a lesson

When you select a lesson (if you accessed the tutorial from a help screen, the tutorial will choose one for you), you'll see an introductory screen for that lesson. This screen tells you what the lesson is about and approximately how long it will take to complete.

To begin the lesson, you simply press [Pg Dn]. When you do this, the tutorial will present the first screen of the lesson. Each lesson consists of a number of screens. Pressing [Pg Dn] moves you to the next screen; pressing [Pg Up] moves you to the previous one. Some screens contain information that you should read; some demonstrate an action; and some require you to perform an action.

If you press the [Ctrl] key while you are running a lesson, the tutorial will display a menu that allows you to print the current screen, advance to later sections of the lesson, return to the menu, quit from the tutorial, and so forth.

Exiting from the tutorial

What happens when you finish a lesson depends on how you entered the tutorial. If you chose the <Lesson> button from the help screen, the tutorial will return you to that help screen. If you selected the Works Tutorial command from the Help menu, you will return to Works when you exit the tutorial. If you accessed the tutorial from DOS, you will return to DOS.

OTHER HELP MENU COMMANDS

The Help menu contains three other commands: Getting Started, Keyboard, and Mouse. When you select any of these commands, you will see the help screen that applies to the topic you selected. The Getting Started command displays the Getting Started in Communications help screen. The Keyboard command displays the Function Keys help screen. Finally, the Mouse command displays the Using the Mouse help screen.

EXITING WORKS

When you have finished with Works for the day, or you want to use your computer to run another program, you should exit Works. To do this, simply pull down the File menu and select the Exit Works command. When you issue this command, Works will give you a chance to save any of your work that you have not yet saved. (We'll talk more about saving your work and the file-saving aspect of the Exit Works command at the end of Chapter 2.) Then, Works will remove itself from your computer's memory, returning you to DOS.

CONCLUSION

In this chapter, we have introduced Works and taught you a number of basic skills that apply to all Works' environments. In the next two chapters, we'll introduce you to some universal Works skills that use the techniques presented in this chapter. In Chapter 2, we'll show you how to save and reopen Works' documents, how to access DOS from within Works, and how to switch between open documents. In Chapter 3, we'll show you how to print your work.

File Basics 2

While you are working with a document, Works holds it in your computer's memory. ▶Works can hold up to eight documents in memory and display them on the desktop at one time.◀ If you want, you can save copies of those documents into a file on a floppy disk or a hard disk drive for future use. Once you have saved a document to disk, you can reopen it into Works at any time.

In this chapter, we'll show you how to create, save, open, and close Works documents and how to switch between them when more than one is open at a time. Like the techniques presented in Chapter 1, the skills you will learn in this chapter apply to all Works environments.

Once you have loaded Works, you can use the Create New File... command on the File menu to create new documents. When you pull down the File menu and issue this command, Works will display the Create New File dialog box shown in Figure 2-1.

CREATING A NEW DOCUMENT

Figure 2-1

You'll see this dialog box when you select the Create New File... command from the File menu.

As we said in Chapter 1, to create a new document, simply choose the type of document you want to create, then press [Enter]. For example, suppose you want to create a new word processor document. To do this, pull down the File menu, select the Create New File... command, choose the <New Word Processor> option from the Create New File dialog box, then press [Enter]. Figure 2-2 shows the result.

Figure 2-2

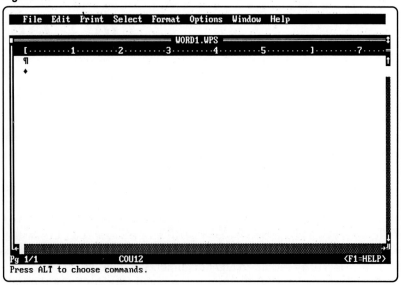

If you choose the <New Word Processor> option from the Create New File dialog box, then press [Enter], Works will create a new word processor document.

Document names

Every Works document has a name that is displayed on the title bar of the document window. Whenever you create a new document, Works assigns a name to it automatically. As you can see in Figure 2-2, Works has assigned the name WORD1.WPS to the word processor document we just created.

The name that Works assigns to a document depends on what type of document it is. The default name of any word processor document begins with the letters WORD and ends with the extension .WPS; the default name of any spreadsheet document begins with the letters SHEET and ends with the extension .WKS; the default name of any database document begins with the letters DATA and ends with the extension .WDB; and the default name of any communications document begins with the letters COMM and ends with the extension .WCM.

The default name of a document also includes a number that identifies how many other documents of that type you have created since you loaded Works. This number appears immediately to the left of the document's extension. Works will use the number 1 for the first document of its type to be created during the current Works session; it will use 2 for the second document of that type to be created during the current session; and so forth. For example, the name WORD1.WPS in the title bar of the document shown in Figure 2-2 indicates that this document was the first word processor document created during the current Works session.

Like most dialog boxes, the Create New File dialog box also has a <Cancel> button. When you choose this button, Works will close the dialog box without creating a new document.

The <Cancel> button

The work you do in any Works document resides only in your computer's random access memory (RAM) until you save it to disk. For example, if you make an entry into a cell of a spreadsheet document, Works will record that entry in a portion of your computer's memory.

SAVING DOCUMENTS

Since Works holds documents in RAM, it can access the information within those documents quickly and easily. However, RAM is volatile. If your computer loses power for any reason, any information stored in RAM will be lost. Consequently, RAM is suitable only for temporary storage of your work.

Fortunately, Works allows you to store "permanent" copies of your work in files on disk. Unlike RAM, files are immune to power failures. Unless you delete the file in which you've stored a document or damage the disk on which that file is stored, you'll be able to open that document back into Works at any time.

Works offers a variety of commands that let you save your documents to disk. In this section, we'll show you how to use those commands to store your documents for future use.

To save a new document for the first time, you can use either the Save or Save As... commands on Works' File menu. When you issue either of these commands from a document that you have not yet saved, Works will present a Save As dialog box like the one shown in Figure 2-3.

Saving a document for the first time

Figure 2-3

You'll see a dialog box like this when you issue the Save or Save As... commands from a document that has not been saved previously.

How you use the Save As dialog box depends on whether you want to save the current document in the default directory (the one listed to the right of the *Directory of* prompt) or in another directory. If you want to save the file in the default directory, you can simply specify a name and choose <OK>. If you want to save the file in another directory, you must choose a directory before you specify a file name and choose <OK>.

We'll show you what happens when Works saves a document after we show you how to specify a name and a destination for the file.

Specifying a name for the file

The Save File As text box is the first element in the Save As dialog box. This text box lets you specify the name of the file in which you want Works to save the current document.

When you save a document for the first time, Works will display the default name of that document in the Save File As text box and highlight that entire name. For example, Figure 2-3 shows the result of issuing the Save or Save As... command from the new word processor document shown in Figure 2-2. Since the default name of that document is WORD1.WPS, Works displays and highlights the name WORD1.WPS in the Save File As text box.

If you want to save a new document under the name that Works assigns it, you won't have to change the entry in the Save File As text box. In most cases, however, you won't want to save a document under its default name. Instead, you'll want to save it under a name that better describes its contents. For example, you might save a spreadsheet document that contains your 1990 budget under the name BUDGET90.WKS.

To specify a name for a document, you can either replace or edit the current entry in the Save File As text box. To replace the current name, simply type the new name while the existing name is highlighted (as it will be when Works first reveals the Save As dialog box). To edit an existing name, use the arrow keys or your mouse to position the cursor, then type new characters or press the [Delete] or [Backspace] keys. For details on how to edit an entry in a text box, refer to Chapter 1.

File name rules. Since Works operates within the DOS system, the names you assign to files must abide by DOS restrictions. Therefore, the name of a Works file cannot contain more than eight characters, exclusive of its extension. For example, CUSTOMER.WKS is a valid name, but CUSTOMERS.WKS is not.

Furthermore, you cannot use any of the following characters in a file name: periods (.)—other than to separate a file name from an extension—asterisks (*), question marks (?), slashes (/), double quotation marks ("), semicolons (;), colons (:), opening brackets ([), closing brackets (]), plus signs (+), and equal signs (=). For example, TEST.WKS is a valid file name, but TEST?.WKS is not.

File extensions. Any file name can have an extension of up to three letters or, if you want, no extension at all. If you do not include either a period or an extension at the end of a file name, Works will add the standard extension for the type of document you are saving. For example, if you specify the name BUDGET for a spreadsheet document, Works will save it into a file named BUDGET.WKS.

If you include an extension at the end of the file name in the Save File As text box, Works will use that extension in the name of the file. If the text box contains the characters TEST.WPS when you choose the <OK> button, for example, Works will save the document under the name TEST.WPS.

If you end a file name with a period but no extension, Works will save the file without an extension. For example, if you choose <OK> while the Save File As text box contains the file name TEMP., Works will save the document TEMP. in a file without an extension.

Importantly, the extension you specify for a file has no effect on the form in which Works saves that file. For example, Works always will save a spreadsheet document as a spreadsheet, a database document as a database, and so forth, no matter what extension you specify.

As you can see, it's relatively easy to assign non-standard extensions to the names of Works files. However, using non-standard extensions makes it harder to open files back into Works. Consequently, we recommend that you let Works add the extension to a file instead of adding it yourself, except when you save files in alternative formats. We'll talk about alternative file formats later in this chapter.

Specifying the directory

When you save a document for the first time, Works lets you specify the directory into which it should be saved. Unless you specify otherwise, Works will save the document to the default directory—the one listed to the right of the *Directory of* prompt. Works automatically looks to the default directory whenever you issue the Save As... or Open Existing File... command.

Unless you've changed the default directory during the current Works session, the default directory will be the one that contains your Works program files. Unfortunately, you usually won't want to save your documents in this directory. If you have a dual-floppy system, you'll want to save your documents to a disk in drive B. If you have a hard disk system, you'll want to save your documents to a subdirectory within the one that contains your Works program files.

You can save a document to an alternative directory in two ways: You can change the default directory, or you can override it. Changing the default directory affects not only where Works will save the current document but also where it will look when you subsequently save and open other files. Overriding the default directory affects only the directory in which Works saves the current document.

You can route a document to any directory simply by making it the default directory—the one Works looks to automatically whenever you issue any File command—and then typing a name for the file into the Save File As text box.

Using the Directories list box. The most common way to change the default directory is to select an alternative directory from the Directories list box, then choose <OK>. At any time, this box will contain a list of the disk drives available on your computer—[-A-] and [-B-] if your computer has two floppy drives, [-A-] and [-C-] if your computer has a hard disk. (Some hard disks are partitioned for [-D-] and [-E-] drives.) If there are any subdirectories within the default directory, Works will display their names in this box as well. If the default directory is not at the root level, Works also will include the option .. in this box.

To change the default directory, move the highlight within the Directories list box to the name of the drive/directory that you want to make current, then choose <OK>. (If you have a mouse, you can double-click the directory name instead.) When you do this, Works will make the directory you selected the current directory and place its name to the right of the *Directory of* prompt.

If you choose the name of a subdirectory from the Directories list box, then choose <OK>, Works will move down one level from the current directory, making that subdirectory the new default. If you choose the .. option from the list box, Works will move up one level from the current subdirectory, making that previous level the new default directory. If you choose one of the drive letters, Works will access the subdirectory of the drive that was current when you last accessed it.

Each time you change the default directory, Works updates the choices in the list box, removing the subdirectories in the old default directory and adding the subdirectories available in the new default directory. However, choices for each of your computer's disk drives will always be available.

Using the list box to move more than one level is a multiple-step process. For example, suppose you want to save a file into the C:\WORKS\FILES subdirectory while C:\ is the default directory. To do this, first highlight the WORKS listing and choose <OK>. This will make C:\WORKS the current directory and cause Works to display the subdirectories in that directory (including FILES). To make C:\WORKS\FILES the current subdirectory, choose FILES from the list box and choose <OK> again.

Typing the new default directory. You also can change the default directory by typing its name (or symbols that lead Works to it from the current directory) into the Save File As text box, then choosing <OK>. When you do this, Works will make that directory the default and display its name to the right of the *Directory of* prompt. Unlike choosing items from the Directories list box, this method allows you to move more than one level at a time.

For example, suppose that C:\WORKS\FILES is the current directory, and you want to save the current document at the root level of drive C (C:\). To do this, you could type *c:* into the Save File As text box, then choose <OK>. When you do, Works will make C:\ the default drive, saving the file to that directory.

Overriding the default directory.   As we have explained, changing the default directory is one way to save a document to another directory. However, changing the default directory doesn't just determine the directory to which Works saves the current document—it changes the directory to which Works looks when you subsequently issue any File command.

In some cases, you may want to save a file into another directory without making that directory the default. To do this, you must enter the name of (or directions to) that directory to the left of the file name in the Save File As text box. If the directory specifications in the text box specify a directory other than the default, Works will save the document in that directory instead of the default.

You can enter a directory specification into the Save File As text box in either of two ways. First, you can type it. For example, suppose you want to save the current document (a spreadsheet) under the name TEST.WKS in the C:\WORKS\FILES subdirectory when C:\WORKS is the default directory. To do this without changing the default directory, you would type either *c:\works\files\test* or simply *\files\test* into the text box, then choose <OK>.

Second, you can select a directory from the Directories list box without pressing <OK>. When you do this, Works will enter your selection into the Save File As text box, overwriting the current entry in that box. At that point, you can move the cursor to the text box, type the name of the file to the right of the directory specification, and choose <OK>.

Once you've selected a file name and/or a destination, you can save the current document to that file by choosing <OK> in the Save As dialog box. (Since <OK> is the default button, you can choose it simply by pressing [Enter].) When you press this button, Works will save the document into the specified file.

Saving the file

While Works is saving a file, it displays an indicator at the left edge of the status line that tells you what percentage of the file has been saved. When Works first begins to save a file, it will display 0%. When it has saved half of the file, it will display 50%. When it finishes saving the file, it will display 100% briefly, then clear the indicator from the status line.

Importantly, specifying a new name for a file changes the name of the document you are saving. For example, if you save a new spreadsheet document with the default name SHEET1.WKS into a file named BUDGET.WKS, Works will change the name of the document to BUDGET.WKS. After the save, the new name will appear on the title bar. Once you save a document, the name of the document will always be the same as the name of the file in which it is stored.

Works does not remove your document from the screen when you save it. Consequently, you can continue working in the document after saving a copy of it to disk. If you want, you can remove a document from RAM after saving it. To do that, you must use the Close command. We'll show you how to use that command later.

Overwriting an existing file.   If you choose <OK> while the entries in the Save As dialog box specify the directory and name of a file that already exists, Works won't save the document immediately. Instead, it will present the alert box shown in Figure 2-4. If you choose <OK> (the default button) in response to the *Replace existing file?* prompt, Works will save the current document on top of the existing file, destroying the original contents of that file. If you choose <Cancel>, Works will return you to the Save As dialog box and let you specify a different name.

Figure 2-4

You'll see this alert box if you choose <OK> when the settings in the Save As dialog box specify the directory and name of an existing file.

Cancelling a save.   If you decide not to save a new document after issuing the Save or Save As… commands, you can choose either the <Cancel> button in the Save As dialog box or simply press [Esc]. Either way, Works will close the Save As dialog box and return you to your former position within the document you were saving.

Resaving a document under the same name in the same directory

Once you have saved a document for the first time, you probably will save it again and again. In most cases, you'll want to save the document into the same file each time. To do this, you should use the Save command. When you issue the Save command while in a document that you have saved previously, Works will save that document into the file to which you saved it before, overwriting the old version of that document with the current version.

Works will resave a document only if you have made changes to that document since the last time you saved it. A change can be as simple as making an entry into a cell or as major as writing several pages of text. If you issue the Save command when there are no changes to save, Works will close the File menu and return you to the document without resaving it.

After you use the Save command to resave a document, that document will remain on the screen—just as it does when you use the Save or Save As… commands to save it for the first time. Consequently, you'll be able to continue exactly where you left off as soon as Works completes the save. Because it's so convenient to save your work, we recommend that you do so after every major change you make to a document or every 15 minutes or so, whichever comes first. That way, you'll never lose a lot of work if your computer loses power. Remember—the changes you make to a document aren't permanent until you save an updated copy of the document to disk.

The Make Backup Copy option

The Make Backup Copy option is a check box that enables you to back up your work after you save a file for the first time. Once you've saved your file to disk, you can protect yourself against changes to your document resulting from an accidental save. When you turn on this option and save your document, Works will rename the extension of the last copy of the document, then save the new changes to your document under its original name.

For example, suppose you have added some information to a spreadsheet document named BUDGET90.WKS, and you have activated the Make Backup Copy option. When you save the changes to your file, Works will first rename the present version on disk BUDGET90.BKS, then save the document with changes under the file name BUDGET90.WKS. In the event that you saved your file with some erroneous changes, you can return to the original file and enter the correct information into it.

Just as Works renames a backup spreadsheet file with the extension .BKS, Works changes the first letter of the other three environment extensions to B as well. The word processor backup file has the extension .BPS; the database backup file .BDB; and, the communications backup file .BCM.

Once you turn on the Make Backup Copy option, you can back up your files merely by issuing the Save command. To turn the option off, you must reissue the Save As… command, then turn off the option. A word of caution: A large backup file will consume a lot of disk space.

When you need to open a backup file, choose the Open Existing File… command. You'll find the backup file listed alphabetically in the Files list box under Other Files.

When you turn on the Save as Template check box in the Save As dialog box, Works will deactivate all other options in the dialog box. When you press <OK>, Works will save your file as a template file. If you create files repeatedly with the same settings (such as printer settings, page margins, or headers and footers) and formats (such as special fonts and styles), the Save as Template option will save these settings in a file that becomes the default document file. For example, if you make a template for a word processor document, that template will become the default file for the word processor environment until you delete it or create another template. We'll discuss the concept of templates later in this chapter in the section "Templates."

The Save as Template option

In most cases, you will want to save each updated version of a document on top of the previous version of that document. However, there may be times when you'll want to save the current version of an existing document into a new file. For example, as you are developing and refining a spreadsheet model, you may want to keep previous versions as an "audit trail" of your work.

The Save As… command allows you to save a document without overwriting the previous version of that document. When you issue the Save As… command within a document that you have saved to disk, Works will present a Save As dialog box like the one shown in Figure 2-5. As you can see, this box looks like the one Works presents when you save a document for the first time.

Resaving a document under a new name and/or in a new directory

Figure 2-5

$Save file as: [WORTH1.WPS.........]

Directory of C:\WORKS2

Directories: Format:

..   (•) Works
[-A-]   ( ) Text
[-C-]   ( ) Printed Text

                   [ ] Make backup copy
                   [ ] Save as template

                   ◄ OK ► <Cancel>

You'll see a dialog box like this one when you issue the Save As... command while working on a previously saved document.

In the Save File As text box, Works enters the name of the file in which the document is currently saved. If that file is in the default directory (the directory that is listed to the right of the *Directory of* prompt), the Save File As text box will contain only the name of the file. If the file is not in the default directory, Works will preface the name in the Save File As text box with the full path to that file.

You can use the elements in this box to resave a previously saved document under a new name, into a new directory, or both. To save a previously saved document under a new name, you must replace or edit the current name of the document that appears in the Save File As text box. To save a previously saved document to a different directory, you can either change the default directory or override it. For an explanation of how to do each of these things, see the section entitled "Specifying the Directory" within the discussion of "Saving Documents" starting on page 45 of this chapter.

Resaving a file

If you want, you can use the Save As... command to save a file on top of itself, just as the Save command does. To do so, simply choose the <OK> button in the Save As dialog box without changing any of the settings in that box. Since the original settings in the Save As dialog box specify the name and directory of the file in which the document is currently stored, choosing <OK> resaves the document into that file. However, since the entry in the Save File As text box specifies the name of an existing file (the previous version of the document you are saving), Works will present the alert box shown in Figure 2-4 instead of resaving the file immediately. If you choose <OK> from this box, Works will save the current version of the document under the existing name, replacing the old version of the document. If you choose <Cancel>, Works will return you to the Save As dialog box and let you specify a different name for the file.

If the Make Backup Copy option is on when you use the Save As... command to overwrite an existing file, Works will save a copy of the old version of the file before overwriting it—just as it does when you issue the Save command.

Unless you specify otherwise, Works will save your documents in the Works format. Files of this sort contain complete working copies of the documents they store. For example, word processor documents will retain their formats, alignments, fonts, and paragraph spacing; spreadsheet documents will retain their formulas, functions, formats, range names, and other structures; database documents will maintain their forms and their report specifications; communications documents will maintain all their settings. You'll almost always want to save your documents in the Works format.

Saving files in alternative formats

In some situations (primarily when you need to use information from a Works document in other programs), you may want to save your Works files in an alternative format. To do this, you must choose one of the options in the Save As dialog box's Format option box.

The type of document you are saving determines how many options the Format option box will contain or whether the Save As dialog box will contain a Format box at all. The Format option box for a word processor document has three options: Works, Text, and Printed Text. The Format boxes for spreadsheet and database documents also have three: Works, Text & Commas, and Text & Tabs. The Save As dialog box for a communications document doesn't have a Format option box.

The Works option saves the current document in the Works format; that is, a complete, working copy of the document. Since you'll want to save your documents in the Works format in almost all cases, Works is the default selection in every Format option box.

The Works format

The Text option saves the information from the current document in the form of an ASCII text file. When you select this option, Works saves the document without any of the special attributes that are saved in a Works file: formatting, margins, range names, formulas, reports, and so forth. Each paragraph of a word processor document is saved on a single line of the file, separated from the next by a carriage return. Spreadsheets and databases are saved in either comma- or tab-delimited form, with formulas and functions converted to their current values.

The Text format

▶The Printed Text option is available only for word processor documents. Like the Text option, the Printed Text option strips formatting codes from the document as it stores it in a file. However, the Printed Text option adds a carriage return at the end of each line as it appears on the screen—that is, at each point where Works wraps text from one line to another and at each end-of-line marker. In addition, the Printed Text option converts left and right margins and tab stops to spaces, and top and bottom margins to blank lines.◀

The Printed Text format
▶WORKS 2◀

**Naming Text-
and Printed Text-
formatted files**

When you save a file in the Text or Printed Text format, you should use an extension and/or name other than the one you will use when you save the file in the Works format. For example, you might want to specify the extension .TXT for files you save in the Text format. Similarly, you might want to use the extension .PRT for files you save in the Printed Text format. Using another extension identifies the format of the file and prevents Works from overwriting a Works-formatted version that you have saved previously.

Specifying a new name for a file when you save a document in another format does not change the name of the document itself. For example, suppose you have previously saved a spreadsheet document in the Works format under the name BUDGET.WKS. If you issue the Save As... command, specify the name TEST.TXT, and choose the Text format, Works will save the document in the Text format into a file named TEST.TXT. After the save, however, the name BUDGET.WKS will still appear on the title bar.

A note

Saving a document in another format does not affect how and where Works will save that document when you next issue the Save command. If you have saved the document in the Works format previously, Works will resave it in the Works format on top of that file. If you have not yet saved the document in the Works format, Works will present the Save As dialog box.

Closing a document

When you issue the Save or Save As... command, Works will save the current document but keep it in RAM. Consequently, you can continue working on the document as soon as Works has finished saving it.

To remove a document from RAM, you must issue the Close command or click the close box for the window that contains the document. When you do, Works will give you the chance to save any changes you have made since you last saved it in the Works format. Depending on your response, Works either will save the changes, then remove the document from RAM, or close the document without saving the changes.

**Closing a previously
saved document**

If you issue the Close command or click the close box in a document that contains unsaved changes, Works will display an alert box like the one shown in Figure 2-6. As you can see, this box asks if you want to save the changes to the document before Works closes it. If you choose <Yes> (the default button), Works will save the document on top of the previous version of that document—just as if you had issued the Save command—then remove it from RAM. If you choose <No>, Works will close the file without resaving it. Any changes you have made to the document since the last time you saved it will be lost. If you choose <Cancel>, Works will cancel the Close command, leaving the document in memory and returning you to it on the screen.

Figure 2-6

You'll see a dialog box like this one when you issue the Close command or click the close box in a document that contains unsaved changes.

If you click the close box or issue the Close command without making any changes to a document, Works will close the document without resaving it.

Works also will display the alert box shown in Figure 2-6 when you issue a Close command within a document that you have not previously saved. If you choose <Cancel>, Works will cancel the Close command, leaving the document open. If you choose <No>, Works will close the document without saving it. If you choose <Yes>, Works will present the Save As dialog box and allow you to specify a name, directory, and format for the file. If you choose <OK> from the Save As dialog box, Works will save the document, then close it. If you choose <Cancel> from the dialog box, Works will cancel the Close command, leaving the document open.

Closing a new document

If you store your files on floppy disks, you're likely to encounter a disk-full problem at one point or another. If the disk becomes full as you're saving a file, Works will display an alert box like the one shown in Figure 2-7. The message in this box, *Disk full. B:\18TXT.PRT*, tells you that there is not enough empty space on the disk to save the file, then tells you the destination of the file and its name. You must choose <OK> to remove the box from the screen.

Disk-full errors

If you encounter the alert box shown in Figure 2-7 while using the Save or Close commands to resave a file, Works will cancel the command when you choose <OK>, returning you to the document. Since these commands overwrite the previous version of the file, but the save is not complete, the disk to which you are trying to resave the document won't contain a usable copy of the file at this point. Faced with this situation, you should insert a disk that has enough room to hold the file into the drive to which you are trying to save the document, then reissue the Save command. When you do, Works will display the Save As dialog box, since the previous version of the file does not appear on that disk. Since Works will display the name of the document in the Save File As text box, you can save it under its original name simply by choosing <OK>.

Figure 2-7

You'll see this alert box when Works runs out of room while saving a file.

If Works is saving the document as a result of a Save As... command (or a Close command from an unsaved document), it will return you to the Save As dialog box as soon as you acknowledge the disk-full alert. At that point, you should insert a disk that has enough room to hold the file into the drive to which you are trying to save the document, then choose <OK>.

You usually will encounter a disk-full alert only when you are saving to a floppy disk. However, you may occasionally encounter one when saving to a hard disk. When that happens, you can save the document into a file on a floppy disk. Alternatively, you can use the Run Other Programs... command to access DOS within Works, delete some files from the hard disk (backup files are a good place to start), return to Works, and try again. We'll show you how to use the Run Other Programs... command near the end of this chapter.

OPENING FILES: THE OPEN EXISTING FILE... COMMAND

So far, we've shown you how to create, save, and resave documents. Once you have saved a document into a file, you can reopen the document into Works. To do this, you must use the Open Existing File... command—the second command on any File menu. When you issue this command, you'll see an Open Existing File dialog box like the one shown in Figure 2-8.

To open a file, you must enter its name into the File to Open text box, then choose <OK>. Unless you specify otherwise, Works will look in the directory for the file you have specified. If the file you want to open is not in the current directory, you'll need to change the default directory (or override the default) before you open the file.

Figure 2-8

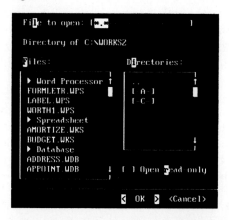

You'll see this dialog box when you issue the Open Existing File... command.

Specifying the file name

There are two ways to enter a file name into the File to Open text box. First, you can select the name of the file you want to open from the Files list box. Alternatively, you can type the name of that file into the File to Open text box.

You'll usually select the file you want to open by choosing its name from the Files list box. This list box always contains the names of the Works files in the current directory and organizes the file types in the following order: word processor, spreadsheet, database, and communications. After all the Works files are listed, Works lists all other files in the directory. To select a file name from the list, you can use the ↓, ↑, [Pg Dn], [Pg Up], [End], or [Home] keys to move the highlight to it. To move into view the portion of the list that contains the file name, you can type the first letter of that name. If you have a mouse, you can use the scroll bar to bring the file name into view, then click that name to select it.

When you choose a file name from the Files list box, Works will enter the name of that file into the File to Open text box. Once the file name is in the text box, you can open it by choosing <OK>. (Since <OK> is the default button, you can choose it simply by pressing [Enter].)

If you want, you can limit the list in the Files list box to files of a certain type (for example, .WPS files) before you select one. To do this, you must enter into the File to Open text box a wildcard expression that identifies the type of file you want Works to list, then choose <OK> or press [Enter]. When you do, Works will update the list in the Files box to include only files that match the pattern you specify. For example, if you want Works to list only word processor files, enter the expression *.WPS into the File to Open text box. When you choose <OK> or press [Enter], Works will update the list in the Files list box to include only files that have the extension .WPS. Even when you change directories in the Directories list box, Works will display only that directory's specified files until you close the Open Existing File dialog box.

Instead of choosing the file you want to open from the Files list box, you can type the file name into the File to Open text box. To do this, simply move the cursor to the text box and type the name of the file you want to open. Once you've entered the file name, you can open it by choosing <OK>.

Works will look automatically for the file you specify in the current directory— the one whose name appears at the right of the *Directory of* prompt. If the file you want to open is not in that directory, you can make the directory that contains that file the default, or you can override the default directory.

The first way to access a file from a directory other than the current one is to access that directory. To do this, you must enter the name of the new default directory (or directions to it from the current default directory) into the File to Open text box and choose <OK>. You can select the name of that directory from the Directories list box or type it directly into the File to Open box.

For example, suppose C:\WORKS is the current directory, and you want to open a file that is stored in the \FILES subdirectory of that directory. To generate

Choosing a file from the Files list box

Typing the file name

Choosing a directory

Changing the default directory

a list of the files in the C:\WORKS\FILES directory in the Files list box, you have to make that directory the current directory. To do this, you could choose FILES from the Directories list box. Alternatively, you could type *files* or *c:\works\files* into the File to Open text box. In either case, as soon as you choose <OK>, Works would make C:\WORKS\FILES the current directory and update the list in the Files list box to include only the files in FILES.

Overriding the default directory

Instead of changing the current directory, you can command Works to open a file from a directory other than the default. To do this, you must enter both the name of the directory that contains that file (or the path to that directory from the current directory) and the name of that file in the File to Open text box. After you have done this, you should choose <OK> to open the file. Then, Works will look for the file in the directory specified in the File to Open text box.

For example, suppose you want to open a file named LETTER.WPS that is stored in the C:\WORKS\FILES directory when C:\WORKS is the current directory. To accomplish this, you could type either *files\letter.wps* or *c:\works\files\letter.wps* in the File to Open text box and choose <OK>.

Opening the file

When you choose <OK> in the Open Existing File dialog box, Works will read into your computer's memory the document stored in the file you have specified. That document will be stored in RAM along with any other document you have created or opened during the current session. (This document will not appear in full size when other documents are open on the desktop.) Later in this chapter, we'll show you how to switch among the documents that are open within Works.

Trying to open a file that does not exist

When you type the name of a file into the File to Open text box instead of choosing it from the Files list box, you run the risk of specifying a file that does not exist. If this happens, Works will present an alert box when you choose <OK>. When you acknowledge this alert by choosing <OK>, Works will return you to the Open Existing File dialog box and let you try again.

Opening a file that is already open

Although it's unlikely, it's possible to open a file that is already open. When you issue the Open Existing File… command, specify the name of a file that is already open and that contains unsaved changes, and choose <OK>, Works will present an alert box that displays the message *File already open. Opening it again erases changes since last save.* and gives you two choices: <OK> and <Cancel>. If you choose <OK>, Works will open the file, clearing the document with the same name from memory. If you choose <Cancel>, Works will cancel the Open Existing File… command and return you to the current document.

Opening files on a dual-floppy system

If you are using Works on a dual-floppy system, you'll need to swap disks when you want to open a file that is on a floppy disk other than the one that is in drive B at the time. To open a file that is not on the current disk, you should pull down the File menu, select the Open Existing File… command, replace the current disk in drive B with the one that contains the file you want to open, choose <OK> to generate a list of files on the new disk, highlight the name of the file you want to open, and choose <OK> again. You also may have to swap disks when you open files from a disk in drive A of either a floppy or a hard-disk system.

Opening a file automatically when Works loads

If you want, you can command Works to open a file as soon as you load it. To do this, at the DOS prompt simply type *works*, followed by a space and the name of the file you want to open, including its extension, and press [Enter]. If the file is in a directory other than the one containing your Works files, you must type the name of the path to that directory as well.

For example, suppose your Works program files are stored in the C:\WORKS directory. If you want Works to open the file named BUDGET.WKS, which is stored in the same directory as your Works program files, you'd load Works by typing *works budget.wks* at the DOS prompt for that directory. If the file is stored in the C:\WORKS\APPS directory, you would type *works\apps\budget.wks*.

Opening non-Works files

Before Works opens a file, it checks to see if that file is a valid Works file; that is, a word processor, spreadsheet, database, or communications document saved in the Works format. If the file is in the Works format, Works will open it into a document of the correct type.

Figure 2-9

You'll see this dialog box when you attempt to open a file that has not been saved in the Works format.

Whenever you attempt to open a non-Works file, Works will display a dialog box like the one shown in Figure 2-9. The options in this box allow you to choose the type of document into which Works will open the file. If you choose Word Processor, Works will load the file into a word processor document; if you choose Spreadsheet, Works will load the file into a spreadsheet document; if you choose Database, Works will load the file into a database document.

Importantly, because a file's extension does not always indicate what sort of document it contains or in what format it is stored, Works does not determine a file's type by looking at its extension. For example, even if you save a spreadsheet document in the Works format under the name BUDGET.SSC, Works will recognize that file as containing a spreadsheet and open it into a spreadsheet document. Conversely, if you save a word processor document in the Printed Text format under the name LETTER.WPS, Works will display the dialog box shown in Figure 2-9 when you try to open the document into Works.

We'll talk about opening non-Works files into Works in detail in Appendix 1. For now, just realize that if you see the dialog box shown in Figure 2-9, you've selected a non-Works file.

TEMPLATES
▶WORKS 2◀

▶Earlier in this chapter, we discussed the Save as Template check box in the Save As dialog box. We said that if you repeatedly create files with the same settings (such as printer settings, page margins, or headers and footers) and formats (such as special fonts and styles), the Save As Template check box will save these settings in a file that becomes the default document file. As you can imagine, a template can reduce the amount of redundant formatting work you must perform when you initially set up a frequently used document type.

Creating templates

If you use the word processor environment often to create documents that use headers and footers or margins different from Works' default settings, you can create a word processor template that includes these settings in it. To do this, simply open a new word processor file and make all the changes you want to Works' default settings. When you issue the Save As… command, activate the Save as Template check box. When you do this, Works will dim all the other options in the Save As dialog box. When you press <OK>, Works will save all your settings in a template file named TEMPLATE.PS. (Works will name a template file TEMPLATE.KS for a spreadsheet, TEMPLATE.DB for a database, and TEMPLATE.CM for a communications document.)

Using templates

Works will use your template file when you open a new document if the appropriate Use Templates For setting in the Works Settings dialog box is activated. When you issue the Works Settings… command, you'll see the dialog box in Figure 2-10. All four of the Use Templates For settings are activated.

Figure 2-10

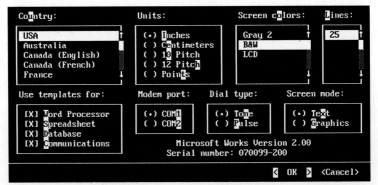

The Use Templates For options in the Works Settings dialog box determine whether Works uses a template as a default document.

In our example about creating a template, if the Use Templates For Word Processor setting is turned on, Works will open the word processor template file each time you choose the Create New File... command and select <New Word Processor>. When you want to replace the template, just create a new one. When you save that file as a template file, Works will present an alert box that asks if you want to replace the existing file. Pressing the <Yes> button will give you a new template file. If you want to return to the original default word processor document, turn off the Use Templates For Word Processor setting in the Works Settings dialog box or delete the template file from the Works directory.◄

►Works 2 provides a command—the File Management... command on the File menu—that lets you execute some of the more common DOS commands, such as Copy File, Delete File, Rename File, Create Directory, Remove Directory, Copy Disk, Format Disk, and Set Date & Time, from within Works.

At some point while you're working in Works, you'll need to use one of these DOS commands. When you do, simply choose the File Management... command from the File menu. When the dialog box shown in Figure 2-11 appears, choose the DOS command you want to use.

FILE MANAGEMENT
►WORKS 2◄

Figure 2-11

From the File Management dialog box, you can issue some common DOS commands without leaving Works.

Each command you choose will cause Works to display a dialog box for you to enter the information necessary to carry out the DOS command. The Copy File command lets you copy a file from one directory to another. The Delete File command allows you to delete a file from a directory. The Rename File command lets you change the name of a file. The Create Directory and the Remove Directory commands let you make and delete a DOS directory. When you need to copy an entire disk of files to back them up or format a disk for copying or saving files, choose the Copy Disk or Format Disk commands. Finally, the Set Date & Time command lets you change the date and time on your computer system's clock.

For example, if you're using a dual-floppy machine—and even on some occasions when you're using a computer with a hard disk—you may run out of room on the disk you're saving your file to. If this problem occurs, you can use the File Management... command to free up some space on your floppy disk without leaving Works. To do this, choose the File Management… command from the File menu. When the File Management dialog box appears, choose the Delete File command, then enter the name of the file into the File to Delete text box shown in Figure 2-12. (In the Delete File dialog box, you choose files from the Files list box in the same way you do in the Open Existing File dialog box.) When you press <OK> or [Enter], Works will present an alert box so you can verify the deletion.

When you are deleting files, be careful not to delete any of your Works program files and never delete any files with the extension .TMP. In some cases, Works uses these temporary files to store portions of a large document while you are working with it. If you delete those files, you'll lose part of the document.◄

Figure 2-12

You'll identify the file to delete from the Delete File dialog box.

ACCESSING OTHER PROGRAMS FROM WORKS
►WORKS 2◄

►You can load and use other programs without exiting Works. If your computer has the memory to run more than one program at a time, you can customize the list of programs in the Run Other Programs dialog box. This dialog box lists one default program: DOS prompt.

Occasionally, you may need to do something that you can do only from DOS or another program. One way to execute a DOS command or load another program is to save all your work, exit from Works, execute the DOS command or work in another program, reload Works, then reopen the document(s) in which you were working. As you can see, this involves a lot of steps—especially if you have a lot of documents open in Works at the same time.

The DOS option

The Run Other Programs... command, which is located on every document's File menu, allows you to access DOS from Works as well as programs you add to the list. When you finish working in DOS or another program, then return to Works, your Works screen will look exactly as it did when you left it.◄

In the previous section, we explained how you can perform some common DOS functions from Works. However, if you need to perform more complex DOS operations, you can enter the DOS environment, complete the tasks, then return to Works, exactly as you left it.

When you pull down the File menu and select the Run Other Programs... command, Works will display the dialog box shown in Figure 2-13. The dialog box always lists *DOS prompt* in its Programs list box. To run DOS, highlight *DOS prompt* by pressing ↑, ↓ or clicking *DOS prompt* with the mouse. When you press <Run> or [Enter], Works will display the message shown in Figure 2-14, telling you that you are about to access DOS. If you choose the <Cancel> button, Works will cancel the command and return you to where you were when you selected the Run Other Programs... command. If you choose <OK>, however, Works will temporarily exit to DOS. (If you are working with Works on a dual-floppy system, Works will ask you to replace the Works Program disk with a DOS disk first.) After Works accesses DOS, the cursor will be at the DOS prompt, which will reflect Works' current default directory.

Figure 2-13

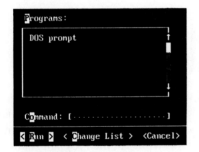

You'll see this dialog box when you select the Run Other Programs... command from the File menu.

Figure 2-14

Works displays this message telling you that you are about to access DOS.

At this point, you can perform any of the DOS commands that Works doesn't list for you in the File Management dialog box. For example, if you need to rearrange some files among the various directories on your hard disk or on one of your floppies, you can do so from the DOS prompt. To return to Works after your work in DOS, simply type *exit* at the DOS prompt and press [Enter].

**Adding other
commands
▶WORKS 2◀**

▶Works equips the Run Other Programs… command to accommodate your need to work in other programs. The dialog box in Figure 2-13 lets you add program names to its list box so you can run those programs directly from Works.

**The <Change List>
and <Add> buttons**

In the Run Other Programs dialog box, you add programs to the Programs list box by choosing the <Change List> button. When you do this, you'll see the dialog box shown in Figure 2-15. To add a program to the Programs list box, type in the Program Name text box the name you want to display in the Programs list box. In the Program Command text box, type the name you enter at the DOS prompt to execute the program. When you press the <Add> button, Works will update the program's list box to include the new program.

Figure 2-15

This dialog box lets you add programs to the Programs list box in the Run Other Programs dialog box.

Suppose you want to access Microsoft Word 5 in the Run Other Programs dialog box. First, choose the Run Other Programs… command from the File menu. Next, select the <Change List> button at the bottom of the dialog box. When the dialog box shown in Figure 2-15 appears, type *Word5* in the Program Name text box. This is the name that identifies the program in the Programs list box. Next, in the Program Command text box, type the exact text you must type at the DOS prompt to execute Word, that is, *WORD*. Finally, select the <Add> button. When you do, you'll notice the program name WORD5 appears in the Programs list box. When you highlight this name, the program name and program command will appear in their respective text boxes. If the program resides in a different directory from Works, then you should type the full path to that program. (On our computer, we keep Microsoft Word in the WORD5 directory, so we would enter *C:\WORD5\WORD* in the Program Command text box.)

**The <Change> and
<Delete> buttons**

You can change any program in the Programs list box by highlighting the program, altering the Program Name text box (or the Program Command text box if you need to change the path to a program), then choosing the <Change> button. For example, if we changed the path to Microsoft Word 5 on our hard disk, we would choose the <Change> button, then edit the path name displayed in the Program Command text box. To delete any program in the Programs list box, highlight the program, then choose the <Delete> button.

When you finish your work in the Run Other Programs dialog box, choose the <Done> button and the dialog box will close, incorporating all the changes you made to the settings in the dialog box.

Returning to Works

Once you have completed all the work you want to do within DOS, you can return to Works simply by typing *exit* at the DOS prompt and then pressing [Enter]. When you work in another program and exit that program normally, your screen will prompt you to press any key to return to Works. When you do this, Works will be reactivated. You'll see the Works document from which you issued the Run Other Programs... command, exactly as it appeared before you issued that command.

When you select the Run Other Programs... command and access DOS, Works' default directory will be the current directory. Similarly, the directory that is current in DOS when you return to Works will become the new default directory. For example, suppose C:\WORKS is the default directory when you issue the Run Other Programs... command. While within DOS, you type *cd ..*, then press [Enter] to switch DOS's attention to the root directory of drive C. If you return to Works at this point, C:\ will be the new default directory.◄

EXITING WORKS

As we explained at the end of Chapter 1, the Exit Works command removes Works from memory and returns you to DOS. Before it does, however, Works first closes each of the documents open at the time. If you have not changed a document since you last saved it, Works will simply close it. If a document contains unsaved changes, however, Works will display the same alert box it presents when you issue the Close command. (Figure 2-6 shows an example of this box.) If you choose <Cancel> from this box, Works will cancel the Exit Works command, leaving you in Works. If you choose <No>, Works will close the document without resaving it, then proceed to the next document in the list.

What happens if you choose <Yes> depends on whether the document has been saved previously. If it has, Works will simply resave the document and then close it. If the document has never been saved, Works will display the familiar Save As dialog box, which lets you specify a name and a destination for the document. If you choose <OK> from the Save As dialog box, Works will save the document, remove it from RAM, then proceed to the next one in the list. If you choose <Cancel>, Works will leave the document open and cancel the Exit Works command.

Works does not give you a single command that closes more than one document at a time. If you want to close several documents, you can close each one individually or choose the Exit Works command.

CONCLUSION In this chapter, we have shown you how to create, save, open, and close Works documents, and how to move among multiple documents that are open at the same time. We also told you how to access other programs without leaving Works. All of these important skills apply equally to all Works environments. In the next chapter, we'll teach you how to print your documents.

Printing Basics 3

*I*n addition to letting you manipulate information and store it on disk, Works allows you to print the information from your documents. In this chapter, we'll demonstrate the basic techniques required to print any Works document.

The commands that make it possible to print a document are located on the Print menu. Every type of document, except communications, has a Print menu.

▶ Figure 3-1 shows a typical Print menu (in this case, the Print menu from a word processor document). Although many of the commands on a particular environment's Print menu are unique to that environment, six commands appear on every Print menu: Print..., Page Setup & Margins..., Preview..., Insert Page Break, Headers & Footers..., and Printer Setup.... These commands control the basic printing process.

▶WORKS 2◀

Figure 3-1

This figure shows the Print menu in a word processor document.

Printing a document is a four-step process. First, you use the Page Setup & Margins... command to set the margins, page dimensions, and header and footer margins for the print-out. Second, you use the Headers & Footers... command to insert the header and footer text, if any, for the document. Third, you use the

Printer Setup... command to specify the printer to which you want to print and the port to which that printer is connected. Finally, you select the Print... command, which instructs Works to print the document.◄

THE PAGE SETUP & MARGINS... COMMAND

The Page Setup & Margins... command on the Print menu lets you define the settings that affect the layout of a printed document. When you select this command, Works will display a Page Setup & Margins dialog box like the one shown in Figure 3-2. The elements in this dialog box allow you to specify the page dimensions, first page number, page margins, and header and footer margins for the print-out.

Figure 3-2

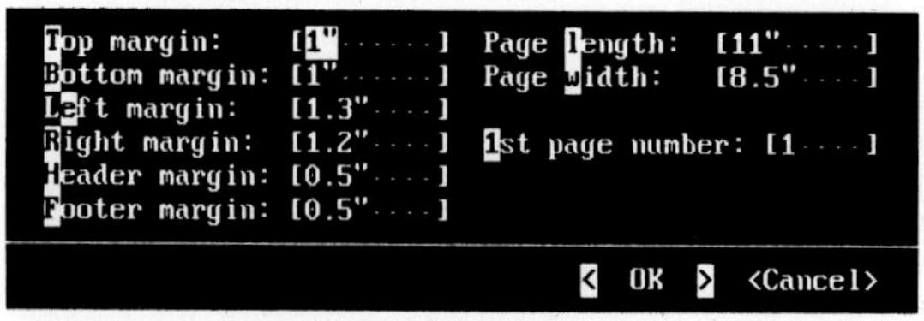

```
 Top margin:      [1"  ·····]   Page Length:   [11"·····]
 Bottom margin:  [1"  ·····]   Page Width:    [8.5"····]
 Left margin:     [1.3"····]
 Right margin:    [1.2"····]   1st page number: [1····]
 Header margin:  [0.5"····]
 Footer margin:  [0.5"····]

                                  ◄  OK  ►   <Cancel>
```

You'll see a dialog box like this one when you select the Page Setup & Margins... command from the Print menu.

The margin settings

The top four text boxes on the left in the Page Setup & Margins dialog box allow you to control the margins of the print-out—the amount of "white space" that Works leaves at the top, bottom, left, and right edges of the page. The Top Margin text box controls the amount of space that Works leaves at the top of the page. As you can see in Figure 3-2, the default Top Margin setting is 1". The Bottom Margin text box controls how much space Works leaves at the bottom of the page. The default Bottom Margin setting is also 1". The Left Margin text box controls the space Works will leave at the left edge of each page. The default value for this setting is 1.3". The Right Margin text box determines the minimum amount of space that Works will leave at the right edge of each page. The default value for this setting is 1.2".

The default values of these four margin settings are appropriate for most applications. However, you can alter them if you want. To do this, simply move the cursor to the setting you want to alter, then either edit or replace it. For example, suppose you want to change the top margin from 1 inch to 2 inches. To do this, you first would move the cursor to the Top Margin text box. Then, you would replace the 1 with a 2, or replace the entire entry with the entry 2". In fact, if the default unit of measure is inches, you could replace the entry 1" with the value 2. In a few pages, we'll show you how to determine the default unit of measure (and how to change it).

The Page Length and Page Width text boxes let you specify the dimensions of the paper on which you are printing. The entry in the Page Length text box indicates the length of the paper. The default value of this setting is 11". The entry in the Page Width text box indicates the width of the paper. The default value of this setting is 8.5". Together, these default values tell Works it will be printing on standard $8^1/_2$-by 11-inch paper.

Like the default margin settings, the default page dimension settings are appropriate for most printing applications. In some cases, however, you may want to print on paper of a different size. For example, you may want to print on legal paper ($8^1/_2$ by 13) or computer paper (14 by 11). To change either of the page dimension settings, simply move the cursor to the appropriate setting and edit or replace the existing entry. If you don't include a unit of measure, Works will use the default (inches).

The margin settings and the page dimension settings work together to determine how much information Works can print on each page. The usable width is equal to the page width minus the left and right margins; the usable height is equal to the page length minus the top and bottom margins. For example, the default margin settings in conjunction with the default page dimension settings leave a 6-inch-wide (8.5-1.3-1.2) by 9-inch-tall (11-1-1) print area.

The page dimension settings

Works has the ability to print the page number on each page of a printed document. The 1st Page Number text box lets you control what number Works prints on the first page of the print-out. In most cases, you'll want Works to start with the number 1—the default value of this setting. However, when you want it to start with another number, you should enter that number into the 1st Page Number text box.

For example, suppose you're about to print a word processor document that contains Chapter 2 of a book you are writing. If Chapter 1 was 25 pages long, you would want Works to begin numbering Chapter 2 with 26—not 1. To instruct Works to do this, you would enter the value 26 into the 1st Page Number text box.

The 1st Page Number setting

The entries in the Header Margin and Footer Margin text boxes control where Works will print the contents of the Header and Footer text boxes in the Headers & Footers dialog box, relative to the top and bottom of the page. The Header Margin text box controls how much space Works will leave between the top of the page and the top of the line on which it prints the header; the Footer Margin text box controls how much space Works will leave between the bottom of the line on which it prints the footer and the bottom of the page. For example, the default Header Margin value of 0.5" tells Works to leave $^1/_2$ inch of space between the top of the page and the line on which it prints the header; the default Footer Margin value of 0.5" tells Works to leave $^1/_2$ inch between the bottom of the footer line and the bottom of the page.

Header and footer settings

The Header Margin and Footer Margin settings must fall within the top margin and bottom margin areas of the page. Consequently, the value you specify for the header margin cannot exceed the value you specify for the top margin. If it does, Works will ignore it and enter a setting that matches the setting for the top margin. For example, if you enter 2 in the Top Margin text box and 3 in the Header Margin text box by mistake, then press <OK> or [Enter], Works will change the 3 in the Header Margin text box to 2. When you reopen the Page Setup & Margins dialog box, you'll see that Works has honored the Top Margin setting and entered 2 in the Header Margin text box.

Your best bet is to specify values for your header and footer margins that are about half of the values you specify for your top and bottom margins, respectively. That way, Works will print the header about midway between the top of the page and the first line of text, and will print the footer about midway between the last line of text and the bottom of the page.

Using alternative units of measure

In most cases, you will use inches as the unit of measure for the entries you make into the Page Setup & Margins dialog box. However, Works lets you use other units of measure. Specifically, you can enter measurements in terms of centimeters, 10-pitch units, 12-pitch units, and points. One centimeter is equal to .394 inches; one 10-pitch unit is equal to $\frac{1}{10}$ of an inch; one 12-pitch unit is equal to $\frac{1}{12}$ of an inch; and one point is equal to $\frac{1}{72}$ of an inch.

Works uses the suffixes *", cm, p10, p12,* and *pt* to identify the five possible units of measure. To ensure that Works interprets a measurement in the units you want, you should follow that unit with one of these suffixes. If you don't follow a value with one of the five suffixes, Works will interpret the value as being stated in the default unit of measure (inches).

To change the default unit of measure, you must select the Works Settings... command from the Options menu. When you do this, you'll see a Works Settings dialog box like the one shown in Figure 3-3. The Units option box within this dialog box controls the default unit of measure. The current default unit will be selected when you first enter the Works Settings dialog box. To change the default unit of measure, simply choose it, then choose <OK>.

Works always displays the measurements in the Page Setup & Margins dialog box in terms of the default unit of measure, and follows each one with the suffix of that unit. If you enter a measurement in units other than the default, Works will display it in the default unit of measure the next time you issue the Page Setup & Margins... command. If you change the default unit of measure, Works will display all the measurements in terms of the new default.

Locking in the settings

Once you have chosen the measurement options in the Works Settings dialog box, you should choose <OK>. When you do this, Works will lock in the settings in that box and remove it from the screen. If you choose <Cancel> instead, Works will remove the Works Settings dialog box, ignoring your changes to the settings.

Figure 3-3

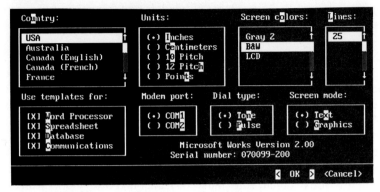

The Units option box in the Works Settings dialog box allows you to change the default unit of measure.

Each document has its own Page Setup & Margins settings. Consequently, the settings you specify within any Page Setup & Margins dialog box apply only to the document from which you issued the Page Setup & Margins... command. When you save a document, Works saves its Page Setup & Margins settings with it. When you reprint a document, therefore, you need to issue the Page Setup & Margins... command only if you want to change the layout settings.

Saving the page settings

Headers and footers are controlled by the Headers & Footers... command on the Print menu. When you choose this command, you'll see a dialog box like the one shown in Figure 3-4.

THE HEADERS & FOOTERS... COMMAND

Figure 3-4

The Headers & Footers dialog box lets you specify header and footer text in your document.

A header is a line of information that appears at the top of each page; a footer is a line of text that appears at the bottom. The header appears within the top margin area of each page; the footer appears within the bottom margin area. Headers and footers commonly contain information such as the title of a report, the number of a chapter, the print date, the page number, and so forth. Works allows you to specify both the contents of headers and footers and the amount of space they occupy on the page.

Specifying the contents of headers and footers

The Header and Footer text boxes let you specify what Works will print as a header and footer on each page of a document. To specify a header for a document, simply move the cursor to the Header text box and type what you want Works to print. For example, if you want Works to print the phrase *Amalgamated Widgets FY 1990 Budget* at the top of each page, you would type that phrase into the Header text box. If you wanted Works to print the phrase *Top Secret* at the bottom of each page, you would type that phrase into the Footer text box.

►WORKS 2◄

►As you can see in Figure 3-4, Works does not supply a default header. Therefore, unless you make an entry into the Header text box, Works won't print a header at the top of each page.

The Use Header & Footer Paragraphs check box appears only in the Headers & Footers dialog box. This check box allows you to enter header and footer text directly into the document. When you activate the Use Header & Footer Paragraphs check box, Works will dim the Header and Footer text boxes, create lines for the header and footer text at the top of the document, and mark these lines with the letters *H* and *F*. You can type your text directly on these lines. We'll cover this option in Chapter 6.◄

Special codes

In addition to containing text, headers and footers can contain any of the special codes listed in Table 3-1. These codes consist of an ampersand followed by a single letter. Some of these codes divide headers and footers into left-aligned, centered, and right-aligned portions. Others command Works to print special information, such as the current page number or the current date.

Dividing headers and footers into parts. The first three codes in Table 3-1—&l, &c, and &r—allow you to divide your headers and footers into left-aligned, centered, and right-aligned portions. Characters that follow the &l code will be aligned with the left margin of the document; characters that follow the &c code will be centered between the two margins; and characters that follow the &r code will be aligned with the right margin. Works will center any information not preceded by one of these three codes.

For example, suppose you want to create a header that has the phrase *Amalgamated Widgets, Inc.* aligned with the left margin, the phrase *F 1990 Budget* centered between the left and right margins, and the word *CONFIDENTIAL* aligned with the right margin. To do this, you would enter *&lAmalgamated Widgets, Inc.&cF 1990 Budget&rCONFIDENTIAL* into the Header text box.

You don't need to divide a header or footer into parts to take advantage of these alignment attributes. For example, you might want your header to consist only of the phrase *Amalgamated Widgets, Inc.*, aligned with the right margin of the page. To do this, you would enter *&rAmalgamated Widgets, Inc.* into the Header text box.

Table 3-1

Code	Effect
&l	Left-aligns following portion of header/footer
&c	Centers following portion of header/footer
&r	Right-aligns following portion of header/footer
&d	Prints the current date
&f	Prints the name of the document
&p	Prints the current page number
&t	Prints the current time

You can use these codes to align the information in headers and footers and insert variable information within them.

Printing variable information in headers and footers. The remaining codes in Table 3-1 let you include variable information—such as the current date and page number—within headers and footers.

The first of these codes, &d, commands Works to print the current date (the date on which the current page is printed) in mm/dd/yy form. For example, if you print a report on March 15, 1990, Works will print the date as 3/15/90.

The second of these codes, &f, commands Works to print the name of the document, just as it appears in the title bar at the top of the window. For example, if the document you are printing is named BUDGET.WKS, the code &f would cause it to print *BUDGET.WKS*.

The third of these codes, &p, commands Works to print the number of the current page as a simple digit. In most cases, for example, Works would print the number 1 on the first page of a print-out, the number 2 on the second page, and so forth. As we explained earlier, however, the entry in the 1st Page Number text box in the Page Setup & Margins dialog box controls which number Works will print on each page. If that box contains the number 1, Works will print 1 on the first page, 2 on the second page, and so forth. If the 1st Page Number text box contains a number other than 1, however, Works will print that number on the first page, that number plus 1 on the second page, and so forth.

The final code, &t, commands Works to print the time at which it began printing the report, using the hh:mm AM/PM form. Importantly, Works prints the time at which it began printing the report—not the time at which it began printing the current page—on each page of the report. Consequently, the same time will be printed on each page.

Since the ampersand signals the beginning of a special code, you must use two & symbols, side by side, to include a literal & symbol in a header or footer. For example, you would have to use the phrase *Profit&&Loss* to make the phrase *Profit&Loss* appear in a header or footer.

Length restrictions

You can enter as many characters as you want into the Header and Footer text boxes. However, Works will print only as much of the header or footer as will fit between the left and right margins of the page. If the header or footer is too long to fit between the margins, Works will cut off the portion that extends beyond the right margin.

Things get a little complicated when you use alignment codes within your headers and footers. As a general rule, Works prints all of the left-aligned portion of a header or footer before it prints the centered portion. If the left-aligned portion encroaches on the space that should be occupied by the centered portion, Works will shift the centered portion to the right. Consequently, it won't be centered. Similarly, Works prints the centered portion in its entirety before it prints any of the right-aligned portion. If the centered portion encroaches on the space that should be occupied by the right-aligned portion, Works will truncate the right-aligned portion. Overall, if the combined length of the parts of a header or footer is greater than the distance between the margins, Works will cut the right-aligned portion first, followed by the centered portion, then the left-aligned portion.

Although Works will print as many characters of the left-aligned and centered portions of a header or footer as will fit between the margins, it will print only as much of the right-aligned portion as will fit in half of that width. For example, if the page dimension and margin settings in the Page Setup & Margins dialog box allow a maximum of 60 characters to fit across a page, Works will never print more than 30 characters of the right-aligned portion of a header or footer—even if the space to the left of that portion is empty.

Other header and footer settings
▶WORKS 2◀

▶In addition to letting you specify the contents of the Header and Footer text boxes, Works allows you to control the printing of the header and/or footer on the first page, and where it should position the header and footer within the top and bottom margins. (We discussed the positioning of headers and footers earlier in the section called "Header and Footer Settings.")

The No Header on 1st Page and No Footer on 1st Page check boxes allow you to control the printing of the Header and Footer text boxes on the first page of a printed document. If you activate the No Header on 1st Page check box, however, Works will not print a header on the first page. Similarly, if you activate the No Footer on 1st Page check box, Works will not print a footer on the first page. You can change the state of these boxes in ways we presented in Chapter 1.

The phrase *1st Page* in the names of these boxes refers to the first page that Works would print if you didn't restrict it to printing certain pages (a concept we'll discuss later). If the 1st Page Number text box in the Page Setup & Margins dialog box contains the number 1, the No Header on 1st Page and No Footer on 1st Page check boxes in the Headers & Footers dialog box will control the printing of headers and footers on the page on which Works will print the number 1. If the 1st Page Number text box contains the number 27, however, the No Header on 1st Page and No Footer on 1st Page check boxes will control the printing of headers and footers on the page on which Works will print the number 27.

When you finish your work in the Headers & Footers dialog box, press <OK> or [Enter] to lock in your settings.◄

►The Printer Setup... command lets you specify which printer you will be using, to which port it is connected, and whether you want Works to pause after printing each page.

When you pull down the Print menu and select the Printer Setup... command, Works will display a dialog box like the one shown in Figure 3-5. As you can see, this box contains three list boxes and two option boxes. The Printers list box lets you select the printer to which you want to print; the Model list box displays different models of the printer type you chose in the Printers list box; the Graphics list box presents a choice of dots-per-inch display if a choice is available for the printer you selected; the Page Feed option box allows you to specify whether you are using continuous-feed paper or individual sheets; and the Connect To option box allows you to specify your printer port.◄

THE PRINTER SETUP... COMMAND
►WORKS 2◄

Figure 3-5

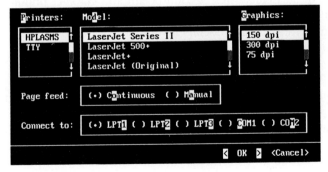

The Printer Setup dialog box lets you define printer settings.

The Printers list box lists the name of every printer you selected in the setup process; that is, every text printer whose driver file is stored in the directory containing your Works program files. If you selected only one printer during the setup process, the name of that printer, plus the generic TTY, will appear in the Printers list box. If you selected two or more printers, the names of those printers

Choosing a printer

will appear in that box, arranged in alphabetical order. In either case, the name of the printer you specified as the default printer will be highlighted. If you want to use that printer, you don't need to do a thing. If you want to use a different printer, you must select its name from the list. The printer whose name is highlighted when you choose <OK> is the one Works will assume you are using.

The text printer driver files listed in the Printers list box contain instructions that tell Works how to communicate with specific printers. Different printers expect different codes to set their margins, invoke special print attributes, and so forth. Unless you select the name of the printer to which you will be printing, Works will send codes that probably won't make any sense to your printer. Consequently, the printed result might not appear the way you would expect. To keep this from happening, always choose the name of the printer to which you will be printing.

▶WORKS 2◀

▶The Model list box enables you to specify which printer model you will use to print your documents. The model you choose will let Works match the configuration settings in your printer so that your documents will appear exactly as you want. In Figure 3-5, you'll notice that the printer HPLASMSL offers a number of models you can choose. You should select the model that matches the actual printer you'll use to print your document. If the printer you use is a LaserJet Series II, you would select that option for optimum results.

The Graphics list box allows you to specify how fine a resolution you want when you print your documents. Depending on the way you will use your print-outs, you can vary the type of resolution you want those documents to display. The Graphics list box in Figure 3-5 shows three choices of dots-per-inch settings. A higher number indicates greater resolution in chart and graphics printing. A lower number indicates a lower resolution. You might use the lower numbers when you are printing draft-quality documents for editing purposes. Also, the lower quality settings will save toner in your printer.◀

Choosing manual or continuous page feed

The Page Feed option box allows you to specify whether Works should pause for you to insert a new sheet of paper after it prints each page. If you are printing on continuous-feed (form-feed) paper, choose Continuous. That way, Works will advance to the next page and continue printing automatically. If you are printing on single sheets of paper ("cut-sheets") choose Manual instead. If the Manual setting is active, Works will pause after it prints each page.

Choosing a connection

In the Connect To option box, you can specify the port to which your printer is connected. This box always contains five options: LPT1, LPT2, LPT3, COM1, and COM2. The first three choices identify parallel ports; the final two choices identify serial ports.

The port that is activated when you choose <OK> is the one through which Works will print. Initially, the default port (the one you selected when you ran the Setup program) will be highlighted. If the printer specified in the Printers list box is attached to that port, you don't need to do a thing. If the printer is attached to a different port, you should select that port.

Saving the Printer
Setup settings

Unlike the Page Setup & Margins settings, the settings in the Printer Setup dialog box do not apply only to the document from which you issue the Printer Setup... command. Instead, those settings automatically apply to every document you subsequently print until you change them again.

Since the Printer Setup settings do not apply to any document in particular, Works does not save those settings in your document files. Instead, it saves those settings in the WORKS.INI file—the same file in which it saves other general Works settings, such as those in the Works Settings dialog box. It is important to note that Works does not save these settings in the WORKS.INI file as soon as you change them—it waits until you next use the Exit Works command to leave Works.

PRINTING
DOCUMENTS

Once you have set your margins, headers, and footers, and have chosen a printer, a port, and a page-feed option, you are ready to print the current document. To do this, you must issue the Print... command—the first command on any Print menu. When you pull down the Print menu and select this command, Works will display a Print dialog box like the one shown in Figure 3-6.

Figure 3-6

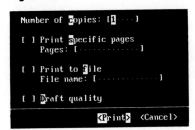

This is the Print dialog box for a word processor document.

The elements in the Print dialog box let you specify how many copies of a document you want Works to print, which pages to print, whether to print to a printer or a file, respectively, and if you want to print a draft-quality document. After you adjust these settings, you must choose the <Print> button, which tells Works to print the current document according to the settings in the Page Setup & Margins, Headers & Footers, Printer Setup, and Print dialog boxes.

Specifying the
number of copies

The Number of Copies text box lets you specify how many copies of the document you want Works to print. The default value in this box, 1, tells Works to print a single copy. If you want to print more than one copy, you must change this entry. For example, if you wanted to print two copies, you would replace the value 1 with the value 2. Works can print as few as one copy or as many as 32,767 with a single Print… command.

When Works prints multiple copies of a document, it prints one complete copy before it begins the next. It doesn't print several copies of the first page, then several copies of the second page, and so forth. When Works finishes printing, you'll have as many copies as you specified.

Printing specific pages

The Print Specific Pages check box and the related Pages text box work together to determine if Works will print an entire report or only certain pages of it. If the Print Specific Pages check box is empty (meaning that it is off), Works will print the entire document. If the Print Specific Pages check box contains an X (meaning that it is on), Works will print only the pages specified in the Pages text box.

If you want Works to print only specific pages of a document, you must do two things. First, you must turn on the Print Specific Pages check box. Then, you must move the cursor to the Pages text box and enter the numbers of the pages you want Works to print. Since Works won't allow you to access the Pages text box unless the Print Specific Pages check box is on, you must perform these two tasks in this order.

The Pages text box gives you a great deal of flexibility in selecting the pages you want to print. If you want to print a single page, you enter the number of that page. For example, if you want to print only page 7, you would type the value 7. If you want to print several non-adjacent pages, you must separate the numbers of those pages by commas. That is, if you want to print pages 1, 3, 5, and 7, you would type 1,3,5,7 into the Pages text box. If you want to print some adjacent pages, you should separate the numbers of the first and last pages in the group with either a hyphen or a colon. For example, if you want to print pages 3, 4, 5, 6, and 7, you would type either 3-7 or 3:7 into the Pages text box.

You can combine references to individual pages and ranges of adjacent pages into a single Pages text box. To do this, simply include the range reference with the references to single pages, separating them by commas. For example, the entry 1, 3, 5-9, 26 would instruct Works to print pages 1, 3, 5, 6, 7, 8, 9, and 26.

In some cases, you'll want Works to start printing at a page other than the first page of a document and continue printing all the way to the end. To do this, you should enter into the Pages text box a range that begins with the first page you want to print and ends with a page number greater than (or equal to) the final page of the document. For example, to print from page 3 through the end of a 50-page document, you could enter 3-50, 3-100, 3-1000, or even 3-10000 into the Pages text box. To avoid seeing an alert box, don't use a page number greater than 32767 as the high value.

No Works document can have fewer than one or more than 32,767 pages. If you specify a number outside of this range (less than or equal to 0, greater than or equal to 32,768), then choose <Print>, Works will present an alert box. As soon as you choose <OK> from this box, Works will return you to the Pages text box and allow you to specify a new page. If you specify a page that is within these limits but exceeds the length of the current document, Works cannot print the page. For example, if you specify page 15 within the Pages text box for a document that is only 12 pages long, Works cannot print that page.

Specifying
non-existent pages

The 1st Page Number setting in the Page Setup & Margins dialog box affects the entries you make into the Pages text box. The page numbers you enter into the Pages text box correspond to the numbers that Works prints (or would print) on each page. If you enter a number other than 1 into the 1st Page Number text box in the Page Setup & Margins dialog box, you'll need to change the settings in the Pages text box to match.

Interactions with
the 1st Page
Number setting

Since the Print Specific Pages check box controls whether Works pays attention to the entries in the Pages text box, you can alternate between printing an entire report and printing only the pages specified in the Pages text box simply by turning the Print Specific Pages check box off and on. However, be careful not to turn on the Print Specific Pages check box while leaving the Pages text box empty. If you do, Works won't print anything when you choose <Print>.

Alternating between
printing specific
pages and printing
the entire document

The Print to File check box and the File Name text box allow you to print the current document to a file rather than to your printer. If the Print to File check box is off, Works will print the document to the printer specified in the Printer Setup dialog box. If the Print to File check box is on, Works will save the print-out to the file name in the File Name text box instead. Works will save the print-out in that file in the same form as it would have printed it to disk, including headers, footers, margins, tabs, print attributes, and so forth.

Printing to a file

Much like printing specific pages, printing to a file is a two-step process. First, you must turn on the Print to File check box. Then, you must move the cursor to the File Name text box and enter the name of the file in which you want to save the print-out. Like any file name, the name you specify can contain up to eight characters, plus an extension of up to three letters.

If, when you choose <Print> to begin printing, you specify an invalid file name or leave the File Name text box empty, Works will display an alert box. When you acknowledge the message in this box by choosing <OK>, Works will return you to the File Name text box and let you enter an alternative name.

If you choose <Print> while the File Name text box contains the name of an existing file, Works will ask if you want to overwrite that file. If you choose <Yes>,

Works will print the document on top of the file with that name. If you choose <No>, Works will return you to the File Name text box and allow you to specify a different name.

Unless you also enter drive/directory information into the File Name text box, Works will save the file into the current default directory. For more on the operations of the File Name text box and the concept of a default directory, see the section entitled "Saving a File for the First Time" in Chapter 2.

Once you have printed a document to disk, you can print it to a printer later by using DOS's Print or Type commands. For instructions on how to use these commands to print a file, see your DOS reference manual.

Other print options

The Print dialog box options we've just described are common to the Print... commands in each Works environment. This dialog box includes one or more options that depend on the particular environment in which you're working. In the word processor environment, the Print dialog box includes a Draft Quality option for quicker printing. The spreadsheet environment adds a Print Row and Column Labels option to the Print dialog box. When you print a chart, the Print dialog box contains a Slow Pen Speed option for higher-quality printing. Finally, the Print dialog box in the database environment varies greatly among the various views of a database: Form, List, and Record. We'll address these other print options when we discuss printing other types of documents.

Commanding Works to print

Once you have specified the correct print settings, you are ready to print your document. To do this, turn on the printer specified in the Printer Setup dialog box, make sure it is connected to the designated port, align the paper within the printer, then issue the Print... command and choose <Print>.

When you do this, Works will print the document, using the margins and the headers and footers you specified. It will print the pages you typed in the Pages text box of the Print dialog box, and print as many copies as you specified. If you have commanded it to print to a file, Works will direct the print-out to the file you specified instead of to the printer selected in the Printer Setup dialog box.

Cancelling printing

Unless you command it to stop, Works will continue printing until it prints the entire document (or, if you instruct it to print only selected pages, until it prints those pages). If you want to pause or stop the printing process before Works is done, you can press the [Esc] key. When you do this, Works will stop sending information to the printer and present the dialog box shown in Figure 3-7. (If your printer has a buffer, it will not stop printing immediately. Instead, it will continue printing until it empties the buffer of information that Works had sent to it previously.)

If you choose <OK> in response to Works' *Printing interrupted: continue printing?* prompt, Works will resume printing exactly where it left off. If you choose <Cancel>, however, Works will advance the paper to the top of the next page, then cancel the Print... command.

Figure 3-7

You'll see this dialog box if you press the [Esc] key while Works is printing a document.

Unlike the settings in the Page Setup & Margins, Headers & Footers, and Printer Setup dialog boxes, the settings in the Print dialog box are not saved either with the document in which you specify them or in the WORKS.INI file. In fact, Works resets the Number of Copies setting to 1, turns off the Print to File setting, and clears the File Name text box when you close the document. Consequently, you'll have to respecify these settings each time you open the document.

However, as long as that document is open in Works, active or not, Works retains the settings in the Number of Copies text box, the Print Specific Pages check box, and the Pages text box. These settings reappear when you activate the document and reissue the Print... command for that document. Later, if you need to, you can alter these settings. When you close the document, Works will reset the Print dialog box settings to their defaults.

Saving the Print settings

▶Works 2 includes a Preview... command that lets you see what your document will look like when it is printed. This Works feature helps you fine-tune the settings of your document before you print it. Figure 3-8 shows the Preview dialog box for the word processor environment.

PREVIEWING DOCUMENTS
▶WORKS 2◀

Figure 3-8

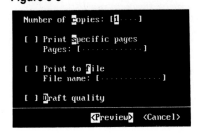

This is the Preview dialog box for a word processor document.

The Preview dialog box is identical to the Print dialog box except for one button: A <Preview> button replaces the <Print> button. When you press the <Preview> button in this dialog box, Works will display a representation of your printed document with correct margin settings, all fonts and styles visible, and any text or charts added from other Works documents shown in their relative printed sizes. For example, suppose you want to print a spreadsheet named BUDGET.WKS, but you want to check the formats, margins, and print settings before you print. You simply choose the Preview… command from the Print menu, then press the <Preview> button or press [Enter]. Figure 3-9 shows this spreadsheet in Preview mode. As you can see, Works gives you a clear indication of how it will arrange your data on the printed page.

Figure 3-9

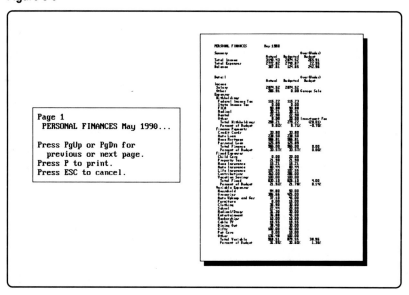

This figure shows a spreadsheet document in Preview mode.

To the left of the preview page, Works displays an information box with the page number and the first line of the document, plus instructions on how to move through the Preview mode, print from it, or leave it. To scan through the entire document, merely press [Pg Up] or [Pg Dn]. When your document looks the way you want it to, you can press *P* to print it directly from Preview mode. If you discover a mistake in your document's settings, you can leave Preview mode by pressing [Esc]. When you do, Works will redisplay your document in its regular window so that you can correct the error.◄

PAGE BREAKS
►WORKS 2◄

►Works inserts page breaks to tell your printer where to begin a new page when it's printing your document. Works sets page breaks automatically when, according to your margin settings, you've entered enough text to fill the page. Works then alters those page breaks when you add or delete text.

As we said at the beginning of this chapter, the Insert Page Break command appears on the Print menu in the word processor, spreadsheet, and database environments. This command allows you to set your own page break. When you use the Insert Page Break command to add a manual page break, Works will readjust the automatic page breaks that follow. If you want to delete a manual page break after you've added one, place the cursor at the beginning of the page break and press [Delete].

We'll further discuss page breaks and the uses of the Insert Page Break command when we discuss printing and handling page breaks in each environment.◄

MORE ABOUT PRINTING

The basics of printing are the same for all Works documents. However, the actual process of printing may involve additional steps, depending on the document's type. For example, before you print a word processor document, you may select various typefaces and styles. In a spreadsheet document, you need to tell Works what portion of the spreadsheet to print. In a database document, you can select the records you want to print. As we mentioned earlier, we'll discuss the specifics of printing within each type of document in the appropriate sections of this book.

CONCLUSION

In this chapter, we demonstrated the basic techniques required to print any Works document. First, we showed you how to use the Page Setup & Margins... command to specify the margin and page dimension settings. Next, we discussed the intricacies of the Headers & Footers… command. Then, we showed you how to use the Printer Setup... command to specify a printer, a port, and a type of page feed (continuous or manual). Finally, we explained how you can use the Print… command to print the document, either to a printer or to disk.

In Chapters 1 through 3, we have shown you a number of "universal" Works skills—techniques that you will use in every type of Works document. In the remaining chapters of this book, we will explore the different types of Works documents in detail. In each of the chapters, we'll assume that you have a working knowledge of the basic skills we just explained to you. For example, we won't explain in detail how to issue a command, choose an item from a list box, open a file, or print a document; we'll simply tell you to use each of those skills. If you need a refresher on any of these skills, please refer to the appropriate sections in Chapters 1 through 3.

Word Processing Basics 4

*P*eople use personal computers more for word processing than for any other purpose. Word processing is the electronic creation and composition of documents such as memos, letters, and reports. Works' word processor environment is designed for word processing. Within the word processor environment, you can compose almost any type of document. Using the commands available within this environment, you can edit, style, and format what you have written. You can copy and move whole blocks of text from one part of a document to another, search for occurrences of certain characters, words, or phrases and, if you want, replace them. You can even merge graphs into a word processor document, compose form letters and mailing labels that draw information from a database, and copy information from a communication document.

In this chapter, we'll introduce Works' word processing powers. First, we'll review the procedure for creating and opening word processor documents. Then, we'll show you how to enter text, move the cursor, and do some simple editing. Next, we'll show you how to select text and how to replace and delete blocks of characters. Finally, we'll show you how to save and print your documents.

To use Works' word processing capabilities, you must either create a new word processor document or open an existing one. As you might expect, the procedure for creating and opening word processor documents is similar to that for creating and opening any other type of Works document. To create a new word processor document, you must pull down the File menu, select the Create New File... command, then choose the New Word Processor option from the Create New File dialog box. To open an existing word processor document in Works, you must pull down the File menu, select the Open Existing File... command, and select the file you want to open from the Open Existing File dialog box. For more on creating and opening documents, refer to Chapter 2.

CREATING AND OPENING WORD PROCESSOR DOCUMENTS

**A TOUR OF A
WORD PROCESSOR
DOCUMENT**

Figure 4-1 shows a new word processor document. This screen includes the elements you'll see when any Works document is active: the menu bar, the message line, the status line, and a window with all of its elements (title bar, scroll bars, work area, and so on).

Figure 4-1

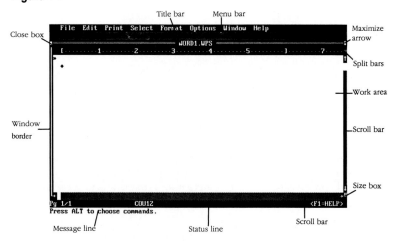

Word processor documents contain the features common to other Works' documents.

The menu bar

The menu bar for a word processor document lists the names of the menus that are available in that environment. These menus contain commands that allow you to manipulate information. Like all types of Works documents, word processor documents have a File menu, a Window menu, and a Help menu. As you learned in Chapter 2, the commands on the File menu allow you to create, save, and open documents. As you learned in Chapters 1 and 2, the commands on the Window menu allow you to use the Windows features and activate other open documents without using a mouse. The Help menu allows you to access Works' Help feature and on-line tutorial. Word processor documents also have five other menus: Edit, Print, Select, Format, and Options. We'll explain what the commands on those menus do in this chapter and the two that follow.

The work area

The work area of a word processor document is where you compose your text. The work area of a new word processor document will not contain any text. However, the work area of any word processor document contains a number of useful elements: a ruler, a page-break marker, an end-of-paragraph marker, an end-of-document marker, and a cursor. Figure 4-2 identifies these elements.

Figure 4-2

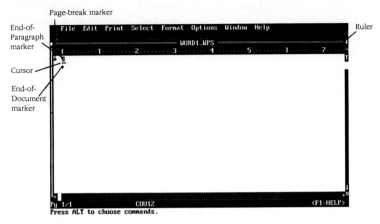

The work area of a word processor document contains a number of useful elements.

The flashing horizontal bar in the work area of a word processor document is the cursor. The cursor marks Works' point of concentration within the document. As you enter text, the characters you type will appear at the cursor, and the cursor will move to the right. When you press the [Delete] key, Works will delete the character above the cursor, and pull any following characters to the left. If you want, you can expand the cursor so that it highlights a block of characters. We'll show you how to do these things later in this chapter.

The cursor

The ruler is the horizontal scale that appears at the top of the work area, immediately below the title bar. This structure provides information about the line length and tab stops for a document. As you can see in Figures 4-1 and 4-2, the ruler is marked incrementally in inches.

The ruler

The 0 point on the ruler marks the left edge of the document. When you enter the document, Works displays a left bracket character ([) at this point. This character marks the left edge of the current paragraph. As we'll explain later, you can indent a paragraph relative to the rest of a document. When you do this, Works will shift the left bracket to the right.

Similarly, Works uses a right bracket character (]) to mark the right edge of the current paragraph. Unless you have commanded Works to indent the right edge of the current paragraph (as we'll show you how to do in Chapter 5), this bracket will mark the right edge of the document. The amount of space between the left bracket and the right bracket is the maximum length of the lines in the current paragraph.

Works allows you to set tab stops for each of the paragraphs in a document. When you do, Works will display special symbols on the ruler to mark the positions of those stops. However, Works does not display the position of the default tab stops for a document (initially, every $1/_2$ inch). We'll talk about tabs in detail in Chapter 5.

Although, Works displays the ruler each time you create a new document or open an existing one, you can turn off the display of the ruler once the document is in view. To do this, simply pull down the Options menu and choose the Show Ruler command. When you do this, Works will remove the ruler from the screen. To bring the ruler back, simply select the Show Ruler command again.

The page-break marker

Works uses a >> icon at the left edge of the work area to mark the page breaks in a document. One of these characters will appear to the left of any line that will be the first line on a page when you print the document. As you can see in Figure 4-2, this symbol appears to the left of the first line of the document. As you create a document, Works repaginates it automatically, placing additional page-break markers where they belong. If you want, however, you can turn off Works' automatic pagination feature. You also can insert "manual" page breaks into a document. We'll show you how to do these things in Chapter 6.

The end-of-document marker

Works uses a small solid diamond (◆) to mark the end of a document. This symbol—the end-of-document marker—appears after the final character in a document. You cannot delete, move, or copy the end-of-document marker, or type any text below it or to its right.

Other markers

Three other types of markers will normally appear in your word processor documents: end-of-paragraph markers, space markers, and tab markers. Works uses the ¶ symbol to mark the end of each paragraph in a document. This character will appear whenever you press the [Enter] key. Works uses a dot (·) to mark each occurrence of a space within a document. Whenever you press the [Spacebar], one of these dots will appear. Works uses a thin right arrow (→) to mark the occurrence of each tab stop in a document. Each time you press the [Tab] key, one of these symbols will appear.

For example, Figure 4-3 shows a word processor document into which we've entered some text, including spaces, carriage returns, and tabs. As you can see, Works has used special markers to represent these characters. Of course, these characters show up only on the screen of your computer; they do not appear in a printed document.

Figure 4-3

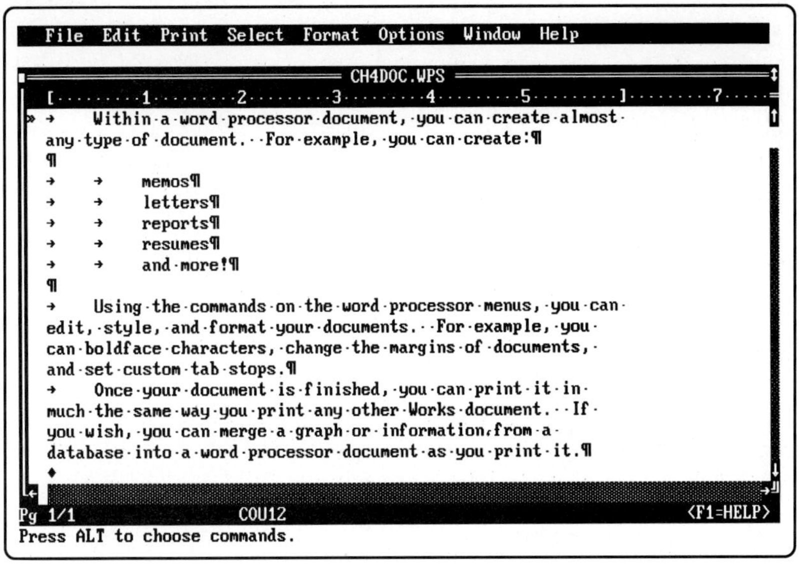

```
 File  Edit  Print  Select  Format  Options  Window  Help

================================= CH4DOC.WPS =================================
  [·········1·········2·········3·········4·········5·········]·········7·····
» →     Within·a·word·processor·document,·you·can·create·almost·
 any·type·of·document.··For·example,·you·can·create:¶
 ¶
 →      →    memos¶
 →      →    letters¶
 →      →    reports¶
 →      →    resumes¶
 →      →    and·more!¶
 ¶
 →      Using·the·commands·on·the·word·processor·menus,·you·can·
 edit,·style,·and·format·your·documents.··For·example,·you·
 can·boldface·characters,·change·the·margins·of·documents,·
 and·set·custom·tab·stops.¶
 →      Once·your·document·is·finished,·you·can·print·it·in·
 much·the·same·way·you·print·any·other·Works·document.··If·
 you·wish,·you·can·merge·a·graph·or·information·from·a·
 database·into·a·word·processor·document·as·you·print·it.¶
       ♦

Pg 1/1                   COU12                          <F1=HELP>
Press ALT to choose commands.
```

Works uses special symbols to mark paragraphs, spaces, and tab stops in a word processor document.

The Show All Characters command on the Options menu allows you to control whether Works displays the end-of-paragraph, space, and tab markers in a document. When this option is on, Works will display these markers on the screen, as shown in Figure 4-3. If you turn it off, however, Works will hide them, as shown in Figure 4-4 on the following page. The Show All Characters command is a toggle command. If the markers are visible, selecting the Show All Characters command will hide them. If these special characters are hidden, selecting the Show All Characters command will reveal them. If you pull down the Options menu while these special characters are visible, a dot will appear to the left of the Show All Characters command, indicating that the option is on.

Unlike the Show Ruler command, the Show All Characters command doesn't affect just the document from which you issue it. Turning off the Show All Characters command hides the special symbols in every word processor document you subsequently open, create, or activate.

When you exit Works, Works saves the current Show All Characters command (as well as a number of other settings) in a special file named WORKS.INI. The settings saved in this file control whether the Show All Characters command will be on or off when you next load Works.

The Show All
Characters command

Figure 4-4

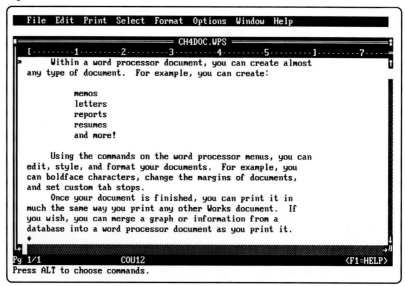

Turning off the Show All Characters command hides the end-of-para-graph, space, and tab markers in a document.

Actually, the Show All Characters command controls the display of more than the end-of-paragraph, space, and tab markers—it also turns the display of symbols for end-of-line characters and optional hyphens on and off. We'll talk about these special characters in Chapter 6. However, the Show All Characters command does not affect the display of page-break and end-of-document markers. For example, as you can see in Figure 4-4, the page-break and end-of-document markers remain visible even when the Show All Characters command is off.

The status line

Works uses the status line in the word processor environment to display a number of important pieces of information about the current word processor document. At the left edge of the status line, Works displays the number of the page on which the cursor is positioned and the number of pages in the document. For example, as we show in Figure 4-4, the message *Pg 1/1* at the left edge of the status line in the document indicates that the cursor is on the first page of a one-page document. In a larger document, you might see a notation like *Pg 4/12*. This notation tells you that the cursor is positioned on the fourth page of a 12-page document.

▶WORKS 2◀

▶Toward the middle of the status line, you'll see an abbreviation that represents the font and font size of the text where the cursor is postioned. The text default is 12-point Courier, abbreviated *COU12*. Whenever you change the font or size of your text, Works will display your current choice on the status line. For example, if the cursor is on a character to which you have assigned the 8-point Line Printer font, Works will display *LIN8* on the status line. Finally, the <F1=HELP> hot key, which we discussed in Chapter 1, appears at the right end of the status line.◄

Works also uses the status line for other purposes. First, it uses the line to display indicators that tell you an editing command is in progress. For example, the word *MOVE* or *COPY* will appear just to the right of the mid-point on the status line while you are moving or copying text within the document. Second, Works displays the abbreviation *EXT* on the status line when it is in the Extend mode. Third, Works displays indicators to the left of the font information on the status line that reveal what print attributes (such as *B*, *I*, and *U* for boldface, italic, and underline type) are assigned to the characters currently marked by the cursor. We'll explain these uses of the status line in detail later in this chapter and in the two that follow.

The message line

The line immediately below the status line is the message line. On this line, Works displays helpful reminders about the effects of different commands as well as notes that will guide you through multi-step commands. For example, Works will display the message *Select new location and press ENTER. Press ESC to cancel.* on the message line when you issue the Move or Copy command. This message tells you what you need to do to complete the command.

ENTERING TEXT

Once you create or open a word processor document, you can begin entering text into it. Each character you type will appear at the position of the cursor. After Works enters a character into the document, it moves the cursor one space to the right. For example, Figure 4-5 on the next page shows the result of typing the phrase *Now is the time* into a new word processor document. As you can see, the phrase now appears on the first line of the document, and the cursor appears immediately to the right of the *e* in *time*—the last character you typed.

If the cursor reaches the end of a line as you are typing, Works will automatically place the cursor at the beginning of the next line. As we mentioned earlier, the end of a line is indicated by the position of the right bracket (]) on the ruler. If you are in the middle of typing a word when the cursor reaches the right edge of the document, Works will push that entire word to the next line. For example, Figure 4-6 on the following page shows the result of typing the remainder of the sentence *Now is the time for all good men to come to the aid of their country.* into the document shown in Figure 4-5. Since the entire word *country* will not fit onto the first line of the document, Works pushes it down onto the second line.

Figure 4-5

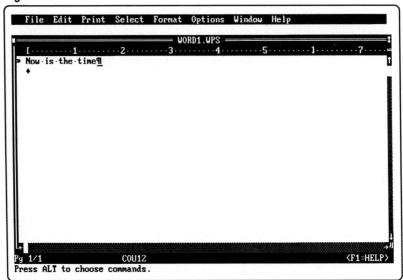

When you type a character, Works will enter that character at the position of the cursor and move the cursor one space to the right.

Figure 4-6

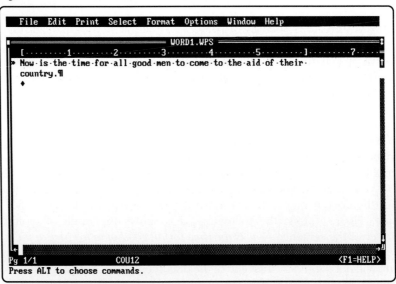

When the cursor reaches the end of a line, Works automatically wraps it to the beginning of the next line.

If you want Works to break a word between lines (that is, to leave part of it on one line and bump the remainder of it onto the next line), you must manually type a hyphen (-) where you want the word to be split. If the portion to the left of the hyphen and the hyphen will fit on the current line, Works will split the word onto two lines. If not, Works will push the entire word (including the hyphen) onto the next line. We'll talk more about hyphens in Chapter 6.

Since Works wraps text automatically, there's no need to press the [Enter] key at the end of each line. In fact, you shouldn't press the [Enter] key except at the end of each paragraph. When you press the [Enter] key, Works places an end-of-paragraph marker (¶) in the text at the position of the cursor and moves the cursor to the beginning of the next line. Since this symbol marks the end of a paragraph, Works won't wrap text past that point. To insert a blank line into a document, you can press the [Enter] key twice. However, we'll show you a better way to add spacing between paragraphs in Chapter 5.

Word processor documents can (and usually will) contain more text than can be displayed on the screen at one time. If you type a character or press [Enter] while the cursor is positioned on the last line of the screen, Works will scroll a new part of the document into view. Specifically, it will scroll the top half of the lines on the screen out of view above the work area and scroll an equal number of lines into view from below the work area.

If you make a mistake as you're entering text, you can press the [Backspace] key to back up the cursor and delete characters, one at a time. Each time you press the [Backspace] key, Works will erase a single character to the left of the cursor. For example, suppose you mistakenly typed *countre* instead of *country.* If the cursor is to the right of the letter *e* (as it would be if you just typed that letter), you can delete the *e* by pressing [Backspace]. Then, you can complete the word by typing a *y.* If the cursor is not to the right of the character you want to delete, you must move it into position before you press [Backspace]. We'll show you how to move the cursor next.

MOVING THE CURSOR

After you've entered some text into a document, you can move the cursor within it. Since Works inserts and deletes characters at the position of the cursor, you'll need to move the cursor in order to edit a document.

The way you move the cursor around within a word processor document depends on whether you are using Works with a mouse. If you do have a mouse, you can use either these keys or the scroll bars to move the cursor around a document. If not, you must use the cursor-movement keys.

Using the cursor-movement keys

The cursor-movement keys include the four arrow keys (→, ←, ↑, and ↓), the [End] key, the [Home] key, the [Pg Up] and [Pg Dn] keys, and combinations of the [Ctrl] key and these keys.

Moving the cursor character by character

The ← and → keys move the cursor to the left or right one character at a time. Holding down either key moves the cursor continuously to the left or right. If you press the → key when the cursor reaches the end of a line, Works will wrap the cursor to the beginning of the next line. Similarly, if you press the ← key when the cursor is under the first character of a line, Works will wrap the cursor up to the end of the previous line. Works will beep but will not move the cursor if you press ← while the cursor is under the first character of a document or if you press → while the cursor is on the last character of a document.

Moving the cursor line by line

Pressing the ↑ and ↓ keys moves the cursor up and down through a word processor document one line at a time. Pressing the ↑ key once moves the cursor up one line; pressing the ↓ key moves the cursor down one line. If you hold down either key, the cursor will move continuously in the indicated direction. If you press the ↓ key while the cursor is on the last line of text that's visible on the screen, but that line is not the last line of the document, Works will scroll the next line into view from beyond the bottom border of the work area and place the cursor in it. Similarly, if you press the ↑ key while the cursor is on the first line of text that's visible on the screen, but that line is not the first line of the document, Works will scroll the next line into view from beyond the top border of the work area and place the cursor in it. Works will beep but not move the cursor if you press the ↑ key while the cursor is on the first line of a document or if you press the ↓ key while the cursor is on the last line of a document.

If the line to which you are moving the cursor has a character in the same position on the line (that is, column) as the character on which it is currently positioned, Works will move the cursor straight up and down the document. If the line to which you are moving the cursor ends to the left of the column in which it is situated, however, Works will move the cursor to the rightmost character of that line. If you continue to move the cursor vertically, it will return to the original column as soon as it encounters a line that has a character in that column. For example, if the cursor is on the letter *c* in the word *commands* on the first line of the second paragraph of the document shown in Figure 4-7, pressing ↑ once will move the cursor to the ¶ character on the line above—the rightmost character of that line. Pressing ↑ again will move the cursor back to the original column—to the letter *o* in the word *more* on the last line of the first paragraph.

Works will continue to remember the column that the cursor was in when you started pressing the ↑ and ↓ keys until you press a key other than ↑, ↓, [Pg Up], or [Pg Dn]. We'll explain what the [Pg Up] and [Pg Dn] keys do in a few pages.

Moving the cursor word by word

You can use the → and ← keys in combination with the [Ctrl] key to move the cursor through a document one word at a time. If you hold down the [Ctrl] key and press →, Works will move the cursor to the first character of the next word in the document. For example, if the cursor is positioned anywhere in the word *processor* on the first line of the second "real" paragraph of the document shown in Figure 4-7, Works will move the cursor to the *m* in *menus* when you press [Ctrl]] If you press the ← key while holding down the [Ctrl] key, Works will move the cursor to the next first character of a word. For example, if the cursor is on the *p* in the word *processor*, Works will move the cursor to the *w* in *word* when you press [Ctrl]←. (If the cursor is on another letter in the word *processor*, Works will move the cursor to the *p* in that same word.)

Figure 4-7

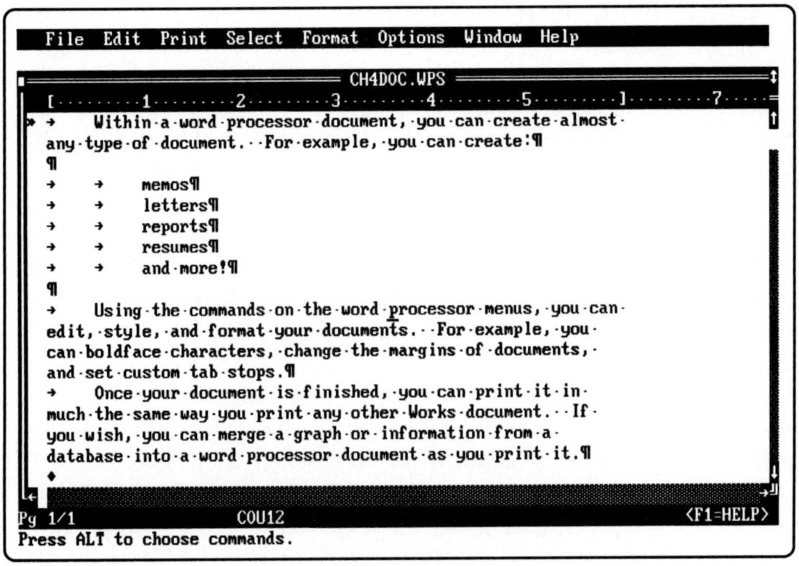

```
 File  Edit  Print  Select  Format  Options  Window  Help

=================== CH4DOC.WPS ===================
[·······1········2·······3·······4·······5········]·······7····
→    Within·a·word·processor·document,·you·can·create·almost·
any·type·of·document.···For·example,·you·can·create:¶
¶
→      →     memos¶
→      →     letters¶
→      →     reports¶
→      →     resumes¶
→      →     and·more!¶
¶
→    Using·the·commands·on·the·word·processor·menus,·you·can·
edit,·style,·and·format·your·documents.···For·example,·you·
can·boldface·characters,·change·the·margins·of·documents,·
and·set·custom·tab·stops.¶
→    Once·your·document·is·finished,·you·can·print·it·in·
much·the·same·way·you·print·any·other·Works·document.···If·
you·wish,·you·can·merge·a·graph·or·information·from·a·
database·into·a·word·processor·document·as·you·print·it.¶
◆

Pg 1/1              COU12                      <F1=HELP>
Press ALT to choose commands.
```

The cursor won't necessarily travel straight up and down as you use the ↑ and ↓ keys to move it through a document.

If you press [Ctrl]→ while the cursor is in the last word on a line, Works will move it to the first character in the first word on the next line. Similarly, if you press [Ctrl]← while the cursor is in the first word on a line, Works will move it to the first character of the last word on the previous line. If you press [Ctrl]→ while the cursor is in the last word of a document, or if you press [Ctrl]← while the cursor is in the first word of a document, Works will beep but will not move the cursor.

The [Home] and [End] keys move the cursor to the beginning and end of the current line, respectively. When you press [Home], Works will move the cursor to the first character on the current line. For example, if you press [Home] while the cursor is anywhere in the second line of the second paragraph of the document

Moving to the beginning or end of a line

shown in Figure 4-7, Works will move the cursor to the *e* in the word *edit* at the beginning of that line. When you press [End], Works will move the cursor to the right of the last character of the current line. For example, if the cursor is on the second line of the second paragraph of the document shown in Figure 4-7, Works will move it to the right of the space character at the end of that line when you press [End].

Moving the cursor paragraph by paragraph

The [Ctrl]↓ and [Ctrl]↑ key combinations move the cursor through a document paragraph by paragraph. If the cursor is anywhere other than in the last paragraph of a document, pressing [Ctrl]↓ will move the cursor to the first character in the next paragraph of the document. If the cursor is in the last paragraph of a document but not on the last character of that paragraph, Works will move it to the last character in that paragraph. If the cursor is already on the last character of the last paragraph, Works will simply beep.

The effect of the [Ctrl]↑ combination also depends on the current position of the cursor within a paragraph and document. If the cursor is on the first character of a paragraph other than the first paragraph in a document, pressing [Ctrl]↑ will move the cursor to the first character of the previous paragraph. If the cursor is on the first character of the first paragraph in a document, Works will simply beep. If the cursor is on a character other than the first one of a paragraph, Works will move the cursor to the first character of that paragraph when you press [Ctrl]↑.

Moving to the beginning or end of the screen

The [Ctrl][Pg Up] and [Ctrl][Pg Dn] key combinations move the cursor to the beginning and end of the text currently visible on the screen. For example, if you press the [Ctrl][Pg Up] combination while your screen looks like the one shown in Figure 4-7, Works will move the cursor to the tab stop (→) in the first line of the document. Pressing the [Ctrl][Pg Dn] combination moves the cursor to the first character in the final line visible on the screen. If you press [Ctrl][Pg Dn] while your screen looks like the one shown in Figure 4-7, Works will move the cursor to the *d* in the word *database* on the final line of the document.

Moving the cursor window by window

The [Pg Dn] and [Pg Up] keys allow you to scroll through a word processor document one screenful at a time. When you press [Pg Dn], Works will scroll a new screenful of text into view from below the bottom border of the work area. The line that was at the bottom of the screen before you pressed [Pg Dn] will appear at the top of the screen. When you press [Pg Up], Works will scroll a new screenful of the document into view from above the top border of the work area. The line that was at the top of the screen before you pressed [Pg Up] will appear at the bottom of the screen. In either case, the cursor will be in the same position relative to the top and bottom borders of the work area as it was before.

If you press the [Pg Dn] key while the final line of the document is visible on the screen, Works won't shift the document within the work area. However, Works will move the cursor to the last line. Similarly, Works won't shift the document if you press [Pg Up] while the first line of a document is visible on the screen. However, it will move the cursor to the first line.

If the line to which Works moves the cursor when you press the [Pg Up] or [Pg Dn] key has a character in the same column as the character on which the cursor is currently positioned, Works will move the cursor straight up and down the document. If the line to which you are moving the cursor ends to the left of the column in which the cursor is situated, however, Works will move the cursor to the rightmost character on that line. If you continue to move vertically, the cursor will return to its original column of movement as soon as it encounters a line that has a character in that column. Works will continue to remember this "default" column until you press a cursor-movement key other than ↑, ↓, [Pg Up], or [Pg Dn].

The [Ctrl][Home] and [Ctrl][End] key combinations move the cursor to the beginning and end of a document, respectively. When you hold down the [Ctrl] key and press [Home], Works will move the cursor to the leftmost character on the first line of the current document. If the first line of the document is not visible on the screen when you press this combination, Works will shift the first screenful of the document into view. When you hold down the [Ctrl] key and press [End], Works will move the cursor to the rightmost character on the last line of the document. If the last line of the document is not visible when you press this combination, Works will shift the final screenful of the document into view.

Moving to the beginning or end of the document

The Go To... command on the Select menu and the [Go To] key ([F5] on the IBM PC) allow you to move the cursor to the top of any page of a word processor document. When you pull down the Select menu and issue this command, Works will present a dialog box like the one shown in Figure 4-8.

The Go To... command

Figure 4-8

You can use the Go To dialog box to move quickly to a particular page in a document.

To move the cursor to a specific page of the document, simply type the number of that page into the Go To text box. For example, if you want Works to move the cursor to the fifth page of the document, type 5 into the Go To text box. (At this point, you have no use for the Names list box; we'll discuss it in Chapter 6.)

As soon as you choose <OK>, Works will move the cursor to the first character of the first line on the indicated page. If that line is not visible on the screen at the time, Works will shift the document so that the first line of the page you specify appears at the top of the work area.

Works repaginates word processor documents automatically as you work within them. The number of lines Works includes on each page of a word processor document is determined by the Top Margin and Bottom Margin settings in the Page Setup & Margins dialog box. We'll show you how to adjust these settings (and, therefore, vary the page length of a document) in Chapter 5.

Using a mouse

If you have a mouse, you can use some alternative techniques for moving around within a word processor document. (Of course, you also can use the keyboard techniques described above.) To move the cursor to any character that is visible on the screen, you can simply point to that character with the mouse pointer and click the left button on your mouse. When you do this, Works will move the cursor from its current position to the character on which you clicked.

If the character to which you want to move the cursor is not visible on the screen, you must scroll it into view before you can click it. To do this, you can use the scroll bars at the right and bottom edges of the screen.

The vertical scroll bar (the one along the right edge of the screen) allows you to shift the document up and down within the work area. If you click the arrow at the top of the vertical scroll bar, Works will bring a new line of the document into view from beyond the top border of the work area and push one line down beyond the bottom edge of the work area. If you click the arrow at the bottom of the vertical scroll bar, Works will bring a new line of the document into view from beyond the bottom border of the work area.

If you click the vertical scroll bar above the scroll box (the dark square within the scroll bar), Works will scroll a new screenful of the document into view from above the top border of the work area, just as it does when you press the [Pg Up] key. Similarly, if you click the vertical scroll bar below the scroll box, Works will scroll a new screenful of the document into view from below the bottom border of the work area, just as it does when you press the [Pg Dn] key.

Dragging the scroll box is another way to shift a word processor document within the work area of the screen. To drag this box, point to it with the mouse pointer, hold down the left button on your mouse, move the box up or down within the scroll bar, and release the mouse button. The position of the scroll box within the scroll bar indicates which portion of the document you will see. For example, if you drag the scroll box to the bottom of the scroll bar, you'll see the final screenful of the document when you release the mouse button.

You can use these three techniques in the horizontal scroll bar (the one along the bottom edge of the work area) to shift a document horizontally within the work area. (You'll need to use the horizontal scroll bar only if you've set up your document with a margin that's wider than the screen. In Chapter 5, we'll show you how to change the margins to suit various needs.) If you click the arrow at the right end of the horizontal scroll bar, Works will shift a new column into view from beyond the right edge of the work area. If you click the arrow at the left end of the horizontal scroll bar, Works will shift a new column into view from beyond the left edge of the work area. If you click the horizontal scroll bar to the right or left of the scroll box, Works will shift the document one screenful to the left or right. You also can shift a document to the right or left by dragging the scroll box within the horizontal scroll bar. Generally, you'll only want to shift a document to the right or left when that document is wider than the screen. For this to happen, you'll have to adjust the page size or the right and left margins of the document—subjects we'll cover in Chapter 5.

Unlike using the cursor keys, using the scroll bars does not move the cursor within a document; it merely brings a new portion of the document into view. Consequently, it's possible to move the portion of the document that contains the cursor off the screen. After using the scroll bars to shift a new portion of a document into view, therefore, you'll need to click a character within that portion to bring the cursor back into view. If you type a character while the cursor is off the screen, Works will shift the portion of the document that contains the cursor back into view when it inserts that character into the document.

SIMPLE EDITING

Now that you know how to position the cursor within a document, you can perform some simple editing tasks, like inserting and deleting characters. First, we'll show you how to insert characters. Then, we'll show you how to delete them one at a time. Later in this chapter, we'll show you how to delete blocks of adjacent characters with a single keystroke.

Inserting individual characters

Unless you're an exceptional typist, you'll occasionally leave letters out of words and words out of sentences as you are typing a document. To correct the document, you'll need to go back and insert the missing characters. To insert text within a document, simply move the cursor to the left of where you want to insert the characters, then type those characters. As you type characters, Works will insert them to the left of the cursor's position.

For example, suppose you want to insert the words *and women* between the words *men* and *to* in the sentence *Now is the time for all good men to come to the aid of their country.* To do this, you would move the cursor to the *t* in *to*, then type *and women* and press the [Spacebar] once. Since the cursor is under the *t* in *to*, Works will insert the characters you type between the *t* and the space that precedes it. The result is the sentence *Now is the time for all good men and women to come to the aid of their country.*

When you insert a character into a line of a document, Works will shift the characters that were on and to the right of the cursor one space to the right. If the final word on the line into which you made the insertion won't fit on that line after the insertion, Works will push it to the beginning of the next line. Works will continue to push words down as necessary until the entire paragraph is justified.

Deleting individual characters

Works also allows you to delete characters from a document. To delete a character, you can use either the [Backspace] or [Delete] key. When you press the [Backspace] key, Works deletes the character to the left of the one on which the cursor is positioned at the time. To delete a character with the [Backspace] key, therefore, you should position the cursor on the character to the right of the one you want to delete, then press [Backspace]. For example, to delete the extra *e* from the word *deleteing*, you would position the cursor on the *i*, then press [Backspace].

The [Delete] key provides a simpler way to delete a character from a document. When you press the [Delete] key, Works deletes the character above the cursor, instead of the character to its left. Consequently, you can delete a character by moving the cursor to it, then pressing [Delete]. For example, to delete the extra *e* from the word *deleteing*, you would position the cursor under that character, then press [Delete].

When you delete a character from a line of a document, Works shifts the characters that were originally to the right of the character one space to the left. If that shift makes enough room on the line from which you deleted the character to accommodate the first word on the next line of the paragraph, Works will pull that word up to the end of that line. Works will continue this process as required to rejustify the entire paragraph.

If you want, you can delete multiple characters by pressing the [Backspace] or [Delete] keys repeatedly, or holding down those keys. Alternatively, you can select the entire block of text you want to delete, then press [Delete] once. We'll show you how to delete characters this way later in this chapter after we show you how to select text.

You can cancel the effects of the [Backspace] or [Delete] key by choosing Undo from the Edit menu. However, you must select the Undo command immediately after you erase the text—before you type any characters, press [Enter], or select a command—in order to recover the deleted characters. (We'll explain the Undo command in more detail in Chapter 5.)

Replacing characters

You can use a combination of these two techniques to replace characters in a document. To replace a character, you first should delete it, using either the [Backspace] or [Delete] keys. After the deletion, the cursor will be on the character that was to the right of the deleted character. Since Works inserts characters to the left of the cursor, you can replace the deleted character simply by typing the new one.

Although this is one way to replace a character, it's not the best way. You can select the character or characters you want to replace, then type the replacement character(s). We'll show you this technique later in this chapter.

In addition to moving the cursor to any single character in a document, you can extend it to select one or more adjacent characters. Selecting text is how you tell Works what part of a document you want to work with before you issue a command or type keystrokes. Selected text appears in inverse video on your screen. You can select anywhere from one character to an entire document. Typically, however, you will select something in between—several words, a couple of sentences, or a paragraph. For example, Figure 4-9 shows the result of selecting the words *any type of document* on the second line of the first paragraph of the document shown in Figure 4-7.

Figure 4-9

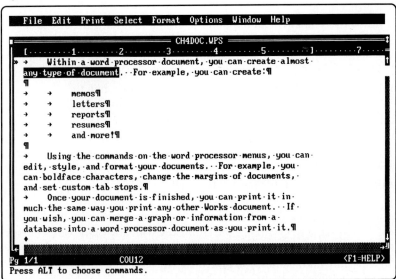

When you extend the cursor to select one or more characters in a document, the selected text appears in inverse video on your screen.

The way you select text in a word processor document depends on whether you have a mouse. If you don't have a mouse, you must use the cursor-movement keys in combination with either the [Shift] or [Extend] keys to select text. If you have a mouse, you can use it to select text.

Using the [Shift] Key   One way to select text is to hold down the [Shift] key while you press any of the keys and key combinations that you can use to move the cursor within a document. If you hold down the [Shift] key and press any of these keys, Works will transform the cursor into a highlight and extend it in the designated direction.

Expanding the cursor one character at a time   Most commonly, you will use the ➡ and ⬅ keys in combination with the [Shift] key. These keys allow you to expand the cursor by highlighting one character at a time. If you hold down the [Shift] key and press the ➡ key once when no text is selected, Works will select the character on which the cursor is positioned. For example, if you hold down the [Shift] key and press ➡ once while the cursor is on the *M* in the word *Microsoft*, Works will highlight the *M*. If you continue to hold down the [Shift] key and press the ➡ key after pressing [Shift]➡ to highlight a character, Works will extend the highlight to the right, one character at a time. For example, if you hold down the [Shift] key and press ➡ eight times after highlighting the *M* in *Microsoft*, Works will extend the highlight to cover the remaining letters in the word.

If you want, you also can expand the cursor in a leftward direction. To do this, simply hold down the [Shift] key and press the ⬅ key. If no characters are selected when you press this combination of keys, Works will highlight the character to the left of the one on which the cursor was positioned at the time. For example, if you hold down the [Shift] key and press ⬅ while the cursor is on the *s* in the word *Microsoft*, Works will highlight the *o* to the left of the *s*—not the *s* itself. If you hold down the [Shift] key and press ⬅ after highlighting a character in this way, Works will expand the highlight to the left, one character at a time. For example, if you hold down the [Shift] key and press ⬅ four times after highlighting the first *o* in *Microsoft*, Works will expand the highlight to the left to cover the letters *r, c, i,* and *M* as well.

Using other cursor keys   In addition to using the ➡ and ⬅ keys in combination with the [Shift] key to expand the highlight, you can use the [Shift] key with any of the other cursor keys and key combinations that move the cursor; for example, ⬆, [Ctrl]➡, [Pg Up], [Ctrl][Pg Up], and [End]. When you hold down the [Shift] key and press any of these keys and key combinations, Works expands the highlight from the current position of the cursor to the character to the right of the one to which it would move the cursor if you were not holding down the [Shift] key. For example, pressing [Ctrl]➡ without holding down the [Shift] key moves the cursor to the first character of the next word in the document. Pressing [Ctrl]➡ while holding down the [Shift] key expands the highlight from the current position of the cursor to the space to the right of that word. For instance, if you press [Shift][Ctrl]➡ while the cursor is on the first *s* in the phrase *Microsoft Works*, Works would highlight the letters *soft* and the space that follows them.

Just as you can expand the cursor by highlighting it, you also can contract it. To do this, hold down the [Shift] key and press a key that moves the cursor in the direction opposite from the direction in which you expanded it. For example, if you hold down the [Shift] key and press ← after extending the highlight to the right, Works will contract the highlight one character at a time. If you hold down the [Shift] key and press [Ctrl]→ after extending the highlight to the left, Works will contract the highlight one word at a time. If you attempt to contract the highlight by more characters than are highlighted at the time, Works will expand the highlight in the opposite direction from the character on which the cursor was positioned originally. For example, suppose you expanded the highlight to cover the letters *soft* in the word *Microsoft* by holding down the [Shift] key and pressing → four times while the cursor was on the *s*. If you then held down the [Shift] key and pressed the ← key nine times, Works would remove the highlight from the letters *soft* and highlight the letters *Micro* in a leftward direction.

If you want to deselect the highlighted text completely, press one of the cursor-movement keys while the [Shift] key is not depressed. When you do this, Works will remove the highlight from the selected text and display a normal cursor.

Contracting the highlight

The [Extend] key provides an alternative to holding down the [Shift] key to select characters in a document. When you press this key ([F8] on the IBM PC), the abbreviation EXT will appear in the status line. This abbreviation indicates that Works is in the Extend mode. While Works is in the Extend mode, the cursor-movement keys and key combinations don't move the cursor around within the document. Instead, they extend the cursor by highlighting it, just as they do when you hold down the [Shift] key. For example, if you press the → key while Works is in the Extend mode, it will extend the highlight one character to the right; if you press [Ctrl]↓, Works will extend the highlight to the end of the current paragraph; if you press [Ctrl][End], Works will extend the highlight all the way to the end of the document; and so forth.

In addition to using the [Extend] key as an alternative to holding down the [Shift] key, you can use it to select text in other ways. Once you've entered the Extend mode, subsequently pressing the [Extend] key will extend the highlight. Pressing the [Extend] key the first time will select the current word; pressing it again will select the current sentence; pressing it a third time will select the current paragraph; and pressing it a fourth time will select the entire document.

Using the [Extend] Key

If you hold down the [Shift] key as you press the [Extend] key, Works will contract the highlight in the same increments by which it expands it when you press the [Extend] key alone. For example, if the entire document is selected and Works is in the Extend mode, pressing [Shift][Extend] once will contract the cursor to the paragraph in which the cursor was positioned before you expanded it. Pressing [Shift][Extend] again will contract the highlight to a single sentence.

Contracting the highlight

Pressing [Shift][Extend] a third time will contract the highlight to a single word. Pressing [Shift][Extend] a fourth time will eliminate the highlight and place the cursor on the character it was marking before you began highlighting text.

Cancelling the Extend mode

Once you press the [Extend] key, Works will be in the Extend mode until you press the [Esc] key. When you do this, Works will remove the abbreviation EXT from the status line, indicating that Works is no longer in the Extend mode. However, any highlighted text will remain highlighted until you press a cursor-movement key. When you do this, Works will remove the highlight from the selected text and display a normal cursor.

The Text command
►WORKS 2◄

►Another way to enter the Extend mode is to choose the Text command from the Select menu. The Text command lets you select a range of text in all the ways we've just discussed. Once the EXT legend appears on the status line, you can use the arrow keys to extend the highlight to cover more characters or you can click the mouse pointer where you want the highlight to end, just as with the [Extend] key. When you want to leave the Extend mode, press [Esc].◄

The Go To... command

If you use the Go To... command (either by selecting it from the Select menu or pressing the [F5] key) while Works is in the Extend mode, Works will expand the highlight from the current position of the cursor to the first character on the page you specify. For example, if you pull down the Select menu, select the Go To... command, type 4 into the Page Number text box, and choose <OK>, Works will extend the highlight from the current position of the cursor to the first character of the fourth page of the document.

The All command
►WORKS 2◄

►When you want to select the entire document, choose the All command from the Select menu. No matter where your cursor is in the document, the All command selects the entire document.◄

Using a mouse

If you are using a Microsoft mouse, you can use it to select text within a Works word processor document. (Of course, you also can use any of the keyboard methods described above.) Dragging is the most fundamental way to select text with a mouse. To select text this way, position the mouse pointer on one end of the block you want to select, hold down the left button on the mouse, drag the pointer to the opposite end of the block, and release the button.

If you drag the mouse pointer to the right and/or downward, Works will expand the highlight from the character you pointed to originally to the character to the left of the one you are pointing to when you release the button. Consequently, you must drag the pointer one character beyond the right edge of the block you want to select. For example, to select the letters *icro* in the word *Microsoft*, you would point to the *i*, hold down the left mouse button, drag to the *s*, then release the button.

If you drag the pointer to the left and/or upward, Works will expand the highlight from the character to the left of the one to which you pointed originally to the character to which you are pointing when you release the button. Consequently, you must begin dragging one character to the left of the leftmost character you want to select. For example, to select the letters *icro* in the word *Microsoft*, you would point to the *s*, hold down the left mouse button, drag to the *i*, then release the button.

In addition to dragging, there are five other techniques you can use to select text with a mouse. First, you can use the right-hand button on your mouse to select text in increments of whole words. If you point to a word and click the right button on your mouse, Works will select that word. If you drag the mouse pointer while holding down the right button, Works will expand the highlight one word at a time.

Second, you can use the mouse to select entire lines of text. If you move the mouse pointer to the blank area to the left of the line you want to select, then click the left button on your mouse, Works will select that line; that is, all the text to the right of the pointer. If you drag the mouse pointer up or down the left edge of the document while holding down the left button, Works will expand the highlight in one-line increments.

Third, you can use the mouse to select full paragraphs. To select a paragraph, you must move the pointer to the blank area to the left of that paragraph and click the right button on your mouse. When you do this, Works will highlight the entire paragraph. If you drag the mouse pointer up or down the left edge of the document while holding down the right button, Works will expand the highlight in full-paragraph increments.

Fourth, you can select the entire document by clicking both mouse buttons simultaneously while the mouse pointer is anywhere in the blank area to the left of the document. When you do this, Works will expand the highlight to cover every character in the document.

Finally, you can use the mouse to expand the highlight from the anchor point to any other point in the document. (If you expand the highlight to the right, the anchor point is the leftmost highlighted character; if you expand the highlight to the left, the anchor point is the rightmost highlighted character.) To do this, you simply point to the character to which you want to expand the highlight, hold down the [Shift] key, and click the left button on your mouse. Pointing and clicking the left button on your mouse while Works is in the Extend mode accomplishes the same task.

EDITING BLOCKS OF TEXT

Once you know how to select blocks of text in a word processor document, you can perform editing tasks other than inserting and deleting one character at a time. Specifically, you can delete whole blocks of text with a single keystroke and replace existing text without deleting it first.

To delete a block of text with a single keystroke, select the characters you want to delete using any of the techniques discussed earlier in this chapter, then press the [Delete] key. When you do this, Works will delete the characters that are highlighted. For example, if you highlight the letters *icro* in the word *Microsoft*, then press the [Delete] key, Works will delete those characters, leaving the characters *Msoft*.

Pressing the [Backspace] key when a block of text is selected does not have the same effect as pressing the [Delete] key. When you press [Backspace], Works will reduce the highlight to a cursor under the leftmost character in the highlighted block and deletes the character to the left of that character. It does not delete the selected text. For example, if you press the [Backspace] key while the letters *icro* in the word *Microsoft* are highlighted, Works will delete the *M* and place the cursor on the *i*.

▶WORKS 2◀

▶When you highlight text and type, Works will remove the highlight, then merely insert the fresh text. If you want to replace a block of text by typing, you must activate the Typing Replaces Selection command on the Options menu. You activate this command by choosing it. If you then highlight text and begin typing, Works will delete the highlighted characters and replace them with the characters you type. For example, suppose you want to replace the word *plain* in the sentence *The rain in Spain stays mainly on the plain.* with the word *coast.* To do this, you would select the characters *plain,* choose the Typing Replaces Selection command (if it is not activated), then type *coast.*

When you first load Works, the Typing Replaces Selection command (a toggle command) is turned off. If you highlight a block of text then type new text when this command is inactive, Works will remove the highlight, and insert the text to the left of the cursor. Once you choose the Typing Replaces Selection command, it stays active. Works saves the command's setting in the WORKS.INI file. Afterward, the Typing Replaces Selection command will remain active until you choose it again, even if you exit and reload Works. Since this command speeds your work in Works, we suggest you activate it. ◀

When you delete or replace a block of text, Works rejustifies the paragraph(s) to which you've made those changes, just as it does when you insert and delete one character at a time. If you add more characters to a line than you remove, Works may push a word or two off the end of that line to the beginning of the next line. If you delete more characters than you add, Works may pull one or more words up from the next line.

In addition to making it easier to delete and replace blocks of text, selecting text is also an essential part of the process of issuing most word processor commands. When you issue most commands, Works operates upon the text that is selected at the time. For example, when you pull down the Edit menu and select the Copy command, Works will copy the text you have selected previously. We'll demonstrate the use of commands that act upon selected text in Chapter 5.

After you've created a word processor document, you probably will want to save it to disk. The process of saving a word processor document is the same as saving any other type of document. To save a word processor document for the first time, you must pull down the File menu and select either the Save or Save As... command. When you select either of these commands, Works will present a Save As dialog box. Within this box, you should specify a name for the document and the directory in which you want Works to save it. When you choose <OK>, Works will save the document to disk. Unless you specify otherwise, Works will save the document under its default name in the default directory. Works will append the extension .WPS to the end of the file name if you don't specify an alternative suffix.

Once you've saved a word processor document for the first time, you can use either the Save or Save As... commands to resave it. If you select the Save command, Works will automatically save the current version of the document on top of the old one. If you select the Save As... command, Works will let you save the current version of the document in another file. You should use the Save As... command if you want to retain copies of the various drafts of your document.

Works allows you to save word processor documents in three different formats: Works, Text, and Printed Text. The form in which Works saves a document depends on which of these three options you choose from the Format option box in the Save As dialog box. If you choose the Works format (the default), Works will retain all the formats and styles you assigned to the document. If you choose Text, Works will strip all the formats and margin information from the file, so that each paragraph is a single line of unformatted text. If you choose Printed Text, Works will strip all the formats from the document but place a carriage return and a line feed at the end of each line of each paragraph. Tabs and left and right margins become spaces; top and bottom margin becomes blank lines. You should use the Text and Printed Text formats only when you need to exchange the information in a Works word processor document with another software package.

Once you have saved a word processor document to disk, you can reopen it into Works. To do this, pull down the File menu, select the Open Existing File... command, specify the name of the file you want to open within the Open Existing File dialog box, then choose <OK>. To limit the list of files that Works displays to only those with the extension .WPS (the default extension Works uses for word processor documents), you can type *.WPS in the File To Open text box in the Open Existing File dialog box. When you choose <OK>, Works will display only word processor document names in the Files list box. For detailed information about saving and opening documents, refer to Chapter 2.

As with any other type of document, printing a word processor document entails a three-step process. First, you use the Page Setup & Margin... command to set the margins, page dimensions, first page number, and header and footer

STORING AND RETRIEVING WORD PROCESSOR DOCUMENTS

PRINTING WORD PROCESSOR DOCUMENTS

margins for the document. (We'll explain in Chapter 5 how the margin and page dimension settings affect the length of the lines in a word processor document itself—not how much of each line will be printed.) Second, you use the Printer Setup... command to select the printer to which you will be printing. (We'll also explain in Chapter 5 how the printer you choose determines what special character fonts are available to Works.) Finally, you select the Print... command to tell Works to print the document.

Figure 4-10

You'll see this dialog box when you select the Print... command from a word processor document's Print menu.

Figure 4-10 shows the dialog box that Works will present when you select the Print... command from the Print menu of a word processor document. The first five elements in this box are the same as they are in the Print dialog boxes for all types of documents. The Number of Copies text box lets you specify how many copies of the document you want Works to print; the Print Specific Pages check box and Pages text box allow you to tell Works which pages of the document you want it to print; and the Print to File check box and File Name text box allow you to direct the print-out to a file. For more on these settings, refer to Chapter 3.

The final element in this dialog box—the Draft Quality check box—is unique to word processor documents. When this setting is off (its default state), Works will print your word processor document complete with all the special styles (such as bold and italic), fonts (such as Times Roman and Helvetica), and type sizes (such as 10 and 12 point) that you assigned to the various characters in the document. When this setting is on, Works will print your document without any of these special attributes. Since most printers can print in draft quality more quickly than they can print a document complete with special fonts and styles, the Draft Quality setting comes in handy when you want to print quickly.

CONCLUSION

In this chapter, we taught you the basics of working in a word processor document: how to create and open word processor documents, how to enter text, how to move the cursor, how to insert and delete characters, how to select text, how to replace and delete blocks of text, and how to save and print word processor documents. In the next chapter, we'll demonstrate some advanced editing techniques and show you how to format a document.

Editing and Formatting 5

*I*n Chapter 4, we taught you skills that are fundamental to everything you do in a word processor document. Once you've mastered those basic skills, you can move on to the more advanced features of Works' word processor.

In this chapter, we'll explore some of these features. We'll begin by discussing Works' powerful editing commands: Copy, Move, Search…, and Replace…. Next, we'll show you how to apply special print attributes—such as boldfacing, superscripting, and special fonts and character sizes—to the text in a word processor document. We'll also explain how to adjust the margins of a document. Then, we'll show you how to control various paragraph formatting features, such as line spacing, indentions, text alignment, tab stops, and borders. Finally, we'll revisit the Edit menu and explain how you can use the Copy Special… command to copy formats and how you can cancel editing and formatting changes with the Undo command.

In Chapter 4, we covered several basic editing skills. We showed you how to delete individual characters using the [Backspace] and [Delete] keys, how to insert new text in a document, and how to replace and delete blocks of text. Although these techniques are enough to get you started in a word processor document, they are not the only editing tools available. In addition to these techniques, Works features commands that let you move and copy blocks of text, that provide an alternative to the [Delete] key for erasing blocks of text, and that automate the process of finding and replacing characters.

Highlighting text is essential to most of these commands. Before you issue the commands that move, copy, and delete text, you must highlight the text on which you want to operate. (The commands that allow you to find and replace text do not require you to highlight text first.) To highlight text, you can use any of the techniques we explained in Chapter 4. Once you have highlighted the text

ADVANCED EDITING TECHNIQUES

you want to act upon, you should issue the command that instructs Works to perform the appropriate action. In the case of the commands that move and copy text, you need to specify a destination after you issue the command.

In the next few pages, we'll show you how to use the editing commands available in a word processor document. First, we'll look at the Move command, which allows you to move text from one position to another in a word processor document. Next, we'll examine the Copy command, which lets you copy text from a word processor document and place it in another location in the same document or a different one. Third, we'll look at the Delete command, which provides an alternative to the [Delete] key for removing blocks of text. All of these commands are located on the Edit menu of any word processor document. Finally, we'll look at the Search… and Replace… commands on the Select menu, which allow you to search for and, if you want, replace blocks of text.

Moving

The Move command allows you to move one or more characters in a word processor document. Moving text is a three-step process. First, you highlight the character(s) you want to move, using any of the techniques presented in Chapter 4. Next, you pull down the Edit menu and select the Move command. (Alternatively, you can press the [Move] key—[F3].) When you issue the Move command in either of these ways, Works will display the word *MOVE* on the status line and the message *Select new location and press ENTER. Press ESC to cancel.* on the message line. At this point, you must tell Works where to move the highlighted text. You can do this either by repositioning the cursor or highlighting a block of text. If you press [Enter] while the cursor is marking a single character, Works will insert the text you selected to the left of that character. If you expand the highlight to cover one or more characters, Works will replace those characters with the text you highlighted prior to issuing the Move command. In either case, Works will remove the text from its original location in the document and rejustify both the source and destination paragraphs.

An example

As an example of the Move command, suppose you want to move the second sentence of the document shown in Figure 5-1 to a position following the third sentence in that document. To move this sentence, begin by highlighting it. (The easiest way to do this is to position the cursor anywhere in the sentence and press [Extend] three times.) Once you have highlighted the sentence, pull down the Edit menu and select the Move command. Then, move the cursor to the first character of the fourth sentence and press [Enter]. Figure 5-2 shows the result. As you can see, Works inserted the second sentence after what used to be the third sentence and closed up the space formerly occupied by the second sentence. Consequently, the original second sentence is now the third sentence, and the original third sentence is now the second sentence.

Figure 5-1

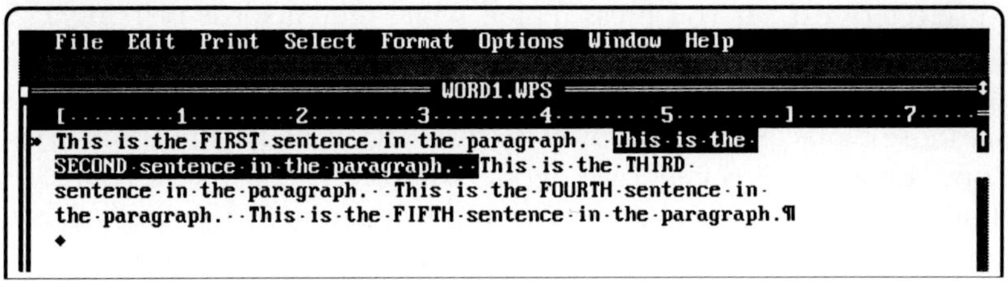

We'll move the second sentence in this document to a position follow-ing the third sentence.

Figure 5-2

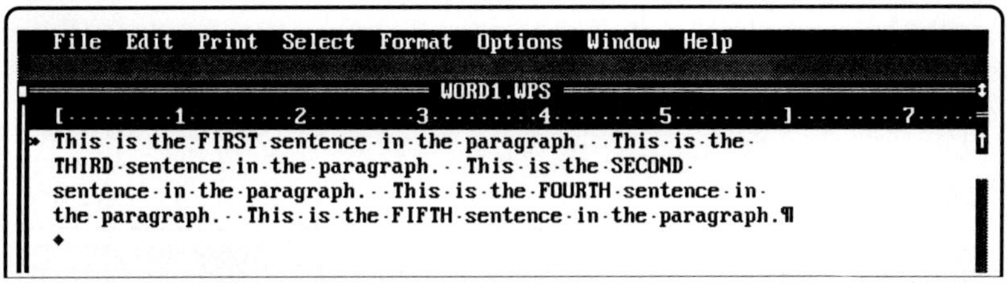

After the move, the original second sentence is the third sentence, and the original third sentence is the second sentence.

If you decide that you don't want to move a block of text after selecting it and issuing the Move command, you can easily cancel the move by pressing [Esc]. (If you press [Enter] while the source text is highlighted, Works will present the message *Cannot move text within selection*.) If you want to "undo" a move after completing it, select the Undo command from the Edit menu. If you select this command after completing the move but before performing any other task, Works will return the document to its original condition. We'll talk more about the Undo command at the end of this chapter.

Cancelling a
Move command

The Copy command allows you to copy a block of text in a word processor document and place it in another location in that document or in another document. After you complete a Copy command, there will be two occurrences of the text you highlighted: the original, which will remain in place, and the copy, which will be wherever you directed Works to place it.

Copying

Like moving text, copying text requires three steps. First, highlight the character(s) you want to move. Next, pull down the Edit menu and select the Copy command. (Alternatively, you can press the [Copy] key—[Shift][F3].) As soon as you issue this command, the word *COPY* will appear on the status line, and the message *Select new location and press ENTER. Press ESC to cancel.* will appear on the message line. At this point, you need to tell Works where to place the copy of the selected text. If you press [Enter] while the cursor is marking a single character, Works will insert a copy of the text you selected to the left of that character. If you expand the highlight to cover one or more characters, Works will replace those characters with a copy of the text that you highlighted prior to issuing the Copy command. In either case, Works will place a copy of the source text at the destination and rejustify the destination paragraph(s). The original text will remain in place.

An example

As an example of the Copy command, suppose you want to copy the word *sentence* from the middle of the first line of the document shown in Figure 5-3 to a place between the words *This is* at the end of the same line. To do this, you would highlight the word *sentence*, pull down the Edit menu, select the Copy command, position the cursor under the *i* in *is*, then press [Enter]. Figure 5-4 shows the result of the copy. As you can see, Works has copied and inserted the word *sentence* between *This* and *is* at the end of the first line of the document.

Figure 5-3

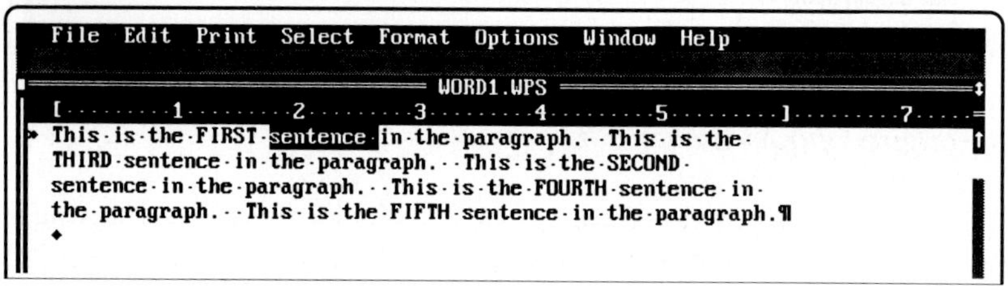

We'll copy the word sentence *on the first line to a place between the words* This *and* is *at the end of the same line.*

Figure 5-4

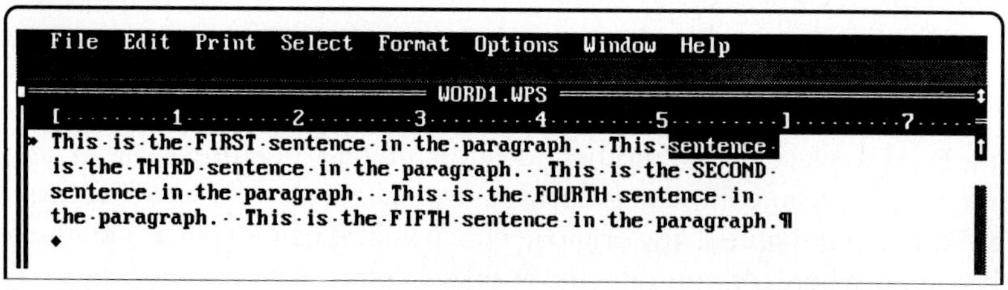

After the copy, there are two occurrences of the source text in the document—the original and the copy.

Repeating a copy

Works makes it easy to copy a block of text repeatedly. Once you have copied a block of text to one location in a word processor document, you can copy the same block of text to another location simply by moving the cursor to or highlighting that location and pressing the [Repeat Copy] key—[Shift][F7]. You can repeat this technique until you issue another command. At that point, you'll have to reissue the Copy command before you can use the [Repeat Copy] key again.

If you decide that you don't want to copy a block of text after selecting it and issuing the Copy command, you can press [Esc] to cancel the Copy command, or you can press [Enter] while the source text is highlighted. Works will copy the source text on top of itself, completing the command. The document will look the same after the copy as it did before. (Interestingly, Works won't let you use the [Repeat Copy] key after you've copied text onto itself.) If you want to "undo" a copy after completing it, you can select the Undo command from the Edit menu before you issue another command, press [Enter], or type any characters.

Cancelling a copy

Although you usually will use the Copy command to copy text from one location to another within a word processor document, you can use it to copy text to other Works documents. To copy text to another document, begin by highlighting the text you want to copy, pulling down the Edit menu, and selecting the Copy command—the same steps you would perform to copy text to another location within the same document. After issuing the Copy command, you must activate the document in which you want to place the copy. If the document is already in RAM, you can do this by pulling down the Window menu and selecting its name. If the document is not in RAM, you must use the Open Existing File... command to open it or the Create New File... command to create it. Once the destination document is active, move the cursor or highlight to the position in the document where you want to place the copy and press [Enter]. When you do this, Works will copy the text you selected in the source document to the specified location in the destination document.

Copying between documents

The result of copying text from one word processor document to another is the same as that of copying from one location to another within a single word processor document. If you press [Enter] while the cursor is marking a single character, Works will insert a copy of the source text to the left of that character; if you expand the highlight to cover more than one character before pressing [Enter], Works will replace those characters with a copy of the source characters. Copying text from a word processor document to other types of documents has different effects. We'll explain those effects in Chapter 19.

In Chapter 4, we showed you how to use the [Backspace] and [Delete] keys to delete individual characters from a word processor document, and how to delete blocks of text by highlighting them, then pressing the [Delete] key. In addition to these techniques, Works gives you one more way to delete characters from a word processor document—the Delete command. This command, which

Deleting

is located on the Edit menu of any word processor document, performs the same function as the [Delete] key—it deletes any text that is highlighted at the time. If no text is highlighted, Works will delete the character under which the cursor is positioned when you issue the Delete command.

Since the action of the Delete command is identical to that of the [Delete] key, and since pressing the [Delete] key is easier than pulling down the Edit menu and selecting the Delete command, we prefer to use the [Delete] key.

If you accidentally delete some text using either the Delete command or the [Delete] key, you can restore that text by selecting the Undo command from the Edit menu. In order for the Undo command to work, you must select it before you type any characters, select a command, or press [Enter].

Searching and replacing

In addition to providing commands that allow you to move, copy, and delete text, Works provides two commands that automate the process of searching for and replacing text: Search... and Replace.... These commands do exactly what their names imply. The Search... command locates occurrences of the text you specify within a word processor document. The Replace... command replaces the occurrences of the text it finds with the replacement text you specify.

The Search... command

To search for text, you first must position the cursor at the point where you want Works to begin the search. When you issue the Search... command, Works will start searching from the current position to the end of the document. If you want Works to search the entire document, you must move the cursor to the beginning of the document before you issue the Search... command.

Once you have positioned the cursor where you want Works to begin the search, pull down the Select menu and issue the Search... command. When you do this, Works will present a dialog box like the one shown in Figure 5-5. If you haven't used either the Search... or Replace... commands in a word processor document during the current Works session, the Search For text box will be blank. If you have used one of these commands during the current Works session (even in another word processor document), the last search string you specified (that is, the text you want to search for) will appear highlighted in this box.

Figure 5-5

Works will display a dialog box like this one when you pull down the Select menu and issue the Search... command.

To command Works to search for a particular search string, you must type that text into the Search For text box, then choose <OK>. The search string can be up to 63 characters long. If you type more than 63 characters into the Search For text box, Works will ignore the extra characters and search for an occurrence of the first 63. Since the Search For text box is only 20 characters wide, Works will display only 19 characters of the search string at a time but will scroll those 19 characters leftward when you type more than 19 characters into the text box. The search string can contain any characters you can type from the keyboard, including spaces, punctuation marks, and mathematical symbols. Additionally, it can contain wildcard characters and codes that instruct Works to search for special characters like end-of-paragraph and tab markers. We'll talk about these special characters in a few pages.

Once you've entered the search string into the Search For text box, you should choose <OK> to begin the search. (Since <OK> is the default button, you can choose it by pressing [Enter].) When you do this, Works will search for the text that you specified, starting at the current position of the cursor. (If you choose <Cancel> or press [Esc], Works will cancel the command.) Works will search down through the document until it finds an occurrence of the search string or until it reaches the end of the document. If Works finds an occurrence of the search string, it will highlight it and close the Search dialog box. (If the occurrence is in a part of the document that is not visible on the screen when you issued the Search... command, Works will scroll that portion of the document into view.) If Works reaches the end of the document without finding an occurrence of the search string, it will replace the Search dialog box with the alert box in Figure 5-6.

Figure 5-6

Works will present this alert box when it can't find an occurrence of the text for which you are searching.

Repeating the Search... command.   Once you have located the first occurrence of the search string, you may want to find another. To do this, you could pull down the Select menu and issue the Search... command again. When you issue the Search... command after issuing it previously during the current Works session, the Search For text box will contain the last search string you entered. Consequently, you don't need to type in the search string each time; you can repeat the search simply by choosing <OK>.

In many cases, one occurrence of the search string will be highlighted when you reissue the Search... command. When this happens, Works won't find the highlighted occurrence of the search string again. Instead, it will find the next occurrence of the string in the document. In general, if you issue the Search... command while a block of text is highlighted, Works will begin the search immediately to the right of that block.

Although reissuing the Search... command might be the most obvious way to search for the next occurrence of a character, it's not the easiest way. Once you have used the Search... command to find the first occurrence of a search string, you can find subsequent occurrences simply by pressing the [Repeat Search] key—[F7]. When you press this key, Works will search for the next occurrence of the search string in the text automatically—it won't present the Search dialog box first. If Works reaches the end of the document without finding another occurrence of the search string, it will display the alert box shown in Figure 5-6.

An example.   Suppose you want to locate every occurrence of the word *the* in the document shown in Figure 5-4. To do this, you would move the cursor to the beginning of the document (the easiest way to do this is by pressing [Ctrl][Home]), pull down the Select menu, issue the Search... command, type the word *the* into the Search For text box, and choose <OK>. When you do this, Works will remove the Search dialog box from the screen and highlight the first occurrence of the word *the* in the text; in this case, the third word on the first line. Figure 5-7 shows this result.

Figure 5-7

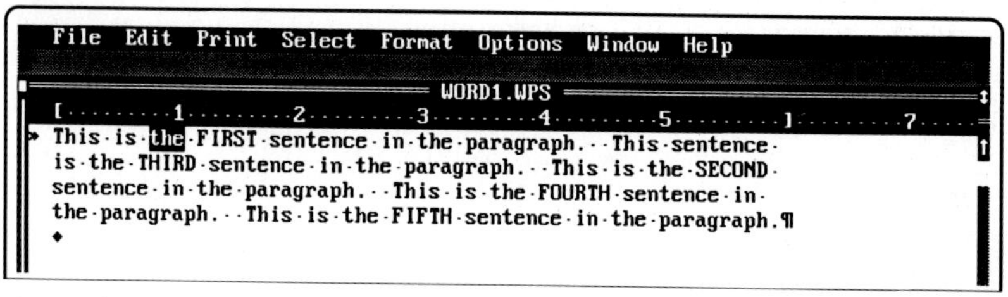

```
 File  Edit  Print  Select  Format  Options  Window  Help

                              WORD1.WPS
 [ · · · · · · · · ·1· · · · · · · ·2· · · · · · · ·3· · · · · · · ·4· · · · · · · ·5· · · · · · · · ] · · · · · · ·?· · · ·
▸ This·is·the·FIRST·sentence·in·the·paragraph.··This·sentence·
  is·the·THIRD·sentence·in·the·paragraph.··This·is·the·SECOND·
  sentence·in·the·paragraph.··This·is·the·FOURTH·sentence·in·
  the·paragraph.··This·is·the·FIFTH·sentence·in·the·paragraph.¶
 ♦
```

Since the cursor was at the beginning of the document, Works located the first occurrence of the word the *in the document.*

To find additional occurrences of the word *the*, you could either reissue the Search... command or press the [Repeat Search] key. The first time you do either of these things, Works will highlight the occurrence of the word *the* to the left of the word *paragraph* in the first line—the second occurrence of that word in the text. The second time, Works will highlight the occurrence of the word *the* to the left of the word *THIRD* near the beginning of the second line—the third occurrence in the document. You can continue through the document like this. Works will display the alert box shown in Figure 5-6 if you reissue the Search... command or press the [Repeat Search] key again after you've reached the last occurrence of the word *the* in the document.

Search options.   Unless you specify otherwise, Works will search within other words for occurrences of the search string you specify as well as search for occurrences that are complete words by themselves. Works also will not be sensitive to capitalization. Fortunately, Works offers two check boxes that control these properties of the Search… command: Match Whole Word and Match Upper/lower Case.

The Match Whole Word check box controls whether Works searches for occurrences of the search string within words. If this option is off (its default state), Works will search for occurrences of the search string within other words in addition to freestanding occurrences of that text (those occurrences that are preceded by a space, a carriage return (¶), or the beginning of the document and that are followed by a space, a punctuation mark, a carriage return (¶), or the end of the document). If this option is on (indicated by an X in the box to its left), Works will search for only freestanding occurrences of that string.

As an example of the effect of this option, suppose you are searching for the word *for* in a document. If the Match Whole Word option is off, Works will look for any character sequence that matches your search text, even if it occurs in the middle of a word. For example, it will find the letters *for* in words like *forecast* and *platform*. If the Match Whole Word option is on, Works will locate only freestanding occurrences of the word *for*.

The Match Upper/lower Case check box controls whether Works considers capitalization when it searches for occurrences of the search string. If this option is off (its default state), Works will ignore capitalization as it conducts its search For example, if you specify the search string *Microsoft*, Works will highlight occurrences such as *microsoft*, *MicroSoft*, and *MICROSOFT*. If this option is on, Works will locate only text that matches the capitalization of the search string. For example, if you specify the search string *Microsoft*, Works will locate the word *Microsoft* but not *microsoft*, *MicroSoft*, *MICROSOFT*, and so forth.

Using wildcards. The question mark (?) is Works' wildcard character. If you include a ? in a search string, Works will match any string that has a character in that position. For example, the search string *b?g* would match any words that begin with the letter b, end with the letter g, and have any single character between; for example, the words *bag, beg, big,* and so forth. If you want Works to search for a string that contains a literal question mark, you must preface the question mark with a caret (^). The caret tells Works to treat the next character literally. For example, you would use the search string *Is this correct^?* to find all occurrences of the question *Is this correct?*. To find occurrences of a literal caret (^), you must use two carets (^^).

Searching for special characters. In addition to finding words and phrases, the Search… command can locate special characters, like end-of-paragraph markers (¶) and tab markers (➡). In order to search for these markers, you must enter special codes into your search text. These codes consist of a caret (^) followed by a single character. For example, the code ^*p* tells Works to search for end-of-paragraph markers, the code ^*t* tells Works to search for tab markers, and so forth. Table 5-1 summarizes these special codes.

Table 5-1

To find:	Type this code:
End-of-paragraph marker (¶)	^ p
Tab marker (→)	^ t
End-of-line marker (↓)	^ n
Page-break marker (manual or automatic)	^ d
Non-breaking space	^ s
Non-breaking hyphen	^ ~
Optional hyphen	^ -
Caret (^)	^ ^
Question mark	^ ?
ASCII character	^ # (# is the ASCII number)
White space	^ w

You can use these codes to locate special characters in a document.

Suppose you want to find every paragraph that begins with the words *For example*. To do this, enter ^*pFor example* as your search text. Works will then search your document for every occurrence of a ¶ marker followed by the two words *For example*.

Although some of the characters mentioned in Table 5-1 will be familiar to you (for example, the caret, the question mark, and the end-of-paragraph, tab, and page-break markers), some will not (for example, ASCII characters, end-of-line markers, non-breaking spaces and hyphens, and optional hyphens). We'll talk about those characters in Chapter 6. The code for finding white space (^w) will find space that has been created by pressing the [Spacebar] or the [Tab] key one or more times. It will not find white space created by indents and line spacing.

The Replace... command

Once you have used the Search... command to locate an occurrence of a particular search string, you can replace that occurrence with another string simply by typing over it. Alternatively, you can edit the occurrence by pressing ← or → to reduce the highlight to a cursor, then using any of the editing techniques discussed in Chapter 4. Replacing text this way is fine if your document contains only a few occurrences of the string you want to replace. If your document contains several occurrences of the search string, however, you'll probably want to use the Replace... command.

Like the Search... command, the Replace... command searches for the search string you specify within the current word processor document, from the current position of the cursor to the end of the document. Unlike the Search... command, however, the Replace... command can replace each occurrence of the search string with the string you specify.

When you pull down the Select menu and issue the Replace... command, Works will display a dialog box like the one shown in Figure 5-8. As you can see, the Replace dialog box contains a Search For text box, just as the Search dialog box does. If you haven't used either the Search... or Replace... commands in a word processor document during the current Works session, the Search For text box will be blank. If you have used one of these commands (even in another word processor document), the last search string you specified will appear highlighted in this box. Within this box, you should enter the string of characters for which you want Works to search. This string can contain any characters you can type from the keyboard, including the ? wildcard and the special codes in Table 5-1.

Figure 5-8

Works will display a dialog box like this one when you pull down the Select menu and issue the Replace... command.

Also, like the Search dialog box, the Replace dialog box has a Match Whole Word check box and a Match Upper/lower Case check box. These boxes control the way Works searches for text the same way they do for the Search... command. If the Match Whole Word option is on (indicated by an X in its box), Works will locate only freestanding occurrences of the search string—not occurrences of that string in other words. If the Match Upper/lower Case option is on, Works will locate only occurrences of the search string that have the same capitalization as the entry in the Search For text box.

Unlike the Search dialog box, the Replace dialog box contains a second text box, labeled Replace With. Within this box, you should enter the character sequence with which you want to replace occurrences of the search string. We'll call the text that you enter into this box the replacement string. Like the search string, the replacement string can contain any character you can type from the keyboard. If you want, you can use any of the special codes shown in Table 5-1 (except ^w) in a replacement string to replace occurrences of the search string with carriage returns, tabs, and so forth. (If you include the characters ^w in a replacement string, Works will treat them as the letter *w*.) Works also will treat the wildcard character ? as a literal character in a replacement string.

Using the Replace... command.   Once you have positioned the cursor where you want Works to begin the search, and issued the Replace... command, you can enter the search string into the Search For text box, enter the replacement string into the Replace With text box, and turn each of the two option boxes on or off. Then, you can begin the process of searching for and replacing text. The first two buttons at the bottom of the Replace dialog box—<Replace> and <Replace All>—control how Works proceeds.

If you choose the <Replace> button, Works will locate the first occurrence of the search string after the cursor, highlight it, and display the dialog box shown in Figure 5-9. If you choose the <Yes> button from this box, Works will replace the highlighted occurrence of the search string with the replacement string, then search for the next occurrence of the search string within the document. If you choose <No>, Works will search for the next occurrence of the search string without replacing the highlighted occurrence. As long as you keep choosing <Yes> or <No>, Works will continue searching until it can't find any more occurrences of the search string, or until you choose the <Cancel> button. If there are no more occurrences of the search string between the current position of the cursor and the end of the document, it will display an alert box like the one shown in Figure 5-10. When you choose <OK> from this box, Works will cancel the Replace... command. It also will cancel the Replace... command if you choose <Cancel> instead of <Yes> or <No> from the dialog box in Figure 5-9.

Figure 5-9

If you choose the <Replace> button, you'll see this dialog box whenever Works locates an occurrence of the search string.

Figure 5-10

When there are no more occurrences of a search string in a replace procedure, Works will display this alert box.

If you want, you can replace every occurrence of the search string in the document by choosing the <Replace> button from the Replace dialog box, then choosing <OK> over and over. Alternatively, you can choose the <Replace All> button from the Replace dialog box. When you choose this button, Works will replace each occurrence of the search string between the position of the cursor and the end of the document automatically, instead of highlighting each one and asking if you want to replace it. As soon as Works has replaced all occurrences of the search string, it will display an alert box that tells you how many occurrences it replaced.

Although the <Replace All> button gives you a fast way to replace the occurrences of a search string within a document, it can be dangerous. If the search string you specified doesn't locate exactly what you wanted it to locate, Works will replace portions of the text that you didn't want it to replace. For example, if you did not turn on the Match Whole Word option before choosing <Replace All> when the Search For text box contained the word *tan* and the Replace With text box contained the word *brown,* Works would convert the words *tangent* and *understand* to *browngent* and *undersbrownd.*

Unfortunately, there's no way to stop the replacement process once you have chosen the <Replace All> button. However, you can undo the results of a "univeral" procedure by selecting the Undo command from the Edit menu before you press any other keys. (Issuing the Undo command after replacing occurrences of the search string individually undoes only the most recent replacement.) To avoid replacing text that you don't want to replace, we recommend that you use the <Replace> command to replace the first few occurrences of the search string within a document. If Works appears to be replacing the correct occurrences, choose <Cancel> to cancel the Replace... command, reissue the command, and choose <Replace All>.

Capitalization effects.   In most cases, Works will match the capitalization of the replacement string when it replaces occurrences of the search string. For example, if you type *Full Name* into the Replace With text box, Works will replace all occurrences of the search string with the characters *Full Name.* Similarly, if you enter the phrase *fuLl nAMe* into the Replace With text box, Works will replace each occurrence of the search string with the characters *fuLl nAMe.*

There are two exceptions to this rule. First, if Works finds the first letter of the search string capitalized in a document, it will capitalize the first letter of the replacement string even if its first letter appears in lowercase in the Replace dialog box. All other letters will appear exactly as they do in the original replacement string. For example, suppose you want to replace all occurrences of the word *name* with the words *full name.* To do this, you would enter *name* into the Search For text box, enter *full name* into the Replace With text box, and choose <Replace All>. If Works finds the word *name,* it will replace it with the words *full name.* If it finds the word *Name,* however, it will replace it with the words *Full name.*

Second, if all the letters of an occurrence of the search string are capitalized, Works will capitalize all the letters of the replacement string when it makes the replacement, regardless of the capitalization of those letters in the Replace dialog box. For instance, if Works encounters the word *NAME* in the previous example, it will replace it with the words *FULL NAME.*

It is important to note that these capitalization changes occur only when the Match Upper/lower Case option in the Replace dialog box is off. When this option is on, Works will use the same combination of uppercase and lowercase letters you entered in the Replace With text box when it replaces occurrences of the search string. (Of course, it will find only occurrences of the search string whose capitalization exactly matches that of the entry in the Search For text box.) For instance, if Works encounters the word *Name* while *Name* is the search string, *full name* is the replacement string, and the Match Upper/lower Case option is on, Works will replace it with the words *full name* (not *Full name*).

The Replace... command and formats. Whenever Works replaces an occurrence of the search string with the replacement string, Works assigns the formats of the first character of the search string to the replacement string. For example, suppose you have instructed Works to replace the word *canine* with the word *dog*. If Works encounters an occurrence of the word *canine* that has been assigned the underline attribute, Works will assign the underline attribute to the replacement text *dog*. There is no way to change the formatting of the text in a document with the Replace... command. We'll talk about formats next.

FORMATTING CHARACTERS

Works allows you to format the characters in a word processor document by assigning attributes that affect the way characters appear when they are printed. You can control three different attributes of any character: its style (for example, Bold, Underline, and Strikethrough), its font (for example, Courier, Times Roman, Line Printer, and Helvetica), and its size (for example, 10-point, 12-point, and 18-point). Figure 5-11 shows the printout of a document that has been assigned various character formats.

Figure 5-11

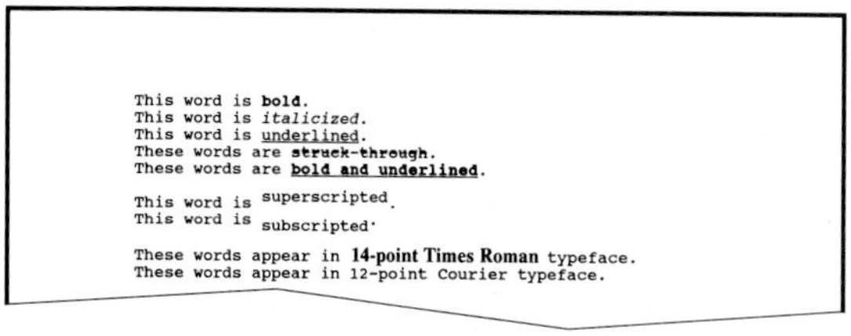

This word is **bold**.
This word is *italicized*.
This word is underlined.
These words are struck-through.
These words are **bold and underlined**.
This word is superscripted.
This word is subscripted.
These words appear in **14-point Times Roman** typeface.
These words appear in 12-point Courier typeface.

The characters in this document have been assigned a variety of character formats.

Assigning character formats

To assign formats to the characters in a document, you must first highlight the characters you want to format, using any of the techniques presented in Chapter 4. Then, select the format you want to assign to those characters. The commands that allow you to specify the styles of the characters in a document are located in the top section of the Format menu, shown in Figure 5-12.

Figure 5-12

The commands in the top section of a word processor document's Format menu allow you to format the characters in that document.

As you can see in Figure 5-12, three styles—Bold, Underline, and Italic—are represented by commands on the Format menu. To assign these attributes to the selected text, simply choose those commands one by one from the menu. The other formats are accessible through the Font & Style... command. ▶Works 2's Font & Style... command replaces the Character... command from Works 1.◀ (The Bold, Underline, and Italic formats are available through this command as well.) When you select this command, Works will present a dialog box like the one shown in Figure 5-13. The elements in the Font & Style dialog box control all of the formats available for the characters in a document. The four Styles check boxes at the upper-left corner of the dialog box control the Bold, Italic, Underline, and Strikethrough attributes. The Position option box controls the position of the selected text: either Normal, Superscript, or Subscript. The Fonts and Sizes list boxes control in what font and size Works will print the selected characters.

▶WORKS 2◀

Figure 5-13

You'll see a dialog box like this one when you select the Font & Style... command.

If the cursor is under a single character or a single character is selected when you issue the Font & Style... command, Works will display the formats of that character in the dialog box. If more than one character is selected, hyphens will appear in the four Styles check boxes, and nothing will be selected in the other boxes, even if all the selected characters have the same formats.

When you choose <OK> in the Font & Style dialog box, Works will assign the specified formats to the characters that are highlighted at the time. Elements that are active will be assigned to those characters; elements that are inactive will be removed from those characters; and elements that are neither on nor off (that is, check boxes that contain hyphens, and option boxes and list boxes in which nothing is selected) will not affect the current characteristics of the highlighted text. Consequently, it's possible to change one format characteristic of a block of text without changing any other characteristics.

Formatting the cursor

In addition to assigning formats to existing characters, you can assign a format to the cursor. That way, the characters you type will have the format(s) you assigned to the cursor. To assign one or more formats to the cursor, position it where you want to begin entering formatted text, pull down the Format menu, and specify the attribute(s) you want, either by choosing them from the menu or by working with the elements in the Font & Style dialog box. Once you do this, Works will assign the format(s) that you assigned to the cursor to the characters you type. Works will continue to do this until you reposition the cursor.

Whenever you position the cursor on an existing character, Works will apply the format settings of that character to the cursor. As you type new characters, Works will assign the format(s) of that character to those new characters. If you replace text by highlighting it and typing, Works will assign the formats of the leftmost highlighted character to every character of the replacement text.

Keyboard shortcuts

In addition to using the commands on the Format menu to assign formats, you can use the key combinations shown in Table 5-2. To use these combinations, simply highlight the text you want to format, then press the appropriate key combination. (To assign the format to the cursor, simply press the appropriate combination while the cursor is positioned where you want to insert text.) For example, to assign the Bold format to a group of characters, you would highlight those characters and press [Ctrl]b.

Repeating formats

Once you have assigned one or more formats to a block of text, you can assign them to other blocks of text simply by highlighting the text you want to format and pressing the [Repeat Format] key—[Shift][F7]. When you press this key, Works will assign the last format you selected to the currently highlighted text. For example, if you last invoked the Bold attribute, either by choosing it from the Format menu or by pressing [Ctrl]b, Works will assign the Bold attribute to the currently selected text when you press the [Repeat Format] key. If you last used the Font & Style... command to assign an attribute, Works will assign all the attributes that were specified in the Font & Style dialog box.

Table 5-2

Attribute	Key combinations
Bold	[Ctrl]b
Underline	[Ctrl]u
Italic	[Ctrl]i
Strikethrough	[Ctrl]s
Superscript	[Ctrl][Shift]=
Subscript	[Ctrl]=
Plain Text	[Ctrl][Spacebar]

You can use these key combinations to assign special format attributes to the text in a document.

Styles

Works offers four special styles that you can assign to the characters in a word processor document: Bold, Italic, Underline, and Strikethrough. The effect of the Bold, Italic, and Underline attributes are obvious; the Strikethrough attribute causes your printer to type a hyphen through each character.

The Bold, Italic, and Underline attributes appear on the Format menu and in the Font & Style dialog box. To assign one of these attributes to a block of text, highlight that text, then invoke the attribute by choosing it from the Format menu, activating it in the Font & Style dialog box, or pressing its special key combination (shown in Table 5-2). The Strikethrough attribute appears only in the Font & Style dialog box. To assign it to a group of characters, you must highlight them, then use the Font & Style dialog box or the [Ctrl]s key combination.

You can format characters with any combination of the four styles. For example, it's possible to have bold, underlined text; italic, underlined, strikethrough text; and so forth. To assign more than one attribute to a block of text, you simply invoke the various attributes individually, or all at the same time within the Font & Style dialog box.

Text mode
►WORKS 2◄

►If you are using Works in the Text mode, what you see depends on whether you have a color or black-and-white display. If you have a color display, entries that have been assigned the Bold, Italic, and Underline attributes will be appear in different colors (the color for each style depends on which of the color options you have selected in the Screen Colors list box in the Works Settings dialog box). If you have a black-and-white display (or a color display and have selected either of the Gray options in the Screen Colors list box), then entries that have been assigned the Bold, Italic, and Underline styles will be displayed in bright characters.

In addition to displaying formatted text in bright video, Works gives you another visual clue about styles. If you forget how you formatted your text or forget which color refers to which formats, you can look at the status line. When you position the cursor (or highlight) on a character that has been assigned a style, Works will display a code on the status line that tells you which attribute(s) are assigned to that character. Works uses the letter *B* to denote the Bold style, *U* to denote the Underline style, *I* to denote the Italic style, and *S* to denote the Strikethrough style. For example, when you position the cursor on a character that has been assigned the Bold and Italic styles, the letters *B* and *I* will appear on the status line. If more than one character is highlighted, Works will display the codes for the styles of the leftmost character of the highlighted text.

Graphics mode

If you have a graphics card, you can display your Works document in Graphics mode. When you display your document in Graphics mode, you'll see the styles you applied to your text just as they appear when you print them out.◄

Position attributes

Works also allows you to control the position at which text is printed relative to its line of the document. Text assigned the Normal Paragraph attribute is printed on its line; text assigned the Superscript attribute is printed slightly above its line; and subscripted text is printed slightly below its line.

The options in the Position option box within the Font & Style dialog box control the position attributes of the characters in a document. Normal is the default attribute. If you want a block of text to be superscripted, you should highlight the text, open the Font & Style dialog box, choose the Superscript option within the Position option box, then choose <OK>. Alternatively, you can highlight the text and press [Ctrl][Shift]=. If you want a block of text to be subscripted, you would choose the Subscript option from the Position option box or press [Ctrl]=. Since these attributes are mutually exclusive, assigning one position attribute to a character cancels whatever position attribute was assigned to that character previously.

►WORKS 2◄

►Like styles, position attributes do not appear on the screen if Works is in the Text mode. For example, characters to which you have assigned the Superscript attribute do not appear shifted above the rest of their lines on the screen. However, characters that have been assigned the Superscript or Subscript attributes appear in bright video on a monochrome screen and in color on a color screen. Additionally, when the cursor is positioned on a character that has a special position attribute, Works will display a code on the status line that tells you what attribute is assigned to that character. If the character has been assigned the Superscript attribute, Works will display a + on the status line; if the character has been assigned the Subscript attribute, Works will display an =.

Of course, if you are in the Graphics mode, Works will display superscript and subscript text on the screen.◄

You can control the font and size of text by making selections from the Fonts and Sizes list boxes in the Font & Style dialog box. To assign a font and size to a block of text (or to the cursor), highlight that block (or position the cursor where you want to insert text), open the Font & Style dialog box, and choose the font and size you want to assign to the block from the lists that Works presents in the Fonts and Sizes list boxes. Since the entries in the Sizes box change depending on which font you select in the Fonts box, you should select a font first. The font and size that are highlighted when you choose <OK> in the dialog box are the ones that Works will assign to the selected characters (or to the cursor).

Fonts and sizes

Since different printers are capable of printing in different fonts and sizes, the choices that Works lists in the Fonts and Sizes boxes vary depending on which printer is selected in the Printer Setup dialog box. Typically, dot matrix printers can print in a wide variety of sizes but only a few fonts; daisy wheel printers can print in a wide variety of fonts but only a few sizes; and laser printers can print in a wide variety of both fonts and sizes. For example, Figure 5-13 shows some of the 23 fonts available for an HP LaserJet printer (a laser printer), Figure 5-14 shows some of the eight fonts available for an Epson LQ-1000 printer (a dot matrix printer); and Figure 5-15 on the following page shows some of the 19 fonts available for a Diablo 630 printer (a daisy wheel printer). (To learn how to use the Printer Setup... command to select different printers, refer to Chapter 3.)

Figure 5-14

The Fonts list box in this Font & Style dialog box lists some of the fonts available for an Epson LQ-1000 printer.

After you assign a font and size to some text, Works will display font and size indicators on the status line. Works will indicate the font by abbreviation and the size by number. For example, if your cursor or a block of text is formatted in 12-point Courier type, you'll see the legend *COU12* near the middle of the status line. (If a block of text contains more than one font and size, Works will indicate the attributes of the leftmost character in the block.) You may also find that Works rejustifies the text in the document to account for the larger or smaller text. In this way, Works indicates which words will appear on each line of the document when it is printed.

Figure 5-15

The Fonts list box in this Font & Style dialog box lists some of the fonts available for a Diablo 630 printer.

For example, Figure 5-16 shows the same sentence with different font and size selections. The sentence on top has been formatted with 8-point Helvetica type; the second sentence has been formatted with 14-point Helvetica type. Although Works displays all the characters in the same size on the screen, it varies the spacing at the end of each line to account for the different fonts and sizes. As you can see, the first sentence doesn't stop at the right margin, while the second sentence wraps well before it.

Figure 5-16

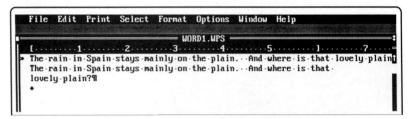

The number of characters that Works places on each line of a document depends on the fonts and sizes assigned to those characters.

The size of the characters in a document also affects how many lines Works can print on each page. Although Works does not vary the spacing between the lines of text on the screen to account for the different sizes of the characters in the text, it does reposition the page-break marker. With the default top and bottom margins, 54 lines of 12-point type will fit on each page. If your document contains only 12-point type, Works will display a page-break marker every 54 lines. If the text is 14 point, however, Works will display a page-break marker every 48 lines.

Cancelling character formats

Although Works gives you several ways to assign formats to the characters in a document, it gives you only two ways to remove them. First, you can highlight the characters whose formats you want to remove and issue the Plain Text command, either by choosing it from the Format menu or by pressing [Ctrl][Spacebar]. When you do this, Works will remove all style attributes (Bold, Italic, and so forth) from the highlighted text, and return it to the Normal position (rather than Superscript or Subscript). However, it will not change the fonts and sizes assigned to those characters.

You can remove formats individually by accessing the Font & Style dialog box and turning off the formats that you want to remove from the selected characters. To turn off a format that is controlled by a check box (Bold, Italic, Underline, and Strikethrough), you simply replace the X's in them (hyphens if more than one character is selected) with blanks, using any of the techniques discussed in Chapter 1. Although you can't turn off a character's Position attribute, you can return it to its default state (Normal). To do this, simply move the dot to the Normal option in the Position option box. Turning off a character's font or size also means returning it to its default state. To do this, you must choose the default font and size from the Fonts and Sizes list boxes. (To determine the default font and size for your printer, position the cursor under a single unformatted character and issue the Font & Style... command. The default font and size will be highlighted in the Fonts and Sizes list boxes.)

Unfortunately, you cannot use the Bold, Underline, or Italic commands on the Format menu or any of the keyboard shortcuts to turn off individual attributes. These commands are not toggles. For example, if you select a block of boldfaced text, pull down the Format menu, and choose Bold, the text will remain boldfaced.

A note about printers

The ease with which you can print in various styles, fonts, and sizes depends on the type of printer you are using. Dot matrix printers and laser printers can switch from one style, font, and size to another without any help from you. Daisy wheel printers cannot. Whenever Works encounters a character assigned a style, font, or size that is not available on the daisy wheel that is currently attached to your printer, it will display an alert box that asks you to install a new wheel and choose <OK> to resume printing. To avoid the inconvenience of switching daisy wheels, we recommend that you use different styles, fonts, and sizes sparingly when printing to a daisy wheel printer.

As we have explained, different fonts and sizes are available on different printers. When you select different printers from the Printer Setup dialog box, Works varies the choices listed in the Font & Style dialog box's Fonts and Sizes list boxes. Occasionally, you may assign fonts and sizes to a document while one printer is selected, then select another printer before you print. If the font you assigned is available on the new printer, Works will use that font. If the font is unavailable, Works will do its best to find a font that approximates the one that is not available.

**SETTING THE
MARGINS FOR
A DOCUMENT**

Works allows you to control the page width and page length of any word processor document. The page width of a document is the maximum amount of space available for text across a page; the page length is the maximum amount of vertical space available for text on a page. The default page width is six inches; the default page length is nine inches.

To set the page width and page lengths, use the Page Setup & Margins... command on the Print menu. When you issue this command, you'll see a Page Setup & Margins dialog box like the one shown in Figure 5-17. The first four text boxes at the upper-left and the two text boxes at the upper-right of this dialog box control the line and page lengths of a document.

Figure 5-17

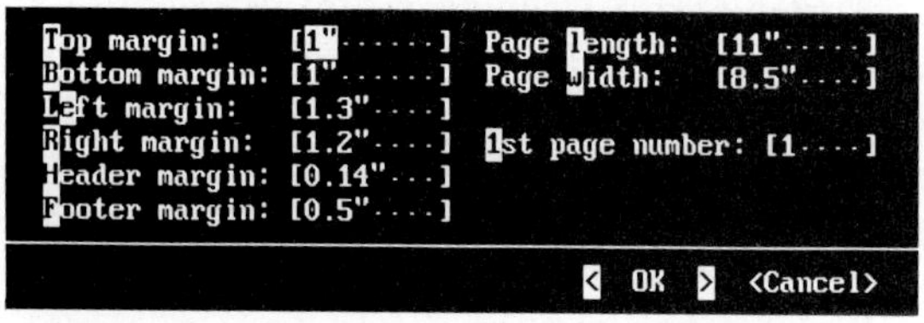

```
Top margin:     [1"·····]  Page Length:  [11"·····]
Bottom margin:  [1"·····]  Page Width:   [8.5"····]
Left margin:    [1.3"····]
Right margin:   [1.2"····]  1st page number: [1····]
Header margin:  [0.14"···]
Footer margin:  [0.5"····]

                              ◄ OK ►   <Cancel>
```

The entries in the text boxes at the upper-right of the Page Setup & Margins dialog box control the page width and page length of a word processor document.

**Setting the
page width**

The entries in the Left Margin, Right Margin, and Page Width boxes control the page width of a word processor document. The page width is equal to the Page Width setting minus the sum of the Left Margin and Right Margin settings. The default settings for page width (8.5"), left margin (1.3"), and right margin (1.2") create a line length of six inches.

When the cursor is on a paragraph that you have not indented relative to the left and right margins (something we'll show you how to do in a few pages), the positions of the [and] symbols on the ruler at the top of a word processor document indicate the page width for that document. The [symbol will appear on the left edge of the ruler—the point at which the left margin of the page begins. The] symbol will appear one page width to the right of the left-margin symbol. The position of the] symbol marks where the right margin of the page ends. This is the point at which Works will wrap text from one line to the next.

Changing the entries in the Page Width, Left Margin, and Right Margin text boxes changes the page width of a document. In most cases, you'll want to keep the Page Width entry set to the width of the paper on which you are printing. To increase or decrease the page width, you'll want to adjust the Left Margin and Right Margin settings. To increase the page width, you must decrease one or both of the settings; to decrease the page width, you must increase the settings.

Figure 5-18

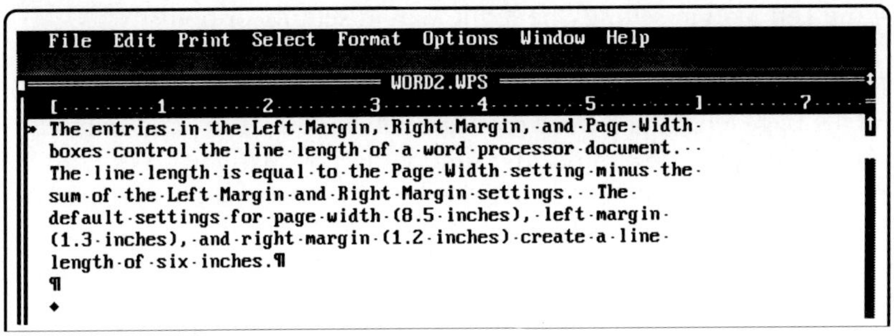

```
 File  Edit  Print  Select  Format  Options  Window  Help
═══════════════════════════ WORD2.WPS ═══════════════════════
[·········1······2·······3·······4········5········]······7····
► The·entries·in·the·Left·Margin,·Right·Margin,·and·Page·Width·
  boxes·control·the·line·length·of·a·word·processor·document.···
  The·line·length·is·equal·to·the·Page·Width·setting·minus·the·
  sum·of·the·Left·Margin·and·Right·Margin·settings.···The·
  default·settings·for·page·width·(8.5·inches),·left·margin·
  (1.3·inches),·and·right·margin·(1.2·inches)·create·a·line·
  length·of·six·inches.¶
  ¶
  ◆
```

This figure shows a word processor document with the standard page width of six inches.

As you adjust these settings, the] indicator will move in or out to reflect the new page width; the [marker will remain at the left edge of the ruler. If the document contains text, Works will adjust it to conform to the new page width. For example, Figure 5-18 shows a word processor document with the standard six-inch page width; Figure 5-19 shows the same document after we've decreased the page width to four inches.

Figure 5-19

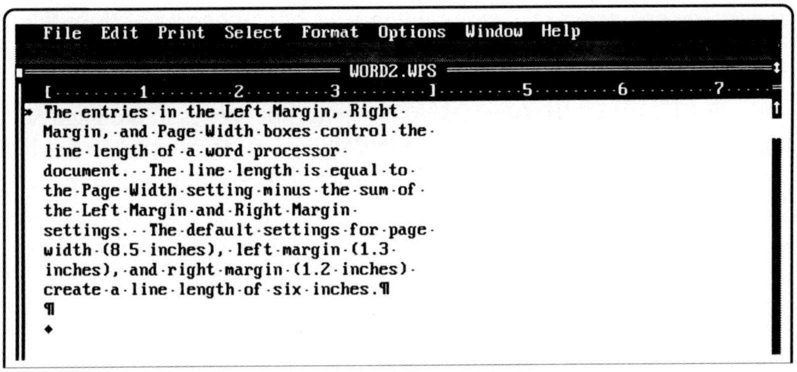

```
 File  Edit  Print  Select  Format  Options  Window  Help
═══════════════════════════ WORD2.WPS ═══════════════════════
[·········1······2·······3·······]·······5········6·······7····
► The·entries·in·the·Left·Margin,·Right·
  Margin,·and·Page·Width·boxes·control·the·
  line·length·of·a·word·processor·
  document.···The·line·length·is·equal·to·
  the·Page·Width·setting·minus·the·sum·of·
  the·Left·Margin·and·Right·Margin·
  settings.···The·default·settings·for·page·
  width·(8.5·inches),·left·margin·(1.3·
  inches),·and·right·margin·(1.2·inches)·
  create·a·line·length·of·six·inches.¶
  ¶
  ◆
```

This figure shows the document shown in Figure 5-18 after we decreased the page width to four inches.

When you alter the page width of a document, remember that you are doing so by adjusting the amount of "white space" that will appear at the left and right edges of the page when Works prints the document. Unless you adjust both the Left Margin and Right Margin settings equally, the printed document will be skewed either to the left or right on the page. However, this change will be obvious. The document will appear the same way on the screen whether you adjust the Left Margin setting, the Right Margin setting, or both.

Setting the page length

The entries in the Top Margin, Bottom Margin, and Page Length text boxes control the page length of a word processor document. The page length is equal to the Page Length setting minus the sum of the Top Margin and Bottom Margin settings. The default settings for page length (11"), top margin (1"), and bottom margin (also 1") create a page length of nine inches.

Changing the entries in the Page Length, Top Margin, and Bottom Margin text boxes changes the page length of a document. In most cases, you'll want to keep the Page Length entry set to the length of the paper on which you are printing. To increase or decrease the page length, you'll want to adjust the Top Margin and Bottom Margin settings. To increase the page length, you must decrease one or both of those settings; to decrease the page length, you must increase them. Remember—you adjust the page length of a document by varying the amount of white space that will appear at the top and bottom of each printed page. To keep the document balanced, you should adjust the Top Margin and Bottom Margin settings equally.

As you increase and decrease the page length of a document, Works will reposition the page-break markers within it so that they correctly mark the first line that will appear on each page. The size attributes of the characters in a document determine how many lines can be printed on each page. Works takes the size attributes of the characters in a document into account when it positions the page-break markers in that document.

Units of measure

As we explained in Chapter 3, Works will accept entries in the Page Setup & Margins dialog box in terms of inches, centimeters, 10-pitch units, 12-pitch units, and points. To specify measurements in terms of these units, you must use the suffixes *"*, *cm*, *p10*, *p12*, and *pt*, respectively. If you don't specify a unit of measure, Works will assume you mean the default unit of measure—the one listed in the Works Settings dialog box. For more on these units of measure and the Works Settings dialog box, refer to Chapter 3 and Appendix 2.

FORMATTING PARAGRAPHS

In addition to letting you format the characters in a word processor document, Works allows you to format paragraphs. By "formatting paragraphs," we mean adjusting attributes like the indention of a paragraph relative to the left and right margins, the alignment of the text in a paragraph, the spacing between the lines of a paragraph, and the spacing between paragraphs; preventing page breaks within a paragraph; positioning the tab stops within a paragraph; and placing borders around a paragraph.

Formatting a paragraph is a two-step process. First, you must position the cursor in or highlight a block of text within the paragraph you want to format. (To Works, a paragraph is any block of text preceded by a ¶ symbol or the beginning of that document and followed by a ¶ symbol.) If you want to format more than one paragraph at a time, you should expand the highlight to cover at least one character in each of those paragraphs. Once you have marked the paragraph(s) you want to format, you should issue the command that controls that format. The commands that control paragraph formats are located in the middle and bottom sections of the Format menu.

▶The four possible alignment formats—Left, Center, Right, and Justified—are represented by commands on the Format menu, as are commands that control two of the possible line-spacing formats: Single Space and Double Space. The remaining paragraph formats are accessible only through the Indents & Spacing..., Tabs..., and Borders… commands. (The six formats that are available from the Format menu are accessible through the Indents & Spacing... command as well. The Right command on the Format menu is new to Works 2. The Indents & Spacing… command replaces the Paragraph… command in Works 1.)◀

▶WORKS 2◀

When you issue the Indents & Spacing... command, Works will present a dialog box like the one shown in Figure 5-20. The elements in the Indents & Spacing dialog box control all of the formats you can assign to a paragraph except the position, alignment, and styling of tab stops, and the location and style of borders. (To set the tab stops in a document, you must use the Tabs... command. To assign a border to a paragraph, you must use the Borders… command.) The first three text boxes control the indention of the paragraph; the next three text boxes control the spacing within and between paragraphs; the last two check boxes control whether Works will split a paragraph or a pair of paragraphs onto separate pages when it prints the document; and the option box controls the alignment of the paragraph.

Figure 5-20

The elements in the Indents & Spacing dialog box control all the formats of a paragraph except the position, alignment, and styling of tab stops and the locations and styles of borders.

If the cursor or highlight is marking a single paragraph when you issue the Indents & Spacing... command, Works will display the formats of that paragraph in the Indents & Spacing dialog box. If more than one paragraph is highlighted, the text boxes will be blank, the check boxes will contain hyphens, and none of the options in the Alignment option box will be chosen, even if all the paragraphs have the same formats.

When you choose <OK> from the Indents & Spacing dialog box, Works will assign the formats specified in that box to the paragraphs that are highlighted at the time. Formats that are on will be assigned to those paragraphs; formats that are off will be removed from those paragraphs; and formats that are neither on nor off (that is, text boxes that are empty, check boxes that contain hyphens, and option boxes in which nothing is selected) will not affect the current characteristics of the selected paragraphs. Consequently, it's possible to change one format characteristic of a group of paragraphs without changing any other characteristics, many of which may be different for the various paragraphs that are selected.

In addition to using the commands in the middle of the Format menu to format the paragraphs in a document, you can use the keyboard shortcuts shown in Table 5-3. To use these key combinations to format a paragraph, position the cursor within the paragraph and press the appropriate key combination. (To format more than one paragraph, you must highlight at least one character within each paragraph.) For example, to center a paragraph, you could move the cursor to it and press [Ctrl]c.

Table 5-3

Paragraph attribute	Keyboard shortcut
Normal paragraph	[Ctrl]x
Left alignment	[Ctrl]l
Justified alignment	[Ctrl]j
Center alignment	[Ctrl]c
Right alignment	[Ctrl]r
Indent left edge of text	[Ctrl]n
Remove indent from left edge of text	[Ctrl]m
Hanging first-line indent	[Ctrl]h
Remove hanging indent	[Ctrl]g
Double spacing	[Ctrl]2
Single spacing	[Ctrl]1
One and one-half spacing	[Ctrl]5
Insert one line above paragraph	[Ctrl]o
Remove space above paragraph	[Ctrl]e

These key combinations provide alternatives to the commands on the Format menu for formatting paragraphs.

The default settings for any paragraph are as follows: left-aligned, single spacing within paragraphs, no indents relative to the left and right margins of the document, no space before or after the paragraph, and default tab stops every $1/2$ inch. If you want the formats of most of the paragraphs in a document to differ from the defaults, you should modify the formats before you begin typing the document. That way, Works will extend the format to the entire document as you create it (whenever you press [Enter] to begin a new paragraph, Works assigns the formats of the previous paragraph to the new paragraph).

Indenting paragraphs

Works allows you to indent paragraphs relative to the left and right margins of a document and indent the first line of a paragraph relative to the remaining lines in the paragraph. The Left Indent, Right Indent, and 1st Line Indent text boxes in the Indents & Spacing dialog box allow you to control the indention of a paragraph. Works also features a number of key combinations that provide faster ways to create standard indentions. We'll show you how to indent paragraphs relative to the left and right margins of a document; then, we'll show you how to indent the first line of each paragraph.

Indenting a paragraph relative to the left and right margins

The Left Indent and Right Indent text boxes in the Indents & Spacing dialog box let you indent a paragraph from the left and right margins of a document. As we explained earlier, the 0 point on the ruler at the top of a document marks the left margin of that document. When the cursor is in a paragraph that is not indented from the left margin of the document, a [symbol appears at that point. The right margin of a document is the point at which text wraps in normal paragraphs. When the cursor is in a paragraph that is not indented from the right margin of a document, a] symbol appears at that point. For example, Figure 5-21 shows a standard document that has three unindented paragraphs.

Figure 5-21

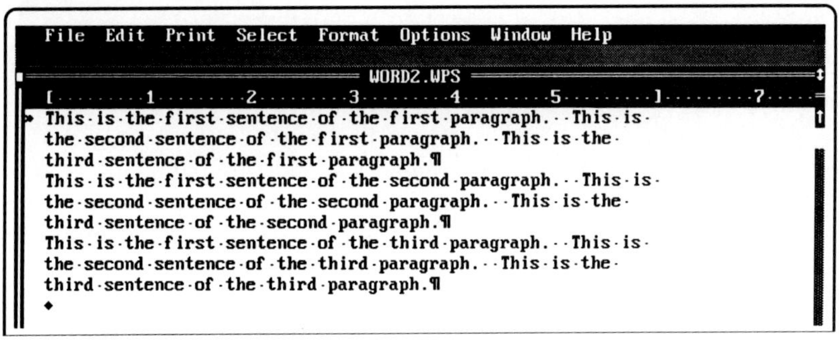

Unless you specify otherwise, the paragraphs in a word processor document will not be indented relative to the left and right margins of that document.

Indenting a paragraph from the left margin.   The entry in the Left Indent text box determines how far the current paragraph will be indented from the left margin of the document. The default entry in this box—0"—specifies no indention at all. To indent a paragraph from the left edge of a document, you must enter a value greater than 0 into this box. For example, if you want an indention of $\frac{1}{2}$ inch relative to the left margin, you would enter .5" into the Left Indent text box. (If the default unit of measure is inches, you can simply enter .5 instead.) You also can use any of the other units of measure that Works understands: centimeters (cm), 10-point units (p10), 12-point units (p12), and points (pt). In any case, the number you enter must be greater than or equal to 0.

Once you enter a positive value into the Left Indent text box and choose <OK>, Works will shift the text to the right in the paragraph(s) you selected. For example, Figure 5-22 shows the sample document from Figure 5-21 after we indented the second paragraph one inch from the left margin of the document. To do this, we positioned the cursor in that paragraph, pulled down the Format menu, selected the Indents & Spacing... command, typed 1 into the Left Indent text box, and pressed [Enter].

Figure 5-22

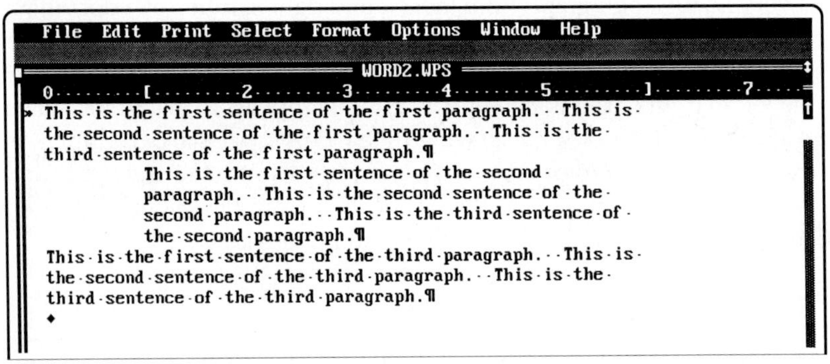

This figure shows the document from Figure 5-21 after we indented the second paragraph one inch from the left margin.

As you can see in Figure 5-22, each line of the second paragraph begins one inch from the left edge of the document. The [symbol also appears one inch from the left edge of the document. Whenever the cursor is in a paragraph that is indented from the left edge of a document, the [symbol will mark the amount of the indention. (If more than one paragraph is highlighted, the [symbol will mark the indention of the top paragraph.)

Works offers a shortcut for indenting a paragraph relative to the left margin of a document. When you press the [Ctrl]n key combination, Works will indent the left margin of the current paragraph an amount equal to the distance from the left edge of the document to the first default tab stop (usually $\frac{1}{2}$ inch). For example, if the current paragraph is not indented relative to the left margin, and the first tab stop is at the $\frac{1}{2}$-inch point, pressing [Ctrl]n will indent it $\frac{1}{2}$ inch; pressing [Ctrl]n again will indent it by another $\frac{1}{2}$ inch; and so forth. If the paragraph is already indented $\frac{3}{4}$ inch from the left margin, pressing [Ctrl]n will increase the indention to $1\frac{1}{4}$ inches.

The [Ctrl]m combination decreases the indention of a paragraph relative to the left margin in increments equal to the distance between the left edge of the document and the first default tab stop. For example, if a paragraph is indented one inch relative to the left margin, and the first default tab stop is at the $\frac{1}{2}$-inch point, pressing [Ctrl]m once will reduce the indention to $\frac{1}{2}$ inch and pressing [Ctrl]m will again reduce the indention to 0.

Indenting a paragraph from the right margin. The entry in the Right indent text box determines how far the current paragraph will be indented from the right margin of the document. The default entry in this box—0"—specifies no indention at all. To indent a paragraph from the right edge of a document, you must enter a value greater than 0 into this box. For example, if you want an indention of $\frac{3}{4}$ inch relative to the right margin, you would enter .75 into the Right indent box. The number you enter must be greater than or equal to 0.

Figure 5-23

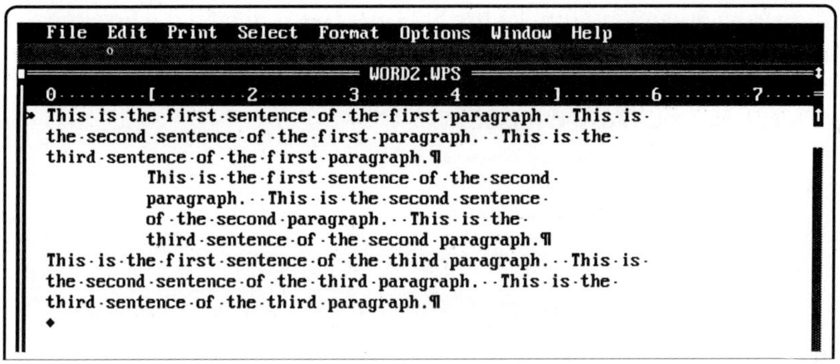

```
 File  Edit  Print  Select  Format  Options  Window  Help
                0
                        ══════════ WORD2.WPS ══════════
 0·······[·······2·······3·······4·······]·······6·······7····
▶ This·is·the·first·sentence·of·the·first·paragraph.···This·is·
  the·second·sentence·of·the·first·paragraph.···This·is·the·
  third·sentence·of·the·first·paragraph.¶
             This·is·the·first·sentence·of·the·second·
             paragraph.···This·is·the·second·sentence·
             of·the·second·paragraph.···This·is·the·
             third·sentence·of·the·second·paragraph.¶
  This·is·the·first·sentence·of·the·third·paragraph.···This·is·
  the·second·sentence·of·the·third·paragraph.···This·is·the·
  third·sentence·of·the·third·paragraph.¶
  ◆
```

This figure shows the document from Figure 5-22 after we indented the second paragraph one inch from the right margin.

When you enter a positive value into the Right indent box and choose <OK>, Works will shift the text in the paragraphs that were highlighted when you issued the Indents & Spacing... command inward from the right margin of the document. For example, Figure 5-23 shows the document from Figure 5-22 after we indented the second paragraph one inch from the right margin. (We indented it one inch from the left margin previously.) To indent this paragraph one inch from the right margin of the document, we positioned the cursor in that paragraph, pulled down the Format menu, selected the Indents & Spacing... command, typed 1 into the Right Indent text box, and pressed [Enter]. As you can see, each line of this paragraph ends at least one inch from the right edge of the document and the] symbol appears one inch from the right edge of the document. Whenever the cursor is in a paragraph that is indented from the right edge of a document, the] symbol will mark the amount of the indention. (If more than one paragraph is highlighted, the] symbol will mark the indention of the top paragraph.)

Indenting the first line of a paragraph

In addition to indenting a paragraph relative to the right or left margins of a document, you can indent the first line of a paragraph relative to the rest of the paragraph. The 1st Line Indent setting in the Indents & Spacing dialog box controls the indention of the first line of a paragraph. The default entry in this box—0"—specifies no indention at all. To indent the first line of a paragraph, you must enter a value greater than 0 into this box. For example, if you want the first line of the paragraph to be indented $1/_4$ inch relative to the remainder of the document, you would enter .25 into the 1st Line Indent text box.

When you enter a positive value into the 1st Line Indent text box and choose <OK>, Works will shift the first line of the paragraphs that were selected when you issued the Indents & Spacing... command inward from the left margin of the document. (If the paragraph is indented from the left margin, Works will indent the first line from the first indention point to the new one.) For example, Figure 5-24 shows the document from Figure 5-23 after we indented the first line of each paragraph $1/_2$ inch. To do this, we expanded the highlight to cover the entire document, selected the Indents & Spacing... command, typed .5 into the 1st Line Indent text box, and pressed [Enter].

Figure 5-24

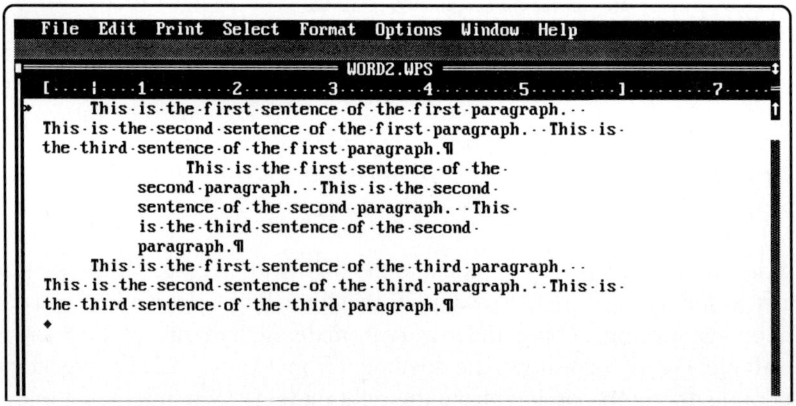

This figure shows the document from Figure 5-22 after we indented the first line of each paragraph $1/_2$ inch.

As you can see, Works has indented the first line of each paragraph $^1/_2$ inch. In the case of the first and third paragraphs, which are not indented relative to the left margins of the document, Works indented their first lines $^1/_2$ inch relative to the left margin of the document. In the case of the second paragraph, which is indented one inch from the left margin of the document, Works indented its first line $^1/_2$ inch from that point. Notice that Works has positioned a | symbol on the ruler. Whenever the cursor is in a paragraph whose first line is indented, Works displays this symbol at the point of the indentation. In this figure, the cursor is positioned in the second paragraph, which is indented one inch relative to the left margin. Consequently, Works positions the first line-indention mark at the $1^1/_2$-inch point.

By using the 1st Line Indent setting in combination with the Left Indent setting, you can create "hanging indents"—situations in which the first line of each paragraph starts to the left of the other lines of that paragraph. You'll commonly use this technique when you list a series of numbered points in a document, like the one shown in Figure 5-25.

Hanging indentions

Figure 5-25

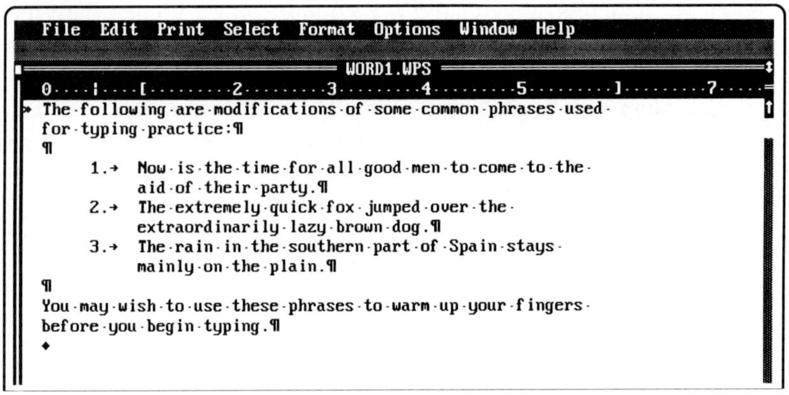

You can use the 1st Line Indent setting in conjunction with the Left Indent setting to create hanging indents.

Creating a hanging indent.   To create hanging indents, you must enter a negative value into the 1st Line Indent text box and enter a positive value into the Left Indent box. The absolute value (that is, positive equivalent) of the value in the 1st Line Indent text box must be smaller than the entry in the Left indent box. For example, to create the hanging indents shown in Figure 5-25, we highlighted the third through fifth paragraphs, pulled down the Format menu, selected the Indents & Spacing… command, typed 1 into the Left indent box, typed -.5 into the 1st Line Indent text box, and chose <OK>. The entry in the Left Indent box tells Works to indent each paragraph one inch relative to the left edge of the document. The entry in the 1st Line Indent box tells Works to "outdent" the first line of each paragraph by $1/2$ inch relative to the left indent of that paragraph. Note that the first line indent marker (|) appears to the left of the left indent marker ([).

Works offers a shortcut for creating a hanging indent. When you press the [Ctrl]h key combination, Works "outdents" the first line of the current paragraph by the distance from the left edge of the document to the first default tab stop (usually $1/2$ inch). If you press [Ctrl]h more than once, Works will continue to indent the left edge of each line of the current paragraph by the same increment, without changing the amount of the hanging indention. For example, suppose you've pressed [Ctrl]h once to create a $1/2$-inch hanging indention. If you press [Ctrl]h a second time, Works will indent the first line of the paragraph by $1/2$ inch and indent all subsequent lines by an additional $1/2$ inch so that they are aligned at the 1-inch point on the ruler.

The [Ctrl]g key combination undoes the effect of the [Ctrl]h combination. If you have pressed the [Ctrl]h combination multiple times, you will have to press [Ctrl]g the same number of times to remove the hanging indent completely.

Aligning paragraphs

By default, the paragraphs in a Works word processor document will be left-aligned; that is, the leftmost character in each line will be aligned with the left margin of the document (or, if the paragraph is indented from the left edge of the document, the point of the left indent). If you want, however, you can assign any of these other alignment attributes to a paragraph: Center, Right, or Justified. Figure 5-26 shows examples of the four possible alignments. As you can see, each line of the centered paragraph is centered relative to the right and left margins of that paragraph. The rightmost character in each line of the right-aligned paragraph is aligned with the right margin of that paragraph. The leftmost character in each line of the justified paragraph is aligned with the left margin of that paragraph, and the rightmost character on each line is aligned with the right margin.

To assign an alignment attribute to a single paragraph, you can either position the cursor in it or highlight one or more characters in it. To assign an alignment attribute to more than one paragraph at a time, you must extend the highlight to cover at least one character in each paragraph.

Once you have selected the paragraphs you want to align, you can assign an alignment attribute to them in a number of ways. You can pull down the Format menu and choose the Left, Center, Right, or Justified commands. Alternatively, you can select the Indents & Spacing... command to reveal the Indents & Spacing dialog box, choose the Left, Center, Right, or Justified options from the Alignment option box, and choose <OK>. Third, you can press the [Ctrl]l, [Ctrl]c, [Ctrl]r, or [Ctrl]j key combinations. Assigning one alignment attribute to a paragraph cancels the one that was assigned to the paragraph formerly.

Figure 5-26

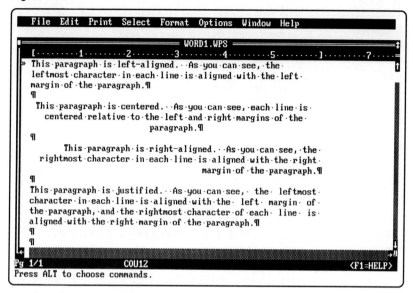

Works offers four paragraph alignment options: Left, Center, Right, and Justified.

Line spacing

Works also allows you to control the spacing between lines in a paragraph; that is, the number of blank lines it inserts between lines of text. The default line spacing is Auto. This value produces single-spaced text—paragraphs that have no blank lines. If you want, however, you can specify different spacing; for example, one blank line between each two lines of text (double-spacing), two blank lines (triple-spacing), and so forth. You can even specify fractional spacing; for example, $1\frac{1}{2}$ and $2\frac{3}{4}$. Unless you specify fractional spacing, Works will display paragraphs on the screen with the spacing you specify. For example, the document shown in Figure 5-27 on the following page contains two paragraphs: The first is single-spaced and the second is double-spaced. The blank lines that Works adds to a document are not usable; you cannot move the cursor to them or type anything on them.

Once you have selected the paragraphs whose spacing you want to alter, you can change their spacing in a number of ways. If you want the paragraphs to be single-spaced or double-spaced, you can select the Single Space or Double Space commands from the Format menu, press [Ctrl]1 for single-spacing or [Ctrl]2 for double-spacing, or select the Indents & Spacing... command to reveal the Indents & Spacing dialog box, type 0, 1, or 2 into the Line Spacing text box, then choose <OK>. A value of 0 or 1 in the box instructs Works not to add any space between lines; a value of 2 commands it to add one blank line.

Figure 5-27

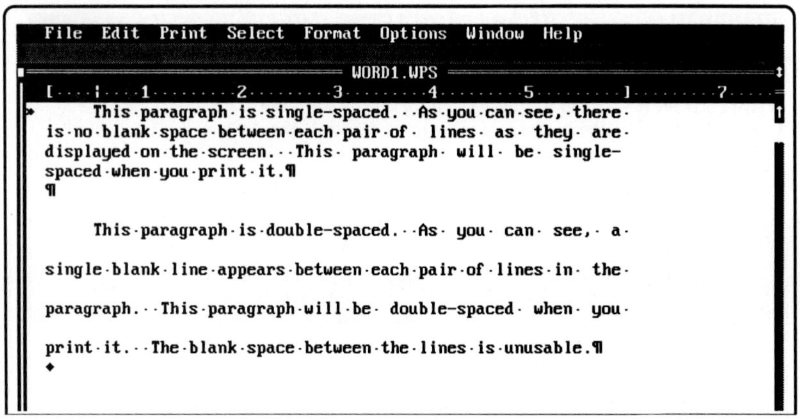

```
   File  Edit  Print  Select  Format  Options  Window  Help

                          WORD1.WPS
  [····¦····1·······2·······3·······4·······5·······]·······7····
     This·paragraph·is·single-spaced.··As·you·can·see,·there·
  is·no·blank·space·between·each·pair·of·lines·as·they·are·
  displayed·on·the·screen.··This·paragraph·will·be·single-
  spaced·when·you·print·it.¶
  ¶

     This·paragraph·is·double-spaced.··As·you·can·see,·a·

  single·blank·line·appears·between·each·pair·of·lines·in·the·

  paragraph.··This·paragraph·will·be·double-spaced·when·you·

  print·it.··The·blank·space·between·the·lines·is·unusable.¶
  ◆
```

The line spacing you select for a paragraph affects the way Works displays the paragraph on the screen.

If you want to specify a number of blank lines other than 0, 1, or 2, you must use the Line Spacing text box. The number you enter into this box is the number of blank lines Works will insert between the lines of the paragraph when it prints the document. For example, to get triple-spacing (two lines between lines of text), you would type 3. (For $1^1/_2$ spaces between each line, you can press [Ctrl]5.)

Fractional line spacing

If you want, you can specify fractional line spacing; for example, $1^1/_2$ or $2^3/_4$ lines between lines of text. Unfortunately, Works cannot display fractional spacing on the screen. When you enter a fractional value into the Line Spacing text box, Works will display the paragraph on the screen according to the rounded value of that entry. For example, if you enter the value 1.4 into the Line Spacing text box, the paragraph will appear single-spaced on the screen. If you enter the value 1.5, however, Works will display the paragraph double-spaced. If your printer supports fractional spacing, it will use the spacing specified in the Line Spacing text box. If not, it will print the paragraph according to the rounded value—precisely the way Works displays it on the screen.

Alternative units

You usually will want to specify line spacing in terms of a number of lines. Works will assume you mean a number of lines when you enter a value without a suffix or with the suffix *li*. If you want, however, you can specify line spacing in terms of inches, centimeters, 10-pitch units, 12-pitch units, or points. To do so, you must follow the value you enter into the Line Spacing text box with the suffixes *"*, *cm*, *p10*, *p12*, and *pt*, respectively.

In addition to allowing you to control the amount of space between the lines of a paragraph, Works allows you to control the amount of space it inserts above and below any paragraph. The default spacing both above and below any paragraph is zero lines. These values produce paragraphs that appear one immediately after each other, both on the screen and in print. However, you can specify any amount of spacing you want. For example, you can specify 1 line before and 1 line after, 1.5 lines before and 2 lines after, and so forth. Unless you specify fractional spacing, Works will display paragraphs on the screen with the intra-paragraph spacing you specify. For example, we've commanded Works to add one line above and two lines below the second paragraph of the document shown in Figure 5-28. Just like the blank lines Works adds within paragraphs, the blank lines it adds above and below paragraphs are not usable.

Paragraph spacing

Figure 5-28

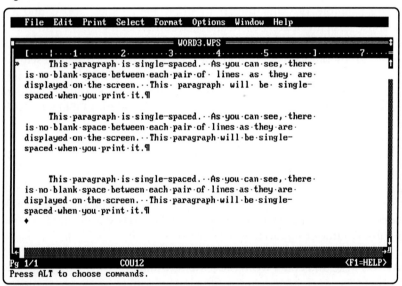

Works allows you to control the amount of space that appears above or below any paragraph in a word processor document.

Once you have selected the paragraphs whose spacing you want to control, you can change the amount of space above and below them in a couple of ways. If you want no lines above each paragraph, you can press [Ctrl]e (unless the paragraph above the highlighted one has been formatted to include a space after, in which case that space will separate the two paragraphs). If you want one line above each paragraph, you can press [Ctrl]o. If you want any other number of lines above each paragraph, or if you want to specify a number of lines below each paragraph, you must pull down the Format menu, select the Indents & Spacing… command to reveal the Indents & Spacing dialog box, make entries into the Space Before and Space After text boxes, then choose <OK>. The value you enter into the Space Before text box determines how much blank space Works will insert above the paragraph; the value you enter into the Space After text box determines how much space it will add after the paragraph. Unless you specify otherwise by using special suffixes, Works will interpret your entry as specifying a number of lines. If you enter a fractional value into either of these boxes, Works will display the paragraph on the screen according to the rounded value of that entry. If your printer supports fractional spacing, it will use the spacing specified in these boxes. If not, it will print the paragraph the way it is displayed on the screen.

The reasons for these options

There are three advantages to using the Space Before and Space After settings rather than simply pressing [Enter] to insert blank lines above and below paragraphs. First, the Space Before and Space After settings allow you to control the amount of space that will appear above or below a paragraph more precisely than you can by pressing the [Enter] key. Second, the Space Before setting will omit the space above any paragraph that happens to fall at the beginning of a new page. Third, it's easier to change the spacing before and after a large group of paragraphs with the Space Before and Space After settings than it is with the [Enter] key.

Line spacing effects

When you enter a value other than 0 into the Line Spacing text box, Works doesn't just insert space between the lines of the paragraph you're formatting— it also inserts space above the first line of the paragraph. This space adds to any space inserted above a paragraph by the Space Before setting. Be sure to keep this additive effect in mind when you use both the Space Before and Line Spacing setting in the same paragraph.

Controlling page breaks

As you write and edit a word processor document, Works keeps track of the positions of the page breaks in that document. Unlike some word processing software, Works will not set a page break in a position that will cause just the first line of a paragraph to appear at the bottom of a page, or that will push the last line of a paragraph to the top of the next page. (In word processing terms, a single line of a paragraph at the bottom or top of a page is a widow.)

In most cases, this ability to handle widows is all the control you'll need over the way Works divides a document into pages. In some cases, however, you may want to keep an entire paragraph or two together on the same page. The Don't Break this Paragraph and Keep this Paragraph with Next check boxes in the Indents & Spacing dialog box make these two things possible.

The Don't Break this Paragraph setting controls whether Works will insert a page break within a paragraph. When this setting is off (its default state), Works may insert a page break anywhere in a paragraph, as long as doing so does not create a widow. When this setting is on, Works will not insert a page break anywhere within the paragraph. If the paragraph will not fit entirely on one page, Works will place the page break ahead of it so that the entire paragraph is printed on the next page. If you don't want a paragraph to be split between pages, you should position the cursor within it, pull down the Format menu, then select the Indents & Spacing... command, and turn on the Don't Break this Paragraph setting, and choose <OK>.

Preventing page breaks within a paragraph

The Keep this Paragraph with Next setting controls whether Works will insert a page break between two paragraphs. When this setting is off (its default state), Works may insert a page break between one paragraph and the paragraph that follows it. When this setting is on, Works will not insert a page break between them. However, it may insert a page break within either of the paragraphs, as long as doing so does not create a widow. Consequently, this setting does not guarantee that all the lines in two adjacent paragraphs will be printed on the same page; it only ensures that at least two lines from one paragraph will appear on the same page as the other paragraph. If you want two paragraphs to appear on the same page in their entirety, you must turn on the Keep this Paragraph with Next setting for the first paragraph as well as turn on the Don't Break this Paragraph setting for both paragraphs.

Keeping two paragraphs together

At some point after you've assigned one or more formats to a paragraph, you may want to return one or more of them to their default state. To return every format to its default state, position the cursor in that paragraph and either pull down the Format menu and select the Normal Paragraph command or press the [Ctrl]x key combination. (If you want to clear the formats from more than one paragraph at a time, you must extend the highlight so that it covers at least one character in each paragraph beforehand.) When you do either of these things, Works will return all the attributes controlled by the elements in the Indents & Spacing dialog box to their default states. For example, it will return all indentions to 0, return line spacing to Auto, return alignment to Left, and so forth. Works also will clear all the custom tab stops and border settings from the paragraph. (We'll talk about custom tab stops and borders next.)

Removing paragraph formats

If you want, you can return any of a paragraph's formats to its default state. In most cases you will have to access the Indents & Spacing dialog box to do this. However, you can use the [Ctrl]l, [Ctrl]1, and [Ctrl]e key combinations to return the alignment, line spacing, and paragraph spacing attributes, respectively, to their default states.

Tab stops

Tab stops are the positions to which Works moves the cursor when you press the [Tab] key in a word processor document. Whenever you press the [Tab] key, Works will move the cursor to the first tab stop to the right of the current position of the cursor. For example, if the cursor is at the left edge of a document, and there are tab stops every $\frac{1}{2}$ inch, Works will move the cursor to the $\frac{1}{2}$-inch point—the first tab stop—when you press the [Tab] key. If the cursor was at the $\frac{3}{4}$-inch point, however, Works would move it to the 1-inch point—the second tab stop. As you can see, pressing the [Tab] key once doesn't necessarily move the cursor to the first tab stop on a line, pressing the [Tab] key a second time doesn't necessarily move the cursor to the second tab stop on a line, and so forth.

Any word processor document can have two types of tab stops: default tab stops and custom tab stops. Default tab stops occur at constant intervals along the ruler (initially, every $\frac{1}{2}$ inch); they are always the same for every paragraph in a document. Custom tab stops can occur at variable intervals. Different paragraphs can have different custom tab stops.

Figure 5-29

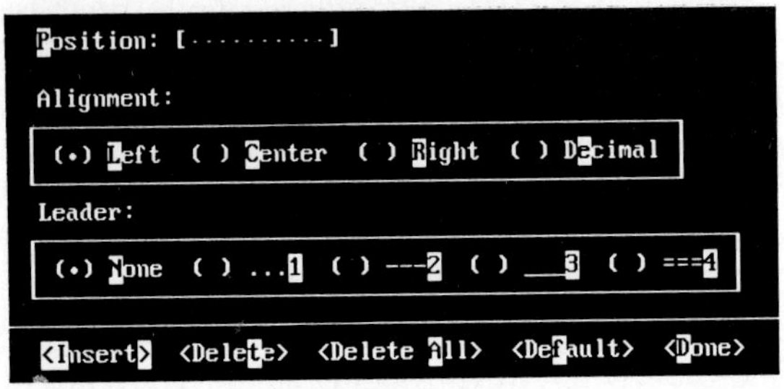

The Tabs dialog box allows you to alter both custom and default tab stops.

The Tabs... command, located at the bottom of the Format menu, allows you to control the default and custom tab stops within a paragraph. When you pull down the Format menu and select this command, Works will display a dialog box like the one shown in Figure 5-29. Using the elements in this box, you can change the default tab interval, and set and remove custom tab stops.

Changing the default tab interval

▶**WORKS 2**◀

Default tab stops occur at constant intervals along the ruler; this increment is always the same for every paragraph in a word processor document. Initially, every word processor document has default tab stops at $\frac{1}{2}$-inch intervals. However, you can change the default tab interval if you want. ▶To do this, pull down the Format menu and select the Tabs... command to reveal the Tabs dialog box. At the bottom of the dialog box, choose <Default>. When you do this, you'll see a second dialog box, like the one in Figure 5-30. For example, to change the default interval to $\frac{3}{4}$ inch, you would type .75". Although you usually will enter this value in terms of inches, you can specify the default tab interval in terms of centimeters, 10-pitch units, 12-pitch units, or points by using the *cm, p10, p12,* and *pt* suffixes. If you don't include a suffix, Works will assume you mean the default unit of measure (usually inches). Now, type the new default tab interval into the Spacing text box. and choose <OK>. When the original Tabs dialog box appears, choose <Done>. Works will then adjust the position of the default tabs in the entire document to the new interval.◄

Figure 5-30

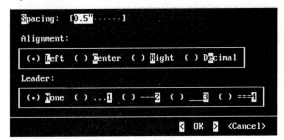

In this Tabs dialog box, you can alter the default Tabs settings.

Custom tab stops

In addition to letting you alter the default tab interval, Works allows you to set custom tab stops. Unlike default tabs, custom tabs do not have to occur at constant intervals along the ruler. For example, you could have one custom tab stop at $^3/_4$ inch, another at $2^1/_3$ inches, another at $2^7/_8$ inches, and so forth. Also, unlike default tabs, custom tabs do not have to be the same for every paragraph in a document. In fact, you can assign custom tab stops on a paragraph-by-paragraph basis.

Setting custom tab stops. Setting custom tabs involves four steps. First, choose the paragraph(s) in which you want to set a custom tab. If you want to set a custom tab in a single paragraph, you should move the cursor into that paragraph or highlight a group of characters within it. If you want to set a custom tab in more than one paragraph, you should expand the highlight so that it touches at least one character in each paragraph.

Once you have selected the paragraph(s) in which you want to set the tab stop, you should pull down the Format menu and select the Tabs... command to reveal the Tabs dialog box. To set the custom tab, type the position of the tab into the Position text box, then choose the <Insert> button. When you do this, Works will set a custom tab stop at the indicated position in each of the paragraphs that were selected when you issued the Tabs... command.

►Alternatively, when you open the Tabs dialog box, you can press [Ctrl][◄] or [Ctrl][►] to move the indicator on the ruler to the point where want to place a tab stop. Each time you press [Ctrl][►], the cursor moves 1/10 inch to the right; each time you press [Ctrl][◄], the cursor moves 1/10 inch to the left. As you move

►WORKS 2◄

the cursor, you'll notice its position appears in the Position text box. When you choose the <Insert> button, Works will set a custom tab stop at the indicated position on the ruler for each of the paragraphs that were selected when you selected the Tabs... command.◄

When specifying the position of the tab, you can use any of the five units of measure that Works accepts. Additionally, you can type as many digits to the right of the decimal place as you want. However, Works will round the position of the tab to the nearest $^1/_{100}$ inch when it sets it in the paragraph. For example, if you enter 2.367 into the Position text box, Works will set the tab stop at 2.37 inches.

After you set a custom tab stop for a paragraph, Works will display a marker on the ruler at the position of the tab whenever the cursor is in that paragraph. The exact marker Works uses depends on which alignment attribute you specified for the tab stop. In most cases, your tab stops will be left-aligned. Works marks left-aligned tabs with the letter *L*. Works uses the letters *C, R,* and *D* to mark centered, right-aligned, and decimal tabs, respectively—the other three alignment options. We'll talk about tab alignment in a few pages.

Once you set a custom tab stop in a paragraph, Works ignores any default tab stops to the left of that tab; that is, it acts as if they don't exist. For example, suppose you set a custom tab stop at the $^3/_4$-inch point in a paragraph when the default tab interval is $^1/_2$ inch. If you press the [Tab] key while the cursor is at the beginning of a line, Works will move the cursor to the $^3/_4$-inch point (the custom tab stop)—not the $^1/_2$-inch point (the default tab stop). However, any default tab stops to the right of the rightmost custom tab stop will remain active.

You can set as many custom tab stops for a paragraph as you want. However, you can set only one at a time. Each time you want to set a custom tab stop, you must pull down the Format menu and select the Tabs... command.

Clearing custom tab stops.   The <Delete> and <Delete All> buttons at the bottom of the Tabs dialog box allow you to clear the custom tab stops from one or more paragraphs. To clear all the custom tab stops from a paragraph at once, position the cursor in that paragraph, pull down the Format menu, select the Tabs... command, and choose the <Delete All> button. When you choose this button, Works will remove all the custom tab stops from the paragraph. At the same time, it will reactivate all the default tab stops in the paragraph and align the information in the paragraph with the appropriate default tab.

The <Delete> button allows you to clear custom tabs one at a time from a paragraph. To clear an individual custom tab stop from a paragraph, you must position the cursor in the paragraph, issue the Tabs... command, type the position of the tab you want to clear into the Position text box, and choose the <Delete> button. When you do this, Works will clear the custom tab whose position you specified without affecting any of the other custom tab stops in the paragraph.

►Alternatively, when you open the Tabs dialog box, you can press [Ctrl][←] or [Ctrl][→] to move the cursor on the ruler to the tab you want to delete. Each time you press [Ctrl][→], the cursor moves 1/10 inch to the right; each time you press [Ctrl][←], the cursor moves 1/10 inch to the left. As you move the cursor, its position appears in the Position text box. When you choose <Delete>, Works will remove the custom tab stop from the indicated position on the ruler for each of the paragraphs that were selected when you issued the Tabs... command.◄

Moving custom tab stops. Although the Tabs dialog box features buttons that allow you to insert and clear custom tab stops, it does not offer a button that allows you to move the positions of existing tabs. To move a custom tab stop from one location to another, you must clear the tab stop at the current location and set a new tab stop at the new location, or vice versa.

Controlling the alignment of custom tab stops. In addition to letting you set the position of a custom tab stop, Works also allows you to control its alignment. Works offers four alignment options: Left, Center, Right, and Decimal. The alignment attribute of a tab stop controls the way Works positions text that you type at that stop. The leftmost character you type at a left-aligned tab will be aligned at the position of that tab; the characters you type at a centered tab will be centered relative to the position of the tab; the rightmost character you type at a right-aligned tab will be aligned at the position of that tab; and the decimal point you type at a decimal tab will be aligned at the position of that tab. Figure 5-31 shows an example of these various alignments. As you can see, Works uses the letter L to mark left-aligned tabs, the letter C to mark centered tabs, the letter R to mark right-aligned tabs, and the letter D to mark decimal tabs.

Figure 5-31

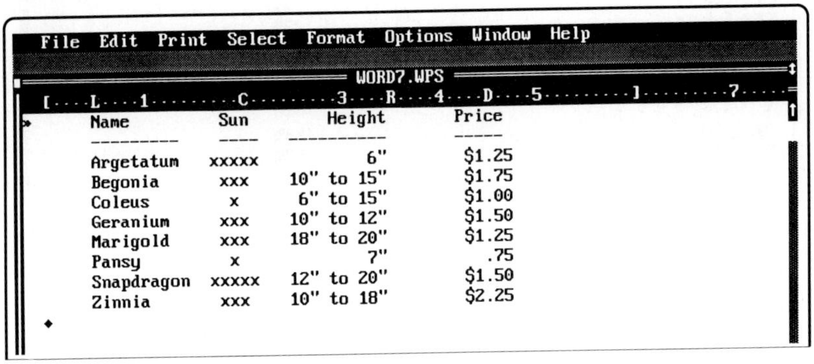

```
 File  Edit  Print  Select  Format  Options  Window  Help

═══════════════════════════ WORD7.WPS ═══════════════════════════
[····L····1·········C·········3···R····4··D····5··········]·······7····
    Name          Sun       Height        Price
    ─────────     ────      ──────────     ─────
    Argetatum    xxxxx             6"      $1.25
    Begonia       xxx      10" to 15"      $1.75
    Coleus         x        6" to 15"      $1.00
    Geranium      xxx      10" to 12"      $1.50
    Marigold      xxx      18" to 20"      $1.25
    Pansy          x               7"       .75
    Snapdragon   xxxxx     12" to 20"      $1.50
    Zinnia        xxx      10" to 18"      $2.25
```

Works allows you to set the alignment of custom tab stops.

Unless you specify otherwise, Works will create left-aligned tabs. To specify an alternative alignment, you must choose one of the other options from the Alignment option box in the Tabs dialog box as you are setting the tab. The option that is chosen when you choose <Insert> is the one Works will assign to the custom tab whose position you typed into the Position text box.

►WORKS 2◄

Although you usually will assign these alternative alignments to custom tabs, you can assign them to the default tabs for a document. ►To do this, choose the <Default> button in the main Tabs dialog box, select the alignment option you want from the Default Tabs dialog box, then choose the <OK> button. This will close the Default Tabs dialog box, at which point you can choose the <Done> button to apply your default tab alteration to the document.◄

Leaders

If you want, you can command Works to display one of four "leaders" to the left of any custom tab stop: a series of periods (...), a series of dashes (———), a series of underlines (___), or a series of equal signs (===). When you assign a leader attribute to a tab, Works will fill the white space to the left of that tab with the appropriate character. For example, we've assigned the .... leader to the right-aligned custom tab at the 5" position of the document shown in Figure 5-32. As you can see, Works has filled the space to the left of each page number with a series of periods.

Figure 5-32

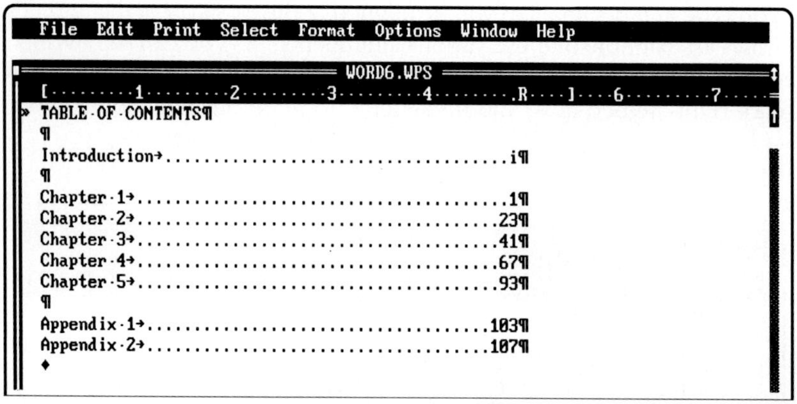

We've displayed the first of Works first four tab leaders.

If you look at the ruler of the document shown in Figure 5-32, you'll see a period to the left of the *R* that marks the right-aligned tab at the 5" mark. This period indicates that you have assigned the .... leader to that tab stop. Works displays the symbols -, _, and = to the left of the markers for tab stops to which you have assigned the ———, ___, and === leaders, respectively.

To assign a leader to a tab stop, you must select it from the Leader option box in the Tabs dialog box as you are creating that tab. The option that is selected when you choose <Insert> is the one that Works will assign to the custom tab whose position you typed into the Position text box. For example, if the ... option is selected, Works will fill the white space to the left of the tab with a series of periods. If you want, you can assign a leader to the default tabs in a document by choosing it from the Leader option box when you are setting the default tab interval.

▶When you want to call attention to a paragraph or section of your document, you can surround that paragraph or section with a border. Works gives you a choice of three types of borders: Normal (single lines), Bold, or Double. You can place a border at the top, bottom, left, or right of a paragraph or you can surround a paragraph or cluster of paragraphs with a border.

Borders
▶WORKS 2◀

Adding a border to a paragraph is simple. First, you place the cursor in the paragraph you want to add a border to, then choose the Borders... command from the Format menu. When you do, you'll see the dialog box shown in Figure 5-33. This box includes a Border option box, which includes five border position options, and a Line Style box that offers three types of line styles. To assign a border, you choose one or more border position options and a line style, then you click <OK>.

Adding borders

To add a border to a number of paragraphs, extend the highlight to cover at least one character in each of the paragraphs you want to border. In other words, to prepare to border three paragraphs, extend the highlight from the last character of the first paragraph to the first character of the third paragraph. Then, choose the Borders... command. When you see the Borders dialog box, you choose one or more Border position options and a Line style, then click <OK>.

Figure 5-33

The Borders dialog box allows you to specify the border position and line style for selected paragraphs.

If you look at the table of contents in Figure 5-32, you'll see three types of chapters: an introduction, five main chapters, and two appendices. Suppose you wanted to separate each section of the table of contents and surround each with outline borders. The Introduction will stand alone as the first section, the five chapters will form the second section, and the appendices, the final section.

To begin, position the cursor in the Introduction paragraph. Select the Borders... command, and activate the Border Outline option. As you will see in Figure 5-34, the Normal line style suits this example well, so we won't alter this setting. When you choose <OK>, Works will draw an outline border around the Introduction paragraph.

Figure 5-34

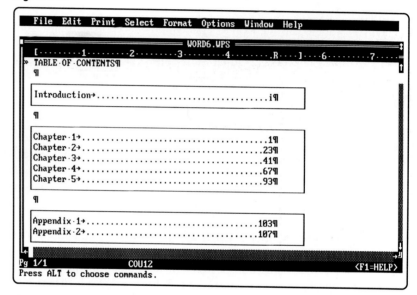

We've added outline borders to this document for emphasis.

Next, you'll want to format the five chapter paragraphs with one outline border for the entire cluster of paragraphs. To begin, expand the highlight to cover at least one character in all five paragraphs. After you do this, activate the Border Outline option in the Borders dialog box, then choose the <OK> button. When you do, the five chapters will be surrounded by one four-sided border.

To put a border around the two appendices, extend the highlight to cover at least one character in each paragraph, then turn on the Border Outline option. Now, your document should look like the one in Figure 5-34.

The border area

A paragraph's margins determine the width of a border area. When you add an outline or left and right border to a "normal" paragraph, the border area will extend from the left to right margin of the paragraph. If you have a normal paragraph with text that doesn't fill the space from the left to right margins, your border will surround blank space along with the text. To reduce that space, you should increase the number in the Right Margin text box in the Page Setup &

Margins dialog box. In Figure 5-34, we widened the right margin so our border wouldn't include much blank space to the right of the paragraphs it surrounds.

If your document has paragraphs with different margins, a border will follow those margins. For example, in Figure 5-35, we've assigned different margins to two paragraphs, then highlighted both paragraphs and placed one outline border around them. The outline follows the widths of the paragraph margins.

Figure 5-35

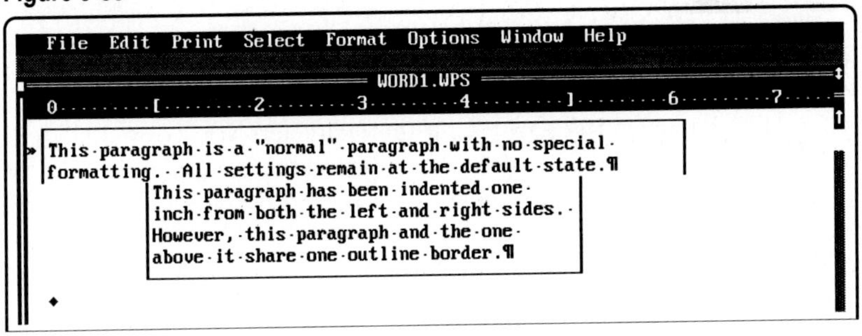

```
  File  Edit  Print  Select  Format  Options  Window  Help
═══════════════════════════ WORD1.WPS ═══════════════════════════
  0········[·········2········3·········4·········]·········6·········7·
 ┌────────────────────────────────────────────────────┐
▶│This·paragraph·is·a·"normal"·paragraph·with·no·special·│
 │formatting.··All·settings·remain·at·the·default·state.¶│
 │        This·paragraph·has·been·indented·one·          │
 │        inch·from·both·the·left·and·right·sides.··      │
 │        However,·this·paragraph·and·the·one·           │
 │        above·it·share·one·outline·border.¶            │
 └────────────────────────────────────────────────────┘
   ◆
```

We've outlined two paragraphs with different margins.

Changing borders

Occasionally, you may want to change a border you've created. To do this, merely position the cursor in the paragraph with the border (or highlight at least one character in each paragraph whose group shares a border), then select the Borders... command. When the Borders dialog box appears, select any additional options you may want to add, or turn off the options you first chose and turn on the ones you now want to use. You can activate one Border option or combine options to create the custom border you want. However, you can use only one line style for each paragraph.

Removing borders

Removing a border is easy. You simply position the cursor or highlight in the paragraph(s) that you formatted with a border. When you open the Border dialog box, turn off the active border options. When you choose <OK>, Works will remove the borders.

If you want to remove an outline border, such as the ones in our previous example, you won't be able simply to deactivate the Border Outline option in the Borders dialog box. Anytime you activate the Border Outline option, close the Borders dialog box, then reopen it, you'll see that Works has turned off the Outline option and has turned on the Top, Bottom, Left, and Right Border options. To turn off an outline border, you'll have to deactivate all the active options. For example, to remove the outline from the introduction paragraph in Figure 5-34, you'll have to turn off four Borders options: Top, Bottom, Left, and Right, instead of the one— Outline—you activated.

To turn off an outline border around a cluster of paragraphs, like the five chapter paragraphs in Figure 5-34, highlight the cluster of paragraphs, and open the Borders dialog box. When you do, you'll see hyphens in the Top, Bottom, Left, and Right check boxes. This happens because you have highlighted more than one paragraph. To remove the outline, you have to click on each check box twice: once to turn it on so that you can click again to turn it off. When you've done this for all four check boxes and have chosen <OK>, Works will remove the outline from the cluster of paragraphs.◄

COPYING FORMATS

When you use the Copy command to copy text in a word processor document, Works will copy the character formats of that text (styles, position, font, and size) as well as the characters themselves. If the characters you copy include the ¶ symbol at the end of a paragraph, Works will copy the paragraph formats of that paragraph (indention, spacing, alignment, tabs, and borders) in addition to the characters you selected.

In some cases, you may want to copy the formats of characters or paragraphs without copying text. The Copy Special... command makes this possible. Using this command is a multiple-step process. To copy the formats of a character, position the cursor on that character or highlight that character or a group of adjacent characters. To copy the formats of a paragraph, simply position the cursor within that paragraph or highlight text within it.

Next, you should pull down the Edit menu and select the Copy Special... command. Then, you should mark the destination of the copy. If you are copying character formats, you should extend the highlight to select the character or characters to which you want to assign those formats. If you are copying the paragraph formats, you should position the cursor in the paragraph to which you want to assign those formats. (If you want to assign the formats to more than one paragraph, extend the highlight so that it includes at least one character of each paragraph.)

Now, press [Enter] and Works will display the Copy Special dialog box shown in Figure 5-36. As you can see, this box contains two options: Character Format and Paragraph Format. If you want to copy character formats, you should choose the Character Format option; if you want to copy paragraph formats, you should choose the Paragraph Format option.

After selecting one of these options, you should choose <OK> from the bottom of the Copy Special dialog box. (Since <OK> is the default button, you can choose it simply by pressing [Enter].) If you choose the Character Format option, Works will format the selected characters with the formats of the characters you highlighted before issuing the Copy Special... command. (If you highlighted more than one character before issuing the Copy Special... command, Works will copy the formats of the leftmost highlighted character.) If you chose the Paragraph Format option, Works will copy the formats of the paragraph in which the cursor was positioned when you issued the command to the paragraph in which it is positioned when you choose <OK>.

Figure 5-36

Works will present this dialog box after you issue the Copy Special... command and specify a destination.

THE UNDO COMMAND

The Undo command, located on the Edit menu, allows you to cancel editing and formatting changes you make to a document. When you select the Undo command, Works will cancel your most recent action—whether that involved typing characters, formatting, or editing. For example, suppose you moved a paragraph from one location to another. If you decide that you don't like what you've just done, you can simply pull down the Edit menu and select the Undo command. When you do this, Works will move the paragraph back to its original location. As another example, suppose you highlight some text and change its position to superscript, then you realize that you don't want to apply superscripting after all. If you issue the Undo command, Works will remove the superscript attribute from the text to which you just assigned it.

You should keep in mind that the Undo command will work only if you issue it immediately after you complete the command you want to undo. To reverse an action with the Undo command, you must choose that command before you issue another command or type any characters.

CONCLUSION

We've covered a lot of ground in this chapter. First, we showed you how to move, copy, and delete text and how to format characters. We showed you how to control the margins of a document. Next, we showed you how to format paragraphs and how to copy the formats of characters and paragraphs. Finally, we explained the action of the Undo command. In Chapter 6, we will complete our look at word processor documents by examining advanced topics, such as the use of special characters, multiple-line headers and footers, and Works' Spell-Checking facility.

Advanced Word Processing Topics 6

*I*n Chapter 4, we taught you the basic skills that you need to work in a word processor document. In Chapter 5, we showed you some other word processor features, including how to move and copy text, format characters, and format paragraphs. In this chapter, we'll explore the remaining features of a Works word processor document. We'll show you how to use special characters to control the appearance of a document, how to control page breaks, you how to insert system and file information in your document, and how to create multiple-line headers and footers. We'll also teach you how to split the work area of a word processor document into two windows, how to use Works' Spell-Checking and Thesaurus facilities, and you how to create footnotes to support your main text and bookmarks to aid in searching through your text.

As we explained in Chapter 4, Works automatically wraps the cursor from one line to the next when the cursor reaches the right edge of a document. If a word is too long to fit at the end of one line, Works will push the entire word to the beginning of the next line.

Although this automatic-wrapping feature works well in most cases, it can cause problems. For example, it can create lines of noticeably different lengths when your text is left-aligned, right-aligned, or centered; if your text is justified, large amounts of white space may appear between words. Hyphens can help; however, they often end up in the middle of a line when you edit or reformat the document. Additionally, Works often breaks lines in awkward places. For instance, if you type a date near the end of a line, Works may place the month name at the end of one line and the day and year at the beginning of the next one.

Fortunately, Works supplies four tools that you can use to control word wrap and line breaks. These tools are special characters: the optional hyphen, the non-breaking hyphen, the non-breaking space, and the end-of-line marker.

CONTROLLING WORD WRAP

Optional hyphens

In Chapter 4, we explained that Works can break a word onto two lines if you hyphenate the word. In many cases, hyphenating one or more words can improve the appearance of a paragraph by making the lengths of its lines more regular. If you want Works to split a word between two lines, you can type a hyphen where you want the word to be split. If the portion to the left of the hyphen and the hyphen will fit on the current line, Works will split the word onto two lines. For example, Figure 6-2 shows the result of inserting a hyphen into the word *paragraph* in the second line of the document shown in Figure 6-1. As you can see, Works has pulled the first part of the word (the letters *para* and the hyphen) up to the first line.

Figure 6-1

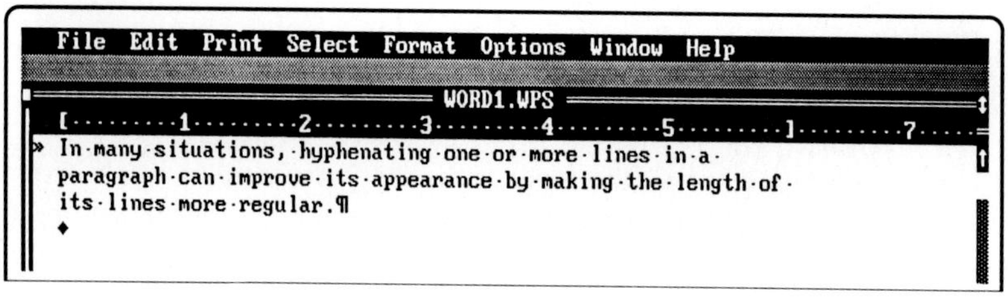

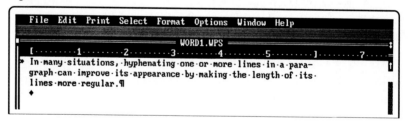

Since the entire word paragraph *won't fit on the first line of this document, Works pushes it down to the beginning of the second line.*

Figure 6-2

Inserting a hyphen into the word paragraph *allows Works to split it between two lines, making the line lengths more even.*

Unfortunately, inserting "regular" hyphens does not always produce the results you want. If the portion of the word to the left of the hyphen plus the hyphen is too long to fit at the end of the current line, Works will push the entire word (including the hyphen) onto the next line of the document. Even if the word breaks correctly when you insert the hyphen, it may not if you subsequently edit or reformat the document.

You can avoid these problems by using optional hyphens instead of regular hyphens. An optional hyphen appears in a printed document only when the word into which you insert it is situated at the end of a line and can be broken at the position of that hyphen. When that happens, Works splits the word at the optional hyphen, makes the hyphen visible, and wraps the second half of the word to the next line. If the hyphenated word falls in the middle of a line, however, or if it falls at the beginning of a line but the portion to the left of the hyphen plus the hyphen is too long to fit at the end of the previous line, Works will print the word without the hyphen. Unless the Show All Characters command is off, the optional hyphen will be visible on the screen. When an optional hyphen is visible on the screen, it looks like a regular hyphen.

To insert an optional hyphen into a word, position the cursor at the point in that word where you want to insert it (under the character to the left of which you want the hyphen to appear). Then, you can insert the hyphen by pressing the [Ctrl]- key combination. Alternatively, you can pull down the Edit menu and select the Insert Special... command, choose the Optional Hyphen option from the Insert Special dialog box (shown in Figure 6-3), and choose <OK>. Either way, Works will insert an optional hyphen to the left of the current position of the cursor.

Figure 6-3

The Insert Special... command enables you to insert a variety of special characters—including optional hyphens—into a word processor document.

Non-breaking hyphens

Occasionally, your document may contain a hyphenated word that you do not want to break between lines. For example, suppose that you work for a company that markets a product called *Taste-O-Honey*. Company policy (and common rules of grammar) requires that you never break this product name onto two lines.

If you were to use regular hyphens when you typed the name of this product, Works could break the name at one of the hyphens should it fall at the end of a line. To make sure that this does not happen, you must use another special type of hyphen—the non-breaking hyphen. Works treats non-breaking hyphens like alphabetic characters—not like regular hyphens. As far as Works is concerned, a word that contains one or more non-breaking hyphens is a single, complete word. If that word will not fit on a line in its entirety, Works will move it to the next line, hyphens and all.

To create a non-breaking hyphen, first position the cursor where you want the hyphen to appear. Then, you can either press [Ctrl][Shift]- or pull down the Edit menu, select the Insert Special... command, choose the Non-breaking Hyphen option from the Insert Special dialog box, and choose <OK>. Either way, Works will insert a non-breaking hyphen to the left of the character on which the cursor is positioned at the time. Non-breaking hyphens look like regular hyphens both on the screen and in a printed document.

Non-breaking spaces

Typically, each word in a paragraph is separated from the one that precedes it by a single space character. Works wraps text from one line to another so that the first letter of a new word appears at the left edge of each line. The space between the first word on a line and the word that precedes it always remains at the end of the previous line.

In some cases, you may not want Works to break a line between two words. For example, you may want a date like July 4, 1776, to appear on one line of a paragraph, rather then being split between the month and the day or the day and the year. You can prevent this from happening by using special non-breaking spaces instead of regular spaces between the words. Works treats non-breaking spaces just like non-breaking hyphens; it considers them to be alphabetic characters—characters which it cannot break. To Works, a pair of words that are separated by a non-breaking space count as a single word. If the words will not both fit at the end of one line, Works will move them to the next line. A non-breaking space looks and prints just like a regular space.

You can create a non-breaking space by pressing the [Ctrl][Shift][Spacebar] key combination. Alternatively, you can pull down the Edit menu, select the Insert Special... command, choose the Non-breaking Space option from the Insert Special dialog box, and choose <OK>. Either way, Works will insert a non-breaking space to the left of the cursor. In many cases, you'll want to replace a regular space with a non-breaking space. To do this, you can either delete the regular space, then insert the non-breaking space or highlight the space before you generate the non-breaking space character.

For example, Figure 6-4 shows how the date July 4, 1776, might appear if you used regular spaces; Figure 6-5 shows the same text after replacing the regular spaces between the month, day, and year components of the date with non-breaking spaces. Since Works cannot break a line at a non-breaking space, it pushed the entire date onto the second line of the document.

End-of-line markers

In some cases, you may want to break a line of text without beginning a new paragraph. That way, you can make one or more of the lines in a paragraph shorter than the remaining lines while still retaining the formats of that paragraph. To do this, you must use an end-of-line marker. When you insert an end-of-line marker into a line of a paragraph, Works will wrap the cursor to the beginning of the next line, just as if you had pressed the [Enter] key to end the paragraph. However, Works won't end the paragraph at that point. Instead, it will continue the same paragraph at the beginning of the next line. If the Show All Characters command is on, the end-of-line marker will appear on the screen as a thin, downward-pointing arrow. If the Show All Characters command is off, you won't be able to see this character. The document in Figure 6-6 contains an end-of-line marker in the second line.

Figure 6-4

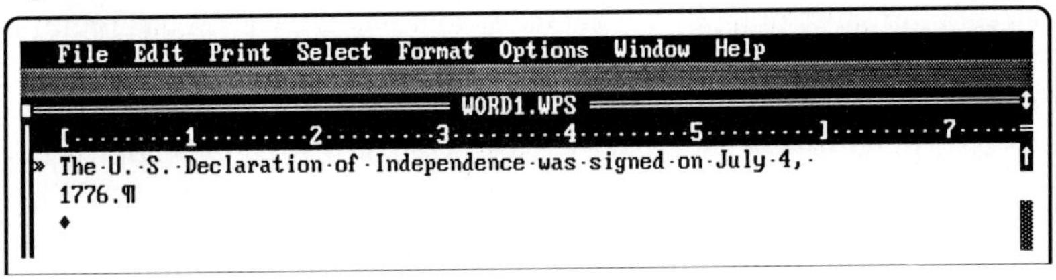

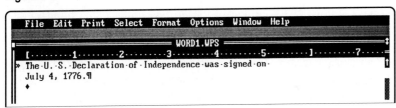

In some cases, Works will break a line between two words that should appear together on the same line.

Figure 6-5

You can prevent Works from breaking a line between two words by replacing the regular space between them with a non-breaking space.

Figure 6-6

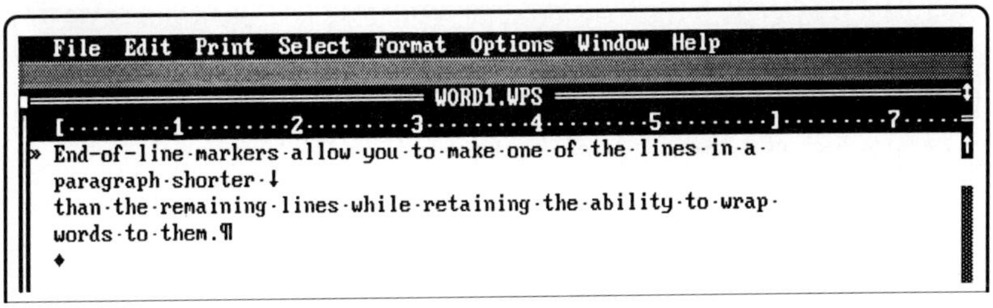

End-of-line markers allow you to make one or more of the lines in a paragraph shorter than the remaining lines.

You can insert an end-of-line marker into a document by holding down the [Shift] key and pressing [Enter]. Alternatively, you can pull down the Edit menu, select the Insert Special... command, choose the End-of-Line Mark option from the Insert Special dialog box, and choose <OK>. In either case, Works will insert an end-of-line marker to the left of the current position of the cursor and move the characters to the right of that marker to the next line of the paragraph.

Fonts and word wrap
▶WORKS 2◀

▶The font and size you select for the text in your documents influences the way Works displays line breaks on your screen. By default, Works will display on each line the same number of characters that will appear on each line when you print your document. As long as you use your printer's default font and size (the default font and size for an HP LaserJet printer is 12-point Courier; the default font on your printer may be different), what you see on the screen is approximately what you'll see when you print. If you choose a smaller point size, Works will be able to squeeze more characters onto each line when you print; therefore, it will display more characters on each line on the screen as well. This means that each line will appear to extend past the right margin you've set and may extend off of your screen. On the other hand, if you choose a larger point size, Works will be able to fit fewer characters onto each line when you print; therefore, it will display fewer characters on each line on the screen as well.

Likewise, if you use a font that is denser than your default font, Works will display less characters on each line on the screen. On the other hand, if you choose a less dense font, Works will display more characters on each line on the screen.

For example, Figure 6-7 shows a sample document formatted in 12-point Courier (the default font and size for our printer). Figure 6-8 shows the same document after we changed the font and size to 8-point Times Roman. Because this font is both smaller and denser than the default font for our HP LaserJet printer, each line extends beyond the right margin and the right edge of the screen.

Figure 6-7

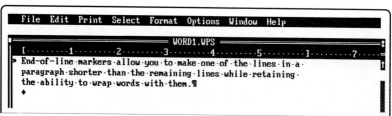

The text in this figure is 12-point Courier.

The Wrap For Screen command on the Options menu causes Works to display text on the screen within the margins you have defined for your document. In effect, this command tells Works to display text as though it were formatted in the default font and size for your printer. Of course, choosing this command will have no effect on the way your document will look when it is printed. This command affects only the display of your document. The Wrap For Screen command comes in handy when you are working in a document that is formatted in a small font and you want to be able to see all your text on the screen at once.

Figure 6-8

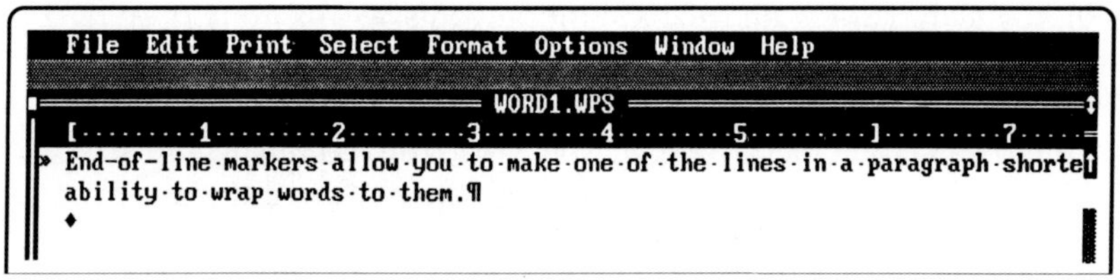

```
 File  Edit  Print  Select  Format  Options  Window  Help
═══════════════════════════ WORD1.WPS ═══════════════════════════
[·········1·········2·········3·········4·········5·········]·········7····
▶ End-of-line·markers·allow·you·to·make·one·of·the·lines·in·a·paragraph·shorter
  ability·to·wrap·words·to·them.¶
  ◆
```

The text in this figure is 8-point Times Roman.

For example, Figure 6-9 shows the document from Figure 6-8 after we selected the Wrap For Screen command. Notice that each line now breaks at the document's right margin. The Wrap For Screen command is a toggle command. To turn this command off, simply select it a second time.◀

Figure 6-9

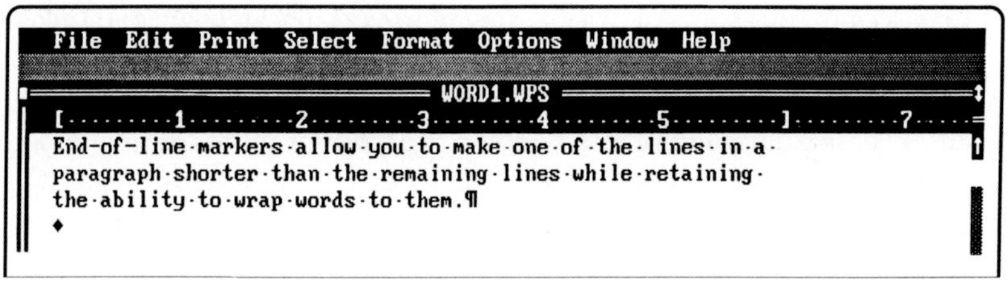

```
 File  Edit  Print  Select  Format  Options  Window  Help
═══════════════════════════ WORD1.WPS ═══════════════════════════
[·········1·········2·········3·········4·········5·········]·········7····
End-of-line·markers·allow·you·to·make·one·of·the·lines·in·a·
paragraph·shorter·than·the·remaining·lines·while·retaining·
the·ability·to·wrap·words·to·them.¶
◆
```

This figure shows the results of activating the Wrap for Screen command in either the document in Figure 6-7 or 6-8.

CONTROLLING PAGE BREAKS

Normally, Works calculates and adjusts the page breaks automatically as you enter, edit, and format data in a word processor document. Works displays the number of the current page on the left side of the status line and displays a page-break marker (>>) on your screen to mark the first line of each new page.

Works' page-break calculations are based on the Page Length, Top Margin, and Bottom Margin settings that you enter into the Page Setup & Margins dialog box. If you change one or more of these settings, Works will reposition the page breaks in your document to adjust for the new page length. The point size of the characters in a document also affects where Works positions page breaks. The larger the point size, the fewer the lines that will fit on each page.

In Chapter 5, we explained that Works never inserts a page break that would cause a widow; it always inserts page breaks so that at least two lines of a paragraph are printed on each page. In that same chapter, we showed you two settings within the Indents & Spacing dialog box that control where Works positions the page breaks in a document: Don't Break this Paragraph and Keep this Paragraph with Next. The Don't Break this Paragraph setting prevents Works from inserting a page break within the paragraph to which you assign that setting; the Keep this Paragraph with Next setting prevents Works from inserting a page break between two paragraphs.

In addition to these two settings, Works gives you a couple of other ways to control the pagination of a document. It lets you turn automatic repagination on and off and allows you to insert manual page breaks into a document.

Adding manual page breaks

Unless you specify otherwise, Works keeps track of the pagination of a document as you create and edit it. Works tries to perform its page-break calculations during pauses; that is, while you aren't typing or issuing commands. For that reason, you usually won't be aware that Works is repaginating your document. If you type for a long time without pausing, however, Works may interrupt you to repaginate the document. If the document is short, Works can reposition the page breaks in a document almost instantaneously. If you're working with a large document, however, you may have to wait several seconds.

In most cases, you won't have any problem with Works' placement of page breaks in a document. In some cases, however, you may want a particular line of a document to be printed at the top of a new page. To make this happen, you can insert a manual page break into a document.

▶WORKS 2◀

To insert a manual page break, you can hold down the [Ctrl] key and press [Enter]. ▶Alternatively, in Works 2, you can pull down the Print menu and select the Insert Page Break command.◀ When you do either of these things, Works will insert a manual page break into the document at the position of the cursor. Works marks the location of a manual page break on your screen with a dotted line that extends across the width of the screen, as shown in Figure 6-10.

Figure 6-10

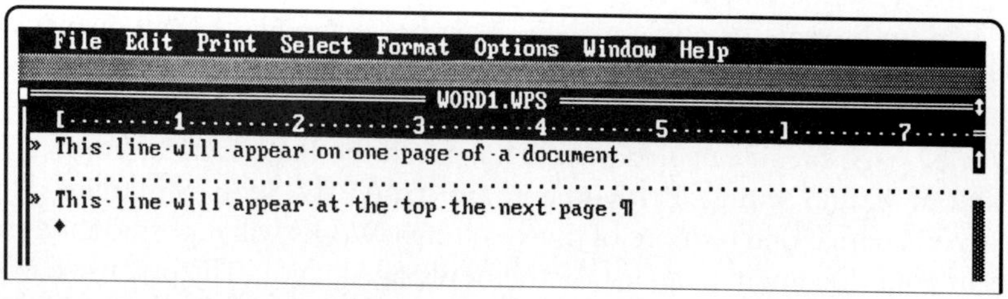

```
 File  Edit  Print  Select  Format  Options  Window  Help
══════════════════════════ WORD1.WPS ══════════════════════════
[········1········2········3········4········5········]········7···
» This·line·will·appear·on·one·page·of·a·document.
·······················································
» This·line·will·appear·at·the·top·the·next·page.¶
  ◆
```

A manual page break appears as a dotted line that extends across the width of the screen.

Before you insert the manual page break, you'll want to position the cursor at the beginning of the first line that you want to appear on the new page or at the end of the last line that you want to appear on the previous page. That way, Works will break the document between lines. If the cursor is in the middle of a line when you insert a manual page break, part of that line will appear at the end of one page, and the remainder will appear at the top of the next page.

Whenever Works repaginates a document that contains a manual page break, it uses the position of the manual page break as the reference point for the next page break. For example, if you use a manual page break to mark the beginning of the fourth page of a document, Works will position the automatic page break that marks the beginning of the fifth page exactly one full page of lines below the manual break.

When you insert manual page breaks into a long document, you may find that Works' automatic repagination feature is slow to catch up to your manual pagination. To make Works repaginate a document after you've inserted manual page breaks, pull down the Options menu and select the Paginate Now command or press [F9]. When you choose this command, Works will recalculate the positions of the manual page breaks in your document and place page-break markers accurately at those points.

Unlike the page breaks that Works inserts into a document automatically, manual page breaks always remain where you inserted them. As a result, if you add or delete lines of text after you have inserted a manual page break, your document may end up with some awkward gaps. You can avoid this problem by waiting until you have completely finished editing and formatting a document before you insert any manual page breaks.

Deleting manual page breaks

You can delete a manual page break in the same ways that you delete any other character from a document. You can move the cursor to it and press [Delete] or pull down the Edit menu and select the Delete command. Alternatively, you can place the cursor on the first character of the line immediately below it and press [Backspace]. You also can move and copy manual page breaks by using the Move and Copy commands.

INSERTING SPECIAL INFORMATION

As you've seen, you can insert a variety of special characters—including optional hyphens, non-breaking hyphens, non-breaking spaces, end-of-line markers, and manual page breaks—into a word processor document. You also can insert six special pieces of information into a document: the current date, the current time, the print date, the print time, the name of the document, and the current page number.

To insert any of these special pieces of information into a document, move the cursor to the point at which you want to insert that information. Then, you can either pull down the Edit menu, select the Insert Special... command, choose the appropriate option from the Insert Special dialog box, and choose <OK>; or you can press one of the key combinations shown in Table 6-1. In either case, Works will insert the special information to the left of the cursor. If one or more characters are selected, Works will replace them with the special information.

Table 6-1

To insert:	Press:
Current date	[Ctrl];
Current time	[Ctrl][Shift];
Print date	[Ctrl]d
Print time	[Ctrl]t
File (document) name	[Ctrl]f
Page number	[Ctrl]p

These key combinations provide an alternative to the Insert Special... command for inserting special information into a word processor document.

Inserting the current date or time

The Current Date and Current Time options in the Insert Special dialog box command Works to type the current date or time into a word processor document. To determine the current date and time, Works looks to your computer system's clock. For these commands to place the correct date or time into a document, your system clock must be set correctly. If it's not, you should use the Set Date & Time Management.. command in the File dialog box to set your computer's clock.

When you choose the Current Date option from the Insert Special dialog box (or when you press the [Ctrl]; key combination), Works will read the date from your computer's clock and type it into the document in mm/dd/yy format at the current position of the cursor. For example, if you selected the Current Date option on December 31, 1989, and your system clock was set correctly, Works would type the characters 12/31/89.

When you choose the Current Time option from the Insert Special dialog box (or when you press the [Ctrl][Shift]; key combination), Works will read the time from your computer's clock and type it into the document in hh:mm AM/PM form at the current position of the cursor. For example, if you selected the Current Time option at 4:53 PM, and your system clock was set correctly, Works would type the characters 4:53 PM into your document.

The characters Works inserts into a document when you select the Current Date and Current Time options are no different from characters that you might type from the keyboard. Consequently, you can delete, copy, move, or format them. Since they are just regular characters, Works will not update them as the date and time on your computer system's clock changes.

As you've seen, the Current Date and Current Time options in the Insert Special dialog box are simply alternatives for looking at a calendar or clock, then typing the time or date into a document yourself. Works offers two other options, Print Date and Print Time, that allow you to enter a *dynamic* date or time into a document—a date or time that Works updates each time it prints the document. To enter a dynamic date into a document, you can either choose the Print Date option from the Insert Special dialog box or press [Ctrl]d. To enter a dynamic time, you can either choose the Print Time option from the Insert Special dialog box or press [Ctrl]t.

Inserting a dynamic date or time

When you use these commands, Works doesn't enter a recognizable date or time into the document. Instead, it enters special placeholders: **date** for the dynamic date, and **time** for the dynamic time. For example, Figure 6-11 shows a document that contains these placeholders. When Works prints the document, it will replace these placeholders with the current date or time, which it draws from your computer system's clock. Works prints the date in mm/dd/yy form; it prints the time in hh:mm AM/PM form. For example, if Works printed the document shown in Figure 6-11 at 3:35 PM on December 31, 1989, it would print the sentence *This document was printed at 3:35 PM on 12/31/89.* Works replaces each occurrence of these placeholders with the date or time at which it began printing the document—not the date or time at which it printed that particular placeholder.

Figure 6-11

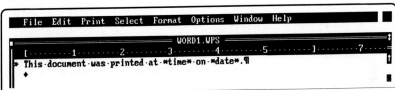

When Works prints a document, it replaces the *time* and *date* placeholders with the current time and date.

The Print Page and Print File options in the Insert Special dialog box allow you to print a document's file name or the current page number anywhere in that document. Typically, you will include this kind of information in headers and footers—sections of a document that we'll cover in the next section of this chapter. However, you can use them in the body of a document as well. Like the Print Date and Print Time options, the Print File and Print Page options insert a special placeholder in your document. When you print the document, Works will replace the placeholder with the current page number or the file name.

Inserting the file name and page number

To insert a document's file name into that document, you can either pull down the Edit menu, select the Insert Special... command, choose the Print file option, then choose <OK>, or you can simply press [Ctrl]f. Either way, Works will insert the placeholder *filename*into the document at the current position of the cursor. When Works prints the document, it will replace this placeholder with the name of the document, printed in all uppercase letters with its full extension. For example, if the name of the document was CHAPTER1.WPS, Works would print the characters *CHAPTER1.WPS* in place of the *filename* placeholder.

To insert the number of the current page into a document, you can either pull down the Edit menu, select the Insert Special... command, choose the Print Page option, then choose <OK>, or you can simply press [Ctrl]p. Either way, Works will insert the placeholder *page* into the document at the current position of the cursor. When Works prints the document, it will replace this placeholder with the number of the page on which it appears. For example, if this placeholder were in the fifth page of the document, Works would print a 5 in its place.

Like the *date*and *time*placeholders, the *filename*and *page*placeholders are treated as single characters. You can edit, format, or delete the entire placeholder just as you would edit, format, or delete any single character in a document. However, you must always act on the entire placeholder—you cannot edit, format, or delete just a portion of it.

HEADERS AND FOOTERS

In Chapter 3, we showed you how to use the Headers & Footers dialog box to specify headers and footers for a printed document. A header is text that appears at the top of every printed page; a footer is text that appears at the bottom of each page. When you use the Headers & Footers dialog box to define your headers and footers, Works limits the amount of text that the header and footer can include to a single line. In addition, Works doesn't allow you to format the header or footer.

▶WORKS 2◀

However, Works does let you define larger and more customized headers and footers in a word processor document. ▶To do this, you should choose the Use Header & Footer Paragraphs option in the Headers & Footers dialog box. (Works dims this option in the spreadsheet and database environments.)◀ When you choose this option, Works will activate two new paragraphs at the beginning of the document, as you can see in Figure 6-12. (If the beginning of your document is not displayed on your screen when you select the Headers & Footers command, Works will scroll it into view in order to display the new header and footer paragraphs.)

The first paragraph, which is marked with an *H*in the left margin, is the header paragraph; the second paragraph, which is marked with an *F*, is the footer paragraph. Notice that the footer paragraph automatically contains the word *Page* followed by a dash and the placeholder *page*, indicating the current page number. In addition, notice that the first page-break marker (the one that marks the top of the document) appears after the header and footer paragraphs.

Figure 6-12

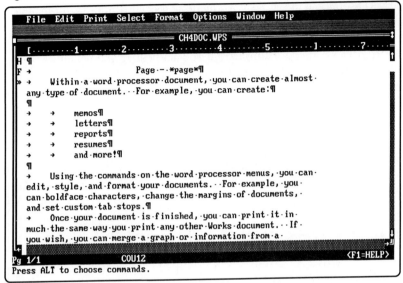

When you select the Use Header & Footer Paragraphs option in the Headers & Footers dialog box, Works will insert a header paragraph and a footer paragraph at the top of your document.

Creating special headers and footers

Once you have turned on the Use Header & Footer Paragraphs option, you can create a header simply by typing it to the left of the ¶ symbol that marks the end of the header paragraph. To create a footer, you type it to the left of the ¶ that marks the end of the Footer paragraph. Anything that you type in the header paragraph will be printed at the top of each page; anything that you type into the footer paragraph will be printed at the bottom of each page.

Because special headers and footers are actual paragraphs that you type into a word processor document, they can be more than one line long. In fact, they can contain as many lines as you want. However, they can be only single paragraphs. While the Use Header & Footer Paragraphs option is on, the first paragraph in a document (that is, the characters to the left of the first ¶ symbol) is the header, and the second paragraph (the characters between the first and second ¶ symbols) is the footer. You can not press the [Enter] key while typing in the header or footer paragraphs. ▶If you do, Works will beep.◀ To create short lines and blank lines within a header or footer, you should use the end-of-line marker, which we examined earlier in this chapter.

▶WORKS 2◀

For your convenience, Works automatically sets two tab stops in the header and footer paragraphs: a centered tab at the 3-inch position, and a right-aligned tab at the 6-inch position. If you're using Works' default margin and page dimension settings, these tabs will occur at the center of the page and at the right margin. These tabs make it easy to divide a special header or footer into left-aligned, centered, and right-aligned portions. (Works also lets you use the [Tab] key to create multiple-line header and footer paragraphs.)

Figure 6-13 shows an example of a special header and footer. The header occupies two lines; the footer occupies only one. The information within this header and footer is aligned at the tab stops that Works sets automatically.

Figure 6-13

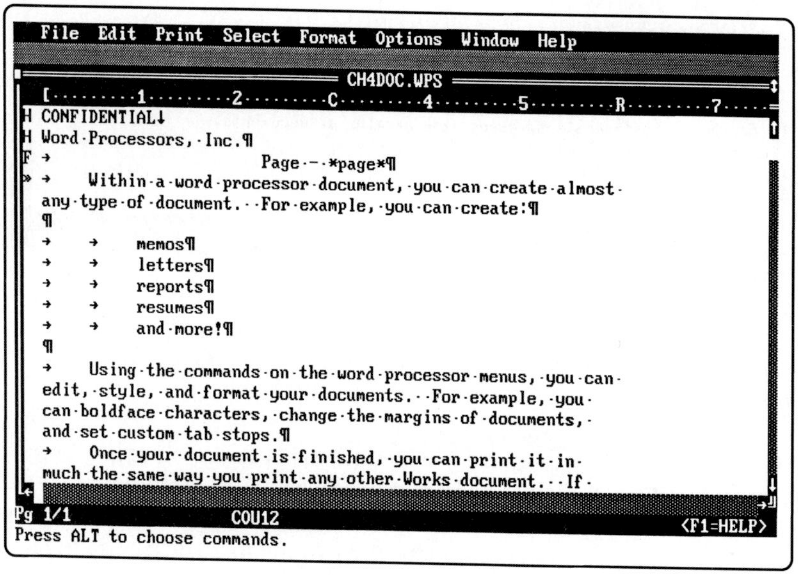

```
 File   Edit   Print   Select   Format   Options   Window   Help

═══════════════════════ CH4DOC.WPS ═══════════════════════
[·········1·········2·········C·········4·········5·········R·········7·····
H CONFIDENTIAL↓
H Word·Processors,·Inc.¶
F  →                       Page·-·*page*¶
→  →      Within·a·word·processor·document,·you·can·create·almost·
any·type·of·document.··For·example,·you·can·create:¶
¶
   →   →    memos¶
   →   →    letters¶
   →   →    reports¶
   →   →    resumes¶
   →   →    and·more!¶
¶
   →      Using·the·commands·on·the·word·processor·menus,·you·can·
edit,·style,·and·format·your·documents.··For·example,·you·
can·boldface·characters,·change·the·margins·of·documents,·
and·set·custom·tab·stops.¶
   →      Once·your·document·is·finished,·you·can·print·it·in·
much·the·same·way·you·print·any·other·Works·document.··If·

Pg 1/1                    COU12
Press ALT to choose commands.                          <F1=HELP>
```

You can use end-of-line markers to create multiple-line headers and footers.

Printing special headers and footers

If the Use Header & Footer Paragraphs option is on (that is, if the header and footer paragraphs are visible), when you choose the Print... command, Works will print the information (if any) in the header and footer paragraphs in place of the information (if any) specified in the Header and Footer text boxes of the Headers & Footers dialog box. (Works will dim the text in the Header and Footer text boxes when you activate the Use Header & Footer Paragraphs option.) If you want Works to use the header and footer specified in the Headers & Footers dialog box instead of the special header and footer, you must turn off the Use Header & Footer Paragraphs option. To do this, simply pull down the Print menu and select the Headers & Footers command, and reselect the Use Header & Footer Paragraphs option. When you do this, Works will hide the header and footer paragraphs. While these paragraphs are hidden, Works will use the header and footer specified in the Header and Footer text boxes when it prints the document. If you ever want to use the header and footer specified in the header and footer paragraphs again, simply turn the Use Header & Footer Paragraphs option back on. When you do this, the header and footer paragraphs will reappear.

Like the headers and footers specified in the Headers & Footers dialog box, Works prints these special headers and footers within the top and bottom margins of each page. Consequently, the Top Margin and Header Margin settings affect the position and appearance of the header, and the Bottom Margin and Footer Margin settings affect the position and appearance of the footer. If either the header or footer paragraph is more than one line long, you probably will need to increase the Top Margin and Bottom Margin values and/or adjust the Header Margin and Footer Margin settings. Otherwise, Works won't be able to print the header or footer completely.

▶To find out if your header or footer text is too large for the margins you've set for it, select the Preview... command, and choose <Preview> at the bottom of the dialog box. When the Preview screen appears, Works will alert you that your header or footer is too tall.◀

▶WORKS 2◀

You can use the No Header on 1st Page and No Footer on 1st Page check boxes in the Headers & Footers dialog box to suppress the printing of special headers and footers on the first page of a document. For more on how these settings work, refer to Chapter 3.

Earlier in this chapter, we showed you the variety of special characters you can insert in a word processor document. The use of these characters is not limited to the body of a document; you can use any of them within a header or footer paragraph. Actually, you will use four special characters—the current time, the current date, current page number, and file name—more in headers and footers than you will in the body of a document. (In fact, Works includes the marker for the current page number in the footer paragraph automatically.)

Using special characters in headers and footers

To insert a special character into a header or a footer, simply move the cursor to the appropriate position within the header or footer paragraph, and either type the key combination that inserts that character, or pull down the Edit menu, select the Insert Special... command, choose the appropriate option from the Insert Special dialog box, and choose <OK>. When you do this, Works will insert a placeholder into the header or footer paragraph. When you print the document, Works will replace the placeholder with the appropriate information.

Because the special headers and footers are paragraphs of characters in a word processor document, you can format them the same way you would any other character or paragraph. For example, you can use the commands in the top section of the Format menu to assign a style (Bold, Italic, etc.), alignment (Normal, Superscript, or Subscript), font (Pica, Elite, Courier, and so forth), and size of any

Formatting headers and footers

of the characters in either a header or footer. You also can use the commands in the second section of the Format menu to control the alignment, spacing, and indention of the Header and Footer paragraphs. ►Furthermore, you can use the Tabs... command to set and clear custom tab stops in the header and footer paragraphs and the Borders... command to format your header and footer text with borders.◄ For an explanation of how to use these commands, refer to the appropriate sections of Chapter 5.

WINDOWS

In most cases, you will view a word processor document through a single window. If you want, however, you can split the work area of a word processor document horizontally into two panes. Through each pane, you can view different parts of the same document. This comes in handy when you need to refer to information in one part of a document while you are working on another part of the same document. Instead of scrolling from one portion of the document to the other, you can position the part of the document to which you need to refer in one pane, and keep the portion in which you are working in the other pane.

Splitting the work area into two panes

The way you split the work area of a word processor window into two panes depends on whether you have a mouse. If you don't, you must pull down the Window menu and select the Split command. When you do this, Works will display a horizontal double line across the top of the work area (directly under the title bar) and display the indicator *SPLIT* in the status line. At that point, you can use the ↑ and ↓ keys to move this line up and down the screen. The position of this line determines the relative size of the two panes. When you press [Enter], Works will split the work area into two panes at the position of the line and remove the word *SPLIT* from the status line.

You can also split a word processor window into two panes with a mouse. To do this, simply point to the = sign that appears at the top of the vertical scroll bar and hold down the left button on your mouse. When you do this, Works will extend the = sign into a double bar that extends all the way across the top of the work area. (If you display your document's ruler, the extended = sign will obscure the ruler.) To split the screen into two parts, simply drag the double line down to the point where you want the split to occur, then release the button on your mouse. When you do this, Works will split the work area into two panes at the position of the line.

Figure 6-14 shows a word processor window that we've split into two panes. As you can see, each pane has its own ruler and its own vertical scroll bar. Initially, the split lines of the document will appear in the top pane, and the lines that were at the top of the work area when you split it will be positioned at the top of the bottom pane.

Figure 6-14

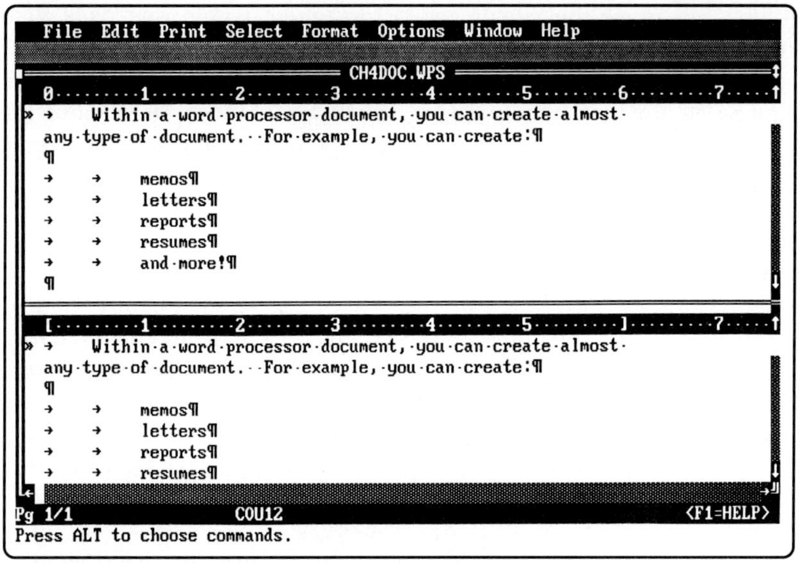

```
┌──────────────────────────────────────────────────────────────────┐
│  File  Edit  Print  Select  Format  Options  Window  Help          │
│ ══════════════════════════ CH4DOC.WPS ══════════════════════════  │
│  0·······1········2········3········4·······5········6·······7····↑ │
│ » →   Within·a·word·processor·document,·you·can·create·almost·      │
│   any·type·of·document.··For·example,·you·can·create:¶              │
│   ¶                                                                 │
│   →    →    memos¶                                                  │
│   →    →    letters¶                                                │
│   →    →    reports¶                                                │
│   →    →    resumes¶                                                │
│   →    →    and·more!¶                                              │
│   ¶                                                                 │
│  [·······1········2········3········4·······5········]·······7····↑ │
│ » →   Within·a·word·processor·document,·you·can·create·almost·      │
│   any·type·of·document.··For·example,·you·can·create:¶              │
│   ¶                                                                 │
│   →    →    memos¶                                                  │
│   →    →    letters¶                                                │
│   →    →    reports¶                                                │
│   →    →    resumes¶                                                │
│ Pg 1/1           COU12                              <F1=HELP>       │
│ Press ALT to choose commands.                                      │
└──────────────────────────────────────────────────────────────────┘
```

If you want, you can split the work area of a word processor window into two panes.

Works regards two panes as parts of one complete window. When you split a window into two panes, then choose the Move or Size command from the Window menu, you'll see that the black-lined border that appears when you choose these commands will surround the document window.

Although you can view a document through two panes at once, you can only work in one at a time. Before you can work within a pane, you must activate it. When you first split a screen into two panes, the bottom pane will be active. Works marks the active pane by displaying the [and] markers on its ruler.

Working within a window

The way you activate a pane depends on whether you have a mouse. If you don't, you must press the Next Pane key ([F6]). Pressing this key deactivates the pane that is active at the time and activates the one that is not. That is, pressing the Next Pane key while the bottom pane is active will activate the top pane; pressing the Next Pane key while the top pane is active will activate the bottom pane. If you have a mouse, you can activate a pane simply by clicking within it.

When you use the [F6] key to activate a pane, the cursor will be on the same character it was on when you last left that pane. If a block of text was selected when you left a pane, the same text will be selected when you return. If you use a mouse, you must click on the ruler of the pane you want to activate if you want the cursor to return to the same place.

Once you have split the work area of a word processor window into two panes, you can move the cursor and/or document within one pane without moving the cursor or document within the other pane. If you don't have a mouse, you can use any of the cursor-movement keys and key combinations we presented in Chapter 4. If you have a mouse, you can use any of the mouse techniques we demonstrated in that chapter. In either case, moving the cursor or document within one pane does not move the cursor or document within the other pane. Each pane provides an independent view of the document. The same is true for selecting text; selecting text in one pane does not alter the position of the cursor or the text that is selected in the other pane.

Although you can move the cursor and select text independently within each pane, remember that you are always positioning the cursor and highlighting text within the same document. Consequently, any editing or formatting changes you make through either pane will affect the entire document—not just the document as it appears through that pane. For example, after you delete a block of text from a document through one pane or the other, that block will no longer be viewable through either pane.

Resizing and deleting windows

Once you have divided the work area of a word processor window into two panes, you can adjust the size of those panes or return to viewing the document through a single window. To do either of these things, you use the same techniques you used to split the window in the first place. If you don't have a mouse, you pull down the Window menu and select the Split command. When you do this, the word *SPLIT* will appear in the status line. When you subsequently press the ↑ or ↓ keys, Works will move the double line from its current position on the screen. The position of the line when you press [Enter] determines the relative sizes of the two panes. If you press [Enter] after moving the line all the way to the top or bottom of the work area, Works will eliminate one of the panes, returning you to a single-window view of the document.

If you have a mouse, you can simply point to the double line that divides the window, hold down the left button on your mouse, drag the line up or down, and release the button. The position of the line when you release the button determines the relative sizes of the two panes. If you release the button after dragging the line all the way to the top or bottom of the work area, Works will return you to a single-window view of the document.

CHECKING SPELLING

In addition to its other features, Works includes a Spell-Checking facility. This easy-to-use feature locates and allows you to correct misspellings and simple grammatical errors, such as incorrect capitalization and back-to-back occurrences of the same word.

To access Works' Spell-Checking facility, you must pull down the Options menu and select the Check Spelling... command. When you choose this command, Works will check for misspellings and simple grammatical errors in the word processor document you were in when you chose it. If the cursor is marking a single character when you choose this command, Works will start at that point and continue through the end of the document. To check the spelling of an entire document, therefore, you must move the cursor to the first character in that document before you select the Check Spelling... command. If you select a block of text before issuing this command, Works will check the spelling of only the words in that block.

As soon as you select the Check Spelling... command from the Options menu, Works will begin the spell-checking process. If you are running Works on a dual-floppy system, Works will ask you to replace your copy of the Works program disk with the Spell and Help disk at this point. If you are running Works from a hard disk, you won't need to do a thing, unless you didn't copy the spell-checking files into your Works directory when you ran the Setup program, or you subsequently deleted them. In either case, you'll have to copy those files to the Works directory before you can use the Spell-Checking facility.

When Works spell-checks a document, it moves through the document one word at a time, starting at the position of the cursor or, if you highlighted a block of text, the character at the beginning of the block. As it checks the document, Works compares each word to the list of 80,000 words in its main dictionary file, MAIN.DIC and, if there is one, an auxiliary dictionary file named PERSONAL.DIC. If Works is unable to locate a word with either of those dictionaries, it will highlight that word and display a dialog box like the one shown in Figure 6-15 on the following page.

Within the Replace With text box at the top of the Check Spelling dialog box, Works will display and highlight a copy of the word it was unable to find in its dictionary file(s)—the same word that is highlighted in the document. It also will display the message *Misspelled Word* above that box.

Once Works locates a misspelled word, you have several options: You can replace the word, add it to the auxiliary dictionary, keep the word as it is, or cancel the Check Spelling... command. We'll cover each of these options one at a time

Correcting a misspelled word

Most commonly, you'll want to correct the spelling of a word that Works has located within your document. You can do this in a couple of ways. First, you can edit or replace the misspelled word in the Replace With text box using any of the text box techniques discussed in Chapter 1, then choose the <Change> button. Since this is the default button, you can choose it simply by pressing [Enter]. For example, if Works flagged the misspelled word *speling*, you could either type the entire word *spelling* into the Replace With text box, or you could insert an additional *l* into the misspelled word.

Figure 6-15

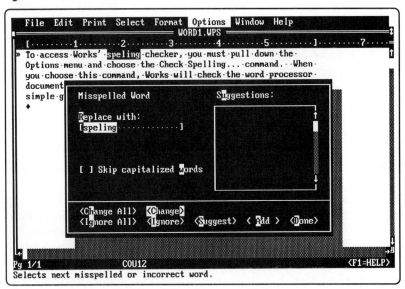

Works presents a dialog box like this one when it encounters a word in a document that doesn't match any of the words in either its main or auxiliary dictionary files.

When you choose the <Change> button, Works will replace the misspelled word in your document with the entry in the Replace With text box (in this case, the word *spelling*). If the replacement word is in its dictionary, Works will close the Check Spelling dialog box and search through the document for the next misspelled word. If the replacement word is not in its dictionary, Works will highlight that word and present the Check Spelling dialog box again. If you choose <Change> without changing the entry in the Replace With text box (that is, while the Replace With text box contains the same misspelling that appears in the document), Works will not recheck the spelling of that word. Consequently, the word will remain as it is, and Works will look for the next misspelled word in the document. Works will, however, stop if it later finds an identical misspelling elsewhere in the document.

Using suggestions

Instead of editing or replacing a misspelled word manually, you can choose the <Suggest> button, then choose the correctly spelled word from the Suggestions list box. When you choose the <Suggest> button, Works will display in the Suggestions list box a list of correctly spelled words similar to the one that is currently in the Replace With text box. For example, if Works finds the misspelled word *speling* in a document, it will display the words shown in Figure 6-16 when you choose the <Suggest> button.

Figure 6-16

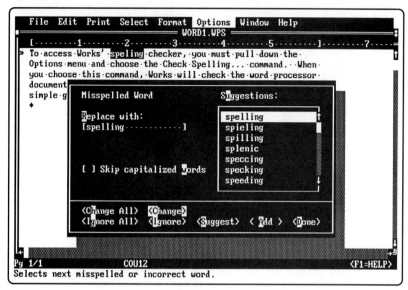

When you choose the <Suggest> button, Works will display within the Suggestions list box a list of correctly spelled words similar to the one that is currently in the Replace With text box.

To replace the misspelled word with one of the words in this list, simply move the highlight to it, then choose the <Change> button. As you move the highlight to the various words in the list, Works will place copies of those words into the Replace With text box. Works will replace the misspelled word with the word that is in the Replace With text box when you choose <Change>. As soon as Works makes the replacement, it will resume the process of searching through the document for the next misspelled word.

In some cases, the list of possible replacements that Works suggests will not contain the word you want. For example, if you had misspelled the word *spelling* as *seplling* instead of *speling*, Works would suggest the words *sapling, zeppelin, sizzling, shelling,* and *shelving.* Since none of those words is the one you want, you would have to correct the misspelling, replacing or editing the entry in the Replace With text box yourself. If you didn't know how to spell the word, you could type a guess into the Replace With text box and press the <Suggest> button again to generate a new list of suggestions. You can continue this process until the list contains the word you are looking for.

Whenever Works replaces a misspelled word, it remembers both the misspelled word and the replacement for the duration of the Check Spelling...

Repeated
misspellings

command. If it encounters another occurrence of that misspelling later in the document, it will automatically enter the word with which it replaced the previous occurrence of that misspelling into the Replace With text box. You can accept the suggestion simply by choosing <Change>.

For example, suppose the misspelled word *speling* occurs twice in the same document. If you commanded Works to replace the first occurrence of that word with the word *spelling*, Works would automatically enter the word *spelling* into the Replace With text box when it found the second occurrence of the misspelled word. To replace the second occurrence of the misspelled word with the word *spelling*, you would simply choose <Change>.

▶WORKS 2◀

▶If there are a number of misspellings throughout your document similar to the one in the Replace With text box, you can choose <Change All> instead of <Change>. When you do this, Works will change the spelling of the currently high-lighted word. From that point on, Works will change the spelling of any identical misspellings in the document automatically. For example, if you commonly misspell the word *occurrence* as *occurance*, you can easily change all instances of the word by pressing <Change All> when Works finds the first misspelling of the word in your document. As Works spell-checks the rest of your document, it will change each instance of the misspelled word *occurance* automatically.◀

Notes

When Works presents you with a misspelled word, you don't have to replace it with the correctly spelled version of the same word. If you want, you can replace it with an alternative word. To do this, simply type the alternative word into the Replace With text box and choose <Change>. For example, suppose you've misspelled the word *the* as *teh*. When Works presents this misspelled word in the Replace With text box, you decide to use the word *a* instead. To replace the misspelled word *teh* with the word *a*, simply type *a* into the Replace With text box, then choose <Change>.

If you choose the <Suggest> button while the Replace With text box contains a word whose first letter is capitalized, Works will capitalize the first letter of each word it provides in the Suggestions list box. For example, if the Replace With text box contained the word *Speling*, Works would display the words *Spelling*, *Spieling*, and so forth in the Suggestions list box. If all the letters in the misspelled word are capitalized, Works will present the words in the Suggestion list box in all uppercase form. For example, if the Replace With text box contained the word *SPELING*, Works would display the words *SPELLING*, *SPIELING*, and so forth.

Using the personal dictionary

Although Works' main dictionary file contains 80,000 words, it probably won't contain all the words that you're likely to use in your writing. For example, it won't contain people's names, abbreviations like NRBQ and ICBM, and many industry-specific terms. Since these words aren't in Works' main dictionary, Works will flag them if it encounters them while spell-checking a document, even if they are spelled correctly, unless you add them to your personal dictionary file.

Whenever Works spell-checks a word processor document, it checks the spelling of the words in the document against the words in both its main dictionary file (MAIN.DIC) and in your personal dictionary file (PERSONAL.DIC). When you begin using Works, there won't be a file named PERSONAL.DIC. Consequently, Works will use only the main dictionary file when it spell-checks a document. However, Works will create a personal dictionary file when you first choose <Add> at the bottom of the Check Spelling dialog box.

The <Add> button allows you to add to your personal dictionary file words that Works flags while it is spell-checking a document. You should use this button whenever Works flags a correctly spelled word in a document. When you choose the <Add> button from the bottom of the Check Spelling dialog box, Works will add the word that is currently in the Replace With text box to your personal dictionary file. Since Works compares each word in a document to the words in both the main dictionary file and your personal dictionary file, it will not flag repeat occurrences of any word you add to your personal dictionary.

Adding words to the personal dictionary

Works does not check the spelling of the words it adds to your personal dictionary file. At some point in your use of Works' spelling checker, therefore, you'll probably add a misspelled word to your personal dictionary. When that happens, you'll want to delete the misspelled word from the dictionary, or edit it so that it is spelled correctly.

Deleting words from the personal dictionary

To delete or edit a word stored in your personal dictionary file, you must open it into a Works word processor document. To do this, pull down the File menu, select the Open Existing File... command, make sure that the directory that contains your Works program files is the current directory, type *personal.dic* in the File Name text box, and choose <OK>. Since PERSONAL.DIC is not a Works file, Works will display an Open As dialog box at this point. To open the file into a word processor document, choose the Word Processor option from this box, then choose <OK>. When you do this, Works will present the contents of your personal dictionary file in a word processor document. Each term in the dictionary will be listed as a single-word paragraph. All the terms will be in alphabetical order. Words that begin with uppercase letters will appear at the beginning.

Once you've opened your personal dictionary file, you can edit or delete any of the terms within it using the same techniques you would use in any other word processor document. When you delete a word from the dictionary, make sure that you delete both the word and the ¶ symbol that follows it; there should be no empty paragraphs within the document. If you want, you can add a word to your personal dictionary by inserting it into the open word processor document. When you do this, be sure to insert the word so that it appears in alphabetical order and on its own line of the document.

When you have finished deleting, editing, and adding words, you should close the document that contains your personal dictionary file, saving the changes. To do this, simply pull down the File menu and select the Close command. Works will then save it into a file named PERSONAL.DIC, then remove it from RAM. When you next use the Check Spelling... command, Works will refer to the updated PERSONAL.DIC file as it searches a document for unrecognized words.

Notes

Although Works will compare the words in a document to the words in your personal dictionary when you choose the Check Spelling... command, it will not include words from that dictionary in the Suggestions list box when you press the <Suggest> button. Consequently, even if the correct spelling of the word is stored in PERSONAL.DIC, you'll have to type the correction into the Replace With text box yourself; you won't be able to choose it from the Suggestions list box.

Cancelling the Check Spelling... command

Once Works has checked every word from the current position of the cursor through the end of the document (or, if you selected a block of text, every word in that block), Works will display an alert box with the message *Spelling check finished.* When you choose <OK> from this box, Works will clear the alert box from the screen and end the spell check. The cursor will be positioned on the first character of the last word that Works flagged during the spell-checking process.

If you want, you can cancel the Check Spelling... command prematurely by choosing the <Cancel> button from the Check Spelling dialog box (or simply by pressing [Esc]). Works will then return control of the document to you, with the cursor positioned on the first character of the last word it flagged. However, while Works is scanning for the next misspelled word, the Check Spelling dialog box will not be visible. Consequently, you can't use the <Cancel> button to cancel the Check Spelling... command. However, you can do so by pressing [Esc].

Non-spelling errors

Although you will use the Spell-Checking facility primarily to catch misspellings, it also alerts you to other problems. First, it will flag certain occurrences of incorrect capitalization. In general, Works will flag any occurrence of a word in which the capitalization is different from the capitalization of that word in either the main or personal dictionary. If a letter in a word stored in either dictionary is capitalized, Works will flag any occurrence of that word in which that letter is not capitalized, and will display the message *Incorrect capitalization.* in the Check Spelling dialog box. For example, if your personal dictionary contains the name *Steve*, Works will flag an occurrence of the word *steve* during the spell-checking process. If a letter in a word stored in either dictionary is not capitalized, Works will flag any occurrence of that word in which that letter is capitalized, and will display the message *Irregular capitalization.* in the Check Spelling dialog box (unless it is the first letter in the word or unless all the letters in the word are capitalized). For example, if the dictionary contains the word *capitalist*, Works won't flag the words *Capitalist* or *CAPITALIST*, but will flag the words *caPitalist*, *CapitalisT*, and so forth.

If Works encounters two occurrences of the same word back-to-back, it will place a single occurrence of that word into the Replace With text box, and display the message *Repeated Word.* above that box. To replace the double occurrence of the word with a single occurrence, simply choose <Change>.

Unfortunately, Works' Spell-Checking facility flags occurrences of words that contain hyphens, even if the hyphens are positioned correctly. If you see that the word is hyphenated incorrectly, you can correct it. If the hyphen is in the correct place, you can choose <Ignore> to resume the spell-checking process without changing the word. ▶(Choose <Ignore All> if there are a number of similarly hyphenated words in your document. Works will then skip each occurrence of the hyphenated word.)◀ Works will not flag hyphenated words if the groups of characters on either side of the hyphen are words that it recognizes. For example, Works would flag the word *su-per*, but not the word *super-script*.

▶**WORKS 2**◀

Sometimes, Works will flag a misspelling that is the result of an error that cannot be corrected directly in the Replace With text box. For example, if you accidentally left a space between the two *l*'s in the word *excellence*, Works would flag the unknown "word" *lence*. To correct this error, you should choose the <Cancel> button to end the spell-checking process, correct the mistake, then rechoose the Check Spelling... command to resume.

If you want, you can command Works not to check the spelling of any words that appear in all uppercase letters. To do this, you simply turn on the Skip Capitalized Words option in the Check Spelling dialog box. While this option is on, Works will not check the spelling of any all-capitalized words for the duration of the current spell-check procedure. This is handy when you are spell-checking a document that contains a number of special codes or acronyms. To resume checking the spelling of all-capitalized words, simply turn this option off again.

Skipping capitalized words

▶Works 2 offers a new command, Footnote..., that you can use to add footnotes (actually endnotes) to your word processing documents. To create a footnote, you first position the cursor at the point where you want the footnote reference to appear in your document. Then, you choose the Footnote... command from the Edit menu. When you choose this command, Works will open a dialog box like the one shown in Figure 6-17. This box lets you choose between using a number or a character reference marker for the footnote. If you choose Numbered (the default option), Works will automatically number the footnote for you. If you choose Character Mark, Works will use a special character instead of a number to reference the footnote. You need to specify the character you want Works to use by entering it into the Mark text box.

FOOTNOTES
▶**WORKS 2**◀

Figure 6-17

The Footnote.. command lets you add foot-notes (actually endnotes) to your word processing documents.

After you choose your marker style, Works will insert a footnote reference marker in the document to the left of the cursor. At the same time, Works will split the screen, opening a footnote pane below the work area of your document window. Works will place the appropriate number or the reference marker you specified in the new window and will place the cursor to the right of the footnote number or marker. At this point, you can type the text of your footnote into the footnote pane. Figure 6-18 shows a word processor document immediately after you choose <OK> in the Footnote dialog box.

Figure 6-18

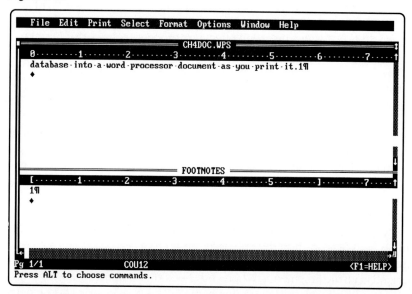

Works adds a footnote reference marker to your document and creates a footnote pane when you choose the Footnote... command.

An example

For example, suppose you wanted to add an explanatory footnote to the document in Figure 6-19. This document describes some of the features of the word processor in Works. You want to add the following footnote to the document's final sentence: *Before we discuss merging database information with a word processor document, we need to discuss database basics.*

Figure 6-19

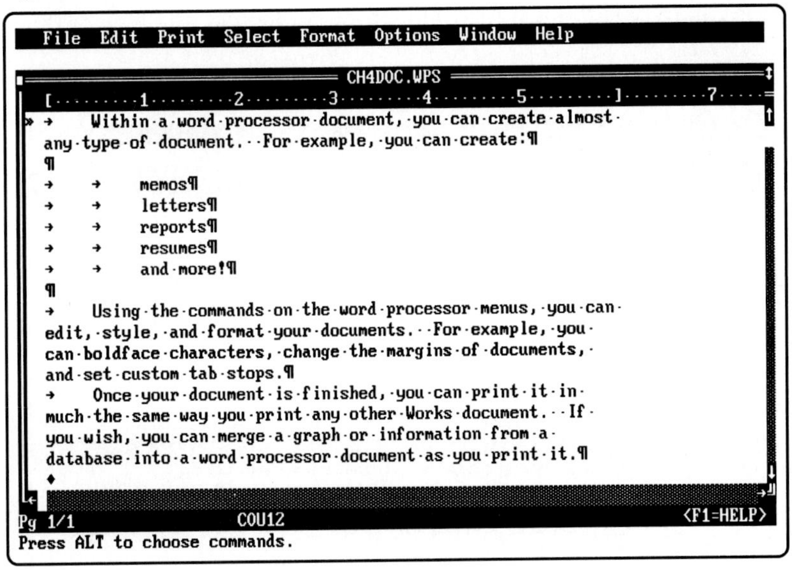

```
  File   Edit   Print   Select   Format   Options   Window   Help
═══════════════════════════════ CH4DOC.WPS ════════════════════════
  [········1·········2·········3········4·········5·········]········7····
» →    Within·a·word·processor·document,·you·can·create·almost·
  any·type·of·document...·For·example,·you·can·create:¶
  ¶
  →    →    memos¶
  →    →    letters¶
  →    →    reports¶
  →    →    resumes¶
  →    →    and·more!¶
  ¶
  →    Using·the·commands·on·the·word·processor·menus,·you·can·
  edit,·style,·and·format·your·documents...·For·example,·you·
  can·boldface·characters,·change·the·margins·of·documents,·
  and·set·custom·tab·stops.¶
  →    Once·your·document·is·finished,·you·can·print·it·in·
  much·the·same·way·you·print·any·other·Works·document...·If·
  you·wish,·you·can·merge·a·graph·or·information·from·a·
  database·into·a·word·processor·document·as·you·print·it.¶
  ◆
Pg 1/1               COU12                          <F1=HELP>
Press ALT to choose commands.
```

We'll add a footnote to this word processor document.

To do this, move the cursor to the right of the period at the end of the last sentence. Then, choose the Footnote... command. Since this document will only have the one footnote, we'll use a special marker, not a number, as the footnote reference. To do this, activate the Character Mark option, type the character * in the Mark text box, and choose <OK> or press [Enter]. At this point, the dialog box will disappear, a footnote pane will appear at the bottom of the screen, and your document will scroll up until the line with the footnote reference appears at the top of the work area. At the end of the sentence, you will see the marker *. The same marker character will appear in the upper-left corner of the new footnote pane, followed by a cursor.

You can now type the text of your footnote directly into the footnote pane. When you are finished, press [F6] or click in the upper pane to resume working with your main document. Figure 6-20 on the following page shows your screen at this point.

Adding more footnotes to a document is simple. You merely repeat the procedure we just described. For example, to add a second footnote to your document, place the cursor in the document where you want the second footnote reference to appear, select the Footnote… command, and choose the Numbered option from the Footnote dialog box. When you do this, Works will reopen the footnote pane (unless it is already open), insert the number 2 at the position of the cursor, activate the footnote pane, scroll the footnote text up one line, and add the number 2 to the upper-left corner of the footnote pane. Now, your screen is ready for you to type the text for your second footnote.

Figure 6-20

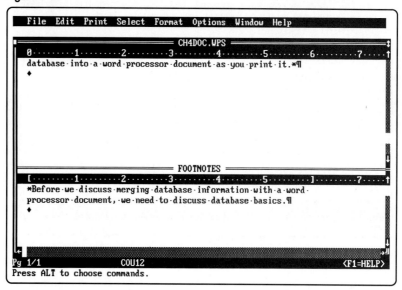

This document shows a footnote pane with footnote text.

If your document will have multiple footnotes, you'll definitely want to use the Numbered option in the Footnote dialog box. Otherwise, it may be difficult to keep up with all of your footnotes.

Notes

You can add footnotes either as you type your document or after you've finished. You can add any number of footnotes to a document, and they can be as succinct or elaborate as you want. Since Works footnotes are actually endnotes, they can extend to multiple pages without disturbing the flow of text in your document. Works will simply append the footnotes to the end of your document, beginning where the main document text ends.

As long as you have the footnote pane open, you can switch between the footnote pane and the document pane. To move from one pane to the other, press the [Next Pane] ([F6]) key or click in the inactive pane. Remember that the active pane is always indicated by the presence of the flashing cursor and the margin brackets on the ruler.

If you use the Numbered option to define your footnote markers, Works will automatically number (and renumber) your footnotes. The first footnote will be number 1, the second will be number 2, and so on. If you add a new footnote above one or more existing footnotes, Works will adjust the numbers of the existing footnotes so that they remain in the correct order.

Occasionally, you may want to open the footnote pane so that you can read or edit your footnotes. You can do this by choosing the Show Footnotes command from the Options menu. When the footnote pane appears, you can activate it by clicking in it or by pressing [F6]. If you have added a number of footnotes to your document and want to check them, you can scroll them into view as you need to by using the scroll bars for the footnote pane. You can also increase the pane size by clicking on the footnote title bar and dragging up.

Opening the footnote pane

If you want to edit the text of your footnotes, first open the footnote pane (if it is not already open) and activate it by pressing [F6] or by clicking in it. Once the footnote pane is active, you can edit the text of your footnotes using the same techniques you use to edit document text.

Editing footnotes

For example, suppose you want to edit the end of your footnote in Figure 6-20 to read *we need to discuss the database environment.* To begin, open the footnote pane (if it's closed) and click in the pane or press [F6] to activate it. When the footnote pane is active, highlight the words *database basics* and type the replacement text *the database environment.* (Be sure that the Typing Replaces Selection command is on before you start typing.)

You can also use the Move command to reposition a footnote and the Copy command to make a copy of a footnote. You do this the same way that you move or copy text in a regular word processing document.

Works always numbers your footnotes sequentially, even if you move or copy them. If you move a footnote, Works will renumber the references in the document and move the entire footnote in the footnote pane. If you copy a footnote, Works will renumber the references in the document and copy the footnote to the appropriate place in the footnote pane. You'll see two versions of the footnote you copied.

Deleting a footnote is simple. First, highlight or place the cursor under the footnote reference in the main document, then press [Delete]. When the reference disappears, so will the text of the footnote and the footnote pane.

Deleting footnotes

Works allows you to change a footnote reference any time you want. To change a footnote reference, highlight it in the document pane or in the footnote pane, and open the Footnote dialog box. If the footnote reference is a number, the Numbered option will be selected. If the reference is a character, the Character

Changing the footnote marker

Mark option will be selected and the reference character will appear in the Mark text box. To change a footnote reference, make sure the Character Mark option is active. Then, click the mouse in the Mark text box or press [Alt]m, and type the replacement text or number for your reference. When you press <OK>, Works will change your footnote reference and open (or activate) the footnote pane. The cursor will appear to the right of the new reference in the upper-left corner of the pane. At this point, you can type your footnote text.

You can even use the Character Mark option in the Footnote dialog box to duplicate a reference number. The procedure is similar to changing a footnote reference. To duplicate a footnote reference, position the cursor in the main document where you want to place your next footnote reference, and open the Footnote dialog box. Activate the Character mark option. Then, click the mouse in the Mark text box or press [Alt]m, and type the character mark or number that duplicates another reference in your document. When you choose <OK>, Works will add that footnote reference to your text at the position of the cursor and open (or activate) the footnote pane. The cursor will appear to the right of the new reference in the upper-left corner of the pane. At this point, you can type your footnote text.

Works will not enter dynamic footnote reference numbers from the Character Mark option. If you duplicate a footnote reference number from the Character Mark option, then add other numbers from the Numbered option, Works will not include in the sequence of numbered footnote references the static footnote number you inserted as a character mark. For example, if your document has a numbered reference 1, then you duplicate that reference from the Character Mark option, you will have two reference 1s. No matter how many numbered references you add to your document, or where you place them, the footnote reference 1 inserted from the Character mark option will remain a 1.◄

THESAURUS
►WORKS 2◄

►In addition to its other features, Works 2 includes a thesaurus. Works' Thesaurus helps you find a synonym for almost any word. This easy-to-use feature will help you find the exact word you need to express a thought.

To use the Thesaurus, first position the cursor under a letter (or to the right of the last letter) in the word you want to look up. (You can also highlight the whole word if you want. You should not, however, highlight a segment of a word. If you do, Works may alert you that it can't find any synonyms for the highlighted letters.) Next, pull down the Options menu and select the Thesaurus… command. When you do, Works will present a Thesaurus dialog box similar to the one shown in Figure 6-21. As you can see, the word you are looking up will appear in the upper-left corner of this box. Under the word, the dialog box includes a Meanings list box, which displays definitions of the highlighted word, along with their parts of speech, and a Synonyms list box, which displays synonyms for the highlighted meaning in the Meanings list box. You can replace the word in your document with either a meaning or a synonym.

Figure 6-21

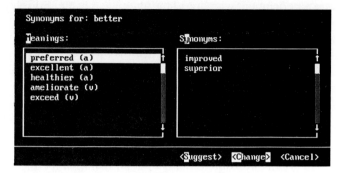

This is the Thesaurus dialog box for the word better.

There are three buttons at the bottom of the dialog box: <Suggest>, <Change>, and <Cancel>. The <Suggest> button and the <Change> button let you replace the highlighted word in your document with one of the meanings or synonyms Works has identified for the word. The <Cancel> button lets you close the Thesaurus and return to your document.

(If you're running Works on a dual-floppy machine, or if you did not install the Thesaurus files during Setup, or if you have deleted them from the Works directory on your hard disk, Works will display an alert box that says *Missing Thesaurus files.* when you select the Thesaurus... command. If you're using a dual-floppy machine, Works will ask you to replace your copy of the Works program disk with the Thesaurus disk. If you are running Works from a hard disk, you'll need to use the DOS COPY command or the Copy File option in the File Management dialog box to copy the Thesaurus files to your Works directory.)

Substituting one word for another

Substituting a word from the Thesaurus dialog box for a word in your document is simple. You can replace the word in your document with either a meaning or a synonym.

Substituting the default meaning

When you first open the Thesaurus dialog box, Works will highlight the first word or phrase in the Meanings list box. If Works' selection is acceptable as a replacement for the word in your document, then you need only press <Change> at the bottom of the dialog box. When you do this, the dialog box will disappear and Works will replace the word in your document with the meaning you chose from the Thesaurus dialog box.

For example, if you highlight the word *better* in your document, then open the Thesaurus dialog box, you'll see that Works highlights the adjective *preferred*. If this is an acceptable synonym, press <Change>. When you do, Works will close the dialog box and replace *better* with *preferred* in your document.

**Selecting
alternate meanings**

Instead of accepting the first meaning Works suggests, you can replace the highlighted word in your document with one of the alternate meanings displayed in the Thesaurus dialog box. To do this, just select one of those other meanings by pointing or clicking and then choosing <Change>. Works will close the Thesaurus dialog box and replace the word with that meaning.

When you highlight an alternate meaning in the Meanings list box, you'll notice that the choices in the Synonyms list box change. If you are trying to decide which word in the Meanings list box offers the most appropriate replacement for the word in your document, you'll want to look at the synonyms for each meaning. They may help you decide which meaning is best. For example, the dialog box shown in Figure 6-21 shows two synonyms for the meaning *preferred*: *improved* and *superior*. If these choices aren't quite right, you can highlight the meaning *excellent*, and you'll see three synonyms in the Synonyms list box: *greater, larger*, and *incomparable*. You can check the synonyms for each meaning in the Meanings list box just by pointing to or clicking on each one.

**Selecting alternate
synonyms**

Just as you can replace the highlighted word in your document with one of the different meanings in the Meanings list box, you can also replace the highlighted word in your document with one of the synonyms in the Synonyms list box. All you have to do is highlight a synonym in the Synonyms list box and choose <Change>. When you do this, Works will close the dialog box and replace the word in your document with the highlighted synonym.

Using suggestions

The <Suggest> button makes it possible to find synonyms of a meaning of a synonym. For example, if you highlight the synonym *improved* in the Synonyms list box shown in Figure 6-21 and choose <Suggest>, Works will list the meanings and synonyms for *improved*. Figure 6-22 shows the Thesaurus dialog box after we highlighted the synonym *improved* and chose <Suggest>. Works lists two meanings for the word *improved*, along with synonyms for the first meaning.◄

**BOOKMARKS
►WORKS 2◄**

►Works 2 lets you insert hidden markers, called bookmarks, in your word processing documents. Bookmarks are very similar to range names in Works' spreadsheets. They mark specific positions in your documents and allow you to move to those locations quickly, easily, and precisely.

The Bookmark feature makes navigating through long documents more certain. If you use the Go To… command without using the Bookmark feature, you'll be able to move only to the top of a page. To look for specific information in this way is haphazard, especially if you are still creating a document and your page breaks are uncertain. If you've inserted bookmarks at specific locations in your documents where the discussion shifts focus or an interesting example appears, you can use the Go To… command to move to that exact location.

Figure 6-22

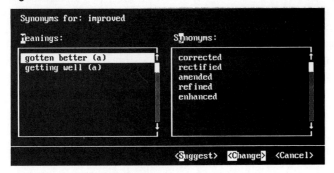

Works presented this dialog box when we pressed <Suggest> after highlighting the synonym improved *in the dialog box shown in Figure 6-21.*

Creating a bookmark

To create a bookmark, you move the cursor to the place in your document where you want to insert the bookmark. When the cursor is in place, choose the Bookmark Name... command from the Edit menu. When you do this, you'll see the Bookmark Name dialog box shown in Figure 6-23. As you can see, the dialog box contains a Name text box, where you type the name of your bookmark, and a blank Names list box, where the names of your bookmarks will appear. (This list box is identical with the one in the Go To dialog box where the same names will appear.)

Figure 6-23

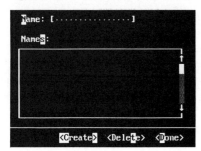

This is the Bookmark Name dialog box.

When the Bookmark Name dialog box appears, you type the name of the bookmark you want to create in the Name text box. The Name text box displays only 15 characters. If your bookmark name contains more characters, Works will scroll the name in the text box as you type, but will display only 15 characters in the text and list boxes when you reopen the dialog box. When you finish typing the bookmark name, choose <Create>.

An example

Most commonly, you'll want to create bookmarks to flag the sections of your documents. For example, in the document shown in Figure 6-24, there are three sections (paragraphs) of text. Each section discusses different features of the Works word processor. The first section discusses creating documents, the second section using word processor commands, and the third section printing and merging documents. To enable you to move easily from one section to another, you can insert bookmarks at the beginning of each.

Figure 6-24

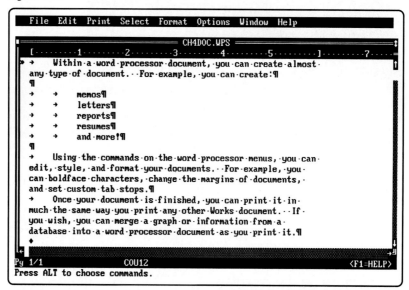

We will insert bookmarks in this document.

To create the first bookmark, move the cursor to the beginning of the first line in the first paragraph in the document. Next, choose the Bookmark Name… command from the Edit menu. When the Bookmark Name dialog box appears, type *Creating docs*, and choose <Create>. When you do this, Works will close the Bookmark Name dialog box and insert a hidden bookmark in your document at the position of the cursor.

To create the next two bookmarks, you can follow the same procedure. First, position the cursor at the left margin of first line of the second paragraph. Next, choose the Bookmark Name… command from the Edit menu. When you do this, the Bookmark Name dialog box shown in Figure 6-25 will appear. Since the document already contains a bookmark name, that name will appear in the dialog box. To create the second name, type *Using commands* and choose <Create>. When you do this, Works will close the Bookmark Name dialog box and insert a hidden bookmark in your document at the position of the cursor. Now, move the cursor to the beginning of the first line of the third paragraph and repeat these steps to add the bookmark name *Print/merge* to the document.

Figure 6-25

This is the Bookmark Name dialog box with three bookmark names in it.

Works doesn't display bookmarks on the screen. When you insert a bookmark into a document, Works will place a hidden marker in your document. The only visible evidence of a bookmark in a word processor document is in the Names list boxes of the Go To and Bookmark Name dialog boxes.

Notes

You'll notice the Names list box has a scroll bar, which is useful when you have a document to which you've added more than six bookmark names—the maximum number the Names list box can display at one time. While there is no limit to the number of bookmarks you can create for a document, we recommend that you consider carefully the placement of bookmarks in your documents. Too many bookmarks defeats the purpose of isolating discrete sections of material.

The Names list box also reveals the order of the bookmarks in your document, thus providing you with a brief outline of your document. If you insert a bookmark ahead of an existing one in your document, Works will insert that bookmark name at the appropriate spot in the list of bookmark names. Likewise, if you move a section of your document to which you've assigned a bookmark, Works will revise the order of the bookmark names in the Names list box to reflect that section's new position in your document. Suppose you have two bookmarks in your document in the following order: *Creating docs* and *Using commands.* If you move the section marked *Using commands* to the beginning of your document, Works will reverse the order of the bookmark names in the Names list box.

Works will not let you duplicate a bookmark name. If you try to create a bookmark for a section of your document by assigning an existing bookmark name, Works will display an alert box that says *Bookmark name already exists.* For this reason, when you copy a section of text that contains a bookmark, Works will not repeat the bookmark name in either the document or the Names list box. Works will list only the original text to which you actually assigned the bookmark.

Works lets you change the name of a bookmark whenever you want. To do this, open the Bookmark Name dialog box, and highlight the bookmark name you want to change. When the bookmark name appears in the Name text box, you can use any of the usual editing techniques to alter the name. Now, press <Create>, and Works will present an alert box that displays the message *Replace existing bookmark?*. Simply press <OK> to change the bookmark name.

Using the Go To... command with bookmarks

In Chapter 4, we showed you how to use the Go To... command and the [Go To] key to move to the top of any page in your document. When you select this command or press this key, the Go To dialog box will appear. This dialog box contains a Names list box that remains empty until you create bookmarks in your document. After you create bookmarks, their names will appear in the Names list box of the Go To dialog box, as you can see in Figure 6-26. To move the cursor in your document to a bookmark, you highlight the bookmark name in the Names list box of the Go To dialog box. When the name appears in the Go To text box, choose <OK>. Works will move the cursor forward or backward to the place in the document where you've inserted a bookmark.

Figure 6-26

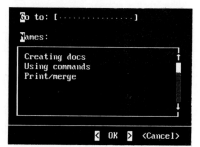

The Go To dialog box includes a Names list box that lists book-mark names.

To move to another bookmark in the document, you can open the Go To dialog box again, highlight the bookmark name you want, then choose <OK>. When you do this, Works will move the cursor to the position of the bookmark in the document. If you have just used the Go To... command to move to a bookmark and you want to move to the next bookmark, simply press the Go to Next Bookmark key combination, [Shift][F5]. Works will move your cursor to the next bookmark.

For example, suppose you want to move the cursor to the section in your document marked *Using commands*. Simply open the Go To dialog box in the sample document. When you do, you'll see the dialog box shown in Figure 6-26. Then, highlight the name *Using commands* in the Names list box. When you do this, Works will place that name in the Go To text box, as shown in Figure 6-27. Now, choose <OK>. As soon as the dialog box closes, Works will move the cursor to the bookmark *Using commands*.

Figure 6-27

When a bookmark name appears in the Go To text box, you can choose <OK> to move the cursor to that bookmark.

Deleting a bookmark

Occasionally, you'll want to delete a bookmark name from a document. To delete a bookmark name, open the Bookmark Name dialog box, highlight the name you want to delete in the Names list box, then choose <Delete>. When you do, the name will disappear from the list box. If you want to delete another name, repeat the procedure. When you finish deleting a name, press <Done> at the bottom of the dialog box. When you reopen either the Bookmark Name or the Go To dialog box, the deleted name(s) will not appear.◄

MERGING INFORMATION INTO WORD PROCESSOR DOCUMENTS

We've covered a lot of material up to this point. However, we haven't demonstrated one important power of Works' word processor documents—their ability to accept information from other types of documents. If you want, you can copy "static" information from spreadsheet and database documents into a word processor document. More importantly, however, you can print form letters and mailing labels by merging information from a database document into a word processor document one record at a time. You also can merge one or more charts into a word processor document. We'll show you how to do these things in Chapter 19.

CONCLUSION

This chapter concludes our coverage of word processor documents. We have shown you the various techniques and commands that you can use to create, edit, format, and print word processor documents. In the next five chapters, we'll explore the uses, powers, and features of spreadsheet documents.

Spreadsheet Basics 7

A Works spreadsheet document is the electronic equivalent of an accountant's columnar pad. Like that pad, a spreadsheet document is designed for financial analysis. You can build financial applications like budgets, tax models, sales forecasts, and so forth, in a spreadsheet document.

In this chapter, we'll cover some basic spreadsheet topics. First, we'll show you how to create and open a spreadsheet document and give you a tour of the screen. Next, we'll show you how to move the highlight around and how to extend it to cover a block of cells. Then, we'll teach you how to enter and edit different types of information. We'll also show you how to recalculate a spreadsheet and how to save, open, and print spreadsheet documents.

You can enter the spreadsheet environment in any of the three ways you can enter any Works environment: by creating a new document, opening an existing document, or making an open document active. To create a new spreadsheet document, you select the Create New File... command from the File menu and choose the New Spreadsheet option. To open an existing spreadsheet document, you select the Open Existing File... command from the File menu and then choose the file you want to open from the list that Works presents. To activate a spreadsheet that is already open, you simply select its name from the bottom of the Window menu.

CREATING AND OPENING SPREADSHEET DOCUMENTS

Figure 7-1 shows a new spreadsheet document. As you might expect, this screen includes the elements you'll see when any Works document is active: the menu bar, the message line, the status line, and a window with all of its elements (title bar, scroll bars, work area, and so forth).

A TOUR OF THE SCREEN

Figure 7-1

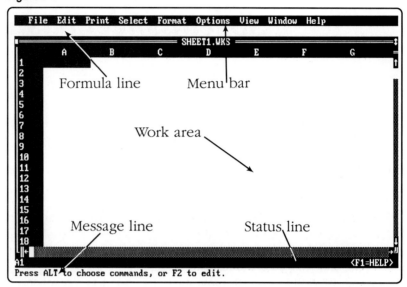

The work area in a spreadsheet document is a gridwork of rows and columns.

As Figure 7-1 shows, the menu bar for a spreadsheet contains the names of nine menus: File, Edit, Print, Select, Format, Options, View, Window, and Help. The commands on several of these menus will already be familiar to you. We'll cover those that are unique to spreadsheets in this and the next three chapters.

The work area in a spreadsheet document is a gridwork of rows and columns bounded by a row of letters at the top and a column of numbers at the left. Every Works spreadsheet has 256 columns and 4,096 rows. Columns are labeled from A to IV. The first column is column A; the 27th column is column AA; the 53rd column is column BA; and so forth. Rows are labeled from 1 to 4,096.

Due to the size of your computer's screen, only a small portion of a spreadsheet (usually seven columns and 18 rows) is visible in a window at one time; the remaining cells are out of view. Works gives you a number of ways to shift different portions of a spreadsheet into view within a window.

When a spreadsheet document is active, the second line of the screen is called the formula line. This bar is unique to spreadsheet documents and comes into play whenever you make or edit cell entries.

Cells

The intersection of any row and column is a cell. Each cell is identified by its column and row coordinates. For example, the cell at the intersection of column A and row 1 is cell A1; the cell at the intersection of column Z and row 100 is cell Z100; and so forth.

Cells are the basic building blocks of any spreadsheet—they hold the information you enter into the spreadsheet. Most spreadsheet commands operate upon the entries in the cells of the current spreadsheet. We'll show you how to make entries and issue spreadsheet commands later in this chapter.

The highlight

If you look again at the spreadsheet shown in Figure 7-1, you'll see that cell A1 is highlighted; that is, displayed in inverse video. In a spreadsheet document, Works uses a highlight to mark the active cell—the cell into which Works will make an entry if you type and press [Enter].

The highlight will always be positioned on cell A1 when you create a new Works spreadsheet. However, you can easily move the highlight to any of the other 1,048,575 cells. We'll show you how to do that next. When you open an existing spreadsheet document, Works will position the highlight on the cell on which it was positioned when you last saved that document.

Although the highlight will mark only a single cell initially, Works allows you to extend it to cover a block of cells. We'll show you how to do that later in this chapter. Even when more than one cell is highlighted, there is still only one active cell. Works identifies the active cell by making its highlight dimmer than the one it uses to mark the remaining cells.

In addition to marking the active cell with the highlight, Works displays the address of that cell at the left edge of the status line. For example, the address *A1* at the left edge of the status line of the spreadsheet document shown in Figure 7-1 indicates that cell A1 is the active cell. When more than one cell is highlighted, Works will display the coordinates of that range instead of the address of the active cell. In that case, only the dim highlight identifies the active cell.

MOVING THE HIGHLIGHT

Works gives you a number of ways to move the highlight around a spreadsheet. If you don't have a mouse, you must use the cursor-movement keys (↑, →, [Pg Up], [End], and so forth). If you have a mouse, you can use it (or the cursor-movement keys) to move the highlight.

The arrow keys

The four arrow keys—←, →, ↑, and ↓—move the highlight one cell at a time in the indicated direction. The ← key moves the highlight one cell to the left; the → key moves the highlight one cell to the right; the ↑ key moves the highlight up one cell ; and the ↓ key moves the highlight down one cell. For example, if the highlight is originally on cell A1, and you press →, ↓, ←, and ↑, Works will move it to cells B1, B2, A2, and then back to A1. You can move the highlight to a succession of cells in any direction, either by holding down the appropriate arrow key or pressing it repeatedly.

If pressing an arrow key moves the highlight to a cell that is visible on the screen, Works will not need to shift the spreadsheet within the work area. For example, if you press → while your screen looks like Figure 7-1, Works will move the highlight to cell B1 and keep columns A through G and rows 1 through 20 on the screen.

If pressing an arrow key moves the highlight to a cell that is not visible on the screen, Works will shift the row or column that contains the cell into view. For example, suppose that columns A through G and rows 1 through 20 are visible on the screen. If you press → while the highlight is anywhere in column G, Works will shift column H into view and position the highlight on the appropriate cell of that column. If you press ↓ while the highlight is in row 20, Works will shift row 21 into view and position the highlight on the appropriate cell of that row.

Whenever Works shifts a column or row into view from beyond one edge of the work area, it shifts a column or row out of view beyond the opposite edge. For example, when Works shifted column H into view from beyond the right edge of the work area in the previous example, it shifted column A off the left edge of the work area. When Works shifted row 21 into view, it shifted row 1 off the top edge of the work area.

The [Pg Up] and [Pg Dn] keys

The [Pg Up] and [Pg Dn] keys move the highlight up and down through a spreadsheet document one windowful at a time. The [Pg Up] key moves the highlight up the spreadsheet; the [Pg Dn] key moves it down. In most cases, 18 rows of the spreadsheet will be visible in the work area at a time. Consequently, the [Pg Up] and [Pg Dn] keys move the highlight 18 rows at a time. In Chapter 11, we'll show you how you can divide the window horizontally into two panes. When the work area is divided horizontally, the [Pg Up] and [Pg Dn] keys move the highlight as many rows as are visible within the current window.

The [Pg Up] and [Pg Dn] keys always shift a new windowful of rows into view. The [Pg Up] key shifts the previous windowful of rows into view; the [Pg Dn] key shifts the next windowful of rows into view. In either case, the highlight stays in place relative to the top and bottom borders of the work area. For example, if the highlight is in the third row from the top of the work area before you press the [Pg Up] or [Pg Dn] keys, it will be in the third row from the top of the work area afterward. Of course, it will be on a different cell, since a different row of the spreadsheet will be in that position in the work area.

The [Ctrl][Pg Up] and [Ctrl][Pg Dn] combinations

The [Ctrl][Pg Up] and [Ctrl][Pg Dn] key combinations move the highlight to the right and left of the spreadsheet in much the same way that the [Pg Up] and [Pg Dn] keys move the highlight up and down the spreadsheet. Pressing [Ctrl]-[Pg Dn] shifts the spreadsheet to the right, bringing a new windowful of columns into view; pressing [Ctrl][Pg Up] shifts the spreadsheet to the left, bringing the previous windowful of columns into view. Unlike the [Pg Up] and [Pg Dn] keys alone, [Ctrl][Pg Up] and [Ctrl][Pg Dn] do not keep the highlight stationary with respect to the borders of the screen. Instead, they position it in the leftmost column of the new windowful of columns.

The [Home] and [End] keys move the highlight to the left and right across the current row. In most cases, the [Home] key moves the highlight into column A. For example, if the highlight is anywhere in row 10, pressing the [Home] key would move the highlight to cell A10. If you have frozen one or more columns onto the screen using the Freeze Titles command, the [Home] key will move the highlight to the first column to the left of the frozen area instead of to column A. We'll show you how to set title columns in Chapter 11.

The [Home] and [End] keys

Before you can understand what the [End] key does, you must understand the concept of the active area. The active area of a spreadsheet is the smallest rectangular area, starting at cell A1, that contains all the cells to which you have made changes since creating the spreadsheet. The active area is bounded on the top by row 1 and on the left by column A. It is bounded on the right by the rightmost column whose width has been adjusted or that contains a non-blank cell, a cell that has been assigned a format, style, or alignment attribute, or a cell that has been unlocked. It is bounded on the bottom by the bottommost row that contains a non-blank, formatted, styled, aligned, or unlocked cell. For example, if you make an entry into cell Z1 of a new, blank spreadsheet, and assign a format to cell A100 of that same spreadsheet, the active area will extend from cell A1 through cell Z100—even though cell Z100 is blank. (We'll show you how to make entries into cells later in this chapter; we'll show you how to alter the widths of columns and how to assign formats, styles, and alignment attributes to cells in Chapter 9.)

The active area

Unfortunately, it's impossible to "shrink" the active area of a spreadsheet while you are working in it. For example, even if you erased the entry from cell Z1 and returned cell A100 to the default format, the active area of our example spreadsheet still would extend from cell A1 to cell Z100. However, you can reduce the active area by saving the spreadsheet after erasing and/or returning cells to their default attributes. For example, if you saved the spreadsheet described above after erasing cell Z1 and removing the format from cell A100, the active area would include only cell A1 when you next opened that spreadsheet.

The [End] key moves the highlight in the current row to the right edge of the active area of the spreadsheet. For example, if the highlight is anywhere in row 15 of a spreadsheet whose active area extends from cell A1 to cell Z100, Works will move the highlight to cell Z15 when you press the [End] key.

The [End] key

The [Ctrl][Home] and [Ctrl][End] key combinations move the highlight to the upper-left and lower-right corners of the active area of a spreadsheet. Unless you have set title rows and columns (a process we'll explain in Chapter 11), Works will move the highlight to cell A1 when you hold down the [Ctrl] key and press [Home]. If you have frozen one or more title rows and/or columns, pressing [Ctrl] [Home] will move the highlight to the upper-left cell outside the title area.

The [Ctrl][Home] and [Ctrl][End] combinations

The [Ctrl][End] key combination moves the highlight to the lower-right corner of the active area of a spreadsheet. For example, if the active area extends from cell A1 to cell Z100, Works will move the highlight to cell Z100 when you hold down the [Ctrl] key and press [End].

[Ctrl] arrow combinations

The [Ctrl] key also adds "power" to the four arrow keys. If you press one of these four keys while holding down the [Ctrl] key, Works will move the highlight in the indicated direction to the cell at the next boundary between a blank cell and an occupied cell, placing it on the occupied cell. If there aren't any more occupied cells in the indicated direction, Works will move the highlight all the way to the edge of the spreadsheet; that is, to column A (unless you have set one or more title columns), column IV, row 1 (unless you have specified one or more title rows), or row 4096.

For example, suppose the highlight is in cell A3 of a spreadsheet as shown in Figure 7-2. As you can see, cells A3, B3, C3, E3, and G3 contain entries. Cells D3 and F3 are blank. If you press [Ctrl]→ while the highlight is on cell A3, Works will move the highlight to cell C3—the first occupied cell at the next boundary between an occupied cell and a blank cell. If you press [Ctrl]→ again, Works will move the highlight to cell E3—the next occupied cell at the next boundary between an occupied cell and a blank cell. As you would expect, pressing [Ctrl]→ again moves the highlight to cell G3. Since cell G3 is the last occupied cell on row 3, pressing [Ctrl]→ again moves the highlight to cell IV3.

Figure 7-2

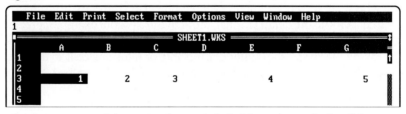

If you press any of the arrow keys while holding down the [Ctrl] key, Works will move the highlight in the indicated direction to the next boundary between a blank cell and an occupied cell.

The [Go To] key

The Go To... command on the Select menu and the [Go To] key ([F5]) move the highlight directly to any cell you specify. When you select this command or press this key, you'll see a dialog box like the one shown in Figure 7-3. To move the highlight to a specific cell, just type the address of that cell into the Go To text box and choose <OK>. (Since <OK> is the default button, you can choose it simply by pressing [Enter].) Works will then move the highlight directly to the cell you specified. For example, if you press the [Go To] key, type Z100, and press [Enter], Works will move the highlight to cell Z100.

Figure 7-3

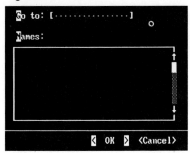

You'll see a dialog box like this one when you issue the Go To... command or press the [Go To] key.

You also can use the Go To... command and [Go To] key to extend the highlight to cover a range of cells. We'll demonstrate this use of the Go To... command and [Go To] key later in this chapter.

If you have a mouse

If you have a mouse, you can use some alternative techniques for navigating within a spreadsheet document. (Of course, you also can use the keyboard techniques described above.) To move the cursor to any cell that is visible on the screen, simply point to that cell with the mouse pointer and click the left mouse button. When you do this, Works will move the highlight from its current position to the cell on which you clicked. For example, if you click on cell B5, Works will move the highlight to cell B5.

If the cell to which you want to move the highlight is not visible on the screen, you must scroll the portion of the document that contains it into view before you can click it. To do this, you can use the scroll bars at the right and bottom edges of the screen. (These scroll bars will be visible only if you have installed Works for use with a mouse.) Figure 7-4 on the following page shows the scroll bars in a spreadsheet document.

Using the vertical scroll bar

The vertical scroll bar (the one at the right edge of the screen) allows you to shift the spreadsheet document up and down within the work area. Each time you click the arrow at the top of the vertical scroll bar, Works will shift the window up one row, so that the bottom row disappears and a new row comes into view at the top of the work area For example, if rows 5 through 22 are visible in the work area before you click the arrow at the top of the vertical scroll bar, rows 4 through 21 will be visible afterwards. Each time you click the arrow at the bottom of the vertical scroll bar, Works will shift the window down one row. For example, if you click this arrow when rows 4 through 21 are in view, Works will shift rows 5 through 22 into view.

Figure 7-4

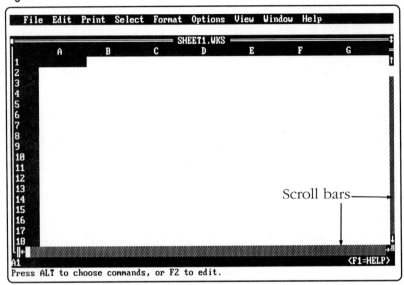

If you installed Works for use with a mouse, you'll see scroll bars at the right and bottom edges of the work area.

If you click the vertical scroll bar above the scroll box (the dark square within the scroll bar), Works will scroll the previous windowful of the spreadsheet (usually 18 rows) into view, just as it does when you press the [Pg Up] key. Similarly, if you click the vertical scroll bar below the scroll box, Works will scroll the next windowful of the spreadsheet into view, just as it does when you press the [Pg Dn] key. Due to the scale of the scroll bar, it is impossible to click above the scroll box when any of the upper 256 rows of the spreadsheet are in view, and impossible to click below the scroll box when any of the last 256 rows are in view. When operating in those regions, you must use the [Pg Up] and [Pg Dn] keys to move the highlight in full-window increments.

Dragging the scroll box is the third way to shift a spreadsheet document within the work area. To drag this box, point to it with the mouse pointer, hold down the left mouse button, move the box up or down within the scroll bar, and release the mouse button. The position of the scroll box within the scroll bar indicates which portion of the spreadsheet you will see. For example, if you drag the scroll box to the bottom of the scroll bar, you'll see the bottommost rows of the spreadsheet when you release the mouse button.

Using the horizontal scroll bar

You can use the same three techniques in the horizontal scroll bar (the one at the bottom edge of the work area) to shift a spreadsheet horizontally within the work area. If you click the arrow at the right end of the horizontal scroll bar, Works will shift the window one column to the right. If you click the arrow at the left end of the horizontal scroll bar, Works will shift the window one column to the left. If you click the horizontal scroll bar to the right or left of the scroll box, Works will shift the window one windowful to the right or left. You can shift the window to the right or left by dragging the scroll box within the horizontal scroll bar.

Unlike the keyboard, the scroll bars do not move the highlight within a spreadsheet; they merely bring a new portion of the spreadsheet into view. Consequently, it's possible (in fact, likely) that you'll move the highlight off the screen when you use your mouse to navigate within a spreadsheet document. After using the scroll bars to shift a new portion of a document into view, therefore, you'll need to click a cell within that portion to bring the highlight back into view.

Moving the highlight off the screen

In addition to letting you move the highlight, Works allows you to extend it to cover more than one cell. You can extend the highlight to cover any rectangular range of cells in a spreadsheet: a single cell, a small block of cells, an entire row or column, or the entire spreadsheet. There are two principal reasons for extending the highlight: to mark the cells a command will act upon and to mark the cells into which you will be making entries.

EXTENDING THE HIGHLIGHT

Figure 7-5

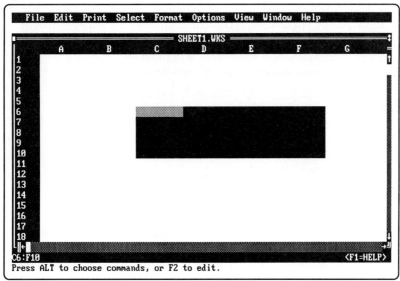

You can extend the highlight to cover any rectangular range of cells.

Figure 7-5 shows a spreadsheet document in which a range of cells is selected. In this case, we've selected cells C6 through F10. When a single cell is highlighted,

Works will display the address of that cell at the left edge of the status line. When more than one cell is highlighted, Works will display the coordinates of the highlighted range instead. Works will display the coordinates of a range in XX:YY form, where XX is the address of the upper-left cell in the range, and YY is the address of the lower-right cell. For example, Works displays the range address *C6:F10* at the left edge of the status line in the spreadsheet shown in Figure 7-5 on the next page.

Even when the highlight covers more than one cell, only one cell is the active cell. Works identifies this cell by displaying it in a different color or with a dimmer highlight than it uses to display the other cells. For example, in the spreadsheet shown in Figure 7-5, cell C6 is the active cell. Later, we'll show you how you can move the active cell within the highlighted range.

The way in which you can extend the highlight in a spreadsheet document depends on whether you have a mouse. If you don't have a mouse, you must use the cursor-movement keys with either the [Shift] or [Extend] keys to select a block of cells. If you have a mouse, you can use it to extend the highlight.

Using the [Shift] key

One way to extend the highlight to cover more than one cell is to hold down the [Shift] key while you press any of the keys or key combinations that move the highlight within a spreadsheet. If you hold down the [Shift] key and press any of these keys, Works will extend the highlight to enclose the active cell plus the cell into which the highlight moves.

You can use the arrow keys in combination with the [Shift] key to extend the highlight one cell at a time in any direction. If you hold down the [Shift] key and press an arrow key when a single cell is highlighted, Works will extend the highlight one cell in the indicated direction. For example, if you hold down the [Shift] key and press ➡ while only cell C6 is highlighted, Works will extend the highlight to cover cell D6 as well.

If you hold down the [Shift] key and press an arrow key while more than one cell is highlighted, Works will either extend or contract the highlight, depending on the position of the active cell in the highlighted range and which key you press. Works always extends or contracts the highlight from the edges of the range opposite the active cell. For example, suppose that the range C5:D5 is highlighted and that the active cell is cell C5 (which is in the upper-left corner of the range.) If you press [Shift]⬇, Works will extend the highlight to cover cells C5:D6. If you then press [Shift]⬅, Works will contract the highlight so it covers cells C5:C6.

Although you usually will use the arrow keys in conjunction with the [Shift] key to extend the highlight, you also can use the [Shift] key with any of the other keys and key combinations that move the highlight: [Ctrl]➡, [Pg Up], [Ctrl][Pg Dn], [End], [Ctrl][Home], and so forth.

▶Instead of using the [Shift] key to highlight a range of cells, you can use the Cells command on the Select menu or the [Extend] key ([F8]). (The Cells command is new to Works 2.) When you select this command or press this key, the word *EXTEND* will appear on the status line, indicating that Works is in the Extend mode. While Works is in this mode, the cursor-movement keys and key combinations don't move the cursor around the spreadsheet. Instead, they extend and contract the highlight, just as they do when you hold down the [Shift] key. For example, if you press the → key while Works is in the Extend mode, it will extend the highlight one cell to the right; if you press [Ctrl][Home], Works will contract the highlight to the upper-left cell in the spreadsheet. The [Extend] key eliminates the need to hold down the [Shift] key.

The [Extend] mode
▶WORKS 2◀

If you want, you can use the Go To... command or the [Go To] key while Works is in the Extend mode to extend the highlight to a remote cell. To do this, select the Cells command or press the [Extend] key to enter the Extend mode, then either press the [Go To] key, or pull down the Select menu and issue the Go To... command to reveal a Go To dialog box like the one shown in Figure 7-3. Once you see this box, type the address of the cell to which you want to extend the highlight into the Go To text box. When you press [Enter], Works will extend the highlight from the active cell to the cell you specified.

You can also use the Search... command while Works is in the Extend mode to extend the highlight to a remote cell. To do this, select the Cells command or press the [Extend] key to enter the Extend mode, then pull down the Select menu and select the Search... command to reveal the Search dialog box. Once you see this box, type the text you want Works to find into the Search For text box and, if you want, choose Rows or Columns to specify the direction of the search. When you choose <OK>, Works will search for the text you specified. If it finds a match with your search text, it will extend the highlight from the active cell to the cell you specified. You extend the highlight to the next occurrence of a matching string by pressing the [Repeat Search] ([F7]) key or by reissuing the Search... command. (We'll cover the Search… command in Chapter 11.)

Once you select the Cells command or press the [Extend] key, Works will be in the Extend mode until you press the [Esc] key. When you do this, Works will remove the word *EXTEND* from the status line, indicating that it is no longer in the Extend mode. However, any highlighted text will remain highlighted until you press [Esc] a second time or press a cursor-movement key.◀

Once you have extended the highlight to cover more than one cell, it will remain extended until you press [Esc] or a cursor-movement key. If you press [Esc], Works will contract the highlight so that it covers only the active cell. If you press a cursor-movement key, Works will contract the highlight to the active cell and then move the highlight. For example, if you press ↑ when the highlight is extended, Works will contract the highlight to the active cell, then move the highlight up one cell

Contracting the highlight to a single cell

Using a mouse

If you are using a mouse, you can select a range by dragging across it. To do this, position the mouse pointer on one of the four corners of the range you want to select, hold down the left mouse button, drag the pointer to the opposite end of the range, and release the button. As you drag, Works will extend the highlight from the cell to which you were pointing when you began to drag. When you release the button, the cell that is highlighted will remain highlighted, and the cell to which you pointed when you began dragging will be the active cell.

You can use the mouse in conjunction with the [Shift] key to extend the highlight from the active cell to any other cell in the spreadsheet. To do this, simply point to the cell to which you want to extend the highlight, hold down the [Shift] key, and click the left mouse button. Works will then extend the highlight from the active cell to the cell on which you clicked. For example, if you hold down the [Shift] key and click on cell Z100 while cell A1 is the active cell, Works will extend the highlight from cell A1 to cell Z100. Pointing and clicking the left mouse button while Works is in the Extend mode has the same effect.

Highlighting entire rows and columns

In many cases, you'll need to highlight one or more entire rows or columns in a spreadsheet. Works gives you a number of ways to do this. First, you can use the [Shift], [Extend], and mouse techniques we have just discussed. However, there are a number of faster ways. If you don't have a mouse, you can use the Row or Column command on the Select menu—or the [Select Row] key ([Ctrl][F8]) or [Select Column] key ([Shift][F8])—to highlight one or more entire rows or columns. If you do have a mouse, you can use it to highlight entire rows and columns with a single click or drag.

Highlighting rows

If you are using Works without a mouse, you can use either the Row command on the Select menu or the [Select Row] key to highlight one or more entire rows in a spreadsheet. When you issue this command or press this key combination, Works will extend the highlight to cover every cell in every row that the highlight occupies at the time. If the highlight is in cell B5, for example, Works will extend it to cover cells A5:IV5—every cell in row 5. If the highlight is covering cells C3:F16, Works will extend it to cover cells A3:IV16.

If you have a mouse, you can highlight a single row simply by pointing to the number of that row and clicking. For example, to highlight every cell in row 17, you would click on the number 17 at the left of that row. To highlight every cell in a number of adjacent rows, you can point to the number of either the top or bottom row that you want to select, hold down the left mouse button, drag the mouse up or down until the rows you want to select are highlighted, then release the button.

Highlighting columns

Highlighting columns is a lot like highlighting rows. If you are using Works without a mouse, you can use either the Column command on the Select menu or the [Select Column] key to highlight one or more entire columns. When you pull down the Select menu and select the Column command, Works will extend the highlight to cover every cell in every column that the highlight occupies at the time. For example, if the highlight is in cell B5, Works will extend it to cover cells B1:B4096—every cell in column B. If the highlight is covering cells C3:F16, Works will extend it to cover cells C1:F4096.

If you have a mouse, you can highlight an entire column simply by pointing to the letter at the top of that column and clicking. For example, if you want to highlight every cell in column C, you would click on the letter C at the top of that column. You can highlight every cell in adjacent columns by pointing to the letter of either the leftmost or rightmost column that you want to select, holding down the left mouse button, dragging the mouse to the right or left until the columns you want to select are highlighted, and then releasing the button.

▶In some cases, you'll want to highlight every cell in a spreadsheet. You can do this easily by using the All command on the Select menu. (The All command is new in Works 2.) When you issue this command, Works will instantly highlight every cell in the spreadsheet.◀

Alternatively, you can use the [Select All] key ([Ctrl][Shift][F8]) to highlight every cell in a spreadsheet. When you press these three keys together, Works will highlight every cell in the spreadsheet.

If you have a mouse, you can highlight every cell in a spreadsheet quickly by clicking in the upper-left corner of the work area—to the left of the leftmost column letter and above the uppermost row number.

Highlighting the entire spreadsheet
▶WORKS 2◀

You also can use the [Go To] key or the Go To... command to extend the highlight to cover a range of cells. To do this, press the [Go To] key, or pull down the Select menu and select the Go To... command to reveal a Go To dialog box, type the address of the range you want to highlight, and press [Enter]. When you do this, Works will move the highlight to the upper-left cell of the range you specified, then extend it to cover the entire range. The cell in the upper-left corner of the range will be the active cell. For example, if you press the [Go To] key, type C5:F11, and press [Enter], Works will highlight cells C5:F11 and make cell C5 the active cell.

Highlighting ranges with the Go To... command

Once you have extended the highlight, you can make a different cell within the highlighted range the active cell. (If you used the Cells command or the [Extend] key to extend the highlight, you must exit from the Extend mode first.) While more than one cell is highlighted but Works is not in the Extend mode, pressing the [Tab] key activates the cell to the right of the active cell. For example, if cells A1:B2 are highlighted, and cell A1 is currently the active cell, cell B1 will become the active cell when you press the [Tab] key. If you press the [Tab] key while a cell in the rightmost column of the highlighted range is active, Works will activate the cell in the leftmost column of the next row. For example, if you press

Moving the cursor within the extended highlight

[Tab] while cells A1:B2 are highlighted and cell B1 is active, Works will make cell A2 the active cell. If you press [Tab] while the cell in the lower-right corner of the highlighted range is active, Works will activate the upper-left cell in the range. For example, if you press [Tab] while cells A1:B2 are highlighted and cell B2 is the active cell, Works will activate cell A1. The [Shift][Tab] combination activates cells in the reverse order.

While more than one cell is highlighted when Works is not in the Extend mode, pressing the [Enter] key activates the cell below the one that is active at the time. For example, if cells A1:B2 are highlighted, and cell A1 is currently the active cell, cell A2 will become the active cell when you press [Enter]. If you press [Enter] while a cell in the bottommost row in the highlighted range is active, Works will activate the cell in the topmost row of the next column. For example, if you press [Enter] while cells A1:B2 are highlighted and cell A2 is the active cell, Works will activate cell B1. If you press [Enter] while the cell in the lower-right corner of the highlighted range is active, Works will activate the upper-left cell in the range. For example, if you press [Enter] while cells A1:B2 are highlighted and cell B2 is the active cell, Works will activate cell A1. The [Shift][Enter] combination activates cells in the reverse order.

As we'll explain later, moving the active cell allows you to make entries into different cells of a highlighted range. Since Works extends or contracts a range from the sides of the range that are opposite the active cell, it also allows you to extend or contract a range from different sides of that range. For example, suppose that after having extended the highlight from cell C5 (the active cell) to cell E7, you want to extend the highlight to cover cells B4:E7. To do this, you would press [Shift][Tab] or [Shift][Enter] to make cell E7 the active cell, press [Shift]← to extend the highlight to cover cells B5:E7, and then press [Shift]↑ to extend the highlight to cover cells B4:E7.

If you press any cursor-movement key other than [Tab], [Enter], [Shift][Tab], or [Shift][Enter] while a range is highlighted, Works will contract the highlight to cover only the active cell and then move it relative to that cell.

A final note

We'll use the words *highlight* and *select* interchangeably in this section to describe the process of extending the highlight to cover a range of cells. When you see either of these terms, understand that we are referring to the techniques explained in the preceding paragraphs.

MAKING ENTRIES INTO CELLS

At the beginning of this chapter, we stated that cells are the basic building blocks of any spreadsheet—the "pockets" that hold the information you enter. Consequently, you must know how to enter information into the cells of a spreadsheet in order to use the document for any productive purpose. In this section, we'll show you how to make entries into a Works spreadsheet.

Making an entry into a cell of a Works spreadsheet is a three-step process. First, you must move the highlight to the cell in which you want to make the entry. Once that cell is the active cell, you should type the entry. ▶As you type, the entry will appear on the formula line at the top of the screen and in the cell on which the highlight is positioned. (In Works 1, the entry did not appear in the cell until after you locked it in.)◀ Additionally, the message *Edit formula.* will appear on the message line. Once you have typed the entry, you should press [Enter] or a cursor-movement key, or click another cell. If you press the [Enter] key, Works will lock the entry into the active cell and keep the highlight on that cell. If you press a cursor-movement key instead, Works will lock the entry into the active cell and move the highlight to a different cell. If you click another cell, Works will make the entry and then move the highlight to the cell you clicked.

If you want to delete the new entry before you lock it in, just press [Esc]. Works will then clear the entry without entering it into the active cell.

Data entry basics

▶WORKS 2◀

Suppose you want to enter the value 123 into cell C3 of a Works spreadsheet and the highlight currently is on cell A1. First, press ➡ and ⬇ two times each to position the highlight over cell C3 (if you have a mouse, simply click that cell). With the highlight in place, type 123. As you type, these characters will appear on the formula line, as shown in Figure 7-6. As you are typing, you'll see a cursor on the formula line. Each character you type appears at the location of the cursor and moves the cursor one space to the right.

An example

Figure 7-6

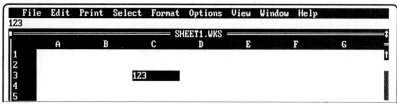

As you type an entry, it will appear on the formula line and in the cell.

Once you have typed this entry, you should lock it into the spreadsheet by pressing the [Enter] key. Figure 7-7 on the next page shows the result. As you can see, the value 123 appears in cell C3, and the highlight remains on that cell. If you pressed ➡ instead, Works would lock the entry 123 into cell C3, then move the highlight to cell D3, all in one step.

Works always displays the contents of the active cell on the formula line. Because cell C3 is the active cell, the characters *123* appear on the formula line in Figure 7-7. While you are making an entry, the cursor will be visible on the formula line. However, it will not be visible when Works is simply displaying the contents of the active cell.

Figure 7-7

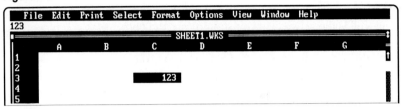

*To lock in an entry, press [Esc] or a cursor-movement key, or click
another cell.*

**Making entries into
occupied cells**

    In most cases, you will make entries into empty cells. However, you also can
make entries into cells that already contain entries. When you position the
highlight on an occupied cell, type an entry, and press [Enter] or a cursor-
movement key, Works will replace the existing entry with the new entry. For
example, if you move the highlight to cell C3 of the spreadsheet in Figure 7-7, type
321, and press [Enter], Works will replace the value 123 with the value 321.

**Making entries when
a range is highlighted**

    Although you usually will make entries into a spreadsheet when only a single
cell is highlighted, you can make entries while a range of cells is highlighted. As
you recall, there is only one active cell even when more than one cell is
highlighted. Works identifies the active cell by giving it a dimmer highlight than
it does the other highlighted cells. When you make an entry while a range is
highlighted, Works will enter it into the active cell.

    To make an entry into a cell of a highlighted range, begin by using the [Tab],
[Shift][Tab], [Enter], or [Shift][Enter] keys to activate the appropriate cell in that
range. After activating that cell, type the entry and press one of these four keys
or key combinations. As you type the entry, it will appear on the formula line.
If you press [Tab], Works will make the entry into the active cell and activate the
cell to its right. If you press [Shift][Tab], Works will make the entry into the active
cell and activate the cell to its left. If you press [Enter], Works will make the entry
into the active cell and activate the cell below it. If you press [Shift][Enter], Works
will make the entry into the active cell and activate the cell above it.

    As long as you keep pressing these keys, Works will activate different cells
in the highlighted range. If you press a "regular" cursor-movement key like ↓,
[Pg Dn], or [Home], Works will make the entry into the active cell, contract the
highlight to cover only the cell, then move the highlight relative to that cell.

    If you want, you can make the same entry into every cell of a highlighted
range. To do this, activate any of the cells in the range, type the entry, and press
[Ctrl][Enter]. For example, if you type 123 and press [Ctrl][Enter] while cells A1:B2
are highlighted, Works will enter the value 123 into all four cells of that range.

You can make six types of entries into a spreadsheet—values, labels, dates, times, formulas, and functions. Value entries are numbers like 123, 99.95, and -53. Label entries are text entries, like *January, Product #1, FY 1990*, and so forth. Date entries are special values that represent a specific day, month, and year. Time entries are special value entries that represent a specific time of day. Formulas are mathematical manipulations of values. Functions are special formulas that allow you to manipulate values in a way that is difficult or impossible to do with traditional operators.

Types of entries

A value is a number Works can manipulate mathematically; that is, a number it can add, subtract, multiply, and so forth. To enter a value into a cell, simply move the highlight to that cell, type the number, and press [Enter] or a cursor-movement key to lock it in. For example, to enter the value 123.45 into cell A1, you would move the highlight to cell A1, type 123.45, and press [Enter].

Entering values

Figure 7-8 shows the result of entering the value 123.45 into cell A1. As you can see, this value appears both in cell A1 of the spreadsheet and, since the highlight is on cell A1, on the formula line as well. Notice that the value is right-aligned; that is, the rightmost digit in the value is aligned with the right edge of the cell (actually, one space to the left of the right edge of the cell). Right alignment is the default alignment of value entries. However, you can specify alternative alignments. We'll show you how to do that in Chapter 8.

Figure 7-8

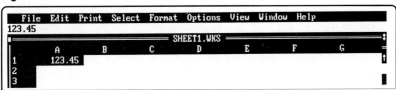

By default, value entries appear right-aligned in their cells.

In most cases, the values you enter into a spreadsheet will contain only digits 0 through 9 and decimal points. However, you can preface a value with a - sign, enclose it in parentheses, include commas within it, enter it in scientific notation, begin it with a $ sign, or end it with a % sign.

To enter a negative value into a spreadsheet, you can preface it with a - sign or enclose it in parentheses. For example, to enter the value -123.45 into cell C3, you would move the highlight to cell C3 and type either -123.45 or (123.45). When you press [Enter], Works will lock the value into the spreadsheet and display it as -123.45. If you want, you can preface positive values with a + sign. However, Works will remove that sign when you lock the value into the spreadsheet.

Negative values

Commas

Commas make it easier to enter large values into a spreadsheet. When you include commas as you enter a value, those commas will appear on the formula line. However, Works will remove the commas when it locks that value into the spreadsheet. For example, although you may type 1,234,567.89 onto the formula line, Works will enter and display the value as 1234567.89 in the spreadsheet.

Scientific notation

Scientific notation is another device that makes it easier to enter large values. Examples of entries in this form include 1.23E+07, 2.56E-10, and 1.01E+24. When you enter a value in scientific notation, it will appear in that form on the formula line. Whether Works displays the value in scientific notation when you lock it into the spreadsheet depends on the magnitude of that value and the width of the cell into which you are making the entry. If the cell into which you are entering the value is wide enough to hold that value in full form, Works will display it in that form. If the cell is not wide enough to hold the value in full form, Works will display it in scientific notation. We'll discuss more about this property of values and the concept of column widths later in this chapter and in Chapter 9.

Automatic formatting the $ and % signs

Works also lets you preface a value with a $ sign or end it with a % sign. When you type entries in either of these forms and press [Enter] or a cursor-movement key, Works will lock the value into the spreadsheet, just as you would expect. However, it does something more—it also assigns a special format to the cell into which it entered the value. A format is a special display characteristic that "filters" your view of the value in a cell. We'll examine this "automatic formatting" briefly now; however, we'll cover formatting in detail in Chapter 8.

When you lock in an entry that is prefaced with a $ sign, Works will assign the Currency format to the cell containing that entry. This format causes Works to display the value in that cell with a leading $ sign and to use commas to separate the hundreds from the thousands, the thousands from the millions, and so forth. For example, if you position the highlight on cell A1, type $1234567.89, and press [Enter], Works will lock the value 1234567.89 into that cell, but display it as $1,234,567.89.

Following a value with a % sign both alters that value and formats the cell containing it. Specifically, Works divides the value by 100 before it enters it into the cell and assigns the Percent format to that cell. The Percent format causes Works to display the value as a percentage. For example, suppose you position the highlight on cell B2 and type 12.3%. When you press [Enter], Works will divide the value 12.3 by 100, lock the result, .123, into cell B2, and display it as 12.3%.

Large and small values

The smallest value that Works lets you enter into a spreadsheet is 1E-306; the largest is 9.99999999999999E+305. If you type a value less than 1E-306 or greater than 9.99999999999999E+305, Works will enter what you type as a label—not a value. We'll talk about labels later in this chapter.

No matter how large or small a value is, Works does not accept values that have more than 15 significant digits. A significant digit is any non-zero numeric character, including any to the right of the first non-zero numeric character in a value, as well as any zeroes sandwiched between two non-zero characters. For example, the values 123000 and .000123 each contain only three significant digits. However, the values 123000.1 and 1.000123 each contain seven significant digits.

When you enter a value that contains more than 15 significant digits, Works will modify that value so that it contains only 15 significant digits. For example, if you type 1234567890123456 and then press [Enter], Works will enter the value 1234567890123450. Note that Works converted the 16th digit to a 0. If you type 1234567890.123456 and press [Enter], Works will lock the value 1234567890.12345 into the spreadsheet.

The width of the column into which you enter a value affects the way Works displays that value in the spreadsheet. If you enter a value into a column that is too narrow to display that value in full, Works will display it in rounded form or in scientific notation. A cell must be at least one character wider than the value you enter into it in order for Works to display that value in full form. Since the default width of the columns in a Works spreadsheet is ten characters, Works can display in full form only values that have nine characters or less—unless you alter the width of the column that contains that value. We'll show you how to change column widths in Chapter 9.

The effect of column widths on values

In most cases, Works will display a value in full form on the formula line, regardless of how it displays that value in a cell. However, Works makes an exception to this rule for very large or very small values. If you enter a value greater than or equal to 1E-252 but less than or equal to 9.99999999999999E+253, Works will display that value in full form on the formula line. For example, if you enter 1.23E+25, Works will display the value 12300000000000000000000000 on the formula line. If you enter a value less than 1E-252 or greater than 9.99999999999999E+253, Works will display that value in scientific notation on the formula line. For example, if you type 1E-300, Works will display the value 1E-300 on the formula line.

How values are displayed on the formula line

As you have seen, you can include non-numeric characters like $ signs, commas, decimal points, the letter E, % signs, + signs, and - signs in numeric entries. As long as those characters are in an appropriate place, Works will accept the entry as a value. If those characters are out of place, or if the entry contains other non-numeric characters, Works will interpret the entry as a label. For example, Works would enter 123$456, 327+52, and *331 Main Street* as labels. We'll talk about label entries next.

Non-numeric entries

Entering labels

Labels are simple text entries. You'll use labels in your spreadsheets as column headers, row labels, spreadsheet titles, notes, messages, and so forth. The process of entering a label is identical to that of entering a value. Just position the highlight on the cell where you want to make the entry, then type the entry. Next, press [Enter] or a cursor-movement key to lock the entry into the spread-sheet.

As an example of making a label entry, suppose you want to enter the label *Widgets* into cell A1 of a spreadsheet. To do this, begin by positioning the highlight on cell A1. Once the highlight is in place, type *Widgets*. As you type, the characters *Widgets* will appear on the formula line. The cursor marks the position at which each character will appear. Once you have typed the entry, you can press [Enter] or a cursor-movement key to lock it in.

Figure 7-9 shows the result of making this entry. As you can see, Works displays the entry *Widgets* in cell A1. On the formula line, however, Works displays *"Widgets*. The leading *"* is Works' label prefix. This prefix tells Works that the entry that follows is a label. In most cases, Works will supply a prefix automatically when you type a label entry.

Figure 7-9

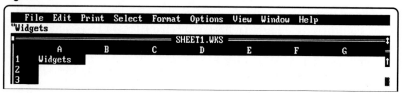

Works includes a label prefix when it displays labels on the formula line.

If you look again at the spreadsheet shown in Figure 7-9, you'll see that the label is left-aligned; that is, the leftmost character in the entry is aligned with the left edge of the cell. Left alignment is the default alignment for label entries. However, you can specify alternative alignments. We'll show you how to do that in Chapter 8.

Using label prefixes

Label entries typically begin with a letter, space, or punctuation mark. However, Works considers a label to be any entry that is not a value, date, time, formula, or function. (We'll discuss dates, times, formulas, and functions later in this chapter.) For example, Works will enter *404-74-1421* as the label *"404-74-1421, 2317 Woodford Place* as the label *"2317 Woodford Place*, and so forth.

In some cases, you may want to enter in label form an entry that Works normally would interpret as a value, date, time, formula, or function. To enter these labels, you must include a label prefix. For example, suppose you want to enter 1990 as a label. If you simply type 1990 and press [Enter], Works will enter the value 1990 into the current cell. If you type *"1990* however, Works will lock in the label *"1990* when you press [Enter].

Works will interpret most entries that contain letters as labels. However, there are some important exceptions to this rule. First, Works interprets the words *True* and *False* as values. If you type *True* and press [Enter], Works will enter the value 1, assign the True/False format to the cell, and display the entry as *TRUE*. Similarly, if you type *False* and press [Enter], Works will enter the value 0, assign the True/False format to the cell, and display the entry as *FALSE*. We'll cover the True/False format in detail in Chapter 8. For now, be aware that you have to preface the words *True* and *False* with a label prefix (") in order to enter them as labels.

Second, if you type the names of months or their abbreviations, Works will enter them as special values that represent dates. To enter a month name as a label, you must include a label prefix. We'll talk about date entries later in this chapter.

Any label can be up to 254 characters long. Although few of your labels will have this many characters, many of them will exceed the width of a typical cell. Unlike values, labels often are not restricted by the boundaries of the cells that contain them. If you enter a label too long to be displayed in a single cell, Works will use any empty cells to the right to display as much of the label as possible.

Long labels

For example, Figure 7-10 shows the result of entering the label *The quick red fox jumped over the lazy brown dog.* into cell A3 of a new spreadsheet. As you can see, Works displays part of this label in cell A3, then displays the rest of the label in cells B3, C3, D3, and E3. Although it looks like different parts of this label are entered into five different cells, the entire label is stored in cell A3. The fact that the entire entry appears on the formula line when the highlight is on cell A3 confirms this. If you move the highlight to cells B3, C3, D3, or E3 and look at the formula line, you'll see that they are empty.

Figure 7-10

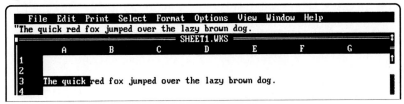

If you enter a label that is too long to be displayed in a single cell, Works will use any empty cells to the right to display as much of the label as possible.

It is important to note that Works allows long labels to overlap only empty cells. If the cell(s) to the right of a long label are occupied, Works will truncate the display of the label. For example, Figure 7-11 shows the spreadsheet in Figure 7-10 after we entered the value 123 into cell C3. As you can see, Works truncated the display of the label at the left edge of cell C3. Even though cells D3 and E3 still are blank, the entry in cell C3 keeps Works from displaying the label in those cells. If you erased the entry in cell C3, the entire long label would reappear.

Figure 7-11

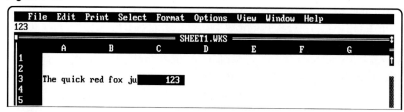

Works will not let a long label overlap cells that contain entries.

Entering formulas

If a Works spreadsheet could do nothing but store values, dates, and times, its usefulness would be limited. The real power of a Works spreadsheet is its ability to use values, dates, and times in mathematical formulas. A formula consists of two or more values or references to value-containing cells connected with one or more of the following operators: +, -, *, /, or ∧. All formulas must begin with an = sign. This sign is Works' signal that what follows is a formula (or, as you will see later, a function).

To demonstrate how formulas work, let's look at a few examples. First, suppose you want to calculate the result of adding 10 and 5 in cell B2. To do this, you would move the highlight to cell B2, type =10+5, and press [Enter] or a cursor-movement key. Figure 7-12 shows the result. As you can see, Works has locked the formula *=10+5* into cell B2, as evidenced by that entry on the formula line. In cell B2 itself, however, Works displays the value 15—the result of that formula. In almost all cases, Works will display the result of a formula—not the formula itself—in the spreadsheet. However, the underlying formula always will appear on the formula line when you highlight a formula-containing cell.

Figure 7-12

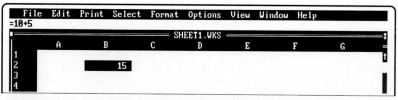

When you enter a formula into a cell of a spreadsheet, Works will display it on the formula line but displays its result in the cell.

You also can use the -, *, /, and ^ operators within formulas. For instance, the formula *=10-5* returns the result of subtracting 5 from 10; *=10*5* returns the result of multiplying 10 and 5; *=10/5* calculates the result of dividing 10 by 5; and *=10^5* returns the result of raising 10 to the fifth power.

So far, we've shown you formulas that contain only a single mathematical operator. However, many of the formulas that you will enter into a Works spreadsheet will contain more than one operator. For example, suppose you want to add 10 to the result of dividing 100 by 4. To do this, you would use the formula *=10+100/4*. When you enter this formula into a spreadsheet, Works will evaluate it and return the result, 35.

In many cases, creating a multiple-operator formula to perform a complex calculation is as easy as connecting the appropriate values with the appropriate operators, as we did in the previous example. In some cases, however, you must use one or more sets of parentheses to override Works' precedence of operators— the order in which Works evaluates the various operators in a multiple-operator formula. As a rule, Works will evaluate powers (^) first, multiplications and divisions next, and additions and subtractions last. If a formula contains both a multiplication and a division, Works will perform the operations in the order that they appear in the formula, moving from left to right. Works also will perform additions and subtractions in the order that they appear in a formula.

When you want to override Works' precedence of operators, you can use parentheses to specify the order in which Works evaluates the individual operations in a complex formula. To understand how this works, suppose you want Works to divide the sum of 10 and 100 by 4. To do this, you must use the formula *=(10+100)/4*. Surrounding 10+100 with parentheses commands Works to evaluate that operation first, contrary to its traditional precedence of operators. As a result, Works divides 110 by 4, and returns the value 27.5.

Multiple operators and the precedence of operators

So far, we've used literal values in our example formulas. Although you will use literal values in formulas every now and then, you will refer to values in other cells of a spreadsheet more often. When you create a formula that contains cell references, you link that formula to other cells in the spreadsheet. Consequently, the result of the formula depends on the current value of the referenced cells. If you change the value in any of the source cells, the result of the formula will change also.

For example, suppose you want to enter a formula into cell B2 that refers to cell A1. To do this, you would move the highlight to cell B2, type *=A1*, and press [Enter]. Figure 7-13 shows the results. As you can see from the formula line, Works has entered the simple formula *=A1* into cell B2. Since cell A1 contains the value 123, Works displays the value 123 as the result of that formula. If you changed the value in cell A1 to 456, Works would display the value 456 in cell B2 as well.

Using cell references in formulas

Figure 7-13

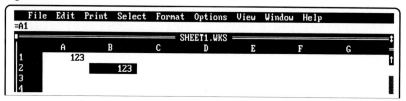

In most cases, your formulas will contain one or more references to other cells.

Of course, formulas usually are more complex than a simple reference to a single cell. Most formulas contain two or more cell references and/or values, connected by a mathematical operator. For example, suppose you want to add the value 987 to the value in cell A1 of the spreadsheet shown in Figure 7-13, and display the result in cell C3. To do this, move the highlight to cell C3 and type *=A1+987*. When you press [Enter] or a cursor-movement key, Works will lock the formula into cell C3 and, since cell A1 contains the value 123, display the result 1110 in cell C3.

As another example, suppose you want to divide the result of the formula *=A1* in cell B2 by the result of the formula *=A1+987* in cell C3, and place the result in cell D4. To do this, move the highlight to cell D4, type *=B2/C3*, and press [Enter] or a cursor-movement key. Whenever a formula references a cell that contains another formula, Works uses the current result of the referenced formula in the calculation. In this case, the formula in cell B2 would return the value 123 and the formula in cell C3 would return the value 1110. Consequently, Works will divide 123 by 1110 and display the result, .1108108, in cell D4.

Of course, you can create formulas that are more complex than the simple examples we've given here. Your formulas can be up to 254 characters long and can contain dozens of operators, values, references, and sets of parentheses.

Pointing

In the previous examples, we entered cell references into formulas by typing them. Although this is perfectly acceptable, Works gives you an alternative way to create cell references—by pointing. Pointing can save time and reduce typing errors. To reference a cell by pointing, simply move the highlight to that cell after typing the = sign or an operator. As you move the highlight, the word *POINT* will appear on the status line, and the address of the current cell will appear to the right of that sign or operator on the formula line. When you press [Enter] or another operator, Works will lock the address of that cell into the formula.

The best way to explain pointing is to demonstrate it. Suppose you want to enter the formula *=B1+B2+B3* into cell B5 of a spreadsheet. To do this, begin by moving the highlight to cell B5—the cell into which you want to enter the formula. With the highlight in place, type = to begin the formula. To include the reference to cell B1, press ↑ four times to move the highlight to that cell. The first time you press ↑, Works will move the highlight to cell B4, the word *POINT* will appear on the status line, and the reference B4 will appear to the right of the = operator on the formula line. The second time you press ↑, Works will move the highlight to cell B3, then replace the reference to cell B4 with a reference to cell B3. After you press ↑ two more times, the highlight will be on cell B1 (the cell you want to refer to), and the formula *=B1* will appear on the formula line.

Once the highlight is on cell B1 (the first cell you want to reference), type a + sign—the first operator in the formula. When you do this, Works will lock in the reference to cell B1, return the highlight to cell B5 (the cell it was on when you started this process), and exit from the Point mode. Then, point to cell B2— the next cell you want to reference—so that the partial formula *=B1+B2* appears on the formula line. Next, type another + to lock in that reference and point to cell B3—the final cell you want to reference. At this point, the formula you want to enter—*=B1+B2+B3*—will appear on the formula line. To lock in this formula, press [Enter] or a cursor-movement key.

You can use any of Works' cursor-movement keys, such as ←, ↑, [End], [Pg Up], [Ctrl]→, [Ctrl][Home], and [Ctrl][Pg Dn], to point to a cell while defining a formula. Each of these keys has the same effect in the Point mode that it has when you are simply moving the highlight around the spreadsheet. If you want, you can even use the [Go To] key and the Go To... command to move the highlight to a cell when building a formula.

In Works, there are three kinds of cell references: relative, absolute, and mixed. The differences between these types of references are important when you copy a formula from one cell of a spreadsheet to another—a technique we'll cover in Chapter 9.

The references you've seen so far are relative references. A relative reference refers to another cell by the position of that cell relative to the one that contains the formula. When you copy a formula that contains a relative reference, Works will alter that reference to reflect the new position of that formula. Absolute references refer to other cells by their exact position in a spreadsheet. When you copy a formula that contains an absolute reference, that reference will not change. Mixed references are half relative and half absolute. Whether Works changes these references when it copies them depends on the position of the copy relative to the original formula.

A dollar sign ($) before the row and/or column coordinates of a reference identify it as being absolute or mixed. The $ sign "fixes" the particular component so that it will not change when you copy the reference. An absolute reference, in which both the column and row coordinates are fixed, has a $ sign before both its column and row coordinates. For example, $A$1 is an absolute reference to cell A1. A mixed reference, in which either the column coordinate or row

Absolute, relative, and mixed references

coordinate is fixed, has a $ sign in front of either its column letter or row number, but not both. For example, $A1 is a mixed reference to cell A1 that fixes its column component; A$1 is a mixed reference to cell A1 that fixes its row component.

Creating absolute and mixed references.   There are two ways to create absolute and mixed references when you type a formula: You can type the $ signs manually at the appropriate places within the formula, or you can use the [Reference] key ([F4]). This key allows you to change a reference from relative to absolute or mixed form as you are building a formula. However, it works only when Works is in the Point mode; that is, when you are pointing to include a reference in a formula. The first time you press the [Reference] key, Works will change the current reference on the formula line from relative to absolute. The second time you press the [Reference] key, Works will make the reference fixed with respect to only its row component. The third time you press the [Reference] key, Works will make the reference fixed with respect to only its column component. The fourth time you press the [Reference] key, Works will return the reference to relative form.

An example.   Suppose you want to create a simple addition formula that fixes both the column and row coordinates of cell A1, fixes only the row component of cell B1, and fixes only the column component of cell C1. To do this, you could type *=$A$1+B$1+$C1*. Alternatively, you could move the highlight to the cell in which you want to enter the formula, type *=*, point to cell A1, press [Reference] once, type *+*, point to cell B1, press [Reference] twice, type *+*, point to cell C1, press [Reference] three times, and then press [Enter].

Referring to blank cells and cells that contain labels

In most cases, the cells you refer to within formulas will contain literal values, formulas, or functions that return values. In some cases, however, your formulas may refer to blank cells and/or cells that contain labels. For purposes of formulas, Works assigns the value 0 both to empty cells and to cells that contain labels. Consequently, referring to a blank cell or a cell that contains a label is the same as referring to a cell that contains the value 0. For example, if cell A1 contains the label *hello* and cell A2 contains the value 123, the formula *=A1+A2* will return the value 123.

Invalid formulas

Works will not allow you to lock in a formula that contains an invalid reference, an incorrect number of parentheses, an illegal operator, and so forth. If you try, Works will display an alert box that identifies the problem. For example, if you press [Enter] after typing *=(1+2/3*, Works will display the alert box shown in Figure 7-14. As you can see, the message in this box tells you that a parenthesis is missing from the formula. When you choose <OK> to acknowledge this message, Works will clear the alert box and place the cursor in the formula on the formula line at the position of the error. At that point, you can correct the formula and then re-enter it.

Figure 7-14

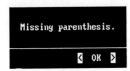

Works will display an alert box if you attempt to enter an invalid formula.

Dates are the third type of entry you can make into a Works spreadsheet. A date entry represents a calendar date, such as July 4, 1956, or August 23, 1986. Works will accept dates from January 1, 1900, through June 3, 2079.

Entering dates

Date entries are not labels—they are values that represent the number of days that have elapsed since Works' base date: December 31, 1899. For example, the value 1 represents January 1, 1900; the value 15317 represents December 7, 1941; the value 23338 represents November 23, 1963, and so forth. We'll refer to the values that Works uses to represent dates as serial date values.

Fortunately, since most people don't think of dates as a number of elapsed days, Works lets you enter dates in forms that are more familiar; for example, 11/24/58, November 24, 1958, and so forth. When you lock a date entry into a cell, Works will convert it to a value and format that cell to display that value as a date. For example, Figure 7-15 shows the result of moving the highlight to cell B2, typing 11/24/58, and pressing [Enter]. Works displays the entry 11/24/58 in that cell. This entry looks like a label; however, a glance at the formula line reveals that it is not. The absence of a label prefix (") before the first character on the formula line means that the entry is not a label. Instead, it is a value (specifically, the value 21513) that has been assigned a Date format. Furthermore, unless you specify otherwise, date entries will appear right-aligned in their cells. By default, label entries will appear left-aligned.

Figure 7-15

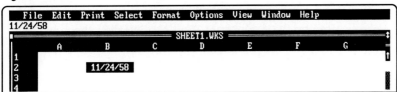

When you make a date entry, Works will transform it into a serial date value and assign a date format to the cell that contains it.

Unlike other formatted values, formatted date values appear in formatted form on the formula line. For example, even though cell B2 in Figure 7-15 contains the value 21513, the characters 11/24/58 appear on the formula line. The fact that date entries show up on the formula line in formatted form makes them easier to edit. We'll show you how to edit entries later in this chapter.

Standard date forms

You can enter dates into a Works spreadsheet in a variety of forms. The six most common forms are Month dd, yyyy; Mon dd, yyyy; Month dd, yy; Mon dd, yy; mm/dd/yy; and mm/dd/yyyy. If you enter a date in any of the first four forms, Works will display it in Mon dd, yyyy form. For example, whether you type January 1, 1990, Jan 1, 1990, January 1, 90, or Jan 1, 90, Works will format the cell into which you enter the date to display it as Jan 1, 1990. The cell would contain the value 32143. If you enter a date into a cell in either of the other two forms (mm/dd/yy or mm/dd/yyyy), Works will format that cell to display the date in mm/dd/yy form.

Alternative forms

Although you usually will enter dates in one of these six "full" forms, you also can enter them in any of these "partial" forms: Month yyyy; Month yy; Mon yyyy; Mon yy; mm/yy; mm/yyyy; Month dd; Mon dd; mm/dd; Month; and Mon. We refer to these as "partial" forms because each leaves out one or more of the three pieces of information (month, day, or year) required to specify a date completely.

When you enter a date in any of these forms, Works will supply the missing information from the date specified by your computer's system clock. For example, suppose your computer's system clock says that it is January 15, 1990. If you enter a date in any of the first six forms, Works will supply the day (in this case, 15). For example, if you type *February 1990*, Works will enter the serial date value for February 15, 1990. If you enter a date in any of the next three forms, Works will supply the year (in this case, 1990). For example, if you type *March 23*, Works will enter the serial date value for March 23, 1990. If you enter a date in either of the final two forms, Works will supply the day and the year (in this case, 15 and 1990, respectively). For example, if you type *April*, Works will enter the date for April 15, 1990. In any case, Works will display the date in the form you specified—only the parts of the date you actually entered will be displayed.

A warning

Since Works interprets entries that consist solely of the full name of a month or the standard three-letter abbreviation of that name, you must preface those entries with a label prefix if you want Works to interpret them as labels. For example, to enter January as a label, you would have to type *"January*.

Works also interprets non-standard month abbreviations as date entries. For example, Works treats the entries *Janu, Janua,* and *Januar,* in the same way it treats the entries *Jan* and *January*—it converts them into a serial date value that represents the current day of the current year in January.

Invalid dates

Whenever you enter a valid date (a date that exists in Works' calendar) in a valid date form (one of the forms that Works recognizes), Works will enter the serial value that corresponds to that date and format the cell accordingly. If you enter an invalid date in a valid form (for example, December 32, 1990), a valid date in an invalid form (like 31-Dec-90), or an invalid date in an invalid form (like 32-Dec-90), Works will not reject the entry; instead, it will enter it as a label. For example, if you type *June 31, 1990*, and press [Enter], Works will enter the label *"June 31, 1990* into the active cell.

Many formatted dates produce results that are more than ten characters wide. If a column is not wide enough to display a formatted date, Works will display a series of # characters instead. For example, Figure 7-16 shows the result of typing *Nov 24, 1958* into cell A1, which is ten characters wide. Because the formatted entry is 12 characters long and the cell is only ten characters wide, Works displays the entry as a series of ten # characters. However, it displays the formatted entry on the formula line. If your formatted dates look this way, you should increase the width of the columns containing them. We'll show you how to change the width of the columns in a spreadsheet in Chapter 9.

Date formats and column widths

Figure 7-16

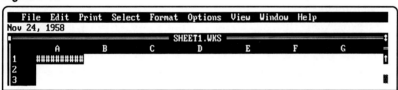

If a formatted date entry is too long to be displayed in its cell, Works will display it as a series of # characters.

In addition to entering dates in any of the 17 standard date forms, you can use either of two special date functions to enter dates into a spreadsheet. The DATE() function lets you enter the serial value for the date you specify. The NOW() function enters the value for the current date. We'll discuss these functions in Chapter 10.

Other ways to enter dates

Works makes it easy to enter the serial date value for the current date into a cell of a spreadsheet. To do this, simply press the [Ctrl] key and a semicolon simultaneously. When you press these keys, Works will extract the date from your computer's system clock and display the date in mm/dd/yy form on the formula line. When you press [Enter], Works will enter the serial date value for that date into the active cell and format that cell to display it in mm/dd/yy form.

Entering the current date

As we mentioned earlier, Works will accept dates from January 1, 1900, through June 3, 2079. When you enter dates prior to January 1, 2000, you can specify the whole year (for example, 1990) or just the final two digits of the year (for example, 90). Works also gives you two ways to specify the year component of a date from January 1, 2000, and beyond. First, just like any other date, you

Dates after December 31, 1999

can specify the entire year. Second, you can add 100 to the final two digits of the year. For example, you could enter the serial date value for June 23, 2005, as either 6/23/2005 or as 6/23/105.

Unfortunately, Works does not follow these rules when it displays dates for the years 2000 and later in the mm/dd/yy and mm/yy formats. Instead of using three or four digits to display the year component of the date, Works uses only two digits. Consequently, it is impossible to tell if the cell contains a date in the 20th or 21st centuries. For example, the serial date values for both August 17, 1958, and August 17, 2058, would appear as 8/17/58 in mm/dd/yy form, and as 8/58 in mm/yy form. Be aware of this shortcoming when your spreadsheet contains dates in both the 20th and 21st centuries.

Changing date formats

Although Works automatically assigns a date format to any cell in which you make a date entry in one of the 17 standard forms, you can change that format if you want. For example, you can make Works display a date that you entered in mm/dd/yy form in Mon dd, yyyy form. You also can command Works to display a date as a serial value (like 30654). In Chapter 8, we'll show you how to change the format of a cell that contains a date entry.

Date arithmetic

Because date entries are values, you can operate upon them in the same way you can any other values in a Works spreadsheet. Most commonly, you will want to calculate the number of days between two dates or calculate the date that is a certain number of days before or after a certain date.

You can compute the number of days that elapse between two dates by subtracting the later date from the earlier one. For example, suppose you want to determine how many days elapsed between October 6, 1957, and November 24, 1958. If cell A1 contains the serial date value for November 24, 1958, and cell A2 contains the serial date value for October 6, 1957, you could use the simple formula =A1-A2 to compute the elapsed days. The result of this function, 414, is the number of days between the two dates.

You also can use a simple formula to compute the date that is a specified number of days removed from a certain date. Suppose you want to find out what date fell 270 days prior to August 23, 1986. If cell A1 contains the serial date value for August 23, 1986, you could use the simple formula =A1-270 to perform this calculation. The result of this formula is the value 31742—the serial date value for November 26, 1986. We'll show you how to format this result in Chapter 8.

Entering times

Times are the fourth type of entry you can make into a Works spreadsheet. Like date entries, time entries are not labels. Instead, they are values that represent the fraction of a day that has elapsed since midnight of the previous day. For example, the value .5 represents 12:00 noon—exactly $1/2$ of a day. Similarly, the value .25 represents 6:00 AM ($1/4$ of a day) and the value .75 represents 6:00 PM ($3/4$ of a day).

Fortunately, since most people don't think of times as fractional days, Works lets you enter times in more familiar forms, like 7:04 AM, 17:05:00, and so forth. When you lock a time entry into a cell, Works will convert it to a value and format that cell to display that value as a time. For example, Figure 7-17 shows the result of moving the highlight to cell C2, typing 4:58 PM, and pressing [Enter]. As you can see, Works displays the entry 4:58 PM in that cell. Although this entry looks like a label, the absence of a label prefix on the formula line reveals that it is not. Instead, it is a value that has been assigned a Time format.

Figure 7-17

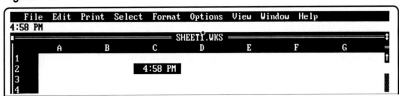

When you type a time in any of the four allowable forms, Works will enter it as a serial time value but display it in formatted form.

Although 4:58 PM appears both in the cell and on the formula line, cell A1 actually contains the value .706944444444444—the fraction of a day that has elapsed since midnight of the previous day. As you can see, Works displays times in formatted form both in the cell and on the formula line, just as it does for date entries. This makes them easier to edit—a topic we'll cover later in this chapter.

Allowable time forms

You can enter times into a Works spreadsheet in any of the following four forms: hh:mm AM/PM, hh:mm (24-hour), hh:mm:ss AM/PM, or hh:mm:ss (24-hour). When you type a time in any of these forms and then press [Enter] or a cursor-movement key, Works will lock a serial time value into the active cell and format that cell so that it displays the value as you entered it. For example, if you type 5:47 PM, then press [Enter], Works will enter .7409722 into the active cell and display that value as 5:47 PM both in that cell and on the formula line.

Invalid times

As you would expect, Works allows you to enter only times from midnight (0:0:00) to 11:59:59 PM, inclusive. Whenever you enter a valid time in one of the four forms Works recognizes, Works will enter the serial value that corresponds to that time and assign the appropriate format to the cell into which it enters that value. If you enter an invalid time in a valid form (like 25:13:07), a valid time in an invalid form (like 3 o'clock), or an invalid time in an invalid form (like 25 o'clock), however, Works will treat the entry as a label instead of as a date value. For example, if you type 25:13:07 and press [Enter], Works will enter the label 25:13:07 into the active cell.

Date formats and column widths

Like a formatted date, a formatted time value will not display properly unless it is at least one character shorter than the width of the cell containing it. When a column is not wide enough to display a formatted time, Works will display a series of # characters instead. For example, if you type 11:23:58 AM into a ten-character-wide cell, Works will display the entry as ########## in the spreadsheet. However, it will display the formatted entry on the formula line. If your formatted times look this way, you should increase the width of the columns that contain them. We'll show you how to alter column widths in Chapter 9.

Other ways to enter times

In addition to Works' four standard time forms, you can use either of two special time functions to enter times into a spreadsheet: TIME() and NOW(). We'll discuss these functions in Chapter 10.

Entering the current time

Works gives you a way to enter the serial time value for the current time into a cell of a spreadsheet. To do this, hold down the [Ctrl] and [Shift] keys while you type a semicolon. When you do this, Works will extract the time from your computer's system clock and display it in hh:mm AM/PM form on the formula line. When you press [Enter], Works will enter the serial time value for that time into the current cell and format that cell to display the time in hh:mm AM/PM form.

Entering times as labels

In some cases, you may want to enter a time as a label instead of as a formatted serial time value. To do this, you must preface the entry with a label prefix. For example, to enter 3:45 PM as a label, you would have to type *"3:45 PM*. If you simply type 3:45 PM, Works will enter the value .15625 instead.

Changing time formats

Although Works automatically assigns a Time format to any cell in which you make a time entry in one of the four standard forms, you can change that format if you want. For example, you can make Works display a time that you entered in hh:mm:ss form in hh:mm AM/PM form. You also can command Works to display a date in serial value form (like .7413194). We'll show you how to change Date formats in Chapter 8.

Time arithmetic

You also can use formulas to operate on time values. Most commonly, you will compute the elapsed time between two times and the time that is a certain amount of time removed from another time.

You can calculate the amount of time that elapses between two times simply by subtracting the smaller time value from the larger one. For example, suppose you want to know how much time elapsed between 8:17 AM and 5:32 PM. If cell A1 contains the serial time value for 8:17 AM, and cell A2 contains the serial time value for 5:32 PM, you could use the formula *=A2-A1* to calculate the elapsed time. The result of this formula is .3854167. Formatting this value (a process we'll explore in Chapter 8) reveals that it represents nine hours and 15 minutes.

You also can subtract one time value from another to determine how much time passes between two times. For example, suppose you want to know what time came four hours and 56 minutes before 5:23 PM. If cell A1 contains the serial time value for 5:23 PM, and cell A2 contains the serial time value for 4 hours and 56 minutes, you could use the function =A1-A2 to perform this calculation. The result, .51875, is the serial time value for 12:27 PM.

Functions

In addition to its standard operators (+, -, *, /, and ^), Works features a variety of functions. Functions are special operators that allow you to perform tasks that would be difficult or impossible to perform with standard operators. For example, the AVG() function calculates the average of a range of values; the IRR() function computes the internal rate of return of a series of cash flows; and the VLOOKUP() function looks up a value from a table. Like formulas, functions must begin with an = sign. When you lock a function into a cell, Works will display the result of that function in the cell and display the function itself on the formula line. We'll explore each of Works' 60 functions in detail in Chapter 10.

EDITING ENTRIES

Once you have made an entry into a spreadsheet, you often will want to erase, replace, or modify it. This process is called editing. In this section, we'll show you how to edit the entries stored in the cells of a Works spreadsheet.

Erasing entries

Works gives you several ways to erase the entries in individual cells of a spreadsheet. First, you can move the highlight to the cell you want to erase, press the [Edit] key ([F2]), press the [Backspace] key once for each character in the entry, and then press [Enter]. After you do this, the cell will be empty. For example, you could erase the value 12345 by highlighting the cell that contains it, pressing [Edit], pressing [Backspace] five times, and then pressing [Enter].

Fortunately, there's an easier way to erase an entry from a cell: Simply position the highlight on the cell that contains the entry you want to erase, press [Backspace] once, and press [Enter]. When you do this, Works will erase any entry from the current cell, no matter how many characters it contains.

The Clear command on the Edit menu gives you an alternative way to erase individual entries and gives you the only way to erase the entries in more than one cell at a time. We'll demonstrate the use of this command in Chapter 9.

Replacing entries

Instead of erasing an entry, you often will want to replace it with another entry. You can use either of the methods described above to erase the cell, then type in the new entry. Alternatively, you can just move the highlight to the cell that contains the entry you want to replace, type the new entry, and press [Enter]. Whenever you lock an entry into a cell, Works automatically replaces the existing entry (if any) in that cell. There is no need to erase the cell first. You can replace an entry of any type with an entry of any other type. For example, you can replace a label with a value, a value with a formula, a function with a label, and so forth.

Modifying entries

You also can modify an existing entry. Modifying an existing entry is a four-step process. First, move the highlight to the cell whose entry you want to modify. Next, press the [Edit] key to enter the Edit mode. When you do this, a cursor will appear immediately to the right of the last character in the entry on the formula line, and the word *EDIT* will appear in the middle of the status line. While Works is in this mode, you can move the cursor within the copy of the entry on the formula line, extend it to highlight groups of adjacent characters, use the [Delete] and [Backspace] keys to erase characters, and use the other keys to type replacement characters. Once you have made the changes you want to make, you can press [Enter] (or any of the cursor-movement keys other than ➡, ⬅, [Home], or [End]) to lock the revised entry back into the spreadsheet. If you press [Esc] instead of one of these keys, Works will clear the revised entry from the formula line without changing the entry in the active cell.

Moving the cursor within an entry on the formula line

When you first enter the Edit mode, Works will position the cursor immediately to the right of the rightmost character in the entry that appears on the formula line. While Works is in the Edit mode, you can use the ⬅, ➡, [Home], and [End] keys to move the cursor around within that entry. The ⬅ and ➡ keys move the cursor one character to the left or right; the [Home] key moves the cursor to the leftmost character in the entry; and the [End] key moves it to the space after the rightmost character in the entry.

If you have a mouse, you can enter the Edit mode and position the cursor where you want it—all in a single step. To do this, simply point to that character within the copy of the entry on the formula line, and click the left mouse button. When you do this, Works will enter the Edit mode and position the cursor under the character that you clicked. Once Works is in the Edit mode, you can point and click to move the cursor to other characters on the formula line.

Highlighting groups of characters on the formula line

In addition to moving the cursor to different characters within an entry on the formula line, you can extend the cursor to highlight any group of adjacent characters on that line. To do this, simply move the cursor to the leftmost (or rightmost) character of the group of characters you want to mark, hold down the [Shift] key, and use the ➡, ⬅, [Home], or [End] keys to extend or contract the highlight. When you press the [Shift] key, the point between the character on which the cursor is positioned and the character to its left becomes the "anchor" point for the highlight. Pressing the ➡, ⬅, [Home], or [End] keys extends or contracts the highlight from that point. Pressing one of these keys without holding down the [Shift] key contracts the highlight back to a cursor. If you have a mouse, you can highlight characters on the formula line simply by dragging across them.

Inserting, deleting, and replacing characters

While an entry is on the formula line, you can add, replace, and delete characters. To insert characters within an entry on the formula line, simply position the cursor on the character to the left of which you want to insert the new characters, and type. To replace characters with other characters, simply highlight the characters you want to replace, and type the replacement characters. To delete a single character, you can use either the [Delete] or [Backspace] key. The [Delete] key erases the character above the cursor; the [Backspace] key erases the character to the left of the cursor. To delete a group of characters, extend the cursor to highlight those characters, then press either [Delete] or [Backspace].

Editing formulas and functions

You can use the same techniques to edit formulas and functions that you use to edit label and value entries. To erase a formula or function, you can use the [Backspace] key. To replace a formula or function with another entry, simply highlight it and type the new entry. To modify a formula or function, use the [Edit] key to enter the Edit mode, then delete characters from it or add characters to it.

As you may recall, you add cell references to a formula or function that you are creating by pointing. You also can point while you are editing a formula or function. To do this, simply move the cursor to the place in the formula or function where you want to insert the reference, press ↑ or ↓ to enter the Point mode, then point to the cell you want to include in the formula.

Importantly, Works won't let you enter the Point mode unless the cursor is marking a position where a cell reference is appropriate: following an = sign, following one of Works' five operators (+, -, *, /, and ^), following an opening parenthesis, or following a colon that separates the endpoints of a range reference. If you press the ↑ or ↓ keys while the cursor is in any other position within a formula, Works will end the edit, lock the entry from the formula line into the active cell, and move the highlight up or down one cell in the spreadsheet.

Although you can use the → and ← keys to move the highlight once you are in the Point mode, you cannot use them to enter that mode. If you press either of these keys before entering the Point mode, Works will move the cursor within the formula on the formula line instead of entering the Point mode and moving the highlight around the spreadsheet.

Editing date and time entries

You can edit date and time entries in much the same way that you edit other types of entries. Unlike formatted value entries, formatted date and time entries appear in formatted form on the formula line. For example, the date value 32143 in a cell that has been assigned the mm/dd/yy date format will appear as 1/1/90—not 32143—on the formula line. This convenience makes it easy to modify date and time entries. For example, suppose that cell A1 of a spreadsheet, which contains the serial date value for November 24, 1990, is formatted to display that date in mm/dd/yy form. To change the entry in this cell into the serial date value for November 24, 1990, you first would move the highlight to that cell and press [Edit] so that the characters 11/24/90 were active on the formula line. To change the entry to the serial date value for November 24, 1990, you would simply press [Backspace], type an 8, and press [Enter].

CALCULATION

Most Works spreadsheets will contain a variety of formulas and functions. Unless you specify otherwise, Works will calculate every formula and function in a spreadsheet whenever you make, edit, copy, or move an entry in that spreadsheet. This method of calculation, called automatic, ensures that every formula and function returns the proper result at all times.

The formulas in many spreadsheets are complicatedly interdependent. For example, a formula in cell A1 may reference formulas in cells F53 and Q104; the formula in cell F53 may reference formulas in cells D17 and AA63; the formula in cell Q104 may reference formulas in cells Z15 and BJ93; and so forth.

For all the formulas and functions in a spreadsheet like this to return the correct result, they must be calculated in a specific order. Works keeps track of this order as you build a spreadsheet. Whenever Works calculates a spreadsheet, it starts by calculating the formulas and functions that do not depend on the results of any other formulas or functions. Next, it calculates the formulas and functions that reference values and the results of the formulas and functions it just calculated. Works continues in this way until every formula and function in the spreadsheet has been calculated. Since Works does not calculate any formula or function until it has calculated all of the formulas or functions on which that formula or function depends, the result is an accurate calculation of the spreadsheet.

Manual calculation

Whenever Works calculates a spreadsheet, it calculates every formula and function in that spreadsheet, even if the value of that formula is not affected by the change(s) you made to the spreadsheet. Consequently, the time required to calculate a spreadsheet depends on how many formulas are in that spreadsheet. For a spreadsheet that contains only a few formulas, calculation is almost instantaneous. For spreadsheets that contain a lot of formulas, however, calculation can take a long time—up to several minutes.

Clearly, waiting for Works to calculate the entire spreadsheet each time you make, edit, move, or copy an entry wastes time. Fortunately, you can avoid this delay by setting your spreadsheet for manual calculation. Once you do this, Works will calculate the spreadsheet only when you tell it to do so—not automatically after each change you make to that spreadsheet.

The Manual Calculation command on the Options menu allows you to specify the manual method of calculation. When a spreadsheet is set for manual calculation, this command will have a dot to its left. When a spreadsheet is set for automatic calculation, the command will appear without a dot. Each time you select this command, it will toggle from one state to the other.

Calculating a spreadsheet set for manual calculation

While a spreadsheet is set for manual calculation, Works will not automatically calculate the formulas and functions within it each time you enter, edit, move, or copy an entry. Instead, it will display the message *CALC* in the center of the status line. This message indicates that the spreadsheet has been changed since it was last calculated.

To calculate a spreadsheet set for manual calculation, either select the Calculate Now command from the Options menu or press the [Calc] key ([F9]). When you do either of these things, Works will calculate the spreadsheet in the same reference-sensitive order that it does when it is set for automatic calculation.

Whether a spreadsheet is set for manual or automatic calculation, Works will calculate the result of formulas and functions as you enter them. If the spreadsheet is set for automatic calculation, Works will calculate all the other formulas in the spreadsheet as well. If the formula you are entering references one or more of those other formulas, Works will calculate those other formulas before it evaluates the one you are entering. Consequently, the result of the formula you are entering will be correct.

Entering formulas and functions into a spreadsheet set for manual calculation

If your spreadsheet is set for manual calculation, Works may not return the correct result of a formula or function when you enter it. If the formula references other formulas whose results are out of date (that is, formulas that reference values that have been changed since the last calculation), Works will use those outdated results when it evaluates the formula you are entering.

If your spreadsheet is set for manual calculation, you can calculate an individual formula or function without calculating the entire spreadsheet. To do this, move the highlight to the cell that contains the formula or function you want to calculate, press [Edit] to activate that formula or function on the formula line, then press [Enter] to lock it back into the spreadsheet. When you do this, Works will calculate the formula or function, just as it does when you enter a new formula or function. Since the spreadsheet is set for manual calculation, Works will not calculate any of the other formulas or functions in the spreadsheet. Consequently, this technique will return the correct result only if the results of the formulas and functions referred to by those you are calculating are up to date.

Calculating part of a spreadsheet

As a general rule, you should not trust the result of any formulas or functions in a spreadsheet that is set for manual calculation until you have calculated that spreadsheet. Be especially careful to calculate a spreadsheet that is set for manual calculation immediately before you print it. Otherwise, the print-out may contain outdated results.

A general warning

Whether a spreadsheet is set for automatic or manual calculation, it is subject to circular references. A circular reference is a situation in which a formula refers to the cell that contains it, either directly or indirectly.

Circular references

Fortunately, Works lets you know when a spreadsheet contains a circular reference. When you enter a formula that is circular in itself, or is circular in conjunction with other formulas in the spreadsheet, Works will display the message *CIRC* on the message line. This message indicates that the spreadsheet contains one or more circular references. Unfortunately, although Works lets you know when a spreadsheet contains circular references, it does not tell you which cells contain those references. You'll have to find them on your own.

The most common circular reference is a SUM() function that refers to itself; for example, the function *=SUM(B3:F3)* in cell F3. If you see a *CIRC* indicator at the bottom of your screen, therefore, you should look at the SUM() functions in your spreadsheet first.

Often, a spreadsheet that contains one circular reference will contain others as well. This happens most often when you enter a circular formula by mistake and then copy it into other cells of a spreadsheet. Unfortunately, Works displays the same indicator—*CIRC*—no matter how many circular references a spreadsheet contains. If the *CIRC* indicator does not go away after you fix one circular reference, then calculate the spreadsheet, you'll know that the spreadsheet contains others. In those cases, you should look for another formula similar to the one that contains the circular reference you corrected.

Circular references are relatively easy to find and correct if you spot them soon after you enter them. If you make a number of entries between the time you enter the circular reference and the time you notice the *CIRC* indicator, however, the circular reference will be hard to find. It's important that you pay attention to the messages on the message line as you work in any Works spreadsheet.

SAVING AND OPENING SPREADSHEETS

After you've created a spreadsheet document, you probably will want to save it to disk. The process of saving a spreadsheet document is the same as that of saving any other type of document. To save a spreadsheet document for the first time, pull down the File menu and select either the Save or Save As... commands. When you select one of these commands, Works will present a Save As dialog box. Within this box, specify a name for the document and the directory in which you want Works to save it. When you choose <OK>, Works will save the document to disk. Unless you specify otherwise, Works will save the document under its default name in the default directory. Works will append the extension .WKS to the end of the file name if you don't specify an alternative suffix.

Once you've saved a spreadsheet document for the first time, you can use either the Save or Save As... commands to save it again. If you select the Save command, Works will automatically save the current version of the document on top of the old one. If you select the Save As... command instead, Works will let you save the current version of the document in another file. You should use the Save As... command if you want to retain copies of the various drafts of your spreadsheet.

You can save spreadsheet documents in three formats: Works, Text & Commas, and Text and Tabs. The form in which Works saves a document depends on which of these options you choose from the Format option box. If you choose the Works format (the default), Works will retain all the formulas, functions, styles, and formats in the spreadsheet. If you choose Text & Commas, Works will save the spreadsheet in a comma-delimited text file. The entries on each row will be separated from one another with commas; label entries will be enclosed in double quotes; and formulas and functions will be transformed into their current values. If you choose Text & Tabs, Works will save the spreadsheet in a text file with tabs separating the entries from each column of the spreadsheet. You should use these last two options only if you use the information from a Works spreadsheet in another software package.

Once you have saved a spreadsheet document to disk, you can open it again into Works. To do this, you must pull down the File menu, select the Open Existing File... command, specify the name of the file you want to open within the Open Existing File dialog box, and choose <OK>. To limit the list of files that Works displays to only those with the .WKS extension (the default extension that Works uses for spreadsheet documents), you can choose the Spreadsheet option from the List Which Files option box. For detailed information about saving and opening documents, see Chapter 2.

PRINTING SPREADSHEET DOCUMENTS

At some point after you create a spreadsheet document, you probably will want to print it. For the most part, the process of printing a spreadsheet is just like the process of printing any other type of document. First, you use the Page Setup & Margins... command to set the margins, page dimensions, and headers and footers for the document. Second, if you have not done so already, you should use the Printer Setup... command to select the printer to which you will be printing. Third, you use the Print... command to print the document.

You can print multiple copies of a spreadsheet, print specific pages of a spreadsheet, and print a spreadsheet to disk, just as you can any other type of document. For a review of how to do these things, refer to Chapter 3. However, you also can do a number of things when printing a spreadsheet that you can't do when printing any other type of document. For example, you can print a specific range of the spreadsheet, print title rows and columns, print row numbers and column letters, and print the spreadsheet in a particular font and size. We'll show you how to do these things in the next few pages.

How Works prints a spreadsheet

Because most spreadsheet documents are too large to print on a single page, Works prints them on multiple pages. On each page, Works will print as many rows and columns as will fit on that page. For example, Figure 7-19 on page 235 shows the result of printing the spreadsheet document partially shown in Figure 7-18 on the following page. Works will never split a column between two pages. If the whole column will not fit onto one page, it will print the entire column on the next page of the print-out.

Figure 7-18

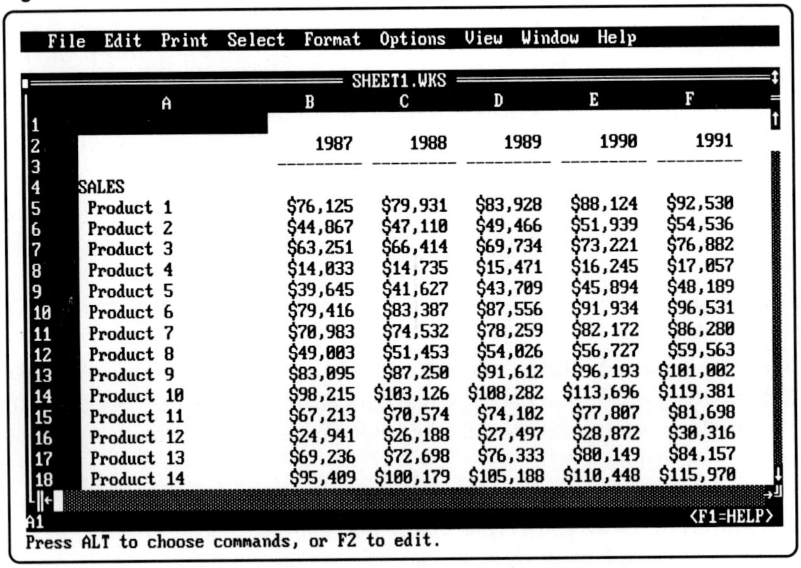

```
╔═══════════════════════════════════════════════════════════════╗
║  File  Edit  Print  Select  Format  Options  View  Window  Help║
║══════════════════════════ SHEET1.WKS ════════════════════════ ║
║          A              B        C        D        E        F   ║
║ 1                                                               ║
║ 2                     1987     1988     1989     1990     1991  ║
║ 3                    _____ _____ _____ _____ _____ ║
║ 4  SALES                                                        ║
║ 5    Product 1       $76,125  $79,931  $83,928  $88,124  $92,530║
║ 6    Product 2       $44,867  $47,110  $49,466  $51,939  $54,536║
║ 7    Product 3       $63,251  $66,414  $69,734  $73,221  $76,882║
║ 8    Product 4       $14,033  $14,735  $15,471  $16,245  $17,057║
║ 9    Product 5       $39,645  $41,627  $43,709  $45,894  $48,189║
║ 10   Product 6       $79,416  $83,387  $87,556  $91,934  $96,531║
║ 11   Product 7       $70,983  $74,532  $78,259  $82,172  $86,280║
║ 12   Product 8       $49,003  $51,453  $54,026  $56,727  $59,563║
║ 13   Product 9       $83,095  $87,250  $91,612  $96,193 $101,002║
║ 14   Product 10      $98,215 $103,126 $108,282 $113,696 $119,381║
║ 15   Product 11      $67,213  $70,574  $74,102  $77,807  $81,698║
║ 16   Product 12      $24,941  $26,188  $27,497  $28,872  $30,316║
║ 17   Product 13      $69,236  $72,698  $76,333  $80,149  $84,157║
║ 18   Product 14      $95,409 $100,179 $105,188 $110,448 $115,970║
║ A1                                                    <F1=HELP> ║
║ Press ALT to choose commands, or F2 to edit.                   ║
╚═══════════════════════════════════════════════════════════════╝
```

When Works prints a spreadsheet, it will print as many rows and columns on each page as it can.

On the first page of a printed spreadsheet, Works will print the topmost rows and leftmost columns of that spreadsheet. If the spreadsheet contains more rows than will fit on this page, Works will print the the next pageful of rows on the second page of the report. This page will contain information from the same columns as those Works printed on the first page. Works will continue in this fashion until it has printed all the information in the leftmost columns in the spreadsheet. At that point, it will begin printing the next page of columns, starting at the top of the spreadsheet.

The Top Margin, Bottom Margin, Left Margin, Right Margin, Page Length, and Page Width text boxes in the Page Setup & Margins dialog box determine how many columns and rows of your spreadsheet Works will print on each page. Most printers will print six lines per inch vertically on a page, and ten characters per inch across a page. Consequently, with the default margins, Page Length, and Page Width settings, Works can print 54 lines of the spreadsheet on each page and 60 characters across each line. These settings are appropriate when you are printing on standard $8^1/_2$- by 11-inch paper. In many cases, however, you will print your spreadsheets on 14- by 11-inch "computer" paper. When you do, you should set the Page Length to 11" and the Page Width to 14". Unless you want to squeeze an extraordinary amount of information onto each page, you should leave the margin settings as they are.

Figure 7-19

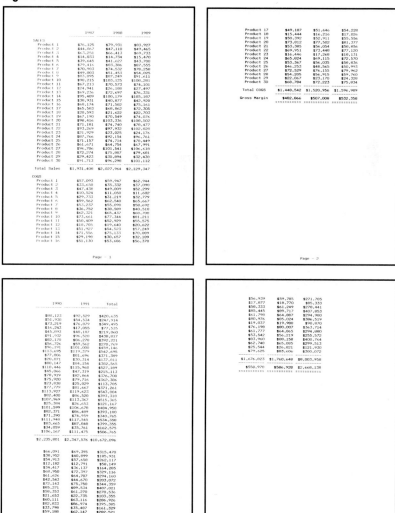

This figure shows the order in which Works prints the spreadsheet shown in Figure 7-18.

Normally, Works will print as many rows of the spreadsheet on each page of the report as the Page Length, Top Margin, and Bottom Margin settings allow. If you want, however, you can command Works to skip to the next page after it prints a certain row by inserting manual page breaks into a spreadsheet. To do this, you must highlight the entire row that you want to appear at the top of the new page,

Controlling page breaks

using any of the techniques we discussed earlier in this chapter. After highlighting this row, you should pull down the Print menu and select the Insert Page Break command. When you select this command, Works will enter a >> marker to the right of the number of the highlighted row. This marker instructs Works to skip to the top of a new page before it prints that row. To remove a manual page break from a row, you must highlight that row, pull down the Print menu, and select the Delete Page Break command. In our example spreadsheet, you might want to force a page break after the row that contains the sales totals. That way, Works will print the SALES and COGS sections of the spreadsheet on separate pages.

Printing a portion of the spreadsheet

Unless you specify otherwise, Works will print the entire active area of a spreadsheet document when you pull down the Print menu and select the Print... command. If you want, however, you can instruct Works to print only a specific part of the spreadsheet. To do this, simply extend the highlight to cover the portion of the spreadsheet that you want Works to print, pull down the Print menu, and select the Set Print Area command. For example, if you want Works to print only the SALES portion of our example spreadsheet, highlight cells A1:G36 and issue this command. When you command Works to print the spreadsheet, it will print only the area you specified. If you want to print the entire active area of a spreadsheet after specifying a smaller print area, you must highlight that active area and reissue the Set Print Area command. (The easiest way to select the active area is to move the highlight to cell A1, hold down the [Shift] key, and press [Ctrl][End].) Works saves a spreadsheet's Set Print Area setting when it saves that spreadsheet.

Printing row and column labels

Normally, Works prints only the information stored in a spreadsheet when it prints from a spreadsheet document. If you want, however, you can command Works to print row numbers at the left edge of each page and column letters at the top of each page. The final element in the Print dialog box—the Print Row and Column Labels check box—controls this feature. When this setting is off (its default state), Works does not include row numbers and column letters in the printed report. When this setting is on, however, Works will print row numbers and column letters at the left and top edges of each page of the report. For example, Figure 7-20 shows the first page of the spreadsheet shown in Figure 7-18 printed while the Print Row and Column Labels setting is on. As you can see, printing row numbers and column letters reduces by one the number of rows and columns of information that Works can print on each page of the report.

Printing title rows and columns

Usually, the information in the first few rows and columns of a spreadsheet identify the information in the spreadsheet. For example, the labels in rows 2 and 3 of the spreadsheet shown in Figure 7-18 identify the various columns in the spreadsheet, and the labels in column A identify the rows. In this case, each column contains values for a particular year; each row contains values for a particular product.

Figure 7-20

		A	B	C	D
1					
2			1987	1988	1989
3			-------	-------	-------
4		SALES			
5		Product 1	$76,125	$79,931	$83,927
6		Product 2	$44,867	$47,110	$49,465
7		Product 3	$63,251	$66,413	$69,733
8		Product 4	$14,033	$14,734	$15,470
9		Product 5	$39,645	$41,627	$43,708
10		Product 6	$79,416	$83,386	$87,555
11		Product 7	$70,983	$74,532	$78,258
12		Product 8	$49,003	$51,453	$54,025
13		Product 9	$83,095	$87,249	$91,611
14		Product 10	$98,215	$103,125	$108,281
15		Product 11	$67,213	$70,573	$74,101
16		Product 12	$24,941	$26,188	$27,497
17		Product 13	$69,236	$72,697	$76,331
18		Product 14	$95,409	$100,179	$105,187
19		Product 15	$38,931	$40,877	$42,920
20		Product 16	$68,174	$71,582	$75,161
21		Product 17	$65,583	$68,862	$72,305
22		Product 18	$20,593	$21,622	$22,703
23		Product 19	$67,190	$70,549	$74,076
24		Product 20	$98,416	$103,336	$108,502
25		Product 21	$71,181	$74,740	$78,477
26		Product 22	$93,269	$97,932	$102,826
27		Product 23	$21,929	$23,025	$24,176
28		Product 24	$87,766	$92,154	$96,761
29		Product 25	$71,157	$74,714	$78,449
30		Product 26	$61,671	$64,754	$67,991
31		Product 27	$96,706	$101,541	$106,618
32		Product 28	$72,274	$75,887	$79,681
33		Product 29	$29,423	$30,894	$32,438
34		Product 30	$91,713	$96,298	$101,112
35			-------	-------	-------
36		Total Sales	$1,931,408	$2,027,964	$2,129,347
37					
38		COGS			
39		Product 1	$57,093	$59,947	$62,944
40		Product 2	$33,650	$35,332	$37,098
41		Product 3	$47,438	$49,809	$52,299
42		Product 4	$10,524	$11,050	$11,602
43		Product 5	$29,733	$31,219	$32,779
44		Product 6	$59,562	$62,540	$65,667
45		Product 7	$53,237	$55,898	$58,692
46		Product 8	$36,752	$38,589	$40,518
47		Product 9	$62,321	$65,437	$68,708
48		Product 10	$73,661	$77,344	$81,211
49		Product 11	$50,409	$52,929	$55,575
50		Product 12	$18,705	$19,640	$20,622
51		Product 13	$51,927	$54,523	$57,249
52		Product 14	$71,556	$75,133	$78,889
53		Product 15	$29,198	$30,657	$32,189

Page - 1

The Print Row and Column Labels check box in the Print dialog box controls whether Works prints row numbers and column letters on each page.

Usually, these title rows and columns will not appear on every page of a printed spreadsheet. For example, in the print-out shown in Figure 7-19, the title columns do not appear on page 2, the title rows do not appear on page 3; and neither the title columns nor the title rows appear on page 4.

If you want, however, you can command Works to print these rows and columns at the top and/or left edge of each page. To do this, shift the upper-left corner of the spreadsheet into view, position the highlight in the cell immediately to the right of the rightmost title column and immediately below the bottommost title row, pull down the Options menu, and select the Freeze Titles command.

For example, to ensure that entries from rows 1 through 3 and column A appear on every page of the spreadsheet shown in Figure 7-18, you would issue this command while the highlight is on cell B4. Figure 7-21 shows the fourth page of the printed result. As you can see, Works printed the appropriate entries from rows 1 through 3 at the top of that page and printed the appropriate entries from column A at the left edge of that page.

Figure 7-21

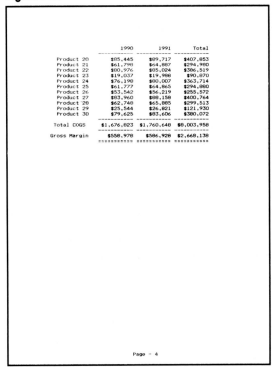

	1990	1991	Total
Product 20	$85,445	$89,717	$407,853
Product 21	$61,798	$64,887	$294,980
Product 22	$80,976	$85,024	$386,519
Product 23	$19,037	$19,988	$90,870
Product 24	$76,198	$80,007	$363,714
Product 25	$61,777	$64,865	$294,880
Product 26	$53,542	$56,219	$255,572
Product 27	$83,960	$88,158	$400,764
Product 28	$62,748	$65,885	$299,513
Product 29	$25,544	$26,821	$121,930
Product 30	$79,625	$83,606	$380,072
Total COGS	$1,676,823	$1,760,648	$8,003,958
Gross Margin	$558,970	$586,928	$2,668,138

Page - 4

The Freeze Titles command allows you to print title rows and columns at the top and left edges of each page.

In addition to locking certain columns and rows onto each page of a printed spreadsheet, the Freeze Titles command locks those rows and columns onto the screen. For a thorough explanation of the use of this command, see Chapter 11.

Alternative fonts and sizes

Unless you specify otherwise, Works will print the information from a spreadsheet document in the default font and size for the printer you are using (the printer you selected with the Printer Setup... command). To print a spreadsheet in a different font and size, pull down the Format menu and select the Font... command to reveal a Font dialog box like the one in Figure 7-22.

As you can see, this dialog box contains two list boxes. In the Fonts list box, Works lists all the fonts available for the current printer (the choices in this box differ for different printers). If you want to print your spreadsheet in an alternative font, you must choose it from this list box. Once you choose a font, you should choose a size from the Sizes list box. Since different fonts are available in different sizes, the choices Works lists within the Sizes list box depend on which font you selected in the Fonts list box.

Figure 7-22

The choices you make in the Font dialog box determine in what font and size Works will print a spreadsheet document.

The choices you make in the Font dialog box affect the way Works prints the entire spreadsheet. They also affect how much information Works can print on each page. You cannot assign different fonts and sizes to different cells or ranges in a spreadsheet document.

Cancelling printing

In most cases, once you command Works to print a spreadsheet, it will continue to print until it has printed every page you specified. If you want to cancel the printing of a spreadsheet before it has printed completely, simply press the [Esc] key. Works will then display a dialog box that contains the message *Printing interrupted. Continue printing?*. If you choose <Cancel>, Works will cancel the Print... command. If you choose <OK>, Works will resume printing exactly where it left off.

CONCLUSION

We've covered a lot of material in this chapter. We showed you how to create a spreadsheet document, move the highlight around a spreadsheet, extend the highlight to cover a range of cells, make various types of entries into the cells of a spreadsheet, edit entries, calculate formulas and functions, save, open, and print spreadsheet documents.

In the next four chapters, we'll explore other powers of spreadsheet documents. In Chapter 8, we'll show you how to format a spreadsheet; in Chapter 9, we'll examine "cut and paste" commands; in Chapter 10, we'll look at each of Works' special functions; and in Chapter 11, we'll look at some additional spreadsheet commands.

Formatting a Spreadsheet 8

*I*n Chapter 7, we explained that the form in which you enter a value determines what, if any, display format Works will assign to the cell containing that value. For example, if you select a cell, type $1234.56, and press [Enter], Works will enter the value 1234.56 into that cell and assign that cell the Currency format with two decimal places. Works will display that value as $1,234.56.

Although formatting a cell as you make an entry is one way to assign a format to a cell, it's not the only way. The commands at the top of the Format menu provide the other. In this chapter, we'll show you how to use these commands to assign formats to the cells in a Works spreadsheet. We'll also show you how to alter the alignment of and assign special print attributes to the entry in a cell.

CELL FORMATS

Formats are display characteristics you assign to the cells in a Works spreadsheet. A cell's format affects the way that Works displays any value stored in that cell. For example, suppose that cell A1 of a Works spreadsheet contains the value 1234.567. If you assign the Currency format with two decimal places to cell A1, Works will display the value as $1,234.57; if you assign the Fixed format with one decimal place to that cell, Works will display the value as 1234.6; if you assign the Exponential format with zero decimal places to the cell, Works will display the value as 1E+03; and so on.

There are two important things you should know about formats. First, formats are characteristics of cells, not of the entries in those cells. If you erase the contents of a formatted cell, the format remains with the cell. Consequently, it will affect the display of any subsequent entries you make into that cell. Second, formats affect only value entries and the results of formulas and functions. Spreadsheet formats do not affect the display of label entries.

Assigning formats

In Chapter 7, we explained that Works automatically assigns formats to cells in which you make value, date, and time entries. In addition to automatic formatting, Works allows you to assign formats to the cells of a spreadsheet, using the commands in the top section of the Format menu. They provide the only way to assign formats to blank cells or cells that contain formulas and functions. You can use these commands to assign formats to more than one cell at a time.

To assign a format to a cell or a group of cells, you must select the cell(s) you want to format, then pull down the Format menu. Figure 8-1 shows a spreadsheet document's Format menu. As you can see, the top section of this menu contains eight commands: General, Fixed..., Currency..., Comma..., Percent..., Exponential..., True/False, and Time/Date.... These commands represent the various formats or families of formats you can assign to the cells of a Works spreadsheet.

Figure 8-1

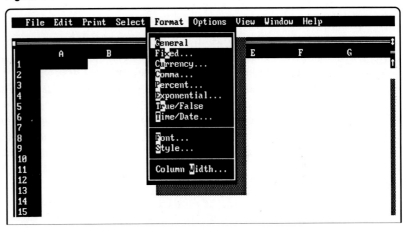

The commands at the top of the Format menu let you assign display formats to the cells in a spreadsheet document.

Once you have pulled down the Format menu, you should select the format you want to assign to the highlighted cell(s). When you choose any command other than General, True/False, or Time/Date..., Works will reveal the dialog box shown in Figure 8-2. This box (called the Decimals dialog box) allows you to specify how many digits you want Works to display to the right of the decimal point in the formatted value. You can specify any number of digits from zero to seven. The default value is 2.

Because the number of digits displayed to the right of the decimal point is an essential component of most formats, we'll include that value whenever we refer to those formats. For example, we'll refer to the Currency format with two decimal places as the Currency 2 format, the Percent format with zero decimal places as the Percent 0 format, and so on.

Figure 8-2

Works will display this dialog box when you choose any command other than General, True/False, or Time/Date....

If you select the Time/Date... command from the Format menu, Works will display a dialog box that lists the various Time and Date formats instead of a box like the one shown in Figure 8-2. Works doesn't display a dialog box when you select the General or True/False commands; it simply assigns the format you have chosen to the selected cell(s).

As an example of assigning a format to a group of cells, suppose you want Works to display the values in cells A1:B5 of a spreadsheet in the Currency 2 format (the Currency format with two digits to the right of the decimal point). To do this, first highlight cells A1:B5, probably by making cell A1 the active cell, holding down the [Shift] key, pressing → once, and pressing ↓ four times. Next, pull down the Format menu and select the Currency... command. At this point, Works will present the Decimals dialog box shown in Figure 8-2. Since the default number of digits to the right of the decimal point is 2, choose <OK> to accept that value. (Since <OK> is the default button, you can choose it simply by pressing [Enter].) Once you do this, Works will assign the Currency 2 format to cells A1:B5. From that point until you change the format, Works will display any values in those cells in the Currency format with 2 digits to the right of their decimal points.

▶Works 2 offers a function key, [Repeat Format] ([Shift][F7]), that allows you to repeat the most recent format you have assigned. This key lets you assign the same format over and over without having to repeatedly select a command from the Format menu.

Before you use this key, you must first use a Format menu command to format a cell or range. Then, to repeat the format, just highlight another cell or range and press [Repeat Format]. Works will assign the same format and number of decimal places to the selected cell or range, just as if you had reissued the command.

You can continue selecting cells and ranges and pressing [Repeat Format] until you have formatted all of the cells you want to format. As soon as you issue another command, however, the chain will be broken. To repeat your format after you have issued another command, you'll have to repeat the command manually.◀

The [Repeat Format] key
▶**WORKS 2**◀

The General format

The General format is Works' default format. The General format instructs Works to display values "as is," whenever possible. If the cell that contains the value is too narrow to display the value in full, however, the General format will display the value in alternative forms.

In Chapter 7, we explained that the maximum number of value entry characters that Works can display in a cell is equal to one less than the width of the cell. For example, Works can display nine characters of a value entry in a ten-character-wide cell, 11 characters of a value entry in a 12-character-wide cell, and so forth.

The width of a cell determines how Works will display an entry in the General format. If the cell is too narrow to display the full value but wide enough to display the integer portion of the value, Works will display the integer portion and as many decimal places as it can. If the cell is too narrow to display the integer portion of the value, Works will display the value in scientific notation. If the cell is too narrow to display the value in scientific notation, Works will display it as a series of # signs.

Figure 8-3

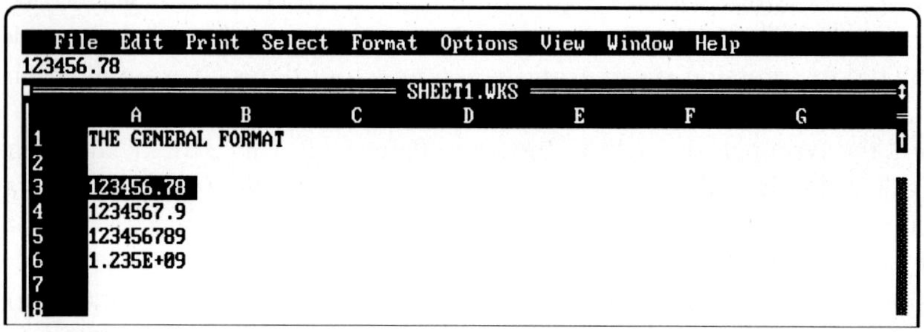

This spreadsheet contains examples of the General format.

Figure 8-3 shows several examples of values in cells that have been assigned the General format. Cell A3 contains the value 123456.78. Because column A is ten characters wide, and this value is only nine characters wide, Works displays it in full form. Cell A4 contains the value 1234567.89. Although this value contains ten characters, Works can display only nine of them in this ten-character-wide cell. Because the integer portion of the value is nine characters wide or less (in this case, seven characters), Works displays the integer portion and as many of the digits to the right of the decimal point as it can, in rounded form. In this case, for example, Works displays the value 1234567.89 as 1234567.9.

Cell A5 contains the 11-digit value 123456789.12. Because this cell is only ten characters wide, Works can display only nine characters of the 11-digit value. Since the integer portion of this value is nine characters wide, Works displays the value in rounded integer form: 123456789. Cell A6 contains the 12-digit value

1234567891.23. Because the integer portion of this value is longer than the width of the cell, less one, Works displays this value in scientific notation: 1.235E+09.

Since General is the default format, you usually will use the General command to assign this format to cells to which you have previously assigned another format. Assigning the General format to a cell will return that cell to the default format for the spreadsheet.

The Fixed format

The Fixed format commands Works to display a value with the number of digits you specify (from zero to seven) to the right of its decimal point. If you specify zero digits to the right of the decimal point, Works will display the number in integer form—it won't even include a decimal point in the value. If you specify a value from 1 through 7, Works will insert a decimal point in the value and display the specified number of digits to the right of that point.

Figure 8-4

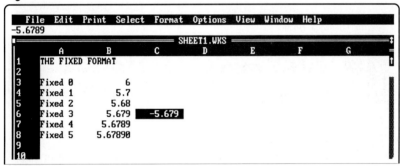

This spreadsheet contains examples of the Fixed format.

Figure 8-4 shows some examples of the Fixed format. Cells B3 through B8 in this spreadsheet all contain the value 5.6789. Cell B3, which has been assigned the Fixed 0 format, displays this value simply as 6. Because this cell is formatted to display 0 decimals, Works rounds the value in the cell, 5.6789, to the closest integer, 6, for display. Cell B4, which has been assigned the Fixed 1 format, displays this value as 5.7. Again, Works has rounded up the rightmost digit in this value. Cell B5, which has been assigned the Fixed 2 format, displays this value as 5.68. Cells B6 through B8 have been assigned the Fixed format with three, four, and five decimal places, respectively. As you can see, Works uses zeroes to fill the appropriate number of decimal places.

Cell C6, to which we have assigned the Fixed 3 format, contains the value -5.679. As you can see, Works displays this value as -5.670. The Fixed format always uses a leading - sign to denote negative values.

Unlike the General format, the Fixed format will not truncate the display of values that are too wide to fit within their cells. If a Fixed-formatted cell is not wide enough to display a value, Works will display a series of # symbols. To display the value, you must alter the format or widen the column that contains the cell. We'll show you how to widen columns in Chapter 9.

The Currency format
▶WORKS 2◀

▶The Currency format instructs Works to display values with a leading $ sign, commas separating the hundreds from the thousands, the hundred thousands from the millions, and so forth, and the number of digits you specify to the right of the decimal point. (In Works 1, this format was called Dollar.) The Currency format displays negative values in parentheses rather than with leading - signs.◀

Figure 8-5

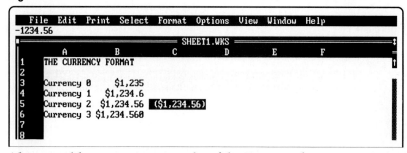

This spreadsheet contains examples of the Currency format.

The spreadsheet shown in Figure 8-5 contains several examples of the Currency format. Cells B3 through B6 in this spreadsheet all contain the value 1234.56. Cell B3, which has been assigned the Currency 0 format, displays this value as $1,235. Cell B4, which has been assigned the Currency 1 format, displays this value as $1,234.6. Cell B5, which has been assigned the Currency 2 format (the variation of the Currency format that you'll use most often), displays this value as $1,234.56. Cell C5, which has been assigned the Currency 2 format, contains the value -1234.56. As you can see, Works displays this value as ($1234.56).

Like the Fixed format, the Currency format displays values that are too long to be shown in full as a series of # signs. We've widened column B to accommodate these formatted values.

The Comma format

Works' Comma format displays values just like the Currency format does, but without the leading $ sign. In other words, the Comma format uses comma separators, displays the number of digits (a maximum of seven) that you specify to the right of the decimal point, and encloses negative values within parentheses. Values too wide to be displayed in full appear as a series of # signs.

Figure 8-6

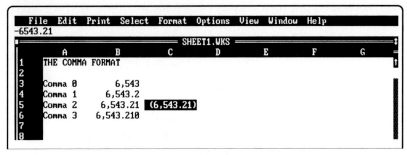

This spreadsheet contains examples of the Comma format.

The spreadsheet shown in Figure 8-6 contains several examples of the Comma format. Cells B3 through B6 in this spreadsheet all contain the value 6543.21. Cell B3, which has been assigned the Comma 0 format, displays this value as 6,543. Cell B4, which has been assigned the Comma 1 format, displays this value as 6,543.2. Cell B5, which has been assigned the Comma 2 format (the default number of digits to the right of the decimal point) displays this value as 6,543.21. Cell C5, which has been assigned the Comma 2 format, contains the value -6543.21. As you can see, Works displays this value as (6,543.21).

The Percent format

The Percent format displays values as percentages. In Percent-formatted cells, Works shifts the decimal point two digits to the right, places the number of digits you specify (up to seven) to the right of the decimal point, and displays a % sign. Negative values are preceded by a - sign.

Figure 8-7

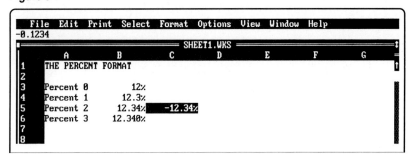

This spreadsheet contains examples of the Percent format.

The spreadsheet shown in Figure 8-7 contains several examples of the Percent format. Cells B3 through B6 all contain the value .1234. Cell B3, which has been assigned the Percent 0 format, displays this value as 12%. Cell B4, which has been assigned the Percent 1 format, displays this value as 12.3%. Cell B5, which has been assigned the Percent 2 format (the default number of digits to the right of the decimal point) displays this value as 12.34%. Cell C5, which has been assigned the Percent 2 format, contains the negative value -.1234. As you can see, Works displays this value as -12.34%.

The Exponential format

The Exponential format commands Works to display values in scientific notation; that is, as a power of 10. Values in Exponential-formatted cells appear with one digit to the left of the decimal point, the number of digits you specify (up to seven) to the right of the decimal point, and the suffix E*x*, where *x* represents a power of 10. For values greater than or equal to 1 or less than or equal to -1, *x* is a positive value, preceded by a + sign. For values less than 1 but greater than -1, *x* is a negative value, preceded by a - sign. Values too long to be displayed in full form are displayed as a series of # signs. Negative values are preceded by a - sign.

Figure 8-8

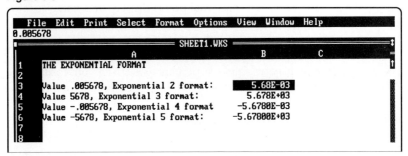

This spreadsheet contains examples of the Exponential format.

The spreadsheet shown in Figure 8-8 contains several examples of the Exponential format. Cell B3, which contains the value .005678, has been assigned the Exponential 2 format. As you can see, this value appears as 5.68E-03. Cell B4, which contains the value 5678, has been assigned the Exponential 3 format. Works displays this value as 5.678E+03. Cell B5, which contains the value -.005678, has been assigned the Exponential 4 format. Works displays this value as -5.6780E-03. Cell B6, which contains the value -5678, has been assigned the Exponential 5 format. This value appears as -5.67800E+03.

The True/False format
▶WORKS 2◀

▶Works 2's True/False format displays all values as either TRUE or FALSE. (In Works 1, this format was called Logical.) The literal value 0 and all formulas and functions that return the value 0 are displayed as FALSE. All other values (both positive and negative) are displayed as TRUE. Since these results are not actually numeric, this format does not allow you to specify a number of digits to the right of the decimal point.◄

Figure 8-9

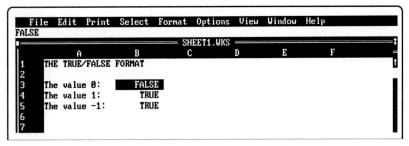

This spreadsheet contains examples of the True/False format.

Cells B3, B4, and B5 in the spreadsheet shown in Figure 8-9 have been assigned the True/False format. Cell B3, which contains the value 0, displays the value FALSE. Cell B4, which contains the value 1, displays the value TRUE. Cell B5, which contains the value -1, also displays the value TRUE. Notice that Works displays these values in formatted form on the formula line.

In addition to the regular value formats described above, Works offers a number of Time and Date formats. These formats let you display serial time and date values in a variety of forms. In Chapter 7, we explained that Works automatically assigns various Time and Date formats to the cells into which you enter times and dates. Although you usually will take advantage of this automatic formatting, you may want to change those formats at some point. You also will need to manually format cells that contain time and date values that are the result of time and date calculations.

Time/Date formats

Figure 8-10

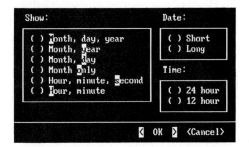

You'll see this dialog box when you select the Time/Date... command from the Format menu.

The Time/Date... command lets you assign Time and Date formats to the cells of a spreadsheet. When you select this option, Works will display the dialog box shown in Figure 8-10. As you can see, this dialog box contains three option boxes: Show, Date, and Time. These three option boxes allow you to choose from a variety of Time and Date formats. Before we show you the various formats, let's take a look at how this dialog box works.

Using the Time/Date dialog box

To assign a Time or Date format to a cell, you choose an option from the Show option box, then choose an option from either the Date or Time option boxes. The first four options in the Show box—Month, Day, Year; Month, Year; Month, Day; and Month Only—represent Date formats. Each of these options (except the final one) offers both a long form, in which the month is stated as an alphabetic abbreviation, and a short form, in which the month is stated as a value between 1 and 12. To fully specify a Date format, you must choose one of the four Date formats from the Show option box as well as one of the two options in the Date option box—Short or Long. (The Time option box is inactive when any of the four date forms are selected.) There are seven Date formats in all.

The final two options in the Show option box—Hour, Minute, Second and Hour, Minute—represent Time formats. Each of these formats has both a 24-hour (military time) form and a 12-hour (AM/PM) form. To fully specify a Time format, you must select one of the two Time formats from the Show option box, as well as one of the two options from the Time option box. (The Date option box is inactive when either of the two Time formats in the Show box is selected.) There are four possible Time formats.

Date formats

Works offers seven Date formats: both short and long forms of the Month, Day, Year; Month, Year; and Month, Day formats, and the long form of the Month Only format. The spreadsheet shown in Figure 8-11 shows the effect of these formats on date values. Cells B3:B9 each contain the serial date value for December 31, 1990—33238. Cell B3, which has been assigned the Month, Day, Year (Short) format, displays this value as 12/31/90. Cell B4, which has been assigned the Month, Day, Year (Long) format, displays this value as Dec 31, 1990. Cell B5, which has been assigned the Month, Year (Short) format, displays this value as 12/90. Cell B6, which has been assigned the Month, Year (Long) format, displays this value as Dec 1990. Cell B7, which has been assigned the Month, Day (Short) format, displays this value as 12/31. Cell B8, which has been assigned the Month, Day (Long) format, displays this value as Dec 31; and cell B9, which has been assigned the Month Only format, displays this value simply as Dec. As you can see, date entries appear in formatted form on the formula line.

Time formats

Works offers four Time formats: the 24-hour and 12-hour forms of the Hour, Minute, Second and Hour, Minute formats. Figure 8-12 shows these four formats.

Cells B3:B6 in this spreadsheet all contain the serial time value for 5:30:19 PM—
.72938657407. Cell B3, which has been assigned the Hour, Minute, Second (24
Hour) format, displays this value as 17:30:19. Cell B4, which has been assigned
the Hour, minute, second (12 Hour) format, displays this value as 5:30:19 PM. Cell
B5, which has been assigned the Hour, Minute (24 Hour) format, displays this
value as 17:30. And cell B6, which has been assigned the Hour, Minute (12 Hour)
format, displays this value as 5:30 PM. Like date entries, time entries appear in
formatted form on the formula line.

Figure 8-11

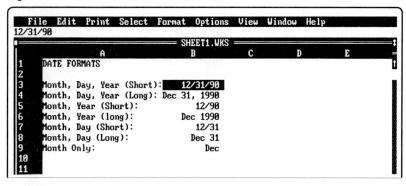

This spreadsheet contains examples of Works' Date formats.

Figure 8-12

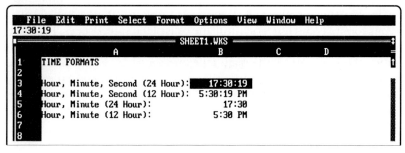

This spreadsheet contains examples of Works' Time formats.

**Making entries into
formatted cells**

As we explained at the beginning of this chapter, formats are characteristics
of cells—not of the values within those cells. If you assign a format to a cell, and
then type a new value into that cell, Works will display the new value according
to the same format it used to display the previous value. However, there is an
exception to this rule. If you type a self-formatting value into a cell that is assigned
another format, that cell will take on the format specified by the new value. For

example, suppose you have assigned the Exponential 2 format to cell C3. If you type 123 into that cell, Works will display that value in the Exponential 2 format. If you type $123, however, Works will assign the Currency 0 format to that cell and display the value according to that format.

Copying and moving entries from formatted cells

When you copy or move an entry from a formatted cell, Works will copy that cell's format as well. After the copy or move, both the source and destination cells will have the format of the source cell. If you move the entry, the destination cell will contain the entry from the source cell, and the source cell will be empty. If you copied the entry, both the source cell and the destination cell will contain the entry that was originally in only the source cell. We'll explain moving and copying in detail in Chapter 9.

THE SHOW FORMULAS COMMAND

The Show Formulas command on the Options menu instructs Works to display the underlying formulas and functions in the cells of a spreadsheet, instead of displaying the results of those formulas and functions. While the Show Formulas attribute is on, you can see the formulas and functions in a screenful of cells at once. When this attribute is off, you can see only the formula or function in the active cell, which appears on the formula line. Unlike formats, the Show Formulas attribute cannot be selectively applied to individual cells or groups of cells; it is a "global" attribute that affects every cell in the spreadsheet.

The Show Formulas command is a toggle. Selecting this command when the Show Formulas attribute is off turns it on; selecting the command when the Show Formulas attribute is on turns it off. If you pull down the Options menu while the Show Formulas attribute is on, you'll see a dot to the left of the command.

When you turn on the Show Formulas attribute, Works will display the underlying formulas and functions in all the cells of the spreadsheet. For example, Figure 8-13 shows a spreadsheet when the Show Formulas attribute is off; Figure 8-14 shows the same spreadsheet after we turn the Show Formulas attribute on. As you can see in Figure 8-14, Works now displays the contents of the cells of the spreadsheet that contain formulas and functions, instead of displaying the results of those formulas and functions. For example, Works now displays the function *=SUM(B4:B7)* instead of the value 330000 in cell B8.

In addition to displaying formulas and functions instead of results, turning on the Show Formulas attribute doubles the width of every column in the spreadsheet. Since formulas and functions are often longer than their results, this expansion usually is required in order for the formulas and functions to be displayed in full. If a formula or function is too wide to be displayed fully in a column, Works will display only as much of that formula or function as will fit in the cell. To display the entire formula or function, you must expand the column. If the column is wider than it needs to be, you can reduce its width. We'll show you how to control the width of columns in Chapter 9.

Figure 8-13

File Edit Print Select Format Options View Window Help
=SUM(B4:B7)
SHEET1.WKS
A B C D E F
1 Qtr 1 Qtr 2 Qtr 3 Qtr 4 Total
2 ------- ------- ------- ------- ---------
3 SALES
4 Product 1 $100,000 $105,000 $110,000 115000 $430,000
5 Product 2 $110,000 $120,000 $130,000 140000 $500,000
6 Product 3 $120,000 $140,000 $160,000 180000 $600,000
7 ------- ------- ------- ------- ---------
8 Total Sales $330,000 $365,000 $400,000 $435,000 $1,530,000
9
10 EXPENSES
11 CGS $250,000 $275,000 $300,000 $325,000 $1,150,000
12 Other $25,000 $30,000 $35,000 $40,000 $130,000
13 ------- ------- ------- ------- ---------
14 Total Expenses $275,000 $305,000 $335,000 $365,000 $1,280,000
15 ------- ------- ------- ------- ---------
16 NET INCOME $55,000 $60,000 $65,000 $70,000 $250,000
17 ======= ======= ======= ======= =========
18
B8 <F1=HELP>
Press ALT to choose commands, or F2 to edit.

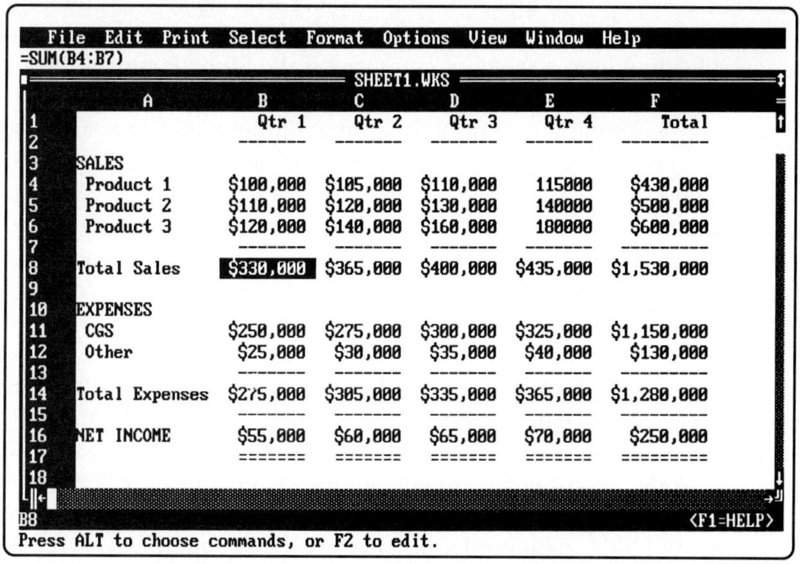

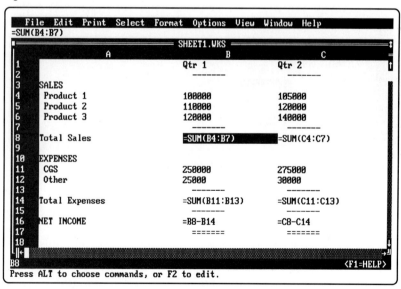

This is a spreadsheet with the Show Formulas attribute off.

Figure 8-14

File Edit Print Select Format Options View Window Help
=SUM(B4:B7)
SHEET1.WKS
A B C
1 Qtr 1 Qtr 2
2 ------- -------
3 SALES
4 Product 1 100000 105000
5 Product 2 110000 120000
6 Product 3 120000 140000
7 ------- -------
8 Total Sales =SUM(B4:B7) =SUM(C4:C7)
9
10 EXPENSES
11 CGS 250000 275000
12 Other 25000 30000
13 ------- -------
14 Total Expenses =SUM(B11:B13) =SUM(C11:C13)
15 ------- -------
16 NET INCOME =B8-B14 =C8-C14
17 ======= =======
18
B8 <F1=HELP>
Press ALT to choose commands, or F2 to edit.

This is the same spreadsheet with the Show Formulas attribute on.

When you turn off the Show Formulas attribute, Works will again display the results of the formulas and functions in the spreadsheet instead of the formulas and functions themselves. It will also reduce the width of each column to half its current width (the width at the time you turn off the Show Formulas attribute).

CELL ALIGNMENT

In addition to letting you control the format of the entries in a spreadsheet, Works allows you to control the alignment of those entries within their cells. To alter the alignment of an entry, you must assign an alignment attribute to the cell that contains that entry. Like formats, alignment attributes are characteristics of cells, not of the entries within those cells. Unlike formats, however, which affect only values, alignment attributes affect all types of entries.

Works offers four alignment attributes: General, Left, Right, and Center. General is the default alignment attribute. Values, dates, and times, whether literals or the results of formulas and functions, appear right-aligned in cells that have been assigned the General alignment attribute; however, text entries appear left-aligned.

The Left, Right, and Center alignment attributes are almost self-explanatory. The Left attribute aligns an entry with the left border of its cell. The Right attribute aligns an entry with the right border of its cell (actually, one space to the left of that border). The Center attribute centers an entry in its cell.

Figure 8-15

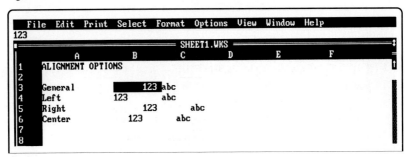

This figure shows examples of various alignments.

The spreadsheet shown in Figure 8-15 demonstrates the effect of the various alignment attributes on value and text entries. Cells B3:B6 contain the value 123; cells C3:C6 contain the text entry *abc*. Cells B3 and C3 are general-aligned; cells B4 and C4 are left-aligned; cells B5 and C5 are right-aligned; and cells B6 and C6 are center-aligned.

Changing alignment attributes

Changing the alignment of an entry is a four-step process. First, highlight the cell(s) whose alignment you want to change. Second, pull down the Format menu and select the Style… command. When you do this, Works will reveal the dialog box shown in Figure 8-16. If you select a single cell, the current alignment attribute will be chosen. If you select more than one cell, none of the alignment options will be chosen, even if all the cells share the same alignment attribute. Third, select the alignment attribute you want to assign from the Alignment option box. Finally, choose <OK> to activate that attribute. (Since <OK> is the default button, you can choose it by pressing [Enter].)

For example, suppose you want to assign the Right alignment attribute to the entries in the range A1:B5 of a spreadsheet. To do this, begin by highlighting cells A1:B5. Next, pull down the Format menu and choose Style.... Then, choose the Right option from the Alignment option box, and choose <OK>.

Figure 8-16

The elements in the Style dialog box allow you to control the alignment, print attributes, and protection status of a cell.

When you copy or move an entry from a cell, Works will copy that cell's alignment attribute as well. After the copy or move, both the source and destination cells will have the alignment attribute of the source cell. We'll explain copying and moving in detail in Chapter 9.

Copying and moving alignment attributes

Works also lets you assign special styles to the cells in a spreadsheet. These styles—Bold, Underline, and Italic—affect the way Works displays and prints the contents of the cells to which they are assigned. Like formats and alignment attributes, styles are attached to cells of the spreadsheet, but are copied and moved with the contents of those cells. Like alignment attributes, styles affect all types of entries. Provided that your printer can print bold, underlined, and italic characters (most can), any styles you assign to a spreadsheet will appear in the printed version of the spreadsheet.

STYLES

To assign a style to a cell or group of cells, you select those cells, pull down the Format menu, and select the Style... command. When you do this, Works will reveal a Style dialog box like the one shown in Figure 8-16. (This is the same box you use to align a cell.)

Assigning styles

The Bold, Underline, and Italic check boxes in the Styles list box control styles. To assign a style to the cell(s) you have selected, simply activate that style and choose <OK>. You can use any of the techniques discussed in Chapter 1 to activate and deactivate these boxes.

For example, if you want to assign the Bold style to a cell, first highlight that cell, then select the Style... command from the Format menu. When the Style dialog box appears, activate the Bold style and then choose <OK>.

You can assign any two or all three of the styles to a single cell or range if you want. To do this, just choose more than one of the options in the Style dialog box before you choose <OK>. For instance, to assign the Bold and Italic styles to a cell, highlight that cell, then select the Style... command from the Format menu. When the Style dialog box appears, make sure the Bold attribute is on and the other two styles are off, then choose <OK>.

When you highlight a single cell and then select the Style... command, each of the three style boxes will either be blank (indicating that that style is not active) or will contain an X (indicating that that style is active). If you highlight a group of cells and select the Style... command, a hyphen will appear in all three check boxes, even if all the cells share the same style. These hyphens simply mean that more than one cell is selected.

What you see
►WORKS 2◄

►What you will see when you assign a style to a cell depends on the type of display you have and whether you are using Works in the Text or Graphics mode. If you are using Works in the Graphics mode, the entries you have styled will appear in the style you selected. For instance, cells B2, B3, and B4 in Figure 8-17 have been assigned the Bold, Italic, and Underline styles, respectively. This ability to display styled entries is one of the significant advantages to using the Graphics mode.◄

Figure 8-17

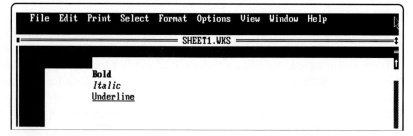

In the Graphics mode, Works can display styles on-screen.

If you are using Works in the Text mode, what you see depends on whether you have a color or black-and-white display. If you have a color display, entries that have been assigned the Bold, Underline, and Italic styles will be displayed in different colors. (The exact color for each style depends on which of the color options you have selected in the Screen Colors list box in the Works Settings dialog box.) If you have a black-and-white display (or if you have a color display and you have selected either of the Gray options in the Screen Colors list box in the Works Settings dialog box), then entries that have been assigned the Bold, Underline, and Italic styles will be displayed in bright characters. This is your only indication that a cell has been assigned a style. To determine which attribute(s) the cell has, you must select the cell individually, pull down the Format menu, select the Style… command, and look at the three style check boxes.

CONCLUSION

In this chapter, we've shown you how to customize the appearance of a Works spreadsheet. Specifically, we showed you how to assign a format to a cell, how to change the alignment of an entry in a cell, and how to assign styles.

In the next chapter, we'll continue our exploration of spreadsheet documents by looking at cut and paste commands.

Cut and Paste Commands 9

*E*diting a paper spreadsheet is a tedious process. To erase entries, you use an eraser. To copy entries, you use a pencil. To move entries, you use both an eraser and pencil. To insert and delete columns, you use scissors and glue. To do any of these things, you need lots of patience.

Fortunately, editing a Works spreadsheet is much easier. Instead of using an eraser, a pencil, scissors, and glue, you use the commands located on the Edit menu. To erase an entry, you use the Clear command. To move an entry, you use the Move command. To copy an entry, you use the Copy, Fill Down, Fill Right, and Copy Special... commands. To insert and delete columns and rows, you use the Insert Row/Column and Delete Row/Column commands. To change the width of a column, you use the Column Width... command (which is located on the Format menu). In this chapter, we'll show you how to use these commands to edit Works spreadsheets.

You'll often want to erase the entries in one or more cells of a spreadsheet. **ERASING** In Chapter 7, we showed you one way to erase an entry: Select the cell that contains the entry, press [Backspace] once, and then press [Enter]. The only problem with this method is that it allows you to erase only one cell at a time.

To erase the entries in a group of cells simultaneously, you must use the Clear command. (If you want, you also can use the Clear command to erase the entry in a single cell.) To use this command to erase the entries in one or more cells, simply select the cell(s) whose entries you want to erase, pull down the Edit menu, and select the Clear command. As soon as you select this command, Works will erase the entries in the selected cells.

The Clear command and the backspace method remove only the entry from a cell. They do not affect any other characteristics of that cell, including formats, alignment attributes, and print attributes. These attributes remain with a cell after you erase the entry from it.

An example

As an example of using the Clear command, suppose you want to erase the entries in the range C6:F6 of the spreadsheet shown in Figure 9-1. To do this, begin by selecting that range, using any of the techniques presented in Chapter 7. Once you have selected these cells, simply pull down the Edit menu and select the Clear command. Figure 9-2 shows the result. As you can see, Works has erased the entries from all four cells that were selected when you issued the Clear command.

Figure 9-1

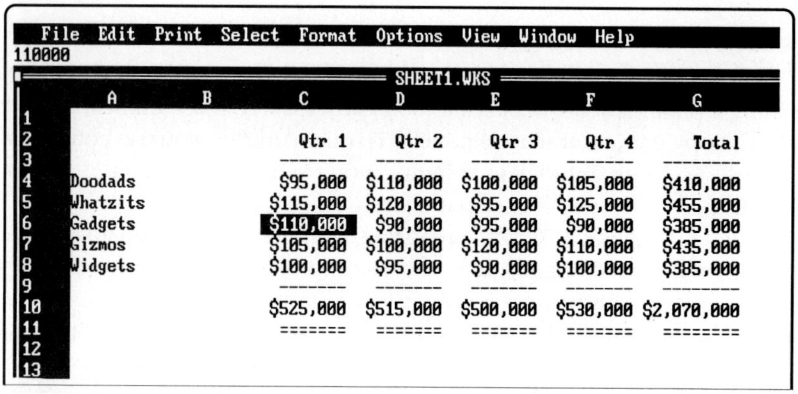

We'll use this spreadsheet to show the effects of the Clear command.

Figure 9-2

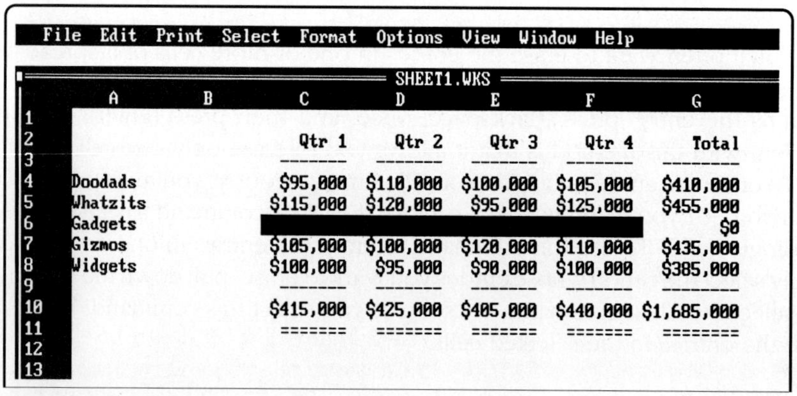

This figure shows the result of erasing the range C6:F6 from the spreadsheet shown in Figure 9-1.

In Chapter 7, we explained that Works assigns the value 0 to blank cells. Since the Clear command produces blank cells, any formulas or functions that refer to those cells will return the same results they would return if those cells contained the value 0.

In our example spreadsheet, the cells in the range G4:G8 contain SUM() functions that add the quarterly sales values for each product. For instance, cell G6 contains the function =SUM(C6:F6). The cells in the range C10:G10 contain SUM() functions that add the product sales for each quarter. For example, cell C10 contains the function =SUM(C4:C8). In Figure 9-1, the cells in the range C6:F6 contain the values 110000, 90000, 95000, and 90000, respectively. As a result, the function =SUM(C6:F6) in cell G6 returns the value 385000. After erasing the range C6:F6, this function returns the value 0, as shown in Figure 9-2. The results of the functions in the cells in the range C10:G10 also change as a result of erasing the range C6:F6.

Reference effects

In some cases, you may want to erase every cell in a spreadsheet. To do this, select the entire spreadsheet by selecting both the Row and Column commands from the Select menu. Then, pull down the Edit menu and select the Clear command. When you do, Works will clear the entries from every cell in the spreadsheet. Of course, any formats, alignment attributes, and print attributes will remain. If you want a spreadsheet that is completely clear of those attributes, you should close the current document and create a new one.

Erasing the entire spreadsheet

The Move command lets you move the contents of a cell or range within the same spreadsheet. Moving a cell or range is a three-step process. First, you select the cell or range you want to move (the source). Next, you either pull down the Edit menu and select the Move command, or press the [Move] key ([F3]). When you do either of these things, Works will display the message *Select new location and press ENTER. Press ESC to cancel.* on the message line. When you see this message, you should point to the location where you want Works to move that cell or range (the destination) and press [Enter]. Works will then move the entries from the source cells into the destination cells. If the destination cells contain entries, those entries will be overwritten by the entries from the source cells.

As we mentioned in Chapter 8, the Move command doesn't just move the entries from the cells you select—it also copies any formats, alignment attributes, and print attributes assigned to those cells. After a move, the destination cells will contain the entries, formats, alignment attributes, and print attributes of the source cells; the source cells will retain these values but will be blank.

MOVING

To move a single cell, you select only that cell, pull down the Edit menu, choose the Move command, select the destination cell, and press [Enter]. For example, suppose you want to move an entry from cell A1 into cell B5. To do this, select cell A1, choose the Move command, select cell B5, and press [Enter].

Moving a single cell

When you move a single cell, you must specify a single cell as the destination. If you expand the highlight to cover more than one cell, Works will display an alert box that contains the message *Destination does not match source.* when you press [Enter] to complete the move. When you choose <OK> to acknowledge this message, Works will clear the alert box from the screen and allow you to respecify a destination. If you want to cancel the Move command, you should press [Esc] instead.

Moving a range

To move a multiple-cell range, select that range, choose the Move command, select the destination, and press [Enter]. For the destination of a multiple-cell move, you can select either a single cell or a range with the same dimensions as the range you are moving. If you specify a single cell, Works will use that cell as the upper-left corner of the destination range, and move the contents and attributes of the source cells into that cell and the cells below it and to its right. If you select a range with the same dimensions as the source range, Works will move the contents and attributes of the source range to those cells.

If you specify a destination range that is larger than a single cell, but does not match the dimensions of the source range, Works will not perform the move. Instead, it will display an alert box that contains the message *Destination does not match source.* If you select <OK> in response to this message, Works will give you another chance to specify the destination of the move. If you press [Esc] instead, Works will cancel the move. To avoid this problem, don't highlight a range as the destination of a move; always select a single cell.

As an example of moving a multiple-cell range, suppose you want to move the contents and attributes of cells A1:B2 in the spreadsheet shown in Figure 9-3 into the range C3:D4 of that spreadsheet. To do this, select the range A1:B2, pull down the Edit menu, and select the Move command. After issuing this command, move the highlight to cell C3 (the upper-left cell of the destination range) and press [Enter]. Figure 9-4 shows the result. As you can see, Works has moved the contents and copied the formats, alignments, and print attributes of the cells in the range A1:B2 into the cells in the range C3:D4.

Figure 9-3

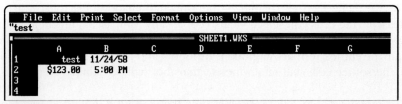

We'll use this spreadsheet to demonstrate the Move command.

Figure 9-4

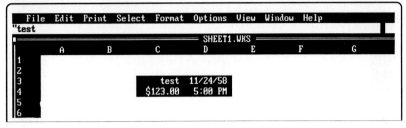

This figure shows the spreadsheet after we moved the entries from the range A1:B2 into the range C3:D4.

When you move a formula or function to another cell in a spreadsheet, Works will not change its references. For example, suppose you want to move the formula *=B2*C3* from cell A1 to cell Z100. If you look at cell Z100 after moving this formula from cell A1 to cell Z100, you'll see that it contains the formula *=B2*C3*— the same formula that was in cell A1.

Moving formulas and functions

After you move an entry from a cell that is referred to by a formula or function, the new location of that entry will be reflected in that formula or function. For example, suppose cell A1 contains the formula *=B2*C3*. If you move the contents of cell C3 into cell Z100, Works will adjust the formula in cell A1 to *=B2*Z100*.

Moving referenced cells

If you move a cell that is included in the range argument of a function, the effect on that function depends on whether that cell is in the middle of the range or is one of its endpoints. If the cell is in the middle of the range, the range reference will not change; consequently, the function will no longer include the entry that was in that cell.

We'll use the simple spreadsheet shown in Figure 9-5 on the next page to demonstrate this effect. As you can see, cell B8 of the spreadsheet contains the function *=SUM(B2:B6)*. Cells B2 and B6 are the endpoints of this range; cells B3, B4, and B5 are between those points. Figure 9-6 on the following page shows the result of moving the entry from cell B4 to a cell outside the range (in this case, to cell C4). Notice that cell B8 still contains the function *=SUM(B2:B6)*. (Since cell B4 is now empty, however, the function in cell B8 returns a lower result than it did before.)

If you move a cell that serves as an endpoint of the range argument of a function, Works will expand the range referred to by that function to include that cell. For example, Figure 9-7 on the following page shows the result of moving the entry in cell B2 (the upper-left cell of the range referred to by the function *=SUM(B2:B6)* in cell B8) into cell A1. As you can see, cell B8 now contains the function *=SUM(A1:B6)*.

Figure 9-5

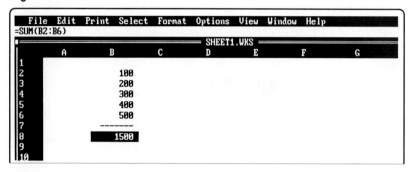

We'll use this spreadsheet to demonstrate the effect of moving cells referred to by the range argument of a function.

Figure 9-6

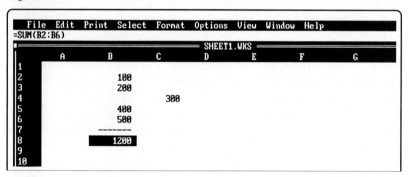

This figure shows how moving the entry from cell B4 into cell C4 affects the function in cell B8.

Figure 9-7

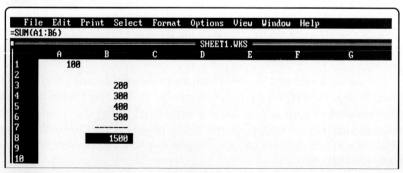

This figure shows how moving the entry from cell B2 into cell A1 affects the function in cell B8.

When you move an entry into a cell that is referred to by a formula, Works replaces the reference to the cell with the value ERR. Consequently, the formula itself will return the value ERR. For example, suppose cell A7 of a spreadsheet contains the formula *=A1+A2+A3+A4+A5*. If you use the Move command to move a value from cell Z100 into cell A3, the formula in cell A7 will become *=A1+A2+ERR+A4+A5*, which returns the value ERR.

Moving entries into referenced cells

When you move an entry into a cell that serves as the endpoint of the range argument of a function, Works will lose track of the range reference, and replace it with the value ERR. Consequently, the function will return the value ERR. For example, suppose cell A7 contains the function *=SUM(A1:A5)*. If you move an entry into cell A1 or cell A5 (the endpoints of the range argument), Works will convert the range argument to the value ERR. The resulting function, *=SUM(ERR)*, will return the value ERR. If you move an entry into cells A2, A3, or A4 (the cells in the interior of the range), the function will remain intact and will use the new entry in its calculation.

You also can use the Move command to move entire rows and columns. To do so, you first must highlight every cell in each of the rows or columns you want to move (the Row and Column commands on the Select menu provide the easiest way to do this). After selecting these rows or columns, you can move them by pulling down the Edit menu, selecting the Move command, specifying the destination, and pressing [Enter].

Moving entire rows and columns

The effect of moving entire rows and columns is different from that of moving individual cells and ranges. When Works moves a row or column, it doesn't just move the contents, formats, and so forth, of the cells in that row or column—it actually moves the row or column itself, cells and all. Works lifts the row or column from the spreadsheet, closes the space it occupied, opens a space for the row or column at the destination, and places the row or column in that space. After moving a row, Works renumbers all the rows in the spreadsheet. After moving a column, Works reletters all the columns.

The effect of moving rows and columns

To specify the destination of a row or column move, you need to select only a single cell. If you are moving one or more rows, you must select a cell in column A (the leftmost column in the spreadsheet). When you press [Enter] to complete the move, Works will insert the rows immediately above the row that contains the cell you selected. For example, if you select cell A5 as the destination of a one-row move, Works will insert that row between rows 4 and 5.

Specifying the destination of a row or column move

If you are moving one or more columns, you must point to a cell in row 1 (the topmost row in the spreadsheet) as the destination of the move. When you press [Enter] to complete the move, Works will insert the columns it is moving to the left of the column in which that cell is located. For example, if you point to cell D1 as the destination of a two-column move, Works will insert those columns between columns C and D.

If you want, you can highlight entire rows or columns as the destination of a row or column move. For the move to be successful, however, you must highlight the same number of rows or columns you are moving. For example, if you are moving one column, you must select all the cells in a single column as the destination; if you are moving two rows, you must select all the cells in two rows; and so forth. If you highlight an incorrect number of rows or columns, incomplete rows or columns, or single cells in other than the first row or column of the spreadsheet, Works will display an alert box that contains the message *Destination does not match source.* when you press [Enter] to complete the move. If you choose <OK> in response to this message, Works will let you respecify the destination. If you press [Esc], Works will cancel the Move command.

An example

As an example of moving entire rows and columns, suppose you want to move row 5 of the spreadsheet shown in Figure 9-8 to a location between the rows that contain the entries for Gizmos and Widgets (rows 7 and 8). To do this, begin by selecting row 5. (If you have a mouse, you can do this simply by pointing to the left of that row and clicking; if you don't, select any cell in that row, pull down the Select menu, and select the Row command.) After selecting row 5, pull down the Edit menu and choose the Move command. Finally, select cell A8 (the leftmost cell in the row above which you want to move row 5) and press [Enter].

Figure 9-8

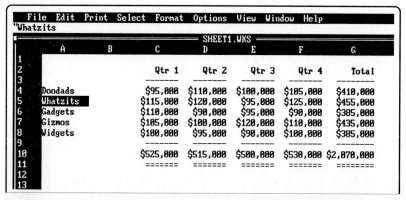

We'll use this spreadsheet to demonstrate the process of moving an entire row.

Figure 9-9 shows the result of this move. As you can see, Works has moved row 5 to a position immediately above row 8. As a result of this move, the original row 5 (the one that we moved) is now row 7; the original row 6 is now row 5; and the original row 7 is now row 6.

Figure 9-9

File Edit Print Select Format Options View Window Help

"Whatzits

SHEET1.WKS

	A	B	C	D	E	F	G
1							
2			Qtr 1	Qtr 2	Qtr 3	Qtr 4	Total
3			-------	-------	-------	-------	--------
4	Doodads		$95,000	$110,000	$100,000	$105,000	$410,000
5	Gadgets		$110,000	$90,000	$95,000	$90,000	$385,000
6	Gizmos		$105,000	$100,000	$120,000	$110,000	$435,000
7	Whatzits		$115,000	$120,000	$95,000	$125,000	$455,000
8	Widgets		$100,000	$95,000	$90,000	$100,000	$385,000
9			-------	-------	-------	-------	--------
10			$525,000	$515,000	$500,000	$530,000	$2,070,000
11			=======	=======	=======	=======	========
12							
13							

This figure shows the result of moving row 5 to a position between rows 7 and 8.

Reference effects

Moving a column or row affects the formulas and functions that reference cells in that column or row. If moving the column or row moves an entry that is referenced individually by a formula or function, that formula or function will reference the new location of that entry after the move. If moving the column or row moves a cell that serves as an endpoint of the range argument of a function, Works will expand the range referenced by that function to include the new location of that cell. If moving a column or row moves a cell that is in the middle of a range that is referenced by a function, the range reference will not change. Since Works makes room for a column or row when you move it, there is no chance of destroying a reference to a cell by overwriting that cell.

COPYING

Works provides four commands that allow you to make copies of the information in a spreadsheet: Copy, Copy Special..., Fill Right, and Fill Down. All of these commands are located on the Edit menu of any spreadsheet document. Like the Move command, these four copy commands overwrite the contents and attributes (formats, alignment attributes, and print attributes) of their destination cell(s) with the contents and attributes of their source cells. Unlike the Move command, however, these copy commands do not remove the entries from their source cells. After a move, the source cells are empty, except for their attributes. After a copy, the source cells contain the same entries and attributes they did before the copy.

Although all of these commands make copies of the information in a spreadsheet, each is designed for a different situation. For that reason, and due to some complexities inherent in the copying process, we'll cover these commands one at a time.

The Copy command

The Copy command and the [Copy] key ([Shift][F3]) let you make single copies of the contents and attributes of cells and ranges in a Works spreadsheet. To use this command, first select the cell(s) whose contents and attributes you want to copy. Second, pull down the Edit menu and select the Copy command or press the [Copy] key. As soon as you do this, Works will display the message *Select new location and press ENTER. Press ESC to cancel.* on the message line and wait for you to highlight the copy destination. When you see this message, point to where you want Works to place the copy, then press [Enter] to complete the process.

Copying from a single cell

To copy from a single cell to another single cell, simply select the cell you want to copy, choose the Copy command, select another single cell as the destination of the copy, then press [Enter]. For example, suppose you want to copy the entry from cell A1 into cell B5. To do this, select cell A1, choose the Copy command, select cell B5, and press [Enter].

You can't use the Copy command to copy from a single cell into a range of cells. If you select a multiple-cell destination, Works will make a single copy of the contents and attributes of the source cell in the upper-left cell of the destination range. To copy from one cell to a range of cells, you must use the Fill Down and Fill Right commands. We'll explain those commands later in this chapter.

Copying from a multiple-cell range

To copy a multiple-cell range, expand the highlight to select that range, select the Copy command, highlight the destination, and press [Enter]. As the destination of a multiple-cell copy, you can select either a single cell or a range with the same dimensions as the range you are copying. If you specify a single cell, Works will use that cell as the upper-left corner of the destination range, and copy the contents and attributes of the source cells into that cell and the cells below it and to its right. If you select a range with the same dimensions as the source range, Works will copy the contents and attributes of the source range to those cells. If you specify a destination range that is larger than a single cell, but does not match the dimensions of the source range, Works will copy as much of the source range as will fit into that range.

Copying value and text entries

When you specify cells that contain text and value entries as the source of a copy, Works will place exact copies of the entries in those cells into the cells of the destination range. For example, suppose cell A1 contains the text entry *TEST*, and cell A2 contains the value 123. If you select the range A1:A2, select the Copy command, highlight D5, and press [Enter], Works will place a copy of the text entry *TEST* into cell D5 and a copy of the value entry 123 into cell D6.

In addition to copying text and values, you can copy formulas and functions. Because formulas and functions typically contain references to other cells, however, copying them is a bit trickier than copying text entries and values. When you copy formulas and functions, Works alters many of the references in them to reflect their new location in the spreadsheet. The way that Works adjusts a reference depends on whether that reference is relative, absolute, or mixed. In the following sections, we'll show you how Works adjusts each of these types of references during the copy process.

Copying relative references. Most of the references in your Works spreadsheets will be relative. Relative references do not have a $ sign in front of either their column letter or row number. When you copy a formula or function to another location in a spreadsheet, Works adjusts the relative references in it to reflect the location of the copy. Consequently, the relative references in the copy will not be the same as the relative references in the original formula or function.

As an example of copying relative references, suppose that you want to enter the functions =*SUM(B8:B9)* and =*SUM(C8:C9)* into cells B11 and C11, respectively, of the spreadsheet shown in Figure 9-10. To do this, you could type each of these functions individually or you could enter the function =*SUM(B8:B9)* into cell B11 and use the Copy command to copy it into cell C11. Figure 9-11 shows the result of this copy. As you can see, cell C11 contains the function =*SUM(C8:C9)*. Instead of referring to cells B8 and B9 like the function in cell B11 does, this function refers to cells C8 and C9.

Copying formulas and functions

Figure 9-10

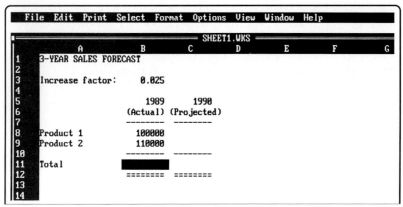

We'll use this spreadsheet to demonstrate the effects of copying relative and absolute references.

Figure 9-11

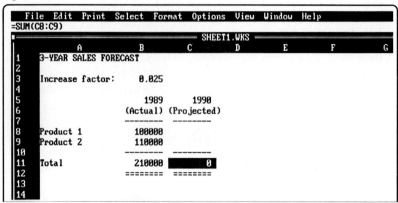

This figure shows the result of copying the formula =SUM(B8:B9) *from cell B11 into cell C11.*

As you can see, Works changed the references B8 and B9 into the references C8 and C9 as it copied the function from cell B11 into cell C11. To understand why this happens, you must understand how Works interprets a relative reference. Instead of thinking of a relative reference in terms of a specific cell, Works thinks of that reference as a map to a cell from the cell that contains the reference. For example, the reference B8 in cell B11 tells Works to pull the value from the cell three cells above cell B11; the reference B9 tells it to pull the value from the cell two cells above that cell.

When you think about relative references in this way, the changes to the formulas in cell C11 make sense. In Figure 9-11, both the function in cell B11 and the copy of that function in cell C11 reference the cells two and three cells above themselves. Although the references refer to different cells, they refer to cells in the same location relative to the cells that contain them.

Copying absolute references. Unlike relative references, absolute references always refer to the same cell no matter where you copy them in a spreadsheet. As we explained in Chapter 7, absolute references are denoted by a single dollar sign preceding their column and row components. For example, $A$1 is an absolute reference to cell A1. To create an absolute reference, you can either type the $ signs manually or press the [Abs] key ([F3]) as you are pointing to a cell while building a formula.

As an example of copying absolute references, suppose you want both cells C8 and C9 of the spreadsheet shown in Figure 9-11 to contain formulas that multiply the entries in the cells immediately to their left by the value in cell B3. To do this, you could enter the formula *=B8*(1+B3)* into cell C8 and enter the formula *=B9*(1+B3)* into cell C9. As an alternative, you could enter the formula *=B8*(1+$B$3)* into cell C8, then use the Copy command to copy it into cell C9.

Figure 9-12

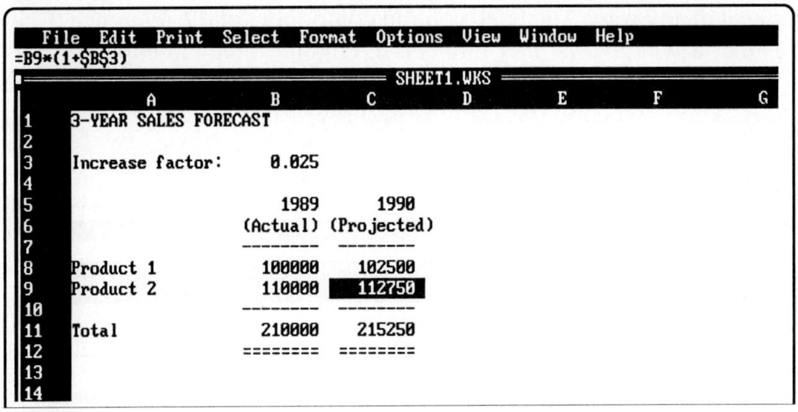

```
  File  Edit  Print  Select  Format  Options  View  Window  Help
=B9*(1+$B$3)
|                                   SHEET1.WKS
|         A            B          C        D       E       F       G
1  3-YEAR SALES FORECAST
2
3  Increase factor:     0.025
4
5                        1989       1990
6                     (Actual) (Projected)
7                     -------- --------
8  Product 1           100000     102500
9  Product 2           110000     112750
10                     -------- --------
11 Total               210000     215250
12                     ======== ========
13
14
```

This figure shows the result of copying the formula =B8*(1+$B$3) from cell C8 into cell C9.

Figure 9-12 shows the result. As you can see, cell C9 contains the formula *=B9*(1+$B$3)*. Because the reference to cell B3 (the increase factor) within the formula in cell C8 is absolute, that formula will refer to cell B3 no matter where you copy it. Since the reference to cell B8 is relative, however, Works changed it to a reference to cell B9 when it copied the formula into cell C9.

Copying mixed references.   Mixed references have either a fixed column component or a fixed row component, but not both. As with absolute references, Works uses $ signs to denote which component of a mixed reference is fixed. A dollar sign in front of the column letter (like $A1) denotes a reference whose column coordinate is fixed; a dollar sign in front of the row component (like A$1) denotes a reference whose row coordinate is fixed.

Mixed references whose column components are fixed will always refer to the same column no matter where they are copied in the spreadsheet, although they may refer to different rows. Mixed references whose row components are fixed will always refer to the same row no matter where they are copied, but they may refer to different columns.

You'll want to use mixed references in situations where you want either a reference's column or row coordinate (but not both) to remain fixed as you copy it. The spreadsheet in Figure 9-13 on the next page illustrates such a situation. This spreadsheet shows a simple unit and dollar sales forecast for two products. The dollar sales for each product in each quarter can be computed by multiplying the product's price (from column B) by the unit sales for that product in that quarter.

The formula in cell C6, *=$B6*C5*, makes this computation for Product 1 in the first quarter. Notice that the reference to cell B6 in this formula is mixed: absolute with regard to column B but relative with regard to row 6. We defined the formula in this way so that we can copy it into the ranges D6:F6 and C10:F10 without having to change it in any way. The fixed column component of the reference to cell B6 ensures that it will always refer to a cell in column B as you copy it across the spreadsheet. The relative row component of this reference allows the row value to change when you copy this formula into row 10.

Figure 9-13

File Edit Print Select Format Options View Window Help

=$B6*C5

SHEET1.WKS

	A	B	C	D	E	F	G
1	SALES FORECAST						
2		Price	Qtr 1	Qtr 2	Qtr 3	Qtr 4	Total
3		-------	-------	-------	-------	-------	-------
4	Product 1						
5	Units		1000	2000	3000	4000	10000
6	Dollars	$24.95	$24,950				$24,950
7							
8	Product 2						
9	Units		500	2000	1500	1000	5000
10	Dollars	$14.95					$0
11							
12							

We'll use this spreadsheet to show the copying of mixed references.

Figure 9-14 shows the result of copying this formula into the range D6:F6 and the range C10:F10. As you can see, these formulas correctly compute the price of both products in every quarter. Notice that the formula in cell F10, *=$B10*F9*, refers to column B (just as the original formula did) but now refers to row 10 instead of row 6. The use of mixed references made it possible to enter a single formula into one cell and copy it into the remaining cells, rather than entering a different formula into each cell individually.

Figure 9-14

File Edit Print Select Format Options View Window Help

=$B10*F9

SHEET1.WKS

	A	B	C	D	E	F	G
1	SALES FORECAST						
2		Price	Qtr 1	Qtr 2	Qtr 3	Qtr 4	Total
3		-------	-------	-------	-------	-------	-------
4	Product 1						
5	Units		1000	2000	3000	4000	10000
6	Dollars	$24.95	$24,950	$49,900	$74,850	$99,800	$249,500
7							
8	Product 2						
9	Units		500	2000	1500	1000	5000
10	Dollars	$14.95	$7,475	$29,900	$22,425	$14,950	$74,750
11							
12							

This figure shows the result of copying mixed references.

Unlike moving entries on top of cells that are referred to by formulas and functions, copying entries into cells that are referred to by formulas and functions does not affect the structure of those formulas. However, it does affect their results. If you copy a value into a cell that is referred to by a formula or function, Works will use the copied value when it evaluates the formula or function that references that cell. For example, suppose cell A1 contains the value 1, cell A2 contains the value 2, cell A3 contains the value 3, and cell A5 contains the formula $=A1+A2+A3$, which returns the value 6. If you copy the value 10 from another cell (say, cell Z100) into cell A2, cell A5 still will contain the formula $=A1+A2+A3$. Because cell A2 now contains the value 10, however, that formula will return the value 14.

Other reference effects

Because the Copy command makes copies of entries rather than relocating them, formulas and functions that refer to cells from which you have copied information will still refer to those cells after the copy. For example, if cell A5 contains the formula $=A1+A2+A3$ before you copy the entry from cell A2 into cell G10, it will contain the same formula afterward.

In most cases, you will copy information from one cell or range in a Works spreadsheet into another cell or range in that same spreadsheet. However, Works allows you to copy information from the cells of one spreadsheet into the cells of another spreadsheet, and even to a Works database or word processor document.

Copying information into another Works document

Copying information from a spreadsheet to another document is a four-step process. First, select the cells whose contents you want to copy. Next, pull down the Edit menu and select the Move command. Then, activate the document into which you want to copy the information from the spreadsheet. If the document is already open, simply pull down the Window menu and select its name. If the document is not open, pull down the File menu, and use the Open Existing File… command to open an existing document, or use the Create New File… command to create a new one. Once you have activated the document into which you want to copy the spreadsheet information, you should position the cursor where you want Works to place that information. When you press [Enter], Works will copy the information into that document.

Copying information into another spreadsheet. The effect of copying information from one spreadsheet to another is the same as that of copying information within a single spreadsheet. When you copy from a cell in one spreadsheet into another spreadsheet, Works will copy the contents of that cell as well as its format, alignment, and print attributes. When you copy a formula, Works will adjust the relative and mixed references in that formula to suit the location of the copy within the new spreadsheet; any absolute references will refer to the same cell in the new spreadsheet that they referenced in the old spreadsheet. For example, if you copy the formula $=A1+\$B2+C\$3+\$D\$4$ from cell E5 of one spreadsheet into cell J10 of another, cell J10 of the destination spreadsheet will contain the formula $=F6+\$B7+H\$3+\$D\$4$.

Copying information from one spreadsheet to another does not link them in any way. The formula in the source spreadsheet references cells in the source spreadsheet; the copy of that formula references cells in the destination spreadsheet. Formulas in one spreadsheet can never refer to cells in another.

Copying spreadsheet information into other types of documents.   Works also allows you to copy information from a spreadsheet into a word processor or database document. You do this the same way you copy information from one spreadsheet to another: by selecting the information you want to copy, issuing the Copy command, activating the document to which you want to copy, and pressing [Enter]. However, the results of copying information into other types of documents differ from those of copying information from one spreadsheet to another. We'll talk about copying information from a spreadsheet into another type of document in Chapter 19.

The [Repeat Copy] key
►WORKS 2◄

►Works 2 offers a function key, [Repeat Copy] ([Shift][F7]), that allows you to repeat the most recent copy you have performed. This key lets you make the same copy over and over without having to select the Copy command repeatedly.

Before you use this key, you must first use the Copy command to copy an entry or entries from one cell or range into another. Then, to repeat the copy, just highlight another cell or range and press [Repeat Copy]. Works will instantly create another copy of the original source cell or range in the the selected cell or range, just as if you had repeated the command.

You can continue selecting cells and ranges and pressing [Repeat Copy] until you have created all the copies you want. When you issue another command, however, the chain will be broken. If you want to repeat your copy after you have issued another command, you'll have to repeat the Copy command manually.◄

The Fill Right and Fill Down commands

As you have seen, the Copy command can make only a single copy of a cell or range at a time. In many cases, however, you'll want to make more than one copy of the information in a cell or range. Most commonly, you'll want to copy the contents and attributes of a single cell into a range of adjacent cells. For example, you may want to copy from cell A1 into the range A2:A4, into the range B1:D1, or even into the range A2:D4.

To make these copies, you could use the Copy command repeatedly. For example, to copy the contents and attributes of cell A1 into the range A2:A4, you could copy from cell A1 into cell A2, copy from cell A1 or A2 into cell A3, and then copy from either cells A1, A2, or A3 into cell A4. You could, however, copy from cell A1 into cell A2, then copy from the range A1:A2 into the range A3:A4.

Fortunately, Works provides two commands that make it easy to copy the contents and attributes of one cell into a range of cells adjacent to that cell. The Fill Right command copies information from one cell into a group of cells on the same row as that cell; the Fill Down command copies information from one cell into a range of cells in the same column as that cell. Although these commands are similar, we'll cover them one at a time.

The Fill Right command

The Fill Right command allows you to copy information from one or more adjacent cells in a single column into a range of cells in the same rows as those cells, starting with those immediately to the right of the source cells. To use this command, first select the source cell(s) for the copy. Second, extend the highlight to the right from the source cells to cover the range into which you want to copy the contents and attributes of those cells. Third, pull down the Edit menu and select the Fill Right command. When you do this, Works will copy the contents and attributes of the source cell(s) into the highlighted cells to their right.

For example, suppose you want to fill the range A1:J1 of a spreadsheet with the values 1988, 1989, 1990, 1991, and so forth. To do this, you could type the correct values into each of these ten cells. Alternatively, you could enter the value 1988 into cell A1, enter the formula $=A1+1$ into cell B1, then use the Fill Right command to copy that relative formula into the range C1:J1. To perform this copy, begin by selecting cell B1—the cell that contains the formula you want to copy. Next, extend the highlight to cover cells C1:J1 as well. With cells B1:J1 selected, pull down the Edit menu and select the Fill Right command. When you do this, Works will copy the formula $=A1+1$ from cell B1 into cells C1:J1.

Since the reference to cell A1 in the original formula is relative, Works will adjust it during the copy process so that each formula refers to the cell immediately to its left. For example, cell C1 will contain the formula $=B1+1$, cell D1 will contain the formula $=C1+1$, cell E1 will contain the formula $=D1+1$, and so on. Since cell A1 contains the value 1988, the formula in cell B1 will return the value 1989; since the formula in cell B1 returns the value 1989, the formula in cell C1 will return the value 1990; and so on. (Later in this chapter, we'll show you how to use the Copy Special… command to replace the formulas in these cells with their values.)

The Fill Down command

The Fill Down command allows you to copy information from one or more adjacent cells in a single row into a range of cells immediately below those cells. As with the Fill Right command, using the Fill Down command is a three-step process. First, select the cell(s) whose contents and attributes you want to copy. Next, expand the highlight downward to cover the cells into which you want to copy the information from the source cells. Finally, while the source and the destination cells are highlighted, pull down the Edit menu and select the Fill Down command. When you select this command, Works will copy the contents and attributes from the source cell(s) into the highlighted cells below those cells.

For example, suppose you want to fill the range A1:A5 of a spreadsheet with the series 1, 2, 4, 8, 16 and fill cells B1:B5 of the same spreadsheet with the series 1, 3, 9, 27, 81. To create these series, begin by entering the value 1 into cells A1 and B1, entering the formula *=A1*2* into cell A2, and entering the formula *=B1*3* into cell B2. After entering these formulas, you can use the Fill Down command to copy them into the ranges A3:A5 and B3:B5, respectively. To do this, select the range A2:B5, pull down the Edit menu, and select the Fill Down command. When you do this, Works will copy the formula from cell A2 into the range A3:A5 and copy the formula from cell B2 into the range B3:B5.

Since the references to cells A1 and B1 in the formulas in cells A2 and B2 are relative, Works will adjust them as it copies those formulas into cells A3:A5 and B3:B5. For example, cell A3 will contain the formula *=A2*2*. Similarly, cell B4 will contain the formula *=B3*3*. Since each formula refers to the value of the cell above it, these copies produce the appropriate geometric series.

Combining the Fill Right and Fill Down commands

Using the Fill Right command or Fill Down commands alone, you can copy information in only a single direction—either to the right of the source cell or below it. However, you can use these two commands together to copy information from a single cell into a multiple-row, multiple-column range that has the source cell in its upper-left corner. For example, you could copy information from cell A1 into cells B1, A2, and A3.

To copy from a single cell into a range, first select the source cell—the cell that contains the entry you want to copy. Second, expand the highlight downward and rightward from the source cell so that it also covers the cells to which you want to copy that entry. While the range is highlighted, select the Fill Right command and then the Fill Down command, or vice versa. Either way, Works will fill every cell of the range with a copy of the contents and attributes of the source cell.

Copying from a single cell to a remote range

As you have seen, you can use the Fill Right and Fill Down commands in combination to copy the information from a single cell into a range that has that cell in its upper-left corner. But what if you want to copy the information from a single cell into a remote range—for example, from cell A1 into cells D5:F7? To do this, you must first use the Copy command to copy the information from that cell into the single cell at the upper-left corner of the destination range. After making this copy, you can use the Fill Right and Fill Down commands in combination to copy the information from that cell into the remaining cells of the destination range.

The Copy Special... command

Works' Copy command lets you copy a value, text entry, formula, or function from one cell or range in a spreadsheet into another cell or range. When you copy text entries and values, the destination cells will contain exact copies of the contents of the source cell. When you copy formulas and functions, the destination cells will contain copies of those formulas and functions, adjusted for the position of the copy.

Like the Copy command, the Copy Special... command allows you to make a single copy of a cell or range. The difference between these two commands is what Works does with the information it copies. Unlike the Copy command, the Copy Special... command copies the current results of formulas and functions—not the formulas and functions themselves. Works can use those values in three ways. First, it can overwrite the contents of the destination cells with the copied values; second, it can add the copied values to the values in the destination cells; third, it can subtract the copied values from the values in the destination cells.

Using the Copy Special... command is a three-step process. First, highlight the cell or range whose value you want to copy. Next, pull down the Edit menu and select the Copy Special... command. Third, select the destination of the copy and press [Enter]. Works will then display a dialog box like the one shown in Figure 9-15. Finally, choose an option from the Copy Special dialog box and choose <OK> to complete the copy.

Using the Copy Special... command

As you can see, the Copy Special dialog box lists three options: Values Only, Add Values, and Subtract Values. If you choose Values Only, Works will overwrite the entries in the destination range with the values from the source range. If you choose Add Values, Works will add the copied values to the values in the destination range. If you choose Subtract Values, Works will subtract the copied values from the values in the destination range.

Figure 9-15

The Copy Special...command lets you copy just the results of formulas and functions.

The destination of a Copy Special... command is like the destination of a Copy command. If you are copying the value from a single cell, you should highlight only a single cell as the destination. If you are copying a range, you can either point to the upper-left corner of the destination range or highlight all or part of that range. (If you point to a single cell or highlight a range with the same dimensions as the source range, Works will copy from every cell in the source range. If you highlight a range that is smaller than the source range, Works will copy from only part of the source range. For more on this, see the discussion of the Copy command that appears earlier in this chapter.) The destination of a Copy Special... command can be in the same spreadsheet as the source or in another Works document.

The Values Only option

The Values Only option allows you to "freeze" the current values of formulas and functions. When you select this option, Works overwrites the entries (if any) in the cells of the destination range with the current values of the formulas and functions in the source range. Unlike the other options in the Copy Special dialog box, the Values Only option copies the format, alignment, and print attributes as well as the values of its source cells.

An example.   The principal use of the Values Only option is for freezing the result of a formula or function so you can compare that result to an updated result of the same formula or function. For example, suppose you want to compare the results of the formulas in cells B8:E8 of the spreadsheet shown in Figure 9-16 at an inflation rate of 3% per year (the current assumption) with the values of those same formulas at an inflation rate of 4% per year. Cells B5 and B6 contain values that represent rent and utilities expenses for 1988; cells C5:D6 contain formulas like *=B5*(1+$B$1)* that calculate expenses for 1989 and 1990 based on the previous year's expense and the inflation rate assumption in cell B1. Cells B8:E8 contain functions like *=SUM(B5:B6)* that sum the expense values for each year; cells E5 and E6 contain functions like *=SUM(B5:D5)* that sum each expense category for the three years; and cell E8 contains the function *=SUM(E5:E6)*, which returns a grand total.

Figure 9-16

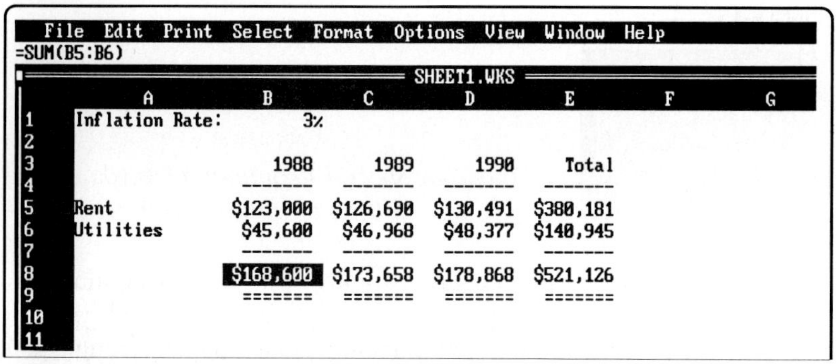

```
      File  Edit  Print  Select  Format  Options  View  Window  Help
 =SUM(B5:B6)
 ┌──────────────────────── SHEET1.WKS ════════════════════════
 │           A              B         C         D         E       F       G
 │ 1   Inflation Rate:        3%
 │ 2
 │ 3                       1988      1989      1990      Total
 │ 4                      -------   -------   -------   -------
 │ 5   Rent             $123,000  $126,690  $130,491  $380,181
 │ 6   Utilities         $45,600   $46,968   $48,377  $140,945
 │ 7                      -------   -------   -------   -------
 │ 8                     $168,600  $173,658  $178,868  $521,126
 │ 9                     =======   =======   =======   =======
 │ 10
 │ 11
```

We'll use this spreadsheet to demonstrate the usefulness of the Copy Special... command's Values Only option.

To begin this analysis, we'll copy the current values of the formulas in cells B8:E8 into cells B10:E10. To do this, select cells B8:E8, pull down the Edit menu, select the Copy Special... command, highlight cell B10, press [Enter], choose Values Only from the Copy Special dialog box, and choose <OK>. Figure 9-17 shows the results. As you can see, cells B10:E10 now contain the values 168600, 173658, 178868, and 521126, respectively—copies of the results of the formulas in cells B8:E8 at an inflation rate of 3%.

Figure 9-17

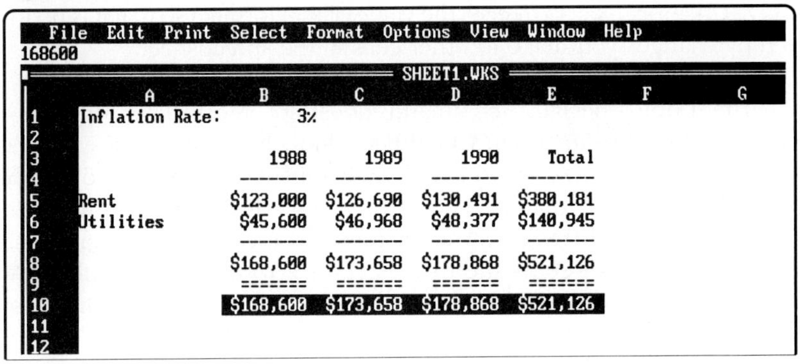

```
 File  Edit  Print  Select  Format  Options  View  Window  Help
168600
┌──────────────────────── SHEET1.WKS ════════════════════
        A          B        C        D        E       F       G
1  Inflation Rate:     3%
2
3                    1988     1989     1990    Total
4                   ───────  ───────  ───────  ───────
5  Rent           $123,000 $126,690 $130,491 $380,181
6  Utilities       $45,600  $46,968  $48,377 $140,945
7                  ───────  ───────  ───────  ───────
8                  $168,600 $173,658 $178,868 $521,126
9                  =======  =======  =======  =======
10                 $168,600 $173,658 $178,868 $521,126
11
12
```

This is the result of using the Copy Special… command's Values Only option to copy the current values of the functions in cells B8:E8 into cells B10:E10.

After you copy the results of these functions when evaluated at an inflation rate of 3%, you can change that rate to 4% and compare the results of those functions to the frozen values. To change the inflation assumption to 4%, simply enter the value .04 into cell B1. Figure 9-18 shows the result. As you can see, the functions in cells B8:E8 now return the values 168,600, 175344, 182358, and 526302, respectively. Since the values of these functions at an inflation rate of 3% are frozen in cells B10:E10, you can easily compare their results at the two rates.

Figure 9-18

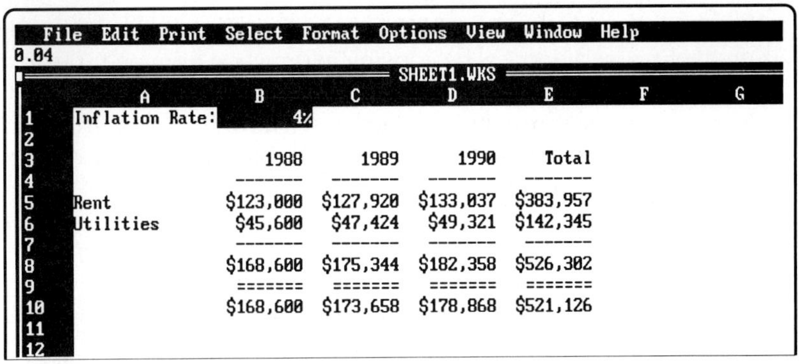

```
 File  Edit  Print  Select  Format  Options  View  Window  Help
0.04
┌──────────────────────── SHEET1.WKS ════════════════════
        A          B        C        D        E       F       G
1  Inflation Rate:     4%
2
3                    1988     1989     1990    Total
4                   ───────  ───────  ───────  ───────
5  Rent           $123,000 $127,920 $133,037 $383,957
6  Utilities       $45,600  $47,424  $49,321 $142,345
7                  ───────  ───────  ───────  ───────
8                  $168,600 $175,344 $182,358 $526,302
9                  =======  =======  =======  =======
10                 $168,600 $173,658 $178,868 $521,126
11
12
```

This figure shows the result of altering the inflation rate after copying the values of the formulas in cells B8:E8 into cells B10:E10.

Replacing formulas and functions with their current values.   You also can use the Values Only option to replace formulas and functions with their current values. To replace a formula with its current value, simply specify the same range as the source and destination of a Values Only option. Since it takes more memory to store a formula than it does to store a value, replacing a formula with its current value saves memory. It also freezes the value of that formula so that it is no longer affected by changes you make to other cells in the spreadsheet.

Notes.   The Copy Special… command does not recalculate formulas and functions before it makes copies of their values; it simply copies the values returned by those formulas and functions at the time you select the command. If your spreadsheet is set for manual recalculation, the value returned by that formula or function may not reflect the current values of the cells that it references. To make sure that Works freezes the true value of a formula or function, always recalculate your spreadsheet before issuing the Copy Special… command in any spreadsheet that is set for manual calculation.

Although the Copy Special… command's Values Only option is designed for copying the current results of formulas and functions, it also copies text entries and literal values. When it acts upon cells that contain value or text entries, the Copy Special… command does the same thing the Copy command does: It makes an exact copy of the contents and attributes of the value- or text-containing cells.

The Add Values option

The Copy Special… command's Add Values option adds the values from the cells of the source range to any values in the corresponding cells of the destination range. The Add Values option copies only literal values and the results of formulas and functions—it does not copy text entries. In addition, the Add Values option affects only the cells of the destination range that contain literal values; it does not alter cells that contain formulas, functions, or text entries. Furthermore, the Add Values option does not copy the format, alignment, and print attributes of its source cells—it copies only their values.

The most common use for the Add Values option is for creating consolidated budgets or other financial models by copying information from one spreadsheet to another. For example, suppose you want to consolidate the information from the simple budgets in the spreadsheet named East (shown in Figure 9-19) and the spreadsheet named West (shown in Figure 9-20) into the spreadsheet named Consol (shown in Figure 9-21).

Figure 9-19

```
 File  Edit  Print  Select  Format  Options  View  Window  Help
100000
┌──────────────────────────────── EAST.WKS ────────────────────────────────┐
│           A           B        C         D         E         F            │
│ 1  FY 1990 BUDGET: EASTERN DIVISION                                       │
│ 2                                                                         │
│ 3                  Qtr 1     Qtr 2     Qtr 3     Qtr 4     Total          │
│ 4                 --------  --------  --------  --------  --------        │
│ 5  Revenues       $100,000  $110,000  $120,000  $130,000  $460,000       │
│ 6  Expenses        $70,000   $75,000   $80,000   $85,000  $310,000       │
│ 7                 --------  --------  --------  --------  --------        │
│ 8  Gross Margin    $30,000   $35,000   $40,000   $45,000  $150,000       │
│ 9                 ========  =======   =======   =======   =======        │
│10                                                                         │
│11                                                                         │
└───────────────────────────────────────────────────────────────────────────┘
```

This is the East spreadsheet.

Figure 9-20

```
 File  Edit  Print  Select  Format  Options  View  Window  Help
150000
┌──────────────────────────────── WEST.WKS ────────────────────────────────┐
│           A           B        C         D         E         F        G   │
│ 1  FY 1990 BUDGET: WESTERN DIVISION                                       │
│ 2                                                                         │
│ 3                  Qtr 1     Qtr 2     Qtr 3     Qtr 4     Total          │
│ 4                 --------  --------  --------  --------  --------        │
│ 5  Revenues       $150,000  $160,000  $170,000  $180,000  $660,000       │
│ 6  Expenses        $95,000  $100,000  $105,000  $110,000  $410,000       │
│ 7                 --------  --------  --------  --------  --------        │
│ 8  Gross Margin    $55,000   $60,000   $65,000   $70,000  $250,000       │
│ 9                 ========  =======   =======   =======   =======        │
│10                                                                         │
│11                                                                         │
└───────────────────────────────────────────────────────────────────────────┘
```

This is the West spreadsheet.

Figure 9-21

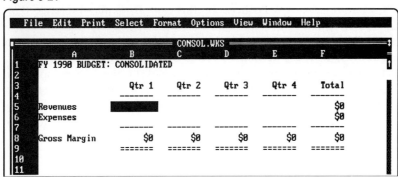

```
 File  Edit  Print  Select  Format  Options  View  Window  Help
┌──────────────────────────────── CONSOL.WKS ──────────────────────────────┐
│           A           B        C         D         E         F            │
│ 1  FY 1990 BUDGET: CONSOLIDATED                                           │
│ 2                                                                         │
│ 3                  Qtr 1     Qtr 2     Qtr 3     Qtr 4     Total          │
│ 4                 --------  --------  --------  --------  --------        │
│ 5  Revenues                                                     $0        │
│ 6  Expenses                                                     $0        │
│ 7                 --------  --------  --------  --------  --------        │
│ 8  Gross Margin        $0        $0        $0        $0        $0         │
│ 9                 ========  =======   =======   =======   =======        │
│10                                                                         │
│11                                                                         │
└───────────────────────────────────────────────────────────────────────────┘
```

We will consolidate information from East and West into the Consol spreadsheet.

To perform this consolidation, begin by opening all three spreadsheets. This ensures that they will be easily accessible during the consolidation process. If you want, however, you can open each one as it is needed. Next, use the Copy command to copy the information from the range B5:E6 of the spreadsheet shown in Figure 9-19 (East) into the range B5:E6 of the spreadsheet shown in Figure 9-21 (Consol). To do this, pull down the Window menu and choose East to make it the active spreadsheet, highlight range B5:E6, pull down the Edit menu and select the Copy command, pull down the Window menu and select the Consol spreadsheet to make it active, then point to cell B5 in that spreadsheet, and press [Enter]. When you do this, Works will copy the values from the range B5:E6 of the East spreadsheet into the same cells of the Consol spreadsheet. Figure 9-22 shows this result.

Figure 9-22

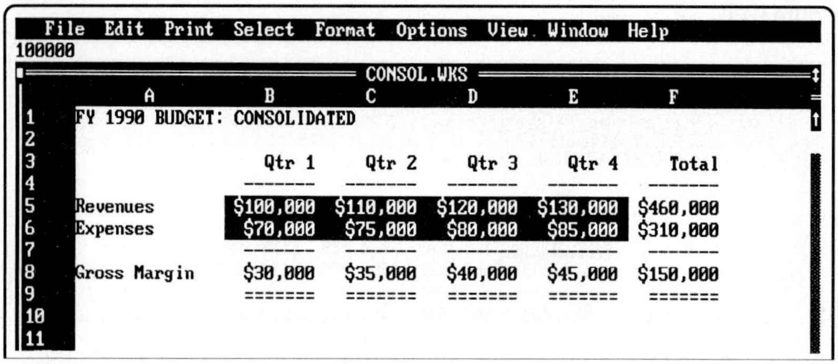

```
 File  Edit  Print  Select  Format  Options  View  Window  Help
100000
═══════════════════════════════ CONSOL.WKS ═══════════════════════════
          A            B          C          D          E          F
1  FY 1990 BUDGET: CONSOLIDATED
2
3                    Qtr 1      Qtr 2      Qtr 3      Qtr 4      Total
4                   --------   --------   --------   --------   --------
5  Revenues        $100,000   $110,000   $120,000   $130,000   $460,000
6  Expenses         $70,000    $75,000    $80,000    $85,000   $310,000
7                   --------   --------   --------   --------   --------
8  Gross Margin     $30,000    $35,000    $40,000    $45,000   $150,000
9                   ========   ========   ========   ========   ========
10
11
```

This spreadsheet shows the results of copying the entries from a range in the East spreadsheet into the same range of the Consol spreadsheet.

After using the Copy command to copy the values from the range B5:E6 of one of the two regional spreadsheets (in this case, East) into the range B5:E6 of the consolidated spreadsheet, you should use the Copy Special… command's Add Values option to add the information from the range B5:E6 of the other spreadsheet (in this case, West) on top of those copied values. To do this, pull down the Window menu and select *West* to make it the current spreadsheet. Next, highlight the range B5:E6 within that spreadsheet, pull down the Edit menu, select the Copy Special… command, pull down the Window menu and select Consol to make it the current spreadsheet, point to cell B5, press [Enter], choose the Add Values option, and choose <OK>.

Figure 9-23

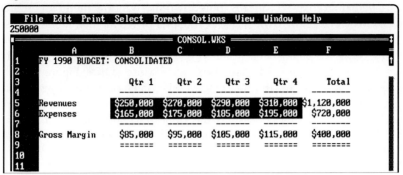

```
   File  Edit  Print  Select  Format  Options  View  Window  Help
 250000
┌══════════════════════════ CONSOL.WKS ══════════════════════════╗
│        A          B         C         D         E         F      ║
│ 1  FY 1990 BUDGET: CONSOLIDATED                                  ║
│ 2                                                                ║
│ 3                Qtr 1     Qtr 2     Qtr 3     Qtr 4     Total    ║
│ 4              --------  --------  --------  --------  --------   ║
│ 5  Revenues    $250,000  $270,000  $290,000  $310,000 $1,120,000 ║
│ 6  Expenses    $165,000  $175,000  $185,000  $195,000  $720,000  ║
│ 7              --------  --------  --------  --------  --------   ║
│ 8  Gross Margin $85,000   $95,000  $105,000  $115,000  $400,000  ║
│ 9              ========  ========  ========  ========  ========  ║
│10                                                                ║
│11                                                                ║
└═════════════════════════════════════════════════════════════════╝
```

This figure shows the result of using the Copy Special... command's Add Values option to add the values from the West spreadsheet to the values already in the same range of the Consol spreadsheet.

Figure 9-23 shows the result of these two special copies. As you can see, Works has added the values from the range B5:E6 of the West spreadsheet to the values in the range B5:E6 of the Consol spreadsheet (the values previously copied from the East spreadsheet). The final values represent the total of the values from the two regions. The formulas and functions in the remainder of the Consol spreadsheet use those consolidated values to produce consolidated totals.

The Copy Special... command's Subtract Values option works in much the same way as the Add Values option. Like the Add Values option, the Subtract Values option copies only literal values and the results of formulas and functions—it does not copy text entries. Also like the Add Values option, the Subtract Values option affects only the cells of the destination range that contain literal values, and it does not alter the attributes of those cells. Unlike the Add Values option, however, the Subtract Values option subtracts the values in the source range from the values in the destination range, instead of adding them.

To demonstrate the effect of this command, let's use it to "unconsolidate" the Consol spreadsheet shown in Figure 9-23. First, we'll subtract the values in the range B5:E6 of the West spreadsheet, shown in Figure 9-20, from the values in the range B5:E6 of Consol, shown in Figure 9-23. To do this, pull down the Window menu and select the West spreadsheet, highlight the range B5:E6 in that spreadsheet, pull down the Edit menu, and select the Copy Special... command. Next, pull down the Window menu again and select the Consol spreadsheet, point to cell B5, press [Enter], choose Subtract Values from the Copy Special dialog box, and choose <OK>. When you do this, Works will subtract the values in the range B5:E6 of the West spreadsheet from the values in the range B5:E6 of the Consol spreadsheet to produce the results shown in Figure 9-22.

The Subtract
Values option

After subtracting the West values from the Consol spreadsheet, let's subtract the East values from it. To do this, pull down the Window menu and select the East spreadsheet, highlight the range B5:E6, pull down the Edit menu, and select the Copy Special… command. Next, pull down the Window menu again and select the Consol spreadsheet, point to cell B5, press [Enter], choose Subtract Values from the Copy Special dialog box, and choose <OK>. Figure 9-24 shows the result. As you can see, the cells in the range B5:E6 of the Consol spreadsheet contain zeroes instead of being empty (as they were before we began the consolidation). Since Works assigns the value 0 to empty cells, however, this spreadsheet is functionally equivalent to the one shown in Figure 9-21.

Figure 9-24

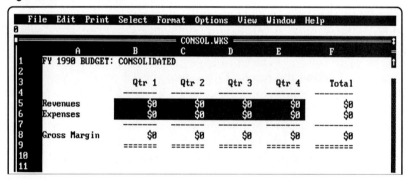

This spreadsheet shows the result of the "unconsolidation."

INSERTING COLUMNS AND ROWS

The Insert Row/Column command allows you to insert new columns and rows into a Works spreadsheet. You'll use this command to make room for additional information in the middle of an existing spreadsheet.

Whether the Insert Row/Column command inserts columns or rows depends on what cells are selected when you issue it. If you select this command while one or more entire columns are selected, Works will insert one or more new columns into the spreadsheet. If you select this command while one or more entire rows are selected, Works will insert one or more new rows into the spreadsheet.

If neither an entire column nor an entire row is highlighted when you select this command, Works will display the dialog box shown in Figure 9-25. This box lets you tell Works whether you want to insert the rows included in the highlighted range or the columns contained in that range. If you choose Row and choose <OK>, Works will insert one or more rows into the speadsheet. If you choose Column, Works will insert one or more columns into the spreadsheet. (You will usually want to select one or more entire rows or entire columns before you select the Insert Row/Column command.)

Figure 9-25

*If you select the Insert Row/Column command
without first highlighting one or more complete rows or columns, Works will display this
dialog box.*

To insert one or more columns into a spreadsheet, first select every cell in the
column(s) to the left of which you want Works to insert the new blank column(s).
If you select one column, Works will insert a single blank column to the left of that
column. If you select two columns, Works will insert two columns to the left of
the leftmost highlighted column. If you select three columns, Works will insert
three columns to the left of the leftmost highlighted column, and so on.

Inserting columns

After selecting these columns, pull down the Edit menu and select Insert Row/
Column. When you select this command, Works will insert the indicated number
of columns immediately to the left of the leftmost highlighted column, then reletter
those columns and the columns to their right.

For example, suppose you want to insert a column for 1989 between the
columns that hold the information for 1988 and 1990 in the spreadsheet shown
in Figure 9-26. To do this, begin by selecting column C—the column to the left
of which you want to insert the new column. If you have a mouse, you can select
this column simply by clicking its letter. If you don't have a mouse, you must select
this column by selecting any cell within it, pulling down the Select menu, and
choosing the Column command.

Figure 9-26

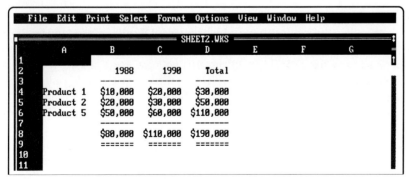

We'll use this spreadsheet to show how to insert columns and rows.

Once you have selected this column, pull down the Edit menu and select the Insert Row/Column command. Figure 9-27 shows the result. As you can see, Works has inserted a new, blank column to the left of the original column C. This new column becomes column C, the former column C becomes column D, the former column D becomes column E, and so forth.

Figure 9-27

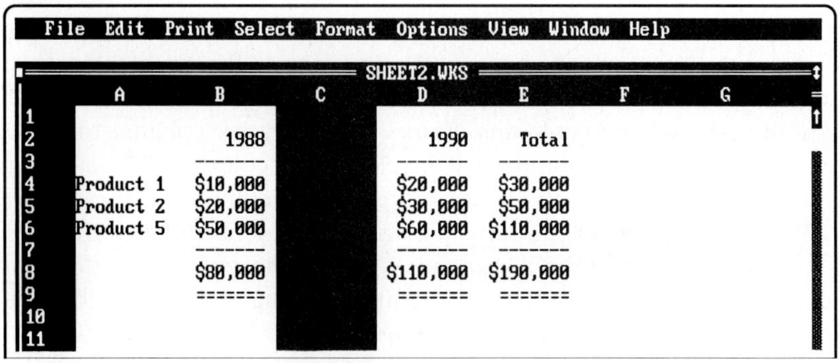

```
 File  Edit  Print  Select  Format  Options  View  Window  Help
═══════════════════════════ SHEET2.WKS ═══════════════════════
        A         B         C         D         E        F        G
 1
 2                1988                1990      Total
 3               --------            --------  --------
 4   Product 1   $10,000             $20,000   $30,000
 5   Product 2   $20,000             $30,000   $50,000
 6   Product 5   $50,000             $60,000   $110,000
 7               --------            --------  --------
 8               $80,000             $110,000  $190,000
 9               =======             =======   =======
10
11
```

This figure shows the result of inserting a new column between columns B and C of the spreadsheet shown in Figure 9-26.

After Works has inserted this new column, you can make entries into it, format it, and assign alignment and print attributes to it. In this case, you'll want to enter the value 1989 into cell C2, copy the entry from cell B3 into cell C3, enter values into the range C4:C6, copy the entries from the range B7:B9 into the range C7:C9, and assign the Currency 0 format to the range C4:C6 and cell C8.

Inserting rows

As with inserting columns, inserting rows is a two-step process. First, you select every cell in the row(s) above which you want Works to insert the new blank row(s). If you select one row, Works will insert a single blank row above that row. If you select two rows, Works will insert two new rows above the topmost highlighted row, and so forth. After selecting these rows, simply pull down the Edit menu and select Insert Row/Column. When you select this command, Works will insert the indicated number of rows immediately above the selected rows, then renumber those rows and the rows below them.

For example, suppose you want to insert two new rows between rows 5 and 6 of the spreadsheet shown in Figure 9-27—one for Product 3 and the other for Product 4. To insert these rows, begin by selecting rows 6 and 7 in that spreadsheet. (Selecting two rows ensures that Works will insert two new rows into the spreadsheet.) Selecting row 6 as the topmost row ensures that Works will insert those rows immediately above that row.

After selecting these rows, pull down the Edit menu and select the Insert Row/Column command. Figure 9-28 shows the result. As you can see, Works has inserted two new blank rows between row 5 and the former row 6. In the process, it has assigned row numbers 6 and 7 to those rows, assigned row number 8 to the former row 6, assigned row number 9 to the former row 7, and so forth.

Figure 9-28

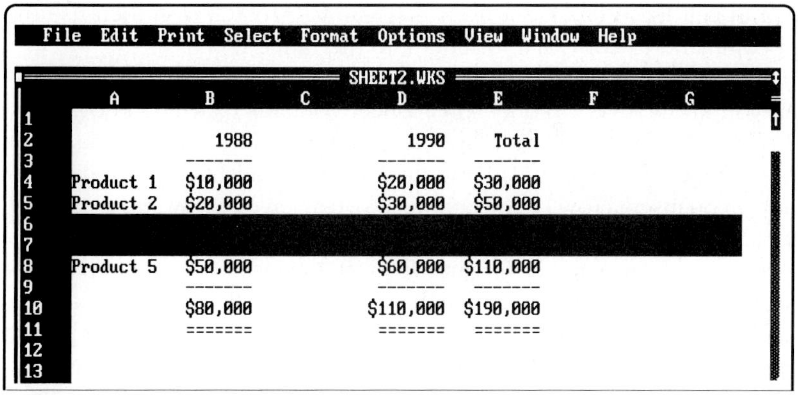

File Edit Print Select Format Options View Window Help						
			SHEET2.WKS			
A	B	C	D	E	F	G
1						
2	1988		1990	Total		
3	-------		-------	-------		
4 Product 1	$10,000		$20,000	$30,000		
5 Product 2	$20,000		$30,000	$50,000		
6						
7						
8 Product 5	$50,000		$60,000	$110,000		
9	-------		-------	-------		
10	$80,000		$110,000	$190,000		
11	=======		=======	=======		
12						
13						

This figure shows the result of inserting two new rows between rows 5 and 6 of the spreadsheet shown in Figure 9-27.

After you insert these rows, you probably will want to fill and format them. In this case, you'll want to enter *Product 3* into cell A6, enter *Product 4* into cell A7, enter values into the range B6:D7, copy the formula from cell E5 into cells E6 and E7, and assign the Currency 0 format to the range B6:E7.

Reference effects

When you insert a column or row between the endpoints of the range argument of a function, Works will expand that argument to encompass that new row or column. For example, cells B8, D8, and E8 of the spreadsheet shown in Figure 9-27 contain SUM( ) functions that add the values in rows 4 through 6 of columns B, D, and E. When we inserted the two new rows into the spreadsheet, Works modified those functions to add the values in rows 4 through 8. For example, the function *=SUM(B4:B6)* in cell B8 became the function *=SUM(B4:B8)* in cell B10. (Of course, rows inserted outside a referenced range have no effect on the reference to that range.)

As you have seen, inserting rows and columns into a spreadsheet shifts some of the existing information in that spreadsheet into different rows and columns. As you would expect, Works adjusts any references to this shifted reference to account for the insertion. For example, the cells in the range D4:D6 of the spreadsheet shown in Figure 9-26 contain simple addition formulas that add the values in columns B and C. For example, cell D4 contains the formula *=B4+C4*.

As a result of the insertion of the new column (shown in Figure 9-27), column C became column D, and column D became column E. Consequently, after the insertion, cell E4 contains the formula *=B4+D4.*

Although Works adjusted the references in the formulas in the range E4:E6 to suit the new position of the cells to which they refer, it did not expand those formulas to encompass the new column, as it would if they had been SUM() functions. After inserting this row, therefore, you probably would want to edit the formula in cell E4 to change it from *=B4+D4* to *=B4+C4+D4,* then use the Fill Down command to copy that formula into the range E5:E8.

Potential problems

As you know, every Works spreadsheet contains exactly 256 columns and 4,096 rows. To maintain this number of columns and rows, Works deletes a column whenever you insert a column into a spreadsheet and deletes a row whenever you insert a row. For example, if you insert one row into a spreadsheet, Works will delete row 4096—the last row of the spreadsheet. If you insert two rows, Works will delete rows 4095 and 4096. If you insert one column, Works will delete column IV—the last column in the spreadsheet. If you insert two columns, Works will delete columns IU and IV.

Fortunately, Works pushes only *empty* columns and rows off the right and bottom edges of a spreadsheet. If an insertion would involve deleting a column or row that contains a non-blank cell (that is, a cell that contains an entry, or that is assigned a format, an alignment attribute, or a print attribute), Works will display an alert box instead of performing the insertion.

DELETING COLUMNS AND ROWS

Works also allows you to delete columns and rows from a spreadsheet. First, select every cell in the column(s) or row(s) that you want to delete. After doing this, pull down the Edit menu and select the Delete Row/Column command. If you have selected one or more columns, Works will remove those columns. If you have selected one or more rows, Works will remove those rows.

If neither an entire column nor an entire row is highlighted when you select this command, Works will display the dialog box shown in Figure 9-29. This box allows you to tell Works whether you want delete the rows included in the highlighted range or the columns contained in that range. If you choose Row and choose <OK>, Works will delete the row or rows that are included in the highlighted range. If you choose Column, Works will delete the column or columns included in the range. (You will usually want to select one or more entire rows or entire columns before you select the Delete Row/Column command.)

Figure 9-29

If you select the Delete Row/Column command without highlighting one or more complete rows or columns, Works will display this dialog box.

Deleting a column or row from a spreadsheet doesn't simply erase the contents and attributes of the cells in that column. Instead, it removes those columns and rows from the spreadsheet entirely.

Whenever you delete a column, Works inserts a new, blank column at the right edge of the spreadsheet; whenever you delete a row, Works inserts a new, blank row at the bottom of the spreadsheet. These actions ensure that every spreadsheet has the full complement of 256 columns and 4,096 rows at all times.

To delete one or more columns from a spreadsheet, highlight the column or columns you want to delete, pull down the Edit menu, and select the Delete Row/Column command. For example, suppose you want to delete column B from the spreadsheet shown in Figure 9-30. To do this, begin by selecting that column, either by clicking its letter with a mouse or selecting a cell in that column, pulling down the Select menu, and selecting the Column command. After you select this column, pull down the Edit menu and choose Delete Row/Column.

Deleting columns

Figure 9-30

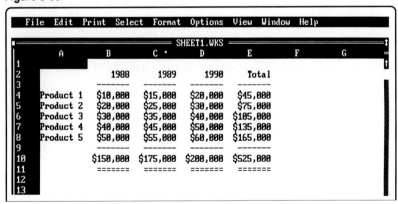

We'll use this spreadsheet to show how to delete columns and rows.

Figure 9-31 shows the result of this deletion. As you can see, Works has deleted column B from the spreadsheet. It also has relettered the remaining columns in that spreadsheet. For example, the former column C is the new column B; the former column D is the new column C; and so forth.

Figure 9-31

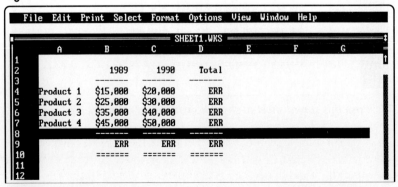

```
 File  Edit  Print  Select  Format  Options  View  Window  Help
==================================== SHEET1.WKS ====================================
         A          B          C          D          E      F      G
 1
 2                 1989       1990      Total
 3                -------    -------    -------
 4   Product 1   $15,000    $20,000      ERR
 5   Product 2   $25,000    $30,000      ERR
 6   Product 3   $35,000    $40,000      ERR
 7   Product 4   $45,000    $50,000      ERR
 8   Product 5   $55,000    $60,000      ERR
 9                -------    -------    -------
10               $175,000   $200,000      ERR
11               =======    =======    =======
12
13
```

This figure shows the result of deleting column B from the spreadsheet shown in Figure 9-30.

Deleting rows

To delete one or more rows from a spreadsheet, you must select those rows, pull down the Edit menu, and select the Delete Row/Column command. As an example of deleting rows, suppose you want to delete row 8 from the spreadsheet shown in Figure 9-30. To do this, select every cell in that row, either by clicking on its number with your mouse or by selecting a cell within it, pulling down the Select menu, and selecting Row. After selecting this row, pull down the Edit menu and select the Delete Row/Column command. Figure 9-32 shows the result.

Figure 9-32

```
 File  Edit  Print  Select  Format  Options  View  Window  Help
==================================== SHEET1.WKS ====================================
         A          B          C          D          E      F      G
 1
 2                 1989       1990      Total
 3                -------    -------    -------
 4   Product 1   $15,000    $20,000      ERR
 5   Product 2   $25,000    $30,000      ERR
 6   Product 3   $35,000    $40,000      ERR
 7   Product 4   $45,000    $50,000      ERR
 8                -------    -------    -------
 9                 ERR        ERR        ERR
10               =======    =======    =======
11
12
```

This figure shows the result of deleting row 8 from the spreadsheet shown in Figure 9-31.

When you delete a column or row from a spreadsheet, Works converts all individual references to cells of that column or row to the value ERR. That's why Works displays the value ERR in the cells in the range D4:D8 of our example spreadsheet after the deletion of column B, as shown in Figure 9-31. Before the deletion of column B, the cells in the range E4:E8 contained formulas that added the values in columns B, C, and D. For instance, cell E4 contained the formula *=B4+C4+D4.* When we deleted column B, Works converted all the references to cells of column B within these formulas to the value ERR. For example, cell D4 contains the formula *=ERR+B4+C4* after the deletion. Since formulas that contain the value ERR always return the value ERR, these formulas return the value ERR after the deletion of column B.

When you delete a column or row that contains a cell that serves as the endpoint of the range reference of a function, Works converts that range reference to the value ERR. Consequently, the function itself returns the value ERR. That's why Works displays the value ERR in the cells in the range B9:D9 after the deletion of row 8, as shown in Figure 9-32. Before the deletion of row 8, the cells in the range B10:D10 contained SUM() functions that added the values in rows 4 through 8. For example, cell B10 contained the function *=SUM(B4:B8).* Since row 8 contained the endpoint of the range references of these functions, Works converted those references to the value ERR when we deleted row 8. For example, cell B9 contains the function *=SUM(ERR)* after the deletion.

Although deleting a row or column that contains the endpoint of a range reference destroys that reference, deleting a row or column that contains a cell in the middle of a range reference does not. When you delete a row or column that contains a cell in the middle of a referenced range, Works will contract the reference to account for the deletion of the column or row. For example, Figure 9-33 on the next page shows what the spreadsheet shown in Figure 9-31 would look like if we deleted row 6 instead of row 8. Before the deletion, cells B10, C10, and D10 contained functions that added the values in rows 4 through 8. For example, cell B10 contained the function *=SUM(B4:B8).* After the deletion, these cells contain functions that add the values in rows 4 through 7. For example, cell B9 contains the function *=SUM(B4:B7)* after the deletion. Because the cells in the range B4:B7 and C4:C7 contain non-ERR values after the deletion, the functions in cells B9 and C9 return non-ERR values. Because the formulas in the cells in the range D4:D7 return the value ERR, the function *=SUM(D4:D7)* in cell D9 returns the value ERR.

The width of a column affects the way Works displays the entries you make into the cells of that column. If the cell that contains a value is too narrow to display that value in the format you have assigned to that cell, Works will display the value as a series of # signs. If a label is longer than the width of the cell that contains it, and a cell to the right of that cell is occupied, Works will truncate the display of that label.

Figure 9-33

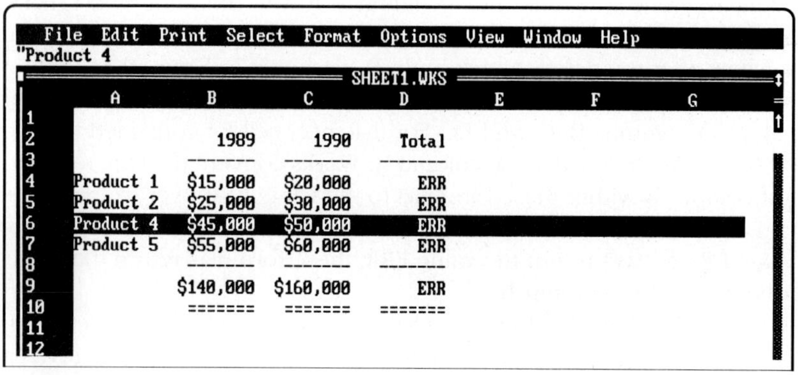

```
  File  Edit  Print  Select  Format  Options  View  Window  Help
"Product 4
================================= SHEET1.WKS =================================
        A         B         C         D         E       F       G
 1
 2                1989      1990      Total
 3               --------  --------  --------
 4  Product 1   $15,000   $20,000      ERR
 5  Product 2   $25,000   $30,000      ERR
 6  Product 4   $45,000   $50,000      ERR
 7  Product 5   $55,000   $60,000      ERR
 8               --------  --------  --------
 9              $140,000  $160,000      ERR
10               =======   =======   =======
11
12
```

*This figure shows the result of deleting row 6 from the spreadsheet
shown in Figure 9-31.*

Fortunately, Works allows you to adjust the widths of the columns in a
spreadsheet. In most cases, you will adjust the widths of the columns to improve
the way labels and formatted values are displayed. However, you also may adjust
the widths of the columns in a spreadsheet for other reasons. For example, you
may want to widen a column to separate the information it contains from the
information in an adjacent column. On the other hand, you might decrease the
width of one or more columns so that you can see more information on the screen
at one time.

**The Width...
command**

The Width... command, located at the bottom of the Format menu, allows you
to alter the width of the columns in a Works spreadsheet. You can use this
command to change the width of one or more adjacent columns at a time.

To alter the widths of one or more columns, you must select at least one cell
in each of the columns whose width you want to adjust, pull down the Format
menu, and select the Width... command. When you do this, you'll see a dialog
box like the one shown in Figure 9-34. If the highlight is marking only a single
column, the current width of that column will appear in the Width text box. If the
highlight is marking more than one column, the value 10 will appear in that space,
regardless of the widths of the columns that are selected. Either way, the entire
entry will be highlighted.

Once you see the Width dialog box, you can specify the width you want to
assign to the selected column(s). Since the current entry will be highlighted, you
can overwrite it simply by typing a new width. Alternatively, you can edit the entry
in that box using any of the techniques we presented in Chapter 1. The minimum
allowable width is 0; the maximum allowable width is 79.

Figure 9-34

*You'll see this dialog box when you select the
Width... command.*

After you have specified a new width, you must choose <OK> to complete
the command. If the Width text box contains an allowable width value, Works
will adjust the width of the highlighted columns, remove the dialog box, and return
to the spreadsheet. If the Width text box contains a value less than 0 or greater
than 79, Works will present an alert box. If you choose <Cancel> instead of <OK>,
Works will cancel the command without altering the column width.

An example

As an example of altering the width of some columns in a spreadsheet,
suppose you want to increase the widths of columns A and B in the spreadsheet
shown in Figure 9-35 to 20 spaces each. Currently, each column is ten spaces wide.
To do this, move the highlight to any cell in column A, then hold down the [Shift]
key and press ➡ to expand the highlight to cover a cell in column B as well. Once
you have highlighted at least one cell in each column, pull down the Format menu,
select the Width... command, type 20, and choose <OK>. Figure 9-36 on the
following page shows the result. As you can see, Works has expanded the width
of columns A and B to 20 spaces each, revealing the long labels and formatted
values in their cells.

Figure 9-35

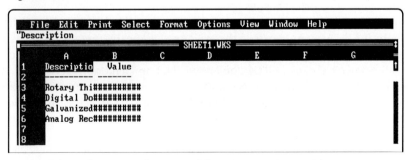

*Each of the columns in this spreadsheet is ten spaces wide —too
narrow to accommodate the labels in column A and the formatted
values in column B.*

Figure 9-36

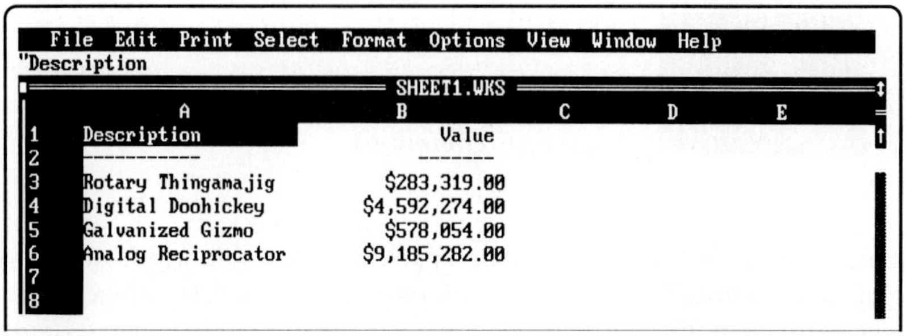

Expanding columns A and B to 20 spaces each reveals the labels in column A and the formatted values in column B.

Altering the width of every column simultaneously

If you want, you can alter the width of every column in a spreadsheet simultaneously. To do this, begin by pulling down the Select menu and choosing the Row command. This selects at least one cell in every column of the spreadsheet. After doing this, pull down the Format menu, select the Width... command, type the width you want to assign, and choose <OK>. Since every column is selected, Works will assign the width you specify to every column in the spreadsheet.

Hiding a column

The minimum column width Works allows you to specify is 0. Setting the width of a column to this minimum value hides it from view, so that the columns to the left and right of it appear adjacent. Hiding a column does not remove it from the spreadsheet, of course. Consequently, formulas that refer to cells in a hidden column return the correct results.

For example, suppose you want to hide column C in the spreadsheet shown in Figure 9-37. As you can see, the cells of column D contain formulas that reference the values in column C. To hide column C, move the highlight to any cell within it (we'll choose cell C4), pull down the Format menu, select Width, type 0, and choose <OK>. Figure 9-38 shows the result. As you can see, Works has hidden column C. Consequently, columns B and D appear adjacent to one another in the spreadsheet. Even though column C is hidden, the formulas in column D still use the values from the cells in that column.

If you look closely at Figure 9-38, you'll see that none of the cells are highlighted. Why? Because the cell that was selected when you issued the Width... command (in this case, cell C4) is hidden. When you press either the → or ← key, however, Works will bring the highlight back into view. Once you've moved out of the hidden column, Works will skip that column as you continue to move around the spreadsheet. For example, if you press → while cell B4 is the active cell of a spreadsheet in which column C is hidden, Works will skip cell C4 and activate cell D4.

Figure 9-37

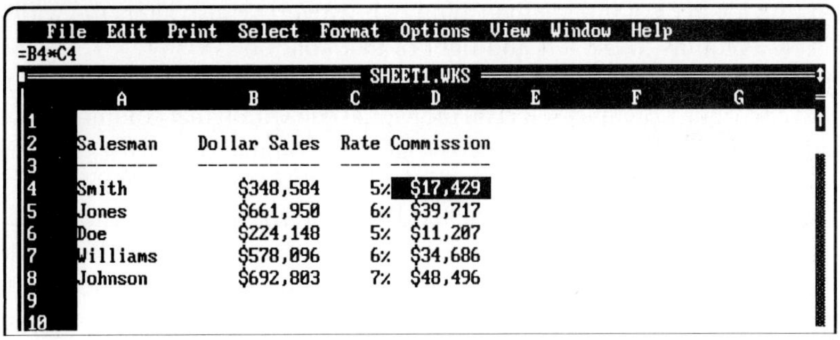

```
 File  Edit  Print  Select  Format  Options  View  Window  Help
=B4*C4
                            ═══════ SHEET1.WKS ═══════
          A           B        C      D         E       F       G
 1
 2  Salesman    Dollar Sales  Rate Commission
 3  --------    ------------  ---- ----------
 4  Smith          $348,584    5%  $17,429
 5  Jones          $661,950    6%  $39,717
 6  Doe            $224,148    5%  $11,207
 7  Williams       $578,096    6%  $34,686
 8  Johnson        $692,803    7%  $48,496
 9
10
```

This figure shows a spreadsheet with no columns hidden.

Figure 9-38

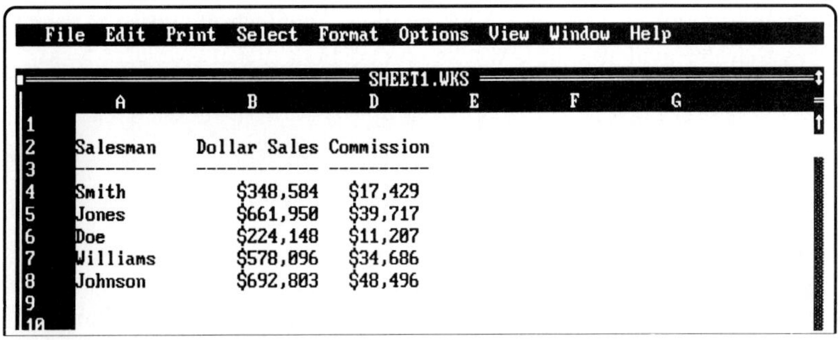

```
 File  Edit  Print  Select  Format  Options  View  Window  Help

                            ═══════ SHEET1.WKS ═══════
          A           B        D         E       F       G
 1
 2  Salesman    Dollar Sales  Commission
 3  --------    ------------  ----------
 4  Smith          $348,584   $17,429
 5  Jones          $661,950   $39,717
 6  Doe            $224,148   $11,207
 7  Williams       $578,096   $34,686
 8  Johnson        $692,803   $48,496
 9
10
```

This figure shows the same spreadsheet after we have hidden column C.

Although you cannot use the arrow keys to highlight an individual cell in a hidden column, you can use them to highlight a range that includes a cell in a hidden column. To do this, you simply highlight a cell in the column to one side of the hidden column or the other, then either press the [Extend] key or hold down the [Shift] key, and use either the ➡ or ⬅ keys to expand the highlight into a cell in a column on the other side of the hidden column. While the highlighted range includes cells in the hidden column, any commands you select will affect the hidden cells as well as the ones that are visible.

"Unhiding" a column

To "unhide" a column, you increase its width to greater than 0. To do this, you must select the column, select the Width... command, type the new width, and choose <OK>.

Unfortunately, selecting a hidden column is a bit tricky. As we just explained, you can select a cell in a hidden column by expanding the highlight from the cell to its left into the cell to its right or vice versa. Unhiding a column you've selected in this way doesn't just unhide that column, however—it also alters the widths of the visible columns to the left and right of that column.

If you want to unhide a column without affecting the width of the columns to its left and right, you must select an individual cell within that column. To select a cell in a hidden column, either select the Go To... command from the Select menu or press the [Go To] ([F6]) key to reveal the Go To dialog box. Within this box, type the address of any cell within the hidden column. When you choose <OK>, Works will select the cell you specified. Although that cell will not be visible on the screen, its address will appear at the left edge of the status line. Once you have selected a cell within a hidden column, you can unhide that column by pulling down the Format menu, selecting the Width... command, typing a width greater than zero, then choosing <OK>.

CONCLUSION

In this chapter, we've shown you how to use cut and paste commands in a spreadsheet document. In the next chapter, we'll show you the variety of functions that are available in a Works spreadsheet.

Functions 10

*I*n addition to its standard operators (+, -, *, /, and ∧), Works offers a variety of functions. Functions are special mathematical operators that allow you to perform calculations that would be difficult or impossible to perform with traditional formulas. For example, Works' AVG() function calculates the average of the values in a range; the NPV() function calculates the net present value of a stream of cash flows; and the VLOOKUP() function looks up a value from a table.

Works has 60 functions in all. In this chapter, we will examine each one individually, explaining what it does and showing you how it works. Before we do, however, let's take a moment to examine the basics of Works' functions.

Although different functions perform different tasks, they all share a similar form. First, all Works functions have names. The name of a function is a short series of letters (usually three or four) that identifies what that function does. For example, the SQRT() function calculates the square root of a value; the TAN() function calculates the tangent of an angle; the PV() function calculates the present value of a stream of cash flows; and so forth.

THE FORM OF FUNCTIONS

Second, most Works functions require or accept one or more arguments. These arguments provide the information that the function uses in the calculation it performs. For example, the SQRT() function, which calculates the square root of a value, requires one argument—the value whose square root you want to calculate. Some functions require more than one argument. For example, the ROUND() function, which rounds a value to a certain number of decimal points, requires two—the value you want to round and the number of digits you want to the right of the decimal point. The arguments of a multiple-argument function must be separated from one another with a single comma.

All Works functions operate on values. In some cases, the arguments of your Works functions will be literal values. To round the value 12.345 to two decimal points, for example, you could use the function *=ROUND(12.345,2)*. In most cases, however, your arguments will be references to cells that contain values, either by address or range name. For example, if cell A1 contained the value 12.345 and cell A2 contained the value 2, the functions *=ROUND(A1,2)*, *=ROUND(12.345,A2)*, and *=ROUND(A1,A2)* all would return the same results as the function *=ROUND(12.345,2)*.

Works also allows you to use formulas and even other functions as the arguments of its functions. For example, the first argument of the function *=ROUND(SUM(A1:A5),2)* is a SUM() function. The technique of using one function as the argument of another is called nesting. When Works evaluates a nested function, it always calculates the functions from the inside out so that the entire function calculates completely.

Many Works functions require range arguments. Other functions accept either multiple single arguments or a range argument. For example, the SUM() function, which adds a group of values, typically sums a range. Within a function, a range can be represented as two cell addresses separated by a colon or by the name you have assigned to that range. If the range A1:A5 is named RANGE, for example, you could sum the values in that range with the function *=SUM(A1:A5)* or the function *=SUM(RANGE)*.

ENTERING FUNCTIONS

When you enter a function into a cell, you must preface it with an = sign. Otherwise, Works will interpret it as a text entry. For example, if you move the highlight to cell A1, type *ROUND(12.345,2)*, and press [Enter], Works will enter the text entry *"ROUND(12.345,2)* into that cell. If you type *=ROUND(12.345,2)* instead, Works will enter the function *=ROUND(12.345,2)* into that cell.

If you want, you can preface a function with an @ sign instead of an = sign. If you do, Works will accept the function. However, it will convert the @ sign into an = sign when you lock the function into its cell.

As we mentioned earlier, the arguments of most functions will reference cells or ranges. You can enter these references into functions either by typing or by pointing, just as you can when you create formulas. For example, suppose you want to enter the function *=ROUND(A1,2)* into cell B1 of a spreadsheet. To do this, you could highlight cell B1, type *=ROUND(A1,2)*, and press [Enter]. Alternatively, you could highlight cell B1, type *=ROUND(*, use the arrow keys to point to cell A1, type *,2)*, and then press [Enter]. If you have a mouse, you could highlight cell B1, type *=ROUND(*, move the mouse pointer to cell A1 and click, type *,2)*, and then press [Enter].

As another example, suppose you want to enter the function *=SUM(A1:A5)* into cell A7 of a spreadsheet. To do this, you could move the highlight to cell A7, type *=SUM(A1:A5)*, and press [Enter]. Alternatively, you could move the highlight to cell A7, type *=SUM(*, use the arrow keys to point to cell A1, press *:* to anchor the highlight, expand the highlight to cover cells A1:A5, type *)*, and then press [Enter]. If you have a mouse, you could highlight cell A7, type *=SUM(*, drag through the range A1:A5, type *,2)*, and then press [Enter].

When you enter a function into a cell, Works evaluates that function and displays the result in the cell that contains the function. If you entered the function *=ROUND(12.345,2)* into cell A1 of a spreadsheet, for example, Works would not display *=ROUND(12.345,2)* in that cell unless the Show Formulas attribute was on. Instead, it would evaluate the function and display the result—in this case, the value 12.35. Works will recalculate the function whenever you press the [Calc] key ([F9] on the IBM PC), choose Calculate Now from the Options menu, or make or edit an entry while Works is set for automatic recalculation.

Works will not allow you to lock in a function that has an invalid name, the wrong number of arguments, the wrong type of arguments, and so forth. If you try, Works will display an alert box that identifies the problem. As soon as you choose <OK> to acknowledge this message, Works will clear the alert box and position the highlight in the function on the formula line at the position of the error. At that point, you can correct the function and then re-enter it.

INVALID FUNCTIONS

Works' mathematical functions are its simplest functions. The six functions in this group—ABS(), MOD(), RAND(), SQRT(), ROUND(), and INT()—perform simple manipulations of values. For example, the ABS() function calculates the absolute value of a value; the RAND() function returns a random value; and the INT() function truncates a value to integer form.

MATHEMATICAL FUNCTIONS

Works' ABS() function returns the absolute value (that is, the positive equivalent) of the value on which it operates. The form of the ABS() function is ABS(*value*) where the single argument refers to the value that the function will operate on. As an example of the use of this function, suppose that cell A1 of a Works spreadsheet contains the value -123. To calculate the absolute value of the entry in this cell, you would enter the function *=ABS(A1)* into another cell of the spreadsheet. Since cell A1 contains the value -123, this function will return the value 123—the positive form of that value. The absolute value of a positive value is that value. Consequently, this ABS() function would have returned the same result if cell A1 had contained the value 123.

The ABS() function

Works' MOD() function returns the remainder that results from dividing one value by another. The form of this function is MOD(*dividend,divisor*), where *dividend* is the value you want to divide, and *divisor* is the value by which you want to divide it. The result of this function is the remainder of the division.

The MOD() function

Figure 10-1

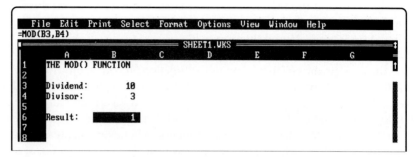

This spreadsheet contains an example of the MOD() function.

The spreadsheet shown in Figure 10-1 contains an example of the MOD() function. As you can see, cell B3 contains the value 10, and cell B4 contains the value 3. Cell B6 contains the function *=MOD(B3,B4)*. Since 3 goes into 10 three times with 1 left over, this function returns the value 1. If cell B4 had contained the value 4, this function would have returned the value 2; if that cell had contained the value 5, it would have returned the value 0.

The RAND() function

The RAND() function lets you generate random numbers for use in a Works spreadsheet. This function returns a random value greater than or equal to 0, but less than 1, accurate to 15 digits to the right of the decimal point. The form of this function is simply RAND(); it does not accept any arguments.

Each time you recalculate a RAND() function, it returns a different value. When you first enter a RAND() function into a cell, for example, it might return the value .209581984377849. Each time Works recalculates this function (as it will whenever you make a change to a spreadsheet set for automatic recalculation, press [Recalc], or choose the Calculate Now command from the Options menu), it will return a different value. For example, the RAND() function might return .803867610457928 after the first recalculation, .402933293306887 after the second recalculation, and so forth.

Although Works' RAND() function returns a value between 0 and 1, you can use it to generate random values in other ranges. To do this, you simply multiply the result of the function by another value. To generate a random value between 0 and 10, for example, you would use the formula *=RAND()*10*. To generate a random value between 0 and 100, you would use the formula *=RAND()*100*, and so forth.

The SQRT() function

Works' SQRT() function calculates the square root of a value; that is, the value that, when multiplied by itself, returns the original value. The form of the SQRT() function is SQRT(*value*), where *value* is a reference to the value whose square root you want Works to calculate.

Figure 10-2

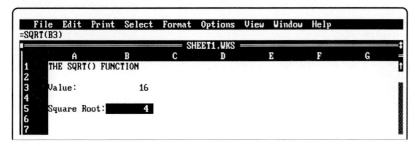

This spreadsheet contains an example of the SQRT() function.

Figure 10-2 shows an example of the use of the SQRT() function. As you can see, cell B5 contains the function =*SQRT(B3)*. Since B3 contains the value 16, this function returns the value 4—the square root of that value.

Works' ROUND() function makes it easy to round any value to a specified number of decimal places. The form of this function is ROUND(*value,decimals*), where *value* is a reference to the value you want to round and *decimals* specifies the number of digits you want to appear to the right of the decimal point. The ROUND() function follows the traditional rules for rounding. If it encounters a digit less than 5, it does not alter the digit to the left of that digit. If it encounters a digit of 5 or greater, it increases the digit to the left of that digit by 1. For example, rounding the value 1.234 to two decimal places produces the value 1.23; but rounding the value 1.235 to two decimal places produces the value 1.24.

The ROUND() function

Cells C5 through C9 in Figure 10-3 on the following page contain some basic examples of the ROUND() function. Cells A5:A9 of this spreadsheet contain the value 123.456. Since cell B5 contains the value 2, the function =*ROUND(A5,B5)* in cell C5 returns the value 123.46. Since cell B6 contains the value 1, the function =*ROUND(A6,B6)* in cell C6 returns the value 123.5. Similarly, since cell B7 contains the value 0, the function =*ROUND(A7,B7)* in cell C7 returns the value 123.

Although the decimals argument of most ROUND() functions will be a positive number, it can be a negative number. A negative decimals argument instructs Works to round to the left of the decimal point. For example, since cell B8 contains the value -1, the function =*ROUND(A8,B8)* in cell C8 returns the value 120. Similarly, since cell B9 contains the value -2, the function =*ROUND(A9,B9)* in cell C9 returns the value 100.

You can also use ROUND() to round negative numbers. Since rounding a number up always means rounding away from zero, rounding a negative value produces a larger negative value. For example, the function =*ROUND(-123.45,1)* would return the value -123.5.

Figure 10-3

```
  File  Edit  Print  Select  Format  Options  View  Window  Help
=ROUND(A5,B5)
                              SHEET1.WKS
        A           B          C         D        E       F       G
 1  THE ROUND() FUNCTION
 2
 3        Value  Decimals     Result
 4
 5      123.456         2    123.46
 6      123.456         1    123.5
 7      123.456         0    123
 8      123.456        -1    120
 9      123.456        -2    100
10
11
```

This spreadsheet contains several examples of the ROUND() function.

The INT() function

Works' INT() function truncates the value you specify to integer form; that is, to a value with no decimal and no digits to the right of the decimal point. The form of this function is INT(*value*), where *value* is the value that Works will convert to an integer.

Figure 10-4

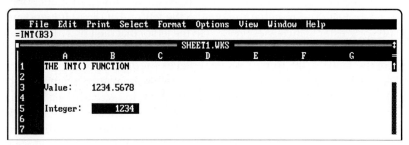

```
  File  Edit  Print  Select  Format  Options  View  Window  Help
=INT(B3)
                              SHEET1.WKS
        A           B          C         D        E       F       G
 1  THE INT() FUNCTION
 2
 3  Value:     1234.5678
 4
 5  Integer:      1234
 6
 7
```

This spreadsheet contains an example of the INT() function.

Figure 10-4 contains an example of the INT() function. As you can see, cell B5 of this spreadsheet contains the function *=INT(B3)*. Since cell B3 contains the value 1234.5678, this function returns the value 1234.

It is important to note that the INT() function does not round values like the ROUND() function does. The function *=INT(B3)* returns the value 1234; the function *=ROUND(B3,0)* would return the value 1235.

In addition to its mathematical functions, Works features a group of three logarithmic functions. These functions—LOG(), LN(), and EXP()—allow you to work with base 10 and natural logarithms. These functions are of interest primarily to scientists and engineers.

LOGARITHMIC FUNCTIONS

The LOG() function calculates the base 10 logarithm of a specified value. A value's base 10 log is the power of 10 that equals that value. For example, since $10^2=100$, the base 10 log of 100 is 2. The form of the LOG() function is LOG(*value*), where *value* is the value whose base 10 log you want to calculate.

The LOG() function

Figure 10-5

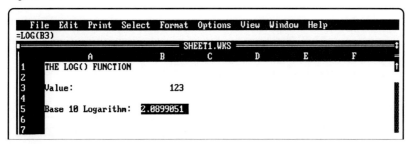

This spreadsheet contains an example of the LOG() function.

Figure 10-5 contains an example of the LOG() function. As you can see, cell B5 of this spreadsheet contains the function *=LOG(B3)*. Since cell B3 contains the value 123, this function returns the value 2.0899051—the base 10 logarithm of 123.

To calculate a value from a base 10 logarithm, you simply raise 10 to that power. For example, you would use the formula *=10^B5* to calculate the value whose base 10 logarithm is calculated in cell B5 of our example spreadsheet. As you would expect, this formula returns the value 123.

The LN() function calculates the natural, or "base e", logarithm of a value. The natural logarithm of a value is the power of the constant e (approximately 2.71828) that produces that value. The form of this function is LN(*value*), where *value* is the value whose natural logarithm you want to calculate.

The LN() function

Figure 10-6 on the next page contains an example of the LN() function. As you can see, cell B5 of this spreadsheet contains the function *=LN(B3)*. Since cell B3 contains the value 123, this function returns the value 4.8121844—the base e logarithm of 123.

The EXP() function makes it easy to calculate a value from its natural logarithm. The form of this function is EXP(*natural log*), where the single argument is the natural logarithm of the value you want the function to return.

The EXP() function

Figure 10-6

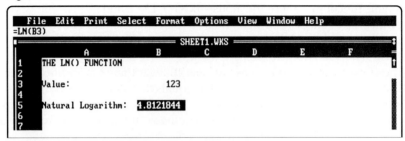

The LN() function calculates the natural logarithm of a value.

Cell B7 of the spreadsheet shown in Figure 10-7 contains an example of the EXP() function. This function, *=EXP(B5)*, acts upon the value in cell B5 (4.8121844)—the natural logarithm of the value in cell B3 (123). As you can see, this function returns the value 123—the original value.

Figure 10-7

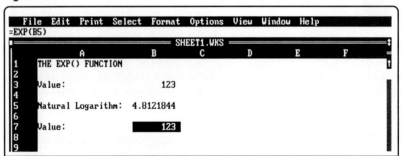

This spreadsheet contains an example of the EXP() function.

You can calculate the exponential of a value by raising e (approximately 2.71828) to that value. For example, you could use the formula 2.71828^B5 to calculate the exponential of the value in cell B5. Since the exact value of e is hard to remember, however, you probably will want to use the EXP() function instead.

TRIG FUNCTIONS

Works features eight trigonometric functions. These functions—PI(), SIN(), COS(), TAN(), ASIN(), ACOS(), ATAN(), and ATAN2()—allow you to compute common trigonometric values.

The PI() function

Works' PI() function does not perform a calculation. Instead, it returns the value of π—a common trigonometric constant. The form of this function is simply

PI()—it accepts no arguments. When you enter this function into a spreadsheet, Works returns the value 3.1415926536—the value of the constant π, accurate to ten digits to the right of the decimal point.

The SIN(), COS(), and TAN() functions

Works' SIN(), COS(), and TAN() functions compute the sine, cosine, and tangent, respectively, of the angle specified by their arguments. The forms of these functions are: SIN(*angle*), COS(*angle*), and TAN(*angle*), where *angle* is the measure, in radians, of the angle whose sine, cosine, or tangent you want Works to calculate. The measure of an angle in radians is equal to the measure of that angle in degrees, multiplied by $\pi/180$ (approximately .0175). For example, 30 degrees is equal to .5235988 radians.

Figure 10-8

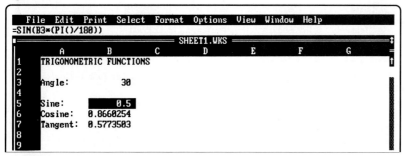

This spreadsheet contains examples of the SIN(), COS(), and TAN() functions.

The Works spreadsheet shown in Figure 10-8 contains examples of these functions. As you can see, cell B3 contains the value 30—the measure in degrees of a 30-degree angle. Cells B5, B6, and B7 contain the functions *=SIN(B3*(PI()/ 180))*, *=COS(B3*(PI()/180))*, and *=TAN(B3*(PI()/180))*, respectively.

The argument of each of these functions, *B3*(PI()/180)*, converts the measurement of the angle in cell B3 to radians. Since cell B3 contains the value 30, these arguments return the value .5235988 (radians). The functions in cells B5, B6, and B7 use this result to return the values .5, .8660254, and .5773503, respectively—the sine, cosine, and tangent of a 30-degree angle.

The inverse trigonometric functions

To complement the SIN(), COS(), and TAN() functions, Works features four functions that perform the opposite tasks: They return an angle, given its sine, cosine, or tangent. These functions are ASIN(), ACOS(), ATAN(), and ATAN2().

The ASIN(), ACOS(), and ATAN() functions

Works' ASIN(), ACOS(), and ATAN() functions return the measure, in radians, of the angle whose sine, cosine, and tangent are specified by their arguments. The forms of these functions are ASIN(*sine*), ACOS(*cosine*), and ATAN(*tangent*). The single argument of each of these functions is the sine, cosine, or tangent, respectively, of the angle whose radian measure you want to calculate.

Figure 10-9

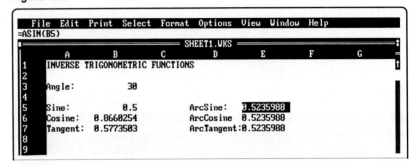

This spreadsheet contains examples of the ASIN(), ACOS(), and ATAN() functions.

The spreadsheet shown in Figure 10-9 contains an example of each of these functions. The function *=ASIN(B5)* in cell E5 returns the value .5235988—the radian measure of the angle whose sine is calculated by the SIN() function in cell B5. The function *=ACOS(B6)* in cell E6 and the function *=ATAN(B7)* in cell E7 return this same value.

The ATAN2() function

Works' ATAN2() function computes a four-quadrant arctangent. Like Works' other three arc functions, this function returns the radian measure of an angle. The form of this function is ATAN2(x,y). Unlike the ASIN(), ACOS(), and ATAN() functions, however, the ATAN2() function requires two arguments. These arguments specify the absolute position of a point in relation to the x- and y-axes, respectively. For example, to measure the four-quadrant arctangent defined by a point with an x-coordinate of 3 and a y-coordinate of -3, you would use the function *=ATAN2(3,-3)*, which returns the value -.785398.

STATISTICAL FUNCTIONS

Works features seven statistical functions: SUM(), COUNT(), AVG(), MAX(), MIN(), STD(), and VAR(). These functions offer an easy way to calculate statistics, such as the sum, average, and standard deviation of a group of values.

The form of statistical functions

Works' statistical functions calculate statistics about the information in two or more cells in a spreadsheet. If the cells on which you want the function to operate are adjacent in the spreadsheet, you can use a single argument that specifies the dimensions of that range. To compute the sum of the values in cells A1, A2, and A3 of a spreadsheet, for example, you could use the function *=SUM(A1:A3)*. To compute the average of those values, you could use the function *=AVG(A1:A3)*. You'll use this form of statistical functions most often.

If you want, you can list those cells that you want a statistical function to act upon as separate arguments in the statistical function. For example, you can use the function *=SUM(A1,A2,A3)* instead of the function *=SUM(A1:A3)* to compute the sum of the values in cells A1, A2, and A3. In most cases, you will use this form of Works' statistical functions to compute statistics about the values in a discontinuous range. For example, you'd use the function *=SUM(A1,B10,C20)* to add the values in cells A1, B10, and C20.

You can even use a mixture of range references and cell references as the arguments of a statistical function. For example, *=SUM(A1:A2,A3)* and *=SUM(A1,A2:A3)* return the same result as *=SUM(A1:A3)*.

Works' SUM() function calculates the sum (that is, the total) of a group of values. When you want to add a range of adjacent values, the SUM() function is more efficient than a formula that uses multiple + operators. For example, suppose you want to add the values in cells B5, B6, B7, B8, B9, B10, B11, B12, B13, and B14 of the spreadsheet shown in Figure 10-10. To do this, you can use the function *=SUM(B5:B14)*, as we have in cell E5. Alternatively, you could use the formula *=B5+B6+B7+B8+B9+B10+B11+B12+B13+B14*. Both the formula and the function return the value 801—the sum of the values in cells B5 through B14. However, the SUM() function is 23 characters shorter than the + formula.

Besides efficiency, the SUM() function has another significant advantage over the + operator—the way it responds to the deletion and insertion of rows and columns. If you delete a row or column that contains a cell referenced by a + operator, that reference will change to the value ERR, and the formula will return the value ERR. If you delete a row or column that contains a cell within the boundaries of a SUM() range, however, Works will contract that range and return the adjusted result of the function. Of course, the SUM() function will return an ERR result if you delete a row or column that contains one of the two "anchor" cells of the SUM() range. For a thorough explanation of this effect, see the section entitled "Deleting Columns and Rows" in Chapter 9.

Like all of Works' functions, the SUM() function assigns the value 0 to both blank cells and cells that contain text entries. For this reason, including blank cells or label-containing cells in the SUM() range has no adverse effect on the outcome of the function.

The SUM() function

Works' COUNT() function counts the number of non-blank cells specified by its argument(s). When Works evaluates a COUNT() function, it assigns the value 1 to each occupied cell (any cell that contains either a value, function, formula,

The COUNT() function

or label) and assigns the value 0 to each empty cell (any cell that does not contain an entry). The sum of these values is the result of the function.

Cell E6 of the spreadsheet shown in Figure 10-10 contains an example of the use of a COUNT() function. This function, *=COUNT(B5:B14)*, counts the non-blank cells in the range B5:B14. Since all the cells in this range contain an entry, this function returns the value 10.

Figure 10-10

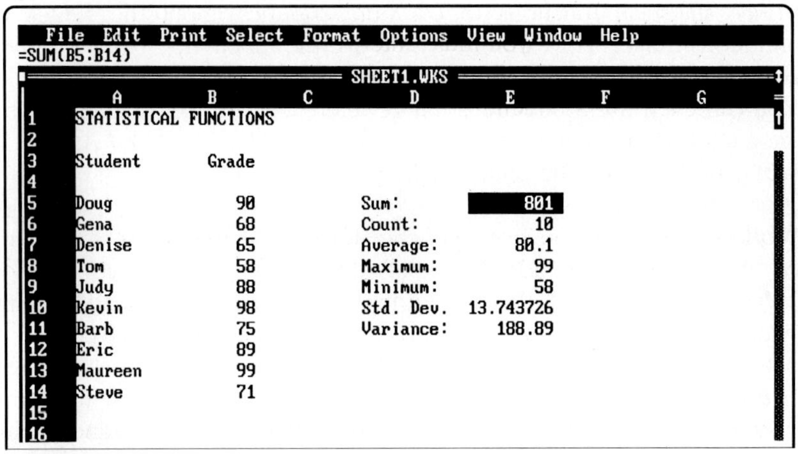

```
  File  Edit  Print  Select  Format  Options  View  Window  Help
=SUM(B5:B14)
                                  ══════ SHEET1.WKS ══════
       A          B         C        D         E       F        G
  1  STATISTICAL FUNCTIONS
  2
  3  Student      Grade
  4
  5  Doug          90              Sum:           801
  6  Gena          68              Count:          10
  7  Denise        65              Average:      80.1
  8  Tom           58              Maximum:        99
  9  Judy          88              Minimum:        58
 10  Kevin         98              Std. Dev.  13.743726
 11  Barb          75              Variance:    188.89
 12  Eric          89
 13  Maureen       99
 14  Steve         71
 15
 16
```

This spreadsheet contains examples of Works' statistical functions.

Since the COUNT() function counts only occupied cells, blank cells in the COUNT() range affect the count. To demonstrate this effect, suppose that cell B9 of the spreadsheet shown in Figure 10-10 was empty. Because only cells B5:B8 and B10:B14 would contain entries, the COUNT() function in cell E6 would return the value 9.

Works' COUNT() function does exhibit one strange behavior—it assigns the value 1 to any cell that it refers to individually, whether that cell is occupied or not. For example, suppose you used the function *=COUNT(B5,B6,B7, B8,B9,B10,B11,B12,B13,B14)* instead of the function *=COUNT(B5:B14)* to count the entries in cells B5:B14 of the spreadsheet in Figure 10-10. Even if one or more of the cells referenced by the COUNT() function were blank, the function would return the value 10.

The AVG() function

Works' AVG() function computes the average (arithmetic mean) of a group of values. The arithmetic mean of a group of values is simply the sum of those values divided by the count of those values. Consequently, the result of an AVG() function is the same as that of dividing the result of a SUM() function by the result of a COUNT() function.

Cell E7 of the spreadsheet shown in Figure 10-10 contains an example of the AVG() function. This function, =AVG(B5:B14), calculates the mean of the values in cells B5 through B14. Since there are ten entries in this range, and the sum of those entries is 801, this function returns the value 80.1.

Like the COUNT() function, the AVG() function does not count empty cells. For example, if cell B9 of the spreadsheet shown in Figure 10-10 had been blank, the AVG() function in cell E7 would have returned the value 79.222222 (713/9). This is the correct result if the student named Judy had been excused from the test. If you want a blank cell to be included in the count (as you would if Judy missed the test without an excuse), you must enter a 0 into it. Since Works assigns the value 0 to blank cells anyway, this entry does not alter the sum. However, it does increase the count. Consequently, the AVG() function will return a lower value than it would if you had left the cell blank. If cell B9 had contained the value 0, the AVG function in cell E7 would have returned the value 71.3 (713/10).

The MAX() and MIN() functions

Works' MAX() and MIN() functions return the highest and lowest values, respectively, from the values specified by their arguments. Cells E8 and E9 of the spreadsheet shown in Figure 10-10 contain examples of these functions. The function =MAX(B5:B14) in cell E8 returns the value 99—the highest value in this ten-cell range. The function in cell E9, =MIN(B5:B14), returns the value 58—the lowest value in the range.

Unfortunately, Works does not point out the location of the cell that contains the value returned by a MAX() or MIN() function. If you want to locate the source of the value, you must track it down yourself. In this case, the maximum value (99) comes from cell B13, and the minimum value (58) comes from cell B8.

When Works evaluates a MAX() or MIN() function, it assigns the value 0 to any cell that contains a text entry. Consequently, any MIN() function that acts upon a range that contains a text entry will return the value 0 unless that range also contains a negative value. Like other statistical functions, the MAX() and MIN() functions ignore blank cells.

The STD() and VAR() functions

Works' final two statistical functions—STD() and VAR()—compute the standard deviation and the variance, respectively, of the values specified by their arguments. Both the standard deviation and the variance measure the dispersion of the values in the specified range.

The STD() function

The STD() function computes the standard deviation of the values in a range. The standard deviation of a group of values is a measure of the extent to which the values in that range are dispersed from the mean for that range. About 68% of the individuals in a normally distributed group will be within one standard deviation from the mean, and about 95% will be within two standard deviations from the mean. A low standard deviation indicates that values in the range are clustered closely around the mean. A high standard deviation means that the values are widely dispersed.

Cell E10 of the spreadsheet shown in Figure 10-10 contains an example of the STD() function. This function, *=STD(B5:B14)*, returns the value 13.743726—the standard deviation of the values in the ten-cell range B5:B14.

The VAR() function

Works' VAR() function calculates the variance of a range of values. The statistical variance is simply the square of the standard deviation. To calculate the variance of the values in the range B5:B14, then, you could use the function *=VAR(B5:B14)*, as we have in cell E11 of the spreadsheet shown in Figure 10-10. Alternatively, you could use the formula *=STD(B5:B14)^2*. Both functions return the value 188.89.

FINANCIAL FUNCTIONS

Works' financial functions allow you to perform sophisticated financial computations, such as calculating the monthly payment on a mortgage, without developing long, complex formulas. Works offers 11 financial functions: PV(), NPV(), IRR(), PMT(), FV(), TERM(), CTERM(), RATE(), SLN(), DDB(), and SYD(). For purposes of explanation, we'll divide these functions into three groups: functions that analyze multiple cash flow investments, functions that analyze single cash flow investments, and functions that calculate depreciation.

Multiple cash flow financial functions

Works' PV(), NPV(), IRR(), PMT(), FV(), and TERM() functions analyze investments that consist of a series of equally spaced cash flows. These types of investments are called annuities. Although the cash flows in an annuity may be of the same or different amounts, they must occur at consistent increments of time. Examples of annuities include bonds, which produce periodic cash inflows in exchange for a single cash outflow (the amount required to purchase the bond) and most consumer loans, like auto loans and home mortgages, which involve periodic payments in exchange for a single cash inflow (the amount borrowed).

The PV() function

Works' most-used financial function, PV(), calculates the present value of a stream of equally spaced constant cash flows. The form of this function is PV(*payment amount, rate, term*), where *payment amount* specifies the amount of each of the equal payments generated by the annuity, *rate* specifies the periodic rate of interest, and *term* specifies the number of cash flows. The rate argument must be based on the term argument. For example, if the term argument specifies a number of months, the rate argument must specify a monthly rate.

An example. As an example of the use of the PV() function, suppose you want to determine the present value of an investment that will pay you five equal yearly payments of $1,000 beginning one year from today. Let's assume that 10% per year is the best rate you can earn elsewhere. The spreadsheet shown in Figure 10-11 solves this problem. As you can see, cell B3 contains the value 1000 (the amount of each payment), cell B4 contains the value .10 (the periodic rate of interest), and cell B5 contains the value 5 (the number of periods). The function =PV(B3,B4,B5) in cell B7 uses the values in these cells to calculate the present value of this investment. The result of this function—3790.79—indicates that you shouldn't pay more than $3,790.79 for this investment opportunity.

Figure 10-11

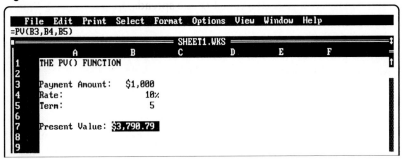

This spreadsheet contains an example of the PV() function.

Timing assumptions. Works' PV() function assumes that the first cash flow of the specified annuity occurs one period from the current date. This is the correct assumption for an ordinary annuity, like the one described above. In some situations, however, the first cash flow of an investment occurs on the date of the analysis, not one year from that date. The payments you make to a set-contribution savings plan (for example, an IRA) exemplify this type of investment.

Although the PV() function does not automatically calculate the present value of this sort of annuity, you can modify it to adjust for this alternative timing assumption. For example, suppose that the cash flow, rate, and term in cells B3, B4, and B5 of the spreadsheet shown in Figure 10-11 describe an investment that will generate five annual payments of $1,000—one today, one a year from today, one two years from today, one three years from today, and one four years from today. To calculate the present value of this opportunity, you would use the formula =PV(B3,B4,B5-1)+B3. This formula calculates the present value over four years instead of five years, and then adds the first year's payment to the result. In other words, this adjusted PV() formula does not discount the first year's payment of $1,000, since that payment occurs today instead of one year in the future. This formula returns the value 4169.87. As you can see, moving each cash flow ahead one period increases the present value of the investment by some $379.

The NPV() function

Like its PV() function, Works' NPV() function calculates the present value of a series of equally spaced cash flows. Unlike the PV() function, however, the NPV() function can compute the present value of a stream of unequal cash flows. The form of the NPV() function is *NPV(rate,range of cash flows)*, where *rate* is the periodic rate of interest and *range of cash flows* is a range that contains the cash flows that occur at each period during the term of the investment. The *range of cash flows* argument must be in the form of a range, such as B5:B8. Unlike Works' statistical functions, the NPV() function will not accept a series of references to single cells.

Because the NPV() function can analyze a stream of unequal cash flows, you can include negative flows in the range of the spreadsheet referred to by the *range of cash flows* argument. Typically, the first cash flow in a net present value analysis—the cash flow required to purchase the investment—will be negative. However, you also can use the NPV() function to calculate the simple present value of a stream of uneven positive cash flows.

An example.   As an example of the use of the NPV() function, suppose that you want to calculate the net present value of the stream of cash flows contained in cells B5 through B8 of the spreadsheet shown in Figure 10-12 at a periodic rate of 12% (the rate returned by an alternative investment). To do this, you would use the function *=NPV(B3,B5:B8)*, as we have in cell B10. The fact that the result of this function is positive (in this case, $277.94) indicates that this investment is a better opportunity than the best available alternative; that is, that its rate of return is better than 12%.

Figure 10-12

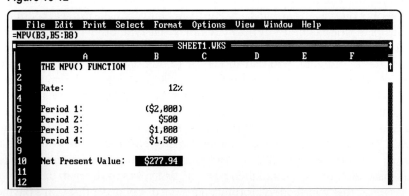

This spreadsheet contains an example of the NPV() function.

Timing assumptions.   Like the PV() function, Works' NPV() function assumes that the first cash flow occurs one period from the date of the analysis, the second cash flow occurs two periods from the date of the analysis, and so forth. When Works evaluates the function in cell B10, then, it assumes that the $2,000 outflow occurs not on the date of the analysis, but one year after the date of the analysis. Similarly, the first inflow ($1,000) occurs two years from the date of the analysis, the second inflow occurs three years from the date of the analysis, and the third inflow occurs four years from the date of the analysis.

To calculate a net present value that assumes that cash flows occur at the beginning of each period, you must adjust Works' basic NPV() formula. Specifically, you should use the NPV() function to calculate the present value of the second through last cash flows, then add the initial flow to the result. To calculate the correct net present value of the cash flows in cells B5 through B8 using the rate contained in B3, you would use the formula *=NPV(B3,B6:B8)+B5*. This formula returns the value 311.29—approximately $33 more than the result of the original calculation.

Works' IRR() function calculates the internal rate of return of an investment. The internal rate of return is the rate of return implied by the cost of an investment and its stream of cash flows. The concepts of internal rate of return and net present value are closely related. Specifically, the internal rate of return is the rate of interest at which the net present value of an investment is zero. Another way to say this is that an investment's internal rate of return is the rate that makes the present value of the cash inflows from that investment exactly equal to the initial cash outflow.

The IRR() function

You can determine the attractiveness of an investment by comparing the internal rate of return on that investment to the best alternative rate. Assuming equal risk, the alternative with the higher rate of return is the better investment.

The form of the IRR() function is IRR(*rate guess, range of cash flows*). The *rate guess* argument must be an approximation of the internal rate of return. Works uses this guess as the starting point of its iterative process of calculating the internal rate of return. The *range of cash flows* argument must be the range of the spreadsheet that contains the cash flows you want to analyze. The first value in this range must be negative, indicating a negative cash flow or investment.

An example.   Cell B10 of the spreadsheet shown in Figure 10-13 on the following page contains an example of this function.   The function in this cell, *=IRR(B3,B5:B8)*, calculates the internal rate of return implied by the cash flows in cells B5:B8. The result, .1943771, indicates that the implied rate of return for the stream of cash flows in the range B5:B8 is approximately 19%.

When Works calculates an IRR() function, it works in much the same way you would if you had to do the calculation by hand. It begins by calculating the net present value of the stream, using your guess as the discount rate. If the result is higher than 0, Works chooses a higher rate and recalculates the NPV. If the result is lower than 0, Works chooses a lower rate and recalculates the NPV. Works continues this iterative process until it pinpoints the rate that produces an NPV of 0. If Works is able to produce an NPV of less than .0000001 within 20 iterations, it returns the rate that produces that NPV as the internal rate of return. If Works is not able to achieve this result within 20 tries, it returns the value ERR. When this happens, you should specify a different guess and calculate the function again. (Fortunately, this problem rarely arises.)

Figure 10-13

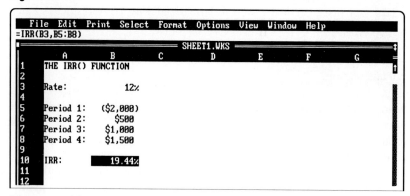

This spreadsheet contains an example of the IRR() function.

Timing assumptions. The IRR() function calculates the internal rate of return as if the first cash flow occurred one year from the date of the analysis, and each subsequent cash flow occurred in one-year increments from that point. However, this assumption makes no difference in the outcome of the analysis. The result of an internal rate of return calculation would be the same no matter what timing assumption was used.

The PMT() function

Works' PMT() function calculates the periodic payment required to amortize (pay off) a loan. The form of this function is PMT(*amount borrowed,interest rate,term*), where *amount borrowed* is the amount borrowed, *interest rate* is the periodic interest rate, and *term* is the number of periods over which you will pay off the loan.

An example. As an example of the use of the PMT() function, suppose you want to calculate the monthly payments on a 30-year, 11.5% APR, $100,000 mortgage. The spreadsheet shown in Figure 10-14 is set up for this calculation. Cell B3 contains the value 100000 (the amount borrowed); cell B4 contains the value .115 (the annual rate); and cell B5 contains the value 30 (the term of the loan, in years). The function =PMT(B3,B4/12,B5*12) in cell B7 uses these values to calculate the monthly mortgage payments: $990.29. Because the payments occur on a monthly basis, we divided the annual rate by 12 to produce a monthly rate of interest. We multiplied the term of the loan in years by 12 for the same reason.

Figure 10-14

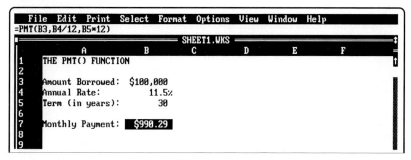

This spreadsheet contains an example of the PMT() function.

Timing assumptions.   Like all of Works' financial functions, the PMT() function assumes that the payments required to amortize the principal amount start one period from the date of the analysis and occur at the end of each period thereafter. This assumption is correct for most installment loans, such as auto loans and home mortgages. In some cases, however, you may be required to make the first payment immediately.

To correct for this alternative timing assumption, you must adjust the result of the PMT() function by dividing it by the sum of 1 plus the periodic interest rate. In this case, then, you would use the formula *=PMT(B3,B4/12,B5*12)/(1+B4/12)*. The result of this formula—$980.89—is $9.40 less than the result of the unadjusted PMT() function.

The FV() function

Works' FV() function calculates the future value of an annuity—a series of equal, evenly spaced cash flows. The future value of an investment is its value at some specified future date, including all of the interest it has earned up to that time. The form of the FV() function is FV(*payments,rate,term*), where *payments* specifies the amount of each of the equal cash flows, *rate* specifies the rate of interest you can earn on the investment, and *term* specifies the number of cash flows that will occur.

An example.   As an example of the use of this function, suppose that you want to calculate the future value of contributing $2,000 to an IRA each year for 30 years, given a 7.5% annual rate of interest. We have set up the spreadsheet shown in Figure 10-15 to perform this calculation. As you can see, cell B3 contains the value 2000—the amount of each contribution to the IRA. Cell B4 contains the value

.075—the annual interest rate. Cell B5 contains the value 30—the term of the investment. The function in cell B7, *=FV(B3,B4,B5)*, calculates the future value of this investment: $206,798.81.

Figure 10-15

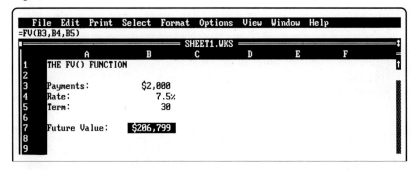

```
    File  Edit  Print  Select  Format  Options  View  Window  Help
=FV(B3,B4,B5)
================================== SHEET1.WKS ==================================
            A              B          C          D        E        F
1   THE FV() FUNCTION
2
3   Payments:          $2,000
4   Rate:                7.5%
5   Term:                  30
6
7   Future Value:    $206,799
8
9
```

This spreadsheet contains an example of the FV() function.

Timing assumptions.   Like Works' other financial functions, the FV() function assumes that the first cash flow in the investment being analyzed occurs one period in the future—not on the date of the analysis. When Works evaluates the function in cell B7, for example, it assumes that the first contribution of $2,000 occurs not at the time of the analysis, but rather one year from that point.

Unfortunately, this is not the assumption you are likely to want to use when performing future value analysis. However, it is relatively easy to adjust this function to match the up-front timing assumption. To do this, just calculate the future value over one more period than you normally would, and then subtract an undiscounted payment from that result. In this case, you would use the formula *=FV(B3,B4,B5+1)-B3*. This formula returns $222,308.72—$15,509.91 more than the result of the unadjusted function.

The TERM() function

Works' final multiple-cash flow financial function, TERM(), calculates the number of periods required for a stream of equal, evenly spaced investments to compound to a target amount, given a constant rate of interest. The form of this function is TERM(*payments,rate,target value*), where *payments* specifies the amount of each equal periodic investment, *rate* specifies the periodic rate of interest, and *target value* specifies the amount of money you want to have at some point in the future.

As you can see, the TERM() function is closely related to the FV() function. Whereas the FV() function solves for a future value, given a rate of interest, a number of periods, and the amount of each payment, the TERM() function solves for the number of periods, given a rate of interest, the amount of each payment, and a future value.

An example. As an example of the use of this function, suppose you want to determine how many years it would take for contributions of $2,000 per year to an IRA to grow to $500,000, given a 7.5% rate of interest. We have set up the spreadsheet shown in Figure 10-16 to solve this problem. In cell B3, we have entered the amount to be invested each period: 2000. In cell B4, we have entered the annual rate: .075. Cell B5 contains the value 500000—the target value. In cell B7, we have entered the function *=TERM(B3,B4,B5)*, which returns the value 41.25. This value indicates that it will take a little over 41 years for annual contributions of $2,000 to compound to a value of half a million dollars at a rate of 7.5% per year.

Figure 10-16

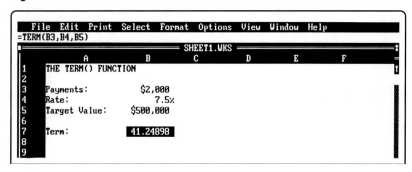

```
 File  Edit  Print  Select  Format  Options  View  Window  Help
=TERM(B3,B4,B5)
========================== SHEET1.WKS ==========================
         A              B         C        D        E        F
1  THE TERM() FUNCTION
2
3  Payments:         $2,000
4  Rate:              7.5%
5  Target Value:   $500,000
6
7  Term:           41.24898
8
9
```

This spreadsheet contains an example of the TERM() function.

Timing assumptions. Like Works' other financial functions, the TERM() function assumes that the cash flows being analyzed occur at the end of each period and that the first cash flow occurs at the end of the first period. Consequently, the TERM() function in cell B7 returns a value that is higher than it would be if it assumed that the first cash flow occurred on the date of the analysis.

To modify the TERM() function to fit this assumption, just divide the result of the function by the sum of 1 plus the periodic rate. For example, the formula *=TERM(B3,B4,B5)/(1+B4)* would calculate the number of periods required for our example investment to grow to $500,000, assuming that the first contribution occurs on the day of the analysis. This formula returns the value 38.37—about three years less than the result returned by the ordinary TERM() function.

The six financial functions that we have discussed so far analyze annuities— investments that involve series of cash flows. Works features two other financial functions—CTERM() and RATE()—that analyze investments that involve only a single cash flow. Investments of this type include the purchase of stock that is not expected to pay dividends or the purchase of a work of art. In either of these cases,

Single cash flow financial functions

you would invest a lump sum of money at one time and withdraw it at another. Unlike most of Works' other financial functions, the CTERM() and RATE() functions are not affected by timing considerations.

The CTERM() function

Works' CTERM() function calculates the number of periods required for a single lump-sum investment to compound to a target value, given a fixed rate of interest. The form of this function is CTERM(*rate,target amount,amount invested*), where *rate* specifies the fixed periodic rate of interest, *target amount* specifies the desired future value of the investment, and *amount invested* specifies the lump sum invested.

Figure 10-17

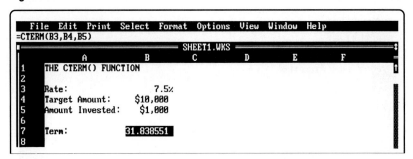

This spreadsheet contains an example of the CTERM() function.

To demonstrate the use of this function, suppose you want to determine how many years it will take for $1,000, invested at 7.5% per year, to grow to a value of $10,000. We have set up this problem in the spreadsheet shown in Figure 10-17. As you can see, cell B3 contains the value .075—the fixed rate of return. Cell B4 contains the value 10000—the target amount. Cell B5 contains the value 1000—the lump sum invested. The function =*CTERM(B3,B4,B5)* in cell B7 uses the values in these cells to compute the result 31.84—the number of years required for the initial amount to grow to the target.

The RATE() function

Works' RATE() function calculates the periodic rate of interest required to compound a lump-sum investment to a target amount over a fixed number of periods. The form of this function is RATE(*target amount, amount invested,term*), where *target amount* specifies the desired future value of the investment, *amount invested* specifies the lump sum invested, and *term* specifies the number of periods over which the investment will compound.

As an example of the use of the RATE() function, suppose you want to know the rate of return that would be required to increase an investment of $1,000 to $10,000 in only ten years. We've set up Figure 10-18 to make this computation.

Cell B3 contains the value 10000—the target amount. Cell B4 contains the value 1000—the amount of the initial investment. Cell B5 contains the value 10—the number of periods over which the investment will compound. Cell B7 contains the function =RATE(B3,B4,B5). The result of this function—.2589—indicates that the investment will have to compound at a rate of nearly 26% per year to reach a total value of $10,000 in just ten years.

Figure 10-18

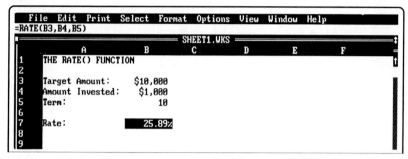

This spreadsheet contains an example of the RATE() function.

Depreciation functions

Works' final group of financial functions provides convenient ways to calculate depreciation. Each of the three functions in this group—SLN(), DDB(), and SYD()—calculates depreciation according to a different method. The SLN() function calculates straight-line depreciation; the DDB() function calculates depreciation by the double-declining balance method; and the SYD() function calculates depreciation by the sum-of-the-years'-digits method.

Unfortunately, the methods of depreciation calculated by these functions have, for the most part, been replaced by the Accelerated Cost Recovery System of depreciation (ACRS). While you can create formulas that compute ACRS depreciation, Works does not offer functions that will make the required computations automatically.

To demonstrate Works' depreciation functions, we'll use the spreadsheet in Figure 10-19 on the next page. Cell B3 of this spreadsheet contains the value 1000—the depreciable value of an asset. Cell B4 contains the value 100—the salvage value of that asset. Cell B5 contains the value 5—the life of the asset.

The SLN() function

Works' SLN() function calculates the straight-line depreciation for an asset. The form of this function is SLN(*cost of asset,salvage value,life of asset*), where *cost of asset* specifies the depreciable value of the asset, *salvage value* specifies the value of the asset at the end of its depreciable life, and *life of asset* specifies the life of the asset.

Figure 10-19

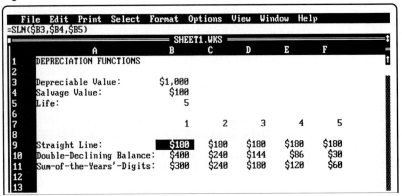

```
     File  Edit  Print  Select  Format  Options  View  Window  Help
=SLN($B3,$B4,$B5)
========================== SHEET1.WKS ===============================
                    A              B      C       D       E       F
1   DEPRECIATION FUNCTIONS
2
3   Depreciable Value:          $1,000
4   Salvage Value:                $100
5   Life:                           5
6
7                                   1      2       3       4       5
8
9   Straight Line:               $180   $180    $180    $180    $180
10  Double-Declining Balance:    $400   $240    $144     $86     $30
11  Sum-of-the-Years'-Digits:    $300   $240    $180    $120     $60
12
13
```

This spreadsheet contains examples of Works' depreciation functions.

Cells B9 through F9 in the spreadsheet shown in Figure 10-19 contain examples of this function. The function in cell B9, =*SLN($B3,$B4,$B5)*, computes the first-year straight-line depreciation for an asset with a $1,000 depreciable value, a $100 salvage value, and a five-year life: $180.00. Since under the straight-line method, the depreciation expense is the same for all periods in the life of the asset, the functions in cells C9 through F9, which compute the depreciation for the second through fifth years in the asset's life, return the same result. (We used mixed references in the formula in cell B9 so that we could copy it into cells C9:F9.)

The DDB() function

Works' DDB() function calculates depreciation using the double-declining balance method. Under this method, the depreciation expense for the first period will be higher than for the second period; the depreciation expense for the second period will be higher than for the third period; and so forth. For this reason, double-declining balance is called an *accelerated* method of depreciation.

Because the double-declining balance method produces a different depreciation expense for each period during the life of an asset, the DDB() function requires an extra argument. The form of this function is DDB(*cost of asset,salvage value,life of asset,current period*). The first three arguments are the same as the three arguments of the SLN() function. The fourth argument, *current period*, specifies the period for which you want to calculate the depreciation.

Cells B10 through F10 in Figure 10-19 contain examples of this function. The function in cell B10, =*DDB($B3,$B4,$B5,B7)*, calculates the first-year double-declining balance depreciation for a $1,000 asset with a $100 salvage value and a five-year life. As you can see, this function returns the value 400.00—significantly greater than the 180.00 returned by the SLN() function in cell B9. The function in cell C10, =*DDB($B3,$B4,$B5,C7)*, computes the second-year depreciation for this asset: 240.00. The functions in cells D10:F10 compute the depreciation for the remaining three years in the life of the asset: 144.00, 86.40, and 29.60, respectively.

The SYD() function

Works' third depreciation function, SYD(), calculates depreciation by the sum-of-the-years'-digits method. Like the double-declining balance method, sum-of-the-years'-digits is an accelerated method of depreciation. Consequently, it requires the same four arguments as the DDB() function. The form of this function is SYD(*cost of asset,salvage value,life of asset,current period*).

Cells B11 through F11 in Figure 10-19 contain examples of the use of the SYD() function. The function in cell B11, =*SYD($B3,$B4,$B5,B7)*, computes the first-year depreciation for a $1,000 asset with a salvage value of $100 and a life of five years. The result, $300.00, indicates that the sum-of-the-years'-digits method does not accelerate depreciation quite as much as the double-declining balance method. The function in cell C11, =*SYD($B3,$B4,$B5,C7)*, computes the second-year depreciation for this asset: 240.00. The functions in cells D11:F11 compute the sum-of-the-years'-digits depreciation for the remaining three years in the life of the asset: 180.00, 120.00, and 60.00, respectively.

LOOKUP FUNCTIONS

Works features four functions that we call lookup functions: CHOOSE(), INDEX(), VLOOKUP(), and HLOOKUP(). These functions "look up" a value from a list or range. Unlike some other Works functions, which make it easier to perform tasks that you could do with a complex formula, these functions let you do things within Works that you simply could not do otherwise.

The CHOOSE() function

Works' simplest lookup function, CHOOSE(), allows you to select a value from a list, based on the position of the result within that list. The form of this function is CHOOSE(*offset,item 1,item 2,item 3,...item n*), where *item 1,item 2,item 3,...item n* is the list of results from which Works will choose, and *offset* specifies the position within that list of the item you want to choose. The items in the list may be literal values, functions or formulas that return values, or references to cells that contain or return values. The individual elements in the list must be separated from one another by commas.

The offset argument also may be a literal value, a formula or function that returns a value, or a reference to a cell that contains or returns a value. This argument must specify a value between 0 and *n*-1, where *n* is the number of items in the list. The offset argument specifies the offset, or position relative to the first item, of the item in the list you want the function to return. The first item in the list has an offset of 0, the second item has an offset of 1, and so on. If you specify an offset of 0, Works will choose the first item from the list; if you specify an offset of 1, Works will choose the second item from the list; and so forth.

Cell B5 of the spreadsheet shown in Figure 10-20 contains an example of the CHOOSE() function. This function, =*CHOOSE(B3,D3,D4,D5,D6,D7)*, returns the value 12345 from cell D6. Since cell B3 (the offset argument) contains the value 3, Works selects the item from the list with an offset of 3. In this case, the argument with an offset of 3 is the cell reference *D6*, so Works returns the value from that cell: 12345.

Figure 10-20

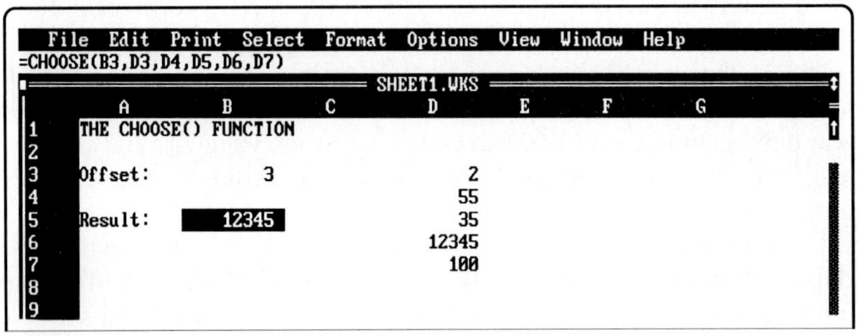

```
    File  Edit  Print  Select  Format  Options  View  Window  Help
=CHOOSE(B3,D3,D4,D5,D6,D7)
                           ===== SHEET1.WKS =====
          A        B        C        D        E      F      G
1    THE CHOOSE() FUNCTION
2
3    Offset:         3                2
4                                    55
5    Result:     12345               35
6                                 12345
7                                   100
8
9
```

This spreadsheet contains an example of the CHOOSE() function.

Although we used cell references as the arguments for the first CHOOSE() example, Works does not require you to do so. For example, the functions *=CHOOSE(3,B3,D3,D4,D5,D6,D7)*, *=CHOOSE(B3,2,55,35,12345,100)*, and *=CHOOSE(3,2,55,35,12345,100)* return the same result as the function in cell B5. You will often use literal values as the arguments of a CHOOSE() function.

The INDEX() function

INDEX() is the second of Works' lookup functions. Unlike the CHOOSE() function, which locates a result from a one-dimensional list based on a single offset argument, the INDEX() function locates a result from a rectangular range of cells, based on both vertical and horizontal offset arguments. The form of this function is INDEX(*range,column offset,row offset*), where *range* specifies the rectangular range of cells from which you want Works to select a result, *column offset* specifies the column of the range that contains the result, and *row offset* specifies the row of the range that contains the result. The column and row offset arguments may be literal values, references to cells that contain or return values, or formulas or functions that return values. These arguments represent the offset, or position relative to the upper-left corner of the range, of the item you want to look up. Works considers the first row and first column in the range to have offsets of 0.

Cell B6 of the spreadsheet in Figure 10-21 contains an example of the INDEX() function. This function, *=INDEX(D2:F6,B3,B4)*, returns the value 777 from cell E4. Since the column offset argument refers to cell B3, and B3 contains the value 1, Works looks in column E—the column with an offset of 1 relative to the first column in the range. Since the row offset argument is a reference to cell B4, which contains the value 2, Works looks in row 4—the row with an offset of 2 relative to the first row. Because cell E4 lies at the intersection of the second column and third row of the index range, Works returns the value 777 from that cell.

Figure 10-21

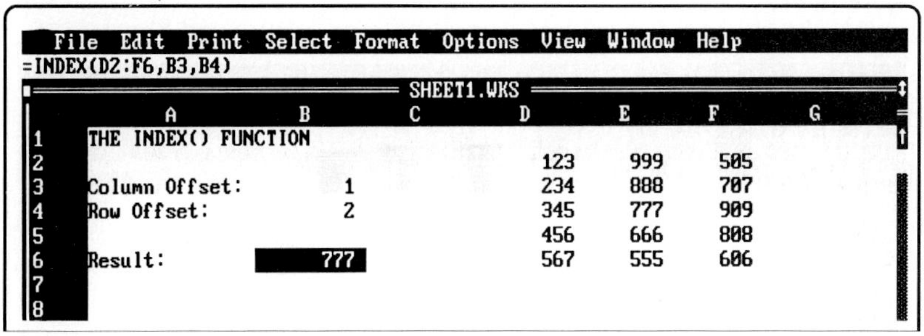

```
 File  Edit  Print  Select  Format  Options  View  Window  Help
=INDEX(D2:F6,B3,B4)
━━━━━━━━━━━━━━━━━━━━━━━━ SHEET1.WKS ━━━━━━━━━━━━━━━━━━━━
        A          B         C       D        E       F       G
1  THE INDEX() FUNCTION
2                                     123     999     505
3  Column Offset:     1                234     888     707
4  Row Offset:        2                345     777     909
5                                      456     666     808
6  Result:          ▐  777  ▌          567     555     606
7
8
```

This spreadsheet contains an example of the INDEX() function.

The VLOOKUP() and HLOOKUP() functions

VLOOKUP() and HLOOKUP() probably are Works' two most commonly used lookup functions. These functions allow you to look up a value from a table based on the match of a key value. Although these functions are very similar, they are easier to understand if tackled one at a time. We'll begin by using the VLOOKUP() function to explain the general principles of table lookups. Then, we'll show you how to use the HLOOKUP() function.

The VLOOKUP() function

Works' VLOOKUP() function looks up a value from a range based on the match of a value in a key column. The form of this function is VLOOKUP(*key value,table range,offset*). The first argument, *key value*, specifies the value Works will look up. The second argument, *table range*, must specify the coordinates of the range that contains the possible results of the function. This table should include at least two partial columns. The entries in the table range must be literal values, or references, formulas, or functions that return values. If the table range includes text entries, they will be assigned the value 0 by the VLOOKUP() function. The final argument, *offset*, specifies the column of the table that contains the function's result.

The VLOOKUP() function works by comparing the key value to the values in the leftmost column of the table range—the "key column." The key value and the entries in the key column must be values.

An example.   Cell B6 in the spreadsheet shown in Figure 10-22 contains an example of a VLOOKUP() function. This function, =*VLOOKUP(B3,D3:F7,B4)*, returns the value 303 from cell E4. Works uses the key value to determine which row of the table contains the function's result. To do this, Works searches the key column for the first value that matches or exceeds the key value. If Works finds a match for the key value, the function's result will be in the row that contains that match. If Works finds a value that exceeds the key value, the function's result will be in the row above the one that contains that value.

Figure 10-22

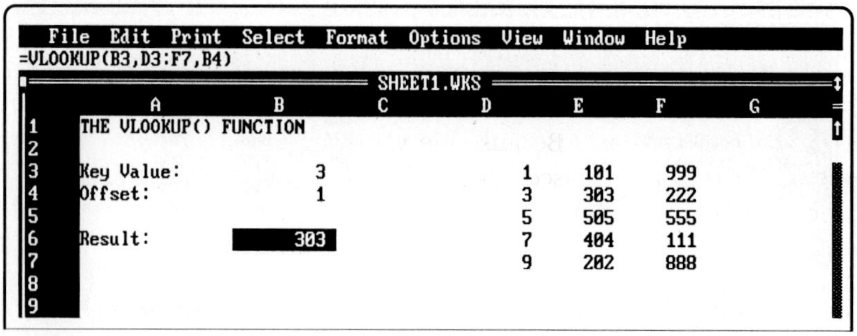

```
    File  Edit  Print  Select  Format  Options  View  Window  Help
=VLOOKUP(B3,D3:F7,B4)
                              SHEET1.WKS
         A          B          C       D       E       F       G
 1  THE VLOOKUP() FUNCTION
 2
 3  Key Value:          3                1     101     999
 4  Offset:             1                3     303     222
 5                                       5     505     555
 6  Result:      [    303]               7     404     111
 7                                       9     202     888
 8
 9
```

This spreadsheet contains an example of the VLOOKUP() function.

In this case, Works begins evaluating the VLOOKUP() function by searching down the index column (cells D3 through D7 in this example) for the first value that meets or exceeds the key value. The key value in this example is a reference to cell B3, which contains the value 3. As you can see, cell D4 (the second cell of the key column) also contains the value 3. Therefore, Works identifies the row that contains that value—row 4—as the row that contains the result of the function.

Once Works has identified the row that contains the result, it uses the offset argument to determine which column contains the result. The first column of the table (the index column) has an offset of 0; the column immediately to the right of this column has an offset of 1; and so on. In this case, the offset of 1 tells Works to look in the second column in the table—column E—for the result. Consequently, Works returns the value from cell E4—303—as the result.

Another example.   It is important that you understand that the VLOOKUP() function does not just look for an exact match between the key value and one of the values in the key column—it looks for the first value that meets or exceeds the key value. In many cases, therefore, the VLOOKUP() function will return a non-ERR result even when the key column does not contain an exact match for the key value. For example, if you replaced the value 3 in cell B3 of the spreadsheet shown in Figure 10-22 with the value 4, the function in cell B6 still would return the value 303 from cell E4. The value in cell D5, 5, is the first index value that meets or exceeds the key value. Since this value exceeds the key value, Works looks for the result of the function in row 4—the row above the one that contains the first value that exceeds the key. Since the offset argument in cell B4, 1, has not changed, the function still returns the entry from cell E4—the value 303.

Rules.   Since the result of a VLOOKUP() function is determined by locating the first value in the index column that is greater than the key value, it is important that the values in the index column be arranged in ascending numeric order. Although Works can evaluate a VLOOKUP() function even if the values in the index column of its table are not in ascending order, the result of that function usually will not be what you expect.

The spreadsheet shown in Figure 10-23 demonstrates such a situation. As you can see, this spreadsheet is set up in much the same way as the one shown in Figure 10-22. In fact, both spreadsheets have the same function in cell B6: =*VLOOKUP(B3,D3:F7,B4)*. Because the values in the key column of the table range are not arranged in ascending order, however, the results of these two functions are not the same.

Figure 10-23

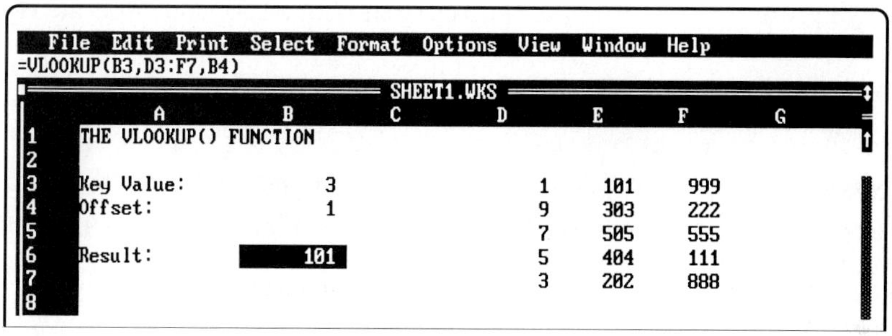

```
    File  Edit  Print  Select  Format  Options  View  Window  Help
=VLOOKUP(B3,D3:F7,B4)
                                    SHEET1.WKS
        A            B        C        D        E      F        G
 1   THE VLOOKUP() FUNCTION
 2
 3   Key Value:       3                 1       101    999
 4   Offset:          1                 9       303    222
 5                                      7       505    555
 6   Result:        101                 5       404    111
 7                                      3       202    888
 8
```

For a VLOOKUP() function to work properly, the entries in the key column must be in ascending numeric order.

When Works evaluates this function, it begins at the top of the key column (cell D3) and searches for the first value that is greater than the key. In this case, Works finds the value 9 in cell D4. Consequently, Works determines that the result of the function is in row 3. Since the offset argument is 1, Works returns the entry from cell E3—the value 101. Because the values in the key column are not arranged in ascending order, Works stops searching before it finds the correct index value, 3.

Other things to know.   If the key value you specify is less than the first value in the key column, the VLOOKUP() function will return the value ERR. If you entered a value less than 1 into cell B3 of the spreadsheet in Figure 10-22, for example, the function =*VLOOKUP(B3,D3:F7,B4)* in cell B6 will return the value ERR.

If the key value you specify is greater than the largest value in the key column, the VLOOKUP() function will assume the result of the function is in the last row of the table. If you enter a value greater than 9 into cell B3 of the spreadsheet shown in Figure 10-22, for example, the function =*VLOOKUP(B3,D3:F7,B4)* will return the value 202 from cell E7.

Works' VLOOKUP() function also will return the value ERR if you specify an offset less than 0 or greater than the number of columns in the range, minus one. For example, the function =*VLOOKUP(B3,D3:F7,B4)* will return the value ERR if you enter a value greater than 2 or less than 0 into cell B4.

If the offset argument in a VLOOKUP() function is 0, the function will return a value from the index column. For example, if you changed the entry in cell B4 to 0, the function =*VLOOKUP(B3,D3:F7,B4)* in cell B6 would return the value 3 from cell D4.

Although the key columns of all the examples we have looked at so far have contained positive values, they also can contain negative values. For the function to work correctly, however, the values in the key column should be arranged in ascending order: negative values followed by positive values.

Finally, the key column of a lookup table should not contain duplicate values. If it does, and the VLOOKUP() function matches one of the duplicate values, it always will return a result from the row that contains that value that is closest to the top of the table.

The HLOOKUP() function

Works' HLOOKUP() function is identical to its VLOOKUP() function in every way except one: The table is rotated 90 degrees. In other words, the HLOOKUP() function locates values in a horizontal lookup table. In a horizontal lookup table, the index values are in the top row of the table, and the data items being looked up are in the rows below.

The form of Works' HLOOKUP() function is HLOOKUP(*key value,table range,offset*). The first argument, *key value*, specifies the value Works will look up in the first row (not column) of the table. The second argument, *table range*, specifies the coordinates or name of the range that contains the entries you want to look up. The final argument, *offset*, specifies the column (not the row) of the table that contains the function's result.

The spreadsheet shown in Figure 10-24 contains an example of the HLOOKUP() function. This function, =*HLOOKUP(B3,C8:G10,B4)*, uses the value from cell B3 as the key value and the value from cell B4 as the offset, just as the function in Figure 10-22 does. In fact, this function is the horizontal equivalent of the vertical lookup function in cell B6 of Figure 10-22.

When it evaluates the function in cell B6, Works searches the key row (C8:G8) from left to right for the first value that meets or exceeds the key value. Since the value 3 in cell D8 meets the key value (the entry in cell B3), Works determines that column D contains the result. The offset argument of 1 then pinpoints the second row of the table range (row 9) as the one that contains the result of the function. Consequently, this function returns the value 303 from cell D9.

Figure 10-24

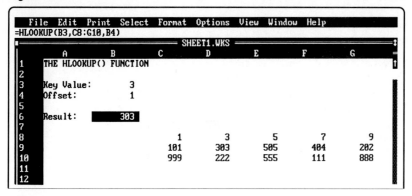

This spreadsheet contains an example of the HLOOKUP() function.

LOGICAL FUNCTIONS

Logical functions allow you to build decision-making capabilities into your Works' spreadsheets. Works' principal logical function is IF(). Its other logical functions are ISERR(), ISNA(), TRUE(), and FALSE().

The IF() function

Works' principal logical function, IF(), allows Works to make decisions based on the result of a conditional test. The form of this function is IF(*conditional test,true result,false result*). The first argument is a conditional test—an expression that is either true or false. If the conditional test is true, Works will evaluate the second argument of the IF() function—the true result. If the test is false, Works will evaluate the third argument of the IF() function—the false result. The true and false arguments should be literal values, or references, formulas, or functions that return values. If the argument is a literal value, the IF() function returns that value. If the argument is a reference, formula, or function, the IF() function evaluates it and returns the value result. If the argument is a reference to a cell that contains a text entry, the IF() function will return the value 0.

Conditional tests

A conditional test is an expression that compares two values or that tests the contents of a particular cell or range for some characteristic. The simplest conditional tests are expressions that make comparisons using one of the six conditional operators listed in Table 10-1 on the next page. For example, the expressions *A1>5, A1=A10, ((A1+10)/A3)<=100,* and *=COUNT(TEST)>=A1* are all conditional tests.

Any expression that uses one of these conditional operators to make a comparison must be either true or false. For example, consider the conditional test A1>5. If A1 contains a value that is less than 5 (such as 3), this test will be false. If cell A1 contains the value 5, this test also will be false. If cell A1 contains a value greater than 5, however, this test will be true.

Table 10-1

Operator	Definition
>	Greater than
<	Less than
=	Equal to
<>	Not equal to
>=	Greater than or equal to
<=	Less than or equal to

Works' conditional operators let you compare two values.

If you enter this test into a cell of a spreadsheet (to do so, you must preface it with an = sign), you might be surprised at the result. If the conditional test is true, Works will display the value 1 in the cell that contains the test. If it is false, Works will display the value 0 in that cell. Works always uses the value 1 to represent a True condition and the value 0 to represent a False condition.

An example

Cells C4 through C6 of the spreadsheet shown in Figure 10-25 contain examples of the IF() function. The function in cell C4, *=IF(B4<30000,0.03,0.05)*, compares the entry in cell B4 with the value 30000. This function says: "If the value in B4 is less than 30000, then return .03; otherwise, return .05." Since cell B4 contains the value 45000, and since 45000 is not less than 30000, this function returns the value .05—the false result. The formula in cell D4, *+B4*C4*, uses this result to compute the total commission for the first salesperson.

Figure 10-25

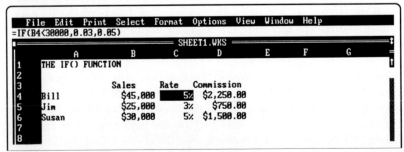

This spreadsheet contains an example of the IF() function.

The function in cell C5, *=IF(B5<30000,0.03,0.05)*, compares the entry in cell B5, 25000, to the value 30000. Since 25000 is less than 30000, this function returns the value .03—the True value. Similarly, the function in cell C6, *=IF(B6<30000,0.03,0.05)*, tests to see if the entry in cell B6 is less than 30000.

Since the entry in that cell is not less than 30000 (they are equal), the function returns .05—the False value.

Complex conditional operators

In addition to the six basic logical operators (=, >, <, >=, <=, and <>), Works offers three "complex" logical operators: #AND#, #OR#, and #NOT#. These operators allow you to join simple conditional tests, like *A1>5*, into compound conditional tests like *#NOT#(A1>5#AND#(B1<10#OR#C1=3))*.

The #AND# operator.   Works' #AND# operator allows you to join two conditional tests in a "logical AND" fashion. When you join two tests in this way, the combined test is true only when both of the component tests are true. If either or both of the component conditions are false, the combined test will be false.

As an example of the use of this operator, suppose you want Works to return the value 777 if both of the following conditions are true: Cell A1 contains a value greater than 100, and cell A2 contains a value less than or equal to 50. Otherwise, Works should return the value 666. To do this, you would use the function *=IF(A1>100#AND#A2<=50,777,666)*. If both of the conditions are true (that is, if cell A1 contains a value greater than 100 *and* cell A2 contains a value less than or equal to 50), this function will return the value 777—the true result. If either or both conditions are false (that is, if cell A1 contains a value less than or equal to 100, cell A2 contains a value greater than 50, or both), this function will return the value 666—the false result.

The #OR# operator.   Works' #OR# operator allows you to join two conditional tests in a "logical OR" fashion. When you use this operator to join two conditions, the combined conditional test will be true if either or both of the component conditions are true. A logical OR test will be false only when both component conditions are false.

As an example of the use of this operator, suppose you want Works to return the value 777 if cell A1 contains a value greater than 100, if cell B2 contains a value less than or equal to 50, or both. Otherwise, it should return the value 666. To achieve this effect, you would use the function

   =IF(A1>100#OR#B2<=50,777,666)

This function will return the value 777 if either one or both of these conditions are true. Works will return the false result (the value 666) only when both conditions (*A1>100* and *B2<=50*) are false.

The #NOT# operator.   Works' #NOT# operator gives you an alternative way to negate a conditional test. Unlike #AND# and #OR#, #NOT# does not join two conditions. Instead, it must preface the condition that you want to negate.

For example, suppose you want Works to return the value 777 if the value in cell A1 is not equal to the value 123, and return the value 666 otherwise. To do this, use the function *=IF(#NOT#A1=123,"777","666")*. The functions *=IF(A1<>123,"777","666") and =IF(A1=123,"666","777")* return the same result.

Other logical functions

In the previous examples of the IF() function, we used basic conditional operators (=, >, <, >=, <=, and <>) and complex conditional operators (#AND#, #OR#, and #NOT#) to create conditional tests. You also can use either of two special functions—ISERR() and ISNA()—as the conditional test of an IF() function. In addition, Works provides two functions—TRUE() and FALSE()—that give you alternative ways to represent True and False conditions within a spreadsheet.

The ISERR() and ISNA() functions

Works' ISERR() and ISNA() functions allow you to test whether a formula or function returns the special values ERR and NA, respectively. Works returns the value ERR when it is unable to evaluate a formula or function due to incorrect syntax, the improper mixing of values and text entries, and so forth. NA, which stands for *not available*, is a placeholder value. The NA() function (which we'll cover later in this chapter) provides the only way to enter this value into a cell.

The forms of these two special functions are ISERR(*argument*) and ISNA(*argument*), where *argument* is the formula or function you want to test, or a reference to a cell that contains that formula or function. The ISERR() function is true when its argument returns the value ERR and is false otherwise. The ISNA() function is true only when its argument returns the value NA. For example, if cell A1 contains a function that returns the value ERR, the function *=IF(ISERR(A1),777,666)* will return the value 777. Similarly, the function *=ISNA(A1)* will be true if cell A1 returns the function NA().

TRUE() and FALSE()

Works' TRUE() and FALSE() functions give you alternative ways to represent the values 1 and 0 (the logical conditions True and False). The TRUE() function returns the value 1, while the FALSE() function returns the value 0. These functions accept no arguments.

DATE AND TIME FUNCTIONS

In Chapter 7, you learned that you can enter date and time values into a spreadsheet simply by typing them in one of several forms. When you press [Enter] to lock in the date or time entry, Works will display that entry in the format you used to enter it. However, the cell will contain a serial date or time value. A serial date value of any date is equal to the number of days that have elapsed between December 31, 1899, and that date. The serial time value of any time is the fraction of a day represented by that time. You can enter the current date or the current time by pressing the [Ctrl]; and [Ctrl]: key combinations, respectively.

In Chapter 7, we showed you how to work with date and time entries in a number of ways. For example, we showed you how to calculate a future date by adding a value to the serial date value in a cell of a spreadsheet and how to calculate an elapsed time by subtracting the time value in one cell from the time value in another cell.

In Chapter 8, we showed you how to change the format of a date or time entry once it's been made. Works supports ten date formats and four time formats.

The tools for entering and manipulating date and time values that we have covered so far are sufficient for many date and time manipulations. However, Works provides even more date/time tools. Specifically, Works features four special functions that allow you to enter and manipulate dates and four special functions that allow you to enter and manipulate times.

Works' four date value functions are: DATE(), DAY(), MONTH(), and YEAR(). The DATE() function gives you an alternative way to enter date values into a spreadsheet; the DAY(), MONTH(), and YEAR() functions extract the day, month, and year components from a serial date value.

Date functions

Works' DATE() function gives you an alternative way to enter date values into a spreadsheet and gives you the only way to include date values directly within a formula or function. The form of this function is *DATE(year,month,day)*, where *year* specifies the year of the date you want to enter, *month* specifies the month, and *day* specifies the day. The year, month, and day arguments may be literal values, references to cells that contain values, or formulas or functions that return values. The year argument should specify a value between 0 (for the year 1900) and 179 (for the year 2079). For example, the year argument 86 would specify a date in the year 1986, and the year argument 105 would specify a date in the year 2005. The month argument should specify a value between 1 (for January) and 12 (for December). For example, the month argument 2 would specify a date in the month of February. The day argument should specify a valid day for the month and year indicated by the first two arguments.

The DATE() function

The result of a DATE() function is the serial value of the date specified by year, month, and day arguments. For example, the function *=DATE(87,7,4)* returns the value 31962—the number of days that have elapsed between December 31, 1899, and July 4, 1987. Similarly, the function *=DATE(72,12,25)* returns the value 26658 (the serial date value of December 25, 1972), the function *=DATE(110,1,1)* returns the value 40179 (the serial date value of January 1, 2010), and so forth.

Using the DATE() function. The principal use of the DATE() function is for including date values directly within formulas and functions. For example, suppose you want to calculate the number of days that elapsed between July 4, 1956, and November 24, 1958. To do this, you could type the date 11/24/58 into one cell (for example, cell A1), type the date 7/4/56 into another cell (for example, cell A2), and use the formula *=A1-A2* to calculate the number of days that have elapsed between those two dates. As you can see, this method requires you to enter the two dates into individual cells of the spreadsheet, then reference those cells within a formula.

In some cases, you may want to include the date values directly within the formula, rather than referencing them from other cells. To do this, you might attempt to use the formula *=11/24/58-7/4/56*. Unfortunately, this formula will not produce the result you intended. Although Works interprets an entry in the form 11/24/58 (or any other date form for that matter) as a date when you type it directly into a cell of the spreadsheet, it will not recognize entries in that form as dates in the middle of a formula or function. In this case, 11/24/58 tells Works to divide 11 by 24, then divide the result by 58. Similarly, 7/4/56 tells Works to divide 7 by 4, then divide the result by 56. The result of the entire formula is -0.023348—the difference between the results of these divisions.

To include date values directly within a formula or function, you must use the DATE() function. For example, to calculate the number of days that elapsed between July 4, 1956, and November 24, 1958, you would use the formula *=DATE(58,11,24)-DATE(56,7,4)*. When Works evaluates this formula, it first evaluates the function *=DATE(58,11,24)*, which returns the value 21513. Then it evaluates the function *DATE(56,7,4)*, which returns the value 20640. Finally, it subtracts the second result from the first to produce the result 873—the number of days that elapsed between the two dates.

If you want, you also can use the DATE() function to enter dates into the cells of a spreadsheet. When you do this, Works will display the serial value for the date in an unformatted (General) form. In most cases, however, you'll probably find it easier simply to type the date in one of the many forms Works recognizes.

Entering invalid dates.   In most cases, the arguments of your DATE() functions will specify valid dates. In some cases, however, you may inadvertently enter an invalid month or day argument—for example, *=DATE(90,13,24)* or *=DATE(90,2,29)*. In these cases, the DATE() function will not return the value ERR, as you might expect. Instead, Works will interpret your entry, transforming it into a valid date.

As an example of this transformation, suppose you entered the function *=DATE(90,4,31)* into a cell of a Works spreadsheet. The arguments of this function specify April 31—a date that does not exist, since April has only 30 days. Instead of rejecting this function, or returning the result ERR, Works carries the extra day forward into the next month (May) and returns the value 31837—the serial date value for May 1, 1987.

The DAY() function

Works' DAY() function returns the day of the month represented by a serial date value. The form of this function is DAY(*serial date value*), where *serial date value* is a reference to a cell that contains a serial date value, a formula that returns a serial date value, or a function that returns a serial date value.

The result of any DAY() function is a value between 1 and 31. For example, if cell A1 of a spreadsheet contains the serial date value for April 15, 1988, the function *=DAY(A1)* will return the value 15. The function *=DAY(DATE(88,4,15))* would return the same value.

Works' MONTH() function returns a value between 1 and 12 that specifies the month of the year in which the date referred to by the function's argument falls. For example, if cell A1 of a spreadsheet contains the serial date value for August 31, 1988, the function *=MONTH(A1)* will return the value 8. The function *=MONTH(DATE(88,8,31))* would return the same result.

The MONTH() function

Works' YEAR() function returns a value between 0 and 179 that specifies the year in which the date referred to by the function's argument falls. For example, if cell A1 contains the serial date value for any date in the year 1987, the function *=YEAR(A1)* will return the value 87. The function *=YEAR(DATE(87,1,1))* would return the same value.

The YEAR() function

As you can see, Works' YEAR() function returns a two-digit number that represents the year portion of a date. If you want to get the full year number, you must add 1900 to the result. For example, if cell A1 contains the serial date value for December 31, 1987, the function *=YEAR(A1)* will return the value 87, but the formula *=YEAR(A1)+1900* would return the value 1987.

Works features four functions that allow you to enter and manipulate time values: TIME(), HOUR(), MINUTE(), and SECOND(). The TIME() function gives you a way to enter an unformatted time value into a cell. The HOUR(), MINUTE(), and SECOND() functions extract the various components of a serial time value.

Time functions

Works' TIME() function gives you an alternative way to enter time values into the cells of a spreadsheet and the only way to include time values directly within a formula or function. The form of this function is TIME(*hours,minutes,seconds*), where *hours*, *minutes*, and *seconds* describe the time you want to enter into the spreadsheet. The *hours* argument should specify a value between 0 and 23, where 0 is midnight, 6 is 6:00 AM., 12 is 12:00 noon, 18 is 6:00 PM., and so on. The minutes and seconds arguments should specify values between 0 and 59.

The TIME() function

The result of a TIME() function is the serial value of the time specified by the hours, minutes, and seconds arguments. For example, the function *=TIME(12,0,0)* returns the value .5 (the fraction of a day that elapses between midnight and noon). Similarly, the function *=TIME(8,30,0)* returns the value .354167—the fraction of a day that elapses between midnight and 8:30 AM.

Using the TIME() function.   The principal use of the TIME() function is for including time values directly within formulas and functions. For example, suppose you want to calculate the amount of time that has elapsed between 8:30

AM on a certain day and 5:18 PM on that same day. To do this, you could type the time *17:18:00* into one cell (for example, cell A1), type the time *8:30:00* into another cell (for example, cell A2), and use the formula *=A1-A2* to calculate the elapsed time. As you can see, this method requires you to enter the two times into individual cells of the spreadsheet, then reference those cells within a formula.

In some cases, you may want to include the time values directly within the formula, rather than referencing them from other cells. To do this, you must use the TIME() function. For example, to calculate the elapsed time between 8:30 AM on a certain day and 5:18 PM on that same day, you would use the formula *=TIME(17,18,0)-TIME(8,30,0)*. When Works evaluates this formula, it first evaluates the function *=TIME(17,18,0)*, which returns the value .72083. Then it evaluates the function *=TIME(8,30,0)*, which returns the value .354167. Finally, it subtracts the second result from the first to produce the result .367—the fraction of a day that elapses between the two times. Formatting this value reveals that it represents eight hours and 48 minutes.

Entering invalid times.   In most cases, the arguments of your TIME() functions will specify valid times. In some cases, however, you may inadvertently enter an invalid hour, minute, or second argument; for example, *=TIME(8,61,0)* or *=TIME(15,17,65)*. In these cases, the TIME() function will not return the value ERR, as you might expect. Instead, Works will interpret your entry, transforming it into a valid time.

As an example of this transformation, suppose you entered the function *=TIME(8,61,0)* into a cell of a spreadsheet. The arguments of this function specify 8:61 AM—a time that does not exist. Instead of rejecting this function or returning the result ERR, Works carries the extra minutes forward into the next hour. Consequently, it returns the value .3756944—the serial time value for 9:01 AM.

The HOUR() function   Works' HOUR() function returns the hour represented by a serial date value. The result of this function is always a value between 0 and 23, inclusive. The form of this function is HOUR(*serial time value*), where the single argument specifies the serial time value whose hour component you want to extract. As an example of this function, suppose that cell A1 of a Works spreadsheet contains the serial time value for 5:57 PM. Given this entry, the function *=HOUR(A1)* will return the value 17—the hour of the time represented by the serial time value, on a 24-hour scale. The function *=HOUR(TIME(17,57,0))* would return the same value.

The HOUR() function returns the hour represented by a time value, using a 24-hour scale. If you want a result in 12-hour form, you must use a formula like

   =IF(HOUR(timevalue)>12,HOUR(timevalue)-12,HOUR(timevalue))

where *timevalue* is a serial time value of the time whose hour you want to extract.

Works' MINUTE() function returns the minute represented by a time value. The result of this function is always a value between 0 and 59, inclusive. For example, if cell A1 contains the serial time value for 11:23 PM, the function =MINUTE(A1) will return the value 23. The function =MINUTE(TIME(23,23,0)) would return the same value.

The MINUTE() function

Works' SECOND() function returns the second component of a time value. Like the result of the MINUTE() function, the result of any SECOND() function will be a value between 0 and 59, inclusive. For example, if cell A1 contains the serial time value for 2:17:35 PM, the function =SECOND(A1) will return the value 35. The function =SECOND(TIME(14,17,35) would return the same value.

The SECOND() function

In Chapter 7, we showed you how to create a combined time/date entry by adding a date value from one cell to a time value in another cell. For example, if cell A1 contains the date value for November 24, 1958 (21513), and cell A2 contains the time value for 3:37 AM (.1506944), the formula =A1+A2 will return the combined date/time value 21513.1506944. You can format this combined entry to display as a date or as a time, but not as both a date and time at once.

With the aid of Works' DATE() and TIME() functions, you can create combined date/time entries without first entering the date into one cell and the time into another. For example, the function =DATE(58,11,24)+TIME(3,37,0) produces a combined date/time value for 3:37 AM on November 24, 1958.

Combining DATE() and TIME() functions

Works' NOW() function produces a combined date/time value that reflects the current date and time. The form of this function is just NOW(); it does not accept any arguments.

When you enter a NOW() function into a spreadsheet, Works draws the current date and time from your computer's system clock and enters it into the spreadsheet as a combined date/time value. If you entered the function NOW() into a spreadsheet at precisely 9:37:15 on November 1, 1987, for example, Works would return the value 32082.400868. The integer portion of this value, 32082, specifies November 1, 1987—the day 32,082 days after Works' base date, December 31, 1899. The decimal portion of this entry, .400868, specifies 9:37:15 AM—the additional portion of a day that has elapsed since that base date.

Works updates any NOW() functions in a spreadsheet each time you recalculate that spreadsheet. If Works is in the manual recalculation mode, the value of NOW() will not be updated until you press the [Calc] key ([F9]). To freeze the current result of a NOW() function, you must use the Copy Special... command's Value Only option. (Of course, pressing the [Ctrl]: combination is the easiest way to enter the current time in "static" form.)

The NOW() function

OTHER FUNCTIONS

In addition to the functions we've covered so far, Works contains some other functions that are difficult to categorize. These four functions are COLS(), ROWS(), ERR(), and NA().

The COLS() and ROWS() functions

Works' COLS() and ROWS() functions return the number of columns or rows in the range specified by their arguments. The forms of these functions are COLS(*range*) and ROWS(*range*), where the single argument specifies the range whose columns or rows you want Works to count. To demonstrate the use of this function, suppose that you have assigned the name TEST to cells A1:Z100. Given this range, the function *=COLS(TEST)* would return the value 26, indicating that the range spans 26 columns. The function *=ROWS(TEST)* would return the value 100, indicating that the range named TEST encompasses 100 rows.

The ERR() function

Works' ERR() function allows you to enter the special value ERR into a spreadsheet. This function does not accept an argument. When you enter the ERR() function into a cell, Works will display the value result ERR—the same result it returns when you enter a reference, formula, or function that Works cannot evaluate. Any cell that refers to the cell containing the ERR() function also returns the value ERR.

The ERR() function can be used to signal errors in your spreadsheets. For example, the function *=IF(C10<100,ERR(),C10)* will return the value ERR if cell C10 contains a value less than 100.

The NA() function

Works' NA() function allows you to enter the special value NA into a spreadsheet. Like ERR(), NA() does not accept an argument. Unlike the value ERR, Works will never return the value NA on its own; the NA() function provides the only way to enter this value into the spreadsheet.

The NA() function is useful principally as a "placeholder" in incomplete spreadsheets. If you do not yet have the correct entry for a cell in a spreadsheet, you can enter the function NA() into that cell. Any cell that references that cell also will return the value NA. Those results remind you that the spreadsheet is lacking a critical piece of information.

CONCLUSION

In this chapter, we've talked about functions—special built-in tools that allow you to manipulate values in ways that would be difficult or impossible to do with traditional operators. In the next chapter, we'll look at some advanced spreadsheeting topics.

Other Spreadsheet Topics 11

*I*n the previous four chapters, we've explored the majority of Works' spreadsheet features, including formatting, cut and paste commands, and functions. In this final chapter on spreadsheet documents, we'll cover their remaining features: named ranges, the Fill Series... command, windows, titles, cell protection, searching and sorting.

NAMED RANGES

In Chapters 7 and 10, we showed you how to enter formulas and functions into the cells of a spreadsheet. In those formulas and functions, we referred to cells and ranges by their addresses: A1, B19, J5:L27, and so forth. However, Works does not limit you to referring to cells and ranges this way. If you want, you can assign names to the cells and ranges in a spreadsheet, then refer to those cells and ranges by name.

Naming a range

Assigning a name to a range is a simple process. First, highlight the cell or group of cells to which you want to assign a name. Second, pull down the Edit menu and select the Range Name... command. When you do this, you'll see a dialog box like the one shown in Figure 11-1 on the following page. To assign a name to the highlighted cell or range, just type that name into the Name text box, then choose the <Create> button. (Since <Create> is the default button, you can choose it by pressing [Enter].) Of course, you can use the ←, →, [Home], [End], [Delete], and [Backspace] keys to edit the range name as you type it. If you decide that you don't want to name the selected range, you should choose <Cancel> instead of <Create>.

As an example of naming a single cell, suppose you want to assign the range name *Grand Total* to cell F9 of the spreadsheet shown in Figure 11-2. To do this, move the highlight to cell F9, then pull down the Edit menu, choose the Range

Name... command, type the name *Grand Total*, and choose <Create>. When you do this, Works will assign the name *Grand Total* to cell F9, close up the Range Name dialog box, and return you to the spreadsheet.

Figure 11-1

You'll see a dialog box like this one when you select the Range Name... command from the Edit menu.

As an example of naming a group of cells, suppose you want to assign the range name *Widgets* to the range B5:E5 of our example spreadsheet. To do this, highlight the range B5:E5, pull down the Edit menu, select Range Name..., type *Widgets*, and select <Create>.

Figure 11-2

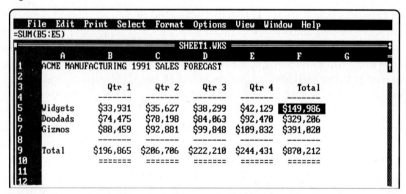

You can use the Range Name... command to assign names to cells and ranges in a spreadsheet.

Default names

In some cases, Works will automatically enter a suggested name into the Name text box of the Range Name dialog box when you issue the Range Name... command. You can accept this name simply by choosing the <Create> button. Since the name will be highlighted, you can overwrite it by typing new text.

When you are naming a single cell that contains a label entry, Works will use that label as the suggested name of the cell. If the cell you are naming contains a value or is blank, Works will look to the cell to the left of the one you are naming for a suggested name. If that cell contains a label entry, Works will use that entry as the suggested name. If that cell contains a value or is blank, Works will look to the cell above the one you are naming. If that cell contains a label entry, Works will use that entry as the suggested name. If it contains a value or is blank, Works will not suggest a name.

If you are naming a group of cells, Works first will look to the active cell for a suggested name. If that cell contains a label entry, Works will suggest that entry as the name. If the active cell contains a value or is blank, the next place Works looks for a suggested name depends on the shape of the range. If you are naming a single-row range, Works will look to the cell to the left of the leftmost cell in that range. If you are naming a single column range, Works will look to the cell above the topmost cell in that range. If you are naming a multiple-row, multiple-column range, Works will look to the cell above the upper-left cell in that range. If that cell contains a label entry, Works will use it as the suggested name for the range. If it contains a value or is blank, Works won't suggest a name.

If the name Works would suggest in a given situation is already assigned to another range in the same spreadsheet document, Works won't suggest that name. Unfortunately, it won't suggest the next choice either. For example, suppose the cell you want to name contains the entry *One*. If another range in the spreadsheet is already named *One*, Works won't suggest a name for that cell, even if the cell to its left or the cell above it contain label entries.

Range names can be up to 15 characters long and can contain any characters you can type from the keyboard, including letters, digits, mathematical symbols, punctuation marks, and spaces. For example, *total*, *Product 1*, and *$#;!!!* are all valid range names. **Range name rules**

When you type a range name, you can use lowercase letters, uppercase letters, or a mixture of the two. For purposes of range names, Works does not differentiate between uppercase and lowercase letters. Consequently, the names *total*, *Total*, *TOTAL*, and so forth, all refer to the same range. Works will display range names in whatever form you entered them.

Works will allow you to type more than 15 characters into the Name text box. However, if you choose <Create> when that box contains more than 15 characters, Works will use only the first 15 characters as the name of the range. For example, if you highlight a range, type *PRODUCT 1 SALES FOR 1990* into the Name text box, then choose <Create>, Works will assign the name *PRODUCT 1 SALES* to that range. The remaining characters will be lost.

Overlapping ranges

Works allows you to assign more than one name to the same range. For example, you could assign both the names *Widgets* and *Test* to the range B5:E5 of the spreadsheet shown in Figure 11-2. As we'll explain later, however, you'll run into problems when you redefine one of the names assigned to a range that has multiple names. Consequently, we recommend that you avoid assigning multiple names to the same range.

It's all right for named ranges to overlap partially. You'd have no problems if you assigned the name *First Qtr.* to the range B5:B7 of the spreadsheet shown in Figure 11-2 and assigned the name *Widgets* to the range B5:E5, even though cell B5 is in both ranges.

**Using range
names in formulas
and functions**

Once you have assigned a name to a cell or range within a Works spreadsheet, you can use that name within formulas that refer to that cell or range. (Of course, you can still use cell coordinates, if you want.) For example, after you assign the name *Grand Total* to cell F9 of the spreadsheet shown in Figure 11-2, you can use either the formula *=F9/3* or *=Grand Total/3* to calculate the result of dividing the value in that cell by 3. As another example, after you assign the name *Widgets* to cells B5:E5, you can use either the function *=SUM(Widgets)* or *=SUM(B5:E5)* to add the values in that range.

Although you can use either coordinates or names to refer to named ranges, Works always refers to a named range by its name. For example, Figure 11-3 shows the spreadsheet shown in Figure 11-2 after we assigned the range name *Widgets* to the range B5:E5. In both figures, cell F5 is the active cell. In Figure 11-2 (the spreadsheet before we assigned the name to the range B5:E5), Works displays the function *=SUM(B5:E5)* on the formula line. In Figure 11-3 (the spreadsheet after we named that range), Works displays the function *=SUM(Widgets)* on that line.

Figure 11-3

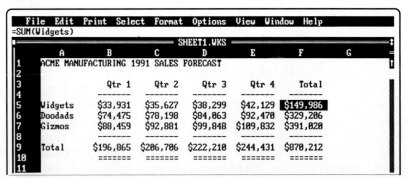

Once you have assigned a name to a range, Works will use that name in all formulas and functions that refer to that range.

**Listing named
ranges**

Once you assign a name to a range, the name and coordinates of that range will appear in the Names list box whenever you issue the Range Name... command. For example, Figure 11-4 shows the Range Name dialog box after we assigned a variety of names to the spreadsheet in Figure 11-3. As you can see, Works doesn't list the range names in alphabetical order. Instead, it lists them in ascending order according to the row location of their upper-left cell. If two ranges begin in the same row, Works will list the one in the leftmost column first.

The Names list box can display only six names at a time. To see the other names, you'll have to use the arrow keys or your mouse to bring them into view. For a review of how to scroll through a list box, refer to Chapter 1.

Figure 11-4

Works lists the names and coordinates of the named ranges in a spreadsheet within the Names list box.

The <List> button at the bottom of the Range Name dialog box gives you another way to view the names and coordinates of the named ranges in a spreadsheet. When you choose this button, Works writes the names and addresses of all the named ranges in the spreadsheet into a group of cells in that spreadsheet. If only one cell is highlighted, Works will enter the list into that cell and the cells below it and to its right. The first column will contain the names; the column to its right will contain the addresses. If more than one cell is highlighted when you choose the <List> button, Works will enter as much of the list as it can into the highlighted range. In either case, the names in the list will appear in the order of the names in the Names list box.

For example, suppose you want to write a list of the named ranges in our example spreadsheet into the spreadsheet. To do this, move the highlight to the upper-left corner of the block of cells into which you want Works to write the list. In this case, we'll select cell A12. After moving the highlight to this cell, pull down the Edit menu, select the Range Name... command, and choose <List>. Figure 11-5 shows the result. Works has written the names of the nine named ranges in the spreadsheet into cells A12 through A20, and has written the coordinates of those ranges into cells B12 through B20.

Figure 11-5

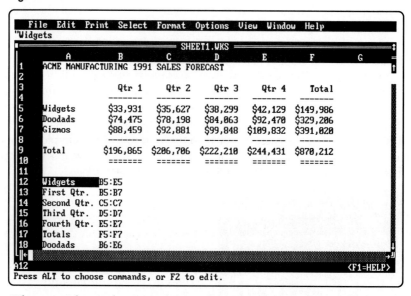

When you choose the <List> button from the Range Name dialog box, Works will enter a list of the names and coordinates of the named ranges into that spreadsheet.

There are a couple of things to keep in mind when you use the <List> button. First, when Works writes a list of range names and their coordinates into a range of cells, it overwrites any entries that already are in those cells. To avoid overwriting existing entries, always position the highlight at the upper-left corner of an empty area of your spreadsheet before you choose the <List> button.

Second, the list produced by the <List> button is not dynamic. That is, it does not change to reflect the creation of new named ranges or the deletion or redefinition of existing named ranges after you create it. Consequently, you must reselect the <List> button each time you want an updated list of the named ranges in a spreadsheet.

Deleting range names

At some point after assigning a name to a range, you may want to delete that name. To delete a range name, first pull down the Edit menu and select the Range Name... command. Next, enter the range name you want to delete into the Name text box, either by highlighting it in the Names list box or by typing it. When the Name text box contains the name you want to delete, simply choose <Delete>. Works will delete that name and return you to the spreadsheet.

For example, suppose you want to delete the range name *Widgets* from our example spreadsheet. To do this, begin by selecting the Range Name... command from the Edit menu to reveal the Range Name dialog box. To delete the name *Widgets*, highlight it in the Names list box, or type the name *Widgets* into the Name text box, then choose <Delete>. When you do this, Works will delete the name and return you to the spreadsheet.

Deleting a range name does not affect the cells to which that name refers. For example, cells B5, C5, D5, and E5 in our example spreadsheet contain the same values after the deletion of the name *Widgets* as they did before. However, deleting a range name does alter the way that Works refers to that range in formulas. After the deletion of a range name, Works will once again refer to the cell or range by its coordinates rather than by its name. For example, after you delete the range name *Widgets* from our example spreadsheet, Works will display the formula in cell F5 as *=SUM(B5:E5)* instead of *=SUM(Widgets)*.

In some cases, you'll need to redefine the coordinates of a range after you have named it. For example, after assigning the name *Test* to cells A1:B5 of a spreadsheet, you may want to expand the range to encompass cells A1:C10, contract it to encompass cells A1:A5, or redefine it completely so that it refers to cells Z100:AA101.

Changing the coordinates of a named range

To redefine the coordinates assigned to an existing range name, follow the procedure you used to name the range originally. To begin, highlight the cell or group of cells to which you want to assign the existing name. After highlighting this range, pull down the Edit menu and select the Range Name... command. When you do this, Works will display the familiar Range Name dialog box. At this point, you should specify the existing range name either by highlighting it in the Names list box or by typing it directly into the Name text box. Once you have selected the name, choose <Create> to assign the new coordinates to it.

Whenever you assign an existing name to a new range, any formulas that referred to the old range will now refer to the new one. In many cases, such as when you are expanding a named range, this is exactly what you want. In other cases, however, such as when you are assigning an existing name to a completely new range, this can produce unintended results.

A problem

For example, suppose that cell A1 of a spreadsheet is named *Test*, and cell B1 contains the formula *=SQRT(A1)*. Since cell A1 is named *Test*, the formula appears as *=SQRT(TEST)* on the formula line. Suppose you want to reassign the name *Test* to cell A3. To do this, move the highlight to cell A3, pull down the Edit menu, select Range Name..., type *Test* in the Name text box, and choose <Create>. After you do this, cell B1 will still contain the formula *=SQRT(TEST)*. Because *Test* now refers to cell A3, however, this function refers to that cell instead of cell A1.

You can avoid this problem by deleting a range name before you assign it to a different range. After you delete a range's name, any formulas or functions that

A solution

refer to that range will refer to it only by its coordinates. When you reassign the name to another range, therefore, the formulas and functions will still refer to the original range.

Renaming a range

In some cases, you may want to change the name that is assigned to a range. To do this, you should delete the old name from the range and then assign the new name to it, or vice versa. For example, suppose you want to change the name of cells F5:F7 of our example spreadsheet from *Totals* to *Product Totals.* To do this, pull down the Edit menu, select the Range Name... command, select the name *Totals* from the Names list box, and choose the <Delete> button. Then, expand the highlight to cover cells F5:F7, select the Range Name... command again, type *Product Totals* into the Name text box, and choose <Create>. At this point, cells F5:F7 will be named *Product Totals.* If you want, you can perform these steps in the opposite order.

If you don't delete the old name from the range you are renaming, it will have two names—in this case, *Totals* and *Product Totals.* Unfortunately, this can cause problems. If you subsequently reassign one of those names to a different group of cells, Works will reassign the other name to that new group as well.

For example, suppose that having assigned both the names *Totals* and *Product Totals* to cells F5:F7 of our example spreadsheet, you want to reassign the name *Totals* to cells B9:E9. To do this, expand the highlight to cover cells B9:E9, pull down the Edit menu, select the Range Name... command, type *Totals* into the Name text box or select it from the Names list box, and choose <Create>.

After doing this, you would expect the name *Totals* to refer to cells B9:E9 and the name *Product Totals* to still refer to cells F5:F7. Unfortunately, that's only half right. Both range names now refer to cells B9:E9. Whenever you redefine the coordinates of a named range, Works will redefine the coordinates of every name assigned to that range. You can avoid this problem by deleting a range name before you assign it to a new range.

How the Move command affects named ranges

The Move command can affect the coordinates of the named ranges in a spreadsheet. If you move a range of cells that contains all the cells of a named range, Works will move the name along with the contents of the cells. For example, suppose that cells A1:A3 are named *Test.* If you highlight cells A1:A3, pull down the Edit menu, select the Move command, move the highlight to cell D5, and press [Enter], the name *Test* will apply to cells D5:D7.

If you move either the upper-left or lower-right cell of a named range without moving the entire range, Works will expand the coordinates of that range. For example, suppose that you've assigned the name *Range* to cells B3:B5. If you move the contents of cell B3 into cell A1, the name *Range* will apply to the range A1:B5. Moving a cell that is within a named range but is not one of its endpoints will not alter the coordinates of that range. For example, if you moved cell B4 into cell Z100, the name *Range* would still refer to cells B3:B5.

If you move an entry into one of the endpoints of a named range (either its upper-left or lower-right cell), Works will lose track of the coordinates assigned to that name. For example, suppose that the range C5:C10 of a spreadsheet is named *Sample*. If you move an entry into either cell C5 or cell C10, Works will lose track of what cells are assigned to the name *Sample*. When you next issue the Range Name... command, the name *Sample* will still appear in the Names list box. However, Works will display ERR instead of the coordinates C5:C10 to the right of that name. More importantly, Works will replace any references to that range with the value ERR. Consequently, any formulas or functions that refer to that range will now return the value ERR.

How inserting and deleting columns affects named ranges

Inserting and deleting columns also can affect the named ranges in a spreadsheet. If you insert a column between the leftmost and rightmost columns of a range, Works will expand that range to include the new column. For example, suppose that you've assigned the name *Temp* to cells A1:B2. If you insert a new column between columns A and B, the name *Temp* will apply to cells A1:C2. Similarly, if you insert a new row between the top and bottom rows of a range, Works will expand the range to encompass the new row. For example, if the name *Temp* applied to cells A1:C2 originally, it will apply to cells A1:C3 after you insert a new row between rows 1 and 2.

Deleting a column or row that contains either the upper-left or lower-right cell of a named range causes Works to lose track of the coordinates assigned to that name. For example, suppose that the range A1:C3 is named *Temp*. If you delete column A, column C, row 1, or row 3, Works will replace any references to *Temp* with the value ERR. Any functions that refer to *Temp* will return the value ERR. If you issue the Range Name... command after deleting one of these rows or columns, Works will still display the name *Temp* in the Names list box but will display ERR instead of a set of coordinates to the right of that name.

If you delete a column or row that contains cells of a named range other than the upper-left or lower-right cells of that range, Works will contract that range. For example, if the name *Temp* originally applied to cells A1:C3, it will apply to cells A1:B3 after you delete column B. If you then delete row 2, the name will apply to cells A1:B2.

Named ranges and the Go To... command

In Chapter 7, we showed you how to use the [Go To] key ([F5]) and the Go To... command on the Select menu to move the highlight to unnamed cells and ranges in a spreadsheet. To do this, you simply issue the Go To... command, type the coordinates of that cell or range, and choose <OK>.

If a spreadsheet contains named ranges, you can use the Go To... command to highlight those ranges. When you press the [Go To] key or select the Go To... command from the Select menu, Works will display a Go To dialog box like the one shown in Figure 11-6. As you can see, Works lists the names and addresses of the named ranges in the spreadsheet in the Names list box. To move the highlight to the coordinates of a named range, choose the name of that range from the Names list box. (Alternatively, you can type the name of that range into the Go To text box.) As soon as you choose <OK>, Works will highlight the range that you specified.

Figure 11-6

The Go To... command lets you highlight a named range.

THE FILL SERIES... COMMAND
▶WORKS 2◀

▶Works 2 offers a new command, Fill Series..., that makes it easier to create series of values. In earlier versions of Works, you have to use formulas to create series. In Works 2, you can use the Fill Series... command to create series quickly and easily.

The Fill Series... command lets you create two types of series: number series and date series. Let's look at how to create each type of series.

Creating number series

To create a number series, you enter the first value of the series into the first cell in the range where you want to create the series. Next, you expand the highlight to include the first cell and all the other cells you want to fill with the series. Once you have highlighted the range you want to fill, select the Fill Series... command from the Edit menu. When you select this command, Works will display the dialog box shown in Figure 11-7. As you can see, this box lets you define the type of series you want to create (Number, Day, Weekday, and so on).

If the entry in the active cell (the first cell of the highlighted range) is a value, then the Number option will be active when the dialog box appears. (In fact, none of the other options in the Units list box will even be available—you cannot choose one of the date options if the first value in the highlighted range is a value.) To create a number series, you simply enter the interval that you want to use to define the series into the Step By text box, then choose <OK> to create the series. If you want to cancel the command without creating the series, choose <Cancel>.

An example

Suppose you want to create a series in the range B2:B11 that begins with the value 10 and has an interval of 10. To create this series, move the highlight to cell

B2 and enter the value 10. Next, highlight the range B2:B11—the entire range you want to fill. When the range has been highlighted, select the Fill Series... command from the Edit menu. When the Fill Series dialog box appears, the Number option will already be active. You need only enter the value 10 into the Step By text box. When you are finished, choose <OK> to create the series. Figure 11-8 shows the result. As you can see, the series begins with the value 10 in cell B2 and "steps" by tens from there to the value 100 in cell B11.

Figure 11-7

You'll see this dialog box when you select the Fill Series... command if the entry in the active cell is a value.

Figure 11-8

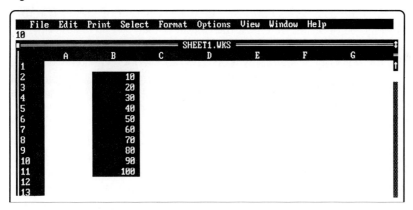

The Number option of the Fill Series... command lets you create a series of values.

Creating date series

To create a date series, enter the first date of the series into the first cell in the range where you want to create the series. Next, expand the highlight to include the first cell and all the other cells you want to fill with the series. Once you have highlighted the range you want to fill, select the Fill Series... command from the Edit menu. When you select this command, Works will display the dialog box shown in Figure 11-9.

Figure 11-9

You'll see this dialog box when you select the Fill Series... command if the entry in the active cell is a date.

If the entry in the active cell (the first cell of the highlighted range) is a date, then only the Day option will be active when the dialog box appears. (The other date series options will be available, but the Number option will be unavailable. You cannot choose the Number option if the first value in the range is a date.) To create a date series, choose the type of date series you want to create—Day, Weekday, Month, or Year—then enter the interval you want to use to define the series into the Step By text box. When you have defined these two parameters, choose <OK> to create the series. If you want to cancel the command without creating the series, choose <Cancel>.

Each of the date series options in the Units option box allows you to create a different type of series. In effect, the option you choose in this box defines the units of the interval you specify in the Step By text box. If you choose the Day option, the units of the interval will be days, and Works will create a simple day series. Similarly, if you choose Month, the units of the interval will be months, and Works will create a month series. Let's take a look at each type of date series in more detail.

Day series

The Day option in the Units option box lets you create a simple day series. For example, suppose you want to create a day series that begins with the date 1/1/90 and that has an interval of one day. You want this series to be entered in the range B2:B11. To create this series, move the highlight to cell B2 and enter the date 1/1/90. Next, highlight the range B2:B11. When the range has been highlighted, select the Fill Series... command from the Edit menu. When the dialog box shown in Figure 11-9 appears, the Day option will already be active and the interval you want to use—1—will already appear in the Step By text box. You need only choose <OK> to create the series. Figure 11-10 shows the result. As you can see, the series begins with the date 1/1/90 in cell B2 and steps by one from there to the date 1/10/90 in cell B11.

Figure 11-10

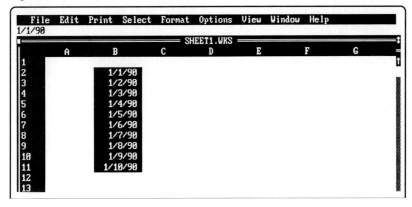

The Day option lets you create a series of dates.

Let's consider another example. Suppose you want to create a series in the range B2:B11 that begins with the date 1/1/90 and that has an interval of seven days. (In other words, you want to create a date series with an interval of seven days, or one week.) To create this series, move the highlight to cell B2 and enter the date 1/1/90. Next, highlight the range B2:B11 and select the Fill Series... command from the Edit menu. When the dialog box in Figure 11-9 appears, the Day option will already be active. To define the series, you need only enter the number 7 into the Step By text box and choose <OK>. Figure 11-11 shows the result. As you can see, the series begins with 1/1/90 in cell B2 and ends with 3/5/90 in cell B11. The interval between the dates in the series is seven days.

Figure 11-11

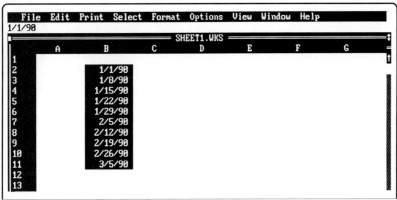

By choosing the Day option and specifying a Step By value of 7, you can create a week series.

Weekday series

The Weekday option in the Units option box lets you create a day series that includes only weekdays. For example, suppose you want to create a weekday series in the range B2:B11 that begins with the date 1/1/90 and that has an interval of one day. To create this series, move the highlight to cell B2 and enter the date 1/1/90. Next, highlight the range B2:B11 and select the Fill Series... command from the Edit menu. When the Fill Series dialog box appears, choose the Weekday option. Since the interval you want to use already appears in the Step By text box, you need only choose <OK> to create the series. As you can see in Figure 11-12, the series begins with the date 1/1/90 in cell B2 and ends with the date 1/12/90 in cell B11. Notice that the series skips the dates 1/6/90 and 1/7/90. If you check a calendar, you'll see that these two dates fall on a Saturday and a Sunday. Since they are not weekdays, they are not included in the series.

Figure 11-12

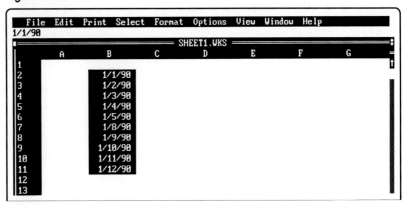

The Weekday option of the Fill Series... command lets you create a series of dates that includes only weekdays.

Month series

The Month option in the Units option box lets you create a series of dates that are a specified number of months apart. For example, suppose you want to create a series that begins with the date 1/1/90 and that has an interval of three months. You want this series to be entered in the range B2:B11. To create this series, move the highlight to cell B2 and enter the date 1/1/90. Next, highlight the range B2:B11 and select the Fill Series... command from the Edit menu. When the Fill Series dialog box appears, choose the Month option, then enter the number 3 into the Step By text box. Finally, choose <OK> to define the series. As you can see in Figure 11-13, the series begins with the date 1/1/90 in cell B2 and ends with the date 4/1/92 in cell B11. The interval between the dates in the series is exactly three full months.

Figure 11-13

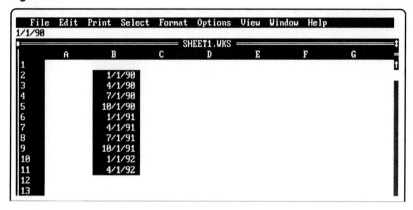

The Month option lets you create a series of dates that are a specified number of months apart.

The Year option in the Units option box lets you create a simple annual series. Year series For example, suppose you want to create a series in the range B2:B11 that begins with the date 1/1/90 and that has an interval of one year. To create this series, move the highlight to cell B2 and enter the date 1/1/90. Next, highlight the range B2:B11 and select the Fill Series... command from the Edit menu. When the Fill Series dialog box appears, choose the Year option. Since the interval you want to use already appears in the Step By text box, you need only choose <OK> to create the series. As you can see in Figure 11-14, the series begins with the date 1/1/90 in cell B2 and ends with the date 1/1/99 in cell B11.

Figure 11-14

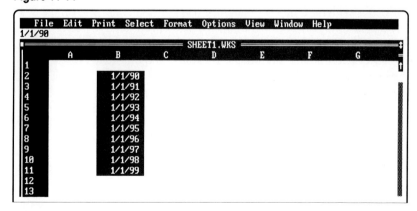

The Year option of the Fill Series... command lets you create an annual date series.

Notes
If the first cell in the highlighted range is empty, Works will display an alert box containing the message *Enter first value.* when you select the Fill Series... command. If the first cell in the highlighted range is not a value, Works will display an alert box containing the message *Starting value must be a number or a date.* when you select the command.

You can use the Fill Series... command to create series in continuous ranges of cells only. If the series you want to create will jump from place to place in your spreadsheet, you'll have to define it using formulas. However, the range you want to fill can be any size. It can include cells in just one row or column, or it can include a rectangular block of cells.

The Step By value you specify can be a negative number. In that case, each number or date in the series will be smaller than the previous number. The Step By value can also be a decimal value. If so, the interval between the numbers or dates in the series will be less than one.◄

SPLITTING WINDOWS INTO PANES
Up to this point, we've viewed spreadsheet documents through a single window. If you want, however, you can divide the work area vertically and/or horizontally into two or four smaller windows. This capability allows you to see up to four different portions of a single spreadsheet on the screen at one time. Just as the windows in your home are probably divided into a number of smaller window panes, a spreadsheet window in Works can be divided into two or four panes. We'll use the word *pane* to describe the smaller windows that result from dividing the work area of a spreadsheet document.

Splitting windows
The way you split the work area of a spreadsheet window into panes depends on whether you have a mouse. If you don't, you must use the Split command to divide the work area. If you do have a mouse, you can use it to create panes.

The Split command
►WORKS 2◄
►If you don't have a mouse, you must use the Split command on the Window menu to split a spreadsheet into multiple panes. (In earlier releases of Works, this command is on the Options menu.)◄ When you select this command, Works will display a set of crosshairs (a double vertical line and a double horizontal line) at the upper-left corner of the screen, display the word *SPLIT* on the status line, and display the message *Use DIRECTION keys to move split, and press ENTER. Press ESC to cancel.* on the message line, as shown in Figure 11-15.

While you see this message at the bottom of the screen, you can use the ←, →, ↑, ↓, [Home], and [End] keys to move the lines around the screen. The ← and → keys move the vertical line across the screen to the left and right one character at a time but do not move the horizontal line. The ↑ and ↓ keys move the horizontal line up and down the screen one row at a time but do not affect the position of the vertical line. The [Home] key moves the intersection of the two lines to the upper-left corner of the screen. The [End] key moves the intersection to the lower-right corner of the screen.

Figure 11-15

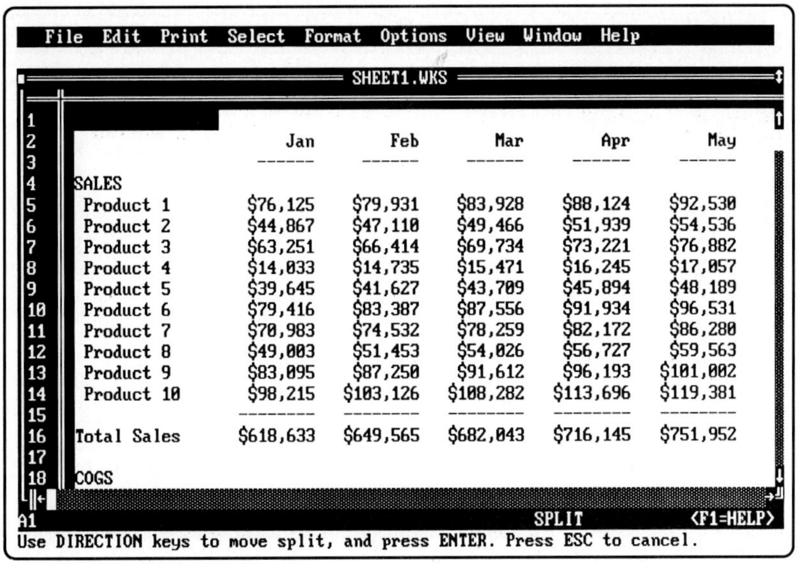

```
┌──────────────────────────────────────────────────────────────────────┐
│   File  Edit  Print  Select  Format  Options  View  Window  Help       │
│                                                                         │
│ ══════════════════════════ SHEET1.WKS ══════════════════════════════   │
│ 1                                                                    ⇡  │
│ 2            Jan       Feb       Mar       Apr       May                │
│ 3          ──────    ──────    ──────    ──────    ──────               │
│ 4  SALES                                                                │
│ 5    Product 1   $76,125   $79,931   $83,928   $88,124   $92,530        │
│ 6    Product 2   $44,867   $47,110   $49,466   $51,939   $54,536        │
│ 7    Product 3   $63,251   $66,414   $69,734   $73,221   $76,882        │
│ 8    Product 4   $14,033   $14,735   $15,471   $16,245   $17,057        │
│ 9    Product 5   $39,645   $41,627   $43,709   $45,894   $48,189        │
│ 10   Product 6   $79,416   $83,387   $87,556   $91,934   $96,531        │
│ 11   Product 7   $70,983   $74,532   $78,259   $82,172   $86,280        │
│ 12   Product 8   $49,003   $51,453   $54,026   $56,727   $59,563        │
│ 13   Product 9   $83,095   $87,250   $91,612   $96,193  $101,002        │
│ 14   Product 10  $98,215  $103,126  $108,282  $113,696  $119,381        │
│ 15              ────────  ────────  ────────  ────────  ────────        │
│ 16  Total Sales $618,633  $649,565  $682,043  $716,145  $751,952        │
│ 17                                                                      │
│ 18  COGS                                                                │
│                                                                         │
│ A1                                     SPLIT           <F1=HELP>        │
│ Use DIRECTION keys to move split, and press ENTER. Press ESC to cancel. │
└──────────────────────────────────────────────────────────────────────┘
```

If you don't have a mouse, you must use the Split command to divide the work area of a spreadsheet document into panes.

The position of the lines when you press [Enter] determines how many panes Works will create and what sizes they will be. If the horizontal line is at the top or bottom of the screen, but the vertical line is somewhere between the left and right sides of the screen, Works will split the window into two vertical panes. If the vertical line is at the left or right edges of the screen, but the horizontal line is somewhere between the top and bottom edges of the screen, Works will divide the window into two horizontal panes. If the horizontal line is somewhere between the top and bottom of the screen, and the vertical line is somewhere between the left and right borders of the screen, Works will divide the window into four panes. The minimum height of a horizontal window is two rows; the minimum width of a vertical window is one space. Figures 11-16, 11-17, and 11-18 on the following pages show examples of these three types of splits.

After you split a window vertically, the same columns will be visible on the screen that were visible before you split it. For example, columns A through F are visible in Figures 11-16 and 11-18, just as they are in Figure 11-15. When you split a window horizontally, all but the last row that was visible before the split will be visible afterward, because the horizontal double line occupies one row. For example, rows 1 through 18 are visible on the screen in Figure 11-15; only rows 1 through 17 are visible in Figures 11-17 and 11-18.

Figure 11-16

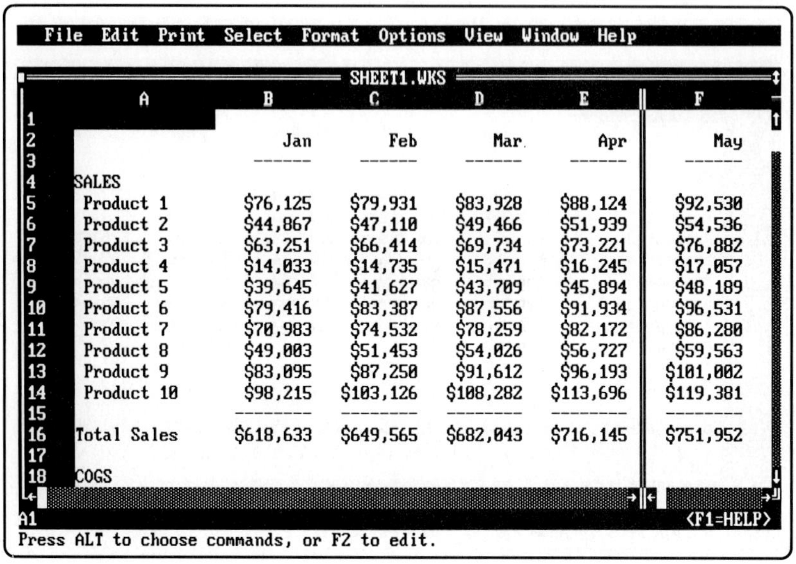

```
  File  Edit  Print  Select  Format  Options  View  Window  Help
══════════════════════════════ SHEET1.WKS ══════════════════════════
          A          B          C          D          E    ║    F
 1
 2                  Jan        Feb        Mar        Apr        May
 3                 ------     ------     ------     ------     ------
 4   SALES
 5     Product 1   $76,125    $79,931    $83,928    $88,124    $92,530
 6     Product 2   $44,867    $47,110    $49,466    $51,939    $54,536
 7     Product 3   $63,251    $66,414    $69,734    $73,221    $76,882
 8     Product 4   $14,033    $14,735    $15,471    $16,245    $17,057
 9     Product 5   $39,645    $41,627    $43,709    $45,894    $48,189
10     Product 6   $79,416    $83,387    $87,556    $91,934    $96,531
11     Product 7   $70,983    $74,532    $78,259    $82,172    $86,280
12     Product 8   $49,003    $51,453    $54,026    $56,727    $59,563
13     Product 9   $83,095    $87,250    $91,612    $96,193   $101,002
14     Product 10  $98,215   $103,126   $108,282   $113,696   $119,381
15                --------   --------   --------   --------   --------
16   Total Sales  $618,633   $649,565   $682,043   $716,145   $751,952
17
18   COGS
A1                                                        <F1=HELP>
Press ALT to choose commands, or F2 to edit.
```

This spreadsheet window is split into two vertical panes.

Figure 11-17

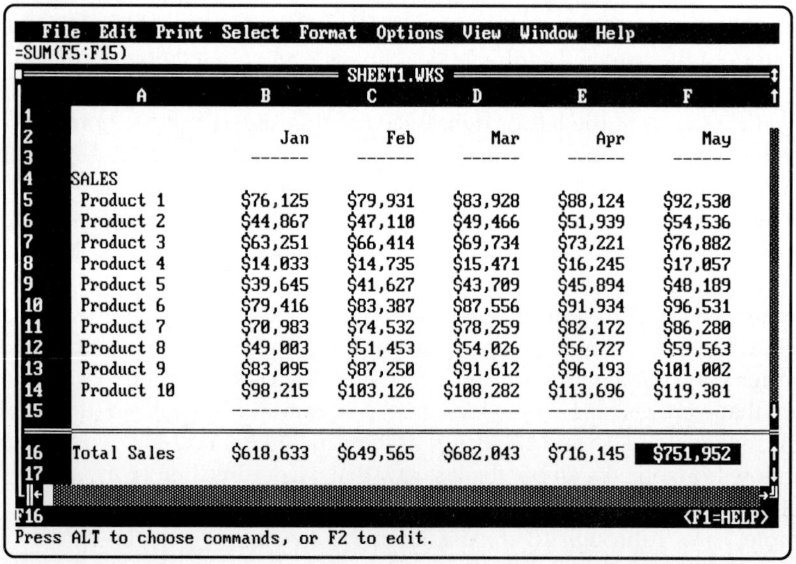

```
  File  Edit  Print  Select  Format  Options  View  Window  Help
=SUM(F5:F15)
══════════════════════════════ SHEET1.WKS ══════════════════════════
          A          B          C          D          E          F
 1
 2                  Jan        Feb        Mar        Apr        May
 3                 ------     ------     ------     ------     ------
 4   SALES
 5     Product 1   $76,125    $79,931    $83,928    $88,124    $92,530
 6     Product 2   $44,867    $47,110    $49,466    $51,939    $54,536
 7     Product 3   $63,251    $66,414    $69,734    $73,221    $76,882
 8     Product 4   $14,033    $14,735    $15,471    $16,245    $17,057
 9     Product 5   $39,645    $41,627    $43,709    $45,894    $48,189
10     Product 6   $79,416    $83,387    $87,556    $91,934    $96,531
11     Product 7   $70,983    $74,532    $78,259    $82,172    $86,280
12     Product 8   $49,003    $51,453    $54,026    $56,727    $59,563
13     Product 9   $83,095    $87,250    $91,612    $96,193   $101,002
14     Product 10  $98,215   $103,126   $108,282   $113,696   $119,381
15                --------   --------   --------   --------   --------
16   Total Sales  $618,633   $649,565   $682,043   $716,145   $751,952
17
F16                                                       <F1=HELP>
Press ALT to choose commands, or F2 to edit.
```

This spreadsheet window is split into two horizontal panes.

Figure 11-18

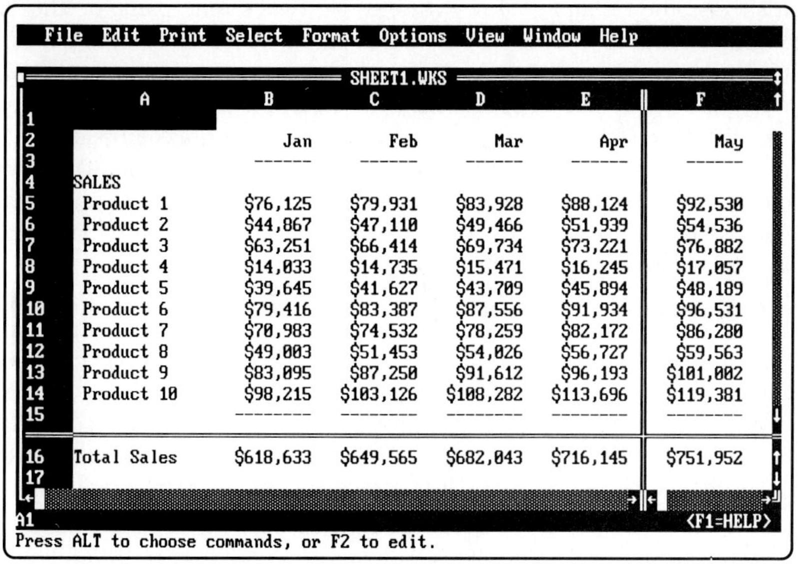

```
┌──────────────────────────────────────────────────────────────────┐
│  File  Edit  Print  Select  Format  Options  View  Window  Help    │
│══════════════════════════════ SHEET1.WKS ════════════════════════  │
│        A         B          C          D          E    ║    F       │
│ 1                                                                   │
│ 2                Jan        Feb        Mar        Apr        May     │
│ 3               ------     ------     ------     ------     ------   │
│ 4     SALES                                                         │
│ 5       Product 1   $76,125   $79,931   $83,928   $88,124   $92,530  │
│ 6       Product 2   $44,867   $47,110   $49,466   $51,939   $54,536  │
│ 7       Product 3   $63,251   $66,414   $69,734   $73,221   $76,882  │
│ 8       Product 4   $14,033   $14,735   $15,471   $16,245   $17,057  │
│ 9       Product 5   $39,645   $41,627   $43,709   $45,894   $48,189  │
│ 10      Product 6   $79,416   $83,387   $87,556   $91,934   $96,531  │
│ 11      Product 7   $70,983   $74,532   $78,259   $82,172   $86,280  │
│ 12      Product 8   $49,003   $51,453   $54,026   $56,727   $59,563  │
│ 13      Product 9   $83,095   $87,250   $91,612   $96,193  $101,002  │
│ 14      Product 10  $98,215  $103,126  $108,282  $113,696  $119,381  │
│ 15               --------   --------   --------   --------   -------- │
│ 16    Total Sales  $618,633  $649,565  $682,043  $716,145  $751,952  │
│ 17                                                                  │
│ A1                                                       <F1=HELP>   │
│ Press ALT to choose commands, or F2 to edit.                        │
└──────────────────────────────────────────────────────────────────┘
```

This spreadsheet window is split into four panes.

If you use a mouse, you do not have to use the Split command to divide a spreadsheet into panes. Instead, you can use the split bars to divide the window. In a single-pane window, the split bars are represented by the = symbol that appears at the top of the vertical scroll bar and the ‖ symbol that appears at the left edge of the horizontal scroll bar. To divide the window into panes, you simply drag these icons onto the work area. When you point to the = symbol and hold down the left button on your mouse, Works will expand that symbol into a double horizontal line that extends all the way across the screen. To split the screen horizontally, just drag this line to the position where you want the split to occur and release the button. When you point to the ‖ symbol and hold down the left button on your mouse, Works will expand that symbol into a double vertical line that extends all the way up and down the screen. To split the screen, drag this line to the position where you want the split to occur and release the button.

If you use a mouse

If you look at Figures 11-16, 11-17, and 11-18, you'll notice that the panes in a spreadsheet window are not completely independent of one another. Panes that are stacked horizontally share the column letters that appear at the top of the upper pane and the horizontal scroll bar that appears at the bottom of the lower pane. Panes that appear side by side share the row numbers that appear to the left of the left-hand window and the vertical scroll bar that appears at the right edge of the right window.

Notes

Panes don't allow you to view a spreadsheet in different ways or view different spreadsheets; they simply allow you to view different parts of the same spreadsheet at one time. After you divide a spreadsheet window into panes, you are still working with just one spreadsheet. Consequently, changes you make in any pane affect the entire spreadsheet, not just the spreadsheet as you see it through that pane. For example, if you delete the entry from cell B5 in one pane, that cell will be blank when you view it through any other pane; if you widen column Z to 20 characters, that column will appear 20 characters wide in every pane; if you assign the Currency format to cell Z26, Works will use that format to display that cell's entry in that format in every pane.

Moving the highlight

You can move the highlight within a pane using any of the techniques you've learned for moving the highlight in a window. For example, pressing the ➡ key moves the highlight one cell to the right; pressing the [Home] key moves the highlight to the left edge of the current row; pressing the [Ctrl][End] combination moves the highlight to the lower-right corner of the active area, and so on. (Recall that a few keys, such as [Pg Up] and [Ctrl]-, move the highlight by windows. These keys have the same action in panes as they do in single windows; however, since panes are typically smaller than single windows, they may move the highlight less distance in panes than in full-screen windows.) As you might expect, if the action you take moves the highlight into a cell that is not visible in the pane, Works will shift the pane so that the cell is in view.

You can also use the mouse and the scroll bars to move around in a paned window. You can use scroll bars in a paned window the same way you use the scroll bars in a single window to move the panes around on the spreadsheet. (For a review of the use of scroll bars in a spreadsheet document, refer to Chapter 7.)

Because related panes share column letters (or row numbers) and scroll bars, Works must display the same columns in both panes of a window that is split horizontally and the same rows in both panes of a window that is split vertically. For example, if columns B through H are visible in the top pane of a horizontal pair, then they will also appear in the bottom pane. Likewise, if rows 2 through 18 are visible in the left-hand pane of a vertical pair, they will be displayed in the right-hand pane as well.

Works automatically synchronizes the scrolling of panes in the direction of the split between them. For example, if you shift columns I through O into view in the top pane of a horizontal pair, Works will automatically shift columns I through O into view in the bottom pane. If you shift rows 21 through 39 into view in the left-hand pane of a vertical pair, Works will shift rows 21 through 39 into view in the right-hand window.

Only panes in the opposite corners of a window that has been split into four panes are completely independent of one another.

Although you can view the spreadsheet through up to four panes at once, you can actually work on the spreadsheet through only one pane at a time. We'll call the pane through which you can work on a spreadsheet the "active" pane. The highlight marks the active pane. The initial active pane depends on how you've split the work area. If you've split the window into two vertical panes, the left-hand pane will be active; if you've split the window into two horizontal panes, the upper pane will be active; and if you've split the window into four panes, the upper-left one will be active.

You can use the [Next Pane] key ([F6]) and the [Prev Pane] key ([Shift][F6]) to activate different panes. If you press the [Next Pane] key when the window is split into two panes, Works will activate the pane that is not active at the time. For example, if you press the [Next Pane] key while the window is split into two horizontal panes and the upper pane is active, Works will activate the lower pane. If you press the [Next Pane] key again, the upper pane will be reactivated.

If the window is split into four panes, Works will activate the panes in a clockwise direction as you press [Next Pane] and in a counterclockwise direction as you press [Prev Pane] ([Shift][F6]). For example, if the window is split into four panes and the upper-left pane is active, Works will activate the upper-right pane when you press the [Next Pane] key. If you press [Next Pane] again, Works will activate the lower-right pane. Pressing [Next Pane] a third time will activate the lower-left pane. If you press [Next Pane] a fourth time, Works will activate the upper-left pane again.

When you use the [Next Pane] key to activate a new pane for the first time, Works will position the highlight in the upper-left corner of that pane. For example, if you split a window horizontally so that cells A1 through G10 are visible through the top pane, and cells A11 through G19 are visible through the bottom pane, Works will position the highlight in cell A11 when you first activate the bottom pane.

When you activate a pane that has been active before, Works won't necessarily move the highlight to the upper-left corner of that pane. If you activate the pane above or below the one that is currently active, the highlight will remain in the same column. However, Works will position it in the row that it was in the last time that pane was active. If you activate a pane to the left or right of the one that is currently active, the highlight will remain in the same row. However, Works will position it in the column it was in the last time that pane was active.

If you have a mouse, you can activate different panes simply by clicking in them. When Works activates the pane, it will position the highlight on the cell on which you clicked.

Once you have divided a work area into multiple panes, you can resize those panes or, if you want, delete them. The way you do these things depends on whether you have a mouse. If you don't, you must reissue the Split command.

Moving the highlight between panes

Resizing panes

When you do this, the word *SPLIT* will appear on the status line, the message *Use DIRECTION keys to move split and press ENTER. Press Esc to cancel.* will appear on the message line, and the split bars will stay where they are. To resize the panes, simply use the ↑, ↓, →, and ← keys to reposition the split bars, then press [Enter].

If you have a mouse, you can drag the double lines into their new positions. If you want, you can drag the lines individually, just as you did to divide the screen into panes in the first place, or you can move both the vertical and horizontal lines together, redefining all four panes at once.

Unsplitting the window

To "unsplit" a window, you must move the appropriate split bar off the work area in the appropriate direction. For example, to unsplit a window that is divided horizontally into two panes, you have to move the split bar up or down until it is off the work area. Similarly, to unsplit a window that is divided vertically into two panes, you have to move the split bar left or right until it is off the work area. The edge or corner to which you move the split bars determines which portion of the spreadsheet will be visible through the resulting window.

The way you move the split bar depends on whether you have a mouse. If you have a mouse, you can drag the split bars off the work area. If you don't, you must reissue the Split command. When you do this, the word *SPLIT* will appear on the status line, and the message *Use DIRECTION keys to move split and press ENTER. Press Esc to cancel.* will appear on the message line. To unsplit the window, simply use the ↑, ↓, →, and ← keys, or the [Home] and [End] keys, to move the split bars off the work area, and then press [Enter].

The [Home] and [End] keys provide the fastest ways to move the split bars to the edges of the window. When you press [Home], Works will move the horizontal split bar to the top of the work area and the vertical split bar to the left edge of the work area. When you press [End], Works will move the horizontal split bar to the bottom of the work area and move the vertical split bar to the right edge of the work area.

TITLES

The first few rows and columns in most of your spreadsheets will contain labels that identify the contents of the spreadsheet. In the spreadsheet shown in Figures 11-16 through 11-18, for example, the labels in rows 2 and 3 identify the various columns in the spreadsheet, and the labels in column A identify the rows. In this case, each column contains values for a particular month; each row contains values for a particular sales or expense category.

There's just one problem: When you scroll away from the upper-left corner of the spreadsheet, the column and row headers in the first few rows and columns will disappear off the top and left sides of the screen. This makes it difficult to determine in what categories entries in the lower-right portions of a spreadsheet belong. For example, Figure 11-19 shows the result of moving the highlight away from the upper-left corner of our example spreadsheet.

Figure 11-19

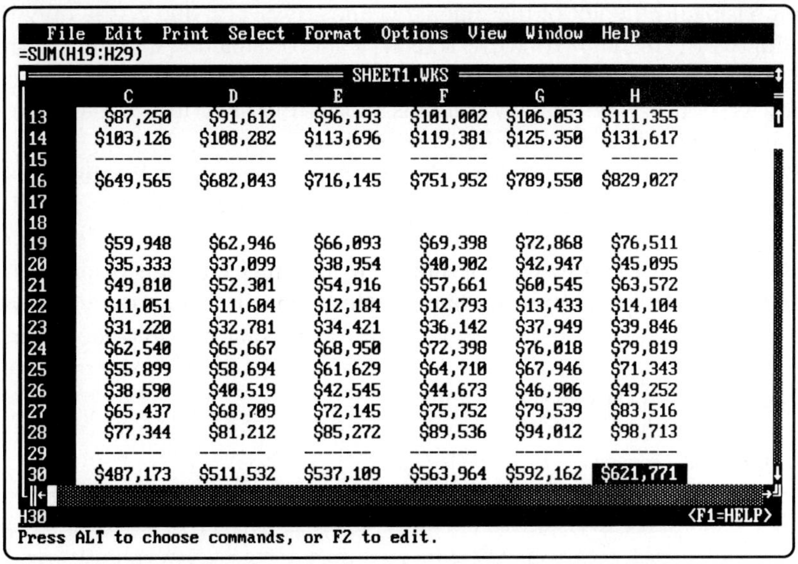

```
  File  Edit  Print  Select  Format  Options  View  Window  Help
=SUM(H19:H29)
                            ═══════ SHEET1.WKS ═══════
          C          D          E          F          G          H
13     $87,250    $91,612    $96,193   $101,002   $106,053   $111,355
14    $103,126   $108,282   $113,696   $119,381   $125,350   $131,617
15    --------   --------   --------   --------   --------   --------
16    $649,565   $682,043   $716,145   $751,952   $789,550   $829,027
17
18
19     $59,948    $62,946    $66,093    $69,398    $72,868    $76,511
20     $35,333    $37,099    $38,954    $40,902    $42,947    $45,095
21     $49,810    $52,301    $54,916    $57,661    $60,545    $63,572
22     $11,051    $11,604    $12,184    $12,793    $13,433    $14,104
23     $31,220    $32,781    $34,421    $36,142    $37,949    $39,846
24     $62,540    $65,667    $68,950    $72,398    $76,018    $79,819
25     $55,899    $58,694    $61,629    $64,710    $67,946    $71,343
26     $38,590    $40,519    $42,545    $44,673    $46,906    $49,252
27     $65,437    $68,709    $72,145    $75,752    $79,539    $83,516
28     $77,344    $81,212    $85,272    $89,536    $94,012    $98,713
29    --------   --------   --------   --------   --------   --------
30    $487,173   $511,532   $537,109   $563,964   $592,162   $621,771
H30                                                        <F1=HELP>
Press ALT to choose commands, or F2 to edit.
```

When you scroll away from the upper-left corner of the spreadsheet, the column and row headers disappear off the screen.

Fortunately, the Freeze Titles command on the Options menu provides a way to "freeze" columns and rows at the top and left edges of a spreadsheet. Columns and rows that are frozen in this way remain visible no matter what part of the spreadsheet you are viewing, much like the column letters and row numbers always do.

To use this command, position the highlight in the column just to the right of the columns you want to freeze and in the row just below the rows you want to freeze. When you select the Freeze Titles command, Works will freeze, or lock onto the screen, the columns to the left of the column that contains the highlight and the rows above the row that contains the highlight.

An example

Suppose you want to lock column A and rows 1 through 3 of the spreadsheet shown in Figure 11-19 onto the screen. To do this, begin by pressing [Ctrl][Home]. Pressing this key combination moves the highlight to cell A1 and, more importantly, ensures that column A will be the leftmost column on the screen and that row 1 will be the top row. Next, since you want to lock column A and rows 1 through 3 onto the screen, move the highlight to cell B4—the cell immediately to the right of column A and immediately below row 3. Once the highlight is on this cell, pull down the Options menu and select the Freeze Titles command.

As soon as you issue this command, Works will lock column A (the only column visible to the left of the highlight) and rows 1, 2, and 3 (the only rows visible above the highlight) onto the screen. Until you shift new columns and rows into view, of course, you won't be able to tell that this column and these rows are frozen. As soon as you shift new columns and/or rows onto the screen, however, the effect of this command will become obvious.

For example, Figure 11-20 shows the result of pressing the ➡ key six times and the ⬇ key 26 times. As you can see, these keystrokes shift columns G and H and rows 19 through 33 onto the screen. Instead of shifting column A off the screen, as it would if that column were not frozen, Works shifts columns B and C off the screen instead. Consequently, the January and February columns are obscured, but the column of sales and expense categories remains. Similarly, instead of shifting rows 1, 2, and 3 off the top of the screen, as it would if they were not frozen, it shifts rows 4 through 18 off the screen.

Figure 11-20

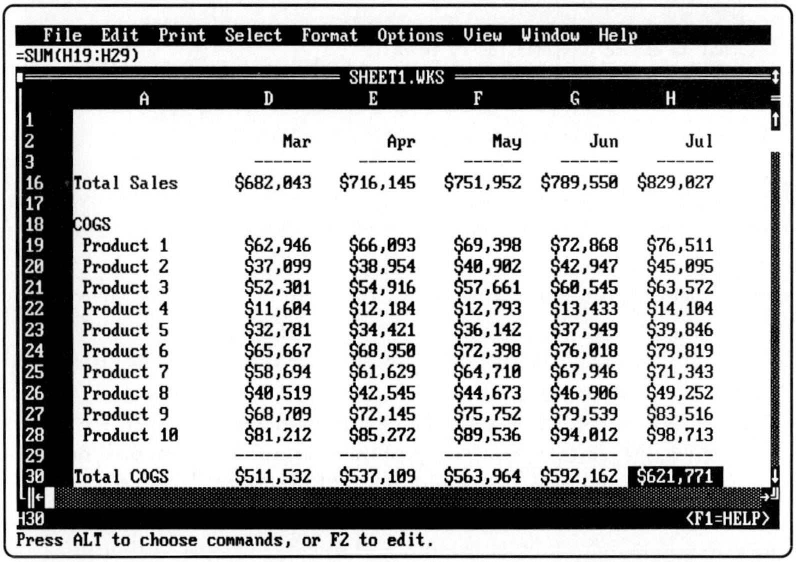

```
   File  Edit  Print  Select  Format  Options  View  Window  Help
=SUM(H19:H29)
═════════════════════════ SHEET1.WKS ═══════════════════════════
        A            D         E         F         G        H
 1
 2                  Mar       Apr       May       Jun      Jul
 3                 ------    ------    ------    ------   ------
16   Total Sales  $682,043  $716,145  $751,952  $789,550 $829,027
17
18  COGS
19    Product 1    $62,946   $66,093   $69,398   $72,868  $76,511
20    Product 2    $37,099   $38,954   $40,902   $42,947  $45,095
21    Product 3    $52,301   $54,916   $57,661   $60,545  $63,572
22    Product 4    $11,604   $12,184   $12,793   $13,433  $14,104
23    Product 5    $32,781   $34,421   $36,142   $37,949  $39,846
24    Product 6    $65,667   $68,950   $72,398   $76,018  $79,819
25    Product 7    $58,694   $61,629   $64,710   $67,946  $71,343
26    Product 8    $40,519   $42,545   $44,673   $46,906  $49,252
27    Product 9    $68,709   $72,145   $75,752   $79,539  $83,516
28    Product 10   $81,212   $85,272   $89,536   $94,012  $98,713
29                ------    ------    ------    ------   ------
30  Total COGS    $511,532  $537,109  $563,964  $592,162 $621,771
H30                                                    <F1=HELP>
Press ALT to choose commands, or F2 to edit.
```

The Freeze Titles command allows you to "freeze" columns and rows at the top and left edges of a spreadsheet.

Moving the highlight into the titles area

Once you have locked one or more rows and/or columns onto the screen, Works will not allow you to move the highlight into the frozen rows and/or columns with the cursor-movement keys. If you press ⬅ while the highlight is in the column just to the right of the bottommost frozen column, or press ⬆ while the highlight is in the row just below the lowest title row, the highlight will not move.

Likewise, if you press [Ctrl][Home], Works will move the highlight to the upper-left cell outside the title area—the cell on which the highlight was positioned when you issued the Freeze Titles command.

However, you can use the [Go To] key or the Go To... command on the Select menu to move the highlight into the title area of a spreadsheet. All you have to do is press [Go To] or select the Go To... command and supply a cell address in a frozen row or column, and Works will move the highlight to that cell. However, you'll see a double image of at least some of the frozen rows and/or columns. For example, Figure 11-21 shows the result of using the [Go To] key to move the highlight to cell A1 of the spreadsheet shown in Figure 11-20 (the one in which column A and rows 1 through 3 are frozen onto the screen). As you can see, Works presents a double image of the frozen rows and columns, and places the highlight on the lower-right occurrence of cell A1.

Figure 11-21

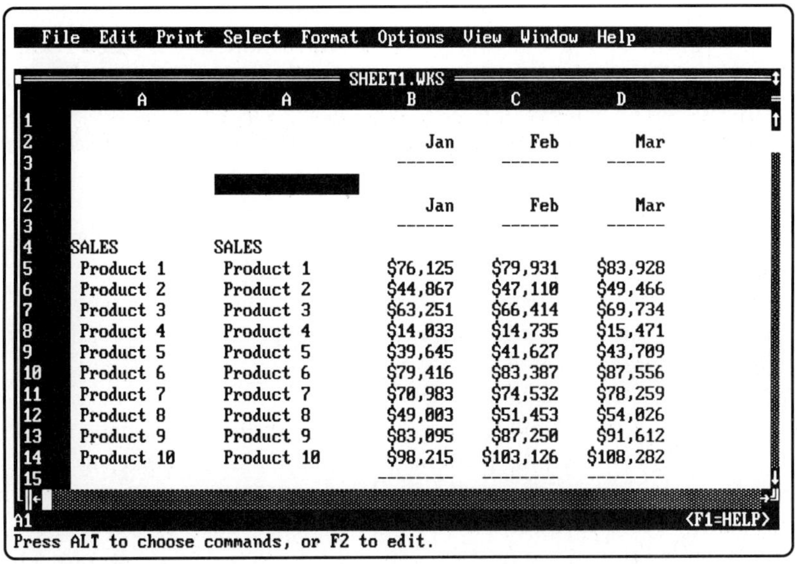

You can use the Go To... command or the [Go To] key to move the highlight into a cell in a title row or column.

If you have a mouse, you can use it to move the highlight to a cell in a frozen row or column. Simply click on the cell to which you want to move the highlight. Works will then display a double image of the frozen rows and columns on the screen, and place the highlight on the lower-right occurrence of the cell on which you clicked.

Works also will allow you to move the highlight into the title area of the screen when it is in the Point mode; for example, when you are building a formula or specifying the destination of a Move or Copy command. In these cases, you can use any of the cursor-movement keys to move the highlight into a frozen row or column. When you do, however, you'll see the same sort of double image shown in Figure 11-21.

Although the double rows and columns do not have any effect on the performance of the spreadsheet, they are confusing. To clear them from the screen, simply press [Pg Dn] and [Ctrl][Pg Dn] a couple of times apiece, then press [Pg Up] and [Ctrl][Pg Up] an equal number of times.

Unfreezing frozen rows and columns

At some point after freezing one or more title rows and/or columns onto the screen, you may want to unfreeze them. To do this, simply pull down the Options menu while the highlight is positioned anywhere in the spreadsheet, and select the Unfreeze Titles command. When you do this, Works will unfreeze the rows and/or columns that are frozen at the time and shift the titles area of the spreadsheet into view. The highlight will remain where it was when you issued the Unfreeze Titles command. In many cases, therefore, the cursor will be in an area of the spreadsheet that is not visible on the screen. However, you can return to the area of the spreadsheet that contains the highlight simply by pressing the [Esc] key.

CELL PROTECTION

Works lets you protect the entries in a spreadsheet from accidental overwriting or erasure. Protection comes in handy both in spreadsheets you will use and in spreadsheets you prepare for others. Using cell protection will keep you or others from destroying valuable entries (especially formulas) in your spreadsheets.

In Works, there are two elements involved in cell protection. First, each cell in a Works spreadsheet can be locked or unlocked individually. Second, Works allows you to enable or disable protection for the entire spreadsheet. While this global protection is on, Works prevents you from making changes to any of the locked cells in the spreadsheet. When global protection is off, you can make changes to any cells, whether they are locked or unlocked.

Originally, all the cells in a spreadsheet are locked, but global protection is turned off. As a result, you can make entries into any cell of a new spreadsheet. If you turn global protection on while each cell is locked, you won't be able to make changes to any of the cells in the spreadsheet. In fact, you won't even be able to unlock locked cells. Consequently, protecting individual cells of a spreadsheet is a two-step process. First, with global protection off, you unlock the cells you don't want protected. Then you turn global protection on. Once you do this, the locked cells will be protected, and the unlocked cells will not.

To lock or unlock a cell, move the highlight to that cell, pull down the Format menu, and select the Style... command. When you do this, you'll see a dialog box like the one shown in Figure 11-22. As you can see, the lower-left corner of this dialog box contains a Locked check box. The X in the brackets to the left of this check box indicates that the highlighted cell is locked.

Figure 11-22

The status of the Locked check box in the Style dialog box determines whether a cell is locked or unlocked.

Choosing the Locked check box changes it to the opposite state. If the Locked check box is on, choosing it will turn it off (and will remove the X from the box). If the Locked check box is off, choosing it will turn it on (and will cause the X to appear). The status of the Locked check box when you select <OK> determines whether the highlighted cell will be locked or unlocked when you return to the spreadsheet.

If you want, you can lock and unlock more than one cell at a time. To do this, simply extend the highlight to cover the cells whose lock status you want to change before you select Style... from the Format menu. If more than one cell is selected when you issue this command, a hyphen (-) will appear in the Locked check box, regardless of whether all the highlighted cells are locked, unlocked, or whether some of the cells are locked and some are not. If you choose the Locked check box at this point, Works will replace the hyphen with an X. Choosing <OK> at this point will lock all of the highlighted cells. If you choose Locked a second time, Works will remove the X from the check box, leaving it blank. Choosing <OK> at this point will unlock all the highlighted cells. If you choose <OK> while the Locked option is marked with a hyphen, Works will return you to the spreadsheet without changing the protection status of the highlighted cells.

Unfortunately, Works does not offer any way to tell which cells in a spreadsheet are protected. It does not display their entries in bold characters or display a marker on the status line when they are highlighted. To determine whether a cell is locked or unlocked, you must highlight it individually, pull down the Format menu, select the Style... command, and look at the Locked check box in the Style dialog box.

In most cases when you use cell protection, you'll want more cells to be protected than unprotected. In those cases, the default protection status of individual cells (locked) is convenient. To protect all but a few of the cells in a spreadsheet, simply unlock those few cells, then turn on global protection. Sometimes, however, you may want to protect only a few of the cells in a spreadsheet and leave the remainder of the cells unprotected. To do this, you must unlock all the cells except the ones you want to protect. Instead of unlocking all the cells around the ones you want to protect (a tedious process at best), unlock every cell in the spreadsheet, then relock the ones you want to protect. To unlock every cell in the spreadsheet, select Row and then Column (or Column and then Row) from the Select menu to select the entire spreadsheet. After doing this, pull down the Format menu, select the Style... command, then choose Locked twice. Once every cell is unlocked, lock the few cells you want to protect, then turn on global protection.

**Turning global
protection on
and off**

The Protect Data command on the Options menu controls the global protection status of the spreadsheet. When global protection is off (its default state), the area to the left of the Protect Data command will be blank. When global protection is on, the Protect Data command will be marked with a dot. If you select the Protect Data command while global protection is off, Works will turn it on. If you select Protect Data while global protection is on, Works will turn it off.

An example

Suppose you want to protect all cells but the ones in the range B4:E5 in the spreadsheet shown in Figure 11-23. That way, you can play "what if" with the values in those cells without accidentally erasing or modifying the formulas in the cells in the ranges B7:F7 and F4:F5. Assuming that global protection is turned off and that every cell in the spreadsheet is currently locked, this is a simple two-step process. First, unlock the cells in the range B4:E5. Second, turn on global protection to protect the worksheet.

Figure 11-23

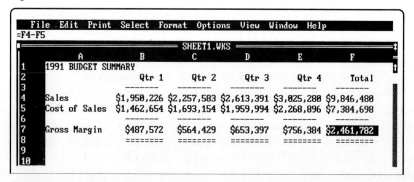

We'll use this spreadsheet to demonstrate the use of cell protection.

To unlock the cells in the range B4:E5, begin by moving the highlight to cell B4, holding down the [Shift] key or pressing the [Extend] key, and then pressing ➡ three times and ⬇ once to highlight those cells. While those cells are highlighted, pull down the Format menu, select the Style... command, and choose Locked twice—once to replace the hyphen with an X, and again to remove the X. When you choose <OK>, Works will unlock the cells in the range B4:E5 and return you to the spreadsheet.

Once you have unlocked the cells in the range B4:E5, you should turn on global protection for the spreadsheet. To do this, simply pull down the Options menu and select the Protect Data command. Now, Works will not allow you to make changes to any cells except those in the range B4:E5—the only unlocked cells in the spreadsheet.

As you would expect, Works will not allow you to do anything to alter the contents of a locked cell when global protection is on. If you try to edit the entry in a locked cell, Works will display the alert box shown in Figure 11-24. It will display the same alert box if you try to type a new entry into a locked cell.

Protection effects

Figure 11-24

Works will display this alert box when you try to edit or type an entry in a locked cell when global protection is on.

In addition to preventing you from editing or replacing the entries in locked cells, global protection deactivates a number of important commands for locked and unlocked cells alike. Specifically, while global protection is on, Works will not allow you to select the Move, Clear, Delete Row/Column, Insert Row/Column, Fill Right, Fill Down, Fill Series..., and Range Name... commands from the Edit menu; the Insert Page Break and Delete Page Break commands from the Print menu; or any of the commands from the Format menu (including the various formats, the Style... command, and the Column Width... command). Consequently, while global protection is on, you cannot move entries to or from any cells, insert or delete any rows or columns, name any cells or ranges, format any cells, or change the width of any columns. These restrictions apply to every cell in a protected spreadsheet—not just to the locked cells. You must turn global protection off before you can use any of these commands.

Unlike many other commands, the Copy and Copy Special... commands remain active while global protection is on. You can use these commands to copy information from both unlocked and locked cells in a protected spreadsheet. However, you cannot specify a destination within that spreadsheet. If you specify any destination within a protected spreadsheet—even an unlocked cell—Works will display the alert box shown in Figure 11-25. These two commands are active to allow you to copy information from the cells of the protected spreadsheet into another Works document—another spreadsheet document, a word processor document, or a database document. (We explained how to copy information from one spreadsheet document to another in Chapter 9; we'll show you how to copy information from a spreadsheet into another type of document in Chapter 19.)

Figure 11-25

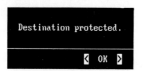

Works will display this alert box when you try to copy an entry into a protected spreadsheet document.

It is important to realize that protecting a cell that contains a formula does not "freeze" the value of that formula. Whenever you make a change to a cell that is referenced by the formula (or press [Calc] if the spreadsheet is set for manual calculation), Works will change the value of that formula—even though it is in a protected cell.

**Erasing
unlocked cells**

Although the Clear command is inactive whenever global protection is on, it still is possible to erase entries from the unlocked cells in a spreadsheet. To do so, move the highlight to the cell whose entry you want to erase, press the [Backspace] key, and then press [Enter]. (You can achieve the same results by pressing [Edit], pressing the [Backspace] key once for each character in the entry, and then pressing [Enter].) Unfortunately, this method allows you to erase only one cell at a time. To erase a group of adjacent cells, you probably will want to turn off global protection and then use the Clear command.

**Activating
unlocked cells**

Works makes it easy to move the highlight to the unlocked cells in a spreadsheet when global protection is on. To do this, simply press the [Tab] key or the [Shift][Tab] combination. When you press [Tab], Works will move the highlight to the right to the next unlocked cell in the current row. If there are no more unlocked cells in the current row, Works will move the highlight down to the leftmost unlocked cell in the next row that contains an unlocked cell. If there are no more unlocked cells between the current position of the highlight and the end of a spreadsheet, Works will wrap the highlight to the first unlocked cell in that spreadsheet.

The [Shift][Tab] combination has the opposite effect. When you press [Shift]-[Tab], Works will move the highlight to the left to the next unlocked cell in the current row. If there are no more unlocked cells in that row, Works will move the highlight up to the rightmost unlocked cell in the first row above the current row that contains an unlocked cell. If there are no more unlocked cells between the current position of the highlight and the beginning of the spreadsheet, Works will wrap the highlight to the last unlocked cell in that spreadsheet.

SEARCHING

The Search… command, which is located on the Select menu, allows you to search through a spreadsheet for a particular entry. When you pull down the Select menu and issue the Search… command, Works will display a dialog box like the one shown in Figure 11-26. When the dialog box appears, you should type the characters for which you want Works to search into the Search For text box. You can specify up to 255 characters We'll call the characters you enter into this box the search string.

Figure 11-26

Works will display a dialog box like this one when you pull down the Select menu and issue the Search… command.

In addition to the Search For text box, the Search dialog box contains a Search By option box. The two options in this box determine the direction in which Works will search the cells of the spreadsheet for the search string. If you choose Rows (the default), Works will search from left to right across each row before it moves down to the next row of the spreadsheet. For example, if you highlight the range A1:B2, Works will look in cell A1, then cell B1, then cell A2, then cell B2. If you choose Columns, Works will search down each column before it moves to the next column. For example, if you again highlight the range A1:B2, Works will look in cell A1, then cell A2, then cell B1, and finally cell B2.

The search process

Once you have entered your search string into the Search For text box and selected a direction in the Search By option box, you should choose <OK>. When you do this, Works will begin searching for the first cell that contains the search string. If the highlight was on a single cell when you issued the Search… command, Works will start searching in the cell to the right of that cell. (If you chose the Columns option, Works will start searching in the cell below the one on which the highlight is positioned.) If you highlighted a range of cells before issuing the Search… command, Works will start at the upper-left corner of that range. (If you chose the Rows option, Works will search row by row; if you chose Columns, Works will search column by column.) As it searches, Works updates an indicator at the left edge of the status line that tells you what percentage of the area it has searched. For example, if you highlight 1000 cells before issuing the Search... command, Works will display *10%* at the left edge of the status line after it searches 100 of those cells.

If Works finds an occurrence of the search string you specified, it will move the highlight to the cell that contains that occurrence and then end the Search... command. If Works searches the entire active area of the spreadsheet (or, if you highlighted a range of cells, the entire range) without finding a match, it will display an alert box that contains the message *No match found.* As soon as you choose <OK> to acknowledge this message, Works will cancel the Search... command. If you want to cancel the Search... command before Works finds an occurrence of the search string or completes its search, simply press [Esc].

What Works searches for

It is important to note that the Search... command locates cells based on what Works displays in them—not what they actually contain. Consequently, you cannot use this command to locate characters within formulas or functions. For example, Works will not locate a cell that contains the formula *=B5+B8* when you specify the search string *B8.* However, it will find characters within the result of formulas and functions. For example, if the formula returned the value 123, Works would locate the cell that contained that formula if you commanded it to search for the characters 123.

Since formats affect the way that values and the results of formulas and functions are displayed, they affect the action of the Search... command. For example, suppose a cell that contains the value 1000 is assigned the Currency format, so that Works displays that value as *$1,000.00.* If you directed Works to search for the string 1000, it would not locate the cell that contains this entry, since due to formatting, the characters 1000 are not adjacent. However, Works would locate this cell if you specified 1,000 as the search string.

When you issue the Search... command, Works won't locate just cells whose display exactly matches the search string; it will also locate cells whose display contains that text. For example, it would locate a cell that contains the text entry *Louisville* if you specified the search string *Louis.* If you specified 0 as the search string, Works would locate all cells whose displayed value contains that character. If you specified the search string $, Works would locate any value-containing cell that was assigned a Currency format.

Finally, the Search... command ignores capitalization. For example, the search string *test* will match the entries *test, TEST, Test,* and so forth. The search string *TEST* will match the same entries.

Repeating a search

As you've seen, Works cancels the Search... command as soon as it locates one occurrence of the search string in the spreadsheet. If you want to find other occurrences, you can reissue the Search... command. When you do this, Works will redisplay the Search dialog box, which will contain the search string you entered the last time you used the Search... command during the current Works session. At this time, you can continue the search simply by choosing <OK>. When you do this, Works will search for the next occurrence of the search string, starting with the cell to the right of or below the one on which the highlight is positioned at the time.

The [Repeat Search] ([F7]) key provides an easier way to repeat the Search... command. When you press this key, Works will search for the next occurrence of the search string automatically (that is, without displaying the Search dialog box and making you choose <OK>).

Works will continue to search for occurrences of the search string as long as you keep issuing the Search... command or pressing the [Repeat Search] key. If you issue this command or press this key after Works has highlighted the last occurrence of the search string in the spreadsheet or highlighted range, Works will resume the search at the top of the spreadsheet or range. Works will continue to cycle through the spreadsheet or range, highlighting the same cells over and over as long as you reissue the Search... command or press the [Repeat Search] key.

Wildcard characters

Works allows you to use two wildcard characters in the search string you specify within a spreadsheet document: ? and *. (As you may recall, you can use only the ? wildcard within a word processor document.) The ? wildcard takes the place of any single character. For example, the search string 1?0 would match the entries 100, 110, 120, and so forth. The * wildcard takes the place of any number of characters, or none at all. For example, the search string 1*0 would match the entries 10, 170, 1950, etc. You can use these characters in place of any characters in search strings.

SORTING ROWS
►WORKS 2◄

►Works 2 offers a new command, Sort Rows..., that allows you to sort tables of information in spreadsheet. Sorting rearranges the rows of the table into ascending or descending order based on the entries in one, two, or three columns. Sorting comes in handy when you want to bring order to a randomly arranged collection of entries; for instance, when you want to arrange a series of entries into date order.

To sort a table, first highlight the range that contains all the entries you want to sort. This range must include at least two rows and can include as many columns as you want. After you highlight the range, select the Sort Rows... command from the Select menu. When you issue this command, Works will display a dialog box like the one shown in Figure 11-27. To sort the highlighted range, simply enter the appropriate column letters into the 1st Column, 2nd Column, and 3rd Column text boxes and choose <OK>. If you plan to sort on only one column, you'll enter a column letter in the 1st Column text box only. (By default, Works will always enter the column letter of the first column in the highlighted range in the 1st Column text box. If you want to sort on that column, you won't need to make a change.) If you plan to sort on two or three columns, you'll enter the letter of the first column in the 1st Column text box, the letter of the second in the 2nd Column text box, and the letter of the third in the 3rd Column text box.

Figure 11-27

The Sort Rows dialog box lets you specify the column(s) on which you want to sort and the sort order for each column.

As you enter each column letter into the Sort Rows dialog box, you will also specify the sort order—Ascend or Descend—that Works will use to arrange the entries in that column. The default sort order, Ascend, tells Works to arrange the entries in that column into ascending order. If you choose Descend, Works will arrange the entries in the sort column into descending order. (We'll talk more about ascending versus descending sort orders later.)

After you have entered the column letters and specified the sort order, press [Enter] or choose <OK> to sort the database. Works will then rearrange the highlighted range by sorting the entries in the column(s) you've specified, then reordering the rest of the table according to these sorted entries.

If you select the Sort Rows... command, then decide not to sort, you can cancel the command by pressing [Esc] or by choosing the <Cancel> button.

An example

Suppose you have created the simple table shown in Figure 11-28. This table lists the last names, first names, and ages of several people. You want to sort this table so that the listings are arranged in alphabetical order by last name. That is, you want the entries in column B to be arranged in alphabetical order. To begin, select the Sort Rows... command from the Select menu. When you see the Sort Rows dialog box, enter the column letter *B* in the 1st Column text box, as shown in Figure 11-29. Since you want to arrange the entries in column B in ascending order, you don't need to change the default sort order, Ascend, after entering the column letter. To execute this sort, just choose <OK> or press [Enter]. Figure 11-30 shows the result.

Figure 11-28

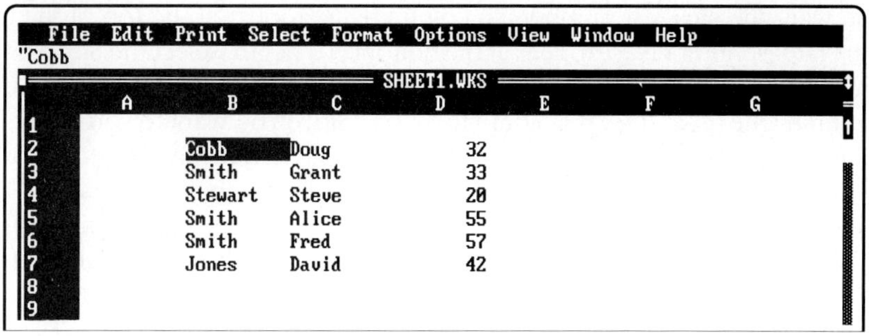

```
  File   Edit   Print   Select   Format   Options   View   Window   Help
"Cobb
╞══════════════════════════════ SHEET1.WKS ══════════════════════════╡
         A          B          C          D          E          F          G
 1
 2                  Cobb       Doug              32
 3                  Smith      Grant             33
 4                  Stewart    Steve             20
 5                  Smith      Alice             55
 6                  Smith      Fred              57
 7                  Jones      David             42
 8
 9
```

We'll use this table to illustrate the process of sorting.

Figure 11-29

This Sort Rows dialog box tells Works to sort the table into ascending order based on the entries in column B.

Figure 11-30

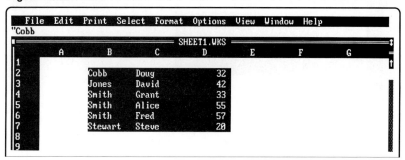

```
  File   Edit   Print   Select   Format   Options   View   Window   Help
"Cobb
╞══════════════════════════════ SHEET1.WKS ══════════════════════════╡
         A          B          C          D          E          F          G
 1
 2                  Cobb       Doug              32
 3                  Jones      David             42
 4                  Smith      Grant             33
 5                  Smith      Alice             55
 6                  Smith      Fred              57
 7                  Stewart    Steve             20
 8
 9
```

Works has rearranged the table so that the entries in column B are in ascending order.

Another example

Suppose you want to sort our sample table into ascending order by age. That is, you want the smallest numbers in column D to appear at the top of the table and the largest numbers to appear at the bottom. To begin, select the Sort Rows... command from the Select menu. When the Sort Rows dialog box appears, enter the column letter *D* in the 1st Column text box. Since you want to sort the entries in column D into ascending order, you don't need to change the default sort order, Ascend. Figure 11-31 shows the completed dialog box. Finally, choose <OK> or press [Enter] to execute the sort. When you do this, Works will sort the table so that the entries in column D are in ascending order, as shown in Figure 11-32.

Figure 11-31

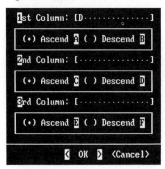

This Sort Rows dialog box tells Works to sort the table into ascending order based on the entries in column D.

Figure 11-32

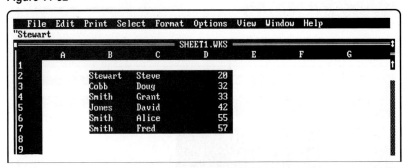

Works has rearranged the sample table so that the entries in column D are in ascending order.

Sort order

As we have mentioned, Works' default sort order is Ascend. If a column contains numbers, the entries will be arranged so that the smallest values come first. If a column contains text, the entries will be sorted into alphabetical order. Entries in the column that begin with a blank space will appear before entries that begin with an alphabetic character.

If the column contains mixed entries (like addresses, which generally contain both numbers and text), then entries that begin with a number will come ahead of entries that begin with an alphabetic character. If the table contains records with no entry in the key column, those records will appear last in the sorted table.

If two or more entries in the sort column begin with the same character, Works will use the second character in those entries to arrange them. If two or more entries begin with the same two characters, then Works will use the third character, then the fourth, then the fifth, and so on, to arrange the entries. If two or more entries in the sort column are identical, then those entries will appear sequentially in the sorted table.

Works also allows you to sort your table into descending order. You can specify descending sort order for a column by choosing Descend in the Sort Rows dialog box. When you select Descend as the sort order for a column, Works will sort the records in the table so that the entries in that column are in descending order. If the column contains values, the entries will be arranged so that the largest values come first. If the column contains text, the entries will be sorted into reverse alphabetical order (Z to A). If the column contains any blank entries, those entries will appear first.

Suppose you want to sort the sample table so that the entries in column D are in descending order. To begin, select the Sort Rows... command from the Select menu. When the Sort Rows dialog box appears, you'll see that the column letter *D* remains in the 1st Column text box. Since this is the column you want to sort, you don't need to change this setting. All you have to do is choose the Descend option below the 1st Column text box. Finally, choose <OK> or press [Enter] to execute the sort. As you can see in Figure 11-33, the table is now sorted so that the entries in column D are arranged in descending order.

Figure 11-33

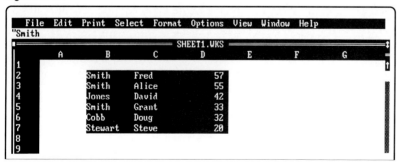

Works has rearranged the sample table so that the entries in column D are in descending order.

**Multiple sort
columns**

So far, we've shown what happens when you sort a table using only one sort column: Works rearranges the table based on the entries in the single sort column you specify. As we have said, if there are two or more identical entries in the sort column, Works will place those entries sequentially in the sorted table. If there are a number of sets of identical entries in the sort column, the sorted table will appear to be "grouped" on those entries.

To make a grouped table easier to use, you may want to sort the table using two sort columns. For instance, you might want to sort each of the last name groups in our example into alphabetical order by first name. That way, the listings in each group would be arranged by first name: *Alice Smith* would come before *Fred Smith*, who would precede *Grant Smith*, and so on.

To achieve this effect, you need to define a second sort column before you sort the table. To sort with two sort columns, first select the Sort Rows… command from the Select menu. When the Sort Rows dialog box appears, enter the column letter of the first sort column in the 1st Column text box and choose a sort order for that column. Then, enter the column letter of the second sort column in the 2nd Column text box and choose a sort order for that column. When you've specified the column letter and sort order for both sort columns, choose <OK> or press [Enter] to sort the table. Works will use the first sort column to arrange the table into the order you've specified. If there are any duplicate entries in the first sort column, Works will group the sorted table around those duplicates and will use the second sort column to arrange the entries in each group.

In some cases, you may even want to specify three sort columns. To sort with three sort columns, first select the Sort Rows… command from the Select menu, enter the column letter of the first sort column in the 1st Column text box, then choose a sort order for that column; enter the column letter of the second sort column in the 2nd Column text box, then choose a sort order for that column; finally, enter the column letter of the third sort column in the 3rd Column text box, then choose a sort order for that column. When you've specified the column letter and sort order for the three sort columns, choose <OK> to sort the table.

A recommendation

While the Sort Rows... command is a very useful addition to the Works spreadsheet, you should not overuse it. This command is intended for sorting simple tables. If you need to sort more complicated tables, you should use the Works database. We'll cover the Works database in Chapters 15, 16, and 17.◄

CONCLUSION

In this chapter, we have completed our look at spreadsheets. In the next three chapters, we'll explore Works' charting capabilities. As you will see, Works can create a variety of different charts from the information in a spreadsheet document.

Chart Basics 12

*W*orks' charts are terrific tools for presenting the information in your spread-sheets in a clear and understandable way. In this chapter, we'll explain how to create, manage, edit, and print charts. In Chapter 13, we'll introduce Works' chart types and show you how to create each. In Chapter 14, we'll show you how to enhance charts by adding titles, legends, data labels, and so on.

In Works, all charts are based on the data in a spreadsheet. In fact, Works allows you to create charts only from within a spreadsheet document. In order to create a chart, then, you must begin with spreadsheet data. This data can be a few simple numbers that you have typed into several cells, or it can consist of a range of cells from a large and complex spreadsheet. You can create up to eight charts for a given spreadsheet.

▶The key to Works' charting abilities is the New Chart and Charts... commands on the spreadsheet environment's View menu. (In Works 1, these commands are located on the Chart menu. There is no Chart menu in Works 2.) You'll use these commands to create and work with charts. The New Chart command allows you to create a new chart, as well as to access Work's chart view. The Charts... command allows you to rename, delete, or copy charts. (Earlier versions of Works offer two other commands: Define and View. These commands are not available in Works 2.)

When you select the New Chart command, Works will enter the chart view. In the chart view, you'll still see your spreadsheet on the screen, but the menu bar at the top of the screen will be different. The commands on the menus in the chart view allow you to modify and enhance your charts. When Works is in the chart view, the legend *CHART* will appear on the status line. To return from the chart

CHART BASICS

▶WORKS 2◀

view to the spreadsheet, press the [View Spreadsheet] key ([F10]) or select the Spreadsheet command from the View menu. (In Works 1, you select the Exit Chart command from the Chart menu to return to the spreadsheet.) ◄

CREATING CHARTS

The quickest way to produce a chart is to let Works create it for you. To create a chart using the automatic method, first highlight the range that contains the numbers you want to graph, then select the New Chart command from the View menu. When you select the New Chart command, Works automatically creates a new chart and defines the data series for that chart from the highlighted data. That's all there is to it.

An example

For example, suppose you want to create a bar chart that illustrates the sales of Widgets in row 4 of the spreadsheet in Figure 12-1. To begin, highlight the values you want to chart—the range B4:E4. Next, select the New Chart command

►WORKS 2◄

from the View menu to create the chart. ►Your new chart will immediately appear on the screen, as shown in Figure 12-2. (In Works 1, the chart does not come into view immediately.)◄ Notice that Works has plotted the data in the range you highlighted, with one bar for each cell in the highlighted range.

Figure 12-1

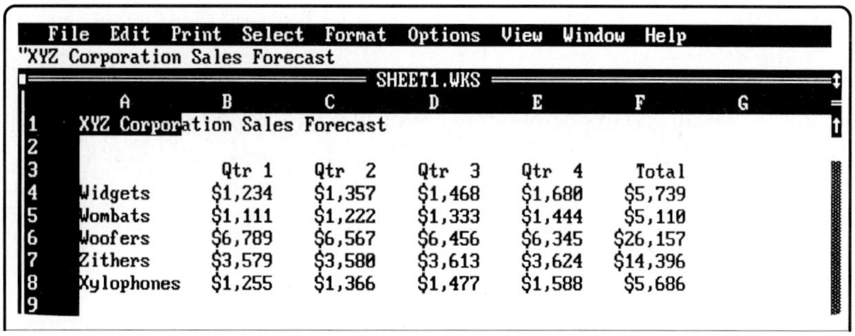

```
  File  Edit  Print  Select  Format  Options  View  Window  Help
 "XYZ Corporation Sales Forecast
 ═══════════════════════════════ SHEET1.WKS ═══════════════════════════
        A          B        C        D        E        F        G
 1    XYZ Corporation Sales Forecast
 2
 3                Qtr 1    Qtr 2    Qtr 3    Qtr 4    Total
 4    Widgets     $1,234   $1,357   $1,468   $1,680   $5,739
 5    Wombats     $1,111   $1,222   $1,333   $1,444   $5,110
 6    Woofers     $6,789   $6,567   $6,456   $6,345   $26,157
 7    Zithers     $3,579   $3,580   $3,613   $3,624   $14,396
 8    Xylophones  $1,255   $1,366   $1,477   $1,588   $5,686
 9
```

In Works, all charts are based on numbers in a spreadsheet.

When you use the automatic method to create a chart, Works automatically defines the data series that makes up the chart and uses the shape of the range you highlight to decide how it should plot the data. If, as in this case, the range includes just a single row (or a single column), then Works will define the values in that row or column as a data series.

When you're finished viewing the chart, press [Esc]. At this point, your screen will look like Figure 12-3. As you can see, your spreadsheet is in view, but the menu at the top of the screen has changed. You are now in the chart view. (We'll

►WORKS 2◄

talk more about the chart view later in this chapter.) ►To return to the spreadsheet, press [F10] or select the Spreadsheet command from the View menu. (In Works 1, this command is called Exit Chart and it appears on the Chart menu.)◄

Figure 12-2

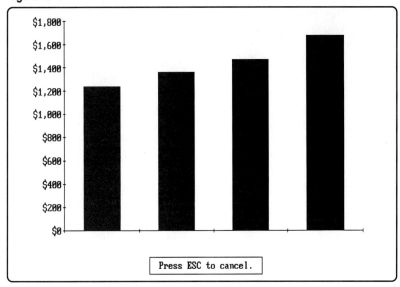

The New Chart command lets you create a chart automatically.

Figure 12-3

File Print Data Format Options View Window Help
1234

```
                              SHEET1.WKS
        A         B         C         D         E         F         G
1  XYZ Corporation Sales Forecast
2
3                Qtr 1     Qtr 2     Qtr 3     Qtr 4     Total
4  Widgets      $1,234    $1,357    $1,468    $1,680    $5,739
5  Wombats      $1,111    $1,222    $1,333    $1,444    $5,110
6  Woofers      $6,789    $6,567    $6,456    $6,345   $26,157
7  Zithers      $3,579    $3,580    $3,613    $3,624   $14,396
8  Xylophones   $1,255    $1,366    $1,477    $1,588    $5,686
9
```

In the chart view, you see your spreadsheet on the screen, but the menu bar will change and the legend CHART will appear on the status line.

Works can chart only values. If you include a cell that contains a label or a **Notes** blank cell in a data series, Works will simply ignore that cell in the chart. If there are no values in one of the data series you specify, Works will not plot that range in the chart. In addition, the values on which each data series in a chart is based must be in adjacent cells of a row or column. There is no direct way to define a data series in a chart from values that are not in adjacent cells.

Whenever you update a spreadsheet on which one or more charts are based, Works will automatically update all the charts that are based on that spreadsheet. The next time you view the chart, it will reflect the changes you have made to the underlying spreadsheet.

When you define a new chart, Works adds its name to the View menus in both the spreadsheet and the chart view. The first chart you create has the default name Chart1, the second Chart2, and so on. You can view the chart at any time just by selecting its name from the View menu in either the spreadsheet or the chart view.

Since every chart you create is part of a spreadsheet, all you have to do to save a chart is save the spreadsheet on which it is based. Works automatically saves all the charts that are based on a spreadsheet when you use the Save or Save As... command to save that spreadsheet.

You can create up to eight charts for a given spreadsheet. If you try to create a new chart when there are already eight charts in a spreadsheet, Works will display an alert box with the message *No more than 8 charts allowed in each Spreadsheet file. To delete charts, use the Charts command in the View menu.* You'll have to delete one or more charts before you can create a new chart. We'll show you how to delete a chart later in this chapter.

The default chart type in Works is a bar chart. As you might expect, you can create several types of charts in Works. We'll show you how to create those in the next chapter.

The manual method

▶WORKS 2◀

You can also create charts manually. To do this, first choose the New Chart command from the View menu in a spreadsheet while the highlight is not extended. ▶When you select this command, Works will display the alert box shown in Figure 12-4. This box warns you that no series has been defined. When you choose <OK> or press [Enter], Works will enter the chart view and create a new chart, adding its name to the View menu.◀ Once in the chart view, highlight the range of values you want to chart, then use the 1st Y-Series command on the Data menu (and, if the chart has more than one range, the other Y-Series commands) to define the ranges of data on which the chart is based. To view the new chart, choose its name from the View menu.

Figure 12-4

Works will display this alert box if you select the New Chart command without first high-lighting a multiple-cell range.

Let's use the manual method to re-create the chart shown in Figure 12-2. To begin, make sure that the highlight is not expanded. (If it is expanded, press [Esc] to contract it to a single cell.) Next, select the New Chart command from the View menu. When Works displays the alert box shown in Figure 12-4, press [Enter] or choose <OK> to enter the chart view. Next, highlight the range you want to chart—B4:E4—then select the 1st Y-Series command from the Data menu.

To view the chart you've just created, select its name—Chart2—from the View menu. (If you select the name of a chart from the View menu before you define any series for the chart, Works will display the alert box shown in Figure 12-4.) The resulting chart will look like Figure 12-2. When you're finished viewing the chart, press [Esc] to return to the chart view. Then, press [F10] or select the Spreadsheet command from the View menu to return to the spreadsheet.

Creating charts in the chart view

Although you will usually begin the process of creating a new chart from within a spreadsheet, you can also create new charts while you are in the chart view. To create a new chart in the chart view using the automatic method, first highlight the range you want to chart then choose New Chart from the View menu. When you do this, Works will create a new chart and add its name to the View menu. To create a new chart in the chart view using the manual method, just choose New Chart from the View menu to create a new chart. Then use the Y-Series commands on the Data menu to define the series for the chart.

Multiple-series charts

So far, we've created graphs with just one data series. Although many of your charts will contain only one data range, any Works chart (except pie charts) can include up to six data ranges. You can define some multiple-series charts using either the automatic method or the manual method. In many cases, however, you'll have to use the manual method to define a multiple-series chart.

The automatic method

To create a multiple-series chart using the automatic method, first highlight the range that contains the numbers you want to graph. This range must include at least two rows or two columns. Next, you choose the New Chart command from the View menu. When you choose this command, Works will create your chart and define its data series.

An example. Suppose you want to create a new chart illustrating the sales of Widgets and Wombats from the spreadsheet in Figure 12-1. To create this chart, highlight the range B4:E5, then select the New Chart command from the View menu. When you do this, Works will create and display the chart shown in Figure 12-5 on the following page.

As you can see, Works has created two sets of bars in this new chart: one set for each of the two rows of data you selected. The chart includes one bar for each cell in the range you highlighted. The bars that represent the corresponding values in the two series are clustered between the tick marks on the x-axis. In Works, the corresponding values in two or more data series are called a category. We'll use this term in this chapter and the next two to describe the corresponding values in the data series in a multiple-series chart.

Figure 12-5

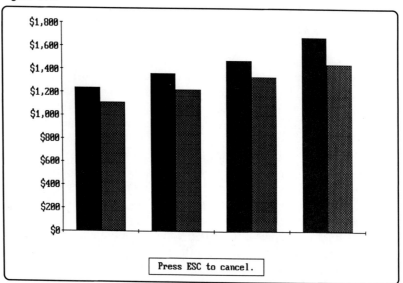

If you highlight multiple rows or columns, then choose the New Chart command, Works will create a multiple-series chart.

How it works.   When you use the automatic method to create a multiple-series chart, Works uses the shape of the range you highlight to decide which values to plot on which axis. If you highlight a range that is wider than it is tall, Works will assume that each row in the range is a data series and will plot the data by row. For example, when you highlighted the four-column by two-row range B4:E5, Works plotted the values by row, as shown in Figure 12-5. Similarly, if the range you highlight is square, Works will assume that each row is a data series. If, on the other hand, you highlight a range that is taller than it is wide, Works will plot the values by column.

Potential problems.   As a result of these rules, the automatic method won't always create the chart you want. For example, watch what happens when you use the automatic method to create a chart that includes Woofers, Zithers, and Xylophones as well as Widgets and Wombats. To create this new chart, highlight the range B4:E8, and select the New Chart command from the View menu. When the chart view menu bar appears, select the chart name—Chart4—from the View menu. Figure 12-6 shows this new chart.

   As you can see, Works has created a bar chart with five clusters of four bars each—in other words, a chart with five categories and four data series instead of four categories and five data series. Because the range we highlighted was taller than it was wide, Works assumed that each column in the range was a data series and turned the chart on its side. The result is not the chart we wanted. To create this chart correctly, you would have to use the manual method.

Figure 12-6

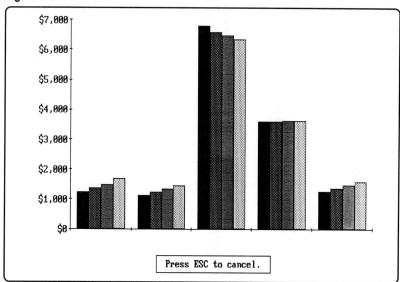

Sometimes the automatic method will not create the chart you want.

As you have seen, the automatic method of creating a chart has a limitation: It works reliably only if your data are arranged correctly. Because the manual method allows you to tell Works exactly what you want to include in the chart and where you want it to be plotted, it overcomes this limitation.

The manual method

To create a multiple-series chart manually, first make sure the highlight is not expanded. Then, select the New Chart command from the View menu in the spreadsheet to create a new chart. Highlight the range you want to use as the first y-series in the chart, and select the 1st Y-Series command from the Data menu to define the first series in the chart. Then, highlight the range that you want to use as the second y-series and select the 2nd Y-Series command to define the second series. You can continue in this way—highlighting individual ranges, then selecting Y-Series commands—until you've defined up to six ranges in the chart. Each of the ranges you highlight to define the data series must include just one row or one column.

For example, suppose you want to create a bar chart manually from the data in rows 4, 5, 6, 7, and 8 in the spreadsheet shown in Figure 12-1. First, make sure that the highlight is not expanded. Then, select the New Chart command from the View menu to create a new chart. When you do this, Works will display the alert message *Series not selected.* When you choose <OK> or press [Enter] to acknowledge this message, you'll be in the chart view.

Now you have to define the chart's series. To do this, highlight the range B4:E4 and select the 1st Y-Series command from the Data menu; highlight the range B5:E5 and select the 2nd Y-Series command.; highlight the range B6:E6 and select the 3rd Y-Series command; highlight the range B7:E7 and select the 4th Y-Series command.; and highlight the range B8:E8 and select the 5th Y-Series command.

Once you've defined all five data series, select the chart's name (Chart5, if you've been working along) from the View menu. Figure 12-7 shows the chart. As you can see, Works has plotted each of the ranges you highlighted as a data series. The result is a clustered bar chart in which each data series represents the sales of a particular product over time, and each cluster compares the sales of all five products at one time.

Figure 12-7

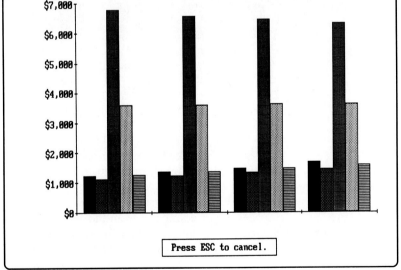

The manual method allows you to create multiple-series charts that correctly represent your data.

Charting data series that are not adjacent

There may be times when you'll want to create a multiple-series chart from data ranges that are not adjacent (discontinuous ranges) in the spreadsheet. For example, suppose you want to chart just the range B4:E4 and the range B8:E8 from the spreadsheet shown in Figure 12-1. Because these rows are discontinuous, you can't use the automatic method to define this chart. To chart discontinuous ranges, you must use the manual method.

For example, to chart the ranges B4:E4 and B8:E8, first make certain that the highlight is not expanded. Then, select the New Chart command from the View menu. When you see the alert message *Series not selected.*, choose <OK> or press [Enter] to enter the chart view. Next, highlight the range B4:E4 and select the 1st Y-Series command from the Data menu. Then, highlight the range B8:E8 and select the 2nd Y-Series command. When you've defined the chart, select the chart's name (Chart6 if you've been working along) from the View menu. Figure 12-8 shows the result.

Figure 12-8

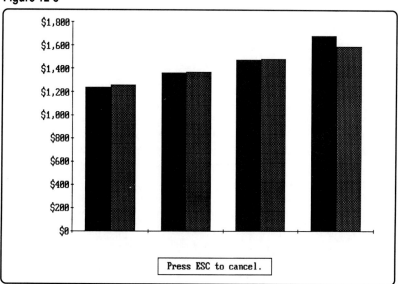

The manual method lets you create multiple-series charts from ranges that are discontinuous.

Automatic vs. manual charting

Now that you're familiar with both the automatic and manual methods for creating charts, the obvious question is which you should use. In general, we recommend the manual method when you need to make absolutely certain that the chart produced is the one you had in mind. This is especially true when you are creating multiple-series charts. On the other hand, for quick charting of just one range, the automatic method will work fine.

MANAGING CHARTS

As we have said, you can create up to eight charts in a single spreadsheet, and Works gives each a default name (Chart1, Chart2, and so on). Works lists the names of the charts for a given spreadsheet at the bottom of the View menu in either the spreadsheet or the chart view. For example, Figure 12-9 shows the View menu for our example spreadsheet after we have created six charts.

Figure 12-9

Works automatically gives each chart you create a name and lists those names on the View menu.

The active chart

The dot next to the name Chart6 on the menu in Figure 12-9 indicates that it is the active chart. Although you can create up to eight charts in a given spreadsheet, only one chart can be active at a time. When you select one of Works' charting commands, Works will execute that command on the active chart. For example, when you select the Titles... command from the Data menu, Works will apply the titles you define to the active chart.

To change the active chart, pull down the View menu, then select the name of the chart you want to activate by pointing to it or by typing the appropriate number: 1 for Chart1, 2 for Chart2, and so on. When you activate a chart, Works will display it on the screen. You can press [Esc] to stop viewing the chart and return to the chart view.

For example, to change the active chart in Figure 12-9 from Chart6 to Chart1, you would pull down the View menu and either type 1 or point to the Chart1 option and press [Enter].

**The Charts...
command**

The Charts... command on the View menu in the spreadsheet and the chart view allows you to rename, delete, and copy your charts. When you select this command, Works will display a dialog box like the one shown in Figure 12-10. As you can see, the names of all of the charts in the current spreadsheet appear in this dialog box, and the name of the active chart is selected. The options <Rename>, <Delete>, and <Copy> at the bottom of this box allow you to rename, delete, and copy charts.

Renaming charts

If you are creating more than one chart for a spreadsheet, you will probably want to give a descriptive name to each chart to make it easier to remember what each represents. You can use the <Rename> option in the Charts dialog box to change the name Works has given to a chart. When you rename a chart, its new name will appear on the View menu and the Charts dialog box in place of Works' default name.

Figure 12-10

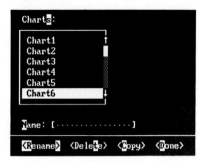

The Charts... command lets you rename, delete, and copy charts.

To rename a chart, first select the Charts... command from the View menu. When the Charts dialog box appears, select the name of the chart you want to rename in the Charts list box. Next, move to the Name text box and type the new name for the chart. As with range names in spreadsheets, chart names can be up to 15 characters long and may include any alphabetic, numeric, or punctuation character. When you've specified the name, choose <Rename>. (Because <Rename> is the default option, you can choose it by pressing [Enter].)

For example, suppose you want to change the name of Chart3 to WIDGETS/ WOMBATS. To begin, first select the Charts... command from the View menu. When the Charts dialog box appears, highlight the name Chart3 in the Charts list box, move to the Name text box and type *WIDGETS/WOMBATS*, and press [Enter] to choose the <Rename> option. If you pull down the View menu at this point, you'll see that Works has changed the name of Chart3 to WIDGETS/WOMBATS.

If the new name you specify for a chart conflicts with the name of an existing chart, Works will display an alert box that contains the message *CHARTNAME already exists.*, where *CHARTNAME* is the name you have specified. If you see this message, you should choose <OK> to acknowledge the error. Then, you should either choose a new name for the chart you are renaming or rename or delete the other chart.

You can use the <Delete> button in the Charts dialog box to delete charts. You might use this command if you create a chart you no longer need or if you want to make room in the current spreadsheet for a new chart.

To delete a chart, first select the Charts... command from the View menu. When you see the Charts dialog box, choose the name of the chart you want to delete from the Charts list box and choose the <Delete> option. Before it deletes the chart, Works will display a dialog box that asks the question *OK to delete: CHARTNAME?*, where *CHARTNAME* is the name of the chart you have chosen. If you choose <OK>, Works will delete the chart. The deleted chart will no longer be listed on the View menu or in the Charts dialog box. If you choose <Cancel>, Works will cancel the Charts... command and will not delete the chart.

Deleting charts

Copying charts

There may be times when you'll want to copy a chart. For instance, suppose you're creating several charts with the same or similar data but different enhancements. It may be easier and faster to create the first chart from scratch, then use the <Copy> option to create the second one, than to create both charts from scratch.

To copy a chart, first select the Charts... command from the View menu. When the Charts dialog box appears, highlight the name of the chart you want to copy in the Charts list box. Then, move to the Name text box and enter the name for the new chart. Finally, choose <Copy> to copy the chart. When you use the <Copy> option to create a new chart, Works will list the new chart on the View menu and in the Charts dialog box, and it will make the new chart the active chart. The new chart will be an exact copy of the source chart.

If you don't specify a name before you copy a chart, Works will assign the new chart a default name. If there are already eight charts in a spreadsheet when you choose the <Copy> option, Works will display an alert box that contains the message *No more than 8 charts allowed in each Spreadsheet file. To delete charts, use the Charts command in the View menu.*

For example, suppose you want to copy Chart1 in the sample spreadsheet into a chart named Number2. To copy this chart, first select the Charts... command from the View menu. When the Charts dialog box appears, choose the name Chart1 from the Charts list box. Then, move to the Name text box and type the name you picked for the new chart: *Number2.* Finally, select <Copy> to copy the chart.

EDITING CHARTS
►WORKS 2◄

►Once you've created a chart, you can modify it or enhance it in a variety of ways. To change the appearance of a chart, first make it the active chart by selecting its name from the View menus of the spreadsheet or the chart view. (When you do, the chart will be displayed on the screen. You have to press [Esc] to stop viewing the chart and gain access to the chart environment menus.)◄

Once you are in the chart view, you can add ranges to a chart or delete ranges from it. We'll show you how to do that next. You can also enhance the chart in a variety of ways. We'll show you how to do this in Chapter 14, by adding titles, legends, and other features.

Adding a series

As we have said, charts in Works can include up to six data series. Sometimes you'll define all of the series for a multiple-series chart when you create it. Other times you'll need to add one or more series to a chart after you have created it. To add a range to a chart, first choose its name from the View menu to make it the active chart and then press [Esc] to access the chart view menus. Next, highlight the range of cells in the spreadsheet that contains the values you want to include in the new series. When the range is highlighted, select the appropriate Y-Series command from the Data menu to add it to the chart. For instance, to make the highlighted range the second series in the chart, select the 2nd Y-Series command.

Suppose you decide to add a range to the chart in Figure 12-5. In addition to charting the sales of Widgets and Wombats, you want to include the sales of Zithers in the chart. To begin, make this chart the active chart by selecting its name—WIDGETS/WOMBATS—from the View menu. When the chart comes into view, press [Esc] to enter the chart view. Next, highlight the range you want to add to the chart—in this example, the range B7:E7. Now, since this is the third range in the chart, select the 3rd Y-Series command from the Data menu to add the new range to the chart.

Now, select the chart's name (WIDGETS/WOMBATS) from the View menu again to view the new chart. As you can see in Figure 12-11, Works has added a third range to the chart. When you're finished viewing the chart, press [Esc] to return to the chart view. Then, press [F10] or select the Exit Chart command from the View menu to return to the spreadsheet.

Figure 12-11

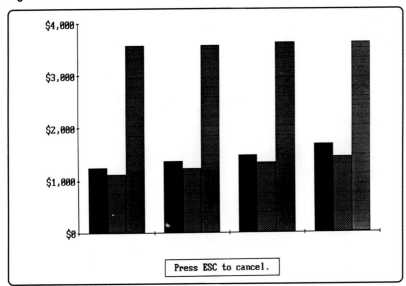

Works lets you add series to an existing chart.

There may be times when you'll want to delete a series from a chart. To delete a range, first choose the chart from the View menu to make it active, and press [Esc] to access the chart view menus. Then, select the Series... command from the Data menu in the chart view to reveal a Series dialog box like the one shown in Figure 12-12. When this box appears, choose the range you want to delete—1st Y-Series, 2nd Y-Series, and so on—from the Series list box. Finally, choose <Delete> to delete the range.

Deleting a series

For example, suppose you want to remove the series for Wombats from the chart in Figure 12-11. To begin, make it the active chart by selecting the name WIDGETS/WOMBATS from the View menu. When the chart comes into view, press [Esc] to enter the chart view. Next, select the Series... command from the Data menu, and choose the 2nd Y-Series (B5:E5) in the Series list box. Finally, choose <Delete> to delete the series. Now, select the chart's name (WIDGETS/ WOMBATS) from the View menu again to view the new chart. As shown in Figure 12-13, the second range is no longer on the chart.

Figure 12-12

The Series... command allows you to delete series from charts.

Figure 12-13

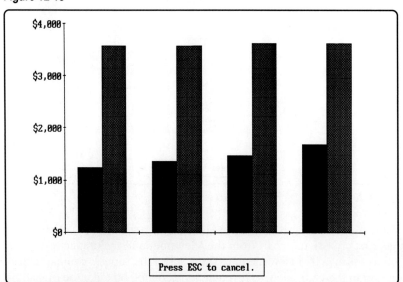

We've deleted the second y-series from the chart in Figure 12-11.

We just showed you how to use the Series... command on the Data menu to delete a series from a chart. This command has a couple of other uses. For one thing, you can use the Series... command to refresh your memory about how you defined a chart. Whenever you select this command, Works will display a list of the definitions of each data series in the active chart.

In addition to showing you the definitions of the series in a chart, the Series... command lets you "go to" (highlight) the range in the spreadsheet that defines a series. To go to a series, first select the Series... command from the Data menu. Then, choose the series you want to go to in the Series list box and choose the <Go To> option. (Since <Go To> is the default choice, you can press [Enter] to choose it.) When you do this, Works will highlight the range that defines the data series you chose.

Listing the series

Once you have created a chart, you can enhance it in many ways. For example, you can add titles, subtitles, legends, x- and y-axis labels, data labels, and other enhancements to your charts. You can also change the color Works uses to display the graph and the symbols or patterns it uses. For example, you could enhance the graph shown in Figure 12-13 to look like the graph shown in Figure 12-14. We'll explain these enhancements, and show you how to use them, in Chapter 14.

Enhancing charts

Figure 12-14

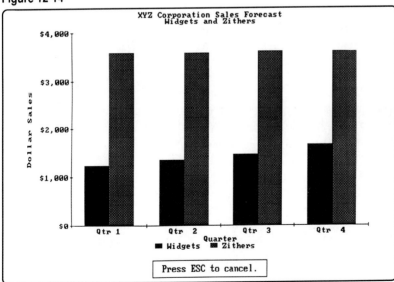

Works allows you to add titles, a legend, data labels, and other enhancements to your charts.

PRINTING CHARTS

So far, you have viewed the charts you have created only on the screen of your computer. While this may be adequate for charts you have created for your own benefit, if you want to share your charts with others—for example, in reports or in presentations—you'll have to print them.

The commands you use to print charts are found on the Print menu in the chart view. To print a chart, first choose its name from the View menu to make it the active chart and then press [Esc] to access the chart view menus. ▶Then, use the Printer Setup... command to choose the printer you want to use. (In Works 1, this command is called Select Chart Printer....) Next, use the the Title Font... and Other Font... commands on the Format menu to select the fonts you want Works to use to print the text in the chart. (In Works 1, these commands are located on the Print menu.) Now, use the Page Setup & Margins... command on the Print menu to specify the layout for the printed chart. (In Works 1, this command is called Layout....) Finally, use the Print... command to print the chart.◀

▶WORKS 2◀

Printing charts is, for the most part, the same as printing other Works documents. In Chapter 3, you learned the basic techniques for printing Works documents. There are, however, some important differences between printing charts and other Works documents. We'll explain those differences in this section as we discuss the process of printing charts.

The Printer Setup... command

The Printer Setup... command on the Print menu in the chart view allows you to specify which printer you will be using to print your charts, which port it is connected to, resolution, and whether you want Works to pause after printing each page. This command is very similar to the Printer Setup... command you use to select a text printer for a spreadsheet. We explained the Printer Setup... command in Chapter 3.

Figure 12-15

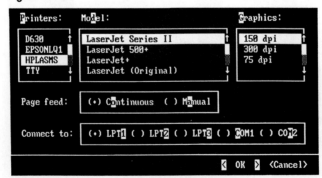

The Printer Setup... command lets you choose a printer.

When you select the Printer Setup... command, Works will display a dialog box like the one shown in Figure 12-15. ▶The Printers and Model list boxes allow you to select the printer to which you want to print; the Graphics list box lets you define the resolution of your printed chart; the Page Feed option box allows you to specify whether you are using continuous-feed paper or individual sheets; and the Connect To option box allows you to tell Works to which port your printer is connected.◀

If you did not select a printer when you installed Works, or if the printer you selected is not capable of printing graphics, you won't be able to print charts. If you want to print charts, you'll have to use the Setup program's Modify Existing Working Copy of Works 2.0 option to add a graphics printer driver to your disk.

As you will see in Chapter 14, you can enhance your Works charts by adding titles, legends, and other text to them. When you print a chart that includes titles and other text, you can choose the font and size Works will use to print the text in the chart. The Title Font... command on the Format menu lets you specify the font and size for the title, and the Other Font... command lets you specify the same for the other text in the chart (such as subtitles, legends, data labels, x-axis labels, y-axis labels, and so on).

Choosing a font

When you select the Title Font... or Other Font... command, Works will display the dialog box shown in Figure 12-16, which lists the fonts and sizes available for printing the current chart. The Fonts list box lists the 12 special fonts supported by Works. The Sizes list box lists the sizes available for the font that is highlighted in the Fonts list box.

Figure 12-16

The Title Font... and Other Font... commands let you choose the fonts and sizes you'll use to print the text in your charts.

To specify the font you want Works to use for the titles in your chart, select the Title Font... command and choose the font you want to use from the Fonts list box. When you select a font, Works will change the list of available sizes in the Sizes list box. You can choose the size you want from this box. When you've selected the font and size, choose <OK> to lock in your selections.

To specify the font you want Works to use for the other text in your chart, select the Other Font... command, choose the font you want to use from the Fonts list box, then choose the size you want to use from the the Sizes box. When you've selected the font and size, choose <OK> to lock in your selections.

For example, suppose you want Works to print the chart title in 28-point, Bold Italic Roman B type and the other text in 18-point, Italic Roman B type. To begin, select the Title Font... command from the Print menu and choose Bold Italic Roman B from the Fonts list box. Then, move to the Sizes list box and choose 28. Finally, choose <OK> to complete the command. Now, select the Other Font... command, choose Italic Roman B from the Fonts list box, choose 18 from the Sizes list box, and choose <OK> to complete the command.

Although Works will print any titles and other text in the fonts you have selected when it prints a chart, it won't automatically display those fonts on your screen. If you want the titles and other text to appear on the screen in the fonts and sizes you've specified, you must select the Show Printer Fonts command from the Options menu in the chart view.

Your ability to use special fonts depends on the choices you make during the Setup program. If you have a hard disk and you choose to copy the font files to the hard disk, you'll be able to use fonts without limitations. The same is true if your working copy of Works is on a floppy disk and you choose to copy the font files to that disk.

If, on the other hand, you have a hard disk and choose not to copy the font files to that disk, you won't be able to use fonts at all. If you select a font other than Screen (the default) and try to print, Works will display an alert box with the message *Invalid or missing font file.* and will not print. If you select a font other than Screen, select the Show Printer Fonts command, then select the View command, Works will display the same alert box and will not display the chart. You won't be able to view the chart until you choose the Screen font again.

If your working copy of Works is on a floppy disk, and you did not copy the font files to that disk, you'll still be able to use the fonts. However, whenever you try to print or view a chart using special fonts, Works will prompt you to place your Printer Disk 2 in the A drive of your computer. After it reads the specified fonts from that disk, Works will display or print your chart.

Chart layout

The Page Setup & Margins... command on the Print menu in the chart view lets you tell Works how to position your chart on a printed page. When you select the Page Setup & Margins... command, Works will display a dialog box like the one in Figure 12-17. This box, which is very similar to the dialog box you see when you select the Page Setup & Margins... command from the Print menu in a spreadsheet, lets you specify the layout of the printed chart: the size of the top and left margins, the height and width of the chart, the length and width of the page, and the orientation of the chart on the page (Landscape or Portrait).

Figure 12-17

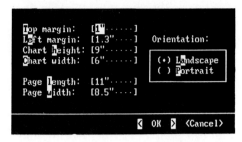

The Page Setup & Margins... command lets you specify the layout for the printed chart.

The settings shown in Figure 12-17 are Works' default settings. To change any of these settings, just move to the appropriate box, then type a new number. When you specify a new setting, be sure to use inches as your unit of measure. When you have finished making your changes, press [Enter] or choose <OK>.

The Top Margin and Left Margin settings define the space between the top edge of the chart and the top edge of the paper, and the left edge of the chart and the left edge of the paper. The Chart Height and Chart Width settings define the actual size of the printed chart. Works will always print your chart so that it fits within the specified dimensions. The Page Length and Page Width settings define the size of the sheet to which you'll be printing.

The sum of the Top Margin setting and the Chart Height setting must always be less than or equal to the Page Length setting you've specified. Similarly, the sum of the Left Margin setting and the Chart Width setting must be less than or equal to the Page Width setting. If you try to define a chart size that won't fit on the paper size you specified, Works will display an alert box that contains the message *Margin or chart too big.* You'll have to specify either a smaller chart, smaller margins, or, if possible, larger paper.

The Orientation option lets you specify the orientation of the chart on the printed page. If Orientation is set to Landscape (the default), Works will print the chart down the page from top to bottom. The chart's title will be printed along the right edge of the page and the x-axis (if any) will be printed along the left edge. (For example, on $8^1/_2$- by 11-inch paper, the title and x-axis would appear on the 11-inch side.) If Orientation is set to Portrait, Works will print the chart across the page from left to right. The chart's title will appear across the top of the page. (For example, on $8^1/_2$- by 11-inch paper, the title will appear on the $8^1/_2$-inch side.)

No matter which Orientation option you select, the relationship between the Chart Height, Chart Width, Page Length, and Page Width settings remains constant. The Chart Height setting always corresponds to the Page Length setting, and the Chart Width setting always corresponds to the Page Width setting.

The settings you specify in the Page Setup & Margins dialog box apply to the active chart only. This means that each chart in a spreadsheet can have a different set of Page Setup & Margins settings. If you activate another chart, then select the

Page Setup & Margins... command, the settings in the Page Setup & Margins dialog box will revert to the default settings. You can then use the options in the Page Setup & Margins dialog box to customize the settings for that chart. When you use the Charts... command to copy a chart, the new chart will have the same layout settings as the original.

The Print...
command
►WORKS 2◄

►Once you've selected the fonts and layout for your chart, you're ready to print. To print a chart, select the Print... command from the Print menu in the chart view. When you select this command, Works will display a dialog box like the one in Figure 12-18. (In Works 1, you can print a chart by selecting the Print Chart... command from the spreadsheet Print menu. This command is not available in Works 2.)◄

Figure 12-18

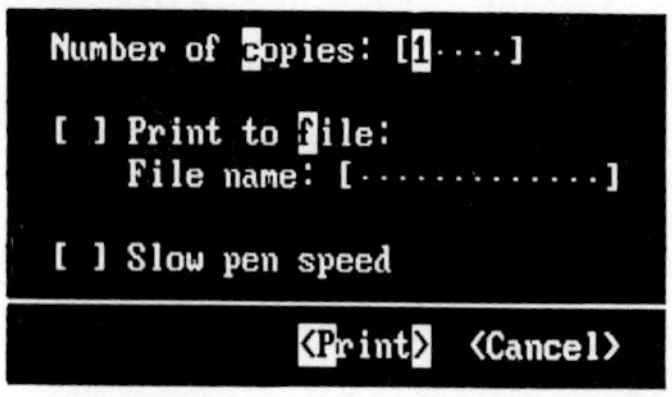

```
┌─────────────────────────────────────┐
│ Number of Copies: [1····]           │
│                                     │
│ [ ] Print to File:                  │
│     File name: [············]       │
│                                     │
│ [ ] Slow pen speed                  │
├─────────────────────────────────────┤
│              <Print>  <Cancel>      │
└─────────────────────────────────────┘
```

The Print... command lets you print the active chart.

When you see the Print dialog box, define the number of copies you want to print, then choose <Print>. (Since <Print> is the default option, you can choose it by pressing [Enter].) The process of printing the chart will probably take several minutes. As the chart is being printed, Works will display in the lower-left corner of the screen the percentage of the chart that has been printed.

If you decide not to print before you choose <Print>, you can choose <Cancel> to abort the command. If you decide to stop while Works is in the midst of printing the chart, just press [Esc].

Printing to a file

Just as Works allows you to print a report to a disk file, it also allows you to print a chart to a file. To print to a file, simply choose the Print to File check box in the Print dialog box and enter the name of the file to which you want to print in the File Name text box. When you choose <Print>, Works will print the chart into the file you have specified. Like the process of printing to a printer, the process of printing to a file is rather slow. Once you've printed a chart to a file, you can use the DOS command PRINT to print the chart from the file at a later time.

Printing to a plotter

If you are printing a multicolor chart to a plotter, when you choose <Print> Works will display a dialog box that lists the colors in the chart and instructs you to mount the appropriate pens on your plotter. When you have mounted the correct pens, just choose <OK>, and Works will begin to print your chart. If the chart has more colors than your plotter can hold at once, this dialog box will reappear when Works has used all of the mounted pens. When you've mounted the next set of pens, choose <OK> again to resume printing.

If you want, you can use the Slow Pen Speed option in the Print dialog box to slow down your plotter's pen speed. Choosing this option will result is a higher-quality graph but will slow down the process of printing.

An example

Suppose you want to print the chart shown in Figure 12-15. To begin, make it the active chart by selecting its name from the View menu. Then, if necessary, use the Printer Setup... command to choose a printer. Once you've selected the printer, use the Title Font... command to set the fonts for the title in the chart—we'll use 14-point, Bold Modern C—and the Other Font... command to set the font for the other text in the chart—we'll use 12-point Modern C. Next, use the Page Setup & Margins... command to change any layout settings (margins, size, and so on) for the printed chart. Finally, select the Print... command, and choose the <Print> option. Figure 12-19 shows the printed chart.

Figure 12-19

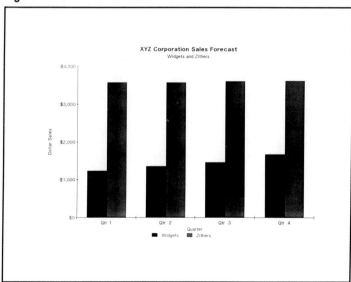

This is an example of a printed Works chart.

CONCLUSION

In this chapter, we have explored the basics of charting. You have learned how to create, manage, edit and print charts. Now that you are familiar with the basics, you're ready to move on. In the next chapter, we will discuss the various types of charts Works can produce: bar, line, mixed line and bar, pie, XY, and hi-lo-close charts. In Chapter 14, we'll show you how to enhance charts.

Chart Types 13

*I*n Chapter 12, you learned the basics of charting. In this chapter, we'll show you how to create each of Works' chart types: bar, line, mixed line and bar, hi-lo-close, pie, and XY charts. We'll begin by showing you how to change the type of a chart. Then, we'll explain the details of each type of chart.

The default chart type in Works is a bar chart. Every chart you create in Works starts out as a bar chart. For example, each of the charts we created in Chapter 12 was a bar chart (or, in the case of multiple-series charts, a clustered bar chart). Once you've created a chart, however, you can change it to any of the other types that Works supports. The key to changing the type of a chart is the chart environment's Format menu, which is shown in Figure 13-1. To change the type of a chart, you simply make that chart active, then choose the new type from the list on the Format menu.

CHANGING
CHART TYPES

Figure 13-1

The commands on the Format menu let you change the type of a chart.

BAR CHARTS

In a bar chart, each bar represents a value in the spreadsheet. Bar charts are best suited for comparing two or more values at a point in time, such as the populations of different cities in a given year.

In fact, you can create four kinds of bar charts with Works: simple bar charts, clustered bar charts, stacked bar charts, and 100% bar charts. Let's examine each of these.

Simple bar charts

Simple bar charts plot the values from one row or column in a spreadsheet (that is, one data series) as a set of bars along the x-axis. To create a simple bar chart, just use either the automatic or manual method to create a chart with one data series. Since bar is Works' default chart type, you don't have to select the Bar command from the Format menu.

For example, suppose you want to create a simple bar chart from the data in the spreadsheet in Figure 13-2, comparing the populations for Lakeside, Barnburg, Autotown, and Silicon City for 1990. To begin, highlight the range C4:C7 and select the New Chart command from the View menu. When you do this, Works will display the simple bar chart shown in Figure 13-3. One bar is centered between each pair of x-axis tick marks. The first bar represents the population of Lakeside, the first value in the data series; the second, Barnburg, the second value in the series; and so on.

Figure 13-2

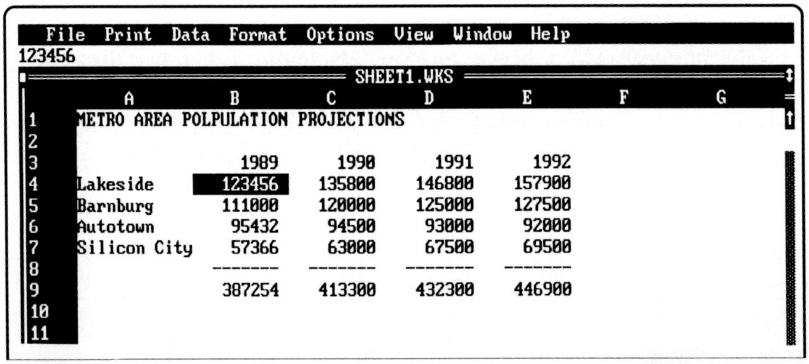

```
 File  Print  Data  Format  Options  View  Window  Help
123456
================================ SHEET1.WKS ================================
         A          B          C          D          E        F        G
 1  METRO AREA POLPULATION PROJECTIONS
 2
 3                  1989       1990       1991       1992
 4  Lakeside       123456     135800     146800     157900
 5  Barnburg       111000     120000     125000     127500
 6  Autotown        95432      94500      93000      92000
 7  Silicon City    57366      63000      67500      69500
 8                 -------    -------    -------    -------
 9                 387254     413300     432300     446900
10
11
```

We'll use this spreadsheet to illustrate most of Works' chart types.

If you plot negative values in a simple bar chart, the bars representing those values will descend below the x-axis.

Once you have created a bar chart, you can add titles, x-axis labels, data labels, and a legend to it. You can also format the values along the y-axis, add a grid, and change the shading patterns and colors We'll show you how to do that in the next chapter.

Figure 13-3

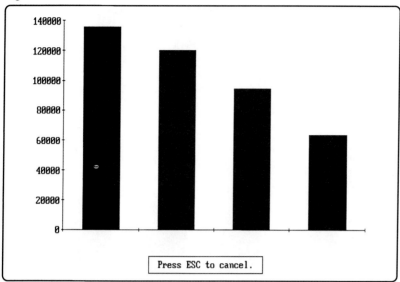

This simple bar chart is based on the values in the range C4:C7 in the spreadsheet in Figure 13-2.

Clustered bar charts

When you plot more than one data series in a bar chart, Works will create a clustered, or side-by-side, bar chart. In a clustered bar chart, the corresponding bars in each data series (that is, the bars for each category) are clustered. Clustered bar charts are useful for comparing several data ranges in one chart.

To create a clustered bar chart, just use the automatic or the manual method to create a chart with more than one data series. Since bar is Works' default chart type, you don't have to select the Bar command.

For example, suppose you want to create a chart comparing the populations of the four towns in Figure 13-2 for the years 1989 through 1992. To create this chart, first make sure that the highlight is not extended. Then, select the New Chart command from the View menu to create a new chart. When Works displays the alert *Series not selected.,* choose <OK> or press [Enter]. Next, highlight the range B4:E4 and select the 1st Y-Series command from the Data menu to define the first data series; highlight the range B5:E5 and select the 2nd Y-Series command to define the second data series; highlight the range B6:E6 and select the 3rd Y-Series command; and highlight the range B7:E7 and select the 4th Y-Series command.

Once you have created the chart, select its name—Chart2—from the View menu to view the chart shown in Figure 13-4. As you can see, the bars in the new chart are clustered between the x-axis tick marks. The first cluster illustrates the populations of all four towns in 1989; the second, the populations of the four towns in 1990; and so on. The first bar in each cluster represents Lakeside's population; the second, Barnburg's, and so on. Works places the bar for the first Y-Series at the left of each cluster, with the bar for the second Y-Series immediately to the right, and so on.

Figure 13-4

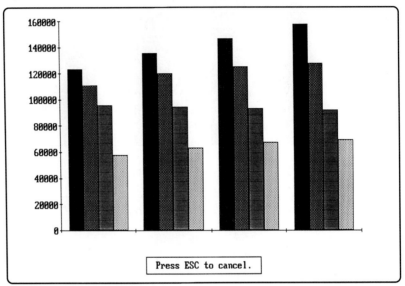

This clustered bar chart is based on the values in the ranges B4:E4, B5:E5, B6:E6, and B7:E7 in the spreadsheet in Figure 13-2.

If you have a color monitor, Works will display each bar in each cluster in a different color. If you have a monochrome monitor, Works will use a different shading for each data series: solid black for the first series, dark gray for the second, medium gray for the third, and light gray for the fourth. Table 13-1 shows the default patterns Works will use for each range in clustered bar, stacked bar, and 100% bar charts.

When you plot negative values in a clustered bar chart, bars representing those values will descend below the x-axis.

Once you have created a clustered bar chart, you can enhance it by adding titles, x-axis labels, data labels, and a legend. You can also format the values along the y-axis, add a grid, and change the shading patterns and colors. We'll show you how to do that in the next chapter.

Stacked bar charts

Stacked bar charts are similar to clustered bar charts. In a stacked bar chart, each bar is made up of two or more segments. Each segment represents a value from one data series. The total height of each column represents the total of the values in a given category. Stacked bar charts are useful for showing how the components of a series of data compare to the total.

Table 13-1

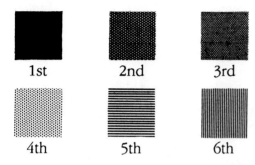

1st   2nd   3rd

4th   5th   6th

Works will use these patterns to shade the bars in clustered bar, stacked bar, and 100% bar charts on a mono-chrome monitor.

To create a stacked bar chart, first create a multiple-series chart using either the automatic or manual method. Then, select the Stacked Bar command from the Format menu to change the chart type to stacked bar.

For example, suppose you want to create a stacked bar chart comparing the total populations of the four towns in the spreadsheet in Figure 13-2 for the years 1989 through 1992. To begin, make sure that the highlight is not extended. Then, select the New Chart command from the View menu to create a new chart. When Works displays the alert *Series not selected.*, choose <OK> or press [Enter]. Next, highlight the range B4:E4, and select the 1st Y-Series command from the Data menu to define the first data series; highlight the range B5:E5 and select the 2nd Y-Series command to define the second data series; highlight the range B6:E6 and select the 3rd Y-Series command; and highlight the range B7:E7 and select the 4th Y-Series command. Once you've created the chart, select the Stacked Bar command from the Format menu.

When you are finished, select the name of the chart—Chart3, in this case— from the View menu to bring the chart shown in Figure 13-5 on the following page into view. Each bar in this chart represents the sum of the populations of the four towns in one year. Each segment in the chart represents the population of one town in one year. For example, the bottom segment in each bar represents the population of Lakeside. The next segment represents the population of Barnburg, and so forth. In a stacked bar chart, Works always plots the first y-series at the bottom of each bar, the second y-series above the first, and so forth.

If you have a color monitor, Works will display each data series in a different color. If you have a monochrome monitor, Works will use a different shading for each data series: solid black for the first series, dense gray for the second, medium gray for the third, and so on.

Figure 13-5

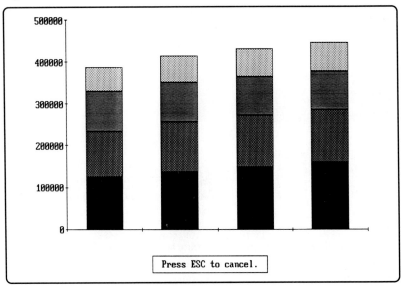

*In a stacked bar chart, Works plots each value as a segment in a bar;
the total height of each bar represents the sums of the values in all data
series in a given category.*

A word of warning: You cannot plot negative values in a stacked bar chart.
If you try, Works will simply ignore the minus sign and will plot the value as though
it were a positive number.

In Chapter 14, we'll show you how to enhance a stacked bar chart by adding
titles, x-axis labels, data labels, legends, and a grid. We'll also show you how to
format the values along the y-axis and change the shading patterns and colors.

100% bar charts

As in a stacked bar chart, each bar in a 100% bar chart is made up of two or
more segments. Unlike stacked bar charts, however, the y-axis in a 100% bar chart
is a percentage scale that begins at 0% and ends at 100%. In addition, each bar
is the same height. Works assumes that each segment in a 100% bar chart
represents the ratio of a value in a data series to the total of the values in that
category in all data series and that the total of the segments in each stack is equal
to 100%. 100% bar charts are useful when you want to illustrate the relationships
between the components of several series of data.

To create a 100% bar chart, first create a multiple-series chart using either the
automatic or manual method. Then, select the 100% Bar command from the
Format menu.

For example, suppose you want to create a 100% bar chart comparing the populations for the four towns in the spreadsheet in Figure 13-2 for the time period 1989 to 1992. First, make sure that the highlight is not extended. Then, select the New Chart command from the View menu to create a new chart. When Works displays the alert *Series not selected.*, choose <OK> or press [Enter]. Next, highlight the range B4:E4 and select the 1st Y-Series command from the Data menu; highlight the range B5:E5 and select the 2nd Y-Series command; highlight the range B6:E6 and select the 3rd Y-Series command; and highlight the range B7:E7 and select the 4th Y-Series command. Next, to change the type of the chart to 100% bar, select the 100% Bar command from the Format menu.

When you are finished, select the name of the chart—Chart4, in this case—from the View menu to bring the chart shown in Figure 13-6 into view. As you can see, the 100% bar chart is similar to the stacked bar chart. However, the bars are the same height and the y-axis is measured in percentages, not values.

Figure 13-6

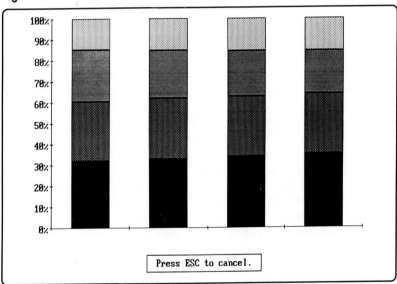

In a 100% bar chart, each segment represents the ratio of a value in a data series to the total of the values in that category in all data series; the total of the segments in each bar is equal to 100%.

If you have a color monitor, Works will display each data series in a different color. If you have a monochrome monitor, Works will use a different shading for each data series.

As with stacked bar charts, you cannot plot negative values in 100% bar charts. If you try, Works will plot the values as though they were positive numbers.

Once you have created a 100% bar chart, you can enhance it by adding titles, x-axis labels, data labels, and legends. You can also format the values along the y-axis, add a grid, and change the shading patterns and colors. We'll show you how to do that in the next chapter.

An aside: Creating one chart from another

The charts in Figures 13-4, 13-5, and 13-6 depict the same data. The only difference is that they are different types of charts. We created the charts shown in Figures 13-5 and 13-6 from scratch so that you could see how to do it. However, we could have created these charts by using the <Copy> option of the Charts... command to create a copy of the chart in Figure 13-4, then selecting the Stacked Bar command or the 100% Bar command from the Format menu to change the type of the copied chart. Whenever you need to create two or more charts that share the same data set, you should consider using the <Copy> option

LINE CHARTS

Line charts are probably the most common business charts. You'll find line charts useful for illustrating trends over time. In a line chart, each value in a data series is represented by a point on a line. Line charts are closely related to bar charts; in fact, in many cases you can use either a line or a bar chart to depict the same information. Generally, you'll find that line charts are preferable for plotting continuous data, while bar charts are useful when you're plotting separate, unconnected data.

You can create three kinds of line charts in Works: simple line charts, multiple-line charts, and area line charts. The multiple-line and area line charts are just variations of the simple line chart.

Simple line charts

Simple line charts let you depict the trend of a single data series over time. To create a simple line chart, first create a chart that includes just a single data series using either the automatic or manual method. Then, select the Line command from the Format menu to change the chart type to line.

For example, suppose you want to create a line chart that shows the growth in the population of Lakeside in the years 1989 to 1992. To do this, highlight the range B4:E4 and select the New Chart command from the View menu to define the first data series. When Works displays the new chart (which will be a bar chart), you should press [Esc], then select Line from the Format menu to change the chart into a line chart.

Once you've defined the chart, select its name—Chart 5—from the view menu to display the chart shown in Figure 13-7. As you can see, each value in the range B4:E4 has been plotted as a point on a line. The first point represents the population of Lakeside in 1989, the first value in the data series; the second, the population in 1990, the second value in the series; and so on.

Figure 13-7

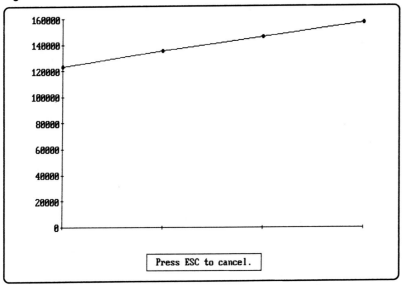

In a simple line chart, the data series is plotted as a line that represents the trend of the values in that series.

You can also plot negative values in a simple line chart. These values will be represented by points below the x-axis.

Once you have created a line chart, you can add titles, x-axis labels, and data labels to it. You can also format the values along the y-axis, add a grid, and change the markers used to represent each value in the chart. We'll show you how to do that in the next chapter.

Multiple-line charts

Multiple-line charts are useful for illustrating the trends in several series of related data over time. To create a multiple-line chart, first create a chart that includes two or more data series using either the automatic or manual method. Then, select the Line command from the Format menu.

For example, suppose you want to create a line chart that shows the population growth of all four towns in Figure 13-2 in the years 1989 to 1992. To create this chart, first make sure that the highlight is not extended. Then, select the New Chart command from the View menu to create a new chart. When Works displays the alert *Series not selected.*, choose <OK> or press [Enter]. Next, highlight the range B4:E4 and select the 1st Y-Series command from the Data menu to define the first data series; highlight the range B5:E5 and select the 2nd Y-Series command to define the second data series; highlight the range B6:E6 and select the

3rd Y-Series command; and highlight the range B7:E7 and select the 4th Y-Series command. Now, select the Line command from the Format menu to make this new chart a line chart.

When you're finished, select the name of the new chart—Chart6—from the View menu. Figure 13-8 shows the multiple-line chart you've created. As you can see, each of the data series you defined has been plotted as a line in the chart.

Figure 13-8

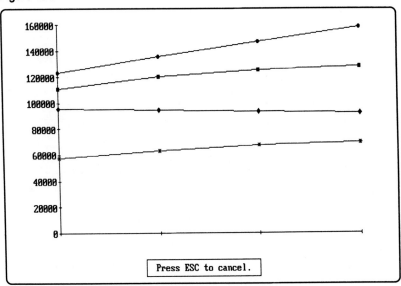

In a multiple-line chart, each data series is represented by a separate line.

If you have a color display, Works will display each line in a different color. If you have a monochrome monitor, Works will use a different marker to represent the data points on each line (● for the first series, ■ for the second, ◆ for the third, and so on. Table 13-2 shows the default markers Works will use for each range in a multiple-line chart.

You can also plot negative values in a multiple-line chart. These values will be represented by points below the x-axis.

In Chapter 14, we'll show you how to enhance a multiple-line chart by adding titles, x-axis labels, data labels, legends, and a grid; by formatting the values along the y-axis; and by changing the colors and markers.

Table 13-2

Y-series	Marker	Y-series	Marker
1st	●	4th	*
2nd	■	5th	○
3rd	◆	6th	□

Works will use these markers for the data series in multiple-line charts.

Area line charts

Area line charts are very much like stacked bar charts. In a stacked bar chart, each data series is represented by a series of bar segments. In an area line chart, each data series is represented by the space, or area, between two lines. The area between the first line and the x-axis represents the first data series, the area between the second line and the first line represents the second series, and so on. Each of the lines represents the cumulative trend of the data series below that line. The top line represents the sum of all the data series that make up the chart. Like stacked bar charts, area line charts are useful for depicting the relationships between the components of several data series and the totals of those components.

To create an area line chart, first create a chart that includes two or more data series using either the automatic or manual method. Then, select the Area Line command from the Format menu to change the chart type to area line.

Suppose you want to create an area line chart that compares the populations of the four towns for the years 1989 through 1992. To begin, make sure the highlight is not extended. Then, select the New Chart command from the View menu to create a new chart. When Works displays the alert *Series not selected.*, choose <OK> or press [Enter]. Next, highlight the range B4:E4 and select the 1st Y-Series command from the Data menu to define the first data series; highlight the range B5:E5 and select the 2nd Y-Series command to define the second data series; highlight the range B6:E6 and select the 3rd Y-Series command; and highlight the range B7:E7 and select the 4th Y-Series command. Now, select the Area Line command from the Format menu to make this new chart an area line chart.

When you're finished, select the name of the new chart—Chart7—from the View menu. Figure 13-9 on the next page shows the area line chart you've created. As you can see, Works has created a chart with four lines. Each data series is represented by the space, or area, between two lines. Each of the lines represents the cumulative trend of the data series below that line.

If you have a color monitor, Works will display each line in a different color. If you have a monochrome monitor, Works will use a different marker to represent the data points on each line.

Figure 13-9

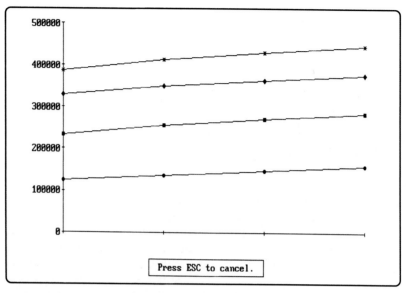

In an area line chart, each data series is represented by the space, or area, between two lines; the top line represents the sum of all the data series.

If you try to plot negative values in an area line chart, Works will simply ignore the minus sign and plot the value as though it were a positive number.

Once you have created an area line chart, you can add titles, x-axis labels, data labels, and a legend to it. You can also format the values along the y-axis, add a grid, and change the markers used to represent each value. We'll show you how to do that in the next chapter.

MIXED LINE AND BAR CHARTS

Mixed line and bar charts allow you to combine lines and bars in the same chart. This type of chart is useful when you are comparing several series and want to plot one or two so that they stand out from the others.

To create a mixed line and bar chart, first create a chart that includes two or more data series using either the automatic or manual method. Then, select the Mixed Line & Bar... command from the Options menu to display the Mixed Line & Bar dialog box shown in Figure 13-10. You use this dialog box to tell Works which data series you want to plot as bars and which you want to plot as lines. If the chart you've created is a bar chart, then the default setting for each data series will be Bar. If the chart is a line chart, then the default for each setting will be Line. To change the setting for a series, just choose the other option (Bar or Line) for that series.

Figure 13-10

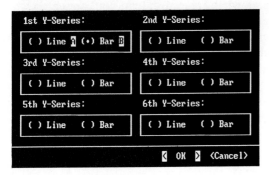

1st Y-Series:

( ) Line 🄰 (•) Bar 🄱

2nd Y-Series:

( ) Line   ( ) Bar

3rd Y-Series:

( ) Line   ( ) Bar

4th Y-Series:

( ) Line   ( ) Bar

5th Y-Series:

( ) Line   ( ) Bar

6th Y-Series:

( ) Line   ( ) Bar

🄺 OK 🄳 〈Cancel〉

*The Mixed Line &
Bar... command lets
you create mixed line
and bar charts.*

If you have a mouse, you can choose any option in the dialog box just by pointing to that option and clicking. If you use your keyboard, you can select an option with the [Tab] and ➡ and ⬅ keys. Alternatively, you can press the [Alt] key. When you do this, Works will display a highlighted letter next to each choice: *A* next to the Line option for the 1st Y-Series, *B* next to the Bar option for the 1st Y-Series, *C* next to the Line option for the 2nd Y-Series, and so on. Once you've pressed [Alt], you can choose any option just by typing the letter that corresponds to that option. When you have defined the type for each series, just choose <OK>.

For example, suppose you want to create a mixed line and bar chart that illustrates the individual populations of the four towns and the total population of the towns. You want to plot the populations of the individual towns as bars and the total population as a line. To begin, make sure that the highlight is not extended. Then, select the New Chart command from the View menu to create a new chart. When Works displays the alert *Series not selected.*, choose <OK> or press [Enter]. Next, highlight the range B4:E4 and select the 1st Y-Series command from the Data menu to define the first data series. Now, highlight the range B5:E5 and select the 2nd Y-Series command to define the second data series; highlight the range B6:E6 and select the 3rd Y-Series command; highlight the range B7:E7 and select the 4th Y-Series command; and highlight the range B9:E9 and select the 5th Y-Series command.

Now select the Mixed Line & Bar... command from the Options menu to display the Mixed Line & Bar dialog box. Since the chart you have created is a bar chart, Works will set the default type for each data series in the chart to Bar. Because you want the first four data series to be plotted as bars, you don't need to change the settings for those series. To change the 5th Y-Series from a bar to a line, either press [Alt] then type the letter *I*, or, if you have a mouse, click the Line option for the 5th Y-Series. When you've made the change, press [Enter] or choose <OK> to lock in your settings.

When you're finished, select the name of the new chart—Chart8—from the View menu to display the chart shown in Figure 13-11. As you can see, the annual population of each town is represented by a bar. The bars that represent the populations of each of the towns in the same year are clustered between the tick marks on the x-axis. Floating above the individual bars is a single line that depicts the trend of the total population of all four towns.

Figure 13-11

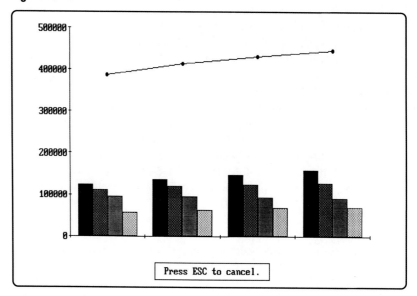

Mixed line and bar charts let you represent some data series by lines and others by bars.

If you have a color monitor, Works will display each bar and the line in a different color. If you have a monochrome monitor, Works will use different shadings for each bar:. The line will include markers that identify the individual data points.

Although the example chart included just a single line, you can combine lines and bars in a mixed line and bar chart any way you want. Once you've defined a chart, you can change the type of any data series just by activating the chart, selecting the Mixed Line & Bar... command, and changing the Line/Bar setting for that data series.

The configuration of the bars in a mixed line and bar chart depends on the underlying type of the chart. If, as in the example, the chart is a bar chart, the bars will be clustered. If the chart is a stacked bar chart, the bars for each data series will be stacked.

Once you have created a mixed line and bar chart, you can add titles, x-axis labels, data labels, and legends to it. You can also format the values along the y-axis; add a grid; and change the markers, colors, and shading patterns used to represent each value. We'll show you how to make these enhancements in the next chapter.

Hi-lo-close charts are designed to illustrate stock-market trends. A hi-lo-close chart typically plots three series: the "high" series, the "low" series, and the "close" series. The three series contain the high, low, and closing prices for a stock (or some other financial instrument) for each day (or week, month, or year) within a longer period of time (such as a week, month, or year). The high series should contain the high price for each increment in the period; the low series the low price for each increment in the period; and the close series the closing price for each increment in the period. While the high series will usually be the first y-series, the low series the second y-series, and the close series the third y-series, you can use any y-series to define the high, low, or close series. Every hi-lo-close chart must contain both a high series and a low series. The close series is optional.

Works plots these series as a collection of vertical lines. Each line represents the range of prices in a given day: The marker at the top of the line represents the high price and the marker at the bottom of the line represents the low value. The closing price (if any) is indicated by a marker somewhere on the vertical line. If the chart has only two ranges, the close price will not appear in the chart.

To create a hi-lo-close chart, create a new chart with up to three series using either the automatic or manual method. Be sure that the range containing the high values is the chart's first y-series, the range that contains the low values is the second y-series, and the range that contains the close values (if any) is the third y-series. When you have defined the chart, select the Hi-Lo-Close command from the Format menu.

Let's create a hi-lo-close chart for the sample spreadsheet in Figure 13-12. This spreadsheet shows the daily high, low, and closing prices for the stock of Close Shave Razors, Inc., across a five-day period. To create the chart, first make sure that the highlight is not extended. Then, select the New Chart command from the View menu to create a new chart. When Works displays the alert *Series not selected.*, choose <OK> or press [Enter]. Now, highlight the range B4:B8, and select the 1st Y-Series command from the Data menu to plot the daily highs of the stock; highlight the range C4:C8 and select the 2nd Y-Series command to plot the daily lows; highlight the range D4:D8 and select the 3rd Y-Series command to plot the daily closes; and select the Hi-Lo-Close command from the Format menu to define the chart type.

Figure 13-12

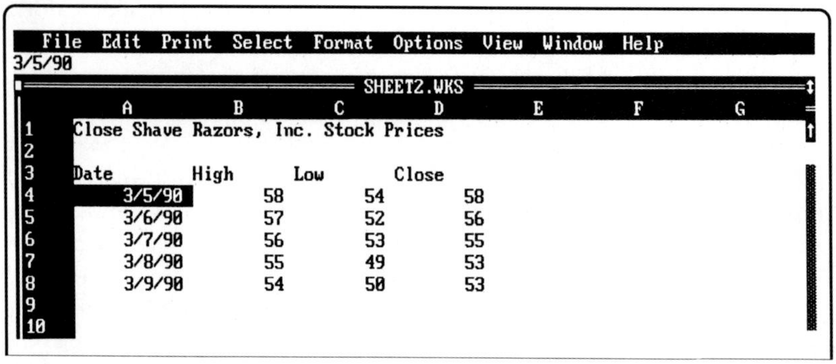

```
   File  Edit  Print  Select  Format  Options  View  Window  Help
  3/5/90
  ═══════════════════════════ SHEET2.WKS ═══════════════════════════
         A          B          C          D        E       F       G
  1 Close Shave Razors, Inc. Stock Prices
  2
  3 Date        High       Low       Close
  4       3/5/90       58        54        58
  5       3/6/90       57        52        56
  6       3/7/90       56        53        55
  7       3/8/90       55        49        53
  8       3/9/90       54        50        53
  9
  10
```

We'll use this spreadsheet to create a hi-lo-close chart.

When you are finished, select the name of the chart—Chart1—from the View menu to display the chart shown in Figure 13-13. As you can see, Works has plotted the chart as a series of vertical lines. The first line represents the range of prices for the stock on March 5, 1990 (the range B4:D4), the second represents the range of prices on March 6, and so on. The markers on each line represent the prices of the stock on that day. The ● represents the highest price, the ■ the lowest, and the ◆ the close. If you have a color monitor, Works will display the line in one color and the high, low, and close markers in other colors. If you have a monochrome monitor, Works will use a different marker for the high, low, and close values.

Although hi-lo-close charts usually have three series, you can create them with just two or with four series. If you create a hi-lo-close chart with two series (the high series and the low series), the chart will simply include a series of vertical lines. If you create a chart with four series, Works will connect the values in the high and low series with a line and will plot two markers on each line—one for the third (low) series and one for the fourth series. Usually, you'll use the fourth series to plot the opening prices for the stock into the chart.

Once you have created a hi-lo-close chart, you can add titles, x-axis labels, and data labels to it. You can also format the values along the y-axis, add a grid, and change the markers used to represent each value. We'll show you how to enhance hi-lo-close charts in Chapter 14.

PIE CHARTS

Pie charts may be the most familiar type of business graph. In a pie chart, each value in a data series is represented by a segment (slice) of a circle (pie). The entire pie represents the total of the values in the data series. Pie charts are similar to

100% bar charts, since both illustrate the ratio of the components to the total. However, a pie chart can depict only a single data series—as much information as a single bar in a 100% bar chart.

Figure 13-13

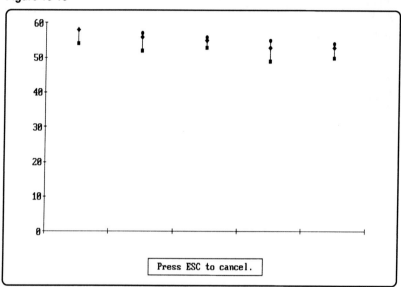

Hi-lo-close charts are designed to illustrate stock-market trends.

To create a pie chart, first use either the automatic or manual method to create a chart with one data series. Then, select the Pie command from the Format menu to make the new chart a pie chart.

For example, suppose you want to create a pie chart that depicts the components of total expenses in the spreadsheet in Figure 13-14 on the following page. To do this, highlight the range C3:C8 and select the New Chart command from the View menu to define the first data series. When Works displays the new chart (which will be a bar chart), press [Esc], then select Pie from the Format menu to change the chart into a line chart.

When you are finished, select the name of the chart—Chart1—from the View menu to view the pie chart shown in Figure 13-15. As you can see, each value in the data series has been plotted as a slice of the pie. The slice to the right of the 12 o'clock position represents the first value; the next slice, the second value; and so on. If you have a color monitor, Works will display each slice in a different color. If you have a monochrome monitor, Works will use different shadings for each slice.

Figure 13-14

```
 File  Edit  Print  Select  Format  Options  View  Window  Help
13200
                              ═══════ SHEET3.WKS ═══════
           A          B          C          D         E        F        G
  1   Jones Family 1990 Expenses
  2
  3   Housing & Utilities  │$13,200│
  4   Food & Supplies          $5,200
  5   Automobile               $9,600
  6   Clothing                 $3,600
  7   Personal                 $1,200
  8   Other                   $12,000
  9                           ────────
 10                           $44,800
 11
 12
```

We'll use this spreadsheet as the basis for a pie chart.

Figure 13-15

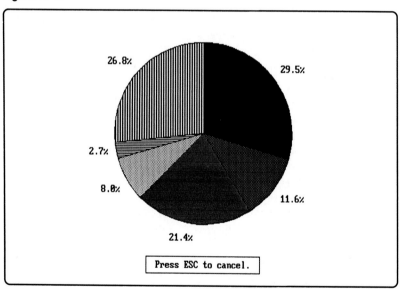

In a pie chart, each value in a data series is represented by a slice of a
pie, and the total of the values is represented by the entire pie.

Works automatically places a percentage next to each slice of the pie to
represent that slice's portion of the total. Works always places these percentages
in your pie charts; there is no way to remove them. If you try to create a pie chart
with one large slice and several smaller slices, the percentages that surround the
chart will overlap.

There is no way to plot a negative value in a pie chart. If you try to include a negative value in a pie chart, Works will ignore the minus sign and chart the value as it does a positive value.

Many of the enhancements you use with other charts—such as data labels and legends—do not apply to pie charts. You can, however, add titles to a pie chart. If you define an x-series for the chart, Works will plot each value in the x-series next to the corresponding slice in the pie. You can also change the color or shading Works uses to shade each segment. You can even "explode" one or more segments. We'll show you how to do these things in Chapter 14.

XY CHARTS

XY charts plot the relationship between two quantifiable characteristics of a set of data. XY charts come in handy when you are using one characteristic (the independent variable) to predict another characteristic (the dependent variable) of a data set. For example, you can use an XY chart to plot the relationship between years of education (the independent variable) and income (the dependent variable) or between height (the independent variable) and weight (the dependent variable).

XY charts—sometimes called scatter charts—are much like line charts, with one important difference: To define a line chart, you simply define one (or more) data series. When you create an XY chart, you must define two data series: the x-series and at least one other series (usually the first y-series). These values work together to determine the position of the points in the chart. The x-series, which determines the horizontal position of each point in the chart, should contain the values for the independent variable. The other range, which determines the vertical position of each point in the chart, should contain the values for the dependent variable.

You can only create an XY chart using the manual method. To create an XY chart, begin by selecting the New Chart command from the View menu to create a new chart. When Works displays the alert *Series not selected.*, choose <OK> or press [Enter]. Next, highlight the series you want to use as the x-series, then select the X-Series command from the Data menu. Then, select the series you want to use as the y-series and select the 1st Y-Series command from the Data menu. Finally, select the X-Y command from the Format menu to define the type of chart.

For example, suppose you have created the spreadsheet shown in Figure 13-16 on the next page, which lists education and income data for a group of people. You want to create an XY chart that depicts the relationship between these two variables. In this case, you would assume that income is dependent upon education. Thus, education is the independent variable and will be plotted as the x-series, while income is the dependent variable and will be plotted as the y-series.

To create the chart, first make sure that the highlight is not extended.- Then, select the New Chart command from the View menu to create a new chart. When Works displays the alert *Series not selected.*, choose <OK> or press [Enter]. Next, highlight the range A5:A16 and select the X-Series command from the Data menu. Then, highlight the range B5:B16 and select the 1st Y-Series command from the Data menu. Finally, select the X-Y command from the Format menu.

Figure 13-16

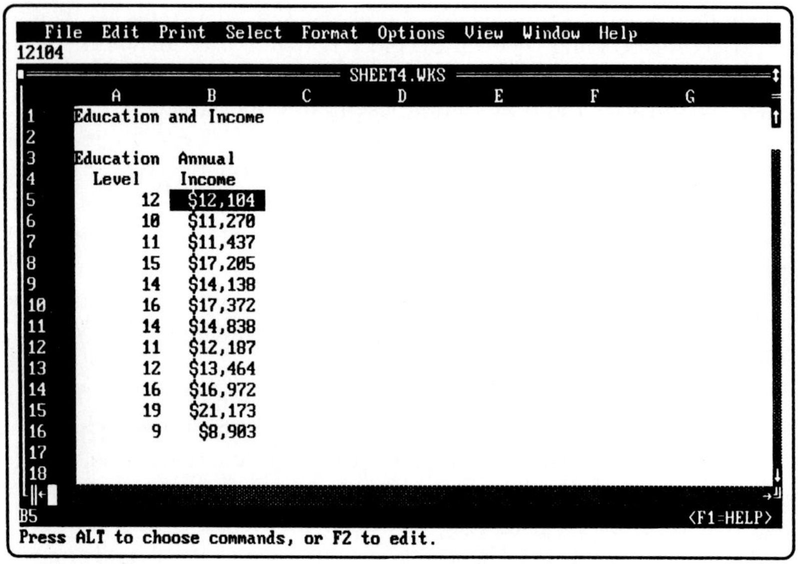

```
    File  Edit  Print  Select  Format  Options  View  Window  Help
  12104
  ═══════════════════════════════ SHEET4.WKS ══════════════════════════
         A         B        C        D        E        F        G
  1  Education and Income
  2
  3  Education  Annual
  4    Level    Income
  5       12   $12,104
  6       10   $11,270
  7       11   $11,437
  8       15   $17,205
  9       14   $14,138
  10      16   $17,372
  11      14   $14,838
  12      11   $12,187
  13      12   $13,464
  14      16   $16,972
  15      19   $21,173
  16       9    $8,903
  17
  18
  B5                                                        <F1=HELP>
  Press ALT to choose commands, or F2 to edit.
```

We'll use this spreadsheet as the basis for an XY chart.

When you've created the chart, select its name—Chart1—from the View menu to bring it into view. Figure 13-17 shows the chart. As you can see, Works has placed a marker in the chart to identify the location of each pair of x-series and y-series values. For example, the upper-right point in the chart is defined by the x-series value in cell A15 (19) and the y-series value in cell B15 (21,173).

Notice that the origin of the x-axis in the chart in Figure 13-17 is 9 and the origin of the y-axis is 8,000. When Works draws an XY chart, it almost never places the start of the x-axis or the y-axis at 0. Instead, it draws the chart so that the top and bottom limits of the two axes are just large enough to hold the points in the chart. This is likely to result in a misleading chart. Fortunately, this problem is easy to correct. You can use the X-Axis... and Y-Axis... commands on the Options menu to set the origin for both axes to 0 manually. We'll show you how in Chapter 14.

Also, notice the labels that appear under the x-axis in this chart. Whenever you include an x-series in a chart, Works will use the values or labels in that range as labels for the x-axis. Since XY charts always have an x-series, they also always have x-axis labels.

Figure 13-17

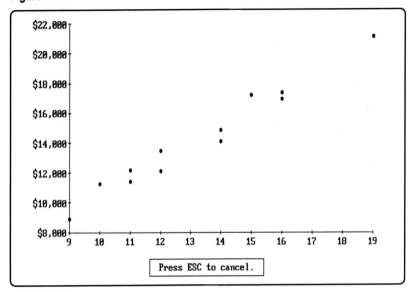

XY charts plot the relationship between two quantifiable characteristics of a set of data.

As you can see, Works has arranged the values along the x-axis in ascending order. In general, the values in the x-series don't have to be evenly spaced or in order in the spreadsheet. Works will automatically order and position the x-series values across the x-axis when it plots the chart. However, the values in the x-series of an XY chart must be values—they cannot be labels.

Once you have created an XY chart, you can enhance it by adding titles, adding a grid, formatting the values along the x- and y-axes, and changing the markers used to represent each point in the chart. We'll show you how to make these enhancements in the next chapter.

CONCLUSION

In this chapter, we've shown you how to create each type of chart supported by Works. Now we're ready to tackle the last topic relating to charting: enhancing charts. We'll show you how to do this in the next chapter.

Enhancing Charts 14

*N*ow that you've grasped chart basics and have learned how to create each type of Works chart, you're ready to learn about enhancing charts. In this chapter, we'll show you how to add titles, x-axis labels, legends, data labels, borders, and grid lines to charts. We'll also explain how to change the color, shading, and markers in your charts, how to adjust the scale of the x- and y-axes in a chart, and how to add a second y-axis to a chart. Finally, we'll explain a few special enhancements that apply only to pie charts.

Figure 14-1 on the following page shows a simple multiple-line chart that is based on the spreadsheet shown in Figure 14-2 on the next page. We'll use this chart to demonstrate most of Works' enhancements. To create this chart, make sure that the highlight is not extended. Then, select the New Chart command from the View menu to create a new chart. When Works displays the alert *Series not selected.*, choose <OK> or press [Enter]. Next, highlight the range B5:E5 and select the 1st Y-Series command from the Data menu to define the first data series; highlight the range B6:E6 and select the 2nd Y-Series command to define the second data series; highlight the range B7:E7 and select the 3rd Y-Series command; highlight the range B8:E8 and select the 4th Y-Series command. Finally, choose Line from the Format menu to make this a Line chart.

TITLES

The most basic enhancement you can make to a chart is to add titles. Works allows you to add five titles to a chart: a title and a subtitle at the top of the chart, one under the x-axis, one along the y-axis, and, if the chart has a second y-axis, one along the right y-axis. (You'll learn about multiple y-axes later in this chapter.) You can add a title and a subtitle to every type of Works chart. You can add an x-axis and y-axis title to any type of chart except a pie chart.

Figure 14-1

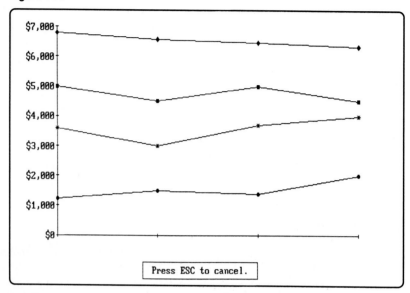

We'll use this chart to demonstrate most of Works' enhancements.

Figure 14-2

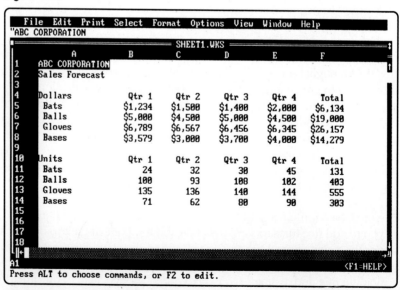

The chart in Figure 14-1 is based on the data in the ranges B5:E5, B6:E6, B7:E7, and B8:E8 in this worksheet.

To add any or all of these titles to a chart, select the Titles… command from the Data menu in the chart view. When you do this, Works will display a dialog box like the one in Figure 14-3. As you can see, this box includes a text box for each of the titles you can define: Chart Title, Subtitle, and so on. To define a title, just make an entry in one of the text boxes and choose <OK>. If you want to define more than one title, just make an entry in each of the appropriate boxes, then choose <OK>.

Figure 14-3

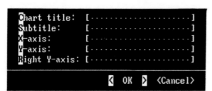

The Titles… command lets you define titles for your chart.

Suppose you want to add titles to the chart in Figure 14-1. To begin, choose the Define command from the spreadsheet Chart menu to enter the chart view. Next, select the Titles… command from the Data menu. When the Titles dialog box appears, enter the title *ABC CORPORATION* into the Chart Title text box. To add a subtitle, move to the Subtitle text box and enter the title *Sales Forecast*. Next, move to the X-axis text box, and enter the title *Quarter*. Finally, move to the Y-axis text box and enter the title *Sales*. Finally, choose the <OK> option to lock in your titles.

An example

When you are finished, select the name of the chart (Chart1) from the View menu to display the chart shown in Figure 14-4 on the following page. As you can see, the chart title and subtitle appear centered at the top of the chart. The x-axis title is centered beneath the horizontal (or x-) axis. The y-axis title is printed sideways and is centered along the vertical (or y-) axis.

Works can display up to 38 characters in the chart title, subtitle, and x-axis title, and up to 25 characters in the y-axis title. Interestingly, you can enter longer titles into the Titles dialog box than Works can display. If you do so, however, Works will simply display the first 38 or (in the case of the y-axis title) 25 characters in the chart.

Notes

There isn't any difference between the initial point size of the chart title and the initial point sizes of the other titles in a chart. However, you can use the Title Font… command on the Format menu to specify the size and font for the chart title, and the Other Font… command on the Format menu to specify the fonts and sizes of the other titles (as well as any other text in the chart). This means that the chart title can appear in a different font and a different size than the other titles. We'll cover each of these commands later in this chapter.

Figure 14-4

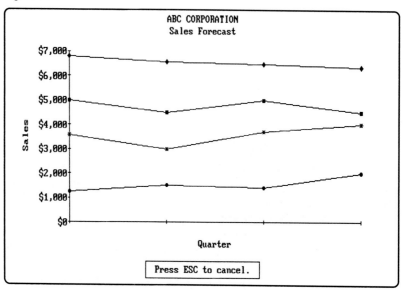

This chart has a chart title, a subtitle, an x-axis title, and a y-axis title.

To remove a title from a chart, just remove the entry you have made in the text box that defines that title. For example, to remove the subtitle from a chart, you would select the Titles... command from the Data menu, highlight the title in the Subtitle text box, press [Backspace] to erase the entry, then choose <OK>. When you choose <OK>, Works will delete the title.

Using cell entries as titles

If you want, you can use the entries in your spreadsheet as titles in your charts. To use a spreadsheet entry as a title, enter the address of the cell that contains the title you want to use into the appropriate text box in the Titles dialog box. If the cell has been given a range name, you can use that name instead of the address to define the title. The cell to which you refer can contain either a label or a value.

For example, instead of typing ABC CORPORATION into the Chart Title text box to define the chart title in the example, you could enter the address A1—which contains the label ABC CORPORATION—into that box.

There is one significant advantage to using cell references instead of literal text to define your titles. If you use cell references, you can change the title of a chart just by entering a new label into the cell. On the other hand, if you erase the entry in the cell, the title of the chart will disappear.

X-AXIS LABELS

When you create a bar, line, mixed bar and line, or hi-lo-close chart, Works will automatically label the tick marks along the y-axis of the chart but will not automatically label the tick marks along the x-axis. However, you can describe the categories represented by the tick marks on the x-axis by using the X-Series command on the Data menu. Works displays the entries in the x-series as labels along the x-axis in a chart.

X-axis labels are always based on values or labels in the spreadsheet on which the chart is based. To add x-axis labels to a chart, first choose the Define command from the Chart menu to enter the chart view. Then, highlight the cells that contain the entries you want to use as x-axis labels and select the X-Series command from the Data menu in the chart view. The cells that you highlight can contain either labels or values.

Suppose you want to add the labels Qtr 1, Qtr 2, Qtr 3, and Qtr 4 along the x-axis of the chart in Figure 14-4. To begin, choose the name of the chart—Chart1—from the View menu to make it active, and press [Esc] to enter the chart view. Next, highlight the range B4:E4, and select the 1st Y-Series command from the Data menu to define the first data series. Then, highlight the range B4:E4 in the spreadsheet that contains these labels. Finally, select the X-Series command from the Data menu to define the x-series.

An example

When you are finished, select the name of the chart—Chart1—from the View menu to display the chart shown in Figure 14-5. As you can see, the labels from cells B4, C4, D4, and E4—the range you defined as the x-series—now appear as labels along the x-axis.

Figure 14-5

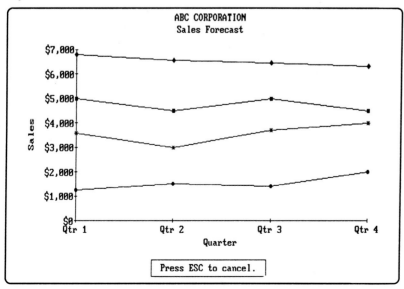

Works uses the entries in the x-series—the range B4:E4—as x-axis labels.

Works always centers x-axis labels at the x-axis tick marks. The alignment of the entries in the spreadsheet on which the x-series is based—left, right, or center—has no effect on the alignment of the labels in the chart. However, if the entries in the x-series are formatted values, the x-axis labels will have the same format as the values.

Usually, your spreadsheet will contain a range of entries that will serve as x-axis labels. If a spreadsheet does not contain an appropriate set of entries, you can simply create those entries in a range in the spreadsheet.

Defining x-axis labels automatically

Normally, you'll add x-axis labels to a chart after you've defined the chart. However, in some circumstances, you can define the x-series for a chart when you define the chart using the automatic method. If the entries in the x-series are labels, and the range you want Works to use as the x-series is adjacent to the range you want Works to use as the first y-series, then you can define the x-series when you define the chart. All you have to do is highlight the range you want Works to use as the x-series and the range(s) you want Works to use as the chart's y-series, then select the New Chart command from the View menu. When you do this, Works will use the cells that contain labels to define the x-series. Works will use the adjacent ranges, which should all contain numbers, to define the chart's y-series.

For example, suppose you want to define a chart from the spreadsheet shown in Figure 14-2 that illustrates the sales of Bats over the four quarters. To begin, highlight the range B4:E5. Notice that this range includes both the labels in row 4 and the values in row 5. Next, select the New Chart command from the View menu to create the new chart shown in Figure 14-6. As you can see, Works has defined the chart and added the x-axis labels to it automatically.

Remember that this technique will work only when the range you want to use to define the x-series contains values and when that range is adjacent to the range you want to use to define the first y-series. If the range you want to use as the x-series contains values, Works will assume that that range should be adjacent to the y-series in the chart. If the range is not adjacent to the range you want to use as the first y-series, you will not be able to highlight both ranges at once.

Setting the label frequency

Normally, Works will display every entry in the x-series as an x-axis label. Sometimes Works won't have enough room to display each label in its entirety on the x-axis. The space available for each x-axis label depends on the number of categories in the chart (that is, the number of tick marks on the x-axis). The more categories there are, the shorter the x-axis labels will have to be. If you define long x-axis labels in a chart with a large number of categories, Works will truncate those labels. Even if Works can display the entire label, the labels may be crowded.

When either of these problems occurs, you can often improve the appearance of the chart by changing the chart's label frequency setting. The default label frequency setting, 1, tells Works to display every entry in the x-series as an x-axis label. A label frequency setting greater than 1 tells Works to print only selected x-axis labels: every second label, every third label, and so on.

Figure 14-6

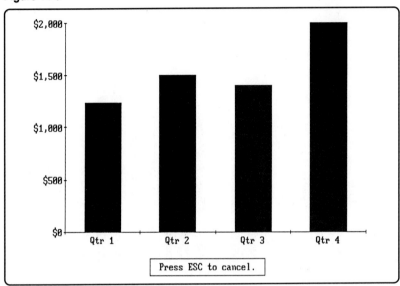

In some cases, you can define the x-series at the same time you define a chart.

You can specify a skip factor by selecting the X-Axis… command from the Options menu in the chart view. When you issue this command, Works will display the dialog box shown in Figure 14-7. To set the skip factor, just enter a number into the Label Frequency text box—2 if you want to display only every other label, 3 if you want to display every third label, and so on—then choose <OK>. The label frequency setting must be greater than or equal to 1 and less than or equal to 20. In most cases, a skip factor of only 2, 3, 4, or 5 will be sufficient to overcome problems with crowded or overlapping labels.

Figure 14-7

The Label frequency option in the X-Axis dialog box lets you specify the frequency of a chart's x-axis labels.

For example, Figure 14-8 shows a chart with 20 categories. You can see that the x-axis labels in this chart are crowded and truncated. Figure 14-9 shows this chart after we used the X-Axis... command to specify a label frequency of 2. As you can see, the labels are no longer truncated.

Figure 14-8

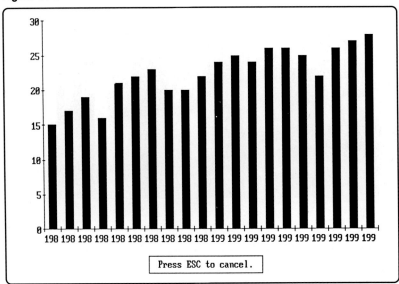

The x-axis labels in this chart are crowded and truncated.

After you have specified a label frequency other than 1, you can change it back to 1 by selecting the X-Axis... command and entering 1 into the Label Frequency text box. The next time you view a chart, Works will display every x-axis label.

Removing x-axis labels

You can use the Series... command to delete the x-axis labels from a chart. To remove x-axis labels, select the Series... command from the Data menu in the chart view, highlight the x-series, then choose <Delete>. When you do this, Works will delete the x-series (and thus, the x-axis labels as well) from the chart.

Pie charts

Pie charts don't have axes so they cannot have x-axis labels. However, you can create labels for the slices in a pie chart by defining an x-series using the X-Series command on the Data menu in the chart view. We'll show you how to do that later in this chapter.

Figure 14-9

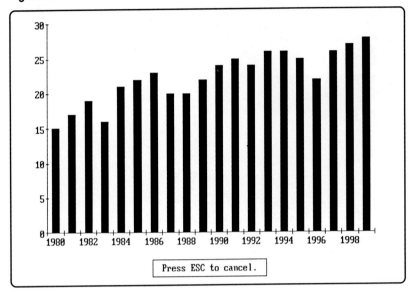

Specifying a skip factor of 2 eliminates overlapping labels.

LEGENDS

Legends make it easier to distinguish one range from another in multiple-series line, clustered bar, stacked bar, and 100% bar charts. When you define a legend for a chart, Works will add text at the bottom of a chart that explains what each range in the chart represents. Since the purpose of legends is to help you differentiate the series in a chart, you will not use legends in single-series charts.

To add a legend to a chart, select the Legends... command from the Data menu in the chart view. When you select this command, the Legends dialog box shown in Figure 14-10 on the next page will appear. Notice that this dialog box lists the six ranges that Works allows you to define in a single chart and includes a Legend text box. To define the legend for a given range in a chart, highlight that range in the list of ranges, type the legend that matches that range into the Legend text box, then choose <Create>.

▶WORKS 2◀

▶In Works 2, you can define legends for all the series in a chart without repeating the Legends... command. To do this, you select the Legends... command, define the legend for the first series, choose <Create>, define the legend for the second series, choose <Create> again, and so on. When you are finished defining legends, choose <Done> to leave the Legends dialog box.◀

An example
▶WORKS 2◀

▶Suppose you want to add legends to the multiple-series line chart in Figure 14-5. To begin, activate the chart by choosing its name from the View menu and then press [Esc] to enter the chart view. Next, select the Legends... command from the Data menu. When the Legends dialog box appears, the 1st Y option will be highlighted. To define the legend for this series, move to the Legend text box and type *Bats*. When you're finished, choose <Create>.

Figure 14-10

The Legends... command lets you define legends for a chart.

To add a legend for the second y-Series to this chart, highlight the 2nd Y option, move to the Legend text box and type *Balls*, then choose <Create>. To add a legend for the third y-Series, highlight the 3rd Y option, move to the Legend text box and type *Gloves*, then choose <Create>. Finally, to add a legend for the fourth y-Series, highlight the 4th Y option, move to the Legend text box and type *Bases*, then choose <Create>. When you have defined legends for all four series, choose <Done>.

Now, select the name of the chart—Chart1—from the View menu to view the chart shown in Figure 14-11. Works has added a legend to the chart. Since this chart is a line chart, each entry in the legend is made up of a marker that identifies each data series. (The markers will be in color if you have a color monitor.) ◄

Notes

The legend text you define for each data series can be up to 19 characters long. However, the practical limit for the legend text for each series is determined by the number of legends in the chart and by the number of characters your monitor can display on a single line. In general, the more series you have, the fewer characters you'll be able to include in the legend text for each series. You'll need to experiment to determine exactly how many characters will fit in your legends. If you create a legend that is more than 19 characters long, Works will simply truncate the legend entry when you choose <Create>.

Since the chart in Figure 14-11 is a line chart, each entry in the legend displays a marker plus one of the legend labels you specified. In bar charts, each entry in the legend is made up of a rectangle that displays the color and/or shading pattern of one of the bars in the chart plus one of the legend labels you specified. (The rectangles will be in color if you have a color monitor and will be shaded if you have a monochrome monitor.) In mixed line and bar charts, Works will display colored or shaded rectangles in the legends for data series that are plotted as bars and markers for the series that are plotted as lines.

Figure 14-11

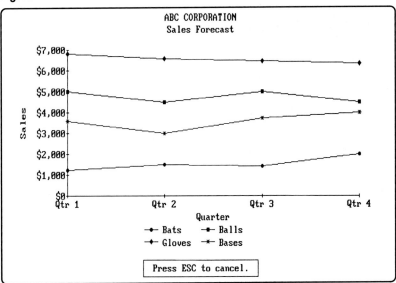

This chart includes a legend for each of its four data series.

If you define the series of a line chart out of sequence, you'll need to be careful when you define legends. You can quickly refresh your memory about the data series in your chart by selecting the Series... command from the Data menu.

Since pie charts have only one data range, you cannot add a legend to a pie chart. To explain the meaning of each segment in a pie chart, you'll need to create an x-series for the chart. We'll show you how to do that later.

If you add a border to a chart that has legends, the legends will lie outside the border. We'll show you how to add a border to a chart later in this chapter.

Using cell entries as legends

Instead of typing the legend text for each legend, you can use entries in your spreadsheet as legend text. To use a cell entry as a legend, first select the Legends... command from the Data menu. Then, highlight the data series for which you want to create a legend. Next, move to the Legend text box and, instead of typing the legend itself, enter the address of the cell that contains the entry you want to use as the legend. If the cell has been given a range name, you can use that name instead of the address to define the legend. The cell to which you refer can contain either a label or a value.

For example, the labels in cells A5, A6, A7, and A8 are identical to the legend text we've defined for the four data series in the example. Instead of typing the legend text for those series, we could refer to those cells. To create the legend for the first data series, we could select the Legends… command, highlight the 1st Y option, then enter the address *A5* into the Legend text box.

Defining legends automatically
►WORKS 2◄

►Normally, you'll add legends to a chart after you've defined the chart. However, in some circumstances you can define the legend for a chart when you define the chart using the automatic method. If the cells that contain the legends for each of the chart's series are located just to the left of the first cells in the series, and if those contain labels, then you can define the legend when you define the chart. All you have to do is highlight the cells that contain the legend text when you highlight the range(s) you want Works to use as the chart's y-series and select the New Chart command from the View menu. When you do this, Works will use the cells to the left of the first cell in each series to define the legend.

For example, suppose you want to define a chart from the spreadsheet shown in Figure 14-2 that illustrates the sales of Bats and Balls over the four quarters. You want to define the legend at the same time you define the chart. To begin, highlight the range A5:E6. Notice that this range includes both the labels in column A and the values in rows 5 and 6. Next, select the New Chart command to create the new chart shown in Figure 14-12. As you can see, Works has defined the chart and added the legend to it automatically.

Figure 14-12

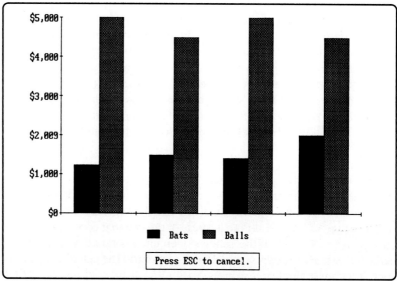

In some cases, you can define the legend when you define a chart.

Remember that this technique will work only when the range you want to use to define the legend contains labels and when that range is adjacent to the ranges you want to use to define the y-series. If the range you want to use as the legend contains values, Works will assume that that range should be part of the y-series in the chart. If the legend range is not adjacent to the range you want to use as the y-series, you will not be able to highlight both ranges at once.◄

Hiding legends

If you decide that you do not want to display any legends in a chart, you can hide them from view. The display of legends is controlled by a toggle command, Show Legends, on the Options menu. If a dot appears to the left of the Show Legends command, the command is on, and Works will display legends on the screen and on the printed chart. The default setting for this command is on.

To prevent a legend from being displayed on your screen or on a print-out, simply select the Show Legends command. When you do this, the dot next to the command will disappear, and Works will not display the legend. If you later want to display the legend, just choose the Show Legends command again.

Deleting legends

Hiding a legend doesn't remove it. If you decide that you want to delete a legend, select the Legends… command from the Data menu, choose the series for which you want to delete the legend, highlight the entire entry in the Legend text box, press [Delete] or [Backspace] to erase the entry, then choose <OK> to complete the command. Just as you must define the legends for each data series in a chart individually, you must delete the legends for each series individually.

DATA LABELS

Data labels are floating labels that you can place next to the data points in line, XY, clustered bar, stacked bar, mixed bar and line, and hi-lo-close charts. (You can't add data labels to pie charts.) Unlike x-axis labels and titles, which appear at the edges of the chart, data labels appear in the chart next to the points or bars that make up the chart.

Like x-axis labels, data labels are always based on entries in the spreadsheet to which the chart refers. Like legends, you can only define the data labels for one data series at a time. To define data labels, first highlight the range of entries you want to use as data labels for one of the series in the chart. The range you highlight should include the same number of cells as the corresponding data series. The range can include values or labels.

Once you've highlighted the range, select the Data Labels… command from the Data menu in the chart view to display a dialog box like the one shown in Figure 14-13. This dialog box lets you define (or delete) data labels for a data series. To define data labels for a data series, choose that series from the Series list box, then choose <Create>. Works will then close the dialog box. If you want to define data labels for all the series in a chart, you have to highlight the data labels range for the first series, select the Data Labels… command, choose <Create>;

highlight the data labels range for the second series, select the Data Labels... command again, choose <Create>; and so on. Works will display the entries from the data labels ranges you've defined next to the data points for the corresponding data series.

Figure 14-13

The Data Labels... command lets you add data labels to a chart.

An example

For example, let's add data labels to the chart shown in Figure 14-11. We'll use the numbers as labels on which to base each of the series. To begin, activate the chart by choosing its name from the View menu, and then press [Esc] to enter the chart view. Next, highlight the range B5:E5 in the spreadsheet—the range that contains the labels for the first data series—and select the Data Labels... command. The 1st Y option in the Series list box will be highlighted when the box appears, so all you have to do is choose <Create> to define the labels for the first data series. Next, highlight the range B6:E6, open the Data Labels dialog box, highlight the 2nd Y option in the Series list box, then choose <Create>. Then, highlight the range B7:E7 in the spreadsheet, open the Data Labels dialog box, highlight the 3rd Y option in the Series list box, then choose <Create>. Finally, highlight the range B8:E8 in the spreadsheet, open the Data Labels dialog box, highlight the 4th Y option in the Series list box, then choose <Create>.

When you're finished, select the name of the chart from the View menu to view the chart shown in Figure 14-14. As you can see, Works has plotted the entries from the ranges you defined into the chart as data labels. Each label has been plotted above the data point in the corresponding data series in the chart.

Notes

Although data labels can add a great deal of clarity to your charts, there are a few problems that can arise. First, the data labels for the first data point in each data series usually overlap the y-axis. For example, in Figure 14-14 the leftmost data label for each series overlaps the y-axis, making both the data label and the y-axis hard to read. Second, if the chart contains more than one series, and the series are close together, the data labels for the different series can overlap.

Unfortunately, there is really no good way to handle this problem. If you can't stand the overlapping characters, you can simply delete the data labels from the chart. We'll show you how to do that in a few paragraphs.

Figure 14-14

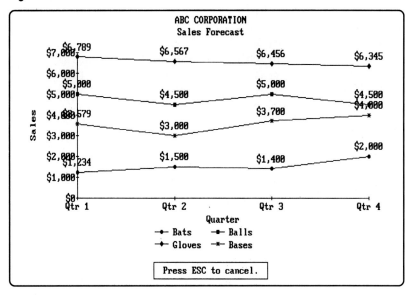

Works positions data labels just above the data points in the chart.

The entries in the data labels ranges you define can be values or labels. The entries can be as long as you want. However, if the entries are too long, they will probably overlap the y-axis, the data series, or one another. If the entries in the data labels ranges are values, then the data labels in the chart will have the same format as the values on which they are based.

After you have defined data labels for a data series, Works will list the range that contains the labels next to that series in the Data Labels dialog box. If you want to move the highlight to the data labels range for a particular data series, just select the Data Labels... command, choose the appropriate data series from the Series list box, then choose the <Go To> option. When you do this, Works will move the highlight to the data labels range for the data series you choose and will expand the highlight to cover that entire range.

Deleting data labels

The Data Labels... command also lets you delete data labels from a chart. To do this, select the Data Labels... command, choose the series for which you want to delete the data labels, then choose the <Delete> option.

►**WORKS 2**◄

►In Works 2, you can delete the data labels from more than one series in a chart without repeating the Data Labels... command.. To do this, select the Data Labels... command, delete the data labels for the first series, choose <Delete>, delete the data labels for the second series, choose <Delete> again, and so on. When you are finished deleting data labels, choose <Done> to leave the Data Labels dialog box.◄

Using data labels
in bar charts

You can also use data labels in simple bar charts and, with a few limitations, in clustered and stacked bar charts. In a single-series bar chart, the data labels for each data point appear at the top of each bar in the chart. In clustered bar charts, the data labels for each data point also appear at the top of each bar in the chart. However, since the bars in the chart are clustered, the data labels for one bar will almost certainly overlap the labels for the adjacent bars or the adjacent bars themselves. The result will be an unattractive graph. For this reason, you'll probably want to avoid using data labels in clustered bar charts.

When you add data labels to a stacked bar chart, Works will position the label for each bar segment above that segment. Since the segments in a stacked bar chart are stacked, the labels for all but the top segment in each bar will overlap the next segment. This makes the labels very hard to read. On the other hand, the label for the top segment will appear at the very top of the bar and should be easy to read. If you want to use data labels in a stacked bar chart, consider defining labels only for the top segment.

CHOOSING AND
DISPLAYING FONTS

So far, we have shown you how to enhance your Works charts by adding titles, subtitles, x-axis labels, legends, and data labels. Until now, all the text you've added to your charts has been displayed in the standard font and size. However, Works gives you the power to choose the font and size of the chart title and the other text (x-axis labels, legends, and data labels) in your charts. The Title Font… command on the Format menu lets you specify the font and size for the chart title, and the Other Font… command lets you specify the font and size for the other text in the chart.

Choosing fonts

When you select the Title Font… or the Other Font… command, Works will display a dialog box that lists the fonts and sizes you can choose. For example, Figure 14-15 shows the dialog box Works will display when you select the Title Font… command. (The Other Font dialog box is identical to the Title Font dialog box.) The Fonts list box will list the 12 special fonts supported by Works. The Sizes list box will list the size options available for the font that is highlighted in the Fonts list box.

Figure 14-15

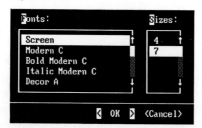

The Title Font… and Other Font… commands let you choose the fonts you'll use to print the text in your charts.

To specify the font you want Works to use for the titles in your chart, select the Title Font... command, then choose the font you want to use from the Fonts list box. When you select a font, Works will change the list of available sizes in the Sizes list box. You can choose the size you want to use by choosing one of the options from this box. When you've selected the font and size, choose <OK> to lock in your selections.

To specify the font you want Works to use for the other text in your chart, select the Other Font... command, choose the font you want to use from the Fonts box, then choose the size you want to use from the Sizes list box. When you've selected the font and size, choose <OK> to lock in your selections.

Displaying fonts

Normally, Works will use only the special fonts you've selected when it prints the chart. Works won't automatically display those fonts on your screen when you view the chart on screen. If you want the titles and other text to appear on the screen in the fonts and sizes you've specified, you can select the Show Printer Fonts command from the Options menu in the chart view. The Show Printer Fonts command is a toggle switch. If a dot appears to the left of this command, the command is on, and Works will display the fonts you have selected in your chart. If no dot appears, the command is off, and Works will use the basic screen font. The default setting for this command is off.

An example

Suppose you want Works to display the title of the chart in Figure 14-14 in 24-point Bold Roman B and the other text in the chart in 14-point Roman B. To begin, activate that chart by choosing its name from the View menu and press [Esc] to enter the chart view. Then, select the Title Font... command from the Format menu, and choose Bold Roman B from the Fonts list box. Then, move to the Sizes box and choose 24. Next, choose <OK> to complete the command. Now, select the Other Font... command, choose Roman B from the Fonts list box, choose 14 from the Sizes list box, and choose <OK> to end the command. Then, to instruct Works to display the fonts you have selected on the screen, choose the Show Printer Fonts command from the Options menu. When you are finished, select the name of the chart from the View menu to display the chart shown in Figure 14-16 on the following page.

Notes

Your ability to use special fonts in charts depends on the choices you made when you set up Works. If you have a hard disk and you choose to copy the font files to the hard disk, you'll be able to use fonts without limitation. The same is true if your working copy of Works is on a floppy disk and you choose to copy the font files to that disk.

If, on the other hand, you have a hard disk and choose not to copy the font files to that disk, you won't be able to use fonts at all. If you select a font other than Screen (the default), select the Show Printer Fonts command, then select the

View command, Works will display an alert box with the message *Invalid or missing font file.* and will not display the chart. The same will occur when you try to print the chart. You won't be able to view or print the chart until you choose the Screen font again.

Figure 14-16

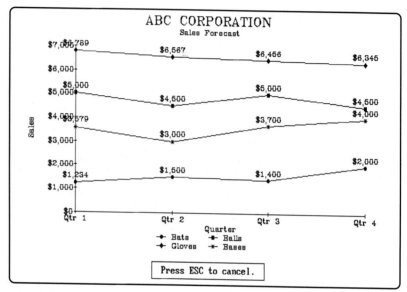

The Show Printer Fonts command tells Works to display the fonts you have selected on the screen.

If your working copy of Works is on a floppy disk, and you did not copy the font files to that disk, you'll still be able to use the fonts. However, whenever you try to print or view a chart using special fonts, Works will prompt you to place your Printer Disk 2 in drive A of your computer. After it reads the specified fonts from that disk, Works will display or print your chart.

ADJUSTING THE Y-AXIS

The Y-Axis... command on the Options menu lets you adjust and format the y-axis of bar, stacked bar, line, hi-lo-close, and XY charts. (This command has no effect on pie charts because pie charts have no axes.) When you issue this command, Works will display a dialog box like the one shown in Figure 14-17. This command allows you to set the maximum and minimum values of the y-axis scale and the interval between the tick marks on the y-axis. It also allows you to change the y-axis in the chart from an arithmetic to a logarithmic scale. You can even use it to change the type of the chart. (This command also lets you create horizontal grid lines in a chart. We'll show you how to do that later.)

Figure 14-17

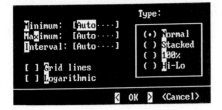

The Y-Axis… command lets you adjust the scale of the y-axis.

The Minimum, Maximum, and Interval options in the Y-Axis dialog box let you adjust the scale of the y-axis in a chart. The default for each of these settings is Auto, which means that Works will set the minimum and maximum values of the y-scale, and the interval between the tick marks on the axis, automatically. While in most cases the scale that Works creates will be satisfactory, you might want to override one or more of these settings. For example, when Works sets the minimum value of the y-axis at a point other than 0, you could use the Minimum option to override the default and place the origin of the y-axis at 0.

Setting the y-Axis scale

To adjust the y-axis scale manually, select the Y-Axis… command from the Options menu. When the Y-Axis dialog box appears, you can specify the lower limit of the y-axis by entering a number representing the new minimum value in the Minimum text box. You can specify the upper limit by entering a number representing the new maximum value in the Maximum text box. If you want to change the interval between the tick marks in the axis, you can enter a number representing the new interval in the Interval text box. You can change any one of these settings individually, or you can change two or all three of them at once. When you've made your changes, choose <OK>.

An example

Let's use the Y-Axis… command to change the upper limit of the y-axis of the chart in Figure 14-16 from 7,000 to 10,000 and to change the interval between the tick marks from 1000 to 2500. To begin, activate that chart and, if you are not in the chart view, select the Define command. Next, select the Y-Axis… command from the Options menu. When the Y-Axis dialog box appears, enter the number 10000 into the Maximum text box and the number 2500 into the Interval text box. Then, choose <OK> to lock in the change.

When you select the name of the chart from the View menu, Works will display the chart shown in Figure 14-18 on the next page. Notice that Works has changed the upper limit of the y-axis to 10,000 and has changed the interval of the tick marks on the y-axis to 2500.

Notes

The upper limit you set for the y-axis must be greater than the lower limit. In addition, the interval you specify must be a positive number. If you break either of these rules, Works will display an alert box that contains the message *Minimum, maximum or interval not valid.* when you choose <OK>. The interval you specify should be less than the difference between the maximum and minimum values. If the interval is greater than the difference between the maximum and the minimum, Works will not plot any tick marks on the y-axis.

Figure 14-18

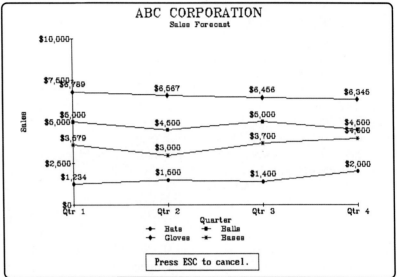

We've used the Y-Axis… command to set the maximum value on the y-axis to 10,000 and the interval to 2500.

You should be careful to choose upper and lower limits for your charts that will allow Works to display all the data in the chart. If you choose a lower limit that is greater than some of the values in the chart or an upper limit that is less than some of those values, Works will truncate your chart. At the same time, you do not want to set the lower limit too low or the upper limit too high. If the limits you set define a range that is too wide, the chart will lose its detail and, therefore, much of its meaning.

Both the upper and lower limits can be negative numbers. You will usually use a negative lower limit only in charts that have some values that fall below 0. You will use a negative upper limit only when every value in the chart is less than 0. Otherwise, the positive values in the chart will not be displayed.

Works uses the interval you specify as a guideline instead of a strict limit. Sometimes Works will change the interval slightly so that it can create nice, even divisions along the y-axis. For example, if you were to use the Y-Axis… command to set the maximum value of the y-axis of the chart in Figure 14-18 to 10,500 and the interval to 2500, Works would change the interval setting to 2625. The tick marks on the y-axis will occur at 2625, 5250, 7875, and 10500.

If the interval you specify is too narrow, the numbers next to the tick marks on the y-axis will overlap. In general, you should define the interval so that there are no more than about ten tick marks on the axis.

To cancel your Minimum, Maximum, or Interval settings, just select the Y-Axis... command and enter the word *Auto* in the Minimum, Maximum, and/or Interval text boxes. When you choose <OK>, Works will automatically redefine any settings you've returned to Auto.

Logarithmic scales

The Logarithmic option in the Y-Axis dialog box lets you convert the usual linear scale on the y-axis to a logarithmic scale. On a logarithmic scale, the intervals along the y-axis will be powers of 10: 10, 100, 1000, and so on. Logarithmic scales are useful for charting series that have wide ranges of values, such as series that depict exponential growth.

To activate this feature, simply choose the Logarithmic option, and an X will appear in the check box. To return to a normal arithmetic scale, just choose the Logarithmic option again to deactivate it.

Changing the chart type

The Type option box in the Y-Axis dialog box allows you to change the type of the y-scale in the current chart. In effect, this option lets you change the current chart type. This box lists four scale types—Normal, Stacked, 100%, and Hi-Lo—and places a dot next to the active type. The active scale type depends on the type of the current chart. The Normal option will be active if the chart you have created is a simple single-series or multiple-series line or bar chart. The Stacked option will be active if the chart is an area line chart or a stacked bar chart. The 100% option will be active if the chart is a 100% bar chart. The Hi-Lo option will be active if the chart is a hi-lo-close chart.

You can use the options in the Type box to change the current chart type. All you have to do is select the Y-Axis... command from the Options menu, then choose the new type from the list of options. The precise type of the resulting chart depends on the basic type of the chart you've created. For example, if the current chart is a multiple-series line chart, choosing Stacked will change the chart into an area line chart. If the chart is a bar chart, choosing the 100% option will turn the chart into a 100% bar chart.

As a rule, you should not set the type of a chart using the Type option box in the Y-Axis dialog box. It's much easier to use the commands on the Format menu to define the type of a chart. However, there is at least one chart type that can only be created using this option. If you create a multiple-series line chart, then choose the 100% type option, Works will change the chart into a 100% area line chart. There is no other way to create this potentially useful chart type.

**ADJUSTING
THE X-AXIS IN
XY CHARTS**

In most types of charts, the values in the x-series are merely labels. In XY charts, however, the x-series defines the scale of the x-axis and helps to determine the position of the points in the chart. In effect, then, the x-axis in an XY chart is like the y-axis in other charts. The X-Axis... command on the Options menu allows you to adjust the scale of the x-axis in an XY chart in much the same way that the Y-Axis... command lets you adjust the scale of the y-axis in other types of charts. When you select the X-Axis... command while the active chart is an XY chart, Works will display a dialog box like the one in Figure 14-19. (If the active chart is not an XY chart when you select the X-Axis... command, Works will display a dialog box like the one shown in Figure 14-7.)

Figure 14-19

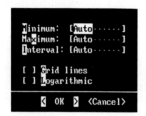

The X-Axis... command lets you adjust the x-axis in an XY chart.

When you see this dialog box, you can set the lower limit of the x-axis by entering the lowest number you want displayed on the x-axis in the Minimum text box. To set an upper limit, enter the highest number you want displayed on the x-axis in the Maximum text box. To set the interval between the tick marks on the x-axis, enter a number representing the interval in the Interval text box.

When Works draws an XY chart, it almost never places the start of the x-axis or the y-axis at 0. Instead, it draws the chart so that the top and bottom limits of the two axes are just large enough to hold the points in the chart. This is likely to result in a misleading chart. Fortunately, this problem is easy to correct. You can use the X-Axis... and Y-Axis... commands on the Options menu to set the origin (lower limit) for both axes at 0 manually.

The X-Axis... command also lets you convert the usual arithmetic scale on the x-axis to a logarithmic scale. To make the x-axis a logarithmic scale, choose the Logarithmic option to activate it. When the Logarithmic option is active, an x will appear in its check box. To change the x-axis back into an arithmetic scale, choose the Logarithmic option again.

BORDERS

The Show Border command on the Options menu in the chart view lets you add a border to a chart. The Show Border command is a toggle switch. If a dot appears next to this command, the command is on, and Works will display a border in your chart. If no dot appears, it is off, and no border will appear in the chart. The default setting for this command is off. To turn this command on and off, simply select it. You can add a border to any type of chart except a pie chart.

For example, to add a border to the chart in Figure 14-18, activate that chart by choosing its name from the View menu and press [Esc] to enter the chart view. Then, select the Show Border command. Figure 14-20 shows the result. To deactivate the border, simply select Show Border again.

Figure 14-20

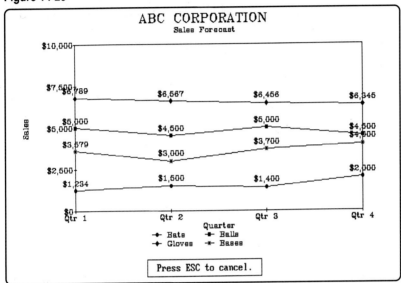

The Show Border command lets you add a border to a chart.

GRID LINES

To help make your charts more readable, you might want to add vertical and/or horizontal grid lines to the chart. To add vertical grid lines, select the X-Axis... command from the Options menu and select the Grid Lines option. To add horizontal grid lines to a chart, select the Y-Axis... command from the Options menu and select the Grid Lines option. When the Grid Lines option in either dialog box is activated, an X will appear in the Grid Lines box.

Suppose you want to add a grid to the chart in Figure 14-20. To begin, activate that chart and, if you are not in the chart view, select the Define command. To create vertical grid lines, select the X-Axis... command, choose the Grid Lines option, then choose <OK>. To add horizontal grid lines to the chart, select the Y-Axis... command, choose the Grid Lines option, then choose <OK>. When you select the View command from the Chart menu, your chart will look like the one shown in Figure 14-21 on the next page.

You can delete the vertical grid lines from a chart by selecting the X-Axis... command and choosing the Grid Lines option again to deactivate it. Similarly, you can delete the horizontal grid lines from a chart by selecting the Y-Axis... command and choosing the Grid Lines option again to deactivate it.

Figure 14-21

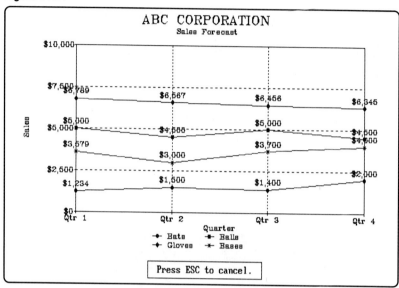

Grid lines help to make your charts easier to read.

FORMATS

Normally, Works will assign the colors, shading patterns, and markers to the data series in your charts manually. The Data Format... command on the Format menu allows you to change the colors, shading patterns, and markers Works uses to plot the data series in your charts. When you select this command, Works will display a Data Format dialog box. The precise appearance of this box depends on the type of the active chart.

If the chart is a line, area line, XY, or hi-lo-close chart, the Data Format dialog box will look like Figure 14-22. In this dialog box, the Series list box lists the six possible series in a chart. The Colors box lists the colors you can use to draw the lines connecting the points in a series. The list will be limited to the colors supported by your computer's graphics card and monitor. (If your computer can display color, the list will include a number of colors; otherwise, it will include just the options Auto and Black.) The Patterns box lists the patterns you can use to draw the lines between the points in each data series. The Markers list box lists the markers you can assign to each data point in a series.

If the active chart is a bar, stacked bar, or 100% bar chart, the dialog box will look like Figure 14-23. As before, the Series list box lists the six possible series in a chart. The Colors list box lists the colors Works allows you to use to color the bars in each data series. The Patterns list box lists the patterns Works allows you to use to shade the bars. The Markers list box is empty.

Figure 14-22

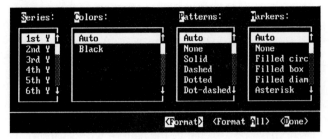

The Data Format... command lets you change the colors, line patterns, and markers Works uses to plot the data series in line, area line, hi-lo-close, and XY charts.

Figure 14-23

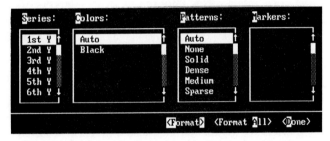

The Data Format... command lets you change the colors and patterns Works uses to plot the data series in bar charts.

Notice that the default settings for Colors, Patterns, and Markers in the Data Format dialog box are always Auto. The Auto setting tells Works to choose the colors, patterns, and markers for the chart automatically. By choosing one of the other options in the Colors, Patterns, and/or Markers list box, you can override the default setting.

To format a data series, select the Data Format... command. When the Data Format dialog box appears, first choose the series you want to format from the Series list box. Then, choose the Color, Pattern, or Marker you want Works to use when it plots that range. (Depending on the type of the chart and on your computer's graphics card and monitor, all these options may not apply to your chart. Some options may have different effects on different types of charts.) When you're finished, you can choose the <Format> option to apply the color, pattern, and/or marker you specified only to the data series you selected. Alternatively, you can choose the <Format All> option to apply the format you specified to all the series in the chart.

**Formatting
data series**

Line charts

If you have a color monitor, Works will display each line in a line, multiple-series line, or area line chart in a different color. If you want, you can use the Colors option to change the color associated with each series. If you choose a data series, choose one of the color options, then choose <Format>, Works will display the line for that series in the selected color. If you choose a color, then choose <Format All>, Works will display the lines for all the series in that color.

If you have a monochrome monitor, Works will use a different symbol to represent the data points on each line— ● for the first series, ■ for the second, ◆ for the third, and so on—and will connect the points in each series with a solid line. You can use the Patterns option to change the pattern Works uses to display the line between the points in any data series and the Markers option to change the marker used to represent the data points of any data series. If you select a data series, choose one of the Patterns options, then choose <Format>, Works will use that pattern to display the line that connects the points in the selected series. If you choose a pattern, then choose <Format All>, Works will display every series in that pattern. If you choose a data series, choose one of the Markers options, then choose <Format>, Works will use that marker to represent the data points in the selected series. If you choose a marker, then choose <Format All>, Works will use that pattern for the points in every series.

If you choose the None option in the Patterns list box, Works will not display a connecting line for the selected data series (or, if you choose <Format All>, for all of the series). If you choose the None option in the Markers list box, Works will not display the data points for the selected data series (or, if you choose <Format All>, for all of the series). By combining these options, you can instruct Works to display just lines without symbols, just symbols without lines, or neither lines nor symbols.

You can also use the Patterns and Markers options if you have a color monitor. If you select a data series, choose one of the Patterns options, then choose <Format>, Works will use that pattern to display the line that connects the points in the selected series. (Of course, the line will also be displayed in color.) If you choose a pattern, then choose <Format All>, Works will display every series in that pattern. If you choose a data series, choose one of the Markers options, then choose <Format>, Works will use that marker to represent the data points in the selected series. If you choose a marker, then choose <Format All>, Works will use that pattern for the points in every series.

Bar charts

If you have a color monitor, Works will display each bar or bar segment in a clustered, stacked, or 100% bar chart in a different color. You can use the Colors option to change the color associated with each series. If you choose a data series, choose one of the color options, then choose <Format>, Works will display the bars for that series in the selected color. If you choose a color, then choose <Format All>, Works will display the bars for all the series in that color.

If you have a color monitor, you can use the Patterns option to add patterns to the bars in a chart. If you choose a data series, choose one of the Patterns options, then choose <Format>, Works will use that pattern to shade the bars in the selected series. (Of course, the bars will also be in color.) If you choose a pattern, then choose <Format All>, Works will use that pattern to shade the bars for all the series.

If you have a monochrome monitor, Works will use different shading for each data series in clustered bar, stacked bar, and 100% bar charts: solid black for the first series, dense gray for the second, medium gray for the third, and so on. You can use the Patterns option to change the pattern associated with any data series. If you select a data series, choose one of the Patterns options, then choose <Format>, Works will use that pattern to display the bars in the selected series. If you choose a pattern, then choose <Format All>, Works will display the bars for every series in that pattern. If you choose the None option in the Patterns list box, Works will not shade the bars for the selected data series (or, if you choose <Format All>, for all of the series).

If you have a color monitor, Works will display the dots representing each data series in a hi-lo-close chart in a different color. You can use the Colors option to change the color associated with each series. If you choose a data series, choose one of the color options, then choose <Format>, Works will display the points for that series in the selected color. If you choose a color, then choose <Format All>, Works will use that color to display the points for every series.

Hi-lo-close charts

If you have a monochrome monitor, Works will use different symbols to display the data points in each data series in a hi-lo-close chart ● for the first series, ■ for the second, ◆ for the third, and ✳ for the fourth. You can use the Markers option to change the symbol associated with any data series. If you choose a data series, choose one of the Markers options, then choose <Format>, Works will use that marker to represent the data points in the selected series. If you choose a marker, then choose <Format All>, Works will use that pattern for the points in every series.

You can use the Patterns option to add connecting lines between the data points in a series in a hi-lo-close chart. The default choice for Patterns in hi-lo-close charts is Auto, which means that Works will not display any lines between the points in each data series. However, if you select a data series, choose one of the other Patterns options, then choose <Format>, Works will use that pattern to draw a line between the points in that series. If you choose a pattern, then choose <Format All>, Works will use that pattern to draw a line between the points in all the series in the chart.

You can also use the Patterns and Markers options if you have a color monitor. If you select a data series, choose one of the Patterns options, then choose <Format>, Works will use that pattern to draw a line between the points in the selected series. (The line will also be in color.) If you choose a pattern, then choose <Format All>, Works will use that pattern to draw a line between the points in every series. If you choose a data series, choose one of the Markers options, then choose <Format>, Works will use that marker to represent the data points in the selected series. If you choose a marker, then choose <Format All>, Works will use that pattern for the points in every series.

XY charts

In almost every case, XY charts will include just one y-series. Works always uses black squares to display the points in the single y-series of an XY chart.

If you have a color monitor, you can use the Colors option to change the color Works uses to display the data points in an XY chart. If you choose one of the color options, then choose <Format>, Works will display the data points in the chart's one data series in the selected color.

You can use the Markers option to change the marker Works uses to plot the data points in an XY chart. If you choose one of the Markers options, then choose <Format>, Works will use the selected marker to draw the data points in chart's one data series.

An example

Let's look at an example of formatting a line chart. Suppose you want to change the pattern and the markers Works uses to display the lines and data points in the chart in Figure 14-21 so that the completed chart looks like Figure 14-24. To begin, activate that chart by choosing its name from the View menu and press [Esc] to enter the chart view. Then, select the Data Format... command from the Format menu in the chart view to reveal the Data Format dialog box shown in Figure 14-22. Next, choose the Dashed option from the Patterns list box, then choose <Format All> to change the line pattern for all data series to dashed.

Now you're ready to format the 1st Y-Series. Since the 1st Y option in the Series list box is already highlighted, just choose Hollow Circle from the Markers box. Then, choose <Format> to lock in the new format. Next, choose the 2nd Y option from the Series list box; choose Hollow Box from the Markers box; then choose <Format> to lock in the new format. Now, choose the 3rd Y option from the Series list box, choose Hollow Diamond from the Markers box; and choose <Format>. Finally, select the Data Format... command; choose the 4th Y option from the Series list box; choose Asterisk from the Markers box; and choose <Format> to lock in the new format. Finally, choose <Done> to lock in your changes.

When you are finished, select the name of the chart from the View menu. Figure 14-24 shows the formatted chart.

Notes

If you use the <Format All> option to specify one format for an entire chart, any new series that you add to the chart will also appear in that format. Of course, you can always use the Data Format... command to reformat those new series.

Figure 14-24

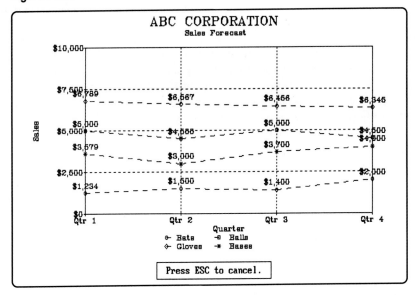

We've used the Data Format... command to change the patterns and markers in this chart.

If the chart you are formatting includes a legend, Works will use the color, pattern, and/or marker you have selected for that series in the legend. If you change the color, pattern, or marker for a series, the legend will also change.

Format For B&W command

If you have a CGA graphics card, or a monochrome graphics card that emulates a CGA card (such as a Compaq monochrome graphics adapter), there may be times when you'll want to display your graphs in black and white (monochrome) graphics instead of in color graphics. In some situations, you may be able to substantially increase the attractiveness and clarity of your charts by turning the Format For B&W command on.

The Format For B&W command on the Options menu in the chart view allows you to do this. The Format For B&W command is a toggle switch. If a dot appears to the left of the command on the Options menu, the command is on, and Works will display your chart in black and white. If no dot appears, the command is off, and the chart will be displayed in color. The default setting for this command is off. To turn this command on and off, simply select it. When you turn the Format For B&W command on, Works will use patterns and/or markers to differentiate the data series in the chart instead of using colors.

When the Format For B&W command is on, the Colors list box in the Data Format dialog box will include just two options: Auto and Black. Since Works is displaying the chart in black and white, none of the other colors supported by your hardware will be available. When you turn the Format For B&W command off, the normal list of colors will return.

**List Printer
Formats command**

The chances are good that your graphics printer has different capabilities than your graphics adapter and monitor. For instance, if you have an EGA color adapter, you'll be able to choose from among 16 colors when you display graphs on your screen. If you have a black-and-white printer, however, you'll only be able to print charts in shades of gray. The opposite may also be true. If you have a monochrome graphics adapter in your computer, you'll only be able to view charts on your screen in black and white. But if you have a color printer or a plotter, you'll have the ability to print charts in color.

The List Printer Formats command on the Options menu allows you to tell Works whether it should format your charts for your screen or for your printer. This command affects the options in the Colors list box in the Data Format dialog box. The List Printer Formats command is a toggle switch. If a dot appears to the left of the command on the Options menu, the command is on, and the Colors list box will include those colors supported by your printer. If no dot appears, the command is off, and the Colors list box will include the colors supported by your graphics card and monitor. To turn this command on or off, simply select it.

If you have a color screen and a black-and-white printer, the List Printer Formats command is only marginally useful. When you print a color chart to a black-and-white printer, Works will simply convert the chart into black and white format as it prints the chart. If you want to see the chart on the screen as it will look after you print it, you can activate the Format For B&W command.

If, on the other hand, you have a monochrome screen but a color printer or plotter, the List Printer Formats command is indispensable. By activating this command, you can change the list of colors in the Data Format dialog box to include all the colors supported by your printer. Once you've added the colors to the list, you can use the Data Format... command to format the chart to include those colors. Although you won't see the colors on the screen, they will show up when you print the chart.

MULTIPLE Y-AXES

Until now, the charts you've created have had only one y-axis. However, there may be times—such as when you want to show two data series in a chart that are related but are measured in different units—when you need to use two y-axis scales in one chart. For example, you might want to plot dollar sales and unit sales of a product in a chart. Since the two ranges in such a chart—dollar sales and unit sales—are measured in different units—dollars and units—you would need two y-axes in the chart.

The Two Y-Axes... command on the Options menu lets you create a second y-axis in a chart and lets you tell Works which series in the chart you want to plot against which axis. When you select this command, Works will display a dialog box like the one shown in Figure 14-25. This dialog box, which is similar to the Mixed Line & Bar dialog box, lets you assign each series to either the left y-axis or the right y-axis in the chart. By default, all the series in a chart are assigned to the left y-axis. All you have to do to create a chart with two y-axes is assign one or more series to the right y-axis. If you have a mouse, you can choose any option in the dialog box just by pointing to that option and clicking. If you use your keyboard, you can select an option with the [Tab] and ➡ and ⬅ keys. Alternatively, you can choose any option just by typing the letter that corresponds to that option. When you've assigned each series to an axis, choose <OK>.

Figure 14-25

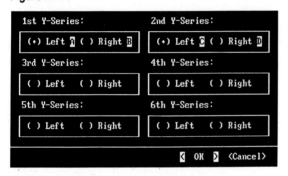

The Two Y-Axes... command lets you create a second y-axis in a chart.

Suppose you want to create a line chart from the spreadsheet shown in Figure 14-2 that shows the dollar sales and unit sales of Bats. Since this chart includes two data series that are measured in different units, you need to create a chart with two y-axes, one measured in dollars and the other in units. **An example**

To create this chart, first make sure that the highlight is not expanded. Then, select the New Chart command from the View menu to create a new chart. When Works displays the alert *Series not selected.*, choose <OK> or press [Enter]. Now, highlight the range B5:E5 and select the 1st Y-Series command from the Data menu. Next, highlight the range B11:E11, and select the 2nd Y-Series command from the Data menu. Then, choose Line from the Format menu to make this a line chart. Now, select the Two Y-Axes... command from the Options menu. When the Two Y-Axes dialog box appears, choose the Right option in the 2nd Y-Series option box to assign the second y-series to the right axis. Finally, choose <OK>.

When you are finished, select the name of the chart—Chart5 if you've been working along—from the menu to display the chart shown in Figure 14-26. As you can see, this chart has two y-axes: one designated in dollars and one designated in units.

Figure 14-26

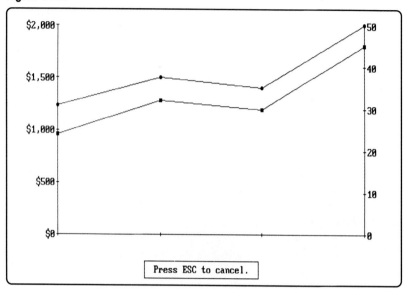

This chart has two y-axes: one designated in dollars, one in units.

In the example, we assigned the 1st Y-Series to the left axis and the 2nd Y-Series to the right axis. In fact, it doesn't matter which y-series you assign to which y-axis. However, you should make certain that all the series you assign to an axis are measured in the same units.

Titling the second axis

If you create a chart with two y-axes, you'll probably want to use the Right Y-Axis option of the Titles… command to title the second axis. To do this, select the Titles… command, enter the title you want to assign to the right y-axis—or a reference to a cell that contains the title you want to use—in the Right Y-Axis text box, then choose <OK>. The title you specify can be up to 25 characters long. When you view the chart, the right y-axis title will be printed sideways and will be centered along the axis.

For example, to title the axes in the example chart, select the Titles… command from the Data menu. When the Titles dialog box appears, move first to the Left Y-Axis box and enter the title *Dollar Sales*. Then move to the Right Y-Axis box and enter the titles *Unit Sales*. Finally, choose <OK>.

Scaling the second axis

The Right Y-Axis… command on the Options menu lets you adjust the scale or change the type of the right y-axis. When you select the Right Y-Axis… command, Works will display a Right Y-Axis dialog box that looks just like the one you see when you select the Y-Axis… command. You can use this dialog box to scale the right y-axis manually, to convert the right y-axis scale to a log scale, to change the type of the right y-axis scale, or to add grid lines to the chart. For more on this command, see the section "Adjusting the Y-Axis" earlier in this chapter.

ENHANCING PIE CHARTS

Many of the enhancements that apply to other types of charts do not apply to pie charts. For example, since pie charts don't have axes, none of the enhancements that apply to the x- or y-axis in a chart—including the x-axis and y-axis titles and the X-Axis... and Y-Axis... commands—are useful in pie charts. Since pie charts include just one data series, you can't add a legend to a pie chart. Some enhancements work differently in pie charts than in other types. For instance, the x-series—which allows you to define x-axis labels in most charts— creates labels for the slices in pie charts. In addition, some enhancements apply only to pie charts. For example, you can explode one or more slices in a pie chart.

In this section, we'll explain the differences between enhancing pie charts and enhancing other types of charts. We'll use the chart shown in Figure 14-27— which is based on the values in the range F5:F8 in the worksheet in Figure 14-2— to demonstrate these techniques. To create this chart, select the New Chart command from the View menu to create a new chart. When Works displays the alert *Series not selected*, choose <OK> or press [Enter]. Then, highlight the range F5:F8 and select the 1st Y-Series command from the Data menu. Now, select the Pie command from the Format menu to change the type of the chart.

Figure 14-27

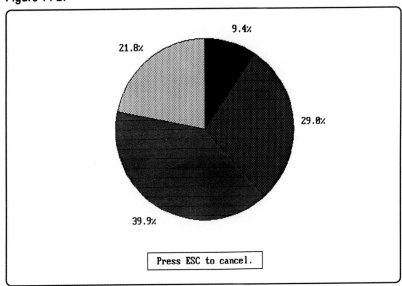

We'll use this chart to demonstrate the process of enhancing pie charts.

Labeling slices

You can label the slices in a pie chart by using the X-Series... command to define an x-series for the chart. Works will display the entries in the x-series in a pie chart as labels next to the various segments in the chart. Works will display the entry in the first cell of the x-series next to the first slice of the pie, the second entry in the x-series next to the second slice, and so on. You define the x-series for a pie chart in the same way you define the x-series in any other chart: Highlight the range of cells in the spreadsheet that contains the entries you want Works to display as slice labels, then select the X-Series command from the Data menu.

For example, let's add slice labels to the pie chart in Figure 14-27. We'll use the entries in the range A5:A8 from Figure 14-2 as labels for the slices in the chart. To begin, activate the pie chart by choosing its name from the View menu (if you've been working along, the pie chart will be Chart6) and press [Esc] to enter the chart view. Next, highlight the range A5:A8 and select the X-Series command from the Data menu. When you select the name of the chart from the View menu, Works will display the enhanced chart shown in Figure 14-28. Notice that the labels from cells A5, A6, A7, and A8 appear as labels next to the slices in the chart.

Figure 14-28

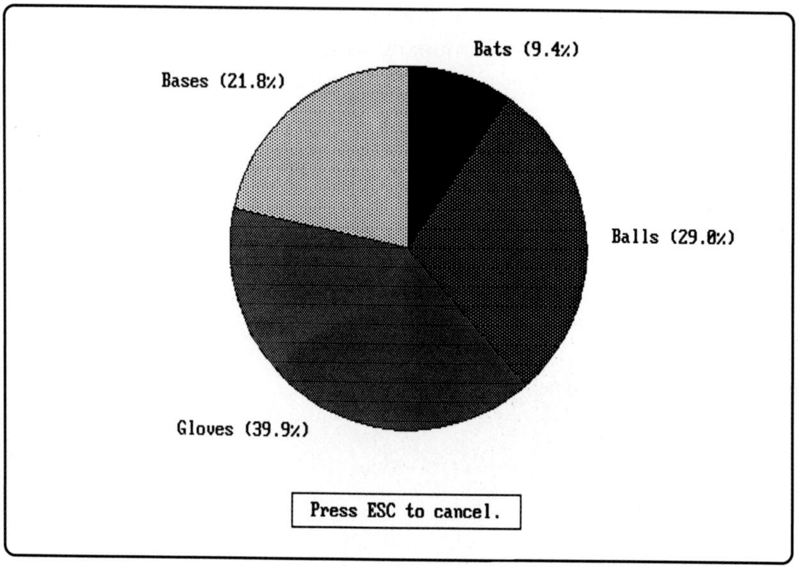

Bats (9.4%)
Bases (21.8%)
Balls (29.0%)
Gloves (39.9%)

Press ESC to cancel.

Works uses the entries in the x-series as slice labels in the pie chart.

In addition to the x-axis labels, Works also displays percentages next to each slice in the chart in Figure 14-28. As we explained in Chapter 13, there is no way to delete these percentages; they will always appear in the chart. If you define slice labels, the percentages for each segment will appear to the right of the labels.

In the example, the x-series we defined contained labels. If you want, the x-series for a pie chart can contain values. If the x-series contains values, Works will use those values as labels for the slices in the chart. You might take advantage of this capability to plot the values as labels for the charts.

If you define long labels for the slices in a pie chart, it is possible that Works will not be able to completely display each label. In that event, Works will include as much of the label as possible and omit the rest. (The percentage that appears to the right of the label will be the first thing to go.) The allowable length of a label depends on where the label appears on the chart (there's more room for labels at the top and bottom of the pie than at the left and right edges) and on the number of labels in the chart. Each chart is different, so you'll need to experiment to see how long your labels and how large your chart can be.

Notes

You can use the Data Format… command on the Format menu in the chart view to control the color and pattern of each slice in a pie chart. It also allows you to explode slices. If you issue this command while a pie chart is active, Works will display a dialog box like the one shown in Figure 14-29. As you can see, the Slices list box at the left of the dialog box lists the slices in the pie. The Colors box lists the colors you can use to color the slices in each data series. This list is limited to the colors supported by your computer's graphics card and monitor. The Patterns box lists the patterns you can use to shade the slices in a pie chart. The Exploded option lets you explode a slice.

Formatting pie charts

Figure 14-29

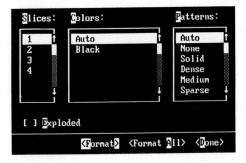

The Data Format… command lets you change the colors and patterns Works uses to plot the slices in pie charts and explode a slice.

If you have a color monitor, Works will display each slice in a pie chart in a different color. You can use the Colors option to change the color associated with each slice. If you choose a slice, choose one of the Colors options, then choose <Format>, Works will display that slice in the selected color. If you choose a color, then choose <Format All>, Works will display all the slices in that color.

If you have a color monitor, you can use the Patterns option to add patterns to the slices in a pie chart. If you choose a slice, choose a pattern, then choose

Formatting slices

<Format>, Works will use that pattern to shade that slice. (Of course, the slice will also be in color.) If you choose a pattern, then choose <Format All>, Works will use that pattern to shade all the slices in the chart.

If you have a monochrome monitor, Works will use a different pattern to shade each slice in the pie: solid black for the first series, dense gray for the second, medium gray for the third, and so on. You can use the Patterns option to change the pattern associated with any slice. If you select a slice, choose one of the Patterns options, then choose <Format>, Works will use that pattern to display that slice. If you choose a pattern, then choose <Format All>, Works will display every slice in that pattern. If you choose the None option in the Patterns list box, Works will not shade the selected slice (or, if you choose <Format All>, all slices).

Exploding slices

In addition to enhancing pie charts with colors and patterns, you can explode one or more slices for emphasis. When you ask Works to explode a slice, it separates that slice slightly from the rest of the pie. To explode an individual slice of a pie chart, select the Data Format… command from the Format menu. When the Data Format dialog box appears, choose the slice you want to explode, then choose the Exploded option to activate it. When the Exploded option is active, an X will appear in the Exploded check box. Then, choose the <Format> option to explode the selected slice.

If, after you have exploded one or more slices of a pie chart, you decide that you don't like the result, you can easily "unexplode" it. To do so, select the Data Format… command from the Format menu, choose the slice you want to unexplode, and choose the Exploded check box to deactivate it. Then, choose the <Format> option to unexplode the selected slice.

Because exploding selected slices draws attention to their data, exploded pie charts are most effective when only one or two slices are exploded. You'll rarely want to explode most or all the slices in a chart.

An example

Suppose you want to set the shading pattern for the third slice in the pie chart in Figure 14-28 to None and that you want to explode that slice. To begin, activate the pie chart by choosing its name from the View menu, and press [Esc] to enter the chart view. Then, select the Data Format… command from the Format menu in the chart view to reveal the dialog box shown in Figure 14-29. When the dialog box appears, choose the number 3 in the Slices section, move to the Patterns section, then choose None. Next, choose the Exploded option to activate it. Finally, choose <Format> to apply your changes to the selected slice.

When you have finished, select the name of the chart from the View menu. The result is a formatted chart like the one shown in Figure 14-30. The third slice now has no shading and is exploded from the other slices. As you can see, exploding a slice of a pie chart adds emphasis to that slice.

Figure 14-30

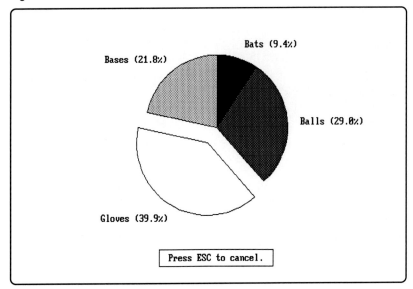

The third slice in this pie chart is formatted and exploded.

CONCLUSION

In this chapter and the previous two, we have shown you how to create and enhance charts in Works. Now that you know the basics, you're ready to begin experimenting on your own. If you begin to use charts in your work with Works, you will soon be creating and enhancing them like a master.

Database Fundamentals 15

*I*n the last three sections, we've looked at Works' word processing, spreadsheet, and charting capabilities. In this chapter, we'll move into a new area: Works' database management facility.

A database is simply a structured collection of information. You probably use databases all of the time, maybe without realizing it. For example, the telephone directory is a familiar database that you use quite often. So is your Rolodex. Works' database makes it possible to store these and other databases—including investment records, employee records, mailing lists, and so on—in your computer in electronic form.

Works' database documents are powerful tools for collecting, organizing, and analyzing information. In addition to storing information electronically, a database document offers tools that allow you to sort and query your databases. For example, if you store your mailing list in a database document, you can sort it so the information is arranged by the last names of the people you write to, by zip code, by city, by state, or in any number of other ways. If you want to write to only those people who live within a certain zip code, you can use Works' querying tools to select just those records. Database documents also feature powerful reporting capabilities that allow you to build sophisticated reports from your data.

In this chapter, you'll learn how to create a database, how to enter information into a database, and how to edit information once you have entered it. We'll also look at the ways you can modify an existing database to display the information you need in a logical and readable manner. In Chapter 16, we'll show you how to sort and query a database. In Chapter 17, we'll cover printing and reporting.

BASICS

Before you create and use a Works database, you should master a few basic concepts. First, let's consider its structure, which is actually very similar to that of a telephone book or a Rolodex directory. Most Rolodexes contain many individual entries, each of which contains individual pieces of information: a name, a street address, a city, a state, a zip code, and a telephone number. In database terminology, the entry for each person in the Rolodex is called a record. The individual pieces of information listed for each record—name, address, and telephone number—are called fields. A typical Rolodex holds many records, each of which contains six fields of information.

A Works database is structured in a similar way. For example, Figure 15-1 shows an address directory database that we've created in Works. In a Works database, each record is stored in a single row. Each field occupies a column. A Works database can have up to 256 fields and 4,096 records. The entries that make up the database occupy the cells that occur at the intersection of each row (record) and column (field)—just like in a spreadsheet. All Works databases have this same basic structure, which allows you to manipulate the information in a database and quickly find any particular piece of information.

Figure 15-1

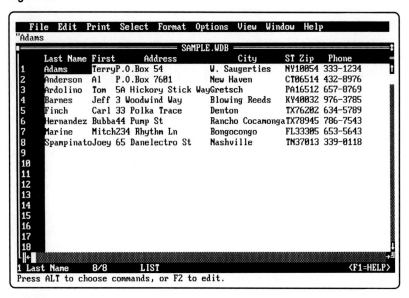

Each record in a Works database occupies a row; each field occupies a column.

Works lets you view your databases in two ways: as a list and through a form. Figure 15-1 shows the List view of our address directory database. In the List view, you see the row-and-column structure of the database we just explained. The name of each field appears at the top of the screen, and each record occupies a single row and has a number. In the List view, you can see a number of records at once, but you can't always see all the fields of those records at the same time.

Figure 15-2 shows the Form view of the database shown in Figure 15-1. Viewing a database in the Form view is similar to browsing through a set of index cards or business forms, in which each card or form contains information about a separate person or item. In the Form view, you see only one record at a time. However, you can see all the fields of that record at once. Forms are quite flexible: You can arrange the fields in a form any way you want and can enter text that offers instructions, notes, and so on.

Figure 15-2

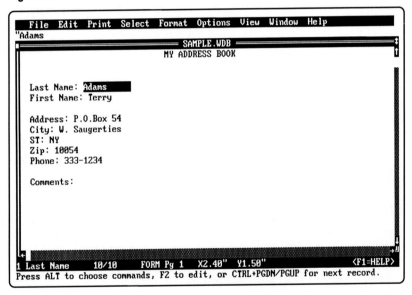

Viewing a database in the Form view is like browsing through a stack of index cards.

To switch from the Form view to the List view, pull down the View menu and select the List command, or press the [View Form/List] key ([F9]). When you do this, Works will display the List view for the current database and will place the highlight on the same field of the same record it was on in the form. To re-enter the Form view, select the Form command from the View menu, or press the [View Form/List] key again. In the form, you'll see the record that contained the highlight in the List view, and the same field will be highlighted.

Although you can view a database in two ways, all Works databases exist in a single database window. This window includes all the elements of a window: title bar, scroll bars, work area, and so on. In addition, when you are working in a database window, you'll see all the standard screen features: a menu bar, a formula line, a status line, and a message line. The formula line, which is immediately below the menu bar, always displays the current cell value in either view. The bottom line on the screen is the message line. Just above the message line is the status line. On this line, Works displays the number of the current record, the name of the current field, the number of records selected and the number of records in the database, the current view (*FORM* or *LIST*), the page number, the coordinates (X and Y) of the cursor relative to the left and top edges of the screen (only in the Form view), and the <F1=HELP> hot key.

In general, you'll use the Form view to enter records and edit existing records, and you'll use the List view when you plan to sort or query the database. However, you can perform any of these tasks in either view. You should use the List view when you want to see more than one record at a time and the Form view when you want to see all the fields of a single record at once.

CREATING A DATABASE

Before you can do anything with a database, you must create one. To create a database, first use the Create New File... command to create a new database document. When the new database document comes into view, you can design an entry form that includes all the fields you want Works to include in the database. When you finish designing the form, Works will create both the form and a database that contains all the fields you have included in the form. At that point, you can begin entering and manipulating information.

Creating a new database document

To create a database document, pull down the File menu, select the Create New File... command, and choose the <New Database> option from the Create New File dialog box. When you do this, Works will present a new Database document screen like the one shown in Figure 15-3. Whenever you open a new database document, Works automatically enters the Form view.

Designing a form

Once you have opened a new database document, you're ready to create a database. In most cases, you'll do this by designing a form. To design a form, move the cursor around the form screen and enter fields and labels at the appropriate places. When you're finished, Works will create both the form you've defined and the database that goes with that form.

Forms
▶WORKS 2◀

▶In Works 2, each form is one large "sheet," 256 characters wide and 256 lines deep. (In Works 1, each form is made up of eight full-screen pages.) You can place fields and labels anywhere you want on this large form work area; however, most forms will use only the first few lines and characters of the form work area.

Figure 15-3

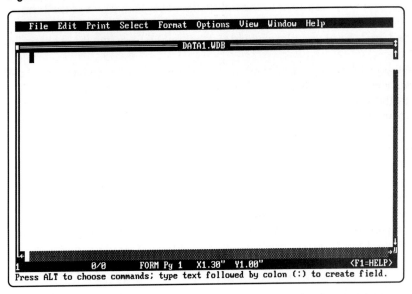

You'll see a screen like this one whenever you create a new database document.

You'll notice a page indicator on the status line to the right of the FORM/LIST indicator. In Works 2, a "page" in the Form view is simply the portion of the form that Works can fit on one printed page. Given Works' default print settings, a Works form is five pages deep. If you change Works' print settings, you'll affect the number of pages in your form, but not the size of the form. For example, suppose you increase your top and bottom margins to three inches each. Your Works form will hold the same amount of information, but when printed, it will be spread over nine pages instead of just the original five. The Pg indicator on the status line always tells you in which page the cursor is positioned.

In order to design a form, you need to know how to move the cursor around the form screen. You can use either the cursor-movement keys or a mouse to move the cursor. The →, ←, ↑, and ↓ keys move the cursor one space in any direction in the Form view. You can use the [Pg Up] and [Pg Dn] keys to move the cursor up and down by windows through the form. You can also use the [Ctrl] key in combination with other keys to move the cursor in a form screen. Pressing [Ctrl]→ moves the cursor one window to the right. Pressing [Ctrl]← moves the cursor one window to the left. Works does not allow the cursor to wrap from one line to the next. When the cursor reaches the edge of a form, it won't go any further.

Moving the cursor

The [Home] key moves the cursor to the beginning of the current line. The [End] key moves the cursor to the right edge of the active part of the form. (The active part of the form is an area that includes all the fields and labels you've placed in the form.) Until you place a field or label on the form, the [End] key will have no effect.

If you have a mouse, you can move the cursor anywhere on the form screen simply by pointing and clicking. You cannot use the scroll bars or scroll boxes to move the cursor up and down or side to side in the form. The vertical scroll bar lets you move from record to record in the database—something we'll show you how to do later—and the horizontal scroll bar moves the window left to right.◄

Placing fields

►**WORKS 2**◄

You can make two types of entries in a form: fields and labels. Field entries define the fields that will appear in the finished form and in the database. To create a field, position the cursor where you want the field to appear in the finished form, type the name of the field, type a colon, and press [Enter]. As you type the name of a field, it will appear on the formula line. ►When you press [Enter], Works will display a Field Size dialog box, like the one shown in Figure 15-4. When this box appears, you can specify the width and height of the field in the Width and Height text boxes. The default width is 20 characters and the default height is one line. The maximum height and width setting is 256 and the minimum is 1. When you choose <OK> or press [Enter] again, Works will place into the form the field name, followed by a colon, a blank space, and a blank for the field equal to the size you specified in the Width and Height text boxes.◄

Figure 15-4

Works displays the Field Size dialog box when you press [Enter] after typing a field name into a form.

The field names you specify can be up to 15 characters long (excluding the colon). The colon after the field name is critical—it tells Works that you're creating a new field as opposed to just entering a label into the form.

►**WORKS 2**◄

►The Height setting in the Field Size dialog box lets you create a field that is more than one line deep. For example, a Height setting of 3 will let you type three lines of text into your field. When you increase the height of the field, it will extend below the line on which the field name is positioned. Multiple-line fields are useful for recording comments and other long entries that are part of a record.◄

Placing labels

In addition to placing fields in a form, you can place labels. You can use labels to include instructions, comments, or other explanatory text in the form. Works considers any entry that is not followed by a colon to be a label. To place a label in a form, you just position the cursor where you want the text to appear, type the label, and press [Enter] to place it in the form. As you type the label, it will appear on the formula line. When you press [Enter], Works will place the label into the form at the position of the cursor and will expand the highlight to cover the label. On the formula line, Works will add the label mark " to the left of the label.

Be sure that you don't include a colon at the end of the label. If you do, Works will think that you're creating a new field instead of entering a label. If you want to include a colon in a label, you must follow the colon with one or more additional characters (such as a single blank space).

An example

Perhaps the best way to learn about designing a new database is to look at an example. Let's walk through the steps you would take to create an address directory database in Works. To begin, you have to create a new database document. To do this, select the Create New File... command from the File menu and choose the <New Database> option. When you do this, a new database file will appear on the screen in the Form view.

Once you've created the new database document, you can design the form shown in Figure 15-2. You'll probably want to begin by entering the label *MY ADDRESS BOOK* at the top of the form. To do this, use the ➡ key to move the cursor 28 spaces to the right, type *MY ADDRESS BOOK*, and press [Enter]. When you press [Enter], Works will place the label into the form at the location of the cursor, as shown in Figure 15-5. As you can see, Works has expanded the highlight to cover the entire label. In addition, Works has placed a double quotation mark (") to the left of the entry on the formula line.

Figure 15-5

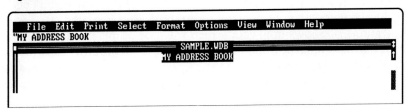

Labels allow you to place titles, comments, and instructions in forms.

Now you're ready to create the fields for this database: Last Name, First Name, Address, City, ST, Zip, Phone, and Comments. To place the Last Name field, press ⬇ three times to move the cursor down three lines, then press [Ctrl]⬅ to position the cursor at the left margin of the form. When the cursor is in place, type *Last*

Name: (the name of the field followed by a colon), and then press [Enter]. When you press [Enter], Works will display the Field Size dialog box. Then, type 10 into the Width text box, and choose <OK> to place the field named Last Name into the form, as shown in Figure 15-6. Works will move the cursor down one line.

Figure 15-6

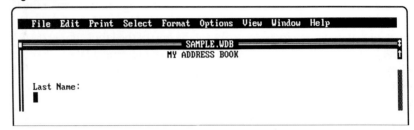

Works defines a field after you determine its width.

After you have placed this field, you should use the same technique to place the other six fields. To place the First Name field, type *First Name:*, press [Enter], type 5 into the Width text box, and choose <OK>. To place the Address field, press ↓ once, type *Address:*, press [Enter] to call up the Field Size dialog box, then choose <OK> to accept the default width. To place the City field, type *City:*, press [Enter], type 16 into the Width text box, and choose <OK>. To place the ST field, type *ST:*, and press [Enter]. When the Field Size dialog box appears, type 2 into the Width text box, then choose <OK>. To place the Zip field, type *Zip:*, and press [Enter]. When the Field Size dialog box appears, type 5 into the Width text box, then choose <OK>. To place the Phone field, type *Phone:*, and press [Enter]. Next, type 8 into the Width text box, and choose <OK>. To place the Comments field, press ↓ once, and type *Comments:*. When you press [Enter], type 40 into the Width text box and 3 into the Height text box, then choose <OK>. Your comments field will now accommodate notes that are up to three lines long and 40 characters wide. Figure 15-7 shows how your screen will look at this point.

As you're designing the form, Works will create both the form you are defining and the database that goes with that form. When you finish designing your form, your screen will look like Figure 15-7. This is the entry form for the database.

To view your new database in the List view, simply pull down the View menu and select the List command or press the [View Form/List] key. Figure 15-8 shows the result of selecting this command. As you can see, Works has assigned the names of the fields that you placed in the form to the first eight columns of the database. The fields appear in the List view in the order that you placed them into the form. Since our example database contains eight fields (whose default widths are 10), you can't see all of them on the screen at once.

Figure 15-7

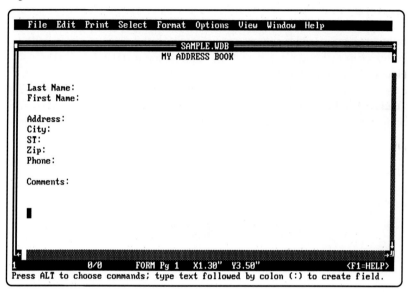

This form includes eight fields—Last Name, First Name, Address, City, ST, Zip, Phone, and Comments—and one label.

Figure 15-8

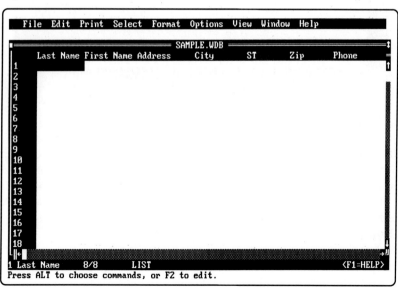

In the List view, field names appear across the top of the screen, and record numbers appear across the left edge.

When you're finished looking at the list, select the Form command from the View menu or press the [View Form/List] key to bring the form back into view.

Creating a database in the List view

In most cases, you'll want to create a database the way we just described: by designing a form. If you want, however, you can create a database in the List view. To do this, you first select the Create New File... command to create a new database document. Then, instead of entering text and field names into the Form view, select the List command on the View menu to enter the List view. When you do this, you'll see a blank list like the one shown in Figure 15-9. No field names appear at the top of the columns.

Figure 15-9

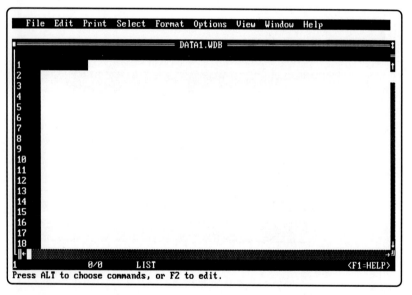

If you want, you can create a database through the List view.

At this point, you can create a database by assigning names to the columns. To do this, use the → or ← keys to move the cursor to the column you want to name, pull down the Edit menu, then select the Field Name... command. Works will then display the dialog box shown in Figure 15-10. To assign a field name to the column in which the cursor is positioned, simply type that name into the Name text box, and choose <OK>. When you do this, Works will enter that name at the top of the current column, creating a field with that name. When you first create a field, it will be 10 characters wide. For example, to name the first field *Last Name*, move the highlight to the first column in the blank document, select the Field Name... command from the Edit menu, type the name *Last Name*, and choose <OK>.

Figure 15-10

To name the columns in the List view of a database, you use the Field Name... command.

If you want, you can let Works assign names to the columns of a database. To do this, simply type an entry into a cell of an unnamed column and press [Enter]. When you do this, Works will lock the entry into the cell and assign a default name to that column. The name will be based on the position of the column relative to the left edge of the document. For example, Works will assign the name Field1 to the first column, Field2 to the second column, and so on. As you might expect, you can use the Field Name... command to change these names if you want. We'll show you how to do that later in this chapter.

Whenever you create a database through the List view, Works will create a default form in which the names of the fields are stacked. After you create the database, you can modify the appearance of the form. We'll also show you how to do that later in this chapter.

Once you have finished working in a new database, you should save it. You save database documents the same way you save every other type of Works document. To save a database document for the first time, select the Save As... command (or the Save command) from the File menu. When the Save As dialog box comes into view, you specify a name and a destination for the file you are about to create. If you want to save the new document to the current directory, just type a name, and choose <OK> to save it. If you want to save the document to a different directory, choose that directory from the Directories list box, and choose <OK> to make that directory the current directory. Then, type a name, and choose <OK> to save the document into a file with that name. To resave a database document under the same name, just pull down the File menu, and select the Save command. To resave a database document under a different name, pull down the File menu, select the Save As... command, type the new name into the Save As dialog box, then choose <OK>. Unless you specify otherwise, Works will add the extension .WDB to the name of any file that contains a database document.

To open an existing database file, pull down the File menu, select the Open Existing File... command, either type the name of the file into the File to Open text box or choose it from the Files list box, then choose <OK>. If the file you want to open is in the current directory, you can either choose its name from the Files list box or type the name into the File to open box, then choose <OK>. If the file is in another directory, choose that directory from the Directories list box, then choose <OK> to make that directory the current directory. Now, choose the name of the file you want to open from the Files list box, or type the name into

Saving and opening a database

the File to Open text box, and choose <OK>. To make Works list only the database files in the Files box, type *.WDB* in the File to Open text box. (For more on saving and opening documents, refer to Chapter 2.)

MOVING THE HIGHLIGHT FROM FIELD TO FIELD

Once you have created a database, you can enter information into it. Before we show you how to enter information, let's take a look at the ways you can move the highlight in a database document. As you will see, moving the highlight in the List view is identical to moving the highlight in a spreadsheet document. However, you'll have to learn some different techniques to move the highlight in the Form view.

The List view

When you're in the List view, pressing →, ←, ↑ or ↓ moves the highlight one cell in the indicated direction. Whenever the highlight moves beyond the boundaries of the window, Works will automatically shift the window in the proper direction to keep the highlight in view. Pressing [End] moves the highlight to the rightmost field of the current record. Likewise, pressing [Home] moves the highlight to the leftmost field of the current record. If you press [Ctrl][End], the highlight will move to the rightmost field of the very last record that contains an entry. As you might guess, pressing [Ctrl][Home] returns the highlight to the first field of the first record. You can move the highlight one screen to the right by pressing [Ctrl][Pg Dn], then one screen to the left by pressing [Ctrl][Pg Up]. You can move the highlight up or down one screen by pressing [Pg Up] or [Pg Dn]. Pressing [Ctrl]→ or [Ctrl]← moves the cursor in the indicated direction to the next boundary between an occupied cell and an empty cell.

If you have a mouse, you can move the highlight simply by clicking the cell to which you want to move it. If the portion of the database that contains the cell is not on the screen, you can use the scroll bars to shift it into view. You can also use the scroll bars to bring other fields into view. To move one field at a time, just click to the left or right of the horizontal scroll box. To move many fields at once, drag the scroll box left or right across the scroll bar. To move one record at a time, just click above or below the vertical scroll box. To move many records at once, drag the scroll box up or down the vertical scroll bar. The scroll bars work in the same way in the List view as they do in a spreadsheet document. (For more on the use of scroll bars, see Chapter 7.)

The Form view

In the Form view, you can use the [Tab] key and the mouse to move through a form. The [Tab] key moves the highlight forward through the fields of a database one field at a time. If there are fields on more than one window of the form, pressing the [Tab] key while the highlight is on the last field on one window will wrap the highlight to the first field on the next window. The same record will remain in view within the form. If you press the [Tab] key while the last field in a record is highlighted, the highlight will move to the first field in the next record.

The [Shift][Tab] key combination moves the highlight up through a form. If the cursor is on the first field of the second or subsequent records in a form, pressing the [Shift][Tab] key combination will wrap the highlight to the last field in the previous record.

Starting from the first field of the second or subsequent record in the form, to move to the first field of the next record, press [Ctrl][Pg Dn] or [Ctrl]↓. Likewise, to move to the first field of the previous record, press [Ctrl][Pg Up] or [Ctrl]↑. You can return to the first field of the first record in your database by pressing [Ctrl][Home]. Pressing [Ctrl][End] will move the highlight to the first field of the first blank record in the database.

If you have a mouse, you can move the highlight from one field to another just by clicking on the new field. You can use the vertical scroll bar to bring other records into view. To move one record at a time, just click above or below the scroll box. To move many records at once, drag the scroll box up or down through the scroll bar. As you scroll through the database, the highlight will stay in the same position relative to the window borders in each record.

The highlight-movement techniques you've learned so far will be appropriate for moving the highlight in most situations. However, you could waste a lot of time finding specific database records using only these techniques. Fortunately, Works' Go To... command lets you move the highlight to any record or any field in the database. This command works in both the List view and the Form view.

▶To use the Go To... command, select it from the Select menu. When you do this, Works will display a Go To dialog box like the one shown in Figure 15-11. This dialog box includes a Go To text box and a Names list box. To move to any record, you just type the number of that record into the Go To text box, then choose <OK>. To move to any field, just point to the name of that field in the Names list box or type the field name in the Go To text box, then choose <OK>.

**The Go To...
command**

▶WORKS 2◀

Figure 15-11

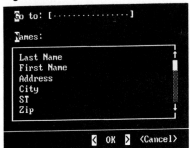

The Go To... command lets you move directly to any record or field.

You cannot use the Go To... command to move directly to a specific field within a record. If you need to move to a specific field in a record, first use the Go To... command to move to that record, then select the command again, and use it to move to the specific field.

Works recognizes only the names in the Names list box. If you try to type a name that doesn't match one of those names, Works will display an alert box with the message *Name does not exist.*◄

ENTERING RECORDS

After you've created a database, the next step is to begin entering records. As you might expect, Works allows you to enter records in either the Form view or the List view. In the Form view, entering data is very similar to filling in the blanks of a paper form: You move from field to field, entering the desired information in each field as you go. Entering records in the List view, on the other hand, is much like making cell entries in a spreadsheet.

Entering records in the Form view

To enter records into a database in the Form view, you move the highlight to the first field of a blank record and begin making entries. (If you have just defined the database, the highlight will be in the first record in the database, which will be blank. Otherwise, you can move the highlight to a new blank record by pressing [Ctrl][End].) Once the highlight is in place, just type the entry for that field. As you type, the characters will appear on the formula line—just as they do when you're making an entry in the spreadsheet. When you're through, press [Enter] or the [Tab] key to lock in the entry and move the cursor to the next field in the form. Once you have entered one record, move the highlight to the first field of the next record by pressing [Tab] and repeat the process.

The entry in any field of a database can be up to 254 characters long. If the entry you type is longer than this, Works will simply truncate the entry to conform to the 254-character rule.

We'll enter the sample data in Table 15-1 into our sample address directory database. Since we just created the database, the highlight is in the first field (Last Name) of the first record, and, as you can see in Figure 15-8, that record is empty. To begin, type the name *Adams* and press [Enter]. Your screen will look like the one in Figure 15-12.

As you would expect, the name *Adams* now appears in the Last Name field. Also, notice that the record counter in the status line has changed from *0/0* to read *1/1*, which indicates that this is the first record in the database and that the database contains one record. When these numbers match, all the records in the database are accessible to you on the screen. If the left number is lower than the right one, then only that number of records is accessible. For example, if you hide 6 records in a database of 10 records, the counter on the status line will read 4/10. Only 4 records are accessible to you on the screen at that point.

Table 15-1

Last Name	First Name	Address
Adams	Terry	P.O.Box 54
Anderson	Al	P.O.Box 7601
Ardolino	Tom	5A Hickory Stick Way
Barnes	Jeff	3 Woodwind Ave.
Finch	Carl	33 Polka Trace
Hernandez	Bubba	44 Pump St.
Marine	Mitch	234 Rhythm Ln.
Spampinato	Joey	65 Danelectro St.

City	ST	Zip	Phone
W. Saugerties	NY	10054	333-1234
New Haven	CT	06514	432-8976
Gretsch	PA	16512	657-8769
Blowing Reeds	KY	40032	976-3785
Denton	TX	76202	634-5789
Rancho Cocamonga	TX	78945	786-7543
Bongocongo	FL	33305	653-5643
Nashville	TN	37013	339-0118

We'll enter this sample data into the database.

Figure 15-12

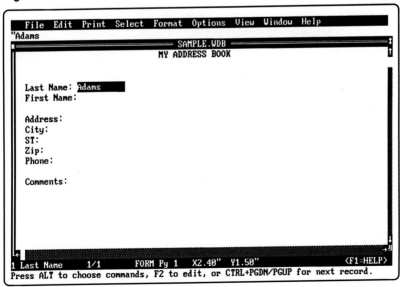

To make an entry in a field, highlight that field, type the entry, then press [Enter].

Now, press the [Tab] key to advance to the First Name field, type *Terry*, and press the [Tab] key to lock in the name and move the highlight to the Address field. Then, enter *P.O.Box 54*, and again press the [Tab] key to lock in the address and move the highlight to the City field. Now, enter the City *W. Saugerties*, and press the [Tab] key to lock in the city and move the highlight to the ST field. Type *NY* in the field and press the [Tab] key to lock in the state and move the highlight to the Zip field. Then, type 10054, and press the [Tab] key to lock in the Zip code and move the highlight to the Phone field. Next, enter the phone number *333-1234*, and press the [Tab] key to lock in the entry and move the highlight to the Comments field. Finally, type *Birthday in August. Likes piano music.*, then press [Enter] to complete the record entry. At this point, your screen should look like Figure 15-13.

Figure 15-13

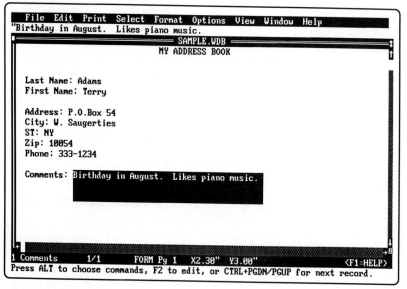

This figure shows a complete record in a form.

To enter the next record, first press the [Tab] key to move the highlight to the first field in the next record. When you do this, the status line will indicate your cursor is in the Last Name field of the second record of the database. When you type an entry into the Last Name field (or any field in the second record), the record counter in the status line will change to *2/2*, indicating that you're in the second record of a two-record database. You can use the techniques we've just described to enter the second record shown in Table 15-1 into the database. Figure 15-14 shows the result.

Figure 15-14

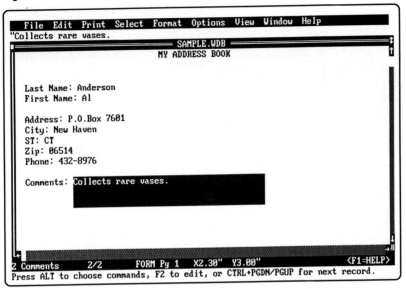

```
 File  Edit  Print  Select  Format  Options  View  Window  Help
"Collects rare vases.
================================ SAMPLE.WDB ================================
                           MY ADDRESS BOOK


    Last Name: Anderson
    First Name: Al

    Address: P.O.Box 7601
    City: New Haven
    ST: CT
    Zip: 06514
    Phone: 432-8976

    Comments: Collects rare vases.




2 Comments        2/2        FORM Pg 1    X2.30"  Y3.00"        <F1=HELP>
Press ALT to choose commands, F2 to edit, or CTRL+PGDN/PGUP for next record.
```

To enter the next record, press [Tab] to move the highlight to the various fields of the database, then enter the information for each.

Entering records in the List view

Entering data into a database through the List view is identical to entering data into a spreadsheet. All you do is move the highlight to the first field in the first blank row in the database. When the cursor is in place, you type the entry for that field. As you type, the characters you enter will appear on the formula line—just as they do when you're making an entry in a spreadsheet. When you're finished, press [Enter] to lock in the entry, or press ➡ to lock in the entry and move the highlight to the next field in the same record. After you have entered all the data into one record, press ⬇ and [Home] to move the cursor to the first field in the next record, then repeat the process.

Let's consider an example. To begin, switch to the List view by choosing the List command from the View menu. Figure 15-15 on the next page shows our two-record address directory database in the List view.

Now, move the highlight to the Last Name field in the third record (the first blank record), type *Ardolino*, and press ➡ to lock in the entry and move the highlight to the First Name field. Type *Tom* and press ➡ to move the highlight to the Address field. Continue this process until you've filled in all of the fields of the third record, as shown in Figure 15-16. After you have entered record 3, press ⬇ then [Home] to move the cursor to the first field in the fourth record, and enter the fourth record. Then, enter the rest of the records shown in Table 15-1.

Figure 15-15

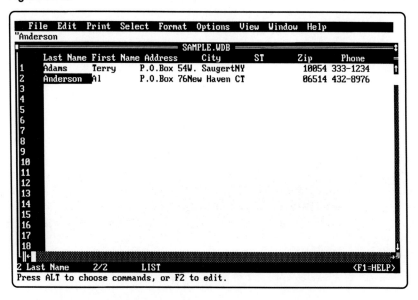

In the List view, you can view up to 18 records at once.

Figure 15-16

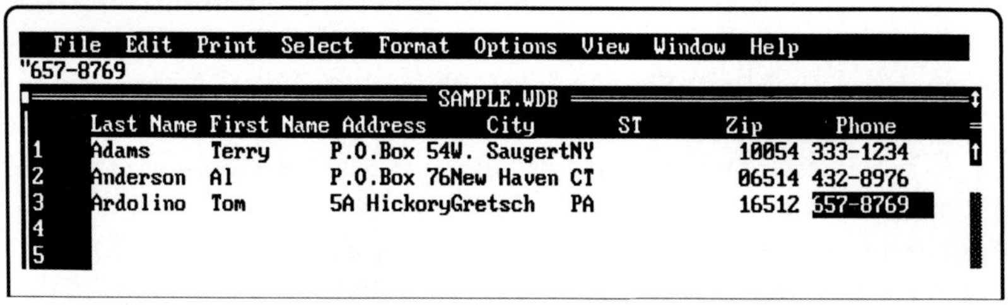

To enter data in the List view, move the highlight to a blank record, then type.

As you can see in Figure 15-16, the Address field entries in our database appear to be missing some characters. In our sample database, the columns are all set to the List view's default width of ten characters, causing Works to truncate the entries in the Address field. As in spreadsheet documents, the number of characters displayed in a column in the List view is limited by the width of the column. Even though each cell may actually contain up to 254 characters, you'll see only as many characters as can be displayed in the current column width. Since you will usually want to view the entire contents of each field, you'll probably want to adjust the widths of the fields in the List view before you begin using the database. We'll show you how to do that later in this chapter.

Once you've entered records into a database, you may need to edit one or more of those records. For example, you may make a few typographical errors as you're entering data, or you may obtain some new information that requires you to update a record. You can edit a record in either the Form view or the List view. Although some editing techniques are the same in both views, each view also offers several different editing commands.

EDITING RECORDS

There are two ways to alter a database entry in either view: You can replace the entry with a new entry, or you can edit the entry. If the entry you want to change is short, it is usually easier to replace it with new data. To do this, position the highlight on the entry you want to change, type the new entry, then press [Enter] or a cursor-movement key to lock in the change. (This is the same technique you use to replace a cell entry in a spreadsheet.)

Editing entries

Instead of replacing an entry, you may want to change only a character or two. As you may have already guessed, you can use the [Edit] key ([F2]) to change a field entry in the same way that you would use that key to edit a cell in a spreadsheet. Since the [Edit] key allows you to edit individual characters, it comes in handy when you need to change long or complicated field entries.

To use the [Edit] key, first move the highlight to the entry you want to change, then press [Edit]. When you press the [Edit] key, an underline cursor will appear at the end of the entry in the formula line. You can use the ➡, ⬅, [Home], and [End] keys to move this cursor to any spot in the entry, then use the [Delete] or [Backspace] key to erase existing characters. You can also type new characters, which will be inserted into the entry at the position of the cursor. When the entry on the formula line appears the way you want it, press [Enter] to lock in the new entry. (Again, you use this same technique to edit a spreadsheet entry.)

▶Often, the changes you'll make to a database involve more than altering individual entries. There may be times when you'll move, copy, or delete a record or an entire field. To perform these tasks, you'll use Works' editing commands: Clear and Clear Field Contents, Move Record, Copy Record, Delete Record, and Insert Record in the Form view; and Move, Copy, Clear, Delete Record/Field, Insert Record/Field, Fill Right, Fill Down, and Fill Series… in the List view.◀

Using editing commands
▶**WORKS 2**◀

In the List view, you can edit text much as you would in a Works spreadsheet. First you must select the text you want to edit, then you can move it, copy it, replace it, and so forth. You can also insert and delete rows, and clear entries. We'll discuss each of these procedures in this section.

List view

Selecting text. In the database environment, Works lets you select a range of cells only when you're working in List view. As you might guess from the appearance of your database in List view, you can select text using the same methods you use in the spreadsheet environment.

You can use the [Shift] key to extend the highlight to cover more than one cell. Just, hold down the [Shift] key while you press any of the keys or key combinations that move the highlight within a database. When you do, Works will expand the highlight from the anchor cell to the destination cell.

You can also use the [Extend] key ([F8]) to highlight a range of cells. When you press this key, the word *EXTEND* will appear on the status line, indicating that Works is in the Extend mode. While Works is in this mode, the cursor-movement keys and key combinations don't move the cursor around the database. Instead they expand and contract the highlight , just as they do when you hold down the [Shift] key.

Once you have extended the highlight to cover more than one cell, it will remain expanded until you press [Esc] or a cursor-movement key. If you press [Esc], Works will contract the highlight so that it covers only the active cell. If you press a cursor-movement key, Works will contract the highlight to the active cell, then move the highlight.

►WORKS 2◄   ►While the techniques you'll use to highlight cells when you work in the List view of a database are similar to the ones you use in a spreadsheet, the terminology changes: a *row* in a spreadsheet is a *record* in a database; a *column* in a spreadsheet is a *field* in a database. Consequently, when you pull down the Select menu in the List view of a database document, you'll see the Cells, Record, Field, and All commands at the top of the menu. These commands correspond to the four commands at the top of the Select menu in a spreadsheet document.

Selecting the Cells command allows you to use the arrow keys to expand the highlight from the anchor cell (the cell in which the cursor is positioned) to any cell you want. Selecting this command is equivalent to pressing the [Extend] key ([F8]) once. Selecting the Record command highlights the entire record in which the cursor is positioned. Selecting this command is equivalent to pressing the [Select Record] key combination ([Ctrl][F8]). Selecting the Field command highlights the entire field in which the cursor is positioned. Selecting this command is equivalent to pressing the [Select Field] key combination ([Shift][F8]). Selecting the All command highlights the entire database. Selecting this command is equivalent to pressing the [Select All Cells] key combination ([Ctrl][Shift][F8]).◄

For more on selecting text, you might want to refer to the section, "Extending the Highlight" in Chapter 7. In that section, we discuss using the [Shift] and [Extend] keys, highlighting columns, rows, and the entire spreadsheet, and so forth.

Moving entries.   To move a record in the List view, first highlight that record with the same techniques you use to highlight a range of cells in a spreadsheet document. Then, select the Move command from the Edit menu. When the word *MOVE* appears on the status line, move the highlight to the blank row where you want the highlighted record to go, then press [Enter]. Works will move the record there. In the List view, you can cancel the Move command by pressing [Esc] before you press [Enter] to complete the move.

For example, suppose you want to move record 4 to record 9 as we've done in Figure 15-17. To do this, move the highlight to any field of the fourth record and select the Record command from the Select menu to highlight the record. Next, select the Move command from the Edit menu. When the word *MOVE* appears on the status line, move the highlight to the ninth record of the database. When you press [Enter] to complete the move, Works will move the highlighted fourth record to the ninth row.

Figure 15-17

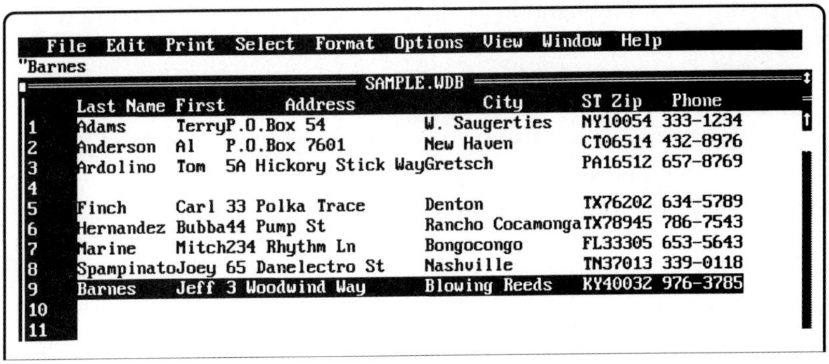

```
   File   Edit   Print   Select   Format   Options   View   Window   Help
"Barnes
═══════════════════════════════ SAMPLE.WDB ═══════════════════════════════
     Last Name First      Address            City       ST Zip    Phone
  1  Adams     TerryP.O.Box 54          W. Saugerties  NY10054 333-1234
  2  Anderson  Al    P.O.Box 7601       New Haven      CT06514 432-8976
  3  Ardolino  Tom   5A Hickory Stick WayGretsch       PA16512 657-8769
  4
  5  Finch     Carl 33 Polka Trace      Denton         TX76202 634-5789
  6  Hernandez Bubba44 Pump St          Rancho CocamongaTX78945 786-7543
  7  Marine    Mitch234 Rhythm Ln       Bongocongo     FL33305 653-5643
  8  SpampinatoJoey 65 Danelectro St     Nashville      TN37013 339-0118
  9  Barnes    Jeff 3 Woodwind Way      Blowing Reeds  KY40032 976-3785
 10
 11
```

You can move records easily in the List view.

In the List view, you can move more than one record at a time. All you have to do is highlight all the records you want to move before you choose the Move command from the Edit menu. To highlight several records, first move the highlight to the record at either the top or bottom row of the group you want to move. ▶Then, select the Cells command on the Select menu or press the [Extend] key ([F8]), and expand the highlight to include each field and record you want to move.◀ Finally, select the Record command from the Select menu to highlight all the records that are touched by the expanded highlight. Once you've highlighted the records you want to move, select the Move command from the Edit menu, move the highlight to the row above which you want the highlighted records to go, then press [Enter]. Works will insert all the records you are moving above the record you point to.

▶WORKS 2◀

Copying entries.   The Copy command allows you to duplicate any number of field entries or records at a new location. You can use this command to copy information from one place to another within a database. In the List view, you can copy any range, from an entry in one cell to an entire record or field or several records and fields. The Copy command in the List view works just like the Copy command in spreadsheet documents. First, highlight the entry or entries you want to copy. If you want to copy a single entry, just move the highlight to the cell that contains that entry. If you want to copy several entries, expand the highlight to include all those entries. If you want to copy an entire record or field, use the Record or Field command on the Select menu to highlight the entire record or field. Then, select the Copy command from the Edit menu.

Next, position the highlight at the spot where you want to duplicate your selection, then press [Enter] to complete the copy. If you are copying a single entry, just position the highlight on the cell in which you want to place the copy. If you are copying several entries, position the highlight on the upper-left cell of the range in which you want to place the copies. If you are copying an entire record or field, position the highlight on the first cell in the row or column in which you want to place the copy. In the Form view (and in spreadsheet documents), if the destination you choose contains any entries, those entries will be overwritten and the data lost.

For example, suppose that the person listed in record 3 of the address directory database is now living at the same address as the person in record 6. To update your listings, you can use the Copy command to copy the Address, City, ST, Zip, and Phone field entries from record 6 to record 3. To begin, highlight the five fields you want to copy, as shown in Figure 15-18. Then, select the Copy command. When the word *COPY* appears on the status line, position the highlight on the Address field of record 3, then press [Enter]. The entries from record 6 will now be duplicated in record 3, as shown in Figure 15-19.

Figure 15-18

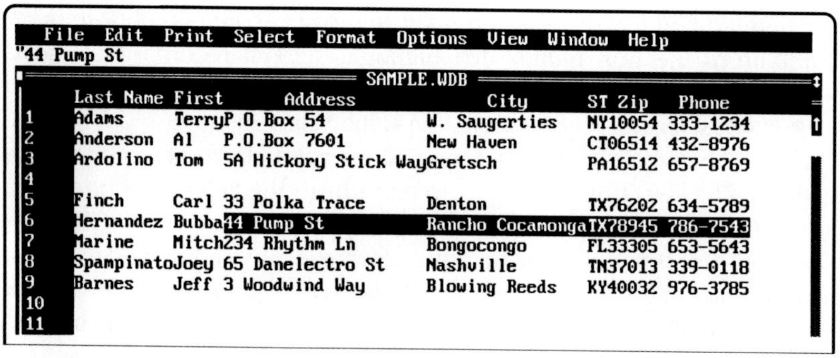

```
  File  Edit  Print  Select  Format  Options  View  Window  Help
"44 Pump St
╔══════════════════════════ SAMPLE.WDB ══════════════════════════╗
    Last Name First      Address           City       ST Zip   Phone
 1  Adams     TerryP.O.Box 54         W. Saugerties  NY10054 333-1234
 2  Anderson  Al   P.O.Box 7601       New Haven      CT06514 432-8976
 3  Ardolino  Tom  5A Hickory Stick WayGretsch        PA16512 657-8769
 4
 5  Finch     Carl 33 Polka Trace     Denton         TX76202 634-5789
 6  Hernandez Bubba44 Pump St         Rancho CocamongaTX78945 786-7543
 7  Marine    Mitch234 Rhythm Ln      Bongocongo     FL33305 653-5643
 8  SpampinatoJoey 65 Danelectro St   Nashville      TN37013 339-0118
 9  Barnes    Jeff 3 Woodwind Way     Blowing Reeds  KY40032 976-3785
10
11
```

To copy in the List view, first highlight the field entry or entries you want to copy, then select the Copy command.

Deleting entries. The Delete commands on the Edit menu allow you to delete a field or a record from a database. In the List view, you must highlight the record or records that you want to delete prior to selecting the Delete command. If you want to delete a field, you must highlight that field.

Figure 15-19

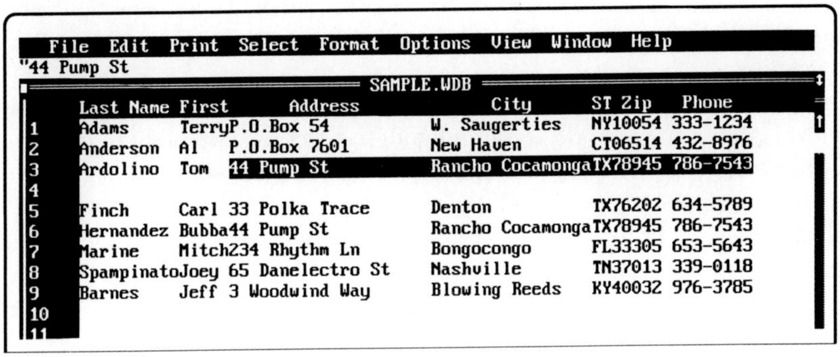

```
 File  Edit  Print  Select  Format  Options  View  Window  Help
"44 Pump St
═══════════════════════════════ SAMPLE.WDB ═══════════════════════════════
    Last Name First      Address           City       ST Zip   Phone
 1  Adams     TerryP.O.Box 54        W. Saugerties   NY10054 333-1234
 2  Anderson  Al    P.O.Box 7601     New Haven       CT06514 432-8976
 3  Ardolino  Tom   44 Pump St       Rancho CocamongaTX78945 786-7543
 4
 5  Finch     Carl 33 Polka Trace    Denton          TX76202 634-5789
 6  Hernandez Bubba44 Pump St        Rancho CocamongaTX78945 786-7543
 7  Marine    Mitch234 Rhythm Ln     Bongocongo      FL33305 653-5643
 8  SpampinatoJoey 65 Danelectro St  Nashville       TN37013 339-0118
 9  Barnes    Jeff 3 Woodwind Way    Blowing Reeds   KY40032 976-3785
10
11
```

To complete the copy, position the highlight where you want to dupli-
cate your selection, then press [Enter].

The Delete Record/Field command in the List view works just like the Delete Row/Column command in a spreadsheet document. To delete a record in the List view, first place the highlight on any field in that record. Then, choose the Record command from the Select menu to highlight the entire record. Finally, choose the Delete Record/Field command from the Edit menu to delete the highlighted record. As it deletes the record, Works will shift up all the records below the deleted record to fill the void in the database. If you select the Delete Record/Field command after highlighting only a single field, Works will delete the field. As it deletes the field, Works will shift left all the fields to the right of the deleted field to fill the void in the database. If you highlight a partial record of a single cell, Works will present the dialog box shown in Figure 15-20. In this dialog box, you choose to delete the record option or the field option. When you choose <OK> or press [Enter], Works will clear the record or field from the database.

Figure 15-20

This is the Delete Record/Field dialog box.

For example, suppose you want to remove record 4 from the address directory database. To delete this record, first bring it into view (you might want to use the Go To… command to move to this record). Now, simply select the Delete Record/ Field command from the Edit menu. When you do this, Works will delete the record from the database and shift all the records that follow it so that record 6 becomes record 5, record 7 becomes record 6, and so forth. After you've executed the Delete Record/Field command, the status line will indicate there are *8/8* records in the database, one fewer than before you selected the Delete Record/Field command.

▶As you might expect, you can delete more than one record at a time in the List view. All you have to do is highlight all the records you want to delete, then select the Delete Record/Field command to delete them.◄

Inserting entries.   In most cases, you'll append new records to the end of your database. However, you may occasionally want to insert a new record between existing records in a database. You use the Insert commands from the Edit menu to insert records into a database.

Inserting a new record in the List view is much like inserting a new row in a spreadsheet document. To insert a record in the List view, you first highlight the record that you want to appear below the new, blank record in the database. Then, choose the Insert Record/Field command from the Edit menu. When you do this, Works will add a new, blank record to the database, then will shift the highlighted record—and all the records below it—down one row in the database. Alternatively, you can highlight one cell in the record, then select the Insert Record/Field command. When you do this, Works will display the dialog box shown in Figure 15-20 that offers you a choice between record and field. At this point, you should just press <OK> to choose the default selection, Record. To insert a field, you can choose the Field option. As it inserts the field, Works will move all of the fields to the right of the highlighted one rightward to make room for the new one.

For example, suppose you want to insert a blank record above record 2 in the example database. First, highlight at least one cell in record 2, then select the Insert Record/Field command on the Edit menu. As you can see in Figure 15-21, a blank record now separates record 1 and record 3.

Figure 15-21

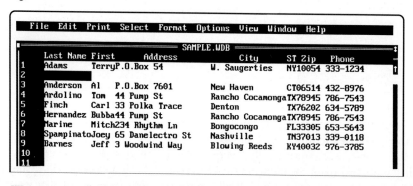

We've inserted a blank record between record 1 and 3.

▶As you might expect, you can insert more than one record at a time. All you have to do is highlight the number of records you want to insert, then select the Insert Record/Field command. When you do this, Works will insert the number of records you have highlighted, then will shift the highlighted records—and all of the records below them—down.◀

Clearing entries.   Occasionally, you'll want to remove the data from a field of one record without deleting the entire record. In the List view, you can use the Clear command on the Edit menu or the [Delete] key to remove a field entry.

The Clear command in the List view works just like the Clear command in a spreadsheet document. To clear an entry in the List view, move the highlight to the cell that contains that entry, then select the Clear command from the Edit menu. When you do this, Works will clear the cell on which the highlight is positioned. If you want to clear several entries at once, highlight all the cells that contain those entries, then select the Clear command.

Suppose the person listed in the third record of our address directory database has moved without leaving a forwarding address. You want to clear his old address from the database. To do this, first bring the third record into view. Then, position the highlight on the Address, City, ST, and Zip fields of this record, as shown in Figure 15-22. Next, select the Clear command from the Edit menu (or press the [Delete] key). Figure 15-23 on the next page shows the result.

Figure 15-22

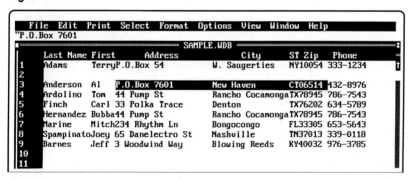

To clear an entry in the List view, first highlight the fields that contain the entries you want to clear.

Fill Down and Fill Right.   The Fill Down and Fill Right commands on the Edit menu offer a quick way to copy data from one cell to an adjacent cell or cells while you're in the List view. These commands are identical to the commands with the same names in the spreadsheet environment: They simply copy one entry into a range of adjacent cells. Fill Down copies the entry in the top cell of a range you have highlighted into the cells below it in the same field. Fill Right copies the entry in the leftmost cell of a range you have highlighted into the cells to its right in the same record.

Figure 15-23

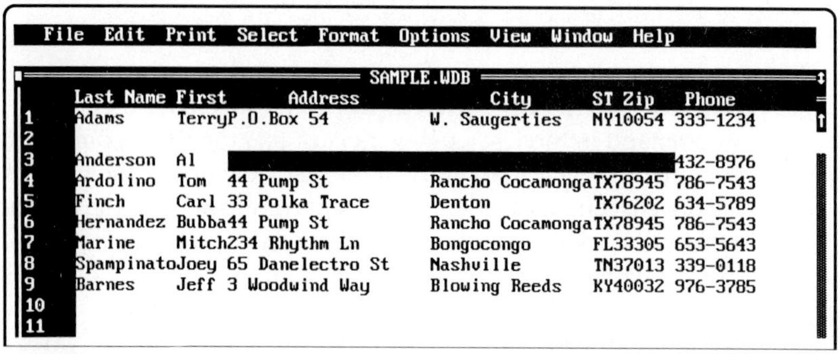

```
┌─────────────────────────────────────────────────────────────────────┐
│  File  Edit  Print  Select  Format  Options  View  Window  Help      │
├─────────────────────────────────────────────────────────────────────┤
│═══════════════════════════ SAMPLE.WDB ═════════════════════════════  │
│      Last Name First        Address          City      ST Zip  Phone │
│   1  Adams      TerryP.O.Box 54          W. Saugerties NY10054 333-1234│
│   2                                                                    │
│   3  Anderson  Al        ▐                              ▌432-8976     │
│   4  Ardolino  Tom  44 Pump St       Rancho CocamongaTX78945 786-7543 │
│   5  Finch     Carl 33 Polka Trace   Denton          TX76202 634-5789 │
│   6  Hernandez Bubba44 Pump St        Rancho CocamongaTX78945 786-7543│
│   7  Marine    Mitch234 Rhythm Ln    Bongocongo      FL33305 653-5643 │
│   8  SpampinatoJoey 65 Danelectro St  Nashville       TN37013 339-0118 │
│   9  Barnes    Jeff 3 Woodwind Way   Blowing Reeds   KY40032 976-3785 │
│  10                                                                    │
│  11                                                                    │
└─────────────────────────────────────────────────────────────────────┘
```

When you select the Clear command, Works will clear the highlighted fields.

The Fill Down command can be particularly helpful if you have a number of records with an identical entry in one field. For example, suppose you need to enter a new record in your database for Betty Jo Adams, who will be rooming with her brother Terry. Since the information for Terry Adams is already in the database and in Figure 15-21 you inserted a blank record between record 1 and 2, you can use use the Fill Down command to enter most of the new record into the blank second row of the database. To copy the information from record 1 to record 2, highlight the cells in the first seven fields in both records, as shown in Figure 15-24. Now, select Fill Down from the Edit menu. Works will repeat the data from the upper record into the lower one, as shown in Figure 15-25. At this point, all you need to do is change the entry in the First Name field to Betty Jo.

The Fill Right command works just like Fill Down, except that it copies data from left to right. You may not use this command as often in databases as you do in spreadsheets since there are few times when you'll want to copy information from one field to another in the same record.

Works offers a special key combination that has a function similar to the Fill Down command: [Ctrl]'. This key copies the contents of the cell above the current cell into the current cell in the List view. After you press [Ctrl]', be sure to press [Enter] to lock the copied information into the new cell.

Form view

Because you see only one record at a time in the Form view, editing your data in the Form view is different from editing data in the List view.

Figure 15-24

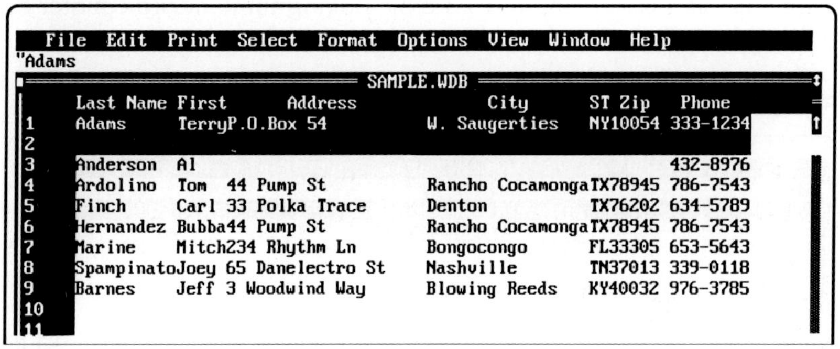

The Fill Down command lets you copy information from one record to the next.

Figure 15-25

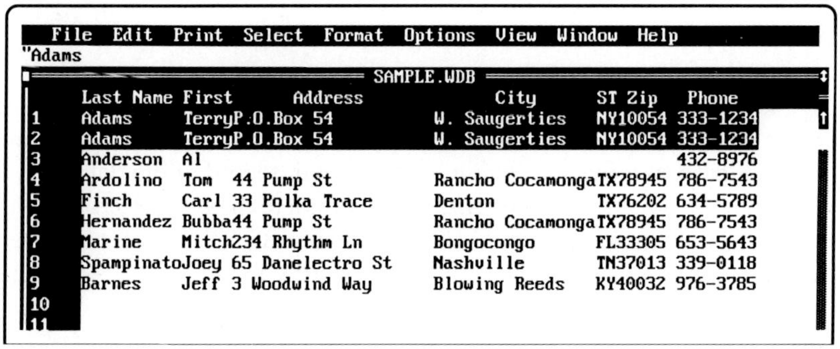

After you highlight the source and destination cells, select the Fill Down command from the Edit menu.

Moving entries. To move a record in the Form view, you first bring that record into view in the form. Then, you select the Move Record command from the Edit menu. When the word *MOVE* appears on the status line, use the [Ctrl][Pg Up], [Ctrl][Pg Dn], [Ctrl][Home], or [Ctrl][End] keys—or the Go To... command using the record number in the Go To text box—to move the cursor to the destination record, then choose <OK>. Works will move the record to that location and shift the other records in the database to account for the move. If you decide not to complete the move, you can cancel the Move Record command by pressing [Esc] before you press [Enter] to complete the move.

Works will always position the record you are moving above the record you see in the form when you press [Enter]. For example, suppose you want to move the ninth record in the address directory database so that it occupies the fifth position in the database. Figure 15-26 shows the ninth record of the database. (You can tell that this is the ninth record by looking at the record counter on the status line.)

Figure 15-26

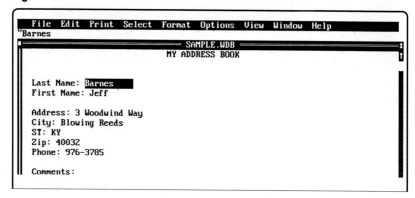

To move a record in the Form view, you first bring that record into view in the form.

With record 9 in view, select the Move Record command from the Edit menu. Now, press [Ctrl]↑ to move the highlight to the sixth record of the database, then press [Enter] to execute the move. After you complete these steps, you'll still see the record you moved in the form, as shown in Figure 15-27. However, the record will now be record 5 as you can tell by the record counter on the status line.

Figure 15-27

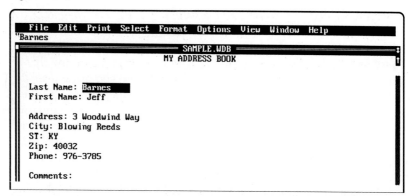

To complete the move, move to the record above which you want to place the record, and press [Enter].

Copying entries. ►The Copy Record command lets you copy an entire record in the Form view. To copy in the Form view, first display the record you want to copy in the form. Then, select the Copy Record command from the Edit menu. When the word *COPY* appears on the status line, move the highlight to the record into which you want to place the copy, then press [Enter]. The record you are copying will now be duplicated at the new location. When the copy is finished, the duplicate record will be in view in the form.

If the destination record contains any entries, those entries will be overwritten and lost. For this reason, you'll usually use the Copy Record command to copy information into a blank record—either a new record you have created with the Insert Record command or a blank record at the end of the database.

For example, suppose you want to create a separate listing in your address directory database for the wife of the person in record 9. To do this, you can simply copy this record to the next record, then change the First Name field of the new record. First, display the record you want to copy in the form, as shown in Figure 15-28. Next, select the Copy Record command from the Edit menu. When the word *COPY* appears on the status line, press [Ctrl]↓ to move the highlight to the new record at the end of the database. Now, press [Enter] to duplicate the original record at this new location. When the copy is finished, the new duplicate record will be in view in the form, as shown in Figure 15-29 on the following page. Now, you can simply edit the entry in the First Name field.

Figure 15-28

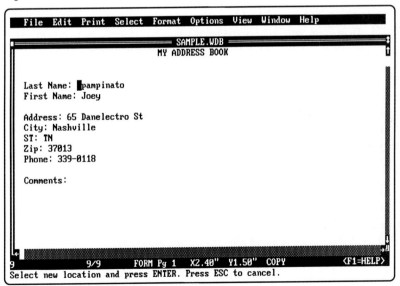

To copy a record in the Form view, first bring that record into view in the form.

Figure 15-29

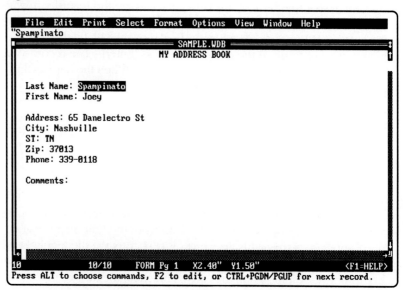

When you press [Enter] to complete the copy, Works will duplicate the original record at the new location and display the new record in the form.

Inserting entries.   In most cases, you'll append new records to the end of your database. However, you may occasionally want to insert a new record between existing records in a database. You can use the Insert Record command on the Edit menu in the Form view to insert a record in a database. In the Form view, Works assumes that you want to insert a new record above the record that currently is displayed on your screen. When you choose the Insert Record command, a new blank record form will appear on the screen. The record that was previously displayed, and those that follow it, will be shifted down one row in the List view.

Now, suppose that you want to insert a new record above the fourth record of the address directory database. Figure 15-30 shows the fourth record of our database displayed in the Form view. To insert a new record, select the Insert Record command from the Edit menu. When you do this, a blank record will appear in the form, as shown in Figure 15-31. If you switch to the List view, you'll see that all subsequent records have been shifted down by one row to open up the new blank record.

Figure 15-30

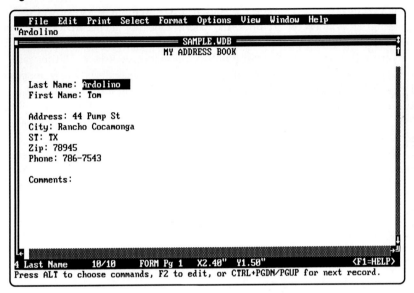

To insert a record in the Form view, first bring the record above which you want to insert the record into view in the form.

Figure 15-31

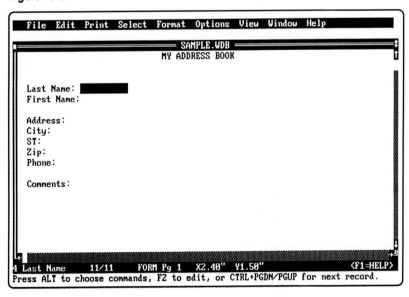

When you select the Insert Record command, Works will insert a blank record in the database and will display that record in the form.

Deleting entries. The Delete commands on the Edit menu allow you to delete a field or a record from a database. To delete a record in the Form view, first move the highlight to that record in the form. Then, select the Delete Record command from the Edit menu to delete the record. When you do this, Works will delete the record from the database and shift all the following records to fill the void.

Suppose you want to remove the blank record (record 4) that we inserted in our previous example. To delete this record, first bring it into view in the form (you might want to use the Go To... command to move to this record). Figure 15-31 shows this record in the form. Now, simply select the Delete Record command from the Edit menu. When you do this, Works will delete the record from the database and shift all the records that follow it so that record 5 becomes record 4, record 6 becomes record 5, and so forth. After you've executed the Delete Record command, the "new" record 4—which formerly was record 5—will be in view in the form.

Clearing entries. Occasionally, you'll want to remove the data from a field of one record without deleting the entire record. In the Form view, you can use the Clear Field Contents command on the Edit menu or the [Delete] or [Backspace] key to clear an entry from a field.◀

To clear an entry in the Form view, first bring the record that contains that entry into view in the form. Then, move the highlight to the field that contains the entry, and select the Clear Field Contents command from the Edit menu. When you do this, Works will clear the highlighted entry.

For example, suppose the person listed in the third record of our address directory database has a new, unlisted phone number. You want to clear his old phone number from the database. To do this, first display the third record on your screen. Then, position the highlight on the Phone field of this record, as shown in Figure 15-32. Next, select the Clear Field Contents command from the Edit menu (or press the [Delete] key). Figure 15-33 shows the result.

Copying between databases

You can also use the Copy command to copy information from one database document to another. In general, copying information from one database to another is similar to copying information within the same database. You can copy from a database in either the Form view or the List view into another database in either view. The source and destination databases do not have to have the same number of fields, and the fields in the databases do not have to share the same names. However, it usually makes sense to copy information from one database to another only if those databases have some common characteristics. For example, you might want to copy an entry from a field in a database to a field in another database that has the same type of entries—say, from one Zip field to another. Likewise, you might want to copy an entire record from a database into another database that has the same structure.

Figure 15-32

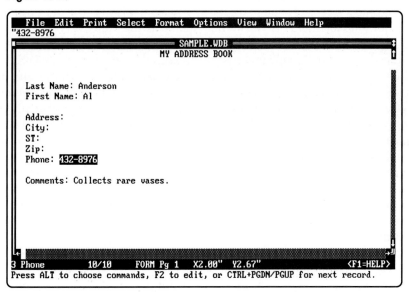

To clear an entry in the Form view, first bring the record that contains that entry into view in the form.

Figure 15-33

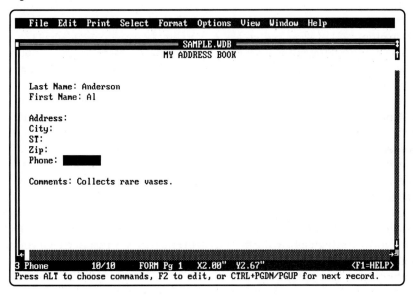

When you highlight the entry and select the Clear Field Contents command, Works will clear the highlighted field.

Copying from the Form view.   If you want to copy a single record from one database into a record of another database, you'll probably want to copy from one Form view into another Form view. If you are copying from the Form view, you must copy an entire record at a time. To copy from the Form view, first display the record you want to copy in the form. Then, select the Copy command from the Edit menu to begin the copy. When the word *COPY* appears on the status line, you need to activate the destination database. If that database is open, you can activate it by selecting its name from the Window menu. If it is not open, you'll have to use the Open Existing File… command to open it.

Once the destination database is active, you should stay in the Form view. Move the highlight to the record into which you want to place the copy, and press [Enter]. The record you selected to copy will now be duplicated at the new location in the destination database. The entry from the first field of the source record will be placed into the first field of the destination record; the entry from the second field of the source will be copied into the second field in the destination; and so on. If there are not as many fields in the destination database as there are in the source, Works will create new fields in the destination database to handle the overflow. These fields will have names like Field5, Field6, and so on. If the fields of the destination record contain information, that information will be overwritten by the copy procedure and will be lost.

Copying from the List view.   If you are copying from the List view, you can copy any range—from an entry in one cell to an entire record or field, several records or fields, or the entire database. Although you don't have to, if you copy from the List view, you'll usually want to copy into the List view. In fact, copying between databases in the List view is identical to copying between spreadsheets.

To copy from the List view, first highlight the field entry or entries you want to copy. Then, select the Copy command from the Edit menu to begin the copy. When the word *COPY* appears on the status line, you must activate the destination database. If that database is open, you can activate it by selecting its name from the Window menu. If it is not open, you'll have to use the Open Existing File… command to open it.

Once the destination database is active, you should enter the List view. Then, move the highlight to the spot in the destination database where you want to insert the copied information. If you are copying a single entry, simply move the highlight to the cell in which you want the copy to be placed. If you are copying a range of entries, move the highlight to the upper-left corner of the range of cells into which you want to place the copies. If you are copying an entire field or record, move the highlight to the first cell in the field or record into which you want to place the copies. If you're copying an entire database, move the highlight to the upper-left corner of the database.

Once the highlight is in place, press [Enter] to complete the copy. Works will place a copy of the entry or entries you highlighted in the source database into the destination database. The entry from the first field in the source range will be placed into the cell that contains the highlight. The other entries from the source range (if any) will be placed in the cells below and/or to the right of that cell. If there are not enough fields in the destination database to accommodate the data you are copying, Works will create new fields in the destination database to handle the overflow. These fields will have names like Field5, Field6, and so on. If the fields of the destination records contain information, that information will be overwritten by the copy and will be lost.

You can also use the Copy command to transfer data from a database to a word processor or spreadsheet document. We'll show you how to do that in Chapter 19.

Copying to other environments

Works lets you protect the entries in a database from being overwritten or erased accidentally. Using protection will keep you and others who might use your databases from destroying valuable entries.

Protection

The process of protecting a database is identical to that of protecting a spreadsheet. There are two elements to this protection. First, each cell in a database can be locked or unlocked individually. Second, Works allows you to enable or disable protection for the entire database. While this global protection is on, Works prevents you from making changes to any of the locked cells in the spreadsheet. When global protection is off, you can make changes to any cells, whether they are locked or unlocked.

When you first create a database, all the cells in that database are locked, but global protection is turned off. As a result, you can make entries in any cell of a new database. If you turn global protection on while each cell is locked, you'll be unable to make changes to any of the cells in the database—you'll also be unable to unlock locked cells. If you want to protect some cells but leave others unprotected, unlock the cells you don't want protected, then turn global protection on. When you do this, the locked cells will be protected, and the unlocked cells will not.

Although you'll sometimes want to have some cells in spreadsheets protected and others unprotected, you'll usually want to protect every cell in a database. When you need to add new information or make changes to existing records, you can briefly unprotect the database, make the change, then reprotect it. Even if you choose not to protect every cell in your databases, you may decide to use protection for columns that contain calculated fields. We'll talk about calculated fields later in this chapter.

Locking cells

The Locked option in the Style dialog box allows you to lock and unlock individual cells. To lock or unlock a cell, move the highlight to that cell, pull down the Format menu, then select the Style… command. When you do this, you'll see the Style dialog box shown in Figure 15-34. The Locked option in the lower-left corner of this dialog box lets you lock and unlock individual cells. An X in the brackets to the left of this option indicates that the highlighted cell is locked. If the brackets are empty, the cell is unlocked. To change the lock status of a cell, just choose the Locked option, then choose <OK> or press [Enter].

Figure 15-34

The Locked option in the Style dialog box lets you lock and unlock cells.

If you want, you can lock and unlock more than one cell at a time. To do this, first extend the highlight to cover the cells whose lock status you want to change. Then, pull down the Format menu, select the Style… command, choose the Locked option, and choose <OK>.

Works does not offer any on-screen indication of a cell's lock status. The only way to determine whether a cell is locked or unlocked is to highlight it and select the Style… command.

Global protection
►WORKS 2◄

►The Protect Data command on the Options menu controls global protection in a database. If you select Protect Data while global protection is off, Works will turn it on. Once you turn global protection on, Works will not allow you to make changes to any of the locked cells in the database. You won't be able to edit an entry in a locked cell or replace the contents of a locked cell using editing commands. In fact, while global protection is on, Works will only allow you to select the Copy command from the Edit menu and will not let you use any of the commands from the Format menu. When global protection is on, the Protect Data option will be marked with a dot.

If you select Protect Data while global protection is on, Works will turn it off. You'll then be able to make changes to every cell in the database. When global protection is off, the area to the left of the Protect Data command will be blank.◄

In a previous section, "Editing Records," we discussed how to use the commands on the Edit menu to manipulate the information in a database. In this section, we will show you how to change the structure of a database by adding and deleting fields, inserting labels, and so forth.

EDITING THE DATABASE

When we created the address directory database, we designed a very simple form (shown in Figure 15-6). Most of your forms will probably be like this one, simple and functional. As you become more proficient in Works, however, you'll probably want to create forms that are more attractive—and more complex—than this one. To do that, you'll need to know more about the process of designing and editing forms. The Form view offers a number of tools for designing and editing forms. You can use the Edit menu commands—Move (Field or Label), Copy (Copy Label), Delete (Text, Field Label, or Line), Insert Line—to change the position of fields and labels, alter the width of a field's text box, insert and delete blank lines, and even delete a field or label.

The Form view

In this section, we'll look at the tools you can use to refine the appearance of a form. To do this, we'll modify the original form we created at the beginning of the chapter. However, it is important that you understand that you can use all of these tools when you are first creating a form, as well as when you are modifying a form. If you know what you want a form to look like when you first create it, there's no need to create a simple version then modify it—you can simply design the form you want from scratch. On the other hand, if you've already created a form, you can use any of the techniques we're about to explain to modify it.

To modify an existing form, select the Form command from the View menu if you are not already in the Form view. When you do this, you'll see the form on the screen. At that point, you can modify the form.

Modifying forms

There may be times when you'll need to edit a label or a field name that you've entered into a form. There are two ways to alter a field name or a label: You can replace the name or label with a new entry, or you can edit it. As long as the entry you are changing is short, it is usually easier to replace the entry with a new entry than it is to edit it. To replace a label or field name, position the highlight on the label or field you want to change, type a new label or field name (don't forget the colon), then press [Enter] to lock in the change. If the entry you are replacing was a label, Works will simply substitute the new label for the old one. If the entry was a field name, Works will replace the old field name with the new name in the Form and in the List view as well.

Editing field names and labels

Instead of replacing a field name or a label, you may want to change only a character or two. As you might expect, you can use the [Edit] key ([F2]) to change a field name or label in a form. To use the [Edit] key, first move the highlight to the entry you want to change, then press the [Edit] key. When you press the [Edit] key, an underline cursor will appear at the end of the current entry in the formula line. You can use the ➜, ◄, [Home], and [End] keys to move this cursor to any spot in the entry and use the [Delete] or [Backspace] key to erase existing characters. You can also type new characters, and those characters will be inserted in the entry at the position of the cursor. When the entry in the formula line appears the way you want it, press [Enter] to lock in the change.

There are a couple of things to watch out for when you are editing field names. First, if you remove the colon from the field name, Works will change the field name to a label. If the field contains any data, the data will be lost. Fortunately, Works will display an alert box with the message *About to delete data in this field?* before it deletes the field. You can choose <OK> to complete the change and delete the field or <Cancel> to abandon the change. Similarly, if you edit a field name and delete all of the characters in the name, Works will assume that you want to delete the field from the form. Once again, Works will give you a chance to cancel the change before it deletes the field.

Changing field sizes
►WORKS 2◄

►When you create a field in a form, Works sets the width and height of that field to match whatever width and height you specify in the Field Size dialog box. (The default height is one row and the default width is 20-characters.) To change the size of a field, highlight that field in the form and select the Field Size... command from the Format menu to display a Field Size dialog box. The Field Size dialog box will display the current width and height of the field. To change the width of the field, type the new width, then choose <OK> to lock in the change. To change the height, type the new height, then choose <OK>.◄

Changing the width of a field in a form does not change the width of that field in the List view. We'll show you how to change the width of a field in the List view later in this chapter.

Assigning formats
and styles

In addition to changing the size of a field, you also can assign a format to each field, field name, and label. The format you assign to a field determines how the entries in that field are displayed in both the Form view and the List view and applies to every entry you make in that field. The format you assign to a field name and label determines how that name and label appear in the form.

To assign a format to a field, highlight it, then use the commands on the Format menu to select the format you want to use. These commands—Fixed..., Currency..., Percent..., Font..., Style... and so on—are identical to those you use to format cells in spreadsheets. When you select any of them, Works will display a dialog box that asks you to specify the number of decimal places to include in the formatted numbers or a dialog box that allows you to choose the font or style you want to assign to that field (Times Roman, Helvetica, Bold, Underline, and so on). After you have made the appropriate choices in these dialog boxes, just choose <OK> or press [Enter] to assign the selected format or style to the field. (For more on each of Works' formats and styles, see Chapter 5.)

To assign a format to a field name or label, highlight it, then use the Font... and Style... commands on the Format menu to select the format you want to use. These commands are identical to the Font... and Style... commands you use to format cells in spreadsheets. When you select either of these commands, Works will display a dialog box that asks you to choose the font or style you want to assign to that field (Times Roman, Helvetica, Bold, Underline, and so on). After you have made the appropriate choices in these dialog boxes, just choose <OK> or press [Enter] to assign the selected format or style to the field.

▶While you're designing your form, you can change the placement of any field by using the Move Field command. To move a field in the Form view, you first highlight that field. Then, you select the Move Field command from the Edit menu. Finally, position the highlight where you want the first character of the field to appear, then press [Enter] to place the field.

Moving fields
▶WORKS 2◀

You can only move one field at a time using the Move Field command. If you want to move more than one field, you have to move each one individually. Works will not let you move a field to the same location as another field. If you do, Works will display an alert box that says *Cannot put item here.* At this point, press <OK>, then move the field to a different location. If you decide not to complete the move, you can cancel the Move Field command by pressing [Esc] before you press [Enter] to complete the move.

To move a label in the Form view, you first highlight that label in the form, just as you do when you move a field. Then, you select the Move Label command from the Edit menu. (The Move Field command changes name to Move Label when you highlight a label.) Finally, position the highlight where you want the first character of the field to appear, then press [Enter] to place the label.

Moving labels

You can only move one label at a time using the Move Label command. If you want to move more than one label, you have to move each one individually. Works will not let you move a label to a position occupied by another label. If you do, Works will display an alert box that says *Cannot put item here.* At this point, press <OK>, then reposition the label away from the existing one. If you decide not to complete the move, you can cancel the Move Label command by pressing [Esc] before you press [Enter] to complete the move.

You can also copy labels from one place to another in a form. To do this, first highlight the label, then pull down the Edit menu, and select the Copy Label command. (When you highlight a label in a form, Works renames the Copy command the Copy Label command.) Next, move the highlight to the position where you want to place the copy, and press [Enter]. Like the Copy Field command, the Copy Label will not allow you to place a copy of a label over an existing label or field.◀

Copying labels

Inserting and deleting lines

The Insert Line and Delete Line commands from the Edit menu allow you to insert and delete blank lines in a form. To delete a line, position the cursor anywhere on an inserted blank line, then select the Delete Line command from the Edit menu to remove that line from the form. If you try to delete a line that contains a field or a label, you will have to delete or move the field or label before Works will allow you to execute the Delete Line command. (We'll talk about deleting fields and labels in a moment.)

You can also insert a blank line anywhere in a form using the Insert Line command. To do this, position the highlight anywhere on the line above which you want Works to insert a new line and select the Insert Line command from the Edit menu. Works will then insert a blank line above the line that contains the highlight and shift all the text below down one line.

If the last line of the form contains a field or label when you issue the Insert Line command, Works will shift that field or label to the second page of the form. Unless you want to place that field or label on the next page, you'll probably want to use the Move (Field or Label) command to change its position before or after you use the Insert Line command.

Works allows you to insert or delete only one line at a time. If you need to insert or delete two or more lines, you must do so one line at a time.

Hiding field names

If you want, you can hide the name portion of any field in a form. To do this, merely highlight the field whose name you want to hide, then select the Show Field Name command from the Format menu. The name will disappear.

The Show Field Name command is a toggle command—its effect changes depending on whether the current field is hidden or visible. If the current field name is in view, you'll see a dot next to the Show Field Name command when you pull down the Format menu. If the field name is hidden, you won't see a dot. To bring a hidden field name back into view, simply place the highlight on the text box for that field and choose the Show Field Name command from the Format menu once more.

If you decide to hide a field name, you will probably want to add a label to the form to identify the contents of the field. Since the field name already appears in the form, you may wonder why you would bother to hide the field name and use a label to identify the field. In fact, there is an advantage to hiding the field name. If you use a label instead of the field name to identify the field, you can place the label above, below, or to the right of the field. (The field name can only appear to the left of the field.) Finally, the label can be longer or shorter than the actual field name. This allows you to use a short field name without creating confusing forms. Overall, we prefer to hide all the field names in our forms.

Deleting fields and labels

If you decide that you don't need one of the fields or labels you've entered on your database form, you can delete it. To do this, move the highlight to the field or label you want to remove and select the Delete (Field or Label) command from the Edit menu. If you are deleting a field, Works will display an alert box with the message *OK to delete data in this field?* before it deletes the field. If you're sure you want to delete the field, choose <OK>. If you don't want to delete the field, choose <Cancel>.

When you delete a field from a form, you delete the field from the database as well. If you've entered any data into the field, it will be lost. Be careful!

As you might expect, you can add fields or labels to a form at any time. To add a field, first position the cursor at the point where you want the field to appear in the finished form, then type the name of the field, followed by a colon. When you're finished, press [Enter], then enter the field width and height in the Field Size dialog box and choose <OK> or press [Enter]. When you add a field to a form, Works will add the field to the List view as well. The field will appear in the List view at the right edge of the database.

To enter a label, just move the cursor to the position where you want the text to appear, type the label, and press [Enter] to place it on the form. Be sure that you don't include a colon at the end of the label. If you do, Works will think that you're creating a new field.

You can place more than one field or label on a single line of a form. However, Works will not let you place a new field directly above an existing field—so the first character in the field you are moving will not fall on the first character in the existing entry. If you place a new label directly above an existing label, Works will display an alert box that says *Cannot put item here.*

▶When you're finished designing the form, you should save your database document. To do this, select the Save As... command from the File menu and save the document just as you would any other Works document.

If you begin to change a form, there is no way to abandon the changes you make. There is no key you can press to return from the Form view to the database without implementing your changes. If you've made a change you want to undo, you'll have to reverse that change. For example, if you add a label to a form, then decide you don't need the label, you'll have to use the Delete Label command to delete it from the Form. You can retrieve the saved form in two ways: by closing the document without saving your changes, then reopening it; or selecting the Save As... command, and renaming the document. Then, you can reopen the original version of the document.◀

Let's use these techniques to modify the simple form for the address directory database, which is shown in Figure 15-7. Notice that we originally grouped the left-aligned fields in our form to convey four types of information: Name, Address (with City, ST, and Zip), Phone, and Comments. Figure 15-35 shows the new

Adding fields and labels

Saving the form
▶WORKS 2◀

An example

address directory form we will create in this example. To create this form, we'll make four changes to our simple form. We'll insert a blank line, add labels, hide field names, and realign fields.

Figure 15-35

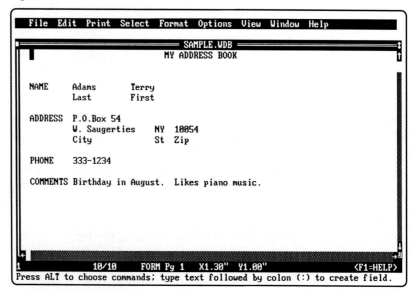

This is how our address directory form will look when we finish modifying it.

To begin modifying our form, you need to insert a blank line above the City field. To do this, place the cursor on the City field. Then, select the Insert Line command from the Edit menu. Figure 15-36 shows the address directory after we inserted a line above the City field.

Now, we want to move the First Name field to the same line as the Last Name field and the ST and Zip fields to the same line as the City field. Figure 15-37 shows the First Name field in the first record of the database.

With the First Name field in record 1 highlighted, select the Move Field command from the Edit menu. When the highlight extends from the field name to cover the field, press → 21 times and ↑ once to move the highlight to the right of the Last Name field or use the mouse to point to the new location of the field. Now, press [Enter] to execute the move. After you complete these steps, the form will look like the one in Figure 15-38 on page 500. The First Name field will now appear on the same line as the Last Name field.

Figure 15-36

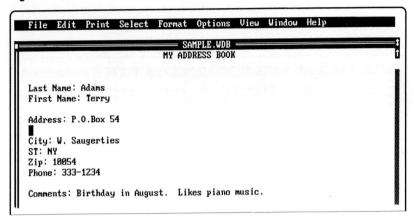

The Insert command lets you insert a blank line.

Figure 15-37

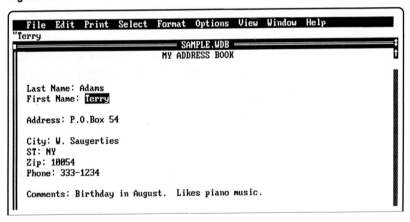

To move a field in the Form view, you first highlight that field in the form.

Next, highlight the ST field and select the Move Field command. Then, press ➡ 22 times and ⬆ once to move the highlight to the right of the City field, or use the mouse to point to the new location of the field. Now, press [Enter] to execute the move.

To move the Zip field, highlight it, select the Move Field command, and press ➡ 28 times and ⬆ twice to move the highlight to the right of the ST field, or use the mouse to point to the new location of the field. Now, press [Enter] to execute the move. After you complete these steps, the form will look like the one in Figure 15-39. The ST and Zip fields will now appear on the same line as the City field.

Figure 15-38

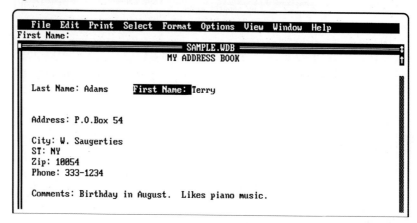

To complete the move, point to a new location and press [Enter].

Figure 15-39

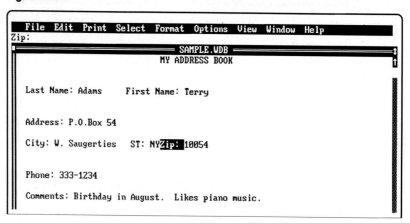

We've moved the ST and Zip fields to the same line as the City field.

Next, we want to add nine labels and delete the field names. (We'll add five labels now, then hide our field names and add the uppercase labels later.) Under the Last Name field, we'll add the label *Last*. Under the First Name field, we'll add the label *First*. Under the City, ST, and Zip field names, we'll add the labels *City, St,* and *Zip*.

Adding a label is easy. First, we'll add the *Last* label. To do this, place the cursor one line below the first character in the Last Name field name. Then, type *Last* and press [Enter]. (Be careful not to insert a colon or Works will think you want to create another field name.) Figure 15-40 shows the Form at this point.

Figure 15-40

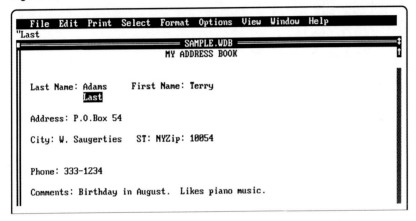

You can use labels to identify fields whose names you will hide.

As you can see in Figure 15-36, we want to add eight more labels: four uppercase (*NAME*, *ADDRESS*, *PHONE*, and *COMMENTS*) and four upper/lowercase (*First*, *City*, *St*, and *Zip*). To create the remaining labels, we need to repeat the simple procedure we just described. We'll position the remaining labels below the first character in the fields rather than below field names.

For example, to add the *City* label, begin by placing the cursor one line below the first character in the City field. When you have the cursor positioned under the City field, type *City,* then press [Enter]. The St and Zip labels also fit in the blank lines directly below their specific fields in the same way.

Before we enter the uppercase labels, we'll hide the field names. (We'll be changing the alignment of the fields after we hide the field names.) The Show Field Name command on the Format menu controls the display of field names. (This command is a toggle command whose default state is on.) To hide the Last Name field name, move the highlight to the field, and select the Show Field Name command from the Format menu. When you do this, the Last Name field name will disappear. Now, repeat these steps to hide the field names for the First Name, Address, City, ST, Zip, Phone, and Comments fields. Figure 15-41 on the following page shows the form at this point.

Next, we'll add the four uppercase labels: *NAME*, *ADDRESS*, *PHONE*, and *COMMENTS*. As you can see in Figure 15-36, we want to left-align each of these labels. The labels occupy the same location as the hidden field names.

Figure 15-41

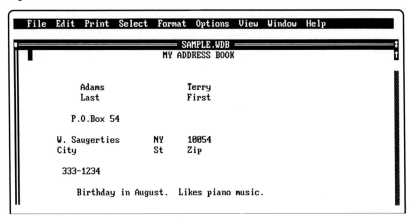

The Show Field Name command lets you hide and display field names.

Now, let's align the fields on the left with the Address field, which begins at an X coordinate of 2.20" from the left of the screen. (We mentioned the X and Y coordinates at the beginning of the chapter.) To begin, move the highlight to the Last Name field, select the Move Field command from the Edit menu, then press the ← key twice to align the highlight with the Address field. Next, press [Enter] to complete the move. Now, highlight the First Name field, select the Move Field command, press the ← key 12 times to close the space between the two name fields, and press [Enter] to complete the move.

Next, we want to align the City field with the Address field, then move the ST and Zip fields leftward to eliminate some unnecessary space between both pairs of fields. To move the City field, highlight it, select the Move Field command, press → three times, then press [Enter]. To move the ST field, highlight the field, select the Move Field command, press ← twice, then press [Enter]. When you get to the Zip field, you'll want to move it three spaces leftward to position it two spaces to the right of the ST field. You'll want to follow the same move procedure to move the Phone field two spaces rightward and the Comments field one space leftward. Figure 15-42 shows the form at this point.

Now, we need to align the labels with the fields they identify. Since we located the remaining field labels directly under the first character in their fields, the instructions for moving the labels are identical to the instructions we just gave for moving the fields.

The last thing we need to do is delete the line above the City field. To do this, position the cursor anywhere on that line above the City, ST, and Zip fields, then select the Delete Line command from the Edit menu. The blank line will disappear and your address directory form will look like the one in Figure 15-35.

Figure 15-42

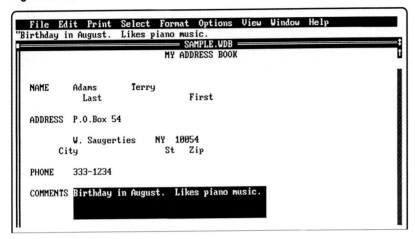

```
 File  Edit  Print  Select  Format  Options  View  Window  Help
"Birthday in August.  Likes piano music.
════════════════════════ SAMPLE.WDB ════════════════════════
                         MY ADDRESS BOOK


   NAME      Adams       Terry
             Last                    First

   ADDRESS   P.O.Box 54

             W. Saugerties    NY  10054
          City               St   Zip

   PHONE     333-1234

   COMMENTS Birthday in August.  Likes piano music.

```

The Move command allows you to reposition fields in a form.

►The Protect Form command on the Options menu protects the database form you create in Form view. If you select this command, you will make it impossible to modify the form in any way. You won't be able to highlight, move, copy, delete, or size field names, field locations, or labels. However, you will still be able to enter and edit information in your fields. This capability is useful if you create forms that many other people will use. When you activate the Protect Form command, Works will place a dot to the left of its name on the Options menu to indicate that the command is on.◄

Form protection
►WORKS 2◄

As you have seen, in the Form view you can add, delete, move, resize and format fields. You can do all of these things and more in the List view as well. We'll continue to use our address directory database to illustrate these List view tools.

The List view

To add a new field in the List view, simply use the Name... command on the Edit menu to name an empty column in the database document. You just move the highlight to an empty column, pull down the Edit menu, and select the Field Name... command. When you do this, Works will display the dialog box shown in Figure 15-10 on page 467. To assign a field name to the column in which the cursor is positioned, simply type that name into the Name text box, then choose <OK>. When you do this, Works will enter that name at the top of the current column, creating a field with that name. Works will also automatically add that field to the form and position it at the end of the form.

If you want, you can let Works assign names to the columns of a database for you. To do this, just type an entry into a cell of an unnamed column, then press

Adding a field

[Enter]. When you do this, Works will lock the entry into the cell and assign a default name to that column. The name will be based on the position of the column relative to the left edge of the document. For example, Works will assign the name Field1 to the first column, Field2 to the second column, and so on. As you might expect, you can use the Field Name... command to change these names if you want. We'll show you how to do that in a few paragraphs.

Let's add a field to the address directory database using this technique. Suppose that you want to create a new field for recording business phone numbers. To do this, place the highlight on the first blank column in the document, then select the Field Name... command from the Edit menu. When the Field Name dialog box appears, type *Bus. Phone,* then press [Enter]. As you can see in Figure 15-43, Works has added the new field to the database and placed the field name at the top of the column, so we could add a business phone number for Mr. Adams.

Figure 15-43

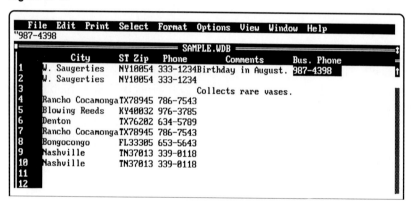

You can use the Field Name ... command to add a field in the List view.

Works automatically adds new fields you create in the List view and positions them at the end of the form. To look at our new field in the Form view, select the Form command from the View menu. Figure 15-44 shows the form. Notice that the Bus. Phone field appears at the bottom of the form. Of course, after you have added one or more new fields to your database, you can reposition those fields anywhere on the form.

Renaming fields

The Field Name... command on the Edit menu in the List view also allows you to change the name of any field in your database. To change a field name in a database, enter the List view, and place the highlight anywhere in the field you want to rename. Then, select the Field Name... command on the Edit menu to bring the Field Name dialog box into view. The current field name will appear highlighted in the Name text box. You should type the new name in the Name box, then choose <OK> or press [Enter] to change the name of the field. (To cancel the Field Name... command without changing the field name, press [Esc] anytime before you choose <OK>.) When the database comes back into view, the new field name will appear at the top of the column. If the name of the field appears in the Form view, it will change there as well.

Figure 15-44

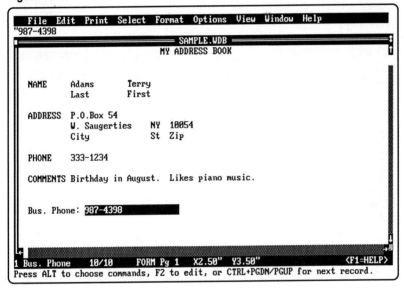

Works automatically adds new fields that you create in the List view to your form.

Changing the field width

Works automatically assigns each new field a default width of ten characters in the List view. As in the spreadsheet, the number of characters displayed in a field in the List view is limited by the column width. This may cause the longer entries in your database to be truncated. By the same token, a width of ten characters may be too wide for fields that contain short entries. To overcome these problems, you'll probably want to adjust the width of the fields so that you can see each entry.

You can use the Field Width... command on the Format menu to change the width of a field in the List view. This command is identical to the Column Width... command in spreadsheet documents. To change the width of a field, move the highlight to that field, then select the Field Width... command from the Format menu to display a Field Width dialog box. To change the width of the field, type the new width, then press [Enter] or choose <OK>. If you decide not to change the width of the field, you can cancel the Field Width... command by pressing [Esc] anytime before you choose <OK>.

For example, suppose you want to widen the Address field from 20 to 25 characters. To do this, first position the highlight anywhere in the Address field. Then, select the Field Width... command from the Format menu. When the Field Width dialog box appears, replace the current width setting (20) with the number 25. Then, choose <OK> to execute the command. Figure 15-45 shows the result.

Figure 15-45

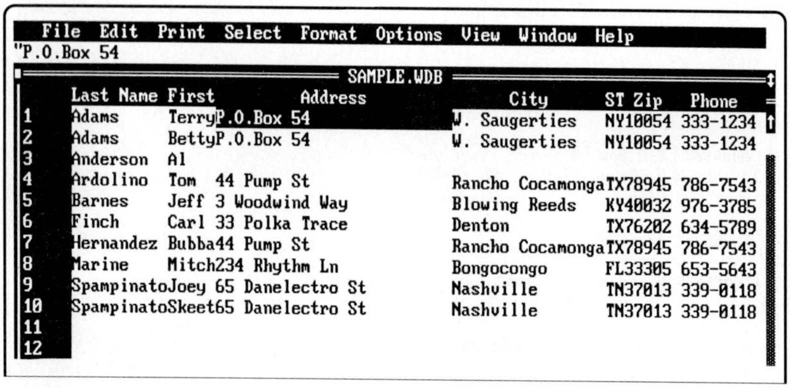

The Field Width... command lets you change the widths of fields in the List view.

Formatting fields

We have already explained that you can assign a format to a field while you are designing a form. You also can assign a format to a field in the List view. The format you assign to a field in the List view determines how the entries in that field are displayed in both the Form view and the List view. The format you give to one cell in a field applies to every cell in that field.

To assign a format to a field, just position the highlight in any cell in that field, then use the commands on the Format menu to select the format you want to use. These commands—Fixed..., Currency..., Font..., Style..., and so on—are identical to those you use to format cells in spreadsheets. When you select any of these commands, Works will display a dialog box that allows you to specify the number of decimal places you want to include in the formatted numbers or, in the case of the Style... command, that allows you to choose the style you want to assign to that field (Bold, Underline, and so on). After you have made the appropriate choices in these dialog boxes, just choose <OK> to assign the selected format or style to the field. (For more on each of Works' formats and styles, see Chapter 5.)

When you first create a database, Works arranges the fields in the List view from left to right in the order in which you created the fields. There may be times when you want to change the order of the fields in the List view. You can make this change using the Move command.

To move a field, highlight it, then select the Move command from the Edit menu. When the word *MOVE* appears on the status line, move the highlight to the first cell in the field that you want to appear to the right of the field you are moving, and press [Enter]. Works will move the field to the location you've chosen. Moving a field in the List view has no effect on the form for that database.

For example, suppose you want the Bus. Phone field to appear between the Zip field and the Phone field. To do this, first position the highlight anywhere in the Bus. Phone field, then choose the Field command from the Select menu to highlight the entire field. Now, select the Move command from the Edit menu. When the word *MOVE* appears on the status line, position the highlight in the first cell in the Phone field (the field that you want to appear to the right of the field you are moving), then press [Enter] to move the field. Figure 15-46 shows the result of the move.

Moving fields

Figure 15-46

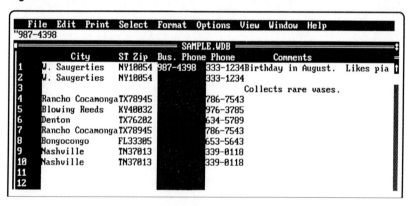

The Move command lets you move a field in the List view.

Earlier, we showed you how to delete fields from a database in the Form view. As you might expect, you also can delete fields in the List view. To delete a field in the List view, highlight the field you want to delete, then select the Delete Record/Field command from the Edit menu. When Works presents the Delete Record/Field dialog box, choose the Field option, then press <OK>. If there are any fields to the right of the deleted fields, those fields will shift to the left to fill the hole left by the deleted field.

Deleting fields

For example, suppose you no longer need the Bus. Phone field in the address directory database. To delete this field, first position the highlight anywhere in the Bus. Phone field, then choose the Delete Record/Field command from the Edit menu. Next, choose the Field option in the Delete Record/Field dialog box, then press <OK>. When you do this, the Bus. Phone column will disappear, and the Phone column will shift to the left to take its place, as shown in Figure 15-47.

Figure 15-47

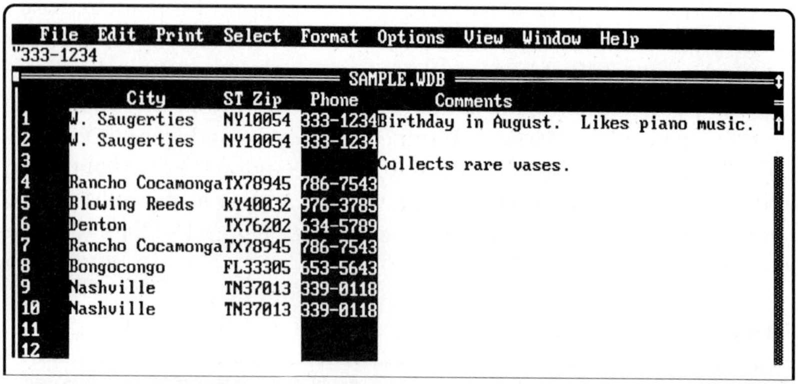

```
 File  Edit  Print  Select  Format  Options  View  Window  Help
"333-1234
                              ══════ SAMPLE.WDB ═══════════════════════════
          City         ST Zip    Phone       Comments
   1    W. Saugerties   NY10054  333-1234 Birthday in August.  Likes piano music.
   2    W. Saugerties   NY10054  333-1234
   3                                       Collects rare vases.
   4    Rancho Cocamonga TX78945 786-7543
   5    Blowing Reeds   KY40032  976-3785
   6    Denton          TX76202  634-5789
   7    Rancho Cocamonga TX78945 786-7543
   8    Bongocongo      FL33305  653-5643
   9    Nashville       TN37013  339-0118
  10    Nashville       TN37013  339-0118
  11
  12
```

The Delete Record/Field command lets you delete a field in the List view.

Deleting a field in the List view deletes the field from the form and—more importantly—deletes all the data you've entered in the field. Be careful!

Splitting the screen

The Split command on the Window menu in the List view offers a handy way to view more than one part of a database on the screen at once. This command, which is available only in the List view, is identical to the Split command in spreadsheet documents. You can use this command to divide your screen display into two or four panes.

To split the screen using the keyboard, first select the Split command from the Window menu. Then, use the arrow keys to position the screen split bars and press [Enter]. To split the screen using a mouse, you don't even need to select the Split command—just use the mouse to drag the screen split bars. To remove the split screen effect, select the Split command once more from the Window menu, then press [Home], and press [Enter]. Once you've split the screen, you can use the [F6] key to move the highlight from window to window. (For more information about splitting the screen, you can refer to the discussion of the Split command in Chapter 11.)

So far, we've entered only labels and values into the fields of our database. **CALCULATED**
Works also allows you to create a special kind of field called a calculated field. **FIELDS**
The main difference between calculated fields and other kinds of fields is that you
do not make entries in a calculated field. Instead, you specify a formula for each
calculated field. Then, Works uses this formula to compute the field entry for each
record automatically.

Typically, the computation in a calculated field is based on the entry in one
or more other fields of the database. For example, you might create a calculated
field that computes sales tax based on the entries in a field called Total Sales.
Formulas in calculated fields refer to the other fields in the database by name.
When a formula in a calculated field refers to another field, each record in the
calculated field will refer to the value in the current record of the other field. The
first record in the calculated field will refer to the first record in the other field, the
second record to the second record in the other field, and so on. There is no way
to create a calculated field formula that refers to an entry in a record of another
field other than the current record.

You can define a calculated field only in the List view. In fact, creating a
calculated field in a database is much like entering a formula in a spreadsheet. You
define a calculated field by entering the formula that defines the field in any cell
in the field. When you press [Enter] to lock in the formula, Works will apply the
formula to every cell in that field. If the formula refers to other fields, you can either
type the names of those fields as you are defining the formula or you can point
to define the field reference.

For example, suppose you have a personnel database that includes the annual **An example**
salary of each person listed. Figure 15-48 on the next page shows such a database
in the List view.

Now, suppose you want to create a new calculated field that computes the
hourly pay rate for each person, using the data in the Salary field. To create this
new field, first position the highlight anywhere in an empty column. Next, select
the Field Name… command from the Edit menu. When you see the Field Name
dialog box, enter a name like *Hourly,* then choose <OK> to create the new field.
Now, type the equation *=Salary/2080* and press [Enter]. This formula will divide
the entry in the Salary field by 2080, the number of hours in a work year based
on 52 forty-hour weeks. When you press [Enter], Works will apply this formula
to each record in the database and display the results as unformatted values, as
shown in Figure 15-49 on the following page.

After creating the calculated field, you'll probably want to format the results.
To begin, select the new field by choosing Field from the Select menu. Then,
choose Currency… from the Format menu to format the results in this field.

Figure 15-48

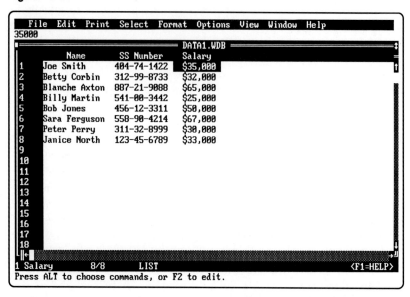

We'll create a calculated field that refers to the Salary field in this sample database.

Figure 15-49

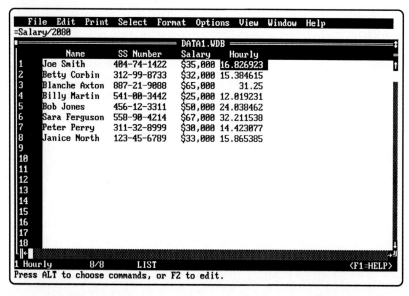

This calculated field is defined by the formula =Salary/2080.

The formula you use to define a calculated field can be up to 64 characters long and can include any of Works' mathematical operators. Like all formulas in Works, the formulas in a calculated field must begin with an equal sign. Typically, a formula will contain at least one field name.

You can use any of Works' spreadsheet functions—SUM(), AVG(), IF(), and so on—in the formulas that define calculated fields. You can also use the date functions DATE(), TIME(), and NOW() in calculated fields to perform date arithmetic. For example, the formula *=Due Date-NOW()* will create a calculated field that computes the difference between the date in the Due Date field and the current date as computed by the NOW() function for each record.

You can edit the formula that defines a calculated field the same way you edit any other formula in Works. All you have to do is move the highlight to any cell in the calculated field, then press the [Edit] key ([F2]) to bring the formula into the formula line. Then, you can move the cursor around in the formula, inserting and deleting characters to modify the formula. When you're finished, press [Enter] to lock in the new formula. The new formula will apply to the entire field. You can also change a formula in a calculated field simply by replacing it with a new formula. To do this, just move the cursor to any cell in the calculated field, then type the new formula.

If you change the name of a field that is referred to by a calculated field, that change will not affect the calculation. Works will automatically update any references to that field in your calculated field formulas.

If you want to override the result of a calculation in a cell of a calculated field, just move the highlight to that cell, then type a new entry. When you press [Enter] to lock in the entry, Works will replace the result of the calculation only in that cell with the value you typed. If you later clear the entry in that cell, Works will redisplay the result of the calculation for that cell. However, you must be sure not to replace the result of a calculated field with a formula. When you press [Enter], Works will redefine the calculated field using the new formula.

Although the formula that defines a calculated field cannot refer to a record other than the current record in another field, it can refer to the previous record in the calculated field. To refer to the previous record in the calculated field, just refer to the field by name. This feature makes it possible to create running totals in a calculated field.

CONCLUSION

In this chapter, you have learned how to create a Works database, how to enter information into a database, and how to edit entries in a database. You've learned about the two views of a database in Works: the Form view and the List view. You've also learned how to modify a form and how to restructure a database in the List view.

In the next chapter, we will show you how to work with the data in a database. You'll learn how to sort a database and how to create queries that select specific records from a database.

Using a Database 16

*I*n Chapter 15, we demonstrated how to create a Works' database, how to enter data into a database, and how to modify the structure of a database. Now that we've explained these basic concepts, we can get on to the real power of Works' database environment: the ability it gives you to manipulate, analyze, and query your data. In this chapter, we will cover the techniques you'll use to work with a database. First, we'll show you how to sort a database. Then, we'll look at the Search… command, which allows you to search for an entry in a database. Finally, we'll show how you can use criteria to query a database.

SORTING RECORDS

Sorting is one of the easiest ways to analyze a database. Sorting rearranges the records in a database into ascending or descending order based on the entries in one, two, or three fields. Sorting comes in handy whenever a record's order will help you find information. For example, suppose you've created a simple telephone book database in Works, and you want to find a friend's number. To find the number, you could sort the database by name. After Works has arranged all the names alphabetically, it's a simpler process to look up the name and find the phone number.

To sort a database, select the Sort Records... command from the Select menu in the Form or List view. (In Works 1, this command is called Sort….) When you issue this command, Works will display the dialog box shown in Figure 16-1. To sort, first enter the names of the fields on which you will sort the database into the 1st Field, 2nd Field, and/or 3rd Field text boxes. If you plan to sort on only one field, you'll enter a single field name in the 1st Field text box. If you plan to sort on two or three fields, you'll enter the name of the first sort field in the 1st Field text box, the name of the second sort field in the 2nd Field text box, and the name of the third sort field in the 3rd Field text box.

Figure 16-1

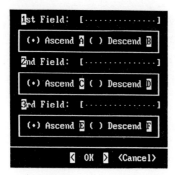

The Sort Records dialog box lets you specify the field that you want to sort and the sort order for each field.

As you enter each field name into the Sort Records dialog box, you will also specify the sort order—Ascend or Descend—Works will use to arrange the entries in that field. The default sort order, Ascend, tells Works to arrange the entries in that sort field into ascending order. If you choose Descend, Works will arrange the entries in the sort field into descending order. (We'll talk more about ascending versus descending sort order later.)

After you have entered the field names and specified the sort order, press [Enter] or choose <OK> to sort the database. Works will then rearrange the database by sorting the entries in the field(s) you've specified, then reordering the rest of the database according to these sorted entries.

If you select the Sort Records… command, then decide not to sort, you can cancel the command by pressing [Esc] or by choosing <Cancel>.

An example

Suppose you have created the real estate listings database shown in Figure 16-2. You want to sort this database so that the listings are arranged alphabetically by state. That is, you want the entries in the ST field to be arranged in alphabetical order. To begin, select the Sort Records… command from the Select menu. When you see the Sort Records dialog box, enter the field name *ST* in the 1st Field text box, as shown in Figure 16-3 on page 516. Since you want to arrange the ST field entries in ascending order, you don't need to specify a sort order after entering the field name. To execute this sort, just choose <OK> or press [Enter]. Figure 16-4 on page 516 shows the result.

Figure 16-2

File	Edit	Print	Select	Format	Options	View	Window	Help

"9311 Taylorsville Road

=========== DATA1.WDB ===========

	Address	City	ST	Zip	Style	BRs	SqFt	FP
1	9311 Taylorsville Road	Louisville	KY	40204	Modern	4	2100	X
2	516 Eline Road	Clarksville	IN	47234	Colonial	3	1400	
3	2321 Trevillian Road	Louisville	KY	40212	Cape Cod	4	2100	X
4	8027 Montero Road	Louisville	KY	40202	Tudor	3	1700	X
5	4206 Churchill Road	New Albany	IN	47123	Cape Cod	4	2300	X
6	223 Royer Court	Louisville	KY	40206	Condo	2	1492	X
7	1242 River Road	Louisville	KY	40202	Houseboat	4	2200	X
8	721 Cannons Lane	St. Matthews	KY	40211	Ranch	4	1900	
9	2900 Carlingford Drive	Louisville	KY	40203	Ranch	4	1900	X
10	316 Clark Station Road	St. Matthews	KY	40211	Ranch	3	1800	X
11	3210 Leith Lane	Louisville	KY	40211	Condo	3	1400	
12	2548 Saratoga Road	Louisville	KY	40206	Cape Cod	3	1789	X
13	4711 Hurstbourne Lane	Louisville	KY	40204	Colonial	4	2000	X
14								
15								

File	Edit	Print	Select	Format	Options	View	Window	Help

2

=========== DATA1.WDB ===========

	Baths	List Date	Price	Term
1	2.0	Jan 16, 1990	$76,000	90
2	3.0	Feb 28, 1990	$72,590	90
3	2.0	Mar 15, 1990	$102,950	90
4	1.0	May 7, 1990	$62,500	30
5	2.5	Jun 20, 1990	$93,795	60
6	1.5	Jun 21, 1990	$32,450	90
7	2.0	Jul 1, 1990	$76,000	30
8	3.0	Jul 1, 1990	$90,595	60
9	1.5	Jul 4, 1990	$58,500	60
10	2.0	Aug 12, 1990	$72,800	60
11	1.5	Aug 26, 1990	$60,900	30
12	2.0	Sep 23, 1990	$76,000	60
13	2.0	Oct 5, 1990	$112,900	90
14				
15				

We'll use this real estate database to illustrate the process of sorting.

Figure 16-3

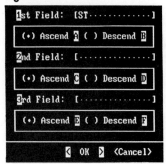

The Sort Records dialog box tells Works to sort the database into ascending order based on the entries in the ST field.

Figure 16-4

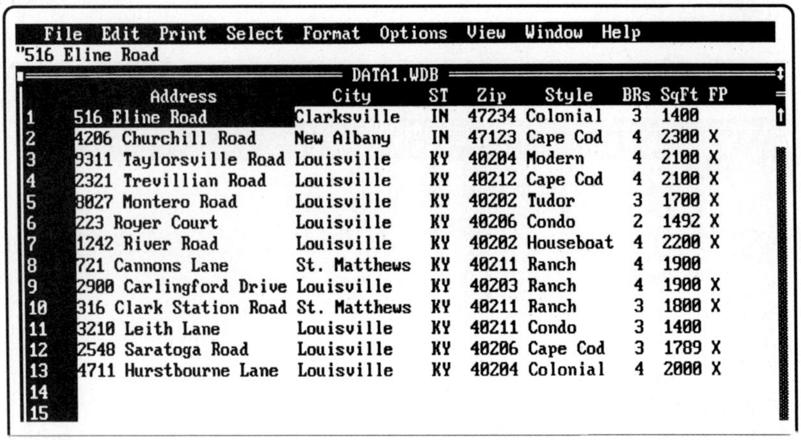

```
 File  Edit  Print  Select  Format  Options  View  Window  Help
"516 Eline Road
======================= DATA1.WDB ====================================
              Address          City         ST   Zip   Style      BRs SqFt FP
1     516 Eline Road        Clarksville    IN  47234 Colonial      3  1400
2     4206 Churchill Road   New Albany     IN  47123 Cape Cod      4  2300 X
3     9311 Taylorsville Road Louisville    KY  40204 Modern        4  2100 X
4     2321 Trevillian Road  Louisville     KY  40212 Cape Cod      4  2100 X
5     8027 Montero Road     Louisville     KY  40202 Tudor         3  1700 X
6     223 Royer Court       Louisville     KY  40206 Condo         2  1492 X
7     1242 River Road       Louisville     KY  40202 Houseboat     4  2200 X
8     721 Cannons Lane      St. Matthews   KY  40211 Ranch         4  1900
9     2900 Carlingford Drive Louisville    KY  40203 Ranch         4  1900 X
10    316 Clark Station Road St. Matthews  KY  40211 Ranch         3  1800 X
11    3210 Leith Lane       Louisville     KY  40211 Condo         3  1400
12    2548 Saratoga Road    Louisville     KY  40206 Cape Cod      3  1789 X
13    4711 Hurstbourne Lane Louisville     KY  40204 Colonial      4  2000 X
14
15
```

Works has rearranged the real estate database so that the entries in the ST field are alphabetized in ascending order.

Sorting for the second time

The first time you select the Sort Records… command, Works will automatically enter the name of the first field in the current database in the 1st Field text box. You can override this default simply by entering a new field name in this text box.

The Sort Records dialog box always "remembers" its most recent Sort settings. In other words, whenever you reselect the Sort Records… command, Works will display the Sort Records dialog box with all the settings you established the last time you sorted the database. For this reason, if you want to re-sort a database using the current settings, merely select the Sort Records… command from the

Select menu, and press [Enter] or choose <OK>. Because Works remembers your most recent Sort settings, it is easy to re-sort a database after you've added a few new records.

Of course, you can easily edit the Sort Records dialog box settings each time you issue the Sort Records... command. Each time the Sort Records dialog box appears, Works automatically extends the cursor to select the current 1st Field entry. You can replace the entry as you would any other selected text simply by typing a new entry. If you have entries in the 2nd Field or 3rd Field text boxes, Works will automatically highlight those entries when you move to those boxes.

For example, suppose you want to sort the real estate database into ascending order by square feet. That is, you want the records with the lowest SqFt field entries to appear at the top of the database and the records with the highest SqFt entries to appear near the bottom. To begin, select the Sort Records... command from the Select menu. When the Sort Records dialog box appears, the previous 1st Field entry, *ST*, will be highlighted. To replace that entry, type *SqFt*. Since you want to sort the entries in the SqFt field into ascending order, you don't need to change the default 1st Field sort order, Ascend. Figure 16-5 shows the completed dialog box. Finally, choose <OK> or press [Enter] to execute the sort. Works will then sort the records so that the entries in the SqFt field appear in ascending order, as shown in Figure 16-6 on the following page.

Figure 16-5

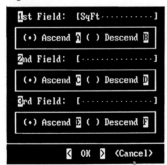

This Sort Records dialog box tells Works to sort the database into ascending order based on the entries in the SqFt field.

Works' default sort order is Ascend. If the field contains numbers, the entries will be arranged so that the smallest numbers come first (large negative numbers first, then small negative numbers, then zero, then small positive numbers, and then large positive numbers). If the field contains text, the entries will be sorted into alphabetical order. Entries in the field that begin with a blank space will appear before entries that begin with a letter

Sort order

Figure 16-6

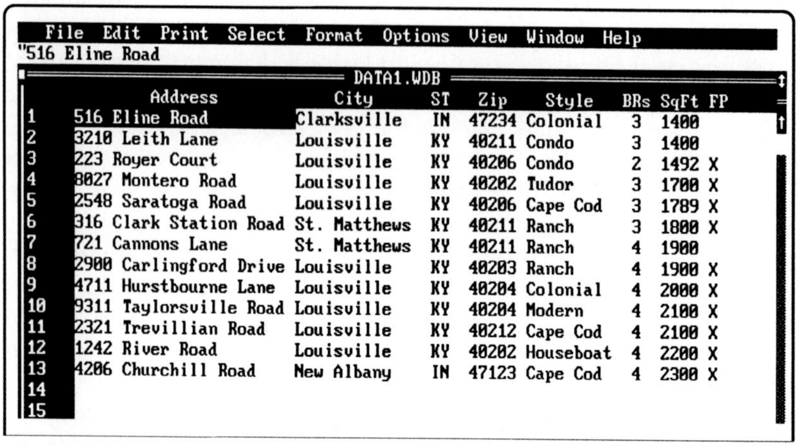

```
  File  Edit  Print  Select  Format  Options  View  Window  Help
"516 Eline Road
══════════════════════════ DATA1.WDB ══════════════════════════
              Address          City        ST   Zip   Style      BRs SqFt FP
1    516 Eline Road          Clarksville   IN  47234 Colonial     3  1400
2    3210 Leith Lane         Louisville    KY  40211 Condo        3  1400
3    223 Royer Court         Louisville    KY  40206 Condo        2  1492 X
4    8027 Montero Road       Louisville    KY  40202 Tudor        3  1700 X
5    2548 Saratoga Road      Louisville    KY  40206 Cape Cod     3  1789 X
6    316 Clark Station Road  St. Matthews  KY  40211 Ranch        3  1800 X
7    721 Cannons Lane        St. Matthews  KY  40211 Ranch        4  1900
8    2900 Carlingford Drive  Louisville    KY  40203 Ranch        4  1900 X
9    4711 Hurstbourne Lane   Louisville    KY  40204 Colonial     4  2000 X
10   9311 Taylorsville Road  Louisville    KY  40204 Modern       4  2100 X
11   2321 Trevillian Road    Louisville    KY  40212 Cape Cod     4  2100 X
12   1242 River Road         Louisville    KY  40202 Houseboat    4  2200 X
13   4206 Churchill Road     New Albany    IN  47123 Cape Cod     4  2300 X
14
15
```

Works has rearranged the real estate database so that the entries in the SqFt field are in ascending order.

If the field contains mixed entries (such as addresses that contain both numbers and text), Works will place entries that begin with a number ahead of entries that begin with a letter. Works will place the entries that begin with the characters

   ! " # $ % & ' ( ) * + , - . /

ahead of any entries that begin with numbers. Works will place entries that begin with the characters

   : ; < > = ? @

after entries that begin with numbers but *before* entries that begin with letters. Any entries that begin with a special character other than those specified above will appear after alphabetic entries in the sorted database. If the sorted database contains records with no entry in the sort field, those records will appear last.

If two or more entries in the sort field begin with the same character, Works will use the second character in those entries to arrange them. If two or more entries begin with the same two characters, Works will use the third character, then the fourth, and so on, to arrange the entries. If two or more entries in the sort field are identical, those entries will appear next to one another in the sorted database.

Works also allows you to sort your database into descending order. You can specify descending sort order for a field by choosing Descend in the Sort Records dialog box. When you do, Works will sort the records in the database so that the entries in that field are in descending order. If the field contains numbers, the entries will be arranged so that the largest numbers come first. If the field contains text, the entries will be sorted into reverse alphabetical order. If the field contains any blank entries, those entries will appear first.

Suppose you want to sort the example real estate database so that the houses are listed from largest to smallest—that is, so that the entries in the SqFt field appear in descending order. To begin, select the Sort Records... command from the Select menu. When the Sort Records dialog box appears, you'll see that the field name *SqFt* remains in the 1st Field text box. Since this is the field you want to sort, you don't need to change this setting. All you have to do is choose the Descend option below the 1st Field text box. Finally, choose <OK> or press [Enter] to execute the sort. As you can see in Figure 16-7, the database is now sorted so that the entries in the SqFt field are arranged in descending order.

Figure 16-7

	Address	City	ST	Zip	Style	BRs	SqFt	FP
File Edit Print Select Format Options View Window Help
"4206 Churchill Road
DATA1.WDB
1	4206 Churchill Road	New Albany	IN	47123	Cape Cod	4	2300	X
2	1242 River Road	Louisville	KY	40202	Houseboat	4	2200	X
3	9311 Taylorsville Road	Louisville	KY	40204	Modern	4	2100	X
4	2321 Trevillian Road	Louisville	KY	40212	Cape Cod	4	2100	X
5	4711 Hurstbourne Lane	Louisville	KY	40204	Colonial	4	2000	X
6	721 Cannons Lane	St. Matthews	KY	40211	Ranch	4	1900	
7	2900 Carlingford Drive	Louisville	KY	40203	Ranch	4	1900	X
8	316 Clark Station Road	St. Matthews	KY	40211	Ranch	3	1800	X
9	2540 Saratoga Road	Louisville	KY	40206	Cape Cod	3	1789	X
10	8027 Montero Road	Louisville	KY	40202	Tudor	3	1700	X
11	223 Royer Court	Louisville	KY	40206	Condo	2	1492	X
12	516 Eline Road	Clarksville	IN	47234	Colonial	3	1400	
13	3210 Leith Lane	Louisville	KY	40211	Condo	3	1400	
14								
15								

Works has rearranged the real estate database so that the entries in the SqFt field are in descending order.

Multiple sort fields

So far, we've shown what happens when you sort a database using only one sort field: Works rearranges the records based on the entries in the single sort field you specify. As we have said, if two or more records have identical entries in the sort field, Works will place those records next to each other in the sorted database. If there are a number of records with identical entries in the sort field, the sorted database will appear to be "grouped" on those records. For example, if you sort a telephone book database on the Last Name field, the sorted database will probably contain several groups of records with the same Last Name field entry: *Smith, Jones, Williams,* and so on.

To make a grouped database easier to use, you may want to sort the records within each group on some other field. For instance, you might want to sort each of the Last Name groups in the telephone book database into order by first name. That way, the listings in each group would be arranged by first name: *Alice Smith* would come before *Fred Smith*, who would precede *Grant Smith*, and so on.

To achieve this effect, you need to define a second sort field before you sort the database. In the Sort Records dialog box, enter the name of the first sort field in the 1st Field text box and choose a sort order for that field. Then, enter the name of the second sort field in the 2nd Field text box and choose a sort order for that field. When you've specified the name and sort order for both sort fields, choose <OK> or press [Enter] to sort the database. Works will use the first sort field to arrange the records in the database into the order you've specified. If there are any records that have the same entry in the first sort field, Works will group those records in the sorted database and will use the second sort field to arrange the records in that group.

In some cases, you may even want to specify three sort fields so that records with the same entry in both the first and second fields will appear in a logical order. For instance, if you were planning to sort a telephone book database, you might want to specify the Middle Initial field as the third sort field. That way, any records with identical entries in both the First Name and Last Name fields will be arranged by the entries in the Middle Initial field.

To sort with three sort fields, first select the Sort Records… command from the Select menu, enter the name of the first sort field in the 1st Field text box, then choose a sort order for that field; enter the name of the second sort field in the 2nd Field text box, then choose a sort order for that field; finally, enter the name of the third sort field in the 3rd Field text box, then choose a sort order for that field. When you've specified the name and sort order for the three sort fields, choose <OK> or press [Enter] to sort the database. Works will use the first sort field to arrange the records in the database in the order you've specified. If there are any records that have the same entry in the first sort field, Works will group those records in the sorted database and will use the second sort field to arrange the records in the group. If there are any records that have the same entry in both the first and second sort fields, Works will group those records in the sorted database and will use the third sort field to arrange the records within that group.

A two-field sort

Let's look at an example of a two-field sort. In the first example, we sorted the real estate listings database using only one sort field: ST. This created two state field groups: one for records with the ST field entry *IN* and one for records with the entry *KY*. Suppose you want the database to be sorted so that the listings in each state group are arranged alphabetically by city. To do this, you would specify the City field as your second field.

To begin, select the Sort Records… command from the Select menu. When the Sort Records dialog box appears, the previous 1st Field entry, SqFt, will be highlighted. To replace that entry, type *ST*. Then, choose the Ascend option below the 1st Field text box. Next, move the cursor to the 2nd Field text box, and enter the field name *City*. By default, the sort order for the 2nd Field should be set to Ascend. Figure 16-8 shows the completed dialog box. Finally, choose <OK> or press [Enter] to execute the sort. When you do this, Works will sort the records so that the entries in the ST field appear in ascending order. Works will group any records that have the same entry in the ST field and will use the City field to arrange the records in each group. Figure 16-9 shows the result.

Figure 16-8

1st Field: [ST·············]
(•) Ascend A ( ) Descend B
2nd Field: [City···········]
(•) Ascend C ( ) Descend D
3rd Field: [···············]
(•) Ascend E ( ) Descend F
< OK > <Cancel>

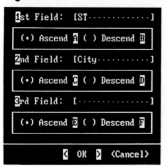

This Sort Records dialog box tells Works to use ST as the primary sort field and City as the secondary sort field.

Figure 16-9

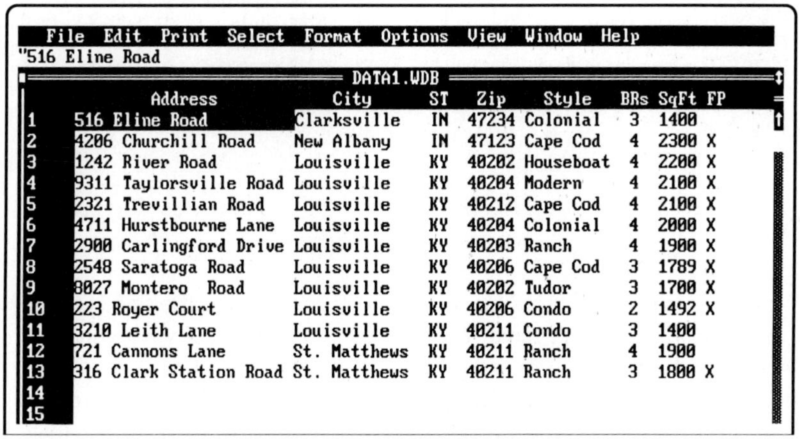

File Edit Print Select Format Options View Window Help
"516 Eline Road
DATA1.WDB
Address City ST Zip Style BRs SqFt FP
1 516 Eline Road Clarksville IN 47234 Colonial 3 1400
2 4206 Churchill Road New Albany IN 47123 Cape Cod 4 2300 X
3 1242 River Road Louisville KY 40202 Houseboat 4 2200 X
4 9311 Taylorsville Road Louisville KY 40204 Modern 4 2100 X
5 2321 Trevillian Road Louisville KY 40212 Cape Cod 4 2100 X
6 4711 Hurstbourne Lane Louisville KY 40204 Colonial 4 2000 X
7 2900 Carlingford Drive Louisville KY 40203 Ranch 4 1900 X
8 2548 Saratoga Road Louisville KY 40206 Cape Cod 3 1789 X
9 8027 Montero Road Louisville KY 40202 Tudor 3 1700 X
10 223 Royer Court Louisville KY 40206 Condo 2 1492 X
11 3210 Leith Lane Louisville KY 40211 Condo 3 1400
12 721 Cannons Lane St. Matthews KY 40211 Ranch 4 1900
13 316 Clark Station Road St. Matthews KY 40211 Ranch 3 1800 X
14
15

The entries in the ST field appear in ascending order, while those in the City field arrange the records within each ST field group.

A three-field sort

Now, let's sort the database using three sort fields. Sorting on a third field helps organize records that have identical entries in both the first and second sort fields. As you can see in Figure 16-9, there are several records that have the entry *KY* in

the ST field and the entry *Louisville* in the City field. These records are grouped together in the sorted database. By adding a third sort field, Zip, you can further arrange these duplicate records.

As before, begin by selecting the Sort Records… command from the Select menu. Since the dialog box retains your prior settings, the 1st Field and 2nd Field text boxes will contain the field names *ST* and *City*. You should not alter those settings. Instead, move the cursor to the 3rd Field text box and enter the field name *Zip*. Since we want to sort the entries in this field into ascending order, we don't have to change the default 3rd Field order setting, Ascend. Finally, execute the sort by choosing <OK> or by pressing [Enter]. When you do this, Works will sort the real estate database records by ST, City, then Zip fields, as shown in Figure 16-10.

Figure 16-10

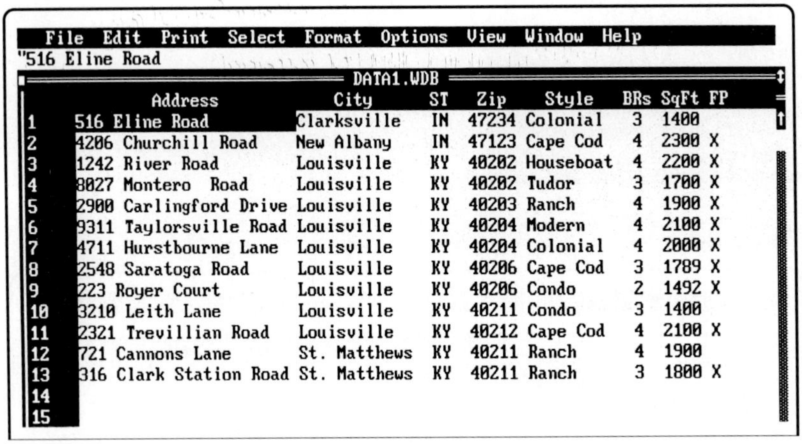

```
 File  Edit  Print  Select  Format  Options  View  Window  Help
"516 Eline Road
══════════════════════════ DATA1.WDB ═══════════════════════════
            Address              City       ST   Zip   Style     BRs SqFt FP
 1   516 Eline Road           Clarksville   IN  47234 Colonial    3  1400
 2   4206 Churchill Road      New Albany    IN  47123 Cape Cod    4  2300 X
 3   1242 River Road          Louisville    KY  40202 Houseboat   4  2200 X
 4   8027 Montero  Road       Louisville    KY  40202 Tudor       3  1700 X
 5   2900 Carlingford Drive   Louisville    KY  40203 Ranch       4  1900 X
 6   9311 Taylorsville Road   Louisville    KY  40204 Modern      4  2100 X
 7   4711 Hurstbourne Lane    Louisville    KY  40204 Colonial    4  2000 X
 8   2548 Saratoga Road       Louisville    KY  40206 Cape Cod    3  1789 X
 9   223 Royer Court          Louisville    KY  40206 Condo       2  1492 X
10   3210 Leith Lane          Louisville    KY  40211 Condo       3  1400
11   2321 Trevillian Road     Louisville    KY  40212 Cape Cod    4  2100 X
12   721 Cannons Lane         St. Matthews  KY  40211 Ranch       4  1900
13   316 Clark Station Road   St. Matthews  KY  40211 Ranch       3  1800 X
14
15
```

Works has sorted the records in the real estate database so that the entries in each ST and City group are arranged by Zip code.

Sort order and multi-field sorts

While you will usually choose the same sort order for the first, second, and third sort fields, you don't have to do so. For instance, if you were sorting a telephone book database, you would probably use ascending order for the first sort field (Last Name), the second sort field (First Name), and the third sort field (Middle Initial). On the other hand, if you were sorting a real estate listings database, you might sort by using the Style field as the first sort field and Price as the second sort field. In that case, you might choose to arrange the entries in the Style field in ascending order and the entries in the Price field into either ascending or descending order.

There is another way to sort a Works database. When you create a report for a database, you can ask Works to group that report on one or more fields. As Works prints a grouped report, it sorts the database on the grouping fields. We'll cover reports in Chapter 17.

The Search... command, which is found on the Select menu in both the Form view and the List view, allows you to search through a database for a particular entry. This command—which is similar to the Search... command on the Select menu in the spreadsheet environment—moves the highlight directly to the first entry in a database that matches the search string you specify.

The main use of the Search... command in databases is to find the record that contains the information for a particular person, place, or thing. For instance, you could use this command to find the record for a friend named *Dave* in a telephone book database.

►When you choose the Search... command, Works will display a Search dialog box like the one shown in Figure 16-11. When the dialog box appears, type the string or value you want Works to locate in the Search For text box and choose either Next Record or All Records from the Match option box. (These options are new in Works 2.) Then, to begin the search, press [Enter] or choose <OK>. When you do this, Works will begin searching the cells of the database for the string you have specified, beginning at the position of the cursor. (If you want to begin searching from the top of the database, you should press [Ctrl][Home] to reposition the highlight before you select the Search... command.)

The Search dialog box in Works 1 included a Search By option box with two options—Rows or Columns—that let you define the order of the search. These options have been eliminated in Works 2.◄

Figure 16-11

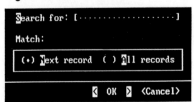

The Search... command lets you find any entry in a database.

Works searches for a match to the search string in the values and labels in the cells of the database, and in the results of formulas—not in the formulas themselves. Works will find any occurrence of the string in the database, including strings that are embedded in a longer entry. For example, if you search for the string *Louis*, Works will match it to the entries *Louis* and *Louisville*. The locale and capitalization of the search string do not matter. For example, the search string *test* will match the entries *test*, *TEST*, *Test*, and so on. The search string *TEST* will match the same entries.

If you highlight a portion of a database before you select the Search...
command, Works will search the highlighted cells only. You can use this
technique to search for an entry in one field of a database. All you need to do
is highlight the column you want to search, select the Search... command, specify
the search string, then press [Enter] or choose <OK> to begin the search.

**The Next
Record option**
►WORKS 2◄

►If you choose the Next Record option in the Match option box, when Works
finds a string that matches the search string you have specified, it will position the
highlight on the cell that contains the string. If Works does not find a matching
entry before it reaches the last entry in the database, it will loop back to the
beginning of the database and continue the search. If Works cannot find a match
to the search string in the database, it will display an alert box containing the
message *No match found*.

For example, suppose you want to find the first record in the database that
has the Style field entry *Cape Cod*. To begin, press [Ctrl][Home] to move the
highlight to the top of the database. Then, select the Search... command from the
Select menu and type the string you want to search for: *Cape Cod*. Since you want
to use the Next Record option, which is the default, you don't need to make a
selection in the Match option box. Now, press [Enter] or choose <OK> to begin
the search. Works will position the highlight on the first occurrence of the string
Cape Cod, as shown in Figure 16-12. ◄

Figure 16-12

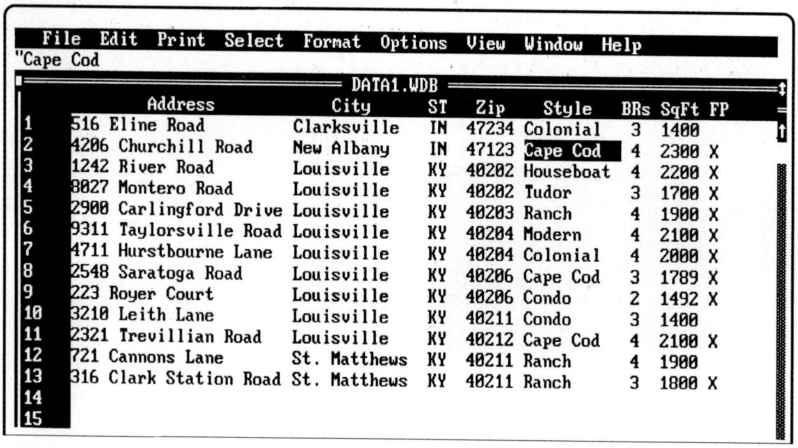

```
 File  Edit  Print  Select  Format  Options  View  Window  Help
"Cape Cod
                       ══════ DATA1.WDB ═══════
            Address          City       ST   Zip    Style      BRs SqFt FP
 1   516 Eline Road          Clarksville  IN  47234 Colonial     3  1400
 2   4206 Churchill Road     New Albany   IN  47123 Cape Cod     4  2300 X
 3   1242 River Road         Louisville   KY  40202 Houseboat    4  2200 X
 4   8027 Montero Road       Louisville   KY  40202 Tudor        3  1700 X
 5   2900 Carlingford Drive  Louisville   KY  40203 Ranch        4  1900 X
 6   9311 Taylorsville Road  Louisville   KY  40204 Modern       4  2100 X
 7   4711 Hurstbourne Lane   Louisville   KY  40204 Colonial     4  2000 X
 8   2548 Saratoga Road      Louisville   KY  40206 Cape Cod     3  1789 X
 9   223 Royer Court         Louisville   KY  40206 Condo        2  1492 X
10   3210 Leith Lane         Louisville   KY  40211 Condo        3  1400
11   2321 Trevillian Road    Louisville   KY  40212 Cape Cod     4  2100 X
12   721 Cannons Lane        St. Matthews KY  40211 Ranch        4  1900
13   316 Clark Station Road  St. Matthews KY  40211 Ranch        3  1800 X
14
15
```

*If you choose the Next Record option, Works will position the highlight
on the cell that contains a match of the search string.*

Once Works has located the first string that matches the search string you have specified, you can use the [Repeat Search] key ([F7]) to search for the next occurrence of the string. Pressing [Repeat Search] after you've used the Search... command to define a search string will move the highlight from its current location to the next cell that contains a matching entry.

The [Repeat Search] key has another application. If the Search For text box in the Search dialog box is empty, pressing the [Repeat Search] key will move the highlight from empty cell to empty cell in the database. If you have already specified a search string, you'll have to delete that string from the Search For text box before you can use the [Repeat Search] key in this way.

▶If you choose the All Records option in the Match option box, Works will display only those records that match the entry and hide all others.

For example, suppose you want to find all the records that have the Style field entry *Cape Cod*. To begin, press [Ctrl][Home] to move the highlight to the top of the database. Then, select the Search... command and type the string you want to search for: *Cape Cod*. Next, choose the All Records option and then press [Enter] or choose <OK> to begin the search. Works will hide all the records that do not contain entries that match the search string you defined, and will position the highlight on the first occurrence of the string *Cape Cod*, as shown in Figure 16-13. ◀

The [Repeat Search] key

The All Records option
▶WORKS 2◀

Figure 16-13

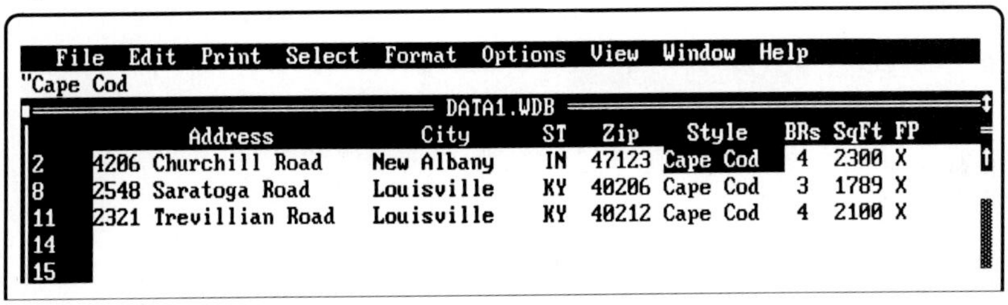

```
 File  Edit  Print  Select  Format  Options  View  Window  Help
"Cape Cod
                        ══════ DATA1.WDB ══════
             Address        City      ST   Zip    Style    BRs SqFt FP
2    4206 Churchill Road  New Albany  IN  47123 Cape Cod   4   2300 X
8    2548 Saratoga Road   Louisville  KY  40206 Cape Cod   3   1789 X
11   2321 Trevillian Road Louisville  KY  40212 Cape Cod   4   2100 X
14
15
```

If you choose the All Records option in the Match option box, Works will display only those records that contain a matching entry.

Queries are tools that allow you to select specific records from a database. In essence, queries let you ask questions about the data in your database. For example, you might use a query to select all the records in a telephone book database that have the entry *Jones* in the Last Name field, or to select all the records in a real estate database for houses of a particular type (such as Cape Cod) or a particular price (such as $85,000). You can use queries to select records that have an entry in a field that is greater than or less than a certain amount. For instance, you could use a query to select all the records in a real estate database for houses

USING QUERIES

that cost more than $100,000 or that have been on the market for less than six months. You can even use queries to select records that meet more than one condition. For example, you can use a query to select the records in a real estate database for houses with three bedrooms and two bathrooms.

We'll begin this section by covering some of the basics of querying. Then, we'll look at a simple example of an exact-match query. After that, we'll move on to some of the more complex rules and procedures for querying and show examples of several kinds of criteria. Along the way, we'll offer tips that you can apply to your own queries.

Query basics
▶WORKS 2◀

▶To define a query, select the Query command from the View menu in either the Form view or the List view. (In Works 1, you defined a query by selecting the Define command from the Query menu. This command no longer exists in Works 2.)◀ When you do this, Works will display a query form that looks just like the data entry form for the database, except that the word *QUERY* will appear on the status line. For instance, Figure 16-14 shows a query form for our sample real estate listings database.

Figure 16-14

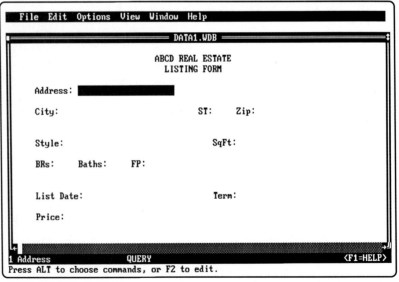

Query forms allow you to define queries that select specific records.

Once this form is in view, you may enter selection conditions, called criteria, into one or more fields in the query form. These criteria tell Works which records you want it to select. ▶When you have finished defining the query, select either the Form or the List command from the View menu, or press [F10]. If you were in the Form view when you began defining the query, then only the Form command on the View menu will be available. Similarly, if you were in the Form view when you began defining the query, pressing [F10] will return you to the Form view. As you might expect, if you were in the List view when you began defining the query, then only the List command on the View menu will be available. Similarly, if you were in the List view when you began defining the query, pressing [F10] will return you to the List view. (In Works 1, you exited from a query form by selecting the Exit Query command from the Edit menu.)◀

▶WORKS 2◀

When you leave the query form, Works will automatically process the query, comparing the entries in each record to the criteria you've specified. When the database comes back into view, Works will display only those records that match the criteria you have defined. Any record whose data doesn't match your criteria will be hidden from view.

If the query you have defined does not select any records, Works will display an alert box that contains the message *No match found*. When you choose <OK> to acknowledge the message, Works will bring the database back into view. All the records then will be in view.

Let's consider a simple example that shows how you might use a query to extract information from a database. Suppose you want to buy a Cape Cod style house. You can set up a query that asks Works to select all the houses in the real estate database that have the entry *Cape Cod* in the Style field. To do this, first select the Query command from the View menu. Works will then display the query form shown in Figure 16-14. Now, move the cursor to the Style field, type *Cape Cod*, and press [Enter] to lock in this criterion. Figure 16-15 on the next page shows the completed query form. Next, press [F10] to leave the Query form and execute the query. The query form will disappear and, in its place, Works will display just those records that have the Style field entry *Cape Cod*. Figure 16-16 on the following page shows the list of selected records.

A simple example

The Select menu offers four commands that allow you to manipulate the record list you've created with a query: Show All Records, Apply Query, Switch Hidden Records, and Hide Record.

The Select menu

The Show All Records command does just what you would expect. When you select this command, Works will show all records in the database, including those that were previously hidden. For example, if you were to select this command after processing the query shown in Figure 16-15, Works would bring all the records in the database back into view. The result would look like Figure 16-12.

Figure 16-15

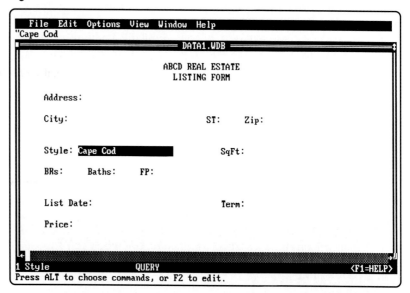

This query tells Works to select those records that have the Style field entry Cape Cod.

Figure 16-16

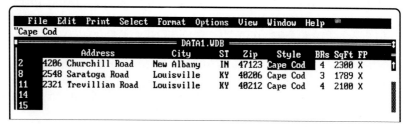

When you apply the query to the real estate database, Works will select and display only those records that have the entry Cape Cod *in the Style field.*

The Apply Query command allows you to reapply a query to a database after you have redisplayed all the records. When you select this command, Works will apply the most recently defined query to the database, displaying those records that are selected by the query and hiding those that are not. For example, if you selected this command after processing the query shown in Figure 16-15 and then selecting the Show All Records command, Works would reapply the query. The result would look just like Figure 16-16.

The Switch Hidden Records command lets you exchange the records currently visible on the screen with the records that are currently hidden. In other words, the Switch Hidden Records command lets you toggle between the records that were selected by the query and those that were not. You might think of the Switch Hidden Records command as a "not equal to" command, since it allows you to see a list of all records that *do not* match your current query. For example, if you select this command when the records shown in Figure 16-16 are in view, Works will hide these records and display those that were previously hidden. Figure 16-17 shows the result. If you select this command again, Works will switch the records again, and the database will look like Figure 16-16 again.

Figure 16-17

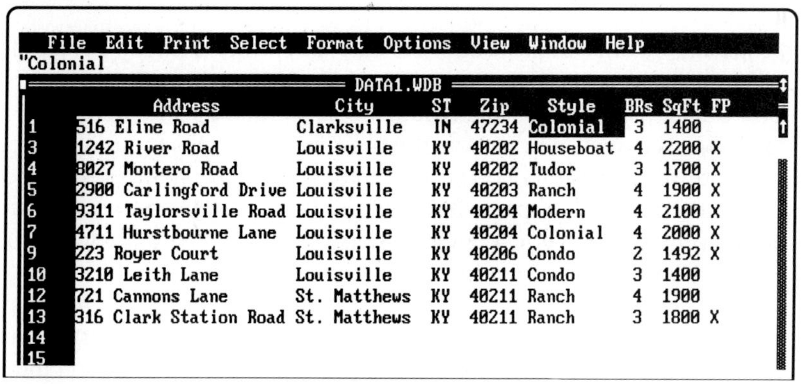

```
 File   Edit   Print   Select   Format   Options   View   Window   Help
"Colonial
========================= DATA1.WDB =========================
          Address            City        ST   Zip    Style    BRs SqFt FP
1  516 Eline Road         Clarksville    IN  47234 Colonial    3  1400
3  1242 River Road        Louisville     KY  40202 Houseboat   4  2200 X
4  8027 Montero Road      Louisville     KY  40202 Tudor       3  1700 X
5  2900 Carlingford Drive Louisville     KY  40203 Ranch       4  1900 X
6  9311 Taylorsville Road Louisville     KY  40204 Modern      4  2100 X
7  4711 Hurstbourne Lane  Louisville     KY  40204 Colonial    4  2000 X
9  223 Royer Court        Louisville     KY  40206 Condo       2  1492 X
10 3210 Leith Lane        Louisville     KY  40211 Condo       3  1400
12 721 Cannons Lane       St. Matthews   KY  40211 Ranch       4  1900
13 316 Clark Station Road St. Matthews   KY  40211 Ranch       3  1800 X
14
15
```

The Switch Hidden Records command hides the records that were previously in view and displays the records that were previously hidden.

The Hide Record command lets you hide records without using a query. To do this, first highlight the record(s) to be hidden by extending the cursor to cover at least one field in every record that you want to hide. Next, select the Hide Record command from the Select menu. When you do this, Works will hide the records you've selected. You can bring them back into view by selecting either Show All Records or Switch Hidden Records.

Working with query forms

As you've seen, the query form is the tool you use to ask Works questions about a database. By entering criteria into the individual fields of the query form, you tell Works what to look for and in which fields to look.

To enter a new criterion into a query form, simply move the cursor to the field on which you want to base your query, then type the criterion. Works will automatically enter the Edit mode as you begin typing, and the message line will display the message *Edit formula*. The characters you type will appear on the formula line until you press [Enter] to lock in the criteria. Instead of pressing [Enter] to lock in your entry, you can cancel it by pressing [Esc].

Capitalization.   Capitalization is not important in criteria. You can enter any criterion in either uppercase, lowercase, or mixed form without changing the records that will be selected by that criterion. For example, suppose you want to select all the records from the real estate database for houses that are located in Louisville—that is, records that have the entry *Louisville* in the City field. To make this selection, you could enter *Louisville, LOUISVILLE*, or *louisville* into the City field of the query form. Any of these criteria will cause Works to find each record with the City field entry *Louisville*.

Editing criteria.   Works offers a couple of ways to change a criterion entry. First, you can easily replace one criterion with another by moving the cursor to the appropriate field in the query form, typing the new criterion, and pressing [Enter]. Works will then automatically remove the old criterion from the formula line, and replace it with the characters you've just entered. If you should decide not to change the criterion, simply press [Esc] before locking in the new criterion.

Alternatively, you can edit a criterion entry just as you would edit any other entry. For example, if you've made a typographical error in a criterion entry, you may want to correct the error by editing the criterion instead of replacing it completely. To edit a criterion, move the cursor to the field in the query form that contains the criterion you want to edit, then press the [Edit] key ([F2] on the IBM PC). When you do this, Works will bring the criterion entry into the formula line and place an underline cursor after the last character in the entry. At that point, you can edit the entry just as you would edit any other entry. Once you've made your changes, press [Enter] to lock in the corrected criterion. You can press [Esc] to cancel the editing process at any time prior to locking in the new text.

Clearing criteria entries.   There may be times when you need to clear criteria entries from a query form. Works provides two commands on the Edit menu— Clear and Delete Query—that allow you to do this. The Clear command lets you clear a criterion from only one field of a query form. To use this command, first use the Query command to activate the query form. Then, move the cursor to the field that contains the criterion you want to delete, and select the Clear command. Works will remove the criterion, leaving the field blank.

The Clear command comes in handy when you need to delete only a single criterion from a form. For example, suppose you have created a query form with three criteria. You now want to alter the query so that only two of the criteria are active. To do this, you could use the Clear command to erase the third criterion from the form.

Of course, you can also clear an entry from a field in a query form by positioning the cursor on that field, pressing either the [Backspace] key or the [Delete] key, then pressing [Enter]. In either case, the results will be identical to using the Clear command: Works will erase the criterion, leaving the field blank.

The Delete Query command allows you to erase the criteria from every field of the query form. You'll use this command most often when you have finished working with one query and want to begin defining a new query. To use this command, first use the Query command to activate the query form. Then, select Delete Query from the Edit menu. When you do this, Works will remove every entry from all the fields of the query form.

Notes

Although you can query a Works database from either the Form view or the List view, you'll probably find that querying in the List view is more efficient. The basic results are the same in both views: Only the records that match your criteria will be visible. However, in the Form view, Works will display the selected records one at a time in the query form. This makes it hard to get a feeling for which records have been selected. (Works will, however, display an indicator at the bottom of the screen in the form X/Y, where X is the number of records that have been selected and Y is the total number of records in the database.) On the other hand, in the List view Works allows you to see up to 18 matching records on the screen at once. This gives you a much better picture of the query results.

Each time you process a query, Works compares the criteria against the entire database, including both hidden and visible records. If any visible records don't match, they will be hidden. Similarly, if any hidden records do match the new criteria, they will be made visible again. This means that if you execute two or more queries successively, the results will not be cumulative.

Once you have defined a query for a database, Works will remember the criteria you have defined. The next time you select the Query command, the previous set of criteria will appear in the query form. Because Works does not clear your criteria from the query form, you can easily modify an existing query and re-execute it.

Once you've processed a query, you can print reports, but they will include only the visible records. As far as the Print… and Print Report… commands are concerned, the database contains only the records that currently are in view. We'll cover the Print… and Print Report… commands in Chapter 17.

If you press [F10] or select the Form or List command while the query form is empty, Works will simply bring the database back into view. All the records will be in view.

A warning about hidden records

You should use caution when performing extended cursor operations if only part of the records in a database are in view. Records that are hidden from view maintain their record number and can be moved, copied, cleared, or deleted without being present on the screen. If you extend the cursor in the List view, and the extended cursor crosses the position of a hidden record, that hidden record will be included in the selection. Even though you cannot see it highlighted, any command you execute will affect it, as well as the visible records. If you choose the Clear command after selecting a range that includes hidden records, both the visible records and the hidden records will be deleted.

Querying with wildcards

Works will allow you to use the DOS wildcard characters ? and * in your criteria. Wildcard characters take their name from their counterparts in card games. In card games, a wildcard can be used in place of any other card. Likewise, a wildcard in a criterion can be used to match any character. The ? wildcard can be used in a criterion to represent any single character. For example, the criterion entry *Sm?th* would match both *Smith* and *Smyth.* The * wildcard can take the place of any number of characters. For example, the criterion entry *Sm** would match *Smith, Smothers, Smog,* and any other entry beginning with the letters *sm.* Clearly, wildcards add a considerable amount of flexibility to your Works queries.

You can use wildcards only in criteria for a field that contains text entries. Whenever you use a wildcard character in a criterion, Works will consider that criterion to be a text entry. If you try to use a wildcard in a criterion for a field that contains numeric data—such as the Price field in our example database—the query will not work properly.

The * wildcard

As we've mentioned, the * wildcard can be used to match any number of characters. Let's suppose you want to select from the real estate database all the houses located on Hurstbourne Lane. Since the Address field entry in each record begins with a different street number, you can't perform an exact-match query using *Hurstbourne Lane* alone as your criterion. However, if you insert the * wildcard at the beginning of the criterion entry, Works will select all records whose Address field begins with any characters and ends with *Hurstbourne Lane.*

To define this query, first select the Query command from the View menu to display the query form. Then, choose the Delete command from the Edit menu to delete any existing criteria. Next, enter the criterion **Hurstbourne Lane* in the Address field. Figure 16-18 shows the completed query form. When you press [F10], Works will display the single record shown in Figure 16-19.

The * wildcard matches any number of characters, including no characters at all. For example, the criterion *Smith** would match the entries *Smithers, Smithson,* and *Smith.* Notice that the * matches no characters at all in the last matching entry.

You can use the * wildcard at any position in a criterion—beginning, middle, or end. Furthermore, the * wildcard may be used more than once in a single criterion. For example, suppose you want to select the record for the one house in your database on Leith Lane, but you're not sure of the address or whether Leith is a lane or a drive. Since you're uncertain of the address, you can use wildcards to find if the house is listed in your database. Just enter the criterion **Leith ** in the Address field of the query form.

Figure 16-18

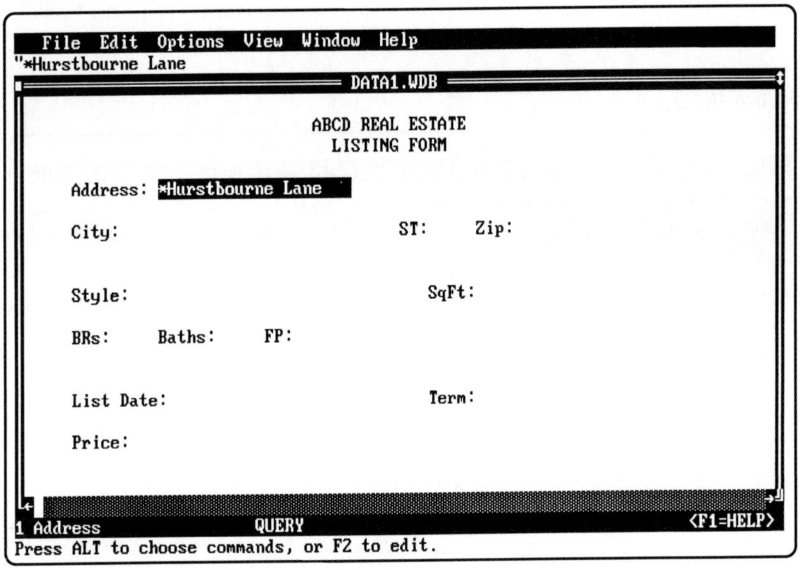

```
 File  Edit  Options  View  Window  Help
"*Hurstbourne Lane
┌─────────────────────── DATA1.WDB ───────────────────────┐
│                                                          │
│                    ABCD REAL ESTATE                      │
│                    LISTING FORM                          │
│                                                          │
│         Address: ▓Hurstbourne Lane                       │
│                                                          │
│         City:                    ST:      Zip:           │
│                                                          │
│                                                          │
│         Style:                   SqFt:                   │
│                                                          │
│         BRs:     Baths:    FP:                           │
│                                                          │
│                                                          │
│         List Date:               Term:                   │
│                                                          │
│         Price:                                           │
│                                                          │
│                                                          │
└──────────────────────────────────────────────────────────┘
1 Address                QUERY                      <F1=HELP>
Press ALT to choose commands, or F2 to edit.
```

*This query uses the * wildcard character.*

Figure 16-19

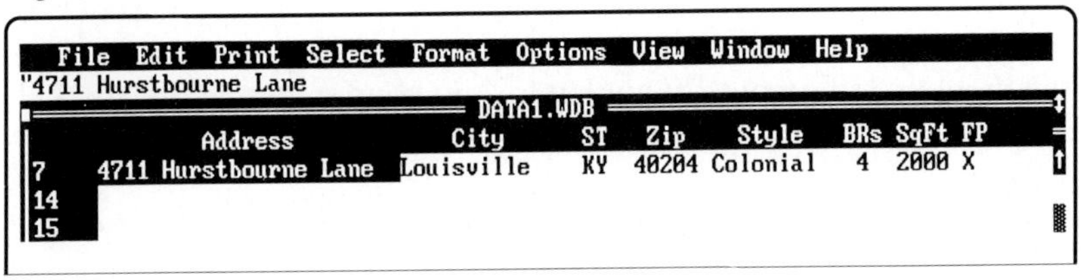

```
 File  Edit  Print  Select  Format  Options  View  Window  Help
"4711 Hurstbourne Lane
┌──────────────────────── DATA1.WDB ────────────────────────┐
│          Address          City      ST  Zip   Style   BRs SqFt FP │
│7   4711 Hurstbourne Lane Louisville KY  40204 Colonial  4  2000 X │
│14                                                         │
│15                                                         │
```

*Works has selected only the record with an Address field entry that
ends with the characters Hurstbourne Lane.*

Of course, when you use one or more wildcards in a query, you may select
some unwanted records. You may need to refine your query by experimenting
with different combinations of wildcards and other characters until you find the
record(s) you're looking for.

Unlike the * operator, the ? wildcard takes the place of only one character in   **The ? wildcard**
a criterion. For example, suppose you want to find the record for the house with
the address on Leith Lane, but you're not sure whether Leith is spelled Leith or
Lieth. To define this query, first select the Query command from the View menu
to display the query form. Then, choose the Delete command from the Edit menu

to delete any existing criteria. Next, move the cursor to the Address field and enter the criterion *L??th * Notice that this criterion uses both the * and the ? wildcards. When you press [F10], Works will display the records shown in Figure 16-20.

Figure 16-20

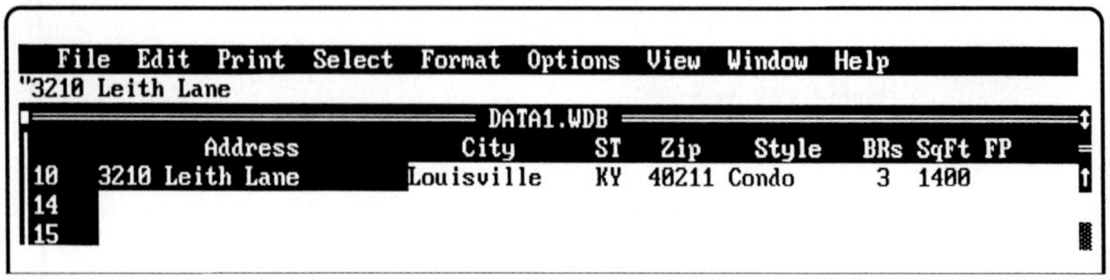

```
  File  Edit  Print  Select  Format  Options  View  Window  Help
"3210 Leith Lane
┌──────────────────────── DATA1.WDB ════════════════════════╗
│              Address            City      ST   Zip    Style    BRs SqFt FP │
│ 10   3210 Leith Lane        Louisville  KY  40211 Condo      3  1400   │
│ 14                                                                       │
│ 15                                                                       │
```

The ? wildcard takes the place of only one character in a criterion.

Numeric queries

As you might expect, you can define queries that use numeric criteria. To do this, simply enter the value you want to match into the appropriate field of the query form. Once you've entered the numeric criterion, select the Form or List command from the View menu or press the [F10] key to return to the database and process the query. When you do this, Works will display only those records with entries in the specified field that exactly match your criteria.

For example, suppose you want to select all the houses with three bedrooms from the real estate database. To do this, select the Query command from the View menu. When Works displays the query form, select the Delete command from the Edit menu to clear any existing criteria. Next, move the cursor to the BRs field, type the number 3, then press [Enter] to lock in your entry. Figure 16-21 shows the completed query form. To execute the query, press [F10]. Figure 16-22 shows the result.

If the numbers you are trying to match include decimals, you should use a decimal point in your criteria. If the numbers you are trying to match have been formatted to include dollar signs ($), commas, or other special symbols, you may omit or include those characters—it's up to you. For example, the criterion *$250,000.00* is functionally identical to the criterion *250000*. If you want, you can enter a number on the query form in exponential form. For example, you could use the criterion *1E6* instead of *1600000*.

Querying date and time values

If your database includes fields that contain date or time entries, you can use date or time criterion to query that database. To create a date criterion, you simply enter a date value into the appropriate field in the query form. You can enter a date or time criterion in any format Works recognizes: mm/dd/yy, mmm dd, yyyy, and so on. For example, you could enter the date April 4, 1990, as Apr 4, 1990 or 4/4/90 or even 32967 (the serial date value for April 4, 1990). If you omit a term from a date, Works will supply the value of that term from the current date to complete the entry. For example, if today is April 4, 1990, and you enter the criterion 8/11, Works will assume you mean the date August 11, 1990. When you press [Enter] to lock in a date criterion, Works will convert it into the format that you've specified for the field.

Figure 16-21

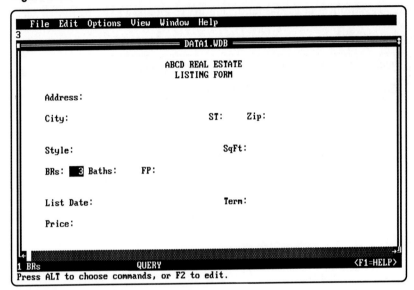

Numeric queries select records that have a particular value in a particular field.

Figure 16-22

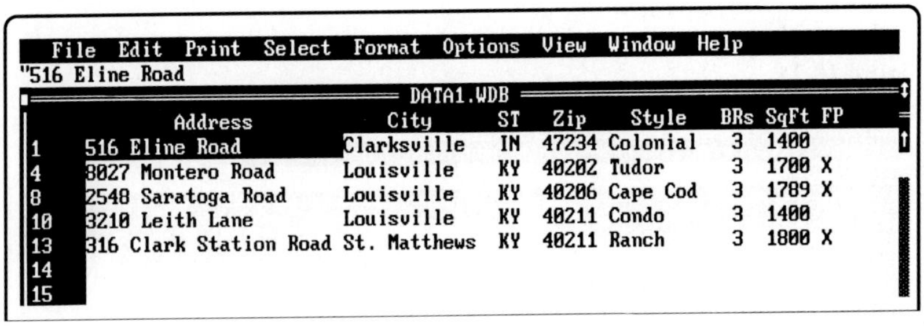

Works has selected every record that has the entry 3 in the BRs field.

For example, suppose you want to find any houses listed on August 12, 1988, in the real estate database. That is, you want to find all of the records that have the entry Aug 12, 1990, in the List Date field. To do this, first select the Query command from the View menu to display the query form. Then, choose the Delete command from the Edit menu to delete any existing criteria. Next, move the cursor to the List Date field, type the criterion 8/12/90 and press [Enter] to lock it in. Since we've formatted this field to display the date in mmm dd, yyyy form, the criterion entry will appear as *Aug 12, 1990* in the query form, as shown in Figure 16-23. When you press [F10], Works will display only the record that has the date entry Aug 12, 1990, in the List Date field. Figure 16-24 shows the result.

Figure 16-23

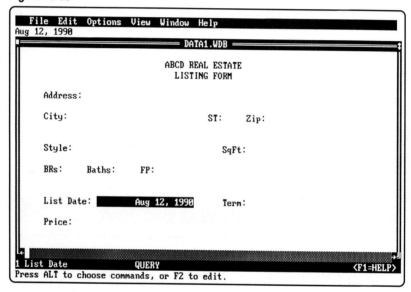

Works automatically displays date criteria in the format you have assigned to the field you are querying.

Figure 16-24

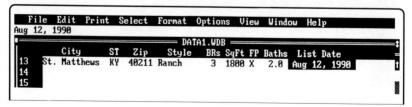

Works has selected just the records with the List Date entry Aug 12, 1990.

As we have said, you can also create time criteria. To create a time criterion, simply enter a time value into the appropriate field in the query form. You can enter a time criterion in any format that Works recognizes: hh:mm:ss AM/PM, hh:mm:ss (24 hour), and so on. For example, you could enter the time 2:15 PM as 2:15 PM; 14:15; 14:15:00; or even .59375 (the serial time value for 2:15 PM). If you omit the seconds portion from a time, Works will assume that the seconds portion is 0. When you press [Enter] to lock in a time criterion, Works will convert it into the format that you've specified for the field.

So far, we've shown how you can create exact-match numeric queries: queries that select records containing a specific value in a given field. Works also will allow you to define queries that select records with entries in a given field that fall within a range. For example, you can locate all the records in the real estate database with a Price field entry that is greater than $70,000 or all the records with a List Date field entry that is less than (before) July 4, 1988. In fact, you will probably use this kind of query more often than you will use exact-match criteria for fields that contain numbers.

Querying with range operators

To create a query that selects values within a given range, use Works' range operators. Table 16-1 summarizes the four range operators.

Table 16-1

Operator	Meaning
>	Greater than
>=	Greater than or equal to
<	Less than
<=	Less than or equal to

The range operators let you select records with entries that fall within a range.

Let's look at an example of how you might use each of these operators. Suppose you want to find all of the houses in the real estate database that have more than three bedrooms; that is, you want to find the records with an entry greater than 3 in the BRs field. To make this selection, first select the Query command from the View menu to activate the query form. Then, choose the Delete command from the Edit menu to delete any existing criteria. Now, move the cursor to the BRs field, type >3, and press [Enter]. Figure 16-25 on the following page shows the completed query form. Finally, press [F10] to process the query. Figure 16-26 shows the resulting database. As you can see, the database displays just those records with an entry greater than 3 in the BRs field.

Figure 16-25

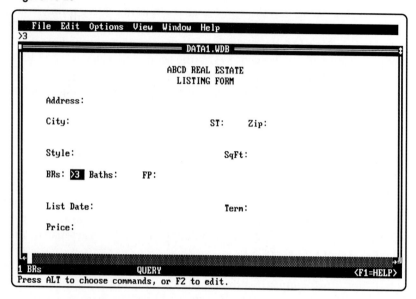

Range operators let you select records that have a value in a field that falls in a range you define.

Figure 16-26

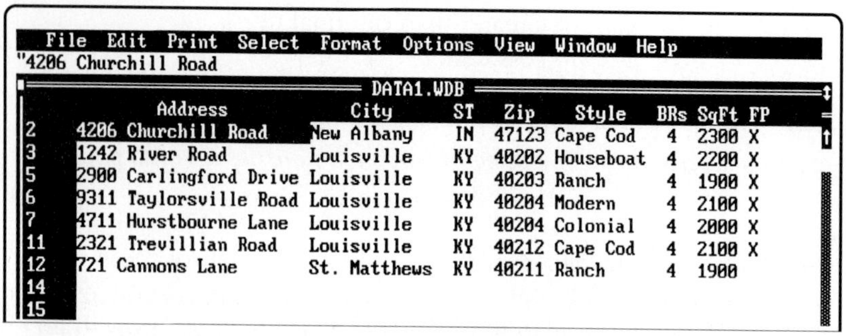

	Address	City	ST	Zip	Style	BRs	SqFt	FP
2	4206 Churchill Road	New Albany	IN	47123	Cape Cod	4	2300	X
3	1242 River Road	Louisville	KY	40202	Houseboat	4	2200	X
5	2900 Carlingford Drive	Louisville	KY	40203	Ranch	4	1900	X
6	9311 Taylorsville Road	Louisville	KY	40204	Modern	4	2100	X
7	4711 Hurstbourne Lane	Louisville	KY	40204	Colonial	4	2000	X
11	2321 Trevillian Road	Louisville	KY	40212	Cape Cod	4	2100	X
12	721 Cannons Lane	St. Matthews	KY	40211	Ranch	4	1900	
14								
15								

Works has selected the records with BRs field entries greater than 3.

Notice that no houses with exactly three bedrooms appear in the database in Figure 16-26. If you decide that you really want to consider houses that have at least three bedrooms—that is, three or more bedrooms—then you can alter the query so that it uses the greater than or equal to operator (>=) rather than the greater than operator. To begin, select the Query command to activate the query form. Next, move the cursor to the BRs field (it should already be there), and use the [Edit] key ([F2]) to change the BRs field entry to >=3, then press [Enter] to lock in your entry. (Instead of editing the existing entry, you could just type the new entry, >=3.) Finally, press [F10] to apply the query. When you do this, Works will display each record with an entry greater than or equal to 3 in the BRs field, as shown in Figure 16-27.

Figure 16-27

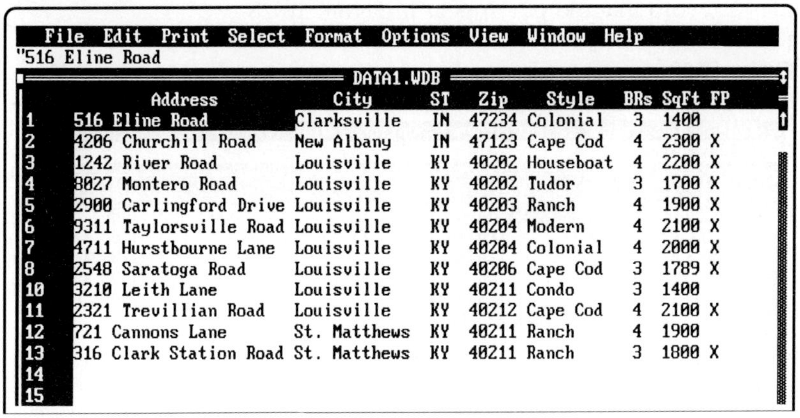

```
 File  Edit  Print  Select  Format  Options  View  Window  Help
"516 Eline Road
                            ══ DATA1.WDB ══
              Address          City      ST   Zip   Style    BRs SqFt FP
 1    516 Eline Road        Clarksville  IN  47234 Colonial   3  1400
 2    4206 Churchill Road   New Albany   IN  47123 Cape Cod   4  2300 X
 3    1242 River Road       Louisville   KY  40202 Houseboat  4  2200 X
 4    8027 Montero Road     Louisville   KY  40202 Tudor      3  1700 X
 5    2900 Carlingford Drive Louisville  KY  40203 Ranch      4  1900 X
 6    9311 Taylorsville Road Louisville  KY  40204 Modern     4  2100 X
 7    4711 Hurstbourne Lane Louisville   KY  40204 Colonial   4  2000 X
 8    2548 Saratoga Road    Louisville   KY  40206 Cape Cod   3  1789 X
10    3210 Leith Lane       Louisville   KY  40211 Condo      3  1400
11    2321 Trevillian Road  Louisville   KY  40212 Cape Cod   4  2100 X
12    721 Cannons Lane      St. Matthews KY  40211 Ranch      4  1900
13    316 Clark Station Road St. Matthews KY 40211 Ranch      3  1800 X
14
15
```

Works has selected only the records with a BRs field entry greater than or equal to 3.

You can use the less than operator (<) to select all records with an entry in a given field that is less than a given value. For example, suppose you want to query the real estate database for homes with less than 1800 square feet. As usual, begin by selecting the Query command to activate the query form. Then, select the Delete command from the Edit menu to clear all existing criteria. Next, move the cursor to the SqFt field, type *<1800*, and press [Enter]. Finally, press [F10] to apply the query. When you do this, Works will display each record with an entry less than 1800 in the SqFt field, as shown in Figure 16-28.

Figure 16-28

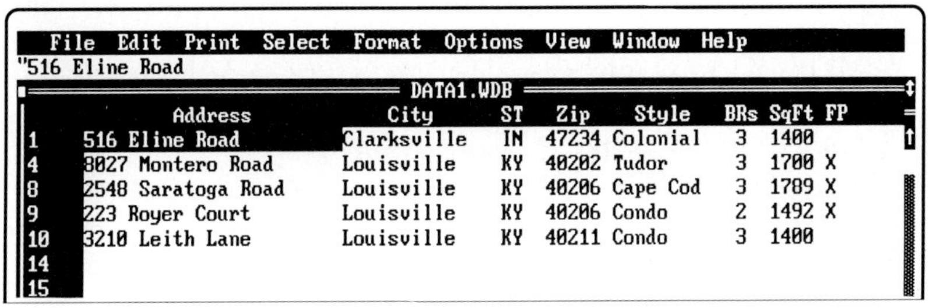

```
 File  Edit  Print  Select  Format  Options  View  Window  Help
"516 Eline Road
                            ══ DATA1.WDB ══
              Address          City      ST   Zip   Style    BRs SqFt FP
 1    516 Eline Road        Clarksville  IN  47234 Colonial   3  1400
 4    8027 Montero Road     Louisville   KY  40202 Tudor      3  1700 X
 8    2548 Saratoga Road    Louisville   KY  40206 Cape Cod   3  1789 X
 9    223 Royer Court       Louisville   KY  40206 Condo      2  1492 X
10    3210 Leith Lane       Louisville   KY  40211 Condo      3  1400
14
15
```

Works has selected the records with a SqFt field entry less than 1800.

If you're interested in listing houses that have 1800 square feet or less, you'll need to use the less than or equal to operator (<=). To define this query, select the Query command to activate the query form. Next, move the cursor to the SqFt field, type <=1800, then press [Enter]. When you press [F10] to apply the query, Works will display the records shown in Figure 16-29. As you can see, this listing includes a record that did not appear in Figure 16-28.

Figure 16-29

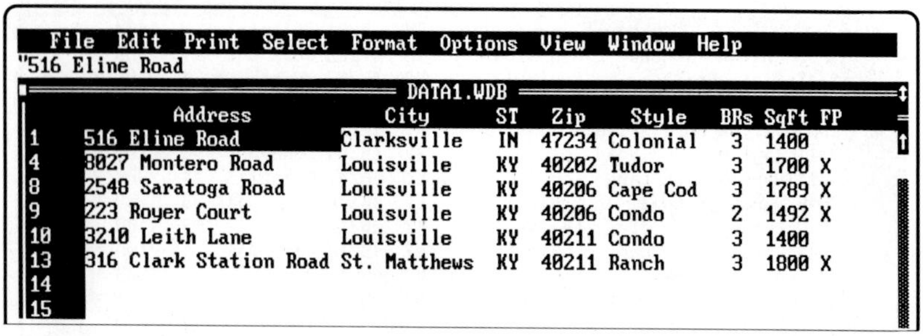

```
┌───────────────────────────────────────────────────────────────────┐
│   File  Edit  Print  Select  Format  Options  View  Window  Help    │
│ "516 Eline Road                                                     │
│ ┌════════════════════════════ DATA1.WDB ═════════════════════════╗  │
│ ║        Address          City        ST   Zip    Style   BRs SqFt FP│
│ ║1   516 Eline Road      Clarksville  IN  47234 Colonial   3  1400  ↕│
│ ║4   8027 Montero Road   Louisville   KY  40202 Tudor      3  1700 X │
│ ║8   2548 Saratoga Road  Louisville   KY  40206 Cape Cod   3  1789 X │
│ ║9   223 Royer Court     Louisville   KY  40206 Condo      2  1492 X │
│ ║10  3210 Leith Lane     Louisville   KY  40211 Condo      3  1400   │
│ ║13  816 Clark Station Road St. Matthews KY 40211 Ranch    3  1800 X │
│ ║14                                                                 ║│
│ ║15                                                                 ║│
│ ╚═══════════════════════════════════════════════════════════════════│
└───────────────────────────────────────────────────────────────────┘
```

Works has selected just the records with a SqFt field entry less than or equal to 1800.

Using range operators with dates and times.   You can also use Works' range operators to query for date and time values. However, when you create range criteria for date and time values, you must use the DATE() or TIME() function to represent the date or time in the criteria. If you use only a formatted date or time value as part of a range expression, Works will not select any records when you apply the query. For instance, the criterion *>=DATE(90,4,4)* will match any date entry greater (after) or equal to April 4, 1988. On the other hand, the criterion *>=4/4/90* will not select any records.

To see how date range criteria work, suppose you want to select every record that has a date after July 4, 1990 in the List Date field. To create this query, select the Query command to activate the query form. Then, select the Delete command to clear all existing criteria. Next, move the cursor to the List Date field, enter the criterion *>DATE(90,7,4)*, and then press [Enter]. Figure 16-30 shows the finished query form. Finally, press [F10] to apply the query. Works will now display each record with an entry greater than July 4, 1990, in the List Date field, as shown in Figure 16-31.

As we have said, you can use Works' range operators to query for time values. When you create range criteria for time values, you must use the function TIME()—and not a formatted time value—to represent the time in the criteria. For instance, the criterion *>=TIME(13,00,00)* will match any time entry that is greater than (after) or equal to 1 PM. But, the criterion *>13:00:00* will not select any records. For more on the DATE() and TIME() functions, see Chapter 10.

Figure 16-30

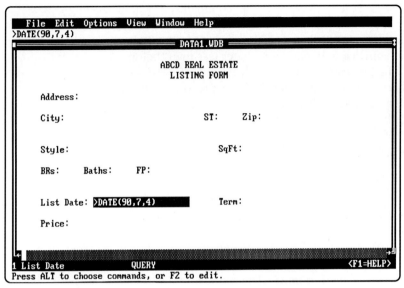

File Edit Options View Window Help
>DATE(90,7,4)
DATA1.WDB
ABCD REAL ESTATE
LISTING FORM
Address:
City:
ST:
Zip:
Style:
SqFt:
BRs:
Baths:
FP:
List Date: >DATE(90,7,4)
Term:
Price:
1 List Date
QUERY
<F1=HELP>
Press ALT to choose commands, or F2 to edit.

Using range operators with DATE() functions lets you select records that have date entries in a field that fall in a range you specify.

Figure 16-31

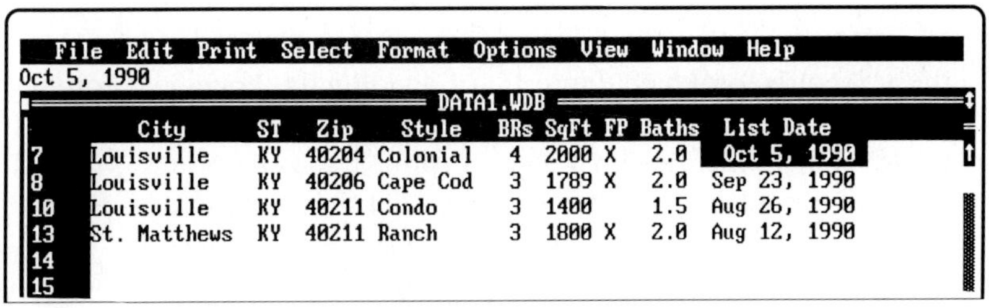

File Edit Print Select Format Options View Window Help
Oct 5, 1990
DATA1.WDB
City ST Zip Style BRs SqFt FP Baths List Date
7 Louisville KY 40204 Colonial 4 2000 X 2.0 Oct 5, 1990
8 Louisville KY 40206 Cape Cod 3 1789 X 2.0 Sep 23, 1990
10 Louisville KY 40211 Condo 3 1400 1.5 Aug 26, 1990
13 St. Matthews KY 40211 Ranch 3 1800 X 2.0 Aug 12, 1990
14
15

Works has selected just the records that have an entry greater than (after) July 4, 1990, in the List Date field.

Using range operators in alphabetic fields. You can even use range operators to set up a criterion for fields that contain alphabetic entries. For example, suppose you are the registrar for a university, and you need to send out notices to all incoming students, instructing them when to register for classes. You decide to divide this list of students into two groups based on last names and assign a different registration time to each group. To do this, you can construct a query that selects all records in which the entry in the Last Name field begins with *A* through *L*. Then, you can construct another query that selects all records in which the entry in the Last Name field begins with the letters *M* through *Z*.

To begin, you would select the Query command to activate the query form. Then, you would select the Delete command to clear all existing criteria. Next, you would move the cursor to the Last Name field and type <*"M*, and press [Enter]. When you press [F10] to apply the query, Works will show all the records with Last Name entries that begin with a letter less than (before) M.

When you are ready to view the records for the rest of the students, you could modify the query and change the expression in the Last Name field to >=*"M*. Instead of creating a new query, however, you could use the Switch Hidden Records command from the View menu. When you issue this command, Works will hide the records that are currently visible and display the records that are currently hidden.

Calculated criteria

You can also define criteria that tell Works to perform a mathematical operation using the values in one or more numeric fields of the database, then use the result of that mathematical operation as a criterion. This type of criterion is called a calculated criterion.

The formula that defines a calculated criterion is called a "field formula." You can use any of the mathematical operators presented in Chapter 7 (+, -, /, *, and ^) to define a field formula. The formula refers to the fields in the database by name and can appear in any field of the query form. However, the field formula is likely to be shorter and simpler if you enter it into one of the fields you're using in the calculation, since there's no need to state the name of the field that contains the formula in the formula.

For example, you could use a calculated criterion to find all of the houses in the real estate database that have a price per square foot of less than $40; that is, to find those records for which the result of dividing the Price field entry by the SqFt field entry is less than 40. You could enter this criterion in the Price field, the SqFt field, or any other field in the query form. If the criterion was in the Price field, it would be =*/SqFt<40*. If it was in the SqFt field, it would be =*Price/<40*. If the criterion was in any other field, it would be =*Price/SqFt<40*.

To create this query, select the Query command to activate the query form. Then, select the Delete command to clear all existing criteria. Next, move the cursor to the Price field, enter the criterion =*/SqFt<40*, then press [Enter]. Figure 16-32 shows the finished query. Finally, press [F10] to apply the query. At this point, Works will evaluate each record in the database, dividing the number in the Price field by the number in the SqFt field. If the result is less than 40, Works will select that record. If the result of the calculation is equal to or greater than 40, Works will not select the record. Figure 16-33 shows the result.

AND and OR queries

All of the queries that we've presented so far have contained only a single criterion. Although this kind of simple query is fine in many circumstances, you're likely to encounter situations where you need to perform more precise queries.

Fortunately, Works allows you to construct queries that select records that meet several criteria simultaneously. These queries are called logical AND queries. In addition, you can construct queries that select records that meet any one of several conditional tests. This kind of query is called a logical OR query. Let's take a look at AND and OR queries.

Figure 16-32

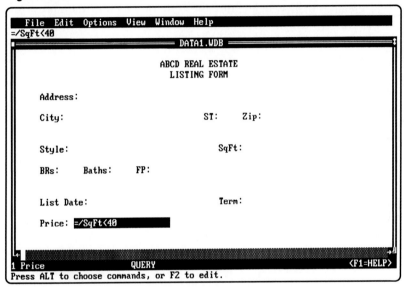

Calculated criteria tell Works to perform a mathematical operation using the values in one or more numeric fields of the database, and then use the result as a criterion.

Figure 16-33

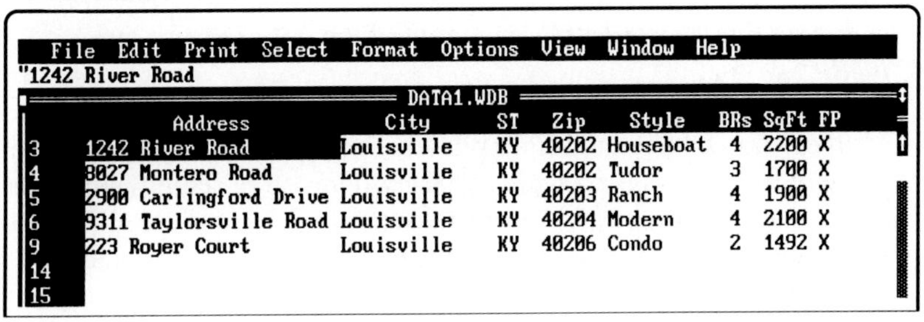

	Address	City	ST	Zip	Style	BRs	SqFt	FP
3	1242 River Road	Louisville	KY	40202	Houseboat	4	2200	X
4	8027 Montero Road	Louisville	KY	40202	Tudor	3	1700	X
5	2900 Carlingford Drive	Louisville	KY	40203	Ranch	4	1900	X
6	9311 Taylorsville Road	Louisville	KY	40204	Modern	4	2100	X
9	223 Royer Court	Louisville	KY	40206	Condo	2	1492	X
14								
15								

Works has selected only the records that have a price per square foot of less than $40.

Logical AND queries

To create a logical AND query, simply enter all criteria that define the records you want to select into the fields of a query form. When you execute this kind of query, Works will select only records that meet every criterion in every field of the form.

For example, suppose you want to find a Colonial style house that has four bedrooms. To create this query, select the Query command to activate the query form. Then, select the Delete Query command to clear all existing criteria. Next, move the cursor to the Style field, enter the criterion *Colonial*, then press [Enter]. Next, move the cursor to the BRs field, enter the criterion 4, then press [Enter]. Figure 16-34 shows the finished query form. Finally, press [F10] to apply the query. Figure 16-35 shows the result.

Figure 16-34

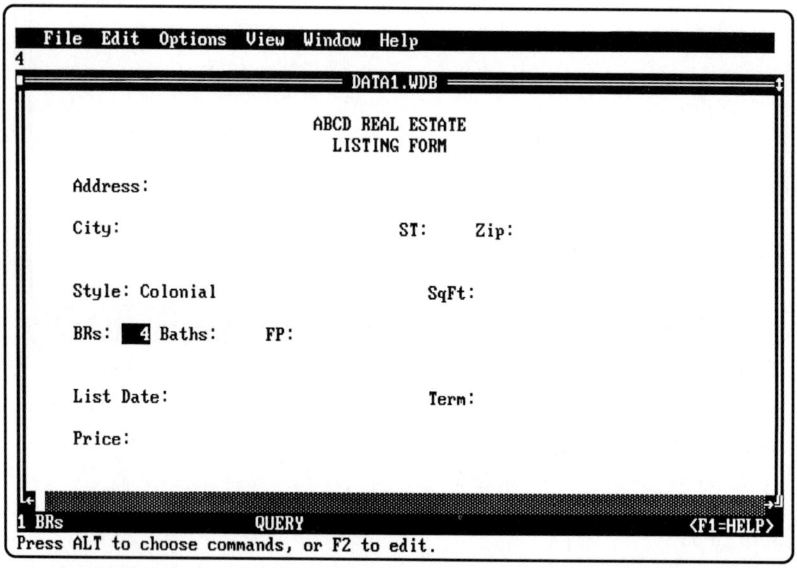

```
┌──────────────────────────────────────────────────────────────────────┐
│   File  Edit  Options  View  Window  Help                              │
│ 4                                                                      │
│ ┌──────────────────────────── DATA1.WDB ════════════════════════════╗ │
│ ║                                                                    ║ │
│ ║                         ABCD REAL ESTATE                           ║ │
│ ║                           LISTING FORM                             ║ │
│ ║                                                                    ║ │
│ ║      Address:                                                      ║ │
│ ║                                                                    ║ │
│ ║      City:                          ST:     Zip:                   ║ │
│ ║                                                                    ║ │
│ ║                                                                    ║ │
│ ║      Style: Colonial                    SqFt:                      ║ │
│ ║                                                                    ║ │
│ ║      BRs: ▮4 Baths:       FP:                                      ║ │
│ ║                                                                    ║ │
│ ║      List Date:                         Term:                      ║ │
│ ║                                                                    ║ │
│ ║      Price:                                                        ║ │
│ ║                                                                    ║ │
│ └█▀▀▀▀▀▀▀▀▀▀▀▀▀▀▀▀▀▀▀▀▀▀▀▀▀▀▀▀▀▀▀▀▀▀▀▀▀▀▀▀▀▀▀▀▀▀▀▀▀▀▀▀▀▀▀▀▀▀▀▀▀▀▀▀▀┘ │
│ 1 BRs                     QUERY                          <F1=HELP>      │
│ Press ALT to choose commands, or F2 to edit.                           │
└──────────────────────────────────────────────────────────────────────┘
```

AND queries select records that match all of the criteria you have defined.

Sometimes you will need to set up two or more conditional tests in the same field of a query form. This is particularly true when you're setting up a criterion in a numeric, date, or time field. To create two or more conditional tests in the same field, you'll use the AND operator (&). You must include the equal sign after the AND operator since Works always looks for a range operator after an AND or an OR conjunction.

Figure 16-35

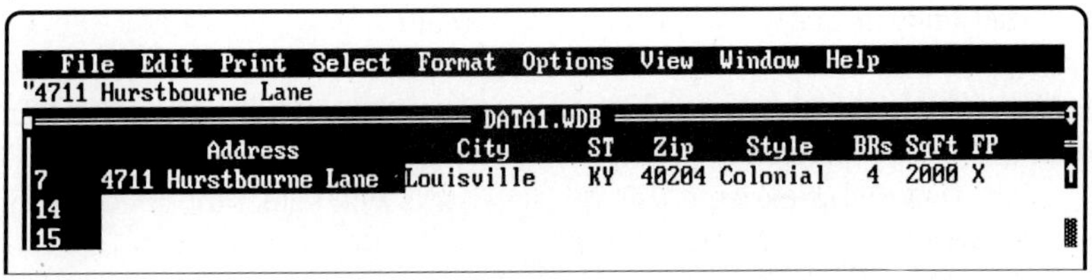

```
 File  Edit  Print  Select  Format  Options  View  Window  Help
"4711 Hurstbourne Lane
═══════════════════════════ DATA1.WDB ═══════════════════════════
            Address          City      ST   Zip    Style    BRs SqFt FP
7    4711 Hurstbourne Lane  Louisville  KY  40204 Colonial   4  2000 X
14
15
```

Works has selected only the records that have the entry Colonial *in the Style field and the entry 4 in the BRs field.*

For example, suppose you want to find a house with a price from $50,000 to $80,000; that is, you want to find the record for a house with a Price field entry greater than or equal to $50,000 and less than or equal to $80,000. To make this selection, you'll enter the criterion *>=50000&<=80000* in the Price field of the query form. Notice that this expression is simply two separate criteria joined with Works' & operator.

To create this query, select the Query command to activate the query form. Then, select the Delete command to clear all existing criteria. Next, move the cursor to the Price field, then enter the expression *>=50000&<=80000*. After you apply this query, Works will select the records shown in Figure 16-36.

Figure 16-36

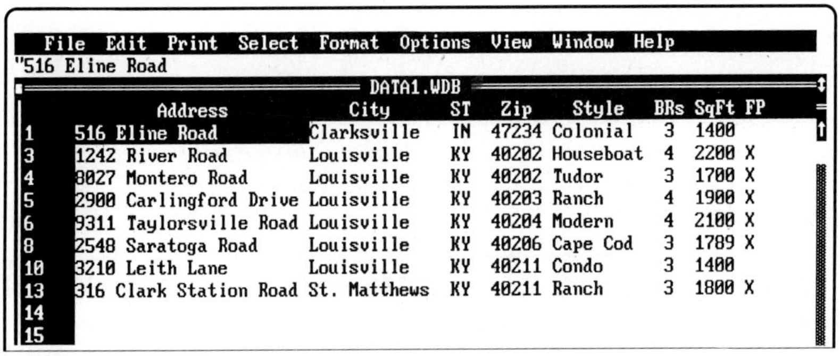

```
 File  Edit  Print  Select  Format  Options  View  Window  Help
"516 Eline Road
═══════════════════════════ DATA1.WDB ═══════════════════════════
            Address             City       ST   Zip    Style    BRs SqFt FP
1    516 Eline Road           Clarksville  IN  47234 Colonial   3  1400
3    1242 River Road          Louisville   KY  40202 Houseboat  4  2200 X
4    8027 Montero Road        Louisville   KY  40202 Tudor      3  1700 X
5    2900 Carlingford Drive   Louisville   KY  40203 Ranch      4  1900 X
6    9311 Taylorsville Road   Louisville   KY  40204 Modern     4  2100 X
8    2548 Saratoga Road       Louisville   KY  40206 Cape Cod   3  1700 X
10   3210 Leith Lane          Louisville   KY  40211 Condo      3  1400
13   316 Clark Station Road   St. Matthews KY  40211 Ranch      3  1800 X
14
15
```

Works has selected only the records that have a Price field entry greater than or equal to 50000 and less than or equal to 80000.

As we have mentioned, Works allows you to select records that meet any one of two or more conditional tests. To set up this kind of query, use Works' OR operator (|) to link two or more criteria. The criteria must refer to the field(s) you want to query by name. The criteria can appear in any field of the query form. However, if both parts of the criteria refer to the same field, you will usually want to enter the criteria into that field in the query form.

Logical OR queries

For example, suppose you want to find all houses in the real estate database that are either Colonial or Cape Cod. To create this query, select the Query command to activate the query form. Then, select the Delete command to clear all existing criteria. Next, move the cursor to the Style field and enter the expression *=Style="Colonial"|="Cape Cod"*. Figure 16-37 shows the completed query form. After you execute this query, Works will select the records shown in Figure 16-38.

Figure 16-37

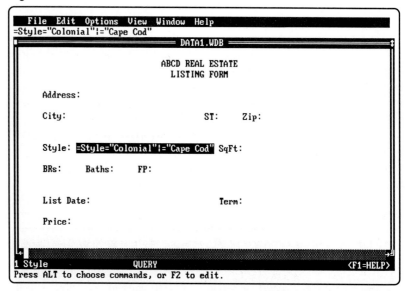

OR queries select records that match either of the criteria you define.

Figure 16-38

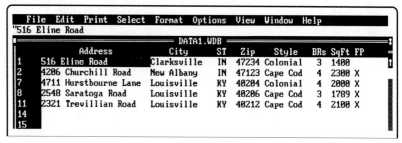

Works has selected just the records that have the entry Colonial *or the entry* Cape Cod *in the Style field.*

There are a couple of things you should notice about the criterion *=Style="Colonial"|="Cape Cod"*. Notice that this criteria refers to the Style field by name even though you entered it in the Style field. If you entered this criteria in any other field, you would have to refer to the Style field twice, like this: *=Style="Colonial"|=style="Cape Cod"*. Also notice that both conditions (*Colonial* and *Cape Cod*) in the criterion must be enclosed in quotation marks. Whenever you create an OR criterion that refers to text entries, the conditions you specify must be enclosed in quotes. If the OR criterion refers to a number field, you don't have to enclose the conditions in quotes. If the OR criterion refers to a field that contains dates or times, you have to use the functions DATE() and TIME() to represent the date or time condition.

Sometimes you'll need to set up a logical OR query in which the conditions refer to different fields. In that case, you'll need to create a query that contains two or more criteria—each of which refers to a specific field by name—linked by the OR operator (|). You can enter the criteria in any field of the query form.

For example, suppose you're interested in finding a house that's either Colonial or that has three or more bedrooms. To create this query, select the Query command to activate the query form. Then, select the Delete command to clear all existing criteria. Next, move the cursor to the Style field and enter the expression *=Style="Colonial"|BRs>=3*. When you press [F10] to apply the query, Works will select the records shown in Figure 16-39.

Figure 16-39

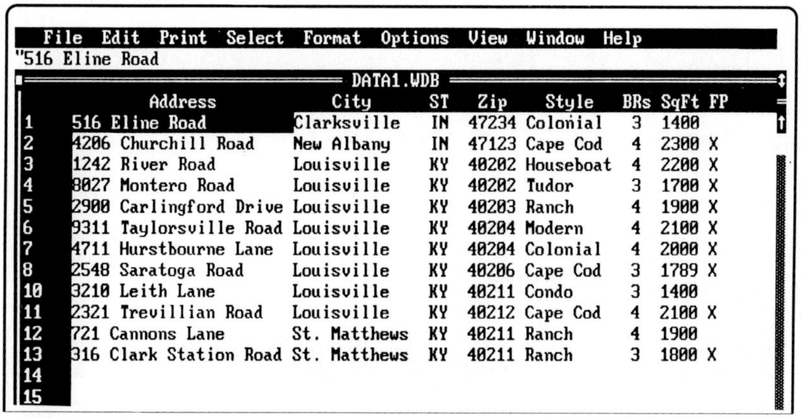

```
┌─────────────────────────────────────────────────────────────────┐
│  File  Edit  Print  Select  Format  Options  View  Window  Help  │
│ "516 Eline Road                                                   │
│ ▐════════════════════════ DATA1.WDB ════════════════════════════ │
│             Address          City        ST   Zip   Style    BRs SqFt FP│
│ 1   516 Eline Road        Clarksville   IN  47234 Colonial   3  1400    │
│ 2   4206 Churchill Road   New Albany    IN  47123 Cape Cod   4  2300 X  │
│ 3   1242 River Road       Louisville    KY  40202 Houseboat  4  2200 X  │
│ 4   8027 Montero Road     Louisville    KY  40202 Tudor      3  1700 X  │
│ 5   2900 Carlingford Drive Louisville   KY  40203 Ranch      4  1900 X  │
│ 6   9311 Taylorsville Road Louisville   KY  40204 Modern     4  2100 X  │
│ 7   4711 Hurstbourne Lane Louisville    KY  40204 Colonial   4  2000 X  │
│ 8   2548 Saratoga Road    Louisville    KY  40206 Cape Cod   3  1789 X  │
│ 10  3210 Leith Lane       Louisville    KY  40211 Condo      3  1400    │
│ 11  2321 Trevillian Road  Louisville    KY  40212 Cape Cod   4  2100 X  │
│ 12  721 Cannons Lane      St. Matthews  KY  40211 Ranch      4  1900    │
│ 13  316 Clark Station Road St. Matthews KY  40211 Ranch      3  1800 X  │
│ 14                                                                │
│ 15                                                                │
└─────────────────────────────────────────────────────────────────┘
```

Works has selected just the records that have the Style field entry Colonial *or the BRs field entry >=3.*

You can also create OR expressions that refer to more than two fields. All you have to do is create a criterion that refers to each field by name and that links them it with the OR operator.

Combining the AND and OR operators

There may be times when you need to combine AND and OR expressions in a query. To create this kind of query, you simply enter the AND and OR operators in separate fields of the query form and process the query. For example, suppose you're interested in houses that have a price below $80,000 and that have three bedrooms or have a price below $100,000 and that have four bedrooms. To create this query, first select the Query command to display the query form. Then, choose the Delete command to delete any existing criteria. Next, move the cursor to the Price field and enter the expression

=(PRICE<80000&BRs=3) | (PRICE<100000&BRs=4)

The query form should now look like Figure 16-40. Stated in English, this criterion says, "Select all records for which the Price field entry is less than 80000 and for which the BRs field entry is equal to 3, OR for which the Price field entry is less than 100000 and for which the BRs field entry is equal to 4." When you execute this query, Works will present the list shown in Figure 16-41.

Figure 16-40

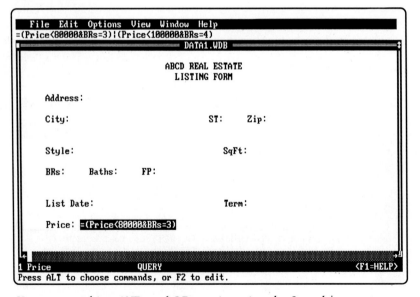

You can combine AND and OR queries using the & and | operators.

The NOT operator

In addition to & and |, Works features another logical operator: ~. This symbol is Works' NOT operator. Prefacing a criterion with this operator negates that criterion. For example, the criterion *=~Age>65* would command Works to select records whose Age field contains a value less than or equal to 65. Similarly,

the criterion *=~First Name="John"* commands Works to select records that have
an entry other than *"John* in their First Name field.

Figure 16-41

```
 File  Edit  Print  Select  Format  Options  View  Window  Help
"516 Eline Road
══════════════════════ DATA1.WDB ══════════════════════
            Address           City        ST   Zip    Style    BRs SqFt FP
1   516 Eline Road          Clarksville   IN  47234 Colonial    3  1400
2   4206 Churchill Road     New Albany    IN  47123 Cape Cod    4  2300 X
3   8027 Montero Road       Louisville    KY  40202 Tudor       3  1700 X
4   1242 River Road         Louisville    KY  40202 Houseboat   4  2200 X
5   2900 Carlingford Drive  Louisville    KY  40203 Ranch       4  1900 X
6   9311 Taylorsville Road  Louisville    KY  40204 Modern      4  2100 X
9   2548 Saratoga Road      Louisville    KY  40206 Cape Cod    3  1789 X
10  3210 Leith Lane         Louisville    KY  40211 Condo       3  1400
12  721 Cannons Lane        St. Matthews  KY  40211 Ranch       4  1900
13  316 Clark Station Road  St. Matthews  KY  40211 Ranch       3  1800 X
14
15
```

*Works has selected only the records that have a Price field entry below
$80,000 and the BRs field entry 3 or that have a Price field entry below
$100,000 and the BRs field entry 4.*

As an example of the use of this operator, suppose you want Works to select
the records from our sample database that have an entry other than KY in their
ST field. To do this, you would select the Query command from the View menu
to reveal the query form. Next, choose the Delete command from the Edit menu
to delete any existing criteria from the form. Third, type *=~ST="KY"* into any field
of the query form, then press [Enter]. Finally, press [F10] to process the query.
Figure 16-42 shows the results. As you can see, Works has selected only those
records that have an entry other than KY in their ST field.

Figure 16-42

```
 File  Edit  Print  Select  Format  Options  View  Window  Help
"516 Eline Road
══════════════════════ DATA1.WDB ══════════════════════
            Address           City        ST   Zip    Style    BRs SqFt FP
1   516 Eline Road          Clarksville   IN  47234 Colonial    3  1400
2   4206 Churchill Road     New Albany    IN  47123 Cape Cod    4  2300 X
14
15
```

Works' ~ operator negates any criterion it prefaces.

CONCLUSION

In this chapter, we've explained how to operate Works databases. We showed
you how to use the Sort Records... command to sort your databases, how to use
the Search... command to search for specific entries in a database, and how to use
queries to select records that match criteria, or selection conditions, you define.

Printing and Reporting 17

*I*n the last two chapters, we've shown you how to create a database and how to manipulate the information in a Works database. In this chapter, we'll show you how to print your databases. First, we'll demonstrate how to use the Print... command to print database documents. Then, we will introduce you to Works' powerful Report view.

SIMPLE PRINTING

The quickest way to print a database is to use the Print... command on the Print menu. This command—which is virtually identical to the Print... command in spreadsheet documents—instructs Works to print a simple listing of the records that are currently visible in a database. You can use this command to print from either the Form or List view.

To print a database, you first use the Printer Setup... command to select the printer and port you will print to. (You need to take this step only if you have not done so before or you want to change the printer or port.) Next, you use the Page Setup & Margins... command to set the margins and page dimensions. Then, use the Headers & Footers... command to set the headers and footers for the document and (if you want) the Font... command to choose the font you want to use. Finally, you select the Print... command to tell Works to print the document.

In general, the process of printing a database is just like the process of printing other documents. For more on printing, see Chapter 3.

An example

As an example of printing a database, let's print a 75-record database, named SALES.WDB, that contains sales results for a company's salespeople. Figure 17-1 shows the upper-left corner of this database. Let's assume that we've already used the Printer Setup... command to select the printer and port we will print to. Let's also assume that we'll use the default layout and fonts for the printout, so we don't need to select the Page Setup & Margins... command or the Font...

command. To begin, select the Print... command from the Print menu. When you do this, Works will display the Print dialog box shown in Figure 17-2. To print the report, make sure that the printer is turned on, then choose the <Print> option. Figure 17-3 shows the completed print-out.

Figure 17-1

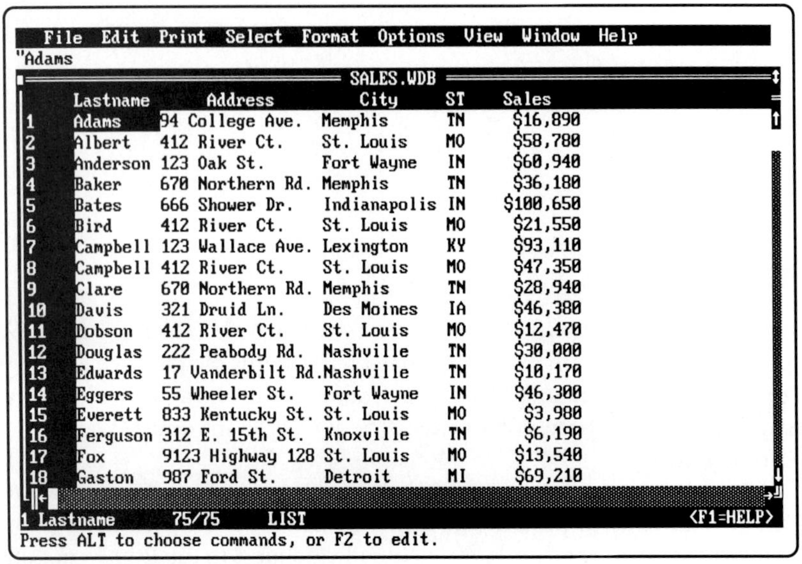

File Edit Print Select Format Options View Window Help
"Adams
SALES.WDB
Lastname Address City ST Sales
1 Adams 94 College Ave. Memphis TN $16,890
2 Albert 412 River Ct. St. Louis MO $58,780
3 Anderson 123 Oak St. Fort Wayne IN $60,940
4 Baker 670 Northern Rd. Memphis TN $36,180
5 Bates 666 Shower Dr. Indianapolis IN $100,650
6 Bird 412 River Ct. St. Louis MO $21,550
7 Campbell 123 Wallace Ave. Lexington KY $93,110
8 Campbell 412 River Ct. St. Louis MO $47,350
9 Clare 670 Northern Rd. Memphis TN $28,940
10 Davis 321 Druid Ln. Des Moines IA $46,380
11 Dobson 412 River Ct. St. Louis MO $12,470
12 Douglas 222 Peabody Rd. Nashville TN $30,000
13 Edwards 17 Vanderbilt Rd.Nashville TN $10,170
14 Eggers 55 Wheeler St. Fort Wayne IN $46,300
15 Everett 833 Kentucky St. St. Louis MO $3,980
16 Ferguson 312 E. 15th St. Knoxville TN $6,190
17 Fox 9123 Highway 128 St. Louis MO $13,540
18 Gaston 987 Ford St. Detroit MI $69,210
1 Lastname 75/75 LIST <F1=HELP>
Press ALT to choose commands, or F2 to edit.

We'll use this simple database to demonstrate the process of printing.

Figure 17-2

Number of copies: [1····]
[ ] Print specific pages
Pages: [·············]
[ ] Print to file
File name: [·············]
[ ] Print record and field labels
<Print> <Cancel>

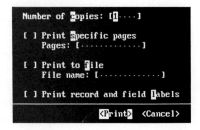

The Print... command allows you to print database documents.

How Works prints databases

Most of the time, your databases will be too long and too wide to print on a single page. In these cases, Works will divide the print-out into page-sized sections, printing as many rows and columns as possible on each page. Works uses the Page Length, Page Width, and margin settings in the Page Setup & Margins dialog box to determine how much data it can print on each page. Works will never split a field between two pages. If a field will not fit onto one page, Works will print the entire field on the next page.

Figure 17-3

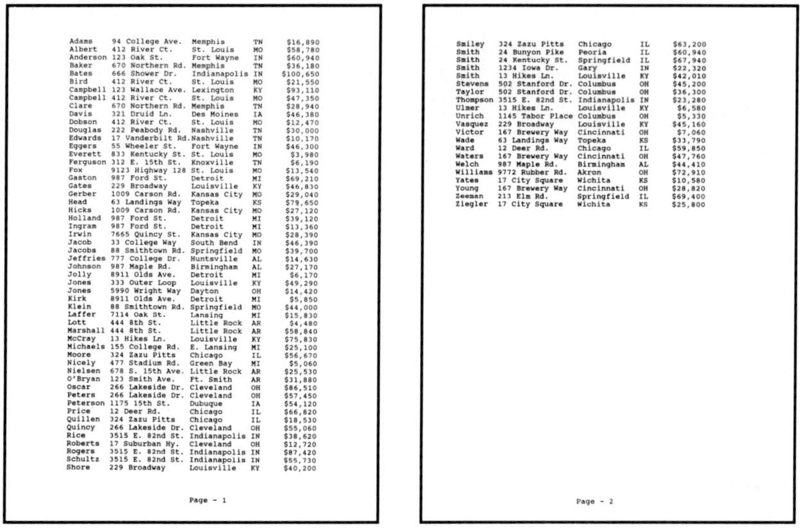

This figure shows the result of printing the database in Figure 17-1.

Works begins by printing as many records and fields as it can from the upper-left corner of the database on the first page of the report. If the database contains more records than will fit on this page, Works will print the next group of records on the second page of the report. This page will contain information from the same fields that Works printed on the first page. Works will continue in this fashion until it has printed all the information in the leftmost fields in the database. At this point, it will begin printing the next full page of fields, starting at the top of the database.

The default Margin, Page Length, and Page Width settings allow Works to print about 54 records on each page and about 60 characters per line on most printers. If you want to print more data on each page, you can increase the page width to 14 inches and print on 14-inch-wide computer paper. Alternatively, you can use the Font... command to choose a smaller font.

When Works prints a database, it prints only the records that are currently visiblep; that is, the records that are not hidden. It prints those records in the order that they appear in the database. If you want to print only selected records from a database, you must first perform a query that hides all the records except those you want to print. If you want to print the records in a certain order, you should sort the database into that order before you print. For instructions on how to query and sort a database, see Chapter 16.

**Controlling
page breaks**

The Insert Page Break command allows you to insert manual page breaks in printed databases. A manual page break in a database causes Works to skip to the top of a new page before it prints another record or to skip to a new page before it prints a marked field.

▶WORKS 2◀

▶To insert a page break into a database, position the cursor over a cell in the record or field where you want the page break to occur. Then, pull down the Print menu and select the Insert Page Break command. When you select this command, Works will present the dialog box shown in Figure 17-4. This dialog box offers you a choice of inserting a page break by record or by field. If you choose Record, Works will insert a horizontal page break in the database. The highlighted cell's record will appear at the top of a new page, and Works will enter a manual page-break marker (>>) to the right of the number of the highlighted record. If you choose Field, Works will insert a vertical page break in the database. The highlighted cell's field will appear along the left margin of a new page, and Works will enter a manual page-break marker (>>) at the left border of the field name. To remove a manual page break, highlight a cell in that record or field, pull down the Print menu, and select the Delete Page Break command.◀

Figure 17-4

You'll see this dialog box if you issue the Insert Page Break command in order to create a manual page break.

To insert a page break quickly into a database, you can highlight the entire record that you want to appear at the top of a new page or highlight the field that you want to appear along the left side of a new page. Then, pull down the Print menu and select the Insert Page Break command. When you select this command, Works will enter a manual page-break marker (>>) to the right of the number of the highlighted record or to the left of the field name. When you print the database, Works will skip to the top of a new page before it prints the marked record or to a new page before it prints the marked field. To remove a manual page break from a record, highlight that record, pull down the Print menu, and select the Delete Page Break command.

**Printing record
numbers and field
names**

You can command Works to include record numbers and field names in a printed database. To do this, just activate the Print Record and Field Labels option in the Print dialog box. When you activate this option, an X will appear to its left. Then, when you choose <Print>, Works will print the database with record numbers and field names.

For example, let's reprint our example database with record numbers and field names. To begin, select the Print… command from the Print menu. When the Print dialog box appears, choose the Print Record and Field Labels option. Then, choose <Print> to print the report with record numbers and field names. Figure 17-5 shows the first page of the printed database.

Figure 17-5

```
        Lastname     Address         City        ST   Sales
    1   Adams      94 College Ave. Memphis       TN   $16,890
    2   Albert     412 River Ct.   St. Louis     MO   $58,780
    3   Anderson   123 Oak St.     Fort Wayne    IN   $60,940
    4   Baker      670 Northern Rd. Memphis      TN   $36,180
    5   Bates      666 Shower Dr.  Indianapolis  IN   $100,650
    6   Bird       412 River Ct.   St. Louis     MO   $21,550
    7   Campbell   123 Wallace Ave. Lexington    KY   $93,110
    8   Campbell   412 River Ct.   St. Louis     MO   $47,350
    9   Clare      670 Northern Rd. Memphis      TN   $28,940
   10   Davis      321 Druid Ln.   Des Moines    IA   $46,380
   11   Dobson     412 River Ct.   St. Louis     MO   $12,470
   12   Douglas    222 Peabody Rd. Nashville     TN   $30,000
   13   Edwards    17 Vanderbilt Rd. Nashville   TN   $10,170
   14   Eggers     55 Wheeler St.  Fort Wayne    IN   $46,300
   15   Everett    833 Kentucky St. St. Louis    MO   $3,980
   16   Ferguson   312 E. 15th St. Knoxville     TN   $6,190
   17   Fox        9123 Highway 128 St. Louis    MO   $13,540
   18   Gaston     987 Ford St.    Detroit       MI   $69,210
   19   Gates      229 Broadway    Louisville    KY   $46,830
   20   Gerber     1009 Carson Rd. Kansas City   MO   $29,040
   21   Head       63 Landings Way Topeka        KS   $79,650
   22   Hicks      1009 Carson Rd. Kansas City   MO   $27,120
   23   Holland    987 Ford St.    Detroit       MI   $39,120
   24   Ingram     987 Ford St.    Detroit       MI   $13,360
   25   Irwin      7665 Quincy St. Kansas City   MO   $28,390
   26   Jacob      33 College Way  South Bend    IN   $46,390
   27   Jacobs     88 Smithtown Rd. Springfield  MO   $39,700
   28   Jeffries   777 College Dr. Huntsville    AL   $14,630
   29   Johnson    987 Maple Rd.   Birmingham    AL   $27,170
   30   Jolly      8911 Olds Ave.  Detroit       MI   $6,170
   31   Jones      333 Outer Loop  Louisville    KY   $49,290
   32   Jones      5990 Wright Way Dayton        OH   $14,420
   33   Kirk       8911 Olds Ave.  Detroit       MI   $5,850
   34   Klein      88 Smithtown Rd. Springfield  MO   $44,000
   35   Laffer     7114 Oak St.    Lansing       MI   $15,830
   36   Lott       444 8th St.     Little Rock   AR   $4,480
   37   Marshall   444 8th St.     Little Rock   AR   $58,840
   38   McCray     13 Hikes Ln.    Louisville    KY   $75,830
   39   Michaels   155 College Rd. E. Lansing    MI   $25,100
   40   Moore      324 Zazu Pitts  Chicago       IL   $56,670
   41   Nicely     477 Stadium Rd. Green Bay     MI   $5,060
   42   Nielsen    678 S. 15th Ave. Little Rock  AR   $25,530
   43   O'Bryan    123 Smith Ave.  Ft. Smith     AR   $31,880
   44   Oscar      266 Lakeside Dr. Cleveland    OH   $86,510
   45   Peters     266 Lakeside Dr. Cleveland    OH   $57,450
   46   Peterson   1175 15th St.   Dubuque       IA   $54,120
   47   Price      12 Deer Rd.     Chicago       IL   $66,820
   48   Quillen    324 Zazu Pitts  Chicago       IL   $18,530
   49   Quincy     266 Lakeside Dr. Cleveland    OH   $55,060
   50   Rice       3515 E. 82nd St. Indianapolis IN   $38,620
   51   Roberts    17 Suburban Hy. Cleveland     OH   $12,720
   52   Rogers     3515 E. 82nd St. Indianapolis IN   $87,420
   53   Schultz    3515 E. 82nd St. Indianapolis IN   $55,730

                    Page - 1
```

The Print Record and Field Labels option tells Works to include field names and record numbers in your print-out.

Alternative fonts and sizes

Unless you specify otherwise, Works will print the information from a database document in the default font and size for the printer you are using (the printer you selected in the Printer Setup dialog box). If you want, however, you can command Works to print using a different font and size. To do this, pull down the Format menu and select the Font… command to reveal a Font dialog box like the one shown in Figure 17-6 on the following page.

As you can see, this dialog box contains two list boxes. In the Fonts list box, Works lists all the fonts available for the currently selected printer. If you want to print your database in one of these fonts, simply choose it. Once you choose a font, you should choose a size from the Sizes list box. Since different fonts are available in different sizes, the choices in the Sizes list box depend on the font you selected in the Fonts list box.

Figure 17-6

The choices you make in the Font dialog box determine the font and size Works will use to print a database document.

The choices you make in the Font dialog box also affect how much information Works can print on each page. If you want to squeeze as much information as possible onto each page of your printed database, you'll probably want to choose a compact font and a small font size.

Other Print ... command options

The Print dialog box includes options that let you specify how many copies of a document you want to print, which pages you want to print, and whether you want Works to print to a file. The Number of Copies option lets you specify the number of copies Works should print. The Print Specific Pages option lets you print only specified pages of a database. The Print to File option lets you print a database to a disk file. We have explained each of these options in detail in Chapter 3.

Printing forms
►WORKS 2◄

►Works 2 lets you print records in the Form view just as they appear on the screen. To do this, press the [View Form] key ([F9]) to make sure your document is in the Form view, then select the Print... command. When you do, you will see an expanded Print dialog box like the one in Figure 17-7. The options in this dialog box allow you to control the printing of forms.

Figure 17-7

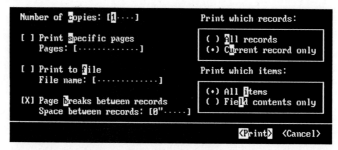

The Print dialog box for the Form view contains special options for printing the database form.

The Print which Records option box controls how many records you can print at one time. You can choose between the All Records option, which prints all the records in the database or the Current Record Only option (the default option), which prints all of the current record.

Specifying the
number of records

If you are printing more than one record, the Page Breaks between Records check box lets you print one record on each page. The default setting for this option is on, which means that Works automatically prints one record on each page. If you do turn off the option, Works allows you to print your records continuously without page breaks.

Specifying a
page break

When you turn off this option, Works lets you determine the amount of space that will appear between records on a page when you print. Simply type into the Space between Records text box the amount of space you want to insert between records. The default amount is 0". (Works will accept up to 22" as a setting in the Space between Records text box.) Only the length of your records and the space between them will determine how many records Works will fit on a page.

The Print which Items option box contains two choices that control the number of items Works will print from the database form: All Items (field labels and contents) and Field Contents Only. By default, the All Items option is activated. If you want to print only the field contents, then activate the Field Contents Only option. When you do this, Works will deselect the All Items option. When you turn on the Field Contents Only option, Works will print the fields in your form aligned exactly as they appear on the screen but without field names or labels. Therefore, if you haven't aligned the fields in your form, your field contents may appear staggered when they're printed out.

Specifying the items

Once you've set the options in the Print dialog box, choose <Print> to print your form. To cancel the printing of a form, press the [Esc] key. When you press this key, Works will display a dialog box that contains the message *Printing interrupted. Continue printing?*. If you choose <Cancel>, Works will cancel the Print... command. If you choose <OK>, however, Works will continue printing where it left off.◄

Printing

An example.   Suppose that you want to print all the forms from the SALES.WDB database in Figure 17-1. Since there are 75 records in the database, you'll want to print more than one form on a page. To do this, make sure the database appears on the screen in the Form view. (If Works is displaying the List view, press the [View Form key], [F9].) Next, select the Print... command from the Print menu. When the Print dialog box appears, choose the All Records option from the Print which Records option box. Then, turn off the Page Breaks between Records check box, and enter 2 into the Space between Records text box. You'll want to print all the items in the form, because the fields will seem randomly distributed across the form if you don't print the field names. As you can see in Figure 17-8, when you choose <Print>, Works will print three forms to a page.

Figure 17-8

```
Lastname: Adams

Address: 94 College
City: Memphis
ST: TN
Sales:        $16,890




Lastname: Albert

Address: 412 River
City: St. Louis
ST: MO
Sales:        $58,780




Lastname: Anderson

Address: 123 Oak
City: Fort Wayne
ST: IN
Sales:        $60,940




                Page - 1
```

This is the first page of a series of forms printed from the SALES.WDB database in Figure 17-1.

DATABASE REPORTING

While the Print... command offers an easy way to print your databases, it only begins to scratch the surface of Works' reporting powers. Works' powerful Report view allows you to create and print sophisticated reports from the information in your databases. You can create reports that include all or part of the fields in a database. You can create reports that are "grouped"—or sorted—on one, two, or three fields and that contain summary statistics for the entries in each group or for the entire report. You can add notes and other explanatory text to the report. In fact, the report generator gives you the power to create just about any report you can imagine from the information in a database.

Report basics
►WORKS 2◄

The key to Works' database reporting abilities is the database environment's View menu. ►You'll use two of the five commands on this menu, New Report and Reports..., to create and work with reports. (In Works 1, you use the four commands on the Report menu: Define, New, View, and Reports.... Works 2 doesn't have a Report menu.) The New Report command allows you to create a new report. The Reports... command allows you to rename, delete, or copy reports. You can create up to eight reports for a given database. We'll explain these commands in greater detail later in this chapter.◄

There are three steps to creating a database report. First, you select the New Report command from the View menu to create a report definition. When you do this, Works will display the default report it creates for you. You have to press [Esc] to see the actual report definition on the screen. Second, if necessary, you use the Sort Records... command on the Select menu to define the fields on which you want to group the report. Third, modify the definition (or even delete it and start from scratch) to define the report you want to print. Although this step is optional, you'll usually want to make at least a few changes to the report definition.

Once you have created a report, you can print it at any time. To do this, select the Print... command on the Print menu in the Report view. This command works the same way when you are printing a report as it does when you are printing a database or any other Works document. (We'll discuss the technique for printing a report later in this chapter.)

Suppose that you want to create a simple report from the example database in Figure 17-1. Select the New Report command from the View menu. When you do this, Works will create the report shown in Figure 17-9 on the next page and will enter the Report view. To view the default report definition, shown in Figure 17-10 on the following page, press the [Esc] key. At this point, you could modify the report definition in a number of ways. For example, you could erase the entries in one or more cells of the definition or add or delete a few rows. You could even delete the entire contents of the definition and start from scratch. We'll show you how to modify a report definition in a few pages.

A simple example

In this example, we'll simply print from the default report definition shown in Figure 17-10. To print from this definition, select the Print... command from the Print menu in the Report view, and, when the Print dialog box appears, choose <Print>. Works will print a report like the one shown in Figure 17-3.

Whenever you use the New Report command to create a new report definition for a database, Works will enter the Report view. When Works is in the Report view, the word *REPORT* will appear on the status line. The commands on the menus in the Report view allow you to modify, enhance, and print your reports.

The Report view

The Report view's work area is divided into a grid of columns and rows. Each column has a letter: A, B, C, and so on. Each row has a type: Intr Report, Intr Page, Record, Summ Report, and others you add later. (We'll explain these in a minute.) The intersection of each row and column is called a cell.

Figure 17-9

```
Lastname Address        City          ST Sales

Adams    94 College Ave. Memphis      TN  $16,890
Albert   412 River Ct.   St. Louis    MO  $58,780
Anderson 123 Oak St.     Fort Wayne   IN  $60,940
Baker    670 Northern Rd. Memphis     TN  $36,180
Bates    666 Shower Dr.  Indianapolis IN  $100,650
Bird     412 River Ct.   St. Louis    MO  $21,550
Campbell 123 Wallace Ave. Lexington   KY  $93,110
Campbell 412 River Ct.   St. Louis    MO  $47,350
Clare    670 Northern Rd. Memphis     TN  $28,940
Davis    321 Druid Ln.   Des Moines   IA  $46,380
Dobson   412 River Ct.   St. Louis    MO  $12,470
Douglas  222 Peabody Rd. Nashville    TN  $30,000
Edwards  17 Vanderbilt Rd.Nashville   TN  $10,170
Page 1                  REPORT
Press ENTER to continue, ESC to cancel.
```

When you select the New Report… command from the View menu,
Works will create a new report for the current database.

Figure 17-10

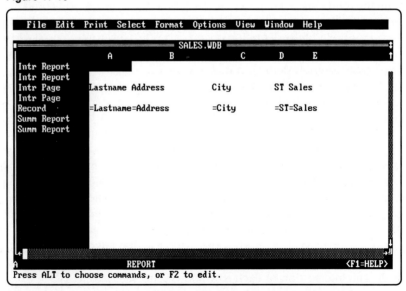

This figure shows the report definition for the report in Figure 17-9.

If you were in the Form view when you began defining the report, the Form command on the View menu will be active. Pressing [F10] will return you to the Form view. If you were in the List view when you began defining the report, the List command will be active. Pressing [F10] will return you to the List view.

When you define a new report, Works adds its name to the View menu. The first report you create has the default name Report1, the second, Report2, and so on. You can view a report at any time just by selecting its name from the View menu in the Form, List, or Report view of the database. Additionally, you can press [Shift][F10] to view the report. (This key combination does not return you to the Report view. It merely shows you the report. When you press [Esc], Works will return you to the previous view. We'll talk about this menu later.)

When you select the New Report command, Works automatically creates a default report definition like the one shown in Figure 17-10. Although the precise contents and appearance of each report definition may differ, all report definitions contain the same types of elements and are arranged in essentially the same way. The cells of a report definition contain various entries that determine what is printed in a report. Any report definition will contain a number of different types of rows. The type of row in which an entry appears determines where that entry will be printed in the report.

Report definitions

Entries.   A report definition can contain four types of entries: labels and values (also called literals), field values, summary functions, and formulas. These entries tell Works what to print in the report. Let's look at each of type of entry.

Literals.   Literal labels and values are simple text and number entries you can use as titles, field names, and explanatory notes in a report. For example, the entries in the Intr Page row in Figure 17-10—*Lastname*, *Address*, and so on—are literal labels. Literals are printed in a report just as they appear in the report definition. As with any type of entry, the position in which literal labels and values appear in a printed report depends on the type of row in which the literals are placed. For instance, since the labels in the definition in Figure 17-10 appear in the Intr Page field, Works printed these labels at the top of every page in the report.

Works automatically includes labels representing the names of the fields in the database in every default report definition. You can add other labels, values, or even dates and times to the definition at any time. We'll show you how to do that in a few pages.

Field values.   Field values are simple formulas that refer to the contents of the fields in the database on which a report is based. For example, the entries in the Record row in Figure 17-10 are field values. Notice that each of these formulas refers to one of the fields in the database: *=Lastname*, *=Address*, and so on.

When Works prints a row that contains a field value, it substitutes the contents of the fields of the database for the field values in the report definition. For example, when Works printed the Record row in the definition in Figure 17-10 for the first time, it printed the entries from the Lastname field, Address field, and so on, in the first record. When Works printed the Record row for the second time, it printed the entries from these fields in the second record.

Summary functions. Summary functions are special calculating tools you can use to compute statistics about the entries in a group, on a page, or in an entire report. Works offers seven summary functions that you can use in database reports: SUM(), COUNT(), AVG(), MAX(), MIN(), STD(), and VAR(). Each of these functions computes a different statistic: SUM() computes a total, COUNT() computes a count, AVG() computes an arithmetic mean, MAX() computes the maximum value, MIN() computes the minimum value, STD() computes the standard deviation, and VAR() computes the variance.

Each of these functions has the form *=FUNCTION(field)*, where *FUNCTION* is the name of the function (SUM, AVG, and so on) and *field* is the name of one of the fields in the database. Each function computes the indicated statistic for the entries in the specified field.

Exactly which entries a function operates on depends on the function's position in the report definition. If a function is in a Summ Group row, it will compute the indicated statistic on the entries in the specified field of the records in each group. If a function is in a Summ Report row, it will compute the indicated statistic on the entries in the specified field of the records in the entire report.

Formulas. Formulas are special entries that manipulate the values in one or more fields to create calculated results. For instance, you could use the formula *=Sales/4* in a report definition to compute quarterly sales from the annual sales values in the Sales field. The results of these formulas will be printed in the report. Works does not include any formulas in its default reports. (We'll show you how to enter formulas into a report definition later in this chapter.)

Rows. A report definition can contain up to six types of rows: Intr Report, Intr Page, Intr Group, Record, Summ Group, and Summ Report. Works prints the contents of each type of row in a different way. For example, it prints the contents of an Intr Report row only once at the beginning of a report. On the other hand, Works prints the contents of a Record row once for each record in the the database. Let's look at each of these types of rows.

►WORKS 2◄   **Intr Report rows.** ►Blank Intr Report rows (two of which are included in default reports in Works 2) are most commonly used to hold labels that serve as report titles. The second Intr Report row tells Works to place a blank row between the title at the top of a page and the field name on that page. Intr Report rows always will be the first rows in the definition.◄

Intr Page rows. Works prints the contents of each Intr Page row in a report definition once at the beginning of each page in the report. Intr Page rows are commonly used to hold labels that serve as names for the fields in the report. For example, the first Intr Page row in the example definition in Figure 17-10 contains a series of field name labels: *Lastname, Address,* and so on. As you can see in Figure 17-12 on the next page, these field names have been printed once at the top of each page in the report. The second Intr Page row tells Works to place a blank row between the field names at the top of each page and the first record on that page.

Record rows. Record rows contain the heart of any report. Works prints the contents of each Record row in a report definition once for each record in the database. Record rows normally contain field values; that is, formulas that refer to the fields of your database. For example, the Record row in the example definition in Figure 17-10 contains a series of field values: *=Lastname, =Address,* and so on. Notice that these formulas cause Works to print the contents of each record in the database in the body of the report.

Summ Report rows. Summ Report rows are commonly used to hold summary functions that calculate statistics for the entries in a given field. For example, the entries we added in the Summ Report row in the example definition in Figure 17-11 on the following page contain a series of summary functions: *=COUNT(Lastname), =COUNT(Address), =COUNT(City), =SUM(Sales),* and so on. As you can see in Figure 17-12, these functions compute summary statistics for each of the fields in the report. Since these functions are in a Summ Report row, Works printed their results once at the end of the report. (We used the Currency… command to display the *=SUM(Sales)* entry in the Currency 0 format.)

To add functions to the report, select the Insert Field Summary… command from the Edit menu. When you do this, the Insert Field Summary dialog box shown in Figure 17-13 on page 565 will appear. For the first field, Lastname, click on Lastname in the Fields list box, then click the COUNT option in the Statistic option box. When you choose <OK>, Works will enter *=COUNT(Lastname)* into the first Summ Report row in field A.

Intr Group and Summ Group rows. Intr Group and Summ Group rows are only relevant in grouped reports. Whenever you create a group in a report, Works creates a Summ Group row for that group. If you want, you can add an Intr Group field to the report definition. The names of these rows depend on the name of the field on which you grouped the report. For instance, if you group a report on a field named *Lastname,* Works will insert a row named Summ Lastname into the report definition.

Figure 17-11

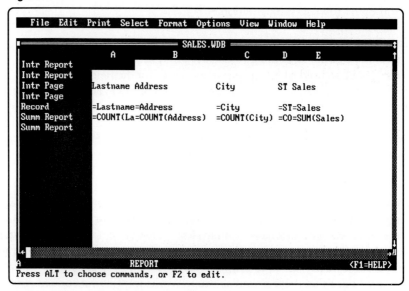

We've added a series of summary functions to the default report definition in Figure 17-10.

Figure 17-12

Lastname	Address	City	ST	Sales
Adams	94 College Ave.	Memphis	TN	$16,890
Albert	412 River Ct.	St. Louis	MO	$58,780
Anderson	123 Oak St.	Fort Wayne	IN	$60,940
Baker	670 Northern Rd.	Memphis	TN	$36,380
Bates	666 Shower Dr.	Indianapolis	IN	$100,650
Bird	412 River Ct.	St. Louis	MO	$21,550
Campbell	123 Wallace Ave.	Lexington	KY	$93,110
Campbell	412 River Ct.	St. Louis	MO	$47,350
Clare	670 Northern Rd.	Memphis	TN	$28,940
Davis	321 Druid Ln.	Des Moines	IA	$46,380
Dobson	412 River Ct.	St. Louis	MO	$12,470
Douglas	222 Peabody Rd.	Nashville	TN	$30,000
Edwards	17 Vanderbilt Rd.	Nashville	TN	$10,170
Eggers	55 Wheeler St.	Fort Wayne	IN	$46,300
Everett	833 Kentucky St.	St. Louis	MO	$3,980
Ferguson	312 E. 15th St.	Knoxville	TN	$6,190
Fox	9123 Highway 128	St. Louis	MO	$13,540
Gaston	987 Ford St.	Detroit	MI	$69,210
Gates	229 Broadway	Louisville	KY	$46,830
Gerber	1009 Carson Rd.	Kansas City	MO	$29,040
Head	63 Landings Way	Topeka	KY	$79,650
Hicks	1009 Carson Rd.	Kansas City	MO	$27,120
Holland	987 Ford St.	Detroit	MI	$39,120
Ingram	987 Ford St.	Detroit	MI	$13,360
Irwin	7665 Quincy St.	Kansas City	MO	$28,390
Jacob	33 College Way	South Bend	IN	$46,390
Jacobs	88 Smithtown Rd.	Springfield	MO	$39,700
Jeffries	777 College Dr.	Huntsville	AL	$14,630
Johnson	987 Maple Rd.	Birmingham	AL	$27,170
Jolly	8911 Olds Ave.	Detroit	MI	$6,170
Jones	333 Outer Loop	Louisville	KY	$49,290
Jones	5990 Wright Way	Dayton	OH	$14,420
Kirk	8911 Olds Ave.	Detroit	MI	$5,850
Klein	88 Smithtown Rd.	Springfield	MO	$44,000
Laffer	7114 Oak St.	Lansing	MI	$15,830
Lott	444 8th St.	Little Rock	AR	$4,480
Marshall	444 8th St.	Little Rock	AR	$58,840
McCray	13 Hikes Ln.	Louisville	KY	$75,830
Michaels	155 College Rd.	E. Lansing	MI	$25,100
Moore	324 Zazu Pitts	Chicago	IL	$56,670
Nicely	477 Stadium Rd.	Green Bay	MI	$5,060
Nielsen	678 S. 15th Ave.	Little Rock	AR	$25,530
O'Bryan	123 Smith Ave.	Ft. Smith	AR	$31,880
Oscar	266 Lakeside Dr.	Cleveland	OH	$86,510
Peters	266 Lakeside Dr.	Cleveland	OH	$57,450
Peterson	1175 15th St.	Dubuque	IA	$54,120
Price	12 Deer Rd.	Chicago	IL	$66,820
Quillen	324 Zazu Pitts	Chicago	IL	$18,530
Quincy	266 Lakeside Dr.	Cleveland	OH	$55,060
Rice	3515 E. 82nd St.	Indianapolis	IN	$38,620
Roberts	17 Suburban Hy.	Cleveland	OH	$12,720
Rogers	3515 E. 82nd St.	Indianapolis	IN	$87,420

Lastname	Address	City	ST	Sales
Schultz	3515 E. 82nd St.	Indianapolis	IN	$55,730
Shore	229 Broadway	Louisville	KY	$40,200
Smiley	324 Zazu Pitts	Chicago	IL	$63,200
Smith	24 Bunyon Pike	Peoria	IL	$60,940
Smith	24 Kentucky St.	Springfield	IL	$67,940
Smith	1234 Iowa Dr.	Gary	IN	$22,320
Smith	13 Hikes Ln.	Louisville	KY	$42,010
Stevens	502 Stanford Dr.	Columbus	OH	$45,200
Taylor	502 Stanford Dr.	Columbus	OH	$36,300
Thompson	3515 E. 82nd St.	Indianapolis	IN	$23,280
Ulmer	13 Hikes Ln.	Louisville	KY	$6,580
Unrich	1145 Tabor Place	Columbus	OH	$5,330
Vasquez	229 Broadway	Louisville	KY	$45,160
Victor	167 Brewery Way	Cincinnati	OH	$7,060
Wade	63 Landings Way	Topeka	KS	$33,790
Ward	12 Deer Rd.	Chicago	IL	$59,850
Waters	167 Brewery Way	Cincinnati	OH	$47,760
Welch	987 Maple Rd.	Birmingham	AL	$44,410
Williams	9772 Rubber Rd.	Akron	OH	$72,910
Yates	17 City Square	Wichita	KS	$10,580
Young	167 Brewery Way	Cincinnati	OH	$28,820
Zeeman	213 Elm Rd.	Springfield	IL	$69,400
Ziegler	17 City Square	Wichita	KS	$25,800

75		75	75	$2,904,800

This figure shows the result of printing the database in Figure 17-10, using the report definition shown in Figure 17-11.

Figure 17-13

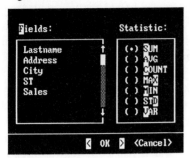

The Insert Field Summary dialog box lets you enter Summ Report rows into the report.

Works prints the contents of each Intr Group row in a report definition once at the beginning of each group. Intr Group rows are commonly used to hold labels that serve as names for the fields in the group. Works prints the contents of each Summ Group row in a report definition once at the end of each group. Summ Group rows are commonly used to hold summary functions that calculate statistics for the entries in a given field or fields of the records in a given group. You have to understand grouping before you can understand Intr Group and Summ Group fields. We'll talk about grouped reports in detail later in this chapter.

Notes.   A report definition does not have to include every type of row. In fact, it is possible for a report definition to have just a single Record row. In most cases, however, you will include several types of rows in a report definition. A report definition can include more than one row of a given type. For instance, the default definition shown in Figure 17-10 includes two Intr Report, Intr Page, and Summ Report rows.

The order of the rows in a report definition is important. All of the Intr Report rows will come first in a report definition, followed by all of the Intr Page rows, then any Intr Group rows, then the Record rows. Any Summ Group rows will come next in the reverse order of the Intr Group rows. Then, any Summ Report rows will follow.

You can print the default report definition Works creates without making any changes to it. In most cases, however, you'll want to modify the default definition by adding or deleting rows, erasing one or more entries, adding labels, field values, or summary functions, or making any of several other changes. We'll show you how to do that later in the chapter.

Formats and column widths.   When Works creates a new report definition, it uses the widths of the columns in the List view of the database document to set the width of the columns in the report definition. For example, the width of column C in the report definition shown in Figure 17-10 is 13 characters—the same as the width of the City field in the database. In addition, Works uses the formats that you assign to a field in the database to format the field values in the report definition. When you print the report, each field in the report will have the same format as the field in the database. As you'll see in a moment, you can change the width of any column or the format of any cell in a report definition.

Previewing a report
►WORKS 2◄

►The Preview… command on the Print menu lets you preview a report on your computer's screen. When you choose the Preview… command, Works will display the report in reduced-sized facsimile "pages" on your computer's screen. Works will display the first page, then pause while you read it. You can move ahead to the next page by pressing [Pg Up]. When you have viewed the entire report, you can exit the preview screen by pressing [Esc].

For example, suppose you want to preview the report you printed in Figure 17-12. To do this, simply select the Preview… command from the Print menu. Works will display a preview of the report, the second page of which is shown in Figure 17-14. When you're finished viewing this page, you can press [Esc] to return to the report definition.◄

Figure 17-14

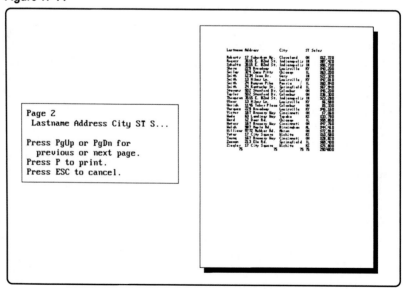

The Preview command lets you preview a report on the screen.

Printing a report

As we said earlier, after you've set your margins and page dimensions, and chosen your printer, there are three steps to creating a database report. First, you select the New Report command from the View menu to create a report definition.

When you do this, Works will preview the default report it creates for you on the screen. You have to press [Esc] to see the actual report definition on the screen. Second, if necessary, you use the Sort Records command on the Select menu to define the fields on which you want to group the report. Next, you can modify the definition (or even delete it and start from scratch) to define the report you want to print. Although this step is optional, you'll usually want to make at least a few changes to the report definition. Once you have created a report, you can print it at any time. To do this, select the Print... command on the Print menu in the Report view. This command works in the same way when you are printing a report as when you are printing a database or any other Works document. For more information on these commands, see Chapter 3.

When you've selected the Print... command in the Report view, Works will display a Print dialog box like the one shown in Figure 17-15. As you can see, this dialog box is similar to Print dialog boxes in other types of documents. You can use the options in this box to specify the number of copies of the report you want to print, to print only specific pages of the report, and to print the report to a file instead of to a printer. You can also tell Works to print all but the Record rows of the report. (We'll explain this option in a few pages.)

Figure 17-15

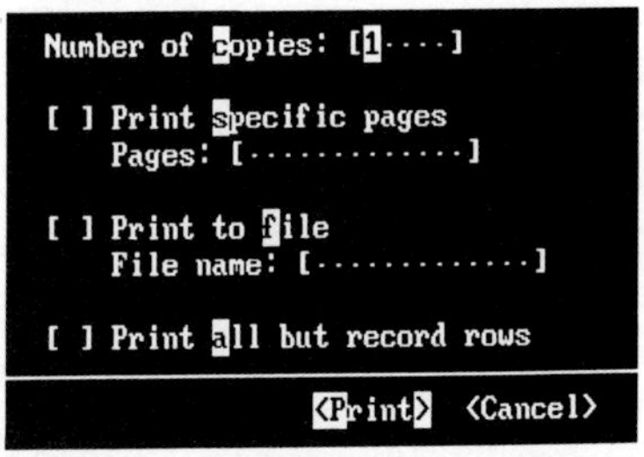

```
Number of Copies: [1····]

[ ] Print Specific pages
    Pages: [·············]

[ ] Print to File
    File name: [·············]

[ ] Print all but record rows

          <Print>  <Cancel>
```

Works will display a dialog box like this one when you select the Print... command from the Print menu in the Report view.

When you're ready to print, make sure that your printer is turned on, then choose the <Print> option. Works will print the report using the margins, page dimensions, font, and print settings you've specified.

To cancel the printing of a database, simply press the [Esc] key. When you do, Works will display a dialog box that contains the message *Printing interrupted. Continue printing?.* If you choose <Cancel>, Works will cancel the Print... command. If you choose <OK>, Works will continue printing where it left off.

In most databases, your reports will be too long or too wide to print on a single page. Then, Works will divide the report into page-sized settings, printing as many rows and columns as will fit on each page. Works uses the Page Length and Page Width settings the Top Margin, Bottom Margin, Left Margin, and Right Margin settings in the Page Setup & Margins dialog box to determine how much of the

How Works prints reports

report to print on each page. Works will never split a field between two pages. If a field will not fit on a page, Works will print the entire field on the next page.

The default Page Length, Page Width, and margin settings allow Works to print about 54 records on each page and about 60 characters per line on most printers. If you want to print more data on each page, you can increase the page width to 14 inches and print on 14-inch-wide computer paper. Alternatively, you can use the Font... command to choose a smaller font.

When Works prints a report, it begins by printing the header you have defined (if any) in the Headers & Footers dialog box at the top of the first page. Next, it prints the contents of any Intr Report rows at the top of the first page, followed by the contents of any Intr Page rows. Then, it prints the contents of as many Record rows as will fit on the rest of the page. (If the report is grouped, Works will print the contents of any Intr Group rows above each group, followed by one Record row for each record in the group, then the contents of any Summ Group rows for the group.) Next, Works will print the contents of any Intr Page rows at the top of the next page, followed by the contents of as many Record rows as will fit on the rest of the page. This will continue until all of the records have been printed. Finally, Works will print the contents of any Summ Report rows at the very end of the report.

Controlling page breaks

The Insert Page Break command allows you to insert manual page breaks in your database reports. A manual page break in a report causes Works to skip to the top of a new page before it prints the contents of the next row in the report definition. To insert a page break in a report, highlight the entire row that you want to appear at the top of a new page, then pull down the Print menu, and select the Insert Page Break command. When you select this command, Works will enter a manual page-break marker (>>) to the right of the row. When you print the database, Works will skip to the top of a new page before it prints the contents of the marked row. To remove a manual page break from a record, highlight that record, pull down the Print menu, and select the Delete Page Break command.

Alternative fonts and sizes

Unless you specify otherwise, Works will print the information from a report in the default font and size for the printer you are using (the printer you selected with the Printer Setup... command). If you want, however, you can command Works to print using a different font and size. For example, to squeeze as much information as possible onto each page of your printed database, you might want to choose a compact font and a small font size.

To change the font and size settings, you must pull down the Format menu and select the Font... command to reveal a Font dialog box like the one shown in Figure 17-6. If you want to print your database in an alternative font, simply choose that font from the Fonts list box. Once you choose a font, should choose a size from the Sizes list box.

The Print dialog box for database reports includes an option, Print All but Record Rows, that lets you print all of the rows in a report definition except for the Record rows. This makes it possible to create summary reports: reports that include all of the introductory and summary rows in the definition (and any summary statistics that are computed in those rows), but no records. Summary reports are useful when you need to obtain summary data—such as the total or average of the entries in a field—but don't want to print the entire report.

The Print All but Record Rows option

To turn on the Print All but Record Rows option, simply choose it in the Report view's Print dialog box. When the Print All but Record Rows option is active, an X will appear in its check box. If you choose <Print> while the Print All but Record Rows option is active, Works will print the report without any Record rows. To return to normal printing, just choose the Print All but Record Rows option again to deactivate it.

Let's use this option to create a summary report from the basic report definition shown in Figure 17-11. To begin, select the Print... command from the Print menu. When the Print dialog box appears, choose the Print All but Record Rows check box. Then, choose <Print> to print the report. Figure 17-16 shows the result. As you can see, Works has printed the database report but has omitted the Record rows. The result is a simple summary report.

Figure 17-16

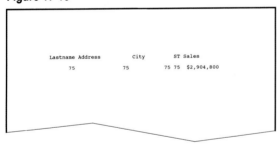

The Print All but Record Rows option lets you create summary reports that do not include any Record rows.

Although you will usually begin the process of creating a new report from within a database document, you can also create new reports while you are in the Report view. To create a new report in the Report view, just select the New Report command from the View menu. When you do this, Works will create and define a new report and activate that report.

Notes

Since every report you create is part of a database, all you have to do to save a report is save the database on which it is based. Works automatically saves all the reports that are based on a database when you use the Save or Save As... commands to save that database.

You can create up to eight reports for a given database document. If you've already created eight reports for the current database and then try to use the New Report command on the View menu to create a new report, Works will display an alert box containing the message *No more than 8 allowed in each Database file. To delete reports, use the Reports command in the View menu.* You'll have to delete an existing report definition before you can create a new report. (For more about deleting report definitions, please refer to the section "Managing Reports" later in this chapter.)

If the database you are working with is empty when you select the New Report command, Works will still create a default report definition for the database. However, it will not make any entries into the cells of the report definition. You'll have to define the report from scratch.

▶WORKS 2◀

If you use a query in the Form or List view to select a portion of the records in a database, then print (view) a report for that database, the report will include only the visible records from the database. ▶In Works 2, you can query directly from a report, something you cannot do in Works 1. We'll discuss this capability later in this chapter.◀

Modifying report definitions
▶WORKS 2◀

Although you can print from the default report definition without making any changes to it, you will usually want to modify it before you print. In most cases, the default report definition will not define the report you want to print. ▶For one thing, in Works 2, default definitions include no summary functions. You'll usually want to add some of these entries.◀ You may also want to add or delete rows at various places in the definition.

To modify a report definition, you first select its name from the database View menu, then press [Esc]. Once you are in the Report view, you can modify a report definition in a number of ways. You can enter new field names, field values, and field summaries in the cells of the definition. You can delete, copy, move, and format entries. You can insert and delete columns and rows. You can change the widths of columns. You can query the database. For the most part, you do these things in a report definition in the same way you do in a spreadsheet or a database.

We'll begin by explaining each of the commands you use to modify a report definition. Then, we'll use those same commands to create a new report for the example database.

Making entries

You can enter a literal, a field value, a summary function, or a formula into any cell of a report definition at any time. We'll show you how to make these types of entries in this section.

Literals. You can enter a literal label, value, date, or time into a report definition in the same way you make an entry into a cell in a spreadsheet or a database in the List view: Simply move the highlight to the cell, and type the entry. For instance, to enter the field name Lastname into a cell, move the highlight to that cell, type *Lastname*, and press [Enter]. Similarly, to enter the value 1000 into a cell, move the highlight to that cell, type 1000, and press [Enter].

If you type a formatted value into a cell, Works will enter the value and format the cell. For example, if you type $1234.45, Works will enter the value into the current cell and give that cell the Currency 2 format. If you type 11/24/58, Works will enter the date value 21513 into the current cell and give that cell the Month, Day, Year (Short) format. If you type 12:15 PM, Works will enter the time value .5104167 into the current cell and give that cell the Hour, Minute (12 Hour) format.

You also can insert the current date or the current time in any cell of a report definition. To insert the current date into a cell, simply move the highlight to that cell, press [Ctrl];, then press [Enter]. When you do this, Works will enter the current date (based on your computer's system clock) into the current cell. The date will appear in the Month, Day, Year (Short) format. To enter the current time into a cell, move the highlight to that cell, press [Ctrl][Shift];, then press [Enter]. When you do this, Works will enter the current time (again, based on your computer's system clock) into the current cell. The time will appear in the Hour, Minute (12 Hour) format. The date and time entries created using the [Ctrl]; and [Ctrl][Shift]; techniques are fixed—they don't change automatically as time moves on.

You can use the Insert Field Name... command on the Edit menu in the Report view to enter a field name label into a definition. To enter a field name label with this command, move the highlight to the cell in which you want to make the entry, then, select the Insert Field Name... command. When you select this command, Works will present a dialog box like the one shown in Figure 17-17 on the following page. As you can see, this dialog box lists the names of all the fields in the active database. When you choose a field name from this list, then choose <OK>, Works will enter the selected field name into the current cell as a label. To cancel the Insert Field Name... command, just choose <Cancel>.

You cannot use any of Works' spreadsheet functions other than AVG(), COUNT(), MAX(), MIN(), STD(), SUM(), and VAR() in a report definition. If you try to enter a spreadsheet function other than one of these seven, Works will display an alert box that contains the message *Only AVG, COUNT, MAX, MIN, STD, SUM, and VAR allowed in report.*

Field contents. You can enter the field contents into a cell of a report definition the same way you enter a formula into a cell in a spreadsheet or a database in the List view: Just move the highlight to the cell and type the field contents. For instance, to enter the field contents *=Lastname* in a cell, move the highlight to that cell, type *=Lastname*, and press [Enter].

Figure 17-17

The Insert Field Name... command lets you enter field names into report definitions.

You can also use the Insert Field Contents... command on the Edit menu in the Report view. To enter the field contents with this command, move the highlight to the cell in which you want to make the entry, then select the Insert Field Contents... command. Works will then present an Insert Field Name dialog box similar to the one shown in Figure 17-17. As you can see, this box contains the names of all the fields in the active database. When you choose a field name from this list, then choose <OK>, Works will enter into the active cell the field contents that refer to the selected field. To cancel the Insert Field Contents... command, just choose <Cancel>.

Summary functions. You can also enter a summary function into a cell of a report definition by moving the highlight to that cell and typing the summary function. For instance, to enter the summary function =*SUM(Sales)* in a cell, you would move the highlight to that cell, type =*SUM(Sales)*, and press [Enter].

You can use the Insert Field Summary... command on the Edit menu in the Report view to enter a summary function into a report definition. To enter a summary function with this command, move the highlight to the cell in which you want to make the entry, then select the Insert Field Summary... command. When you select this command, Works will present a dialog box like the one shown in Figure 17-18. As you can see, this box lists the names of the fields in the active database. It also lists each of the seven summary functions available for use in a report: SUM, AVG, COUNT, and so on. To insert a summary function into a report definition, highlight the name of the field for which you want to compute the summary statistic, highlight the type of summary function, and choose <OK>. When you do this, Works will enter into the current cell a summary function of the specified type that refers to the selected field. To cancel the Insert Field Summary... command, just choose <Cancel>.

A note. Keep in mind that the position of an entry in a report definition determines where and how often that entry will appear in the printed report. You'll usually enter literals in Intr Report, Intr Page, and Intr Group rows (although literals can be used in other types of rows as well); field contents in Record rows (and, in a few cases, Intr Group rows); and summary functions in Summ Group or Summ Report rows.

Figure 17-18

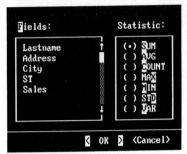

The Insert Field Summary...
command lets you enter summary
functions into report definitions.

Editing entries

There are two ways to change an entry in a report definition: You can replace the entry with a new entry or you can edit the entry. If the entry you want to change is short, it is usually easier to replace it with new data. To do this, position the highlight on the cell that contains the entry you want to change, type a new entry, and press [Enter]. (This is the same technique you use to replace a cell entry in a database.)

Instead of replacing an entry, you may want to change only a character or two. As you might expect, you can use the [Edit] key ([F2]) to change an entry in a report definition in the same way that you would use that key to edit an entry in a database. To edit an entry, first move the highlight to the entry you want to change, then press the [Edit] key. When you press this key, an underline cursor will appear at the end of the entry on the formula line. You can use the ➜, ←, [Home], and [End] keys to move the cursor to any spot in the entry in the formula line and the [Delete] or [Backspace] key to erase existing characters. You can also type new characters, which will be inserted in the entry at the position of the cursor. When the entry in the formula line is the way you want it to be, press [Enter] to lock in the new entry.

Clearing entries

To clear an entry from a cell in a report definition, you should move the highlight to the cell that contains the entry, then select the Clear command from the Edit menu. When you do this, Works will clear the cell on which the highlight is positioned. You also can clear an entry by moving the highlight to it, pressing [Delete] or [Backspace], then pressing [Enter]. If you want to clear several entries at once, you must highlight all the cells that contain those entries and select the Clear command.

Formatting entries

When Works creates a new report definition, it uses the formats (if any) that you assign to a field in the database to format the field contents in the report definition. When you print the report, each field in the report will have the same format as the corresponding field in the database.

If you want, you can change the format or style of any cell or range of cells in a report definition. To format a cell or range, first position the highlight on the cell or extend the highlight to cover the entire range you want to format. Then, pull down the Format menu and select the format command you want to use to format the cell or range. These commands—Currency..., Fixed..., Style..., and so on—are identical to those you use to format cells in spreadsheets and databases. When you select any of these commands, Works will display a dialog box that asks you to specify the number of decimal places to include in the formatted numbers or—in the case of the Font... or Style... command—that allows you to choose the font and size, or style or alignment attribute (Bold, Underline, and so on), you want to assign to that cell or range. After you have made the appropriate choices in the dialog box, just choose <OK> to assign the selected format or style to the cell. For more on Works' formats and styles, see Chapter 8.

Copying entries

The Copy command on the Edit menu allows you to duplicate an entry or a range of entries at a new location in a report definition. This command comes in handy when you are modifying a report definition. For instance, you might use this command to copy a set of summary functions from the cells in one summary row to a different summary row within a report definition.

To copy the contents of a cell or range, begin by highlighting the entry or entries you want to copy. If you want to copy a single entry, you just move the highlight to the cell that contains that entry. If you want to copy several entries, you must extend the highlight to include all of those entries. Next, select the Copy command from the Edit menu. To complete the move, you should position the highlight where you want to duplicate the highlighted cells, and press [Enter]. When you do this, Works will duplicate the entries from the range you highlighted into the destination you specified. If the destination contains any entries, those entries will be overwritten and lost.

Moving entries

The Move command allows you to move an entry or range of entries from one place to another within a report definition. You can use this command to move the field contents from one cell to another or to move field name labels in a definition from one Intr row to another.

To move the contents of a cell or range, first highlight the entry or entries you want to move. If you want to move a single entry, position the highlight on the cell that contains that entry. If you want to move several entries, extend the highlight to include all those entries. Next, select the Move command from the Edit menu. Then, position the highlight where you want your selection to appear, and press [Enter] to complete the move. When you do this, Works will move the entry or entries from their original location to the destination you specified. If the destination contains any entries, those entries will be overwritten and lost.

You can also use the Move command to move an entire row or column (or two or more adjacent rows or columns) in a report definition. For instance, you can use it to reverse the order of two rows in a report definition or to move a column of entries from one place in a report definition to another.

To move a column, first highlight the entire column you want to move. You can do this by moving the highlight to any cell in the column and then selecting the Column command from the Select menu. (If you want to move more than one column, just highlight several adjacent columns before selecting the Column command.) Next, select the Move command from the Edit menu. Then, move the highlight to the first cell in the column where you want the column you are moving to appear, and press [Enter]. When you do this, Works will remove the column you selected from its original location, closing up the space it previously occupied. It will also insert a new column at the position of the highlight and insert the column you highlighted into that new column. Any columns to the right of the new column will be moved one column to the right.

To move a row, first highlight the entire row you want to move. You can do this by moving the highlight to any cell in the row and then selecting the Row command from the Select menu. Next, select the Move command from the Edit menu. Then, move the highlight to the first cell in the row where you want the row you are moving to appear, and press [Enter]. When you do this, Works will remove the row you selected from its original location, close up the space it previously occupied, insert a new row at the position of the highlight, and insert the row you highlighted into that new row. Any rows below the new row will be moved down one row.

You can't move rows from one place to another indiscriminately. Works controls the order of the rows in a report definition: Intr Report rows come first, then Intr Page rows, Intr Group rows, Record rows, and so on. You cannot move a row in violation of this rule. If you try to move a row out of order—for instance, if you try to move an Intr Page row to the bottom of the report definition—Works will display an alert box that contains the message *Cannot insert row here.*

Changing column widths

Works automatically assigns each column in a report definition the width you have assigned to the corresponding field of the database in the List view. Provided that you have set the widths of the fields in the database to display the contents of the database in full, the default widths of the columns in the report definition should be adequate.

If you want, however, you can use the Column Width… command on a report definition's Format menu to change the width of a column in a report definition. To do this, move the highlight to that field, and select the Column Width…

command from the Format menu, type the new width for the column into the Column Width dialog box, and choose <OK>.

Inserting columns

You can use the Insert Row/Column command on the Edit menu to insert a new column into a report definition. To do this, first highlight the entire column to the left of which you want to insert a new one. You can do this by moving the highlight to any cell in the column, then selecting the Column command from the Select menu. Next, select the Insert Row/Column command from the Edit menu. Works will then insert a new column at the position of the highlight. The column you highlighted and any columns to its right will be shifted one column to the right.

▶WORKS 2◀

▶You can also insert a column by highlighting only one cell in the column where you want to insert the new column. When you've highlighted a cell in that column, select the Insert Row/Column command. When you do, you'll see the Insert Row/Column dialog box shown in Figure 17-19. To insert a column, choose the Column option. When you do this, Works will insert a new column at the position of the highlight. The column you highlighted and any columns to its right will be shifted one column to the right.◀

Figure 17-19

The Insert Row/Column command lets you add a new column to a report definition.

Deleting columns

You can use the Delete Row/Column command on the Edit menu to delete columns from a report definition. First, highlight the entire column you want to remove by moving the highlight to any cell in the column, then selecting the Column command from the Select menu. Next, select the Delete Row/Column command from the Edit menu to delete the highlighted column. If there are any columns to the right of the deleted columns, those columns will shift to the left.

▶WORKS 2◀

▶You can also delete a column by highlighting only one cell in the column you want to delete. When you've highlighted a cell in that column, select the Delete Row/Column command, and choose Column from the Delete Row/Column dialog box. When you do this, Works will delete the highlighted column. The column you highlighted and any columns to its right will be shifted one column to the left.◀

Inserting rows

You can use the Insert Row/Column command on the Edit menu to insert a new row into a report definition. To do this, first highlight a single cell above which you want to insert a new row by moving the highlight to any cell in the row, then selecting the Row command from the Select menu. Next, select the Insert Row/Column command from the Edit menu. Works will display an Insert Row/Column dialog box like the one shown in Figure 17-20. As you can see, this box lists all the row types available for the current report definition. Works will automatically highlight the type of row that it thinks you want to insert. Works' selection is based on the position of the row you have highlighted in the report definition. (Of course, the contents of the Type list box will differ from report to report.)

If you select the Insert Row/Column command without highlighting a row, Works will display the dialog box shown in Figure 17-19 before it displays the dialog box shown in Figure 17-20.

Figure 17-20

The *Insert Row/Column command lets you add a new row to a report definition.*

To insert a row, simply select the type of row you want to insert, then choose <OK>. When you do this, Works will insert a new row of the type you've chosen into the report definition. Any rows below the one Works inserts will be shifted down one row. To cancel the Insert Row/Column command without inserting a row, choose <Cancel>.

As we have said, rows in a report definition must be arranged in a specific order: Intr Report rows must come first, then Intr Page rows, Intr Group rows, Record rows, and so on. The Insert Row/Column command automatically obeys this rule when it inserts rows into a report definition. If the type of row you choose in the Insert Row/Column dialog box cannot be placed at the position you have highlighted in the report definition, Works will insert a row of the type you've chosen at the appropriate place in the report definition. For example, if you choose an Intr Report row from the Insert Row/Column dialog box while a Summ Report row is highlighted, Works will not insert the new row at the position you've highlighted. Instead, it will insert the new Intr Report row just below the last Intr Report row in the definition.

Deleting rows

You can use the Delete Row/Column command on the Edit menu to delete a row from a report definition. First, highlight the entire row that you want to remove. Then, select the Delete Row/Column command from the Edit menu. When you do this, Works will delete the highlighted row. If there are any rows below the deleted row, those rows will shift upward. Of course, you can delete a row by highlighting a single cell, then choosing the Row option after you select the Delete Row/Column command.

An example

We'll use these techniques to modify the report definition shown in Figure 17-11. To begin, if Works is not already in the Report view, select the report you want to view from the View menu. Once you are in the Report view, you can begin modifying the report definition.

To begin, let's delete the second Intr Page row from the report. To do this, move the highlight to any cell in that row, then select the Row command from the Select menu to highlight the entire row. Next, select the Delete Row/Column command from the Edit menu to delete the highlighted row from the report definition.

Now let's assign the Bold style and Centered alignment to the field name labels in the Intr Page row. Highlight the entire Intr Page row, pull down the Format menu, and select the Style... command. When the Style dialog box appears, choose the Center option from the alignment box, choose the Bold option from the Styles box, then choose <OK>.

Next, let's change the field name label for the ST field from ST to State. To do this, move the highlight to the first cell in column D, type the label *State*, and press [Enter]. So that this entire label will be visible in the column, let's change the width of column D from three characters to six. To do this, position the highlight in column D (it should already be there), select the Column Width... command from the Format menu, type 6 into the Column Width dialog box, and choose <OK>.

Next, let's delete the COUNT() function from columns A, B, C, and D of the Summ Report row. To do this, expand the highlight to cover all of these cells, then select the Clear command from the Edit menu to delete the highlighted functions. After deleting these functions, move the highlight to column A in the Summ Report row and enter the label *Total*. This entry labels the summary function in column E of this row.

Now, let's move column E so that the Sales field appears just to the right of column A (which contains the Lastname field). To begin, highlight column E. Then, select the Move command from the Edit menu. Next, move the highlight to the first cell in column B in the report definition, and press [Enter]. When you do this, Works will move the contents of column E into column B. The contents of the other columns in the definition will shift one column to the right to make room for the moved column.

Next, let's enter a title for the definition into an Intr Report row. First, move the highlight to column C in the first Intr Report row, type the label *SALES REPORT,* and press [Enter]. To delete the second Intr Report row, using the same techniques we used to delete the Intr Page row we didn't need, highlight the second Intr Report row, then select the Delete Row/Column command from the Edit menu.

Now, let's add to the report definition a new Summ Report row above the existing Summ Report row. To begin, move the highlight to the Summ Report row, and select the Row command from the Select menu to highlight the row. Then, pull down the Edit menu, and select the Insert Row/Column... command. When the Insert Row/Column dialog box appears, choose the Summ Report option (it should be highlighted), and choose <OK> to insert a new Summ Report row above the existing row. When the new row appears, enter the label " - - - - - - - - - (a quotation mark and two spaces followed by nine dashes) in column B.

Finally, in the third Summ Report row, enter the label *AVERAGE* in column A and the summary function *=AVG(Sales)* in column B.

When you're finished, your report definition will look like the one shown in Figure 17-21. To print the report, select the Print... command from the Print menu. When the Print dialog box appears, make sure that the Print All but Record Rows option is off, then choose <Print>. Figure 17-22 shows the resulting report.

Figure 17-21

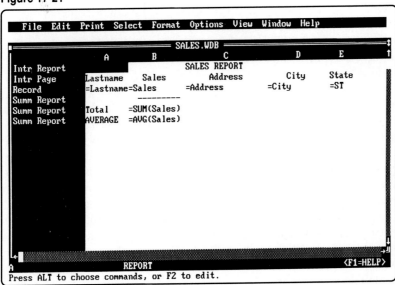

You can modify an existing report definition by adding and deleting columns and rows; erasing, moving, formatting, and copying entries; and entering new literals, field contents, and summary functions.

Figure 17-22

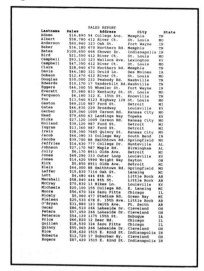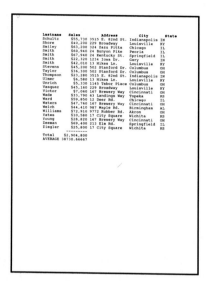

This report is based on the report definition shown in Figure 17-21.

In this example, we modified an existing report definition to create a new definition. In some cases, you'll want to delete the entire contents of a report definition, then create a new definition from scratch. To delete the entire contents of a report definition, highlight all the rows in the report definition, then select the Delete Row/Column command from the Edit menu. Then, you can create a new report definition.

Querying the report
▶WORKS 2◀

▶In Chapter 16, we discussed the use of queries in the database. As we suggested there, Works 2 allows you to query the database from the Report view. To define a query, select the Query command from the View menu in the Report view. When you do this, Works will display a query form that resembles the data entry form for the database. The only obvious difference is that the word *QUERY* will appear on the status line. For instance, Figure 17-23 shows a query form for our example sales database.

Once this form is in view, you may enter selection conditions, called criteria, into one or more fields in the query form. These criteria tell Works which records you want it to select. When you have finished defining the query, select the report you want to view from the View menu, or press [F10]. This will return you to the Report definition. (For a detailed discussion of the Works query feature, refer to the section "Using Queries" in Chapter 16.)

Figure 17-23

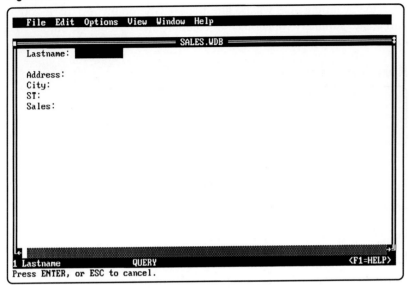

Query forms allow you to define queries that select specific records.

When you leave the query form, Works will automatically process the query, comparing the entries in each record to the criteria you've specified. To review the query, select the report you want to view from the View menu. As you can see in Figure 17-24 on the following page, when the Report comes into view, Works will display only those records that match the criteria you have defined. Any record whose data don't match your criteria will be hidden from view.

If the query you have defined does not select any records, Works will display an alert box with the message *No match found.* When you choose <OK> to acknowledge the message, Works will bring the report definition back into view.

To show all records in the report again after a query, return to the report definition, then select the Form or List command from the View menu. When you're in the Form or List view, select the Show All Records command on the Select menu. The Show All Records command does just what you would expect: It redisplays all hidden records. When you select a report number from the View menu, the report will include all the records in the database.◄

Grouping

As we have mentioned, Works allows you to create sorted, or grouped, reports. You can group it on up to three fields. When a report is grouped on a field, the report will be sorted so that the entries in that field are printed in ascending or descending order. Consequently, each set of records with identical entries in the grouping field will be grouped together in the report. If you want, you can create summary functions that compute statistics on the entries in each group. In this section, we'll show you how to create grouped reports.

Figure 17-24

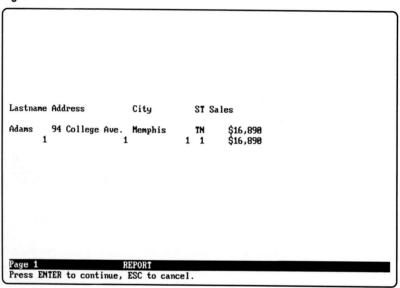

A queried report shows only the records that match the query criteria.

Creating grouped reports

Works uses the settings in the 1st Field, 2nd Field, and 3rd Field text boxes in the Sort Records dialog box to determine how Works should group a new report. To create a grouped report, you simply use the Sort Records... command on the Select menu to sort the database on one, two, or three fields. (As you can see in Figure 17-25, the Sort Records dialog box for the Report view is an expanded version of the Sort Records dialog box we showed you in Chapter 16.) Then, when you press <OK>, Works will automatically update your report definition to define a grouped report. When you print or view the report, the entries in each sort field will be printed in ascending or descending order. Each set of records with identical entries in each sort field will be grouped together in the report.

The Report view's Sort Records dialog box includes a Break option for each sort field setting. The Break option controls whether Works inserts breaks between the groups in a grouped report. When the Break option for a sort field is on, Works will group the report on that sort field and will insert a break after each group. Any summary functions in the Summ Group row for that group will compute statistics for the fields in the group. When you turn the Break option on, an X will appear in the Break check box.

Figure 17-25

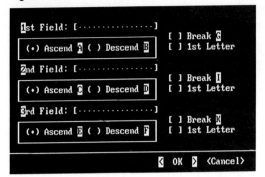

```
1st Field: [················]        [ ] Break S
   (•) Ascend A ( ) Descend B        [ ] 1st Letter

2nd Field: [················]        [ ] Break U
   (•) Ascend C ( ) Descend D        [ ] 1st Letter

3rd Field: [················]        [ ] Break N
   (•) Ascend E ( ) Descend F        [ ] 1st Letter

                              ◄ OK ► <Cancel>
```

The Sort records dialog box lets you group your report information by fields.

An example.   For example, suppose you want to create a report for the SALES database that is grouped by the entries in the ST field. ►To do this, first select the Sort Records... command from the Select menu in the Report view.◄ When the Report view's Sort Records dialog box appears, enter the field name *ST* in the 1st Field text box, activate the Break option for the 1st Field, and choose <OK> to execute the command and sort the database. When your report definition reappears, as shown in Figure 17-26, Works will add a Summ ST row, which contains summary functions.

►WORKS 2◄

Figure 17-26

```
 File  Edit  Print  Select  Format  Options  View  Window  Help

═══════════════════════════════ SALES.WDB ═══════════════════════════════
              A          B            C            D         E
                                SALES REPORT
Intr Report
Intr Page    Lastname    Sales      Address        City      State
Record       =Lastname  =Sales     =Address       =City     =ST
Summ ST      =COUNT(La  =COUNT(Addre=COUNT(City)   =COUNT(ST) =SUM(S
Summ Report             ──────────
Summ Report  Total      =SUM(Sales)
Summ Report  AVERAGE    =AVG(Sales)
```

If you have sorted a database, the default report definition for that database will include Summ Group fields.

Now, let's print the report. To do so, select the Print... command from the Print menu in the Report view. When the Print dialog box shown in Figure 17-15 appears, choose the <Print> option to print the report. When you do this, Works will print the report shown in Figure 17-27 on the next page.

As you can see, the report is printed so that entries in the ST field are in ascending order. Each set of records with identical ST field entries is collected into a group. For example, all of the records with the ST field entry *IA* are in one group, the records with the ST field entry *IL* are in another group, and so on. Works has inserted a break after each group, so that the group for *IA* is separated from the group for *IL*, and so on.

Figure 17-27

This report is grouped on the ST field.

In addition, Works has computed statistics for each of the fields in each group. Each time Works finished printing one group of records, the summary functions in the Summ ST row of the report definition compute the count or sum of the entries in the fields of the records in that group. The results of these functions appear just below the last record in each group.

For example, we turned on the Break option for the 1st Field in Figure 17-26. As a result, when we printed the report, each set of records with identical ST field entries was collected into a group, and Works computed statistics for each of the fields in each group: SUM( ) functions for fields that contain only values and COUNT( ) functions for fields that contain labels. (To display the sales statistics for each group, we had to widen the ST column from six to eight characters.)

Turning off breaks.   If you turn off the Break option for a sort field, Works will not insert a break between each group. However, the report will still be sorted according to the entries in the sort field. As a result, the report will be printed in one continuous stream, just as if it were not grouped.

To turn off the Break setting for a sort field, select the Sort Records… command from the Select menu, choose the Break option, then choose <OK>. When the Break option is off, the Break check box will be empty.

Suppose you want to deactivate the Break option for the first (and only) sort field in the database. To begin, select the Sort Records... command. When the Sort Records dialog box appears, choose the Break option for the 1st Field to deactivate it. Then, choose <OK> to lock in your change.

To print the report, select the Print... command from the Print menu in the Report view. When the Print dialog box appears, choose the <Print> option to print the report. Figure 17-28 shows the first page of the report.

Figure 17-28

```
                 SALES REPORT
Lastname   Sales         Address         City         State
Jeffries    $14,630 777 College Dr.  Huntsville    AL
Johnson     $27,170 987 Maple Rd.    Birmingham    AL
Welch       $44,410 987 Maple Rd.    Birmingham    AL
Lott         $4,480 444 8th St.      Little Rock   AR
Marshall    $58,840 444 8th St.      Little Rock   AR
Nielsen     $25,530 678 S. 15th Ave. Little Rock   AR
O'Bryan     $31,880 123 Smith Ave.   Ft. Smith     AR
Davis       $46,380 321 Druid Ln.    Des Moines    IA
Peterson    $54,120 1175 15th St.    Dubuque       IA
Moore       $56,670 324 Zazu Pitts   Chicago       IL
Price       $66,820 12 Deer Rd.      Chicago       IL
Quillen     $18,530 324 Zazu Pitts   Chicago       IL
Smiley      $63,200 324 Zazu Pitts   Chicago       IL
Smith       $60,940 24 Bunyon Pike   Peoria        IL
Smith       $67,940 24 Kentucky St.  Springfield   IL
Ward        $59,850 12 Deer Rd.      Chicago       IL
Zeeman      $69,400 213 Elm Rd.      Springfield   IL
Anderson    $60,940 123 Oak St.      Fort Wayne    IN
Bates      $100,650 666 Shower Dr.   Indianapolis  IN
Eggers      $46,300 55 Wheeler St.   Fort Wayne    IN
Jacob       $46,390 33 College Way   South Bend    IN
Rice        $38,620 3515 E. 82nd St. Indianapolis  IN
Rogers      $87,420 3515 E. 82nd St. Indianapolis  IN
Schultz     $55,730 3515 E. 82nd St. Indianapolis  IN
Smith       $22,320 1234 Iowa Dr.    Gary          IN
Thompson    $23,280 3515 E. 82nd St. Indianapolis  IN
Head        $79,650 63 Landings Way  Topeka        KS
Wade        $33,790 63 Landings Way  Topeka        KS
Yates       $10,580 17 City Square   Wichita       KS
Ziegler     $25,800 17 City Square   Wichita       KS
Campbell    $93,110 123 Wallace Ave. Lexington     KY
Gates       $46,830 229 Broadway     Louisville    KY
Jones       $49,290 333 Outer Loop   Louisville    KY
McCray      $75,830 13 Hikes Ln.     Louisville    KY
Shore       $40,200 229 Broadway     Louisville    KY
Smith       $42,010 13 Hikes Ln.     Louisville    KY
Ulmer        $6,580 13 Hikes Ln.     Louisville    KY
Vasquez     $45,160 229 Broadway     Louisville    KY
Gaston      $69,210 987 Ford St.     Detroit       MI
Holland     $39,120 987 Ford St.     Detroit       MI
Ingram      $13,360 987 Ford St.     Detroit       MI
Jolly        $6,170 8911 Olds Ave.   Detroit       MI
Kirk         $5,850 8911 Olds Ave.   Detroit       MI
Laffer      $15,830 7114 Oak St.     Lansing       MI
Michaels    $25,100 155 College Rd.  E. Lansing    MI
Nicely       $5,060 477 Stadium Rd.  Green Bay     MI
Albert      $58,780 412 River Ct.    St. Louis     MO
Bird        $21,550 412 River Ct.    St. Louis     MO
Campbell    $47,350 412 River Ct.    St. Louis     MO
Dobson      $12,470 412 River Ct.    St. Louis     MO
Everett      $3,980 833 Kentucky St. St. Louis     MO
Fox         $13,540 9123 Highway 128 St. Louis     MO
```

When the Break option for a sort field is inactive, Works will not insert breaks between the groups.

As you can see, the report is still sorted according to the entry in the 1st Field box in the Sort Records dialog box. However, Works has not inserted breaks between the groups. As a result, the report was printed in one continuous stream.

The 1st Letter option.   Works lets you group reports in two different ways. You can either group the report so that each group contains all of the records with the same entry in the sort field, or you can group a report so that each group contains all of the records with entries in the sort field that begin with the same letter.

The 1st Letter option in the Report view's Sort Records dialog box controls whether Works will insert a break in the report between any two records that have different entries in the sort field. Consequently, the report will be grouped so that each group contains all of the records with the same entry in the sort field. When the 1st Letter option for a sort field is active, Works will insert a break whenever the first letter in the sort field changes. Consequently, each group will include records with entries in the sort field that begin with the same letter. (Of course, if the Break option for a sort field is off, the setting of the 1st Letter option makes no difference. The report will not include any breaks.)

By default, the 1st Letter setting for each sort field in a report is off. When the 1st Letter option is off, the 1st Letter check box will be empty. To activate the 1st Letter setting for a sort field, you must select the Sort Records... command from the Select menu, choose the 1st Letter option for the appropriate sort field, then choose <OK>. When the 1st Letter option is on, an X will appear in the 1st Letter check box.

To show how this option works, let's reprint the last report with the 1st Letter option active. To begin, select the Sort Records... command. When the Sort Records dialog box appears, choose the 1st Letter option for the 1st Field to turn it on. (You should also activate the Break option if it has been deactivated.) Then, choose <OK> to lock in your change.

To print the report, select the Print... command from the Print menu in the Report view. When the Print dialog box appears, choose the <Print> option to print the report. Figure 17-29 shows the first page of the report.

As you can see, the report is still sorted according to the entry in the Sort Records dialog box. This time, however, Works has inserted breaks whenever the first letter of the entries in the ST field change. As a result, the report is now grouped so that each group contains records whose entries in the sort field begin with the same letter.

Notes. In the example, we asked Works to arrange the entries in the ST field in ascending (alphabetical) order. You can also ask Works to sort the entries in a sort field in descending order. Simply select the Descend option when you define the sort field or fields in the Sort Records dialog box. When Works prints the report, it will arrange the entries in the grouping field in descending order.

As we mentioned, when you sort the records in your report, then activate the Break option for the field you sort, Works will automatically add a Summ Group row for the group to the report definition and will enter summary functions for that group in the row. In most cases, you won't want or need all of the functions Works creates for you. If you want, you can erase some or all of the functions just by highlighting them and selecting the Clear command from the Edit menu. Once you've cleared some or all of the functions, you can leave the cells blank, or you can enter explanatory labels or alternative functions into them.

Figure 17-29

```
                    SALES REPORT
 Lastname  Sales      Address         City        State
 Jeffries  $14,630 777 College Dr.  Huntsville    AL
 Johnson   $27,170 987 Maple Rd.    Birmingham    AL
 Welch     $44,410 987 Maple Rd.    Birmingham    AL
 Lott       $4,480 444 8th St.      Little Rock   AR
 Marshall  $58,840 444 8th St.      Little Rock   AR
 Nielsen   $25,530 678 S. 15th Ave. Little Rock   AR
 O'Bryan   $31,880 123 Smith Ave.   Ft. Smith     AR
        7          7                        7    7  $206,940
 Davis     $46,380 321 Druid Ln.    Des Moines    IA
 Peterson  $54,120 1175 15th St.    Dubuque       IA
 Moore     $56,670 324 Zazu Pitts   Chicago       IL
 Price     $66,820 12 Deer Rd.      Chicago       IL
 Quillen   $18,530 324 Zazu Pitts   Chicago       IL
 Smiley    $63,200 324 Zazu Pitts   Chicago       IL
 Smith     $60,940 24 Bunyon Pike   Peoria        IL
 Smith     $67,940 24 Kentucky St.  Springfield   IL
 Ward      $59,850 12 Deer Rd.      Chicago       IL
 Zeeman    $69,400 213 Elm Rd.      Springfield   IL
 Anderson  $60,940 123 Oak St.      Fort Wayne    IN
 Bates    $100,650 666 Shower Dr.   Indianapolis  IN
 Eggers    $46,300 55 Wheeler St.   Fort Wayne    IN
 Jacob     $46,390 33 College Way   South Bend    IN
 Rice      $38,620 3515 E. 82nd St. Indianapolis  IN
 Rogers    $87,420 3515 E. 82nd St. Indianapolis  IN
 Schultz   $55,730 3515 E. 82nd St. Indianapolis  IN
 Smith     $22,320 1234 Iowa Dr.    Gary          IN
 Thompson  $23,280 3515 E. 82nd St. Indianapolis  IN
       19         19                       19   19 #########
 Head      $79,650 63 Landings Way  Topeka        KS
 Wade      $33,790 63 Landings Way  Topeka        KS
 Yates     $10,580 17 City Square   Wichita       KS
 Ziegler   $25,800 17 City Square   Wichita       KS
 Campbell  $93,110 123 Wallace Ave. Lexington     KY
 Gates     $46,830 229 Broadway     Louisville    KY
 Jones     $49,290 333 Outer Loop   Louisville    KY
 McCray    $75,830 13 Hikes Ln.     Louisville    KY
 Shore     $40,200 229 Broadway     Louisville    KY
 Smith     $42,010 13 Hikes Ln.     Louisville    KY
 Ulmer      $6,580 13 Hikes Ln.     Louisville    KY
 Vasquez   $45,160 229 Broadway     Louisville    KY
       12         12                       12   12 $548,830
 Gaston    $69,210 987 Ford St.     Detroit       MI
 Holland   $39,120 987 Ford St.     Detroit       MI
 Ingram    $13,360 987 Ford St.     Detroit       MI
 Jolly      $6,170 8911 Olds Ave.   Detroit       MI
 Kirk       $5,850 8911 Olds Ave.   Detroit       MI
 Laffer    $15,830 7114 Oak St.     Lansing       MI
 Michaels  $25,100 155 College Rd.  E. Lansing    MI
 Nicely     $5,060 477 Stadium Rd.  Green Bay     MI
 Albert    $58,780 412 River Ct.    St. Louis     MO
 Bird      $21,550 412 River Ct.    St. Louis     MO
 Campbell  $47,350 412 River Ct.    St. Louis     MO
```

When the 1st Letter option for a sort field is active, each group will include records with entries in the sort field that begin with the same letter.

►Finally, the changes you make in the Sort Records dialog box in the Report view do not affect the order of the records in the Form or List views of the database document. (In Works 1, the changes you make to the Sort dialog box in the Report view affect the order of the records in the database.)◄

►WORKS 2◄

When you group a report, Works automatically inserts a Summ Group row for each group in the default report definition. If you want, you can add one or more Intr Group rows for each group to the report definition. Intr Group rows are most often used to label groups. You can even use data from within a group as part of the Intr Group row.

You insert an Intr Group row into a database the same way you insert any other type of row. To insert a new Intr Group row, first highlight the entire row above which you want to insert the new row. Next, select the Insert Row/Column... command from the Edit menu. When you do this, Works will display an Insert Row/Column dialog box like the one shown in Figure 17-20. If the report is grouped, the box will include Intr Group and Summ Group options for each grouping field. To insert an Intr Group row, simply select its name from the list,

Inserting Intr Group rows

then choose <OK>. When you do this, Works will insert into the report definition the new Intr Group row you've chosen . As always, Works will not let you insert an Intr Group row out of order. If Works cannot place the Intr Group row at the position you have highlighted, it will insert the row at the apprpriate place in the report definition.

For example, suppose you want to add an Intr ST row to the report definition shown in Figure 17-26. To begin, highlight the Record row in the definition. Next, select the Insert Row/Column command from the Edit menu to display the Insert Row/Column dialog box. Since this report is grouped on the ST field, the box will include an Intr ST and a Summ ST option. To insert the Intr ST row into the definition, highlight the Intr ST option in the list box, and choose <OK>. When you so this, Works will insert an Intr ST row in the definition between the Intr Page and the Record rows, as shown in Figure 17-30.

Figure 17-30

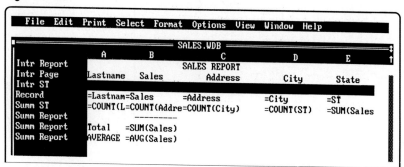

Works inserted an Intr ST row between the Intr Page and Record rows.

Whenever you enter a new Intr Group row into a database, it will be blank. You'll usually want to make an entry in the row that introduces the upcoming group. For example, you might want to place the field contents in the Intr Group row that refers to the grouping field, so that as Works prints the Intr Group row, it will print the entry from the grouping field at the top of each group. For example, since the example report is grouped on the ST field, you might enter the label *State* in column A of the Intr ST row and the field value = *ST* in column B of that row, as shown in Figure 17-31.

To print a report from the definition shown in Figure 17-31, select the Print… command from the Print menu in the Report view, then choose <Print> from the Print dialog box. Figure 17-32 shows the report.

Figure 17-31

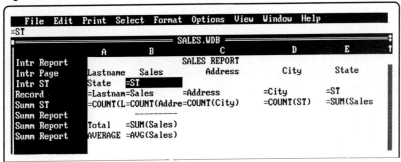

You'll usually want to make an entry in an Intr Group row that introduces the upcoming group.

Figure 17-32

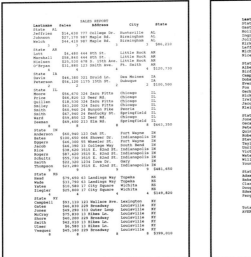 

Works prints the contents of the Intr ST row just before it prints each new group.

As you can see, the report is sorted and grouped on the ST field. This time, however, Works has printed the contents of the Intr ST row just before each new group. The field value in that row, *=ST*, returns the entry from the ST field of the records in the upcoming group.

**Inserting Summ
Group rows**

Works will automatically place one Summ Group row in a report definition for every group field you define. If you want, you can add more Summ Group rows for each group. You can use the second Summ Group row to hold additional summary functions for the group or to hold labels that mark the end of the group.

To insert a new Summ Group row, highlight the entire row at the position you intend to insert a new row. Next, select the Insert Row/Column command from the Edit menu. When you do this, Works will display an Insert Row/Column dialog box. To insert a Summ Group row, simply select its name from the list, then choose <OK>. When you do this, Works will insert a new Summ Group row for the field you've chosen into the report definition. As always, Works will not let you insert a Summ Group row out of order. If Works cannot place the Summ Group row at the position you have highlighted, it will insert the row at the appropriate place in the report definition.

Nesting groups

So far, we've only grouped our reports on one field. However, Works lets you group reports on up to three fields at a time. To create a report that is grouped on two fields, use the Sort Records… command to define two sort fields—the 1st Field and the 2nd Field—for the report. To create a report that is grouped on three fields, you must define three sort fields—the 1st Field, the 2nd Field, and the 3rd Field. Next, activate the Break option for each sort field. Then, when you choose <OK> or press [Enter], Works will include a Summ Group row for each of the sort fields you defined. These rows will include summary functions for each field in the database.

When you group a report on more than one field, the various groups in the report will be "nested." That is, each group of records defined by the first sort field may contain several groups defined by the second sort field. Likewise, each group defined by the second sort field may contain several groups defined by the third sort field. Each group can have its own Intr Group and Summ Group rows. The Summ Group rows for each group may contain summary functions that compute sums and other statistics about the entries in that group. As a result, three levels of subtotals will appear in the report.

An example. Let's create a report for the SALES database that is grouped first by ST, then by City. The resulting report will have a group for each unique ST field entry. These groups will be further grouped by City.

To begin, select the Sort Records… command from the Select menu. When the Sort dialog box shown in Figure 17-25 appears, enter the field name *ST* into the 1st Field text box and the field name *City* in the 2nd Field text box. Next, turn on the Break option for both the 1st Field and the 2nd Field. Then, choose <OK> to execute the command and sort the report. Figure 17-33 shows the new default report definition. Notice that this report definition includes a Summ ST row and a Summ City row and that these rows contain a series of summary functions. Now, from the report definition, select the report you want to see from the View menu.

Figure 17-33

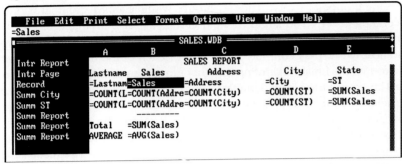

If you've sorted a database on several fields, its default report definition for that database will include a Summ Group row for each sort field.

To print the report, select the Print... command from the Print menu in the Report view. When the Print dialog box appears, choose the <Print> option to print the report. Figure 17-34 shows the first page of the report.

Figure 17-34

```
                SALES REPORT
Lastname    Sales      Address            City          State
Johnson     $27,170 987 Maple Rd.       Birmingham   AL
Welch       $44,410 987 Maple Rd.       Birmingham   AL
     2         2                      2          2    $71,580
Jeffries    $14,630 777 College Dr.     Huntsville   AL
     1         1                      1          1    $14,630
     3         3                      3          3    $86,210
O'Bryan     $31,880 123 Smith Ave.      Ft. Smith    AR
     1         1                      1          1    $31,880
Lott         $4,480 444 8th St.         Little Rock  AR
Marshall    $58,840 444 8th St.         Little Rock  AR
Nielsen     $25,530 678 S. 15th Ave.    Little Rock  AR
     3         3                      3          3    $88,850
     4         4                      4          4   $120,730
Davis       $46,380 321 Druid Ln.       Des Moines   IA
     1         1                      1          1    $46,380
Peterson    $54,120 1175 15th St.       Dubuque      IA
     1         1                      1          1    $54,120
     2         2                      2          2   $100,500
Moore       $56,670 324 Zazu Pitts      Chicago      IL
Price       $66,820 12 Deer Rd.         Chicago      IL
Quillen     $18,530 324 Zazu Pitts      Chicago      IL
Smiley      $63,200 324 Zazu Pitts      Chicago      IL
Ward        $59,850 12 Deer Rd.         Chicago      IL
     5         5                      5          5   $265,070
Smith       $60,940 24 Bunyon Pike      Peoria       IL
     1         1                      1          1    $60,940
Smith       $67,940 24 Kentucky St.     Springfield  IL
Zeeman      $69,400 213 Elm Rd.         Springfield  IL
     2         2                      2          2   $137,340
     8         8                      8          8   $463,350
Anderson    $60,940 123 Oak St.         Fort Wayne   IN
Eggers      $46,300 55 Wheeler St.      Fort Wayne   IN
     2         2                      2          2   $107,240
Smith       $22,320 1234 Iowa Dr.       Gary         IN
     1         1                      1          1    $22,320
Bates      $100,650 666 Shower Dr.      Indianapolis IN
Rice        $38,620 3515 E. 82nd St.    Indianapolis IN
Rogers      $87,420 3515 E. 82nd St.    Indianapolis IN
Schultz     $55,730 3515 E. 82nd St.    Indianapolis IN
Thompson    $23,280 3515 E. 82nd St.    Indianapolis IN
     5         5                      5          5   $305,700
Jacob       $46,390 33 College Way      South Bend   IN
     1         1                      1          1    $46,390
     9         9                      9          9   $481,650
Head        $79,650 63 Landings Way     Topeka       KS
Wade        $33,790 63 Landings Way     Topeka       KS
     2         2                      2          2   $113,440
Yates       $10,580 17 City Square      Wichita      KS
Ziegler     $25,800 17 City Square      Wichita      KS
     2         2                      2          2    $36,380
     4         4                      4          4   $149,820
Campbell    $93,110 123 Wallace Ave.    Lexington    KY
```

This report is grouped on the ST and City fields.

As you can see, the report is grouped by ST. Within each ST field group, the records are grouped by City. The City groups within each ST group are arranged in ascending order. The larger ST field groups are also arranged in ascending order. Works has inserted a break after each City group and after each ST group. In addition, Works has computed statistics for each of the fields in each group. Each time Works finished printing one City group, the summary functions in the Summ City row of the report definition computed the count or sum for the entries in the fields of the records in that group. The results of the functions for each group appear just below the last record in the group. Each time Works finished printing an ST group, the summary functions in the Summ ST row computed the count or sum for the entries in the fields of the records in that group. The results appear just below the last record in each group.

Notes. In the previous example, we grouped the report on two fields. You can also group a report on three fields. To do so, you should select the Sort Records… command, enter the name of the third sort field in the 3rd Field text box, activate the Break option for the third field, and choose <OK> to sort the report. The report will include Summ Group rows for all three sort fields. When you print the report, Works will group the report on all three sort fields.

To add a third group to the report shown in Figure 17-34, we'll use the Address field as the third sort field and begin by selecting the Sort Records… command from the Select menu. When the Sort Records dialog box appears, enter the field name *Address* in the 3rd Field text box, activate the Break option for the third field, then choose <OK>. Figure 17-35 shows the report definition after you issue this command. Notice that the definition now includes a Summ Address row and that this row contains a series of summary functions.

Figure 17-35

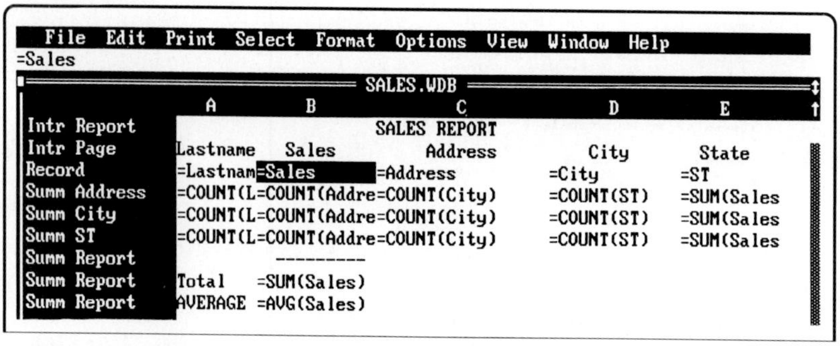

The Sort… command allows you to add a new group to an existing report definition.

To print the report, select the Print… command from the Print menu in the Report view. When the Print dialog box shown in Figure 17-15 appears, choose <Print> to print the report. Figure 17-36 shows the first page of the report.

Figure 17-36

```
                          SALES REPORT
         Lastname    Sales       Address         City       State
         Johnson    $27,170  987 Maple Rd.    Birmingham  AL
         Welch      $44,410  987 Maple Rd.    Birmingham  AL
                2              2                 2           2    $71,580
                2              2                 2           2    $71,580
         Jeffries   $14,630  777 College Dr.  Huntsville  AL
                1              1                 1           1    $14,630
                1              1                 1           1    $14,630
                3              3                 3           3    $86,210
         O'Bryan    $31,880  123 Smith Ave.   Ft. Smith   AR
                1              1                 1           1    $31,880
                1              1                 1           1    $31,880
         Lott        $4,480  444 8th St.      Little Rock AR
         Marshall   $58,840  444 8th St.      Little Rock AR
                2              2                 2           2    $63,320
         Nielsen    $25,530  678 S. 15th Ave. Little Rock AR
                1              1                 1           1    $25,530
                3              3                 3           3    $88,850
                4              4                 4           4   $120,730
         Davis      $46,380  321 Druid Ln.    Des Moines  IA
                1              1                 1           1    $46,380
                1              1                 1           1    $46,380
         Peterson   $54,120  1175 15th St.    Dubuque     IA
                1              1                 1           1    $54,120
                1              1                 1           1    $54,120
                2              2                 2           2   $100,500
         Price      $66,820  12 Deer Rd.      Chicago     IL
         Ward       $59,850  12 Deer Rd.      Chicago     IL
                2              2                 2           2   $126,670
         Moore      $56,670  324 Zazu Pitts   Chicago     IL
         Quillen    $18,530  324 Zazu Pitts   Chicago     IL
         Smiley     $63,200  324 Zazu Pitts   Chicago     IL
                3              3                 3           3   $138,400
                5              5                 5           5   $265,070
         Smith      $60,940  24 Bunyon Pike   Peoria      IL
                1              1                 1           1    $60,940
                1              1                 1           1    $60,940
         Zeeman     $69,400  213 Elm Rd.      Springfield IL
                1              1                 1           1    $69,400
         Smith      $67,940  24 Kentucky St.  Springfield IL
                1              1                 1           1    $67,940
                2              2                 2           2   $137,340
                8              8                 8           8   $463,350
         Anderson   $60,940  123 Oak St.      Fort Wayne  IN
                1              1                 1           1    $60,940
         Eggers     $46,300  55 Wheeler St.   Fort Wayne  IN
                1              1                 1           1    $46,300
                2              2                 2           2   $107,240
         Smith      $22,320  1234 Iowa Dr.    Gary        IN
                1              1                 1           1    $22,320
                1              1                 1           1    $22,320
         Rice       $38,620  3515 E. 82nd St. Indianapolis IN
         Rogers     $87,420  3515 E. 82nd St. Indianapolis IN
```

This report is grouped on the ST, City, and Address fields.

Once you've created a grouped report, you can use the Insert Row/Column command on the Edit menu to add one or more Intr Group rows for each of the groups. You'll usually want to make an entry in each Intr Group row that introduces the next group.

Formulas

Formulas are special entries that manipulate the values in one or more fields to create calculated results. Formulas are much like field contents, since they refer to the fields in a database. However, while field contents simply refer to the entries in a field, formulas manipulate the values in the field. For instance, you could use the formula =*Sales/52* in a report definition to compute the average weekly sales for each salesperson. Works will print the result of these formulas in the report.

Like formulas in databases, formulas in report definitions use the values in one or more fields as the basis for a calculation. Formulas in a report definition can use the same mathematical operators that you use in formulas elsewhere in Works: +, -, *, /, and ^. Formulas can include references to the fields of the database, literal values, and summary functions. In report definitions, they refer to the fields in the database by name.

You can enter a formula into a cell of a report definition in the same way you enter a formula into a cell, in a spreadsheet or a database in the List view: Move the highlight to a cell, and type the formula. For example, to enter the formula =*Sales/52* into a cell of a report definition, you would move the highlight to that cell, type =*Sales/52,* and press [Enter]. Once you've entered a formula into a definition, you can use the commands on the Format menu to format its result.

As with other types of entries, the position of a formula in a report definition determines where it will appear in the report. If you place a formula in a Record row, that formula will act upon the values in the fields of each record, and its result will be printed once for each visible record in the database.

You can also place formulas in Summ Group and Summ Report rows. When you use formulas in Summ rows, you'll usually want the formula to operate on the result of one or more summary functions. That way, the result of the formula will apply to the group, page, or report as a whole, rather than to one specific record.

At first, it's easy to confuse formulas with summary functions. Both are used to compute new information from the existing entries in your database. The key difference is that summary functions compute statistics about the entries in many records but just in one field. Formulas make computations based on the entries in a field that affect more than one record.

An example

Let's look at an example of using formulas in reports. Suppose you want to add formulas to the report definition shown in Figure 17-21 that compute the weekly sales for each salesperson in the report and the total and average weekly sales for all the salespeople. To begin, make that report the active report by selecting its name from the View menu. When the report definition shown in Figure 17-21 appears, highlight column C, and select the Insert Row/Column command from the Edit menu to insert a new column into the worksheet. Next, enter the label *Weekly* into the second cell in the new column (column C), and use the Style… command on the Format menu to assign the Bold style to this cell.

Next, move the highlight to the cell in the Record row in column C, and enter the formula =*Sales/52.* Then, move the highlight down to the cell in the second Summ Report row in column C, and enter the formula =*SUM(Sales)/52.* Next, move the highlight down to the cell in column C of the third Summ Report row, and enter the formula =*AVG(Sales)/52.* Finally, assign the Currency (0) format to the cells that contain these three formulas. Figure 17-37 shows the report definition with these formulas in place.

To print the report, select the Print… command from the Print menu in the Report view. When the Print dialog box appears, choose the <Print> option to print the report. Figure 17-38 shows the first two pages of the report. As you can see, the formulas in the report definition have computed the weekly sales for each salesperson and the total and average weekly sales for the report as a whole.

Figure 17-37

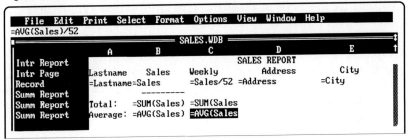

Formulas compute new information from the values in fields or the results of summary functions.

Figure 17-38

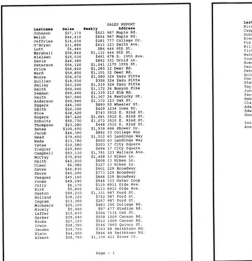
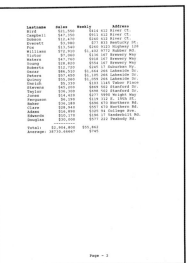

The formulas in the report definition have computed average weekly sales for each salesperson and the total and average weekly sales for the sales report as a whole.

The formula that you use to define a calculated field can be up to 64 characters long, and it can include any of Works' mathematical operators. Like all formulas in Works, the formulas in a calculated field must begin with an equal sign. Typically, a formula will contain at least one field name, although it does not have to.

Notes

You can edit a formula in a report definition the same way you edit any other formula in Works. All you have to do is move the highlight to any cell in the calculated field and press [Edit] ([F2]) to bring the formula onto the formula line. Then, you move the cursor around in the formula, inserting and deleting characters to modify it. When you're finished, press [Enter] to lock in the new formula.

If you change the name of a field that is referred to by a formula, that change will not affect the calculation. Works will automatically update any references to that field in the formula.

A formula in a report definition can refer to any field in the database on which the definition is based, including fields that aren't actually in the definition. For example, if you create a report definition for the SALES database that doesn't include the Sales field, you can still enter a formula in that definition that refers to the Sales field.

Managing reports

As we have said, you can create up to eight reports in a single database. Works gives each report you create a default name. The first report will be named Report1, the second, Report2, and so on. Works lists the names of the Reports you have created for a given database at the bottom of the View menu in either the database document or the Report view. For example, Figure 17-39 shows the View menu for our example database after we have created three reports. Notice that the names of the reports—Report1, Report2, and Report3—appear at the bottom of the menu.

Figure 17-39

Works automatically gives each report you create a name and number and lists them on the Report menu.

The active report

The dot next to the name of Report3 in the list in Figure 17-39 indicates that it is the active report. Although you can create up to eight reports in a given database, only one of those reports can be active at a time. When you issue one of Works' reporting commands, Works will execute that command on the active report. For example, when you select the Print... command from the Report view's Print menu, Works will print the active report.

Each time you create a new report, it becomes the active report. To make another report the active report, just pull down the View menu, and select the name of the report you want to make active. You can select the name of the report by pointing to it or by typing the appropriate number: 1 for Report1, 2 for Report2, and so on. When you select a report, the dot will move to the name you select, signifying that it is now the active report. For example, to change the active Report in Figure 17-38 from Report3 to Report2, you would pull down the View menu and either type 2 or highlight the Report2 option and press [Enter].

The Reports... command on the View menu in database documents and in the Report view allows you to rename, delete, and copy your reports. When you select this command, Works will display a dialog box like the one shown in Figure 17-40. As you can see, the names of all of the reports in the current database appear in this box, and the name of the active report is selected. The options at the bottom of this box—<Rename>, <Delete>, and <Copy>—allow you to rename, delete, and copy reports.

The Reports... command

Figure 17-40

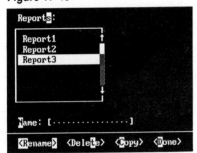

The Reports... command allows you to rename, delete, and copy reports.

Renaming Reports.   If you are creating more than one report from a database, you will probably want to give names to your reports that make it easier for you to remember what they do. You can use the <Rename> button in the Reports dialog box to change the name that Works has given to a report. When you rename a report, its new name will appear on the Report menu and inside the Reports dialog box in place of Works' default name.

To rename a report, first select the Reports... command from the View menu. When the Reports dialog box appears, choose the name of the report you want to rename in the Reports list box. Next, move to the Name text box, and type the new report name. Like range names, report names can be up to 15 characters long and may include any alphabetic, numeric, or punctuation character. Once you've specified the name, choose <Rename> to rename the report. (Since <Rename> is the default choice, you can choose it simply by pressing [Enter].)

If the new name you specify for a report conflicts with the name of an existing report, Works will display an alert box with the message *REPORTNAME already exists.*, where *REPORTNAME* is the name you have specified. If you see this message, you should choose <OK> to acknowledge the error. Then you should either choose a new name for the report you are renaming or rename or delete the other report.

Deleting reports. You can use the <Delete> button in the Reports dialog box to delete reports. You might use this command if you create a report that you no longer need or if you want to make room in the current database for a new report. (Remember, only eight reports can exist at once in a given database.)

To delete a report, select the Reports... command from the View menu. When you see the Reports dialog box, choose the name of the report you want to delete from the list of reports in the Reports list box. Then, choose <Delete> to delete the report. Before it deletes the report, Works will display a dialog box that asks the question, *OK to delete: REPORTNAME?*, in which REPORTNAME is the name of the report you've chosen. This box will offer two buttons: <Yes> and <No>. If you choose <Yes>, Works will delete the report. The deleted report will no longer be listed either on the Report menu or in the Reports dialog box. If you choose <No>, Works will cancel the Reports... command and will not delete the report.

Copying reports. There may be times when you'll want to copy a report. For instance, suppose you're creating several reports that are basically similar but have a few different features. Rather than creating both reports from scratch, it may be easier and faster to create the first report from scratch, then use the <Copy> button to create the second one.

To copy a report, first select the Reports... command from the View menu. When the Reports dialog box appears, highlight the name of the report you want to copy in the Reports list box. Then, move to the Name box, and enter the name for the new report. Finally, choose <Copy> to copy the report. When you use the <Copy > button to create a new report, Works will list the new report on the View menu. The new report will be an exact copy of the source report. To activate it, you can choose the report from the View menu.

If you don't specify a name before you copy a report, Works will assign the new report one of its standard numerical names (such as Report6 or Report7). If there are already eight reports in a database when you choose the <Copy> button, Works will display an alert box that contains the message *No more than 8 reports allowed in each Database file. To delete reports, use the Reports command in the View menu.*

CONCLUSION

In this chapter, we have shown you how to print databases. First, we explained the Print... command on the Print menu in database documents, which lets you print simple listings of your reports. Then, we examined Works' powerful report generator, which lets you create sophisticated grouped reports.

This chapter is the last of three covering database documents. In the next chapter, we'll introduce communications documents and show you how to use Works to communicate with other computers.

Communications 18

*I*n addition to its word processing, spreadsheet, and database powers, Works can communicate with other computers. Within a Works communications document, you can send information to other computers and receive information from them. For example, you can communicate with other PCs, computer bulletin boards, and on-line services like CompuServe, Dow Jones News/Retrieval, and The Source.

Using Works to communicate with another computer involves five steps. First, you create or open a communications document. Next, if you have created a new document, customize the communication settings to match those of the computer with which you will be communicating. Then, connect with the remote computer, either by calling it or answering a call from it. Once you are connected, you can send and receive information in a variety of ways. After you finish communicating, break the connection.

In this chapter, we'll show you how to use Works' communications powers. First, we'll tell you what hardware you need and show you how to configure Works' various communication settings. Then, we'll teach you how to connect with another computer. Finally, we'll show you how to send and receive information once you are on-line.

HARDWARE

Before you can use Works to communicate with another computer, you need certain pieces of hardware. For one thing, your computer must have a serial communication card. This card contains the circuitry that allows your computer to send and receive information through the serial communication port—either a DB-25 or DB-9 connector—that is attached to it. Many multifunction memory boards have built-in serial ports. If you have one of these cards in your computer, you won't need a separate serial communication card.

If you will be communicating over telephone lines, you'll need a modem— a device that converts the binary digits the computer uses to represent characters into audible tones that can be sent across telephone lines, and vice versa. If your modem is Hayes or Hayes-compatible, you'll be able to take advantage of Works' built-in commands that dial and hang up the phone. If not, you'll find the process of making and breaking a connection somewhat more difficult. If you have a Hayes modem, its dip switches should be in their default positions. Table 18-1 shows these default settings.

Table 18-1

Switch number	Position
1	down
2	up
3	down
4	up
5	down
6	down
7	up
8	down

This table shows the proper switch settings for a Hayes modem.

If you'll be communicating with a computer that is close to your computer (for example, in an adjacent room), you won't need a modem. Instead, you can connect the serial ports of the two computers directly with a null-modem cable. Your local computer store probably has these in stock; if not, someone there should be able to make one for you. Table 18-2 contains a diagram of the proper pin connections for a null-modem cable.

Table 18-2

First connector	Second connector
Pin #2	Pin #3
Pin #3	Pin #2
Pin #7	Pin #7

This table shows the proper pin connections for a null-modem cable.

ENTERING THE COMMUNICATIONS ENVIRONMENT

Before you can use Works to communicate with another computer, you must create or open a communications document. To create a new communications document, pull down the File menu, select the Create New File… command, and choose the <New Communications> option. To open an existing communications document, pull down the File menu, select the Open Existing File… command, choose the name of the document you want to open, and then choose <OK>.

Whether you create a new communications document or open an existing one, Works will present an empty communications document like the one shown in Figure 18-1. ▶(If you open an existing document, Works 2 also will display a dialog box that asks if you want it to connect with the remote computer specified by that document. We'll explain more about that later.)

▶WORKS 2◀

Figure 18-1

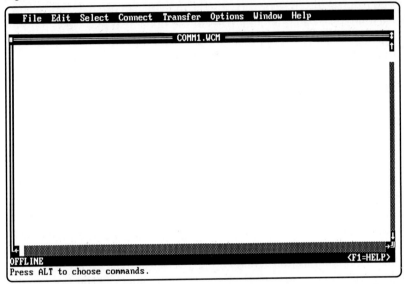

Your screen will look like this when you create or open a communications document.

As you can see, the Communications environment has eight menus: File, Edit, Select, Connect, Transfer, Options, Window, and Help. (Earlier versions of Works do not offer the Edit, Select, and Help menus in their Communications environment.)◀ The File, Window, and Help menus contain the same commands that they do in any other Works environment (commands that allow you to open and close files, switch between active documents, access help, and so forth). The Edit menu contains a single command that allows you to copy text from a communications document; the commands on the Select menu let you select text in a communications document without a mouse; the Connect menu's commands let you connect with a remote computer; the Transfer menu's commands let you send and receive information; and the Options menu's commands let you alter the communication settings for the communications document.

►WORKS 2◄

►At the top of any Works 2 communications document, you'll see the name of that document. For example, the name of the document in Figure 18-1 is COMM1.WCM. (The document name appears at the right edge of the status line in previous versions of Works.)◄ At the bottom of the document, you'll see a status line and a message line. At the left edge of the status line, Works displays the message *OFFLINE* if it is not connected to a remote computer or the elapsed connection time if it is. We'll explain more about this indicator later in this chapter.

►WORKS 2◄

►In Works 2, every communications document appears within a window. You can use your mouse or the commands on the Window menu to resize the window; you can use the close box to close it; and you can use the vertical and horizontal scroll bars to shift different parts of the document into view. In previous releases of Works, communications documents occupy the entire screen, and you can't bring previous portions of a communications document into view.◄

COMMUNICATIONS SETTINGS

Before you can begin to use a new communications document to communicate with another computer, you must adjust the document's communication settings to match those of that computer. The proper settings for most on-line services are published in the documentation you'll receive when you subscribe to those services. If you're going to use the communications document to communicate with another PC, you'll probably want to call the operator of that PC and agree on the settings you'll use. If you don't know what settings to use, 1200 baud, 8 data bits, even parity, and 1 stop bit usually will allow you to make a connection. You can adjust any incorrect settings after you connect.

The Options menu, shown in Figure 18-2, contains the three commands that allow you to adjust the communication settings of a communications document: Terminal..., Communication..., and Phone.... The Terminal settings affect the way the communication session is displayed on your screen. The Communication settings control vital parameters like baud rate, data bits, parity, and stop bits. The Phone settings tell Works what number to dial, the type of phone line to which your modem is connected, and so forth.

Figure 18-2

The commands on the Options menu allow you to adjust the communication settings of a communications document.

The Terminal settings allow you to control the way incoming and outgoing information is displayed in a communications document. To alter the Terminal settings for a communications document, pull down the Options menu and select the Terminal... command. When you do this, Works will present a dialog box like the one shown in Figure 18-3.

The Terminal settings

Figure 18-3

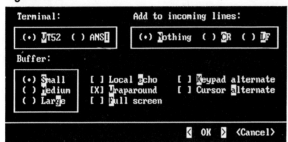

You'll see a dialog box like this one when you select the Terminal... command from the Options menu.

When Works opens the Terminal dialog box, it places the cursor in the Terminal option box. The option you choose in that box determines which type of "dumb" terminal Works will program your computer to emulate. If the computer with which you will be communicating expects your computer to emulate a VT52 terminal, choose *VT52*. If it expects your computer to emulate a VT100 or VT220/240 terminal, choose *ANSI*. If it doesn't care what sort of terminal your computer is emulating, or even whether it is emulating a terminal at all (most won't), you can choose either VT52 or ANSI.

Terminal types

▶The Buffer option box in the Terminal dialog box controls the size of the communications buffer—the amount of RAM that Works reserves for the storage of incoming and outgoing information. (This option box is unique to Works). If you select the Small option, Works will reserve enough room for 100 lines of text; if you select the Medium option, Works will reserve enough room for 300 lines of text; and if you select the Large option, Works will reserve enough room for 750 lines of text.◀

The communications buffer
▶WORKS 2◀

Works uses the communications buffer to store the information that scrolls across the screen during a communication session. This includes the information sent to you by a remote computer, as well as the information you send to a remote computer. ▶(As we'll explain later, you can select all or part of the information in the communications buffer and copy it to another document.)◀ Once the buffer has been filled, Works will remove the first character from the buffer each time you type a character or receive a character from the remote computer. Consequently, at any point in time, the communication buffer will hold only the last

▶WORKS 2◀

portion of the current communication session. Unless you have instructed Works to capture the incoming text to a file (a process we'll explain later), any information that Works removes from the buffer to make room for new information will be lost.

End-of-line characters

The Add to Incoming Lines option box in the Terminal dialog box determines whether Works will add a carriage return (CR), a line feed (LF), or nothing at all to each end-of-line sequence (either a CR, an LF, or a CR/LF) it receives. If the remote computer sends only a CR when the user presses [Enter], you should choose the LF option. Otherwise, each incoming line will overwrite the previous one on your screen. If the remote computer sends only an LF (this is very rare), you should choose the CR option. Otherwise, Works will skip down to the next line but will not return to the left edge of the screen at the end of each line. If the remote computer sends both a CR and an LF, you should choose Nothing.

Importantly, "incoming" characters are not just those characters sent to Works by the other computer—they also include characters sent by your computer and echoed back to it, either by the remote computer or locally. Like many other programs, Works sends a CR only when you press [Enter]. Unless you choose LF, each line you type will overwrite the previous one on your screen. For this reason, you'll almost always want to have the LF option selected. That way, the information you type will be single-spaced on your screen. If the remote computer sends only a CR, the information it sends will appear single-spaced on your screen as well. However, if the remote computer sends CR/LF combinations, the information will be double-spaced. This is better than the result you'll get with the Nothing option: The information sent by the remote computer will be single-spaced, but each line you send will overwrite the previous one.

Local Echo

The Local Echo check box determines whether Works will "echo" to the screen the information you type from the keyboard. If the remote computer echoes each character you send (full-duplex communication), this check box should be inactive. If the remote computer does not provide an echo (half-duplex communication), this check box should be activated.

If you have chosen the incorrect Local Echo setting, you'll see either two occurrences of each character that you type or nothing at all. If Local Echo is on while you are communicating with a computer that provides a remote echo, two occurrences of everything you type will appear on your screen. If you type *test*, for example, you'll see the characters *tteesstt*. To solve this problem, just turn Local Echo off. If Local Echo is off while you are communicating with a computer that does not provide a remote echo, nothing you send will appear on your screen. To solve this problem, simply turn Local Echo on.

Like most communication software, Works does not provide a remote echo. Therefore, Local Echo should be on when you are communicating with another Works system. Many on-line services do provide a remote echo; consequently, Local Echo should be off when you communicate with those services.

The Wraparound setting determines whether Works will wrap lines of text longer than 80 characters (the number of usable columns on Works' communication screen—not necessarily the number of characters visible on each line of a communications window) to the beginning of a new line. If this option is turned on, long lines will wrap around to the beginning of the next line. If this option is off (indicated by a blank check box), long lines will not wrap. Instead, the cursor will remain lodged against the right margin, and each new character will replace the previous one; Works won't wrap back to the left edge of the screen until it receives a carriage return. In almost all cases, you'll want this setting to be on— its default position.

Wraparound

The Full Screen check box controls how many lines of information Works can display on the screen of your computer. When this check box is off, Works will display a menu bar at the top of the screen, both a status line and message line at the bottom of the screen, and a border around the communications window, as shown in Figure 18-1. ►This leaves a maximum of only 19 lines (21 lines in previous releases of Works) available for the display of incoming and outgoing information.◄ When this check box is on, the menu bar, status line, message line, and window borders disappear, making 24 rows available.

Full screen

►WORKS 2◄

Whether you should select the normal view or the full-screen view depends on the computer with which you are communicating. VT52 and VT100 terminals have 80-column by 24-row screens. Therefore, when you are communicating with a computer that expects you to emulate one of these terminals, you should turn on the Full Screen check box. If you are not emulating one of these terminals, this check box can be either on or off. We prefer the normal view, since it allows you to see the messages and indicators on the status and message lines and access the menus easily with a mouse. When Works is in the full-screen view, you must press the [Alt] key (or click anywhere on the screen) to reveal the menu bar.

Interestingly, Works will display a communications document in the full-screen view only when it is in the Connect mode. When Works is off-line, all communications documents appear in the normal view. As soon as you connect to another computer, though, communications documents in which the Full Screen check box is turned on will appear in the full-screen view.

The Keypad Alternate and Cursor Alternate check boxes control the function of the keys on your computer's numeric keypad in a communications document. The Keypad Alternate check box controls the function of the keys on your computer's numeric keypad when the [Num Lock] key is on (that is, when the keypad is in its Number mode) during a communication session. If the Keypad Alternate check box is off, these keys have their normal function: Typing 1 will send the number 1 to the remote computer; typing + will send a + sign; and so forth. If this check box is on, however, Works will send character sequences that have special meanings to VT52 and ANSI host computers when you press those

Keypad Alternate and Cursor Alternate

keys. If the VT52 option is selected in the Terminal option box, Works will send the character sequences shown in the second column of Table 18-3 when you press those keys. If the ANSI option is selected, Works will send the sequences shown in the third column of that table instead. You should not select this option unless you are communicating with a system that expects you to emulate one of these terminals.

Table 18-3

Key pressed	Escape sequence sent VT52	ANSI
0	[Esc]?p	[Esc]Op
1	[Esc]?q	[Esc]Oq
2	[Esc]?r	[Esc]Or
3	[Esc]?s	[Esc]Os
4	[Esc]?t	[Esc]Ot
5	[Esc]?u	[Esc]Ou
6	[Esc]?v	[Esc]Ov
7	[Esc]?w	[Esc]Ow
8	[Esc]?x	[Esc]Ox
9	[Esc]?y	[Esc]Oy
-	[Esc]?m	[Esc]Om
*	[Esc]?l	[Esc]Ol
.	[Esc]?n	[Esc]On
+	[Esc]?M	[Esc]OM

This table shows the escape sequences Works will send when the Keypad Alternate setting is on.

The Cursor Alternate check box controls the function of the four arrow keys when Works is in the ANSI emulation mode (that is, while ANSI is selected in the Terminal option box). If the Cursor Alternate check box is off, these keys function normally. If this check box is on, however, Works will send the character sequences shown in Table 18-4 when you press these keys. Unless you are communicating with a system that expects you to emulate an ANSI terminal (such as a DEC VT-100), you should leave this check box off.

The Communication settings

When you pull down the Options menu and select the Communication... command, Works will display a dialog box like the one shown in Figure 18-4. The settings in this dialog box allow you to control vital communication settings like baud rate, data bits, and parity. Unlike the Terminal settings, these settings don't affect just the way that information is displayed on the screen of your computer—

they affect the way Works sends information to and receives information from the remote computer. If the communication settings do not match those of the remote computer, the information you send and receive may be garbled. In some cases, you won't be able to communicate with the remote computer at all.

Table 18-4

Cursor key	Escape sequence sent
↑	[Esc]OB
←	[Esc]OD
→	[Esc]OC
↓	[Esc]OA

This table shows the escape sequences Works will send when the Cursor Alternate setting is on.

Figure 18-4

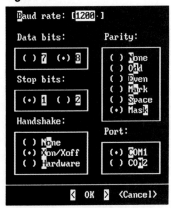

You'll see a dialog box like this one when you select the Communication... command from the Options menu.

The Baud Rate text box in the Communication dialog box allows you to set the speed at which Works will communicate with the remote computer. To specify the communication speed (measured in bits per second), you simply type the speed at which you want to communicate in the Baud Rate text box. ▶Works allows you to specify any speed from 50 bits per second (75 in previous releases of Works) to 9600 bits per second.◀

There are two factors to consider when selecting a baud rate for communicating with another computer via modem. First, you must select a baud rate at which your modem is capable of communicating. Older Hayes modems can communicate at 300 or 1200 baud; the Hayes 2400 can communicate at 300, 1200, or 2400 baud. If you choose a baud rate that your modem cannot handle, your modem will not respond to Works' commands to dial or answer the phone.

Baud rate

▶WORKS 2◀

Selecting the baud rate at which the remote system expects to communicate is as important as selecting a baud rate that your modem can handle. As with most communication settings, you should always select the baud rate that the remote system will use. For most communication via modem, you'll use 1200 baud.

Baud rate mismatches.   When a modem answers an incoming call, it always does so at the baud rate used by the modem that called it. If the baud rate your modem is using does not match the baud rate Works is set for, your computer will not be able to communicate with your modem. Characters sent to you will appear as gobbledygook on your screen. To correct this problem, pull down the Options menu after connecting, select the Communication… command, specify the correct baud rate, and choose <OK>.

Direct connections.   If you are directly connected to a remote computer, your baud rate choices are not limited to the rates that your modem can handle. In these situations, you probably will want to transfer information as rapidly as Works will allow (up to 9600 bits per second). In direct-connect situations, however, you still must select the baud rate for which the remote computer is set. Otherwise, you'll receive strange characters from the remote computer, and that computer will receive strange characters from you.

Data bits

The Data Bits option box in the Communication dialog box lets you specify the number of bits (either 7 or 8) that make up each transmitted character. To specify the number of data bits, simply move the cursor to the Data Bits option box and choose either the 7 option or the 8 option.

It takes 7 bits to represent ASCII characters 0 through 127 (the "normal" characters—letters, numerals, punctuation marks, and so on), but 8 bits to represent characters 128-255 (characters such as £, Ω, and ÷). If you will be sending and receiving only lower-level characters, you may select either 7 bits or 8 bits. If you will be sending and receiving upper-level characters, however, you must select 8 data bits. Otherwise, Works will strip the high-level bit from the character during the transmission, transforming the character into its lower-level equivalent.

As with other communication settings, you should select the number of data bits that the remote computer expects. Since many on-line services require 8-bit communication, which offers the maximum flexibility even when communicating with systems that do not require it, you probably will use an 8-bit character length in most communication sessions.

Stop bits

All asynchronous communication systems use either 1 or 2 stop bits to mark the end of each transmitted character (a series of 7 or 8 data bits). The Stop Bits setting in the Communication dialog box allows you to specify how many stop bits Works will append to each outgoing character and strip from each incoming character. To alter this setting, simply move the cursor to the Stop Bits option box and choose either 1 (the default) or 2. As with other communication settings, the number of stop bits you select should match that used by the remote computer. In most cases, this number will be 1.

Works also allows you to specify what sort of handshaking it should use: either None, Xon/Xoff, or Hardware. Handshaking is a system by which two computers can tell each other when to start and stop sending information. Works supports two methods of handshaking: software (Xon/Xoff) and hardware. Under software handshaking, the receiving computer sends an Xoff signal ([Ctrl]S) to the sending computer when it wants that computer to pause and sends an Xon signal ([Ctrl]Q) when it wants the computer to resume. Under hardware handshaking, the receiving computer tells the sending computer to pause and resume by raising or lowering the voltage on one of the wires that connects them. You can use hardware handshaking only when two computers are directly connected—not when they are communicating via modem.

Handshaking

To specify the type of handshaking Works should use, simply move the cursor to the Handshake option box and choose one of the three options. If you choose None, Works will neither send nor respond to either software or hardware handshaking signals. If you choose Xon/Xoff, Works will use Xon/Xoff (software) handshaking. If you choose Hardware, Works will send and respond to hardware handshaking. Of course, you should choose the type of handshaking the remote computer will be using. In almost all cases, this will be Xon/Xoff.

The Parity option allows you to specify the type of parity checking that Works will use. Parity is an error-checking mechanism that lets the receiving computer identify incorrectly transmitted characters. When two computers use parity checking, the sending computer adds an 8th bit (a parity bit) to the end of each character that it transmits to the receiving computer. If parity is set to Odd, Works adds whichever digit is required to make the sum odd. If parity is set to Even, the sending computer adds a binary 1 or a binary 0 as the 8th bit—whichever is required to make the sum of the digits in the character even. If parity is set for Mark, the sending computer adds a binary 1 as the parity bit. If parity is set for Space, the sending computer uses a binary 0. If parity is set for Mask, Works won't use parity checking and will ignore any used by the remote computer.

Parity

Works checks the parity bit of each character it receives. If the bit is what it is supposed to be, Works will accept that character. If the bit is not correct, Works will reject it and display a * in place of the faulty character.

To select a parity setting, simply move the cursor to the Parity option box within the Communication dialog box and select one of the six options: None, Odd, Even, Mark, Space, or Mask (the default). As with other communication settings, you should match the parity setting of the remote computer.

**Selecting a
communication port**

The final setting in the Communication dialog box allows you to specify which port Works should use for transmitting and receiving information. As you can see, the Port option box contains two options: COM1 (the default) and COM2. These choices correspond to your computer's first and second serial communication ports. If your computer has only one serial port, you should select COM1. If your computer has two serial ports, you can choose either COM1 or COM2. In all cases, you should select the port to which your modem will be connected when you use the current communications document to communicate with a remote computer. If you use a serial mouse, you should not select the serial port to which that mouse is connected.

▶WORKS 2◀

Originally, COM1 will be the default Port setting; that is, the COM1 port will be selected in any new communications document. ▶However, in Works 2, you can make COM2 the default port. We'll show you how in Appendix A2.◀

The Phone settings

When you pull down the Options menu and select the Phone... command, Works will display a dialog box like the one shown in Figure 18-5. The settings in this box control the way Works communicates with your modem. For example, they tell your modem what number to dial, what type of phone line it is connected to, and so forth.

Figure 18-5

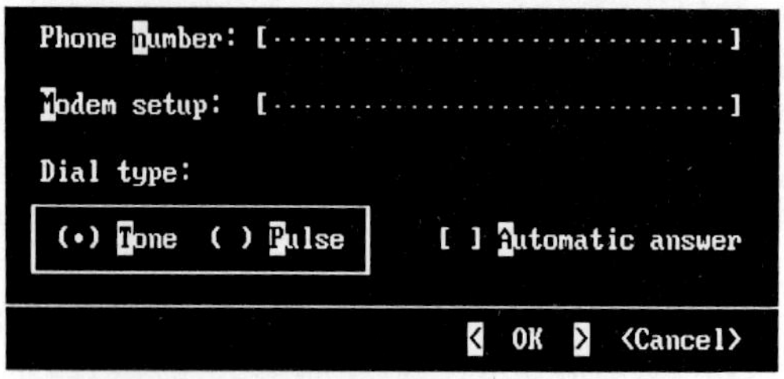

You'll see a dialog box like this one when you select the Phone... command from the Options menu.

**Specifying a
phone number**

The Phone Number text box in the Phone dialog box allows you to specify the number you want Works to dial when you command it to dial the phone. To specify a phone number, simply move the cursor to the text box and type a number. The number you specify can be up to 255 characters long and can contain any characters you want to include. However, your modem will ignore all characters except digits, which it dials, and commas, which introduce two-second delays into the dialing sequence. If you specify the string *9,,1-(800)-555-1212*, your modem will dial a 9, wait four seconds, then dial 18005551212. (Modems that are not Hayes-compatible may use a different pause character.)

The Modem Setup text box in the Phone dialog box allows you to specify a custom setup string that Works will send to your modem whenever you command it to connect with a remote computer. If you have a Hayes-compatible modem, you probably won't have much use for this option. If you have a modem that does not use the Hayes command set, however, you must use this box to communicate with it. If you want a non-Hayes modem to dial the phone, you'll need to enter that modem's dial command and the number you want to dial in this box. If you want to tell a non-Hayes modem to answer the phone automatically, you'll have to type that modem's automatic answer string into this box.

Specifying a modem setup string

The Dial Type option box in the Phone dialog box allows you to specify whether your modem is connected to a pulse (rotary dial) line or to a touch-tone line. The choice you make determines whether your modem will "dial" as if it were using a touch-tone phone or an old-fashioned rotary (pulse) phone. If your modem is connected to a rotary line (rare these days), you must choose Pulse. If your modem is connected to a touch-tone line, you should choose Tone, but you can choose Pulse if you want.

Selecting a phone type

Tone is the default Dial Type setting. ►However, you can make Pulse the default, if you want. We'll show you how to do that in Appendix A2.◄

►WORKS 2◄

The final setting in the Phone dialog box, Automatic Answer, tells Works whether to switch your modem to the Automatic Answer mode. If this check box is on, Works will switch your modem to the Automatic Answer mode—rather than dial the phone—when you issue the Connect command. This setting should be on only when you want Works to answer an incoming call. It must be off in order for Works to dial the phone.

The Automatic Answer setting

As you have seen, you must make a variety of choices to establish the correct settings for communicating with a particular remote computer. Fortunately, you only have to create these settings once. After selecting the appropriate settings for communicating with a particular computer, you can save those settings and reuse them whenever you need to communicate with that computer.

Saving communication settings

How do you save a set of communication settings? By saving the communications document. Saving a communications document is no different from saving any other Works document—you simply pull down the File menu, select either the Save or Save As... command, and specify a name. Works uses the extension .WCM to identify files that contain communications documents.

When you save most Works documents, Works saves both the contents of those documents and their settings. For example, when you save a word processor document, Works saves the text in that document, as well as its margin settings, tab settings, and so forth. Unlike other types of Works documents, communications documents do not store any information—they are simply collections of settings. Consequently, that's all Works saves.

As you use Works to communicate with other computers, you'll find that almost every computer will require a slightly different set of communication settings. For that reason, you'll want to create a different communications document (that is, a different set of settings) for each computer with which you will communicate on a regular basis. For example, you may save the settings for communicating with CompuServe in one document, save the settings for communicating with Dow Jones in another, and save the settings for communicating with The Source in yet another. Whenever you need to communicate with a particular remote computer, you simply open the communications document that contains the settings for that computer and then connect with it.

CONNECTING WITH A REMOTE COMPUTER

Once you have established the correct settings for communicating with a particular computer, you can connect with that computer. There are two ways to connect with a remote computer: by calling it or by answering an incoming call from it. Regardless of how you establish a connection, the result is the same—you'll be on-line with the remote computer.

The Connect command on the Connect menu allows you to make and break connections with a remote computer. What Works does when you issue this command depends on the settings in the Phone dialog box and whether Works is connected to a remote computer at the time. Depending on these factors, Works will either instruct the modem to dial the phone, set the modem to the Automatic Answer mode, or disconnect from the remote computer.

Dialing the phone

In order for Works to dial the phone, it must be off-line; your modem must be connected to a telephone line and to the serial port specified in the Terminal setting; the communications document that contains the settings for the computer you want to connect with must specify the correct phone number; and the Automatic Answer check box must be turned off.

Once those conditions are met, you can command Works to dial the phone. The way you do this depends on whether the communications document that contains the settings you want to use is open. If it is, simply make it the active document, pull down the Connect menu, and select the Connect command. If the communications document that contains the settings you want to use is not open,

▶WORKS 2◀

use the Open Existing File... command to open it. ▶As soon as Works 2 opens the document you specify, it will display the dialog box shown in Figure 18-6. (Earlier versions of Works will not display this box.) To connect with the remote computer, choose the <OK> button; to open the document without connecting, choose <Cancel>. (If you use Works 1 or 1.05, you'll have to issue the Connect command once you open the communications document.)◀

When you do either of these things, Works will instruct your modem to dial the phone. While the modem is dialing, Works will replace the *OFFLINE* indicator at the left edge of the status line with a clock displaying the amount of time that has elapsed since you issued that command. This clock begins before Works actually makes a connection with the remote computer. However, the time it displays at any point usually will be pretty close to the amount of time that Works has been on-line.

Figure 18-6

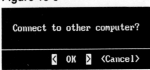

Works 2 displays this dialog box when you open an existing communications document.

After your modem dials the phone, you'll hear it ringing through your modem's speaker. If the remote computer's modem picks up the phone, it will emit a high-pitched tone. When it does, your modem will briefly answer with a lower tone. After a moment, both tones will stop. At that point, you'll be connected with the remote computer.

In some cases, the remote computer's modem may not answer the phone. This will happen mostly when the line is busy or when the remote computer does not instruct its modem to answer the phone. In the first case, you'll hear a busy tone through your modem's speaker; in the other, you'll hear the phone ringing.

If the remote computer's modem does not answer, you can do a couple of things. First, you can redial the number. To do this, simply pull down the Connect menu and select the Dial Again command. When you do, Works will instruct your modem to hang up and then re-dial the number in the Phone Number text box. This does not break Works out of the Connect mode. Alternatively, you can disconnect. To do this, simply pull down the Connect menu, select the Connect command (just as you did to dial the phone), and choose <OK>.

Many on-line services prompt you to provide several pieces of information before you can connect with them. For example, you may be asked for the service to which you want to connect, your account number, and your password. Together, the pieces of information are called a sign-on sequence. Supplying this information in response to the remote computer's prompts is called signing on.

Recording and playing sign-on sequences

Typing a sign-on sequence each time you connect with an on-line service can be tedious. Fortunately, Works doesn't require you to sign-on manually each time. Instead, you can record the sign-on sequence once, then play it back automatically each time you connect.

Works records a sign-on sequence as you actually sign on to the on-line service. To record a sign-on sequence, therefore, you must begin by activating the communications document for the on-line service for which you want to record the sequence, then commanding Works to dial the phone. After your

Recording sign-on sequences

modem has connected with the remote modem, but before you type anything, you should pull down the Connect menu and select the Record Sign-On command. When you do this, the word *RECORD* will then appear in the status line. From this point until you turn the recording off, Works will record what you type, as well as the prompts that the remote computer sends to you.

Once you have turned the recording feature on, you should sign on to the on-line service just as you normally would. As you do, Works will record both the host computer's prompts and your responses. For example, suppose you are signing on to CompuServe—one of the most popular on-line services. After Works dials the local access number of CompuServe and makes a connection, you should begin the sign-on process by pressing [Enter]. When you do, the remote system will respond with the prompt *Host Name:*. In response to this prompt, type *compuserve* and press [Enter]. At this point, the remote system will present the prompt *User ID:*. Type your CompuServe ID number (five digits, a comma, and another four digits) and press [Enter] again. When the remote system presents the prompt *Password:*, type your CompuServe password, and press [Enter] one more time. Finally, you will be connected to CompuServe.

When you have completed the sign-on process, you should turn off the recording feature before you type anything else. To do this, simply pull down the Connect menu and select Record Sign-On again. When you pull down the Connect menu this time, there will be a dot to the left of the Record Sign-On command. Like the *RECORD* indicator in the status line, this dot indicates that Works is currently recording the sign-on sequence. When you select this option, Works will turn off the recording feature and remove the *RECORD* indicator from the status line. The next time you pull down the Connect menu, you'll also see that it removed the dot from the left of the Record Sign-On command.

Since Works recorded the actual process of signing on to the on-line service, you'll be connected to that service once you record the sign-on sequence. At that point, you can use the service or, if the only purpose of the call was to record the sign-on sequence for future use, simply disconnect from it. To disconnect, you should sign off the on-line service, then hang up the phone—a process we'll explain later.

After you have recorded the sign-on sequence, you should make it a permanent part of the communications document by saving (or resaving) that document. To do this, you can use either the Save or Save As... command. You can save or resave the document either while you are on-line or after you have disconnected.

**Playing back
sign-on sequences**

Once you have recorded a sign-on sequence for a particular on-line service, you can play it back each time you need to sign on to that service. To do this, connect with the service and get to the point where you started the recording. (If you start the playback at the wrong point within the sign-on process, the sign-on probably will fail.) Then, pull down the Connect menu and select the Sign-On command. In almost all cases, the first statement in any recorded sign-on sequence will be the first thing you typed after Works began recording. Therefore, as soon as you select the Sign-On command, Works will "type" the first thing you typed during the recording of the sign-on sequence. After Works types this string, it will wait for a prompt from the on-line service. When Works receives that prompt, it will type whatever you typed in response to that prompt. Works will continue in this fashion until it has played back the entire sign-on sequence. At that point, it will turn off the Sign-On command and return control to you.

Most of the prompts that on-line services send during their sign-on sequence will be the same each time you sign on. For example, CompuServe will always present the prompt *Password:* after you respond to the prompt *User ID:*. However, some prompts will be slightly different each time. Usually, this is because the prompt contains the current time or date. In most cases, this slight variation won't make any difference to Works. Since Works only records and uses the final line of each prompt, it usually will respond even to prompts that are not the same as the ones recorded in the sign-on sequence. As long as the last line of the prompt that Works receives is the same as the last line it received when it recorded the sign-on sequence, it will respond to that prompt.

Occasionally, however, Works will not receive the prompt it is looking for. When that happens, Works will not send the next string to the remote computer. Instead, it will wait for the string it expects, which, of course, will not come. In those situations, you should cancel the Sign-On command by pulling down the Connect menu and selecting the Sign-On command again. (When you pull down this menu, you'll see a dot to the left of the Sign-On command, which indicates that Works is currently playing back the recorded sign-on sequence.) After cancelling the Sign-On command, you have two choices: complete the sign-on process manually, or break the connection, reconnect, and play the sign-on sequence again from the start.

Although you usually will use a recorded sign-on sequence to automate only the process of signing on to a remote computer, you can use it to automate other processes as well. If you turn on Works' recording facility before you connect with the remote computer, for example, Works will record the dial instructions and phone number it sends to your modem when you issue the Connect command. When you subsequently issue the Sign-On command, Works will begin by dialing the phone. Consequently, you won't have to issue the Connect command.

If you routinely type the same responses to an on-line service's prompts, you can record those commands in the sign-on sequence. That way, Works will type those responses for you after it signs on. You can even record the process of signing off the remote system and hanging up the phone (reissuing the Connect command). In this way, you can use a recorded sign-on string to automate a complete communication session.

Extending the use of recorded sign-on sequences

A limitation

Works will allow only one recorded sign-on sequence per communications document. If you select the Record Sign-On command from within a document that already contains a recorded sign-on sequence, Works will present an alert box like the one shown in Figure 18-7. If you choose <OK> in response to the *Replace old sign-on script?* prompt, Works will replace the old sequence with the new one. If you choose <Cancel>, Works will cancel the Record Sign-On command and leave the existing recording intact.

Figure 18-7

You'll see an alert box like this one when you select the Record Sign-On command from a document that already contains a sign-on sequence.

Answering incoming calls

Although you usually will use Works to make outgoing calls, you also can use it to receive incoming calls. To answer an incoming call, the Automatic Answer check box in the Phone dialog box must be turned on. As we explained earlier, this setting overrides any phone number that may be listed in the Phone dialog box. Consequently, Works will answer the phone rather than dialing when you command it to connect with a remote computer.

Except for the difference in the Automatic Answer setting, the process of instructing Works to answer an incoming call is the same as that of instructing it to dial. If the communications document that contains the settings for the computer that is (or will be) trying to connect with you is open, simply make it the active document, pull down the Connect menu, and select the Connect command. If the communications document is not open, use the Open Existing

►WORKS 2◄

File... command to open it. ►As soon as Works opens the document you specify, it will display the dialog box shown in Figure 18-6. (Earlier versions of Works will not display this box.) To connect with the remote computer, choose the <OK> button; to open the document without connecting, choose <Cancel>. (If you use Works 1.0 or 1.05, you'll have to issue the Connect command at this point.)◄

As long as the Automatic answer check box is on, Works will send a signal to your modem that places it in the Automatic Answer mode; then it will place itself in the Connect mode and display an *ANSW* indicator on the status line. Although Works will not actually be on-line yet, the clock will appear at the left edge of the status line and begin counting.

If the phone is ringing when you issue the Connect command, your modem will answer the incoming call. Since Works will be in the connect mode, you will be on-line as soon as your modem makes the connection. If the phone is not ringing when you issue the Connect command, your modem will wait for the next incoming call and answer that call after the first ring.

Importantly, you do not have to be in a communications document in order for Works to answer an incoming call. Once you have used the Connect command to place your modem in the Automatic Answer mode, you can activate any other Works document. If you happen to be in a document other than the communications document from which you issued the Connect command when your modem receives an incoming call, the modem still will answer and make a connection. As soon as you activate the communications document, you can begin to send and receive information.

At some point after you have connected with a remote computer, you will want to end the communication session. To do this, you should first sign off from the remote system, if appropriate. Then, to break the connection, pull down the Connect menu and issue the Connect command. When you pull down the Connect menu while Works is in the connect mode, you'll see a dot to the left of the Connect command. This dot indicates that Works is in the Connect mode. If you issue this command while the dot is visible, Works will display the dialog box shown in Figure 18-8. If you select <OK> from this box, Works will instruct your modem to hang up the phone. As soon as the connection is broken, Works will exit from the connect mode, replacing the clock on the status line with the message *OFFLINE*. If you select <Cancel>, Works will continue with the connection.

Disconnecting—hanging up the phone

Figure 18-8

You'll see this dialog box when you select the Connect command while Works is in the connect mode.

The Connect command also instructs your modem to exit from the automatic answer mode, if it is in that mode. (It will be, if you answered an incoming call.) This ensures that the modem will not answer an incoming call when Works is not prepared to receive it.

Although you usually will use the Connect command to break a successful connection, you also will use it to cancel an unsuccessful attempt to connect with a remote computer. For example, suppose you use the Connect command to make a call to a remote computer. If the line is busy, or if the remote computer does not answer, you'll need to reissue the Connect command to stop the attempt. As another example, suppose you used the Connect command to place your modem in the automatic answer mode. If you do not receive the call you expect, reissue the Connect command to cancel the modem's Automatic Answer setting.

Direct connecting

If you want to communicate between two computers that are relatively close to one another (for example, in the same or adjacent offices), you don't need to communicate over telephone lines using modems. Instead, you can connect the computers directly with a special cable, called a null-modem cable. This cable sends signals directly from the serial port of one computer to the serial port of the other computer.

To make a direct connection with a remote computer, simply pull down the Connect menu and select the Connect command. When you do this, Works will enter the connect mode. As soon as the remote computer enters its connect mode, you can start communicating.

Since no modems are involved in a direct connection, Works' Phone settings are superfluous. If the Phone dialog box contains a phone number or a modem setup string, or if its Automatic Answer setting is on, Works will send a few strange characters to the remote computer when you issue the Connect command. Although these characters will not affect the communication session, they are annoying. To avoid the transmission of these characters, empty the Phone dialog box before you establish a direct connection.

Direct connecting has two principal advantages over communicating through phone lines. First, it doesn't tie up a phone line. Second, it lets you communicate faster than you can via modem. Most modems allow you to communicate at a maximum of 2400 bits per second. When connected directly, you can communicate as fast as 9600 bits per second.

SENDING AND RECEIVING INFORMATION

Once you have connected your computer to another computer, you can send information to that computer and receive information from it in a variety of ways. For example, you can send information by typing it, copying it from another Works document, or reading it from a file. You can receive information to the screen, capture it to a text file, or receive it directly into a file.

In most cases, you won't be sending and receiving information constantly while you are connected to a remote computer. Sometimes, you'll issue commands in the communications document; at other times, you'll activate, open, or create other documents. As long as either Xon/Xoff or Hardware handshaking is selected when you do any of these things, Works will send a message to the remote computer that tells it to stop sending information. If the remote computer uses the type of handshaking you selected, it will pause. When you return to the communications document (or exit from one of the Communications menus), Works will send a signal to the remote computer that commands it to resume the transmission of information. At that point, the remote computer will continue where it left off. If the remote computer does not use the type of handshaking you specified, or if you selected the None Handshake option, the remote computer will continue to send information. In that case, all but the first 256 transmitted bytes will be lost.

The Pause command on the Connect menu allows you to send a "stop" signal to the remote computer manually. When you issue this command, Works will send a signal to the remote computer that tells it to suspend the transmission of information temporarily. (Of course, Works won't send a signal if Handshake is set to None.) If you pull down the Connect menu while the transmission of information is paused, you'll see a dot to the left of the Pause command. Also, the word *PAUSE* will appear on the status line. While Works is in the Pause mode, nothing you type will be sent to the remote computer. In fact, Works will display the alert box shown in Figure 18-9 if you type anything within the Communications window. To resume the transmission of information, simply reselect the Pause command.

The Pause and Break commands

Figure 18-9

```
Paused: choose Connect Pause to continue.

                              ◄  OK  ►
```

Works will display this alert box if you attempt to send any information to the remote computer while Works is in the Pause mode.

The Break command (also on the Connect menu) sends a four-second break signal to the remote computer. This signal serves two purposes. It "gets the attention" of the remote computer, and it interrupts that operation if the remote computer is doing something (like sending a file). Many mainframe computers recognize this signal; most PC communication packages do not.

While Works is connected to another computer, you can send information to that computer in four ways. First, you can type from the keyboard. However, since on-line time is expensive, you should use this method primarily for short messages and responses to prompts. To send longer messages, you should compose them in an alternative Works document—preferably before connecting to a remote computer. ►Then, you can send the messages in either of two ways—by copying them into the communications document (this can be done only in Works 2) or by saving them in text files and then using the Send Text... command.◄ To send binary files, you should use the Send File... command.

Sending information

►WORKS 2◄

While Works is connected with another computer, anything you type from the keyboard will be sent to that computer. For example, if you type *The quick red fox jumped over the lazy brown dog.*, Works will send those 49 characters to the remote computer one at a time in the order you type them. At the same time, those

From the keyboard

characters will appear on your screen, either having been echoed to Works by the remote computer or having been sent directly to the screen by Works. (If you see two copies of everything you type, you should turn off the Local Echo setting. If you don't see anything you type, you should turn the Local Echo setting on.)

You'll communicate by typing from the keyboard in a variety of situations. Most commonly, you'll type responses to prompts issued by on-line services, type short messages for posting on computerized bulletin boards, and so forth.

Actually, saying that Works will send everything you type is a bit of an exaggeration. Works will send only characters you type within the communications document from which you issued the Connect command—not anything you type in another document that you may switch to while you are connected. Furthermore, Works will not transmit any keystrokes you execute in the process of issuing a command.

**Copying from
other documents
►WORKS 2◄**

►In Works 2, you can send information to a remote computer by copying it from a word processor, spreadsheet, or database document into a communications document. (You cannot do this in earlier versions of Works.) Simply open the document that contains the information you want to send (or, if the document is already open, activate it), select the information you want to send, issue the Copy command, reactivate the communications document, and press [Enter]. When you do this, Works will copy the information you selected into the communications document and send that information to the remote computer.

Figure 18-10

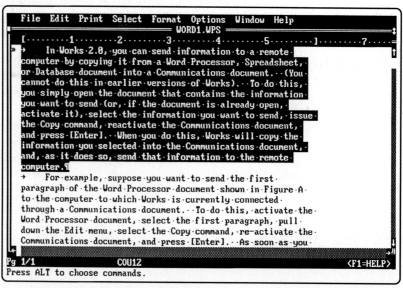

*We'll send the first paragraph of this document to a remote computer
by copying it into a communications document.*

For example, suppose you want to send the first paragraph of the word processor document shown in Figure 18-10 through a communications document to the computer to which Works is currently connected. To do this, activate the word processor document, select the first paragraph, pull down the Edit menu, select the Copy command, reactivate the communications document, and press [Enter]. Works will then "type" the text that you copied from the Word processor document into the communications document, one character at a time. As each character is typed, it will be sent to the remote computer—just as if you were typing those characters yourself. After Works "types" the final character, it will stop. Figure 18-11 shows how the communications document will look at this point.

Figure 18-11

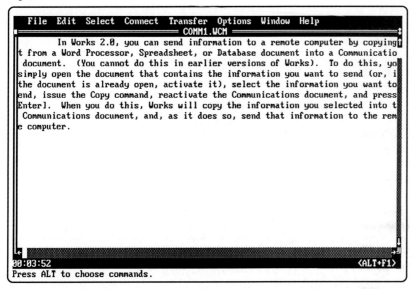

```
 File  Edit  Select  Connect  Transfer  Options  Window  Help
 ════════════════════ COMM1.WCM ════════════════════
           In Works 2.0, you can send information to a remote computer by copying
 t from a Word Processor, Spreadsheet, or Database document into a Communicatio
  document.  (You cannot do this in earlier versions of Works).  To do this, yo
 imply open the document that contains the information you want to send (or, i
 the document is already open, activate it), select the information you want to
 end, issue the Copy command, reactivate the Communications document, and press
 Enter].  When you do this, Works will copy the information you selected into t
  Communications document, and, as it does so, send that information to the rem
 e computer.




 00:03:52                                                              <ALT+F1>
 Press ALT to choose commands.
```

This is how the communications document will look after we copy the first paragraph of the Word processor document shown in Figure 18-10 into it.

Although you usually will copy information from word processor documents, you can copy from spreadsheet and database documents as well. When you do this, Works will "type" a copy of the selected range exactly as it appears on the screen. That is, Works will copy labels, values, and the result of formulas and functions (rather then the formulas and functions themselves). All of this information will be copied in formatted form. For example, if you copy from a cell that contains the value 123 and has the Currency 2 format, Works will send the characters $123.45. Works sends a tab character between the entries in each column and sends a carriage return at the end of the final entry on each row.

Figure 18-13 shows the results of copying the contents of cells A4:D11 of the spreadsheet document shown in Figure 18-12 into a communications document. As you can see, Works has copied the dates in column B and the values in column D in formatted form. Because Works sets tab stops at every eight characters in a communications document (and converts the tab characters to spaces), the information is no longer in perfect columnar form. The way tabular information will appear on the screen of the receiving computer depends on how it deals with tab characters.◄

Figure 18-12

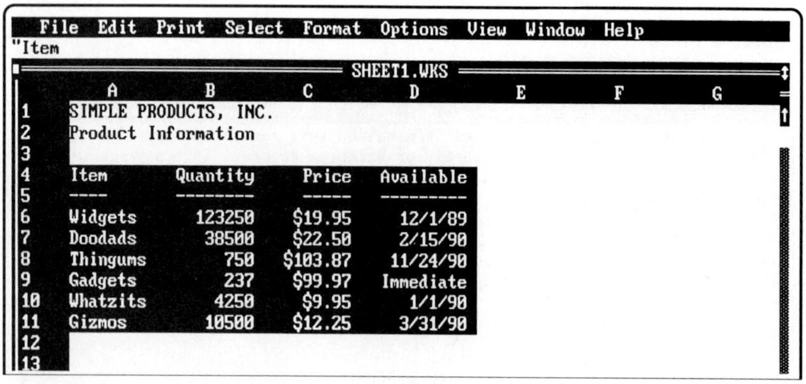

```
 File  Edit  Print  Select  Format  Options  View  Window  Help
"Item
═══════════════════════════ SHEET1.WKS ═══════════════════════════
           A          B          C          D          E        F        G
 1  SIMPLE PRODUCTS, INC.
 2  Product Information
 3
 4  Item        Quantity      Price    Available
 5  ----        --------      -----    ---------
 6  Widgets       123250     $19.95     12/1/89
 7  Doodads        38500     $22.50     2/15/90
 8  Thingums         750    $103.87    11/24/90
 9  Gadgets          237     $99.97    Immediate
10  Whatzits        4250      $9.95     1/1/90
11  Gizmos         10500     $12.25     3/31/90
12
13
```

We'll send the information in cells A4:D11 of this spreadsheet to another computer by copying it into a communications document.

Figure 18-13

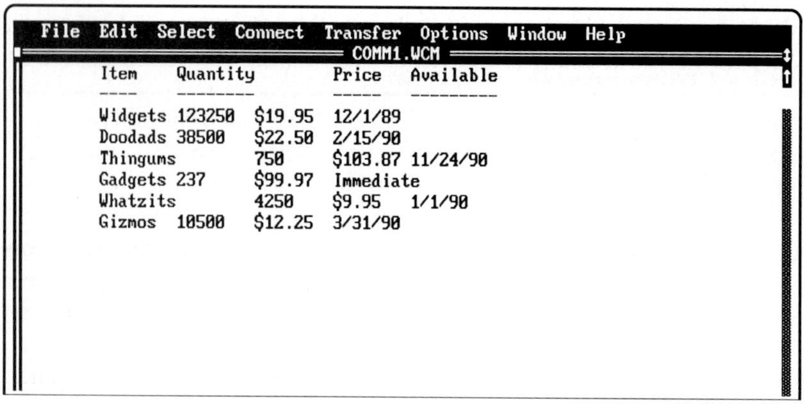

```
 File  Edit  Select  Connect  Transfer  Options  Window  Help
═══════════════════════════ COMM1.WCM ═══════════════════════════
    Item      Quantity        Price    Available
    ----      --------        -----    ---------
    Widgets 123250 $19.95     12/1/89
    Doodads 38500  $22.50     2/15/90
    Thingums         750      $103.87 11/24/90
    Gadgets 237    $99.97     Immediate
    Whatzits        4250      $9.95    1/1/90
    Gizmos  10500  $12.25     3/31/90
```

This figure shows what your communications document will look like after you copy the information from cells A4:D11 of the spreadsheet shown in Figure 18-12 into it.

Although copying is the most convenient way to send prepared messages to a remote computer, it's not the only way. After composing the message in a Works word processor document, you can save it to disk using the Text or Printed Text options in the Save As dialog box. Then, after connecting with the remote computer, you can use the Send Text... command on the Transfer menu to send the message to the remote computer. (To learn how to save a word processor document in an alternative format, see Chapters 2 and 4.)

From text files

Using the Send Text... command to send information from a text file to a remote computer is a relatively simple process. First, pull down the Transfer menu and select the Send Text... command. When you do this, Works will present a dialog box like the one in Figure 18-14. As you can see, this dialog box contains six elements: a File to Send text box, a Files list box, a Directories list box, a Delay text box, an <OK> button, and a <Cancel> button. These structures allow you to select the file whose contents you want Works to send to the remote computer.

Figure 18-14

Works will display a dialog box like this one when you pull down the Transfer menu and select the Send Text... command.

Within the send text dialog box, you should specify the file that contains the text you want to send. You can do this in any of the ways that you can use to select a file from the Open dialog box when you issue the Open... command. First, you can type the name of the file into the File to Send text box. Alternatively, you can highlight the name of the file in the Files list box. If the file that contains the text you want to send is in another directory, you should use the Directories list box to make that directory the default before using the File to Send or Files text boxes.

No matter how you select the file from which you want Works to send text, you should choose <OK> afterward. When you do, Works will begin to read that file from disk and send its contents to the remote computer. As Works sends the information from the file, that information will scroll across the screen of your computer just as if you were typing it yourself—only a lot faster. Works will continue to send information until it reaches the end of the file or until you press [Esc]. If Works reaches the end of the file first, it will simply stop sending text—just as you would want. If you press [Esc] before Works reaches the end of the file, it will display a dialog box with two buttons: <OK> and <Cancel>. If you choose <OK>, Works will stop sending text. If you choose <Cancel>, Works will resume the process.

Importantly, you should use this command only to send information from files you have saved in the Text or Printed Text formats—not regular Works files. Files saved in these formats contain only the information in the document (words, numbers, and so forth) plus carriage returns. Regular Works files contain upper-level characters that specify the structure, formatting, and so forth, for the document. You don't want to include these characters in the message you transmit to the remote computer.

Unless you specify otherwise, Works will send the text from the file you specify one line after the other, without pausing at the end of each line. In a few cases, the receiving computer may have trouble keeping up with Works' pace. If this is the case, you can use the Delay text box at the bottom of the Send Text dialog box to introduce a delay between each line of text Works sends to the remote computer. To do this, simply type into the Delay text box the number of tenths of seconds you want Works to pause after sending each line. If you want a tenth of a second delay, for example, you would type 1 into this box; if you want a half-second delay, you would type 5; if you want a full one-second delay, you would type 10; and so forth.

Using the X-Modem protocol

The Send File... command on the Transfer menu allows you to send complete files from the disk drive of your computer directly to the disk drive of a remote computer. When you use this command, Works will send the files according to the X-Modem error-checking protocol. This common protocol sends files in 128-byte segments, checking the accuracy of the transmission of each segment before sending the next one. In order to send a file this way, both computers must support and use the X-Modem protocol.

Although the Send Text... and Send File... commands both send information from a file to a remote computer, they are radically different commands. Like copying information from another document, the Send Text... command simply provides an alternative to typing messages on-line; the remote computer receives the information Works sends, just as if you were typing it from your keyboard. It can either let that information scroll off the screen or capture it into a text file.

Unlike the Send Text... command, the Send File... command sends complete files from the disk drive of your computer to the disk drive of the remote computer.

The purpose of this command is not to serve as a substitute for typing messages from the keyboard; instead, it is intended for sending working copies of any sort of file from one computer to another.

To send a file to a remote computer using the X-Modem protocol, you must begin by pulling down the Transfer menu and selecting the Send File... command. Works will then display a dialog box like the one shown in Figure 18-15.

Figure 18-15

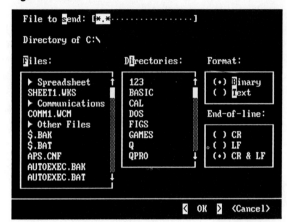

Works will display a dialog box like this one when you select the Send File... command.

When Works presents this box, you should specify the file you want to send to the remote computer. To do this, choose a drive and/or directory from the Directories list box, then either select the file name from the Files list box or type the name of the file into the File to Send text box.

Once you have specified the file you want to transmit, you should make selections from the Format and End-of-Line option boxes. In almost all cases, you'll want to choose the Binary option in the Format box. In fact, you'll only want to choose the Text option when you are sending text files to a computer whose operating system expects only a carriage return or a line feed—but not both—at the end of each line. You'll rarely encounter a situation of that sort.

The options in the End-of-Line option box affect only file transfers for which you have selected the Text option. Consequently, this box is active only when the Text option is chosen in the Format option box. The options in this box allow you to command Works to strip a carriage return, a line feed, or nothing from the file it is transmitting whenever it encounters a carriage return/line feed combination in that file. If you choose CR, Works will strip a line feed from each carriage return/line feed pair, leaving only a carriage return. You should use this option when you send text files to a computer that expects only a carriage return at the end of each line. If you choose LF, Works will strip the carriage return from each pair, leaving only a line feed character. You should choose this option when you send a text file to a computer that expects only a line feed at the end of each line. If you choose CR & LF from the option box, Works will strip nothing from the file. In fact, it will send the file in the same way it would if you had chosen Binary instead of Text from the Format option box. The only difference between the Binary and Text options is that the Text option allows you to access the character-stripping options in the End-of-Line option box.

After you have specified the file you want to send and have chosen the appropriate item from the Format option box (and, if you have chosen Text, from the End-of-Line option box), you should then choose <OK> to begin the file transfer. When you do this, Works will display the dialog box shown in Figure 18-16. This box presents three pieces of information: the status of the transfer (initially WAITING), the number of bytes sent (initially 0), and the number of retries (also 0 initially). This information keeps you apprised of the progress of the transfer.

Figure 18-16

Works will display a dialog box like this one while it is sending a file via the X-Modem protocol.

As soon as you choose <OK> from the Send File dialog box to begin the transfer, Works will send a signal to the remote computer, indicating that it is ready to begin sending the file. If the remote computer is set to receive an X-Modem transfer, it will send a signal back to Works, telling it to send the first 128-byte segment. If the remote computer does not respond, Works will send it the same ready signal every ten seconds until it does. If the remote computer does not respond after 11 tries, Works will abort the transfer.

As soon as the remote computer responds to Works' signal, Works will begin transferring the file. The process of transferring the file goes something like this. Works will send the first 128 bytes from the file, calculate the sum of those bytes (the "checksum"), and send it to the remote computer. When the remote computer receives those 128 bytes, it will calculate the checksum and compare it to the result of Works' calculation. If the two values are the same, the remote computer will signal Works to send the next 128-byte segment. If the values do not match, the remote computer will signal Works to send the same segment again. If the checksums match this time, the remote computer will signal Works to send the next segment of the file. If not, it will signal Works to send the same segment again.

While Works is transmitting a file, it will display the progress of the transfer in the dialog box shown in Figure 18-16. The Status indicator will alternate between the messages *SEND* and *WAITING*. *SEND* means that Works is sending a 128-byte segment of the file; *WAITING* means that Works is waiting for a response from the remote computer. The Bytes Sent indicator will display the number of bytes Works has sent to the remote computer. Since the X-Modem protocol sends files in 128-byte segments, Works will display a value that will always be a multiple of 128 (0, 128, 256, 384, 512, 640, and so forth). The Retries indicator will display the number of times Works has sent the current segment of the file. Each time Works successfully sends a segment of the file, it resets this value to 0. Works does not display the contents of the file it is sending during an X-Modem transfer.

The file transfer will continue in this fashion until one of three things happens: the entire file has been transferred, Works aborts the transfer, or you abort the transfer. In most cases, Works will complete the transfer without any problems. As soon as it has sent the final segment of the file, Works will beep, display the message *Transfer successful* to the right of the Status prompt, and replace the <Cancel> button with an <OK> button. When you choose <OK>, Works will close the dialog box and return control of the communications document to you.

If Works is not able to send any segment of the file successfully after 11 tries, it will abort the transfer. When it does, it will beep, display the message *Transfer ended* within the dialog box, and change the <Cancel> button to an <OK> button. When this happens, you must choose <OK> to break out of the Send File... command. Then, if you want, you can attempt the transfer again.

You can cancel a file transfer yourself by choosing <Cancel> from the dialog box Works displays as it is sending the file (the one in Figure 18-16). When you do this, Works will display a dialog box with two buttons, <OK> and <Cancel>, and pause the transfer until you make a choice. If you choose <OK>, Works will abort the transfer. If you choose <Cancel>, Works will resume the transfer.

Receiving information
►WORKS 2◄

Just as Works can send information in three ways, it can receive information in three ways. First, it can receive information to the screen of your computer. ►(If you use Works 2, you can subsequently copy this information to another Works document.)◄ Second, it can capture that information into a text file. Third, it can receive files that are sent using the X-Modem protocol.

To the screen

While Works is connected to a remote computer, anything sent by that computer will appear on the screen of your computer within the communications window. For example, if the remote computer sends the sentence *Now is the time for all good men to come to the aid of their country.*, those characters will appear on the screen of your computer, starting at the current position of the cursor.

The Terminal settings control the way incoming information (and outgoing information, for that matter) appears on your computer's screen. If the Full Screen setting is off (its default position), Works will give you a 77-column by 18-row work area. If the Full Screen setting is on, the work area will expand to 24 rows. If the Wraparound setting is on (its default position), Works will move the cursor to a new line of the screen whenever it receives a line feed character (or a carriage return, if the Add to Incoming Lines option is set to LF), and whenever the cursor reaches the end of any line. If the Wraparound setting is turned off, Works will move the cursor to a new line only when it receives an LF (or, in some cases, a CR) character.

Importantly, you can receive information from a remote computer only when the communications document through which you connected with that computer is the active document. Whenever you switch from the communications document through which Works is connected to another computer (or pull down a menu), Works will send a handshaking signal to the remote computer that tells it to stop sending information. If the remote computer responds to the type of handshaking Works is using (either Xon/Xoff or Hardware), it will stop sending information. Consequently, it won't send any information while you are away from the communications document. When you switch back to that communications document (or complete the command), Works will send a signal to the remote computer that tells it to resume sending information.

If the remote computer does not respond to the type of handshaking for which Works is set, it will continue to send information after you switch from the communications document or issue a command. In that case, you'll miss almost all of the information that the remote computer sends while you are away from the communications document. (Since Works has a 256-character receive buffer, you'll actually see the last 256 characters that the remote computer sent while you were away.)

Copying information into other documents
▶WORKS 2◀

▶During any communication session, incoming and outgoing information will quickly fill the screen. Once this happens, Works will scroll a line off the top of the screen for each new line that it writes at the bottom of the screen. In earlier versions of Works, that information is lost as soon as it scrolls off the screen. In Works 2, it is not. Instead, it is saved in the communications buffer. As we explained earlier, you can control the size of this buffer. Depending on your selection, Works will retain the last 100, 300, or 750 lines of information that scrolled across the screen.

Once you have received information to the screen of your computer, you can copy it to another Works document. To do this, first bring the information you want to copy back into view. If you have a mouse, you can use the scroll bar at the right edge of the communications window to do this. (As soon as you click on the scroll bar, Works will enter the Pause mode.) If you don't have a mouse, you must enter the Pause mode manually by pulling down the Connect menu and choosing Pause. At that point, you can use the ↑, ↓, [Pg Up], [Pg Dn], [Home], and [End] keys to bring the information you want to copy into view.

Once the information is in view, you should select it. If you have a mouse, you can do this simply by dragging across the text you want to copy. If you don't have a mouse, use the arrow keys to position the underline cursor on the first or last character of the block you want to copy. Then, pull down the Select menu and choose the Text command. Once you do this, Works will begin highlighting text (rather than simply moving the cursor) when you subsequently use the ↑, ↓, →, ←, [Pg Up], [Pg Dn], [Home], and [End] keys. (If you hold down the [Shift] key while using these keys, there's no need to choose Text from the Select menu first.) If you want to select all of the text in the communications buffer, you should choose the All option—rather than the Text option—from the Select menu. When you do this, Works will select the entire contents of the buffer.

Once you have selected the text you want to copy, you can copy it to another Works document. To do this, pull down the Edit menu and choose the Copy command. Then, activate, open, or create the document you want to copy to, position the cursor (or highlight) at the appropriate place within that document, and press [Enter]. When you do this, Works will copy the information you selected in the communications window into the current document.

Copying information into a word processor document. If you copy information from a communications document into a word processor document, the information will look pretty much the same in it as it does in the communications document. For example, Figure 18-18 on the following page shows the result of copying the table of information in the communications document shown in Figure 18-17 on the next page into a word processor document. As you can see, Works uses space characters (rather than tabs) to position the information properly on each line. This happens because Works converts tab characters into spaces when it stores information in the communications buffer.

If you want a table from a communications document to have tabs between the columns when you copy it into a word processor document, copy it into a spreadsheet document first, using the Table option. (See the next paragraph for instructions on how to do that.) Then, copy it from the spreadsheet document into a word processor document, as explained in Chapter 19.

Copying information into a spreadsheet or database document. If you copy information from a communications document into a spreadsheet or database document, Works will present the dialog box shown in Figure 18-19 on page 631. The two options in this box—Text and Table—determine how Works will copy the information.

Figure 18-17

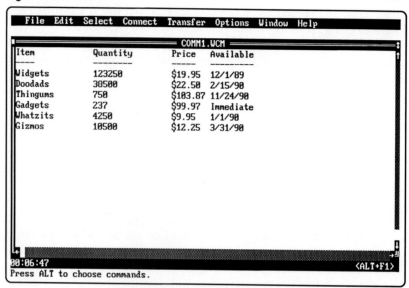

```
┌──────────────────────────────────────────────────────────────────┐
│  File  Edit  Select  Connect  Transfer  Options  Window  Help     │
│╞══════════════════════════ COMM1.WCM ═══════════════════════════╪│
││Item            Quantity        Price   Available                ↑│
││----            --------         -----   ---------               ↑│
││Widgets         123250          $19.95  12/1/89                   │
││Doodads         38500           $22.50  2/15/90                   │
││Thingums        750             $103.87 11/24/90                  │
││Gadgets         237             $99.97  Immediate                 │
││Whatzits        4250            $9.95   1/1/90                     │
││Gizmos          10500           $12.25  3/31/90                   │
││                                                                  │
││                                                                 ↓│
│└4                                                               ↓│
│00:06:47                                               <ALT+F1>    │
│Press ALT to choose commands.                                      │
└──────────────────────────────────────────────────────────────────┘
```

We'll copy the information shown on the screen of this communications document into a word processor and spreadsheet document.

Figure 18-18

```
┌──────────────────────────────────────────────────────────────────┐
│  File  Edit  Print  Select  Format  Options  Window  Help         │
│╞══════════════════════════ WORD3.WPS ═══════════════════════════╪│
││[········1········2·······3········4·······5········]·······7····=│
││» Item·········Quantity·····Price···Available¶                  ↑│
││----·········--------·····-----···---------¶                     │
││Widgets·······123250·········$19.95··12/1/89¶                    │
││Doodads·······38500··········$22.50··2/15/90¶                    │
││Thingums······750············$103.87·11/24/90¶                   │
││Gadgets·······237············$99.97··Immediate¶                  │
││Whatzits······4250···········$9.95···1/1/90¶                     │
││Gizmos········10500··········$12.25··3/31/90¶                    │
││¶                                                                 │
││◆                                                                 │
││                                                                 ↓│
│└4                                                               ↓│
│Pg 1/1                    COU12                        <F1=HELP>   │
│Press ALT to choose commands.                                      │
└──────────────────────────────────────────────────────────────────┘
```

This screen shows the results of copying the table shown in Figure 18-17 into a word processor document.

Figure 18-19

Works will present this dialog box when you copy information from a communications document into a spreadsheet or database document.

If you choose the Text option, Works will enter the information from each line of the communications document as a long label in a single cell. For example, Figure 18-20 shows the result of selecting the information on the screen of the communications document shown in Figure 18-17, issuing the Copy command, activating a new spreadsheet document, positioning the highlight on cell A1, pressing [Enter], choosing the Text option, and clicking <OK>. As you can see, cell A1 contains the long label

```
A1:  "Item          Quantity      Price   Available
```

The remainder of the cells in row 1 are blank. Similarly, cells A2:A8 contain long labels; the remainder of the cells in those rows are blank.

Figure 18-20

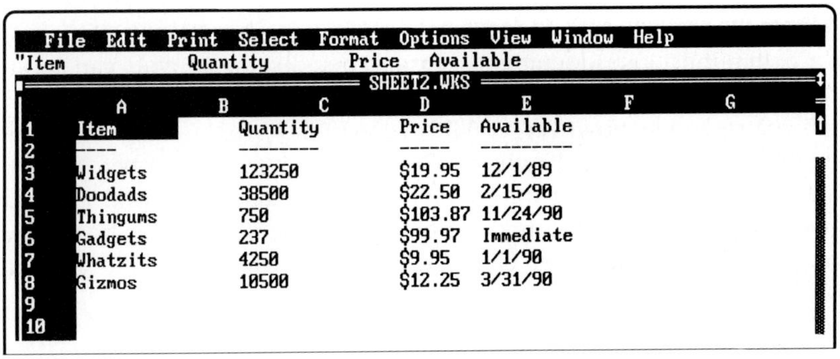

```
  File  Edit  Print  Select  Format  Options  View  Window  Help
"Item             Quantity           Price    Available
========================== SHEET2.WKS ==========================
          A          B          C          D          E        F        G
 1   Item               Quantity        Price    Available
 2   -----              --------        -----    ----------
 3   Widgets            123250          $19.95   12/1/89
 4   Doodads            38500           $22.50   2/15/90
 5   Thingums           750             $103.87  11/24/90
 6   Gadgets            237             $99.97   Immediate
 7   Whatzits           4250            $9.95    1/1/90
 8   Gizmos             10500           $12.25   3/31/90
 9
10
```

This figure shows the result of copying the table from the communications document in Figure 18-17 into a new spreadsheet document, using the Text option.

If you choose the Table option, Works will enter each "column" of the copied information into a different column of the worksheet (or field of the database). It also will look at each piece of information and enter it as the appropriate type of entry (value, text, date, or time) and give it the appropriate format. For example, Figure 18-21 shows the result of copying the table from the communications document shown in Figure 18-17 into a new spreadsheet document, using the Table option. As you can see, Works has entered the information into four columns of the spreadsheet—not just column A. The entries in column A are labels; the entries in column B are values; the entries in column C are values formatted with the Currency 2 format; and the entries in column D are formatted date values.

Figure 18-21

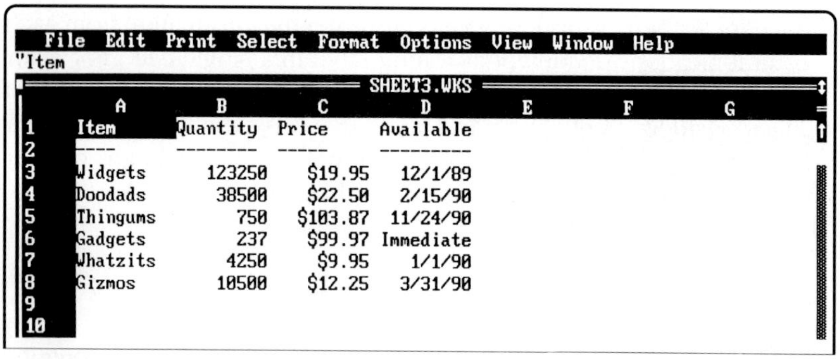

```
 File  Edit  Print  Select  Format  Options  View  Window  Help
"Item
══════════════════════════════ SHEET3.WKS ══════════════════════════
           A        B        C         D        E       F       G
 1   Item      Quantity  Price    Available
 2   ----      --------  -----    ----------
 3   Widgets     123250  $19.95    12/1/89
 4   Doodads      38500  $22.50    2/15/90
 5   Thingums       750 $103.87   11/24/90
 6   Gadgets        237  $99.97  Immediate
 7   Whatzits      4250   $9.95     1/1/90
 8   Gizmos       10500  $12.25    3/31/90
 9
10
```

This figure shows the result of copying the table from the communications document shown in Figure 18-17 into a new spreadsheet document, using the Table option.

Returning to the communications document.   Once you have copied information from a communications document into another document, you can return to the communications document. Because the communications document will be in the pause mode, however, you'll have to pull down the Connect menu and choose the Pause command (which will have a dot to its left) before you can resume sending or receiving information. If you attempt to send information before exiting from the pause mode, Works will present the dialog box shown in Figure 18-9. If you see this box, click OK, then pull down the Connect menu and choose Pause.◀

Capturing to text files

Instead of using the Copy command to copy information to a text file once you have received it, you can command Works to write that information to a text file as it is being received. The process of recording the information that passes through a communications document is called *capturing*.

Capturing information to a text file is relatively simple. To begin, pull down the Transfer menu and select the Capture Text... command. When you select this command, Works will display a dialog box like the one shown in Figure 18-22. Within this box, you should type the name of the file into which you want Works to save the information that scrolls across the communications screen and specify the directory in which you want Works to create that file.

Figure 18-22

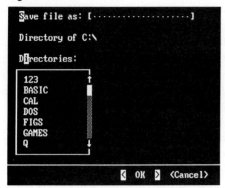

Works will display a dialog box like this one when you select the Capture Text... command.

As soon as you choose <OK>, Works will check to see if there is already another file with the name you specified on the disk in that drive. If not, it will begin capturing information into that file. If there is one, Works will display the dialog box shown in Figure 18-23. If you choose <Append> in response to the *Append to or replace existing file?* prompt, Works will add the information it captures to the end of the existing file. If you choose <Replace>, Works will replace the information in that file with the new information it will capture. If you choose <Cancel>, Works will cancel the Capture Text... command.

Figure 18-23

Works will display this dialog box if you specify an existing file as the one into which you want to capture incoming information.

Once you've turned on Works' capture capability, Works will write every character that is subsequently written to the communications screen into the named file. This includes information sent to you by the remote computer as well as information you send to the remote computer, either from the keyboard, by copying from another document, or with the Send Text... command. It won't capture information that is on the screen when you issue the Capture Text... command.

Works will continue to capture information until one of three things happens: you command it to stop capturing, you disconnect from the remote computer, or Works runs out of space on the disk to which it is capturing information. To command Works to stop capturing information, you must pull down the Transfer menu and select the End Capture Text command, which will appear in place of the Capture Text... command. As soon as you do this, Works will stop capturing information and close the capture file. If you disconnect from the remote computer before issuing the End Capture Text command, Works will close the capture file automatically before it disconnects.

If Works runs out of room on the disk to which it is capturing information, it will display the alert box that contains the warning *Disk full.* When you click <OK> to acknowledge this message, Works will save as much of the captured material as will fit on the disk, then turn off the capture facility. To continue capturing incoming information, you must insert a new disk and reissue the Capture Text... command.

Opening text files.   After you have captured information into a text file, you can open that file into Works as a word processor, spreadsheet, or database document. To open a captured file into Works, pull down the File menu, select the Open Existing File... command, specify the name of the file that contains the captured information, and choose <OK>**.** Works will then present the dialog box shown in Figure 18-24. The choice you make from this box determines into which type of document Works will load the captured information. To learn what happens when you open a non-Works file into Works, see Appendix 1.

Figure 18-24

Works will display this dialog box if you specify a non-Works file in the Open dialog box.

Advantages and disadvantages.   Capturing information directly to a text file has several advantages relative to copying it from the communications buffer. First, it eliminates the chance of missing the information you want to capture. (If you wait too long to copy information from the communications buffer, that information may be gone.) Second, Works does not replace tab characters with spaces when you capture information to disk, as it does when you capture information to the screen.

The principal disadvantage of capturing to disk is speed (or rather, lack of it). Especially if you are capturing to a floppy disk, Works won't be able to receive information as quickly as it can if you are simply capturing information to the communications buffer.

Earlier in this chapter, you learned that Works can send files to a remote computer using the X-Modem protocol. As you might expect, it also can be on the receiving end of X-Modem transfers. The Receive File... command makes this possible. When you pull down the Transfer menu and select this command, Works will display a dialog box like the one shown in Figure 18-25.

Receiving files using the X-Modem protocol

Figure 18-25

Works will display a dialog box like this one when you select the Receive File... command.

When you see this dialog box, you first should specify a name for the file into which you want Works to store the file it will receive. To do this, you can either select a drive and directory from the Directories list box and then type a name for the file into the Save File As text box or type both the drive/directory and file name into that box. Next, select either Binary or Text from the Format option box. If you choose Binary, Works will receive the file just as the remote computer sends it. If you choose Text, Works will ensure that each line of the file ends with both a carriage return and a line feed. You can choose Text if the remote computer is sending an ASCII text file. However, you should never choose the Text option when you are receiving a binary file. A good rule of thumb is to choose Text only in those rare situations in which you will be receiving a text file that does not have both a carriage return and a line feed to end each line.

Once you have selected a file name and a format, you should choose <OK> to begin the transfer. When you do this, Works will replace the Receive File dialog box with the dialog box shown in Figure 18-26. As you can see, this box is similar to the one that Works displays when it is sending a file via the X-Modem protocol. The three indicators in this box—Status, Bytes Received, and Retries—reveal the progress of the transfer at any point during the transmission of the file.

Figure 18-26

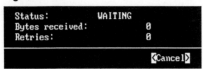

Works will display a dialog box like this one while it is receiving a file via the X-Modem protocol.

Receiving the file.   As soon as you press <OK> to begin the transfer, Works will send a signal to the remote computer, indicating that it is ready to begin receiving the file. If the remote computer is set to send a file via the X-Modem protocol, it will begin the transfer by sending the first 128-byte segment of the file. If the remote computer does not send anything, Works will send it the same ready signal every ten seconds until it does. If the remote computer does not send information after 11 tries, Works will abort the transfer.

As soon as the remote computer knows that Works is ready to receive the file, it will begin to send it. The process of transferring the file goes something like this: The remote computer will send the first 128 bytes from the file to Works, calculate the checksum of those bytes, and then send that checksum. When Works receives those 128 bytes, it will calculate the checksum and compare it to the result of the remote computer's calculation. If the two values are the same, Works will accept those bytes and signal the remote computer to send the next segment. If the values do not match, Works will signal the remote computer to send the same segment again. If the checksums match this time, Works will accept the segment and then signal the remote computer to send the next one. If not, Works will signal it to send the same segment again.

While Works is receiving a file, it will display the progress of the transfer in the dialog box shown in Figure 18-26. (Since Works does not display the contents of the file it is receiving on the screen, these indicators provide the only means of monitoring the progress of the transfer.) While Works is receiving a file, the Status indicator will alternate between the messages *RECEIVE* and *WAITING*. *RECEIVE* means that Works is receiving a 128-byte segment of the file; *WAITING* means that Works is sending a response to the remote computer. The Bytes Received indicator will display the number of bytes Works has received from the remote computer. Since the X-Modem protocol sends files in 128-byte segments, Works will always display a value that is a multiple of 128 (0, 128, 256, 384, 512, 640, and so forth). The Retries indicator will display the number of times the remote computer has sent the current segment of the file. Each time Works successfully receives a segment of the file, it resets this value to 0.

The file transfer will continue in this fashion until one of three things happens: the entire file has been transferred, Works aborts the transfer, or you abort the transfer. In most cases, Works will complete the transfer without any problems. As soon as it has received the final segment of the file, Works will beep, display the message *Transfer successful* to the right of the Status indicator, and replace the <Cancel> button with an <OK> button. When you choose <OK>, Works will close the dialog box and return control of the communications document to you.

If, after 11 tries, Works is not able to receive any segment of a file successfully, it will abort the transfer. When it does, it will beep, display the message *Transfer ended* within the dialog box, and change the <Cancel> button to an <OK> button. When this happens, you must choose <OK> to break out of the Receive File... command, then, if you want, attempt the transfer again.

You can cancel a file transfer yourself by choosing <Cancel> from the dialog box that Works displays as it is receiving the file (the one shown in Figure 18-26). When you do this, Works will display a dialog box with two buttons, <OK> and <Cancel>, and pause the transfer until you make a choice. If you choose <OK>, Works will abort the transfer. If you choose <Cancel>, Works will continue receiving the file.

Using files received with the X-Modem protocol.   In most cases, you will use the Receive Protocol... command to receive binary Works files. Once you have received these files, you can use the Open Existing File... command to load them directly into Works, just as you would a Works file that you created and saved yourself.

However, you also may receive non-Works files via an X-Modem transfer. After receiving these files, you can exit from Works and load them into the programs for which they are intended. In some cases, you may be able to import those files into Works. For an explanation of this process, see Appendix 1 at the end of this book.

In addition to its other powers, Works can communicate with other computers. Using a Works communications document, you can connect with other computers either via modem or directly, send information to them, and receive information from them.

CONCLUSION

Sharing Information Between Environments 19

So far, we've shown you how to work within each of Works' four types of documents: word processor, spreadsheet, database, and communications. In many cases, you will do all your work within a single document. In other cases, however, you will work in more than one type of document at a time and share information between documents—often documents of different types.

Works lets you share information between different types of documents in several ways. First, you can copy information from one type of document to another. For example, you can copy information from a spreadsheet document into a word processor document or from a database document into a spreadsheet document. Second, you can merge one or more charts into a word processor document. Third, you can merge information from a database document into a word processor document to create form letters and mailing labels. In this chapter, we'll show you how to share information in each of these ways.

In previous chapters of this book, we showed you how to copy information from one document to another document of the same type. For example, in Chapter 5 we showed you how to copy information from one word processor document to another; in Chapter 9, from one spreadsheet document to another; and in Chapter 15 from one database document to another. Although you usually will copy between documents of the same type, you can copy information between different types of documents.

The process of copying information between different types of documents is the same as that of copying information between documents of the same type. First, highlight the information you want to copy within the source document, then pull down the Edit menu and select the Copy command. Next, create, open, or

COPYING INFORMATION BETWEEN DIFFERENT TYPES OF DOCUMENTS

activate the document to which you want to copy that information (the destination document). Finally, point to the location within that document where you want Works to place the copy, and press [Enter].

It is important to note that copying information between two documents does not link them. Works simply places a "static" copy of the information from one document into the other document. Updating the document from which you copied information will not change the destination document.

When you copy information from one type of document to another, the destination document's type determines how it will receive that information. In the following paragraphs, we'll explain what happens when you copy information between each type of Works document.

Spreadsheet to word processor

The ability to copy information from a spreadsheet document into a word processor document allows you to integrate tables of values into reports, letters, and memos. When you copy information from a spreadsheet document into a word processor document, Works places a tab (➡) between the entries from each row of the source range, and places a carriage return (¶) after the last entry on each row. Consequently, the entries from each column of the spreadsheet will be arranged in a separate column in the word processor document, and each row of information will be in a separate paragraph.

For example, suppose you wanted to copy the entries from cells A4:E11 of the spreadsheet document shown in Figure 19-1 to a position between the two paragraphs of text in the word processor document shown in Figure 19-2. To do this, you would activate the spreadsheet document, highlight cells A4:E11, pull down the Edit menu, and select the Copy command. Then, you would create, open, or activate the word processor document, position the cursor at the beginning of the eighth line of that document, and press [Enter]. Figure 19-3 on page 642 shows the result.

As you can see, the arrangement and spacing of the information Works copied into the word processor document is the same as the information in the spreadsheet document. To achieve this effect, Works created custom tab stops for each row of information it copied from the spreadsheet document. The position of each tab stop is determined by the width of the columns in the spreadsheet and the alignment of the entries within each cell. The alignment of each tab stop is usually determined by the alignment of the entry in that cell (left, right, or centered). However, if a cell contains a value and is assigned a format that requires you to specify a number of decimal places, Works will set a decimal tab. Since each row of information from the spreadsheet becomes a separate paragraph in the word processor document, the position and alignment of the custom tab stops can be different for each row of information you copied from the spreadsheet. In most cases, you'll want to change the position and alignment of the tab stops in the copied information. For instructions on how to do this, see Chapter 5.

Figure 19-1

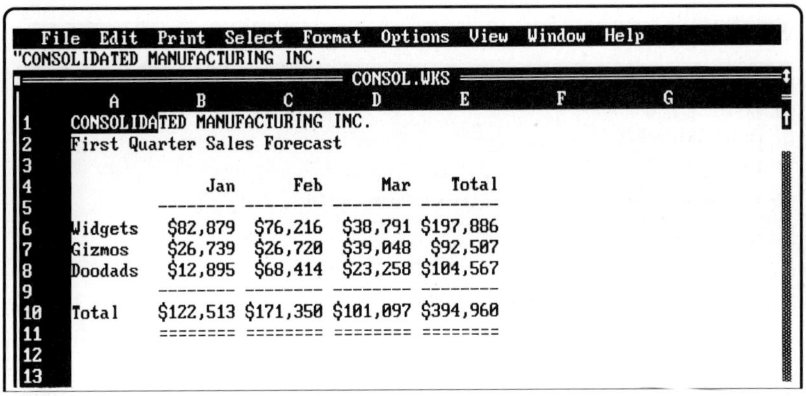

```
  File  Edit  Print  Select  Format  Options  View  Window  Help
"CONSOLIDATED MANUFACTURING INC.
                            ═══════════ CONSOL.WKS ═══════════
       A       B        C        D        E        F        G
1  CONSOLIDATED MANUFACTURING INC.
2  First Quarter Sales Forecast
3
4              Jan      Feb      Mar     Total
5          ———————— ———————— ———————— ————————
6  Widgets  $82,879  $76,216  $38,791 $197,886
7  Gizmos   $26,739  $26,720  $39,048  $92,507
8  Doodads  $12,895  $68,414  $23,258 $104,567
9          ———————— ———————— ———————— ————————
10 Total   $122,513 $171,350 $101,097 $394,960
11         ════════ ════════ ════════ ════════
12
13
```

*We'll copy the information from cells A4:E11 of this spreadsheet
document into the word processor document shown in Figure 19-2.*

Figure 19-2

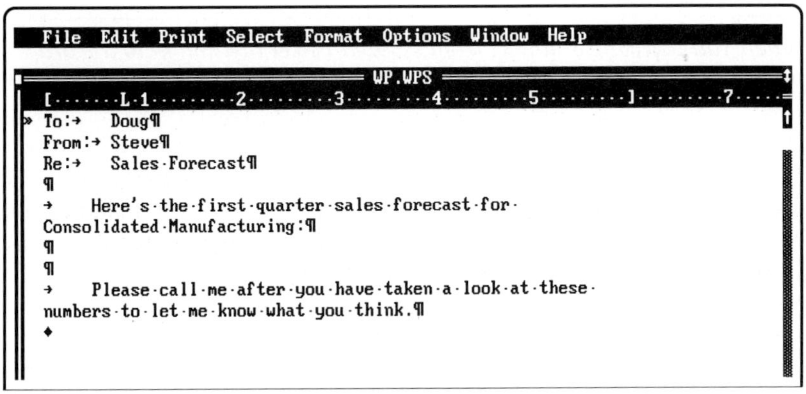

```
  File  Edit  Print  Select  Format  Options  Window  Help
                         ═══════════ WP.WPS ═══════════
  [······L·1·········2·········3·········4·········5·········]·········7·····
» To:→    Doug¶
  From:→  Steve¶
  Re:→    Sales·Forecast¶
  ¶
  →    Here's·the·first·quarter·sales·forecast·for·
  Consolidated·Manufacturing:¶
  ¶
  ¶
  →    Please·call·me·after·you·have·taken·a·look·at·these·
  numbers·to·let·me·know·what·you·think.¶
  ◆
```

*We'll copy information from cells A4:E11 of the spreadsheet document
shown in Figure 19-1 into this word processor document.*

When Works copies information from a spreadsheet document into a word
processor document, it copies labels, values, and the results of formulas and
functions (not the formulas and functions themselves). Additionally, Works
always copies information in formatted form. If you want, you can use the Copy
Special... command instead of the Copy command to copy information from a
spreadsheet document into a word processor document. This command produces
the same results as the Copy command.

Figure 19-3

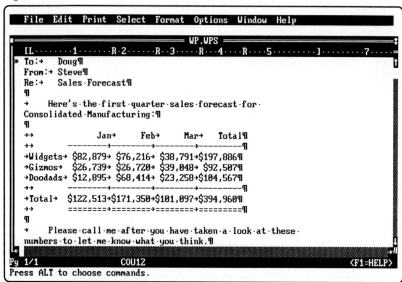

When you copy information from a spreadsheet document to a word processor document, Works arranges the information in tabular form.

Database to word processor

Copying information from a database document into a word processor document is virtually identical to copying information from a spreadsheet document into a word processor document. Each row of information from the database (that is, each record or partial record) becomes a separate paragraph. Works sets custom tab stops for each paragraph according to the width and alignment of the information in each cell on that line (that is, the entry in each field). Works copies all entries in formatted form.

Of course, the amount of information you can copy at one time depends on how you are viewing the database. If you are working with the database in the List view, you can copy as many records or partial records as you like with a single Copy command. If you are working with a database in the Form view, you can copy only one record at a time, and you must copy the information in every field of that record. For more on copying information from a database document, see Chapter 15.

Spreadsheet to database

In some cases, you may want to copy information from a spreadsheet document into a database document. Doing this is essentially the same as copying information from one database document to another. When you copy information from a spreadsheet document into a database document, Works places the information from each column of the source range into a different field of the database. If there are not enough fields in the database to accommodate the information you are copying from a spreadsheet, Works will add new fields to the database to accommodate the additional columns of information.

When you copy information from a spreadsheet to a database, Works copies the formats, styles, and alignment attributes of that information as well. Works copies label entries as labels, value entries as values, and date and time entries as serial values. However, Works doesn't copy formulas and functions. Instead, it copies their current results, just as it does when you copy information from one database to another.

If you are copying information from a spreadsheet into a database in the List view, the position of the highlight determines into which field Works will place the first column of information. If the database is in the Form view, Works will place the first column of information into the first field, the second column of information into the second field, and so forth, no matter which field is highlighted when you press [Enter]. For more on copying information to a database document, see Chapter 15.

You also can copy information from a database document into a spreadsheet document. Copying information from a database document into a spreadsheet document is quite similar to copying information from one spreadsheet document to another. When you copy information from a database into a spreadsheet, Works places the entries from each field into an individual column of the spreadsheet and places the entries from each record into an individual row.

Database to spreadsheet

When you copy information from a database to a spreadsheet, Works copies the formats, styles, and alignment attributes of that information as well. Works copies label entries as labels, value entries as values, and date and time entries as serial values. However, it copies only the current results of formulas and functions.

If you are viewing a database in the List view, you can copy as many records or partial records as you like at one time. If you pull down the Edit menu and select the Copy command while viewing a database in the Form view, Works will copy only the record that is visible in the form at the time, and will copy every field of that record. If the highlight is positioned on a single cell of the spreadsheet when you press [Enter] to complete the move, Works will use that cell as the upper-left corner of the destination range. If you extend the highlight to cover a range of cells, Works will copy as much of the information from the database as will fit in that range. For more on copying from database documents, see Chapter 15. For more on copying to spreadsheet documents, see Chapter 9.

Although you usually will copy information from other types of documents into word processor documents, you can copy information from word processor documents into other types of documents. For example, you can copy information from a word processor document into a spreadsheet document. When you do,

Word processor to spreadsheet

Works will place the contents of each paragraph into an individual row of the spreadsheet. Each tab marker in a paragraph tells Works to skip to the next cell on the current row.

For example, Figure 19-5 shows the result of copying the table from the word processor document shown in Figure 19-4 into a new spreadsheet document. To do this, we activated the word processor document, extended the highlight to cover the entire table, pulled down the Edit menu, selected the Copy command, activated the spreadsheet document, positioned the highlight on cell A1, then pressed [Enter].

Figure 19-4

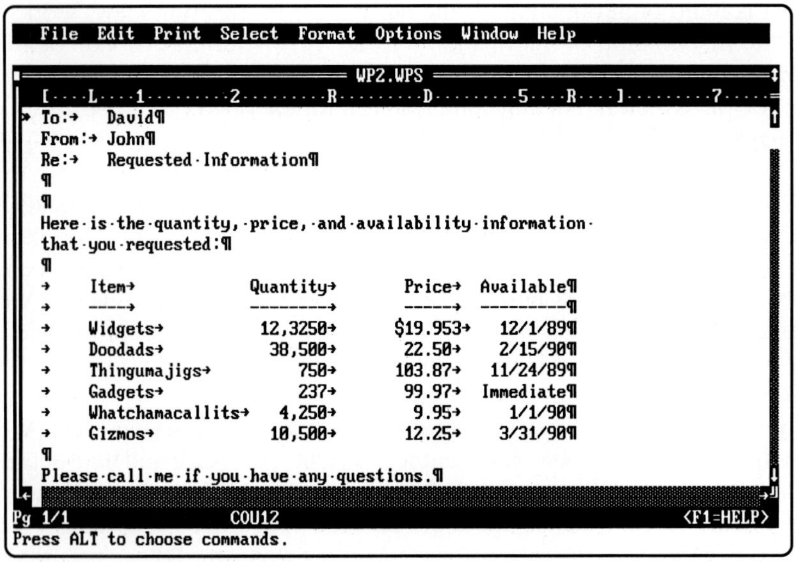

```
   File  Edit  Print  Select  Format  Options  Window  Help

══════════════════════════════ WP2.WPS ══════════════════════════
 [····L····1·········2·········R·········D········5···R···]········7·····
▸To:→    David¶
 From:→  John¶
 Re:→    Requested·Information¶
 ¶
 ¶
 Here·is·the·quantity,·price,·and·availability·information·
 that·you·requested:¶
 ¶
 →    Item→              Quantity→        Price→  Available¶
 →    ----→             --------→        -----→  --------¶
 →    Widgets→           12,3250→       $19.953→  12/1/89¶
 →    Doodads→           38,500→         22.50→   2/15/90¶
 →    Thingumajigs→        750→         103.87→  11/24/89¶
 →    Gadgets→             237→          99.97→  Immediate¶
 →    Whatchamacallits→  4,250→           9.95→   1/1/90¶
 →    Gizmos→           10,500→          12.25→   3/31/90¶
 ¶
 Please·call·me·if·you·have·any·questions.¶

Pg 1/1                      COU12                          <F1=HELP>
Press ALT to choose commands.
```

We'll copy the table from this word processor document into a new spreadsheet document.

Since each column of information that we copied from the word processor document is separated from the next one by a tab, Works placed each column into a different column of the spreadsheet. Works enters text as labels, numbers as values, and date and time entries as serial values (if the dates and times appear in one of the forms that Works recognizes). If a number is preceded by a $ sign, Works will assign the Currency 2 format to the cell into which it enters that value. If a number is followed by a % sign, Works will divide it by 100 and assign the Percent 2 format to the cell into which it enters that value. Works always assigns the appropriate format to date and time entries.

Figure 19-5

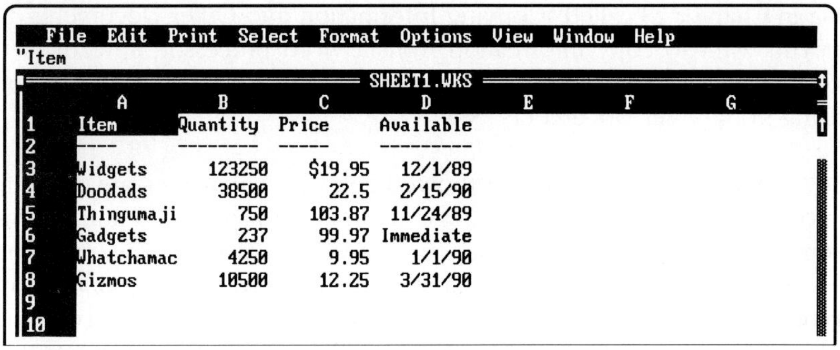

```
   File  Edit  Print  Select  Format  Options  View  Window  Help
  "Item
  ══════════════════════════════ SHEET1.WKS ══════════════════════════╤
        A          B         C          D         E        F        G
   1   Item       Quantity  Price      Available
   2   ----       --------  -----      ---------
   3   Widgets      123250  $19.95     12/1/89
   4   Doodads       38500    22.5     2/15/90
   5   Thingumaji      750  103.87     11/24/89
   6   Gadgets         237   99.97     Immediate
   7   Whatchamac     4250    9.95      1/1/90
   8   Gizmos        10500   12.25      3/31/90
   9
  10
```

Works places each paragraph onto a single row and divides the
information into different cells of the row according to the tab markers.

As you can see, the alignment of the tab stops in the word processor document does not affect the alignment attributes of the cells of the spreadsheet. Furthermore, the positions of the tab stops in the word processor document do not affect the width of the spreadsheet's columns. Consequently, you'll probably want to change the widths of the columns in the destination spreadsheet, then change the alignment of its entries after you copy the information.

Word processor to database

You also can copy information from a word processor document into a database document. When you do this, Works places the contents of each paragraph into an individual row of the database. Each tab marker in a paragraph tells Works to skip to the next field of the database. If there are not enough fields in the database to accommodate the information you are copying to it, Works will add new fields to the database.

When you copy information from a word processor document into a database, Works enters text as labels, numbers as values, and dates and times as serial values. If a value is preceded by a $ sign, Works assigns the Currency 2 format to the cell into which it enters that value. Works always assigns a format to date and time entries. The alignment of the tab stops in the word processor document does not affect the alignment attributes of the cells in the database, and the position of the tab markers in the word processor document does not affect the widths of the columns in the database.

Copying between a communications document and other documents
►WORKS 2◄

►Because Works 2 now includes a communications buffer that holds all the information that comes into a communications document, you can copy information from a communications document directly into word processor, spreadsheet, and database documents. The buffer will retain a variable amount of information depending on your choice of settings. For details on the procedure you use to copy information from a communications document to other documents, see the section in Chapter 18 called "Copying Information into Other Documents.

If you want to copy information from a word processor, spreadsheet, or database into a communications document, see the section in Chapter 18 called "Copying from Other Documents".◄

MERGING A CHART INTO A WORD PROCESSOR DOCUMENT

In Chapters 12, 13, and 14, we showed you how you can create charts from the information in a spreadsheet document. In most cases, you'll simply want to view your charts on the screen of your computer or make a print-out of the charts. However, you can make Works print a chart within a word processor document. To do this, you must use the Insert Chart... command, which is located on the Edit menu of any word processor document. This command inserts a special placeholder for the chart at the position you specify within the document. When Works prints the word processor document, it will replace the placeholder with the chart, thereby printing the chart within the document.

Inserting a placeholder for the chart

To insert a chart into a word processor document, begin by opening both the word processor document into which you want to insert a chart and the spreadsheet document that contains the chart you want to insert. Then, while the word processor document is active, position the cursor at the point within that document where you want Works to insert the chart. Next, pull down the Edit menu and select the Insert Chart... command. When you do this, you'll see an Insert Chart dialog box like the one shown in Figure 19-6.

Figure 19-6

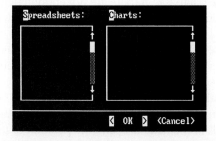

Works will present a dialog box like this one when you select the Insert Chart... command.

As you can see, this dialog box contains two list boxes: Spreadsheets and Charts. Within the Spreadsheets list box, Works will list the names of all the spreadsheet documents that are open at the time. From this list, you should choose the spreadsheet that contains the chart you want to include in the word processor document. Once you highlight the name of that spreadsheet, Works will display in the Charts list box the names of all the charts associated with that spreadsheet.

From this list, you should choose the name of the chart you want to merge into the word processor document. When you choose <OK> from the bottom of this dialog box, Works will insert a placeholder for the chart into the word processor document at the current position of the cursor. This placeholder will be in the form *chart spreadsheet:chartname*, where *chartname* is the name of the chart, and *spreadsheet* is the name of the spreadsheet that contains it.

Sizing the chart

Once you have inserted a placeholder for the chart you want to merge into your word processor document, you should tell Works how large to make that chart when it prints the document. By default, Works will print the chart 4 inches high, leave one blank line above and below it, extend it all the way to the left and right margins of the document, then print it in Portrait orientation.

To change any of these settings, you must position the cursor on the placeholder for the chart, pull down the Format menu, then select the Indents & Spacing… command. When you do this, Works will present a Indents & Spacing dialog box like the one shown in Figure 19-7

Figure 19-7

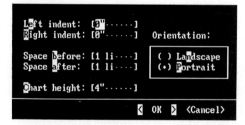

Works will display a dialog box like this one if you select the Indents & Spacing… command while the cursor is on the placeholder for a chart.

The elements in this box allow you to control the size and orientation of the printed chart. The entries in the Left Indent and Right Indent text boxes determine how far Works will indent the chart from the left and right margins of the document. The default value for both settings is 0. The entries in the Space Before and Space After text boxes determine how many blank lines Works will leave above and below the chart. The default value for these settings is 1 li. The entry in the Chart Height text box determines how tall the printed chart will be. The default value of this setting is 4". The option you choose from the Orientation option box determines the orientation of the chart on the page. If you accept the default Portrait option, Works will print the chart up-and-down on the page. If you choose the Landscape option, Works will turn the chart 90 degrees, printing it across the page. The settings specified within this dialog box when you choose <OK> are the ones that Works will use when it prints the chart within the document. The default settings are appropriate in most situations.

Printing the document

Once you have inserted a placeholder for the chart you want to print and, optionally, adjusted the size and orientation of the chart, you can print the word processor document. To do this, you must have a printer that can print both text and graphs. This includes most dot matrix and laser printers but excludes daisy wheel printers. The printer you will use must be specified in the Printer Setup dialog boxes for the Chart and the word processor documents. For information on selecting a chart printer, refer to Chapter 12. For information on selecting a text printer, see Chapter 3.

Once you have specified a printer and a port, opened both the spreadsheet document and the word processor document, and made the word processor document active, you can print the document by pulling down the Print menu, selecting the Print... command, then choosing <Print> from the Print dialog box.

In order for Works to print a chart within a word processor document, the spreadsheet that contains that chart must be open. If it is not, Works will pause printing and display the dialog box shown in Figure 19-8 when it encounters the placeholder for the chart. If you choose <OK>, Works will continue printing the document, leaving blank lines where it would have printed the chart. If you choose <Cancel>, Works will cancel the Print... command without printing the remainder of the document.

Figure 19-8

Works will display this dialog box if the spreadsheet containing the chart referenced within the document you are printing is not open.

An example

As an example of merging a chart into a document, suppose you want to merge a chart named Total Sales Pie, shown in Figure 19-9, between the two paragraphs in the document named SALEMEMO.WPS, shown in Figure 19-10. You want this chart, which is based on the information in a spreadsheet document named SALES1.WKS, to be 3 inches high, indented $^1/_2$ inch from each margin, one line removed from the text above and below it, and printed in Portrait orientation.

To do this, begin by opening both SALES1.WKS and SALEMEMO.WPS. After activating SALEMEMO.WPS, position the cursor at the left edge of the paragraph that begins *As you can see...*, pull down the Edit menu, select the Insert Chart... command, highlight SALES1.WKS in the Spreadsheets list box, highlight Total Sales Pie in the Charts list box, then choose <OK>. Figure 19-11 on the following page shows how your document will look at this point. As you can see, Works has inserted the placeholder *chart SALES1.WKS:Total Sales Pie* at the position of the cursor.

Figure 19-9

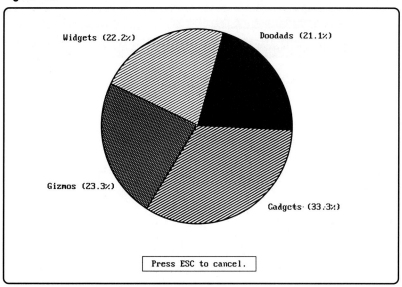

We'll merge this chart into the word processor document shown in Figure 19-10.

Figure 19-10

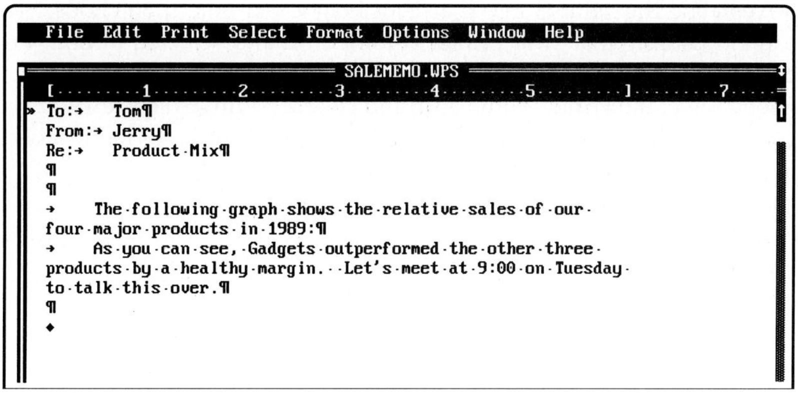

We'll merge the chart shown in Figure 19-9 into this document.

Figure 19-11

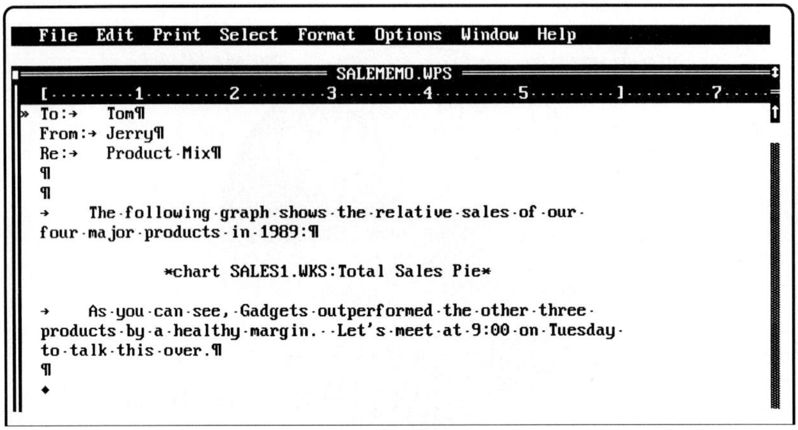

```
 File  Edit  Print  Select  Format  Options  Window  Help

══════════════════════════ SALEMEMO.WPS ══════════════════════════
[........·1·........·2·........·3·........·4·........·5·........]·........·7·....
» To:→    Tom¶
  From:→ Jerry¶
  Re:→    Product·Mix¶
     ¶
     ¶
  →     The·following·graph·shows·the·relative·sales·of·our·
  four·major·products·in·1989:¶

              *chart SALES1.WKS:Total Sales Pie*

  →     As·you·can·see,·Gadgets·outperformed·the·other·three·
  products·by·a·healthy·margin.··Let's·meet·at·9:00·on·Tuesday·
  to·talk·this·over.¶
     ¶
  ♦
```

The placeholder *chart SALES1.WKS:Total Sales Pie* *tells Works to insert the chart named Total Sales Pie from the spreadsheet named SALES1.WKS when it prints this document.*

Once you have inserted this placeholder, you should modify the size of the chart. To do this, position the cursor on the chart placeholder, pull down the Format menu, then select the Indents & Spacing... command. Within the Indents & Spacing dialog box, type the value .5 into both the Left Indent and Right Indent text boxes, type the value 3 into the Chart height text box, then choose <OK>. Now, after ensuring that your printer is turned on and selected in both Printer Setup dialog boxes, pull down the Print menu within the SALEMEMO.WPS document, select the Print... command, and choose <Print>. Figure 19-12 shows the result. As you can see, Works inserted the chart in place of the placeholder when it printed the document.

Notes

Before we end our discussion of merging charts into word processor documents, there are a couple of additional things you should know. First, you can merge more than one chart into a single word processor document; in fact, you can merge as many as you want. The different charts you merge can be from the same or different spreadsheet documents.

Second, inserting a placeholder for a chart into a word processor document creates a dynamic link between the word processor document and the spreadsheet document that contains the chart. If you change values in the spreadsheet that affect the merged chart, the chart will reflect those changes the next time you print the word processor document into which you have merged that chart.

Figure 19-12

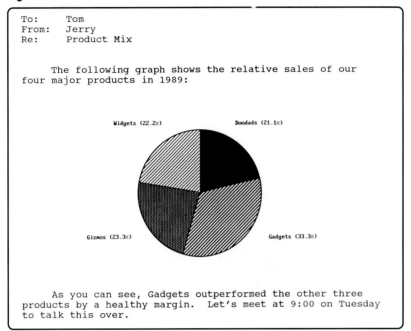

```
To:      Tom
From:    Jerry
Re:      Product Mix


     The following graph shows the relative sales of our
four major products in 1989:
```

Works inserted the pie chart into the printed word processor document.

As you've seen, Works allows you to copy information from a database into a word processor document. When you do this, the copied information appears in the word processor document as a table of entries. The information is "static"; that is, it does not change as you make changes to the database.

Works does, however, allow you to create dynamic links between a database document and a word processor document. To do this, you insert placeholders for the various fields of the database into the word processor document. When you print the word processor document using the Print Form Letters… or Print Labels… command, Works will print one copy of the document for each active record in the database, printing the entries from a different record each time. The Print Form Letters… command allows you to print "mail-merge" letters; the Print Labels… command makes it easy to print mailing labels.

FORM LETTERS AND MAILING LABELS

You can create form letters by merging information from a database document into a word processor document. First, compose the letter in a word processor document, inserting special placeholders for the fields of the database from which you want to extract information. After preparing this "merge document," use the Print Form Letters… command instead of the regular Print… command to print it.

Form letters

When you do this, Works will print one letter for each record that is visible in the database, using the information from a different record in each letter.

Creating a form letter

To create a form letter, begin by typing the letter as you normally would within a word processor document. At the places in the document where you want information from a certain field of a database to appear, you should insert a placeholder for that field, using the Insert Field... command. When you pull down the Edit menu and select this command, Works will present a dialog box like the one shown in Figure 19-13.

Figure 19-13

The Insert Field dialog box lets you insert placeholders for the fields of a database into a word processor document.

As you can see, this dialog box contains two list boxes: Databases and Fields. Within the Databases list box, Works will list the names of all the database documents that are open at the time. In order to insert a placeholder for a field of a database, therefore, that database must be open in Works. From this list, you should choose the database that contains the field you want to include in the word processor document. Once you highlight the name of that database document, Works will display in the Fields list box the names of all the fields in that database. From this list, you should choose the name of the field that you want to merge. (If you want, you can type the name of the field directly into the Field Name text box. In that case, the database from which you will be extracting information does not need to be open.) When you choose <OK>, Works will insert a placeholder for the field you selected at the current position of the cursor in the word processor document. This placeholder will be in the form <<*field name*>>, where *field name* is the name of the field that you selected from the Fields list box. You should repeat this process until you have inserted placeholders for all the fields from which you want to extract information.

An alternative way to insert field placeholders

If you want, you can type field placeholders directly into a document instead of choosing them from or typing them within the Insert Field dialog box. To generate the << character (the character that marks the beginning of a field placeholder), hold down the [Alt] key, type 174 on your computer's numeric keypad, then release the [Alt] key. To generate the >> character (the character that marks the end of a field placeholder), hold down the [Alt] key, type 175 on the numeric keypad, then release the [Alt] key. For example, to insert a placeholder for a field named First Name, you would position the cursor where you want to place that placeholder within the word processor document, hold down the [Alt] key, type 174 on the numeric keypad, release the [Alt] key, type *First Name*, depress the [Alt] key again, type 175 on the numeric keypad, then release the [Alt] key. When you do this, Works will insert the placeholder *<<First Name>>* into the word processor document.

When Works prints a merge document, it prints one copy of the document for each visible record in the database, in the order that those records appear in that database. If you want to print copies of the document for only part of the records in the database, you should hide the records you don't want to print, using any of the techniques presented in Chapter 16. If you want to print the records in an order other than the one in which they are currently arranged, you should rearrange them, either by sorting or by moving. These techniques are also explained in Chapter 16.

Preparing the database

Once you have prepared the form letter (and, if you want, selected the records for which you want to print copies of that letter and sorted them into the order you want the letters to be printed), you can print it. To begin, make sure that both the database document from which you want Works to extract information and the word processor document in which you designed the form letter are open and that the word processor document is active. Then, pull down the Print menu and select the Print Form Letters... command. When you do this, Works first will present a dialog box like the one shown in Figure 19-14 on the following page. As you can see, this box contains a single list box labeled Databases. Within this list box, Works will list the name of every database document that is currently open. From this list, you should choose the database from whose fields you want Works to extract information when it prints the document.

Printing the form letters

When you highlight the name of a database document and choose <OK>, Works will display a dialog box like the one shown in Figure 19-15 on the next page. As you can see, this is the same dialog box Works presents when you select the Print... command from a word processor document's Print menu. The elements in this box allow you to specify how many copies of each letter you want Works to print, which pages you want to print, whether you want it to print to a file instead of a printer, and whether you want it to print in draft quality.

When you choose <Print> from the bottom of this dialog box, Works will print one copy of the document for each visible record in the database document you specified. (Actually, it will print as many copies of the letter for each record as you specified in the Number of Copies text box.) In the first letter, Works will replace the field placeholders with the entries from the first visible record in the database; in the second letter, it will replace the placeholders with the entries from the second visible record; and so forth. Works will continue until it has printed the appropriate number of letters for each of the visible records in the database, or until you press [Esc].

Figure 19-14

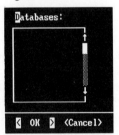

Works will present a dialog box like this one when you select the Print Form Letters... command from the Print menu of a word processor document.

Figure 19-15

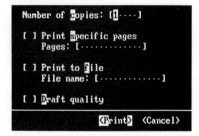

Works will display a dialog box like this one when you choose the name of a database document from the Print Form Letters dialog box, then choose <OK>.

An example

As an example of creating and printing mail-merge letters, suppose you want to print form letters like the one shown in Figure 19-16 for each of the records shown in Figure 19-17 that has the entry *KY* in its State field, in ascending zip code order. As you can see, this database document is named MAILLIST.WDB.

Creating the merge document. To begin, you should create the merge document shown in Figure 19-18 on page 656. To do this, first use the Create New File... command to create a new word processor document. After creating this new document, you can insert field placeholders and type text into it. Since you'll want to insert field placeholders for fields of the database shown in Figure 19-17, make sure that the database is open as well.

Figure 19-16

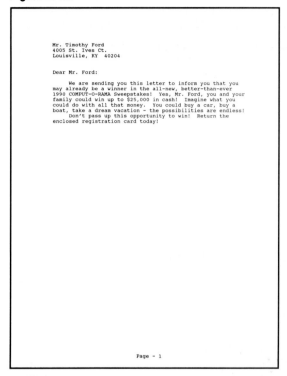

```
        Mr. Timothy Ford
        4005 St. Ives Ct.
        Louisville, KY  40204

        Dear Mr. Ford:

            We are sending you this letter to inform you that you
        may already be a winner in the all-new, better-than-ever
        1990 COMPUT-O-RAMA Sweepstakes!  Yes, Mr. Ford, you and your
        family could win up to $25,000 in cash!  Imagine what you
        could do with all that money.  You could buy a car, buy a
        boat, take a dream vacation - the possibilities are endless!
            Don't pass up this opportunity to win!  Return the
        enclosed registration card today!




                        Page - 1
```

We'll print form letters like this one for each record in the database shown in Figure 19-17 that has the entry KY in its State field.

Figure 19-17

```
  File   Edit   Print   Select   Format   Options   View   Window   Help
"Ms.
═══════════════════════ MAILLIST.WDB ═══════════════════════
     Title First    Last       Street          City       State Zip
1    Ms.  Patricia Shields    2506 Sherry Rd.   Louisville     KY   40207
2    Ms.  Peggy    Zeillmann  1010 Glenridge Dr. New Albany    IN   47132
3    Mr.  Tom      Cottingham 9710 Gandy Rd.    Louisville     KY   40222
4    Ms.  Becket   Ledford    4705 Shady Oak Ln. Jeffersonville IN  47300
5    Ms.  Tara     Billinger  4502 Franklin Ave. Lexington     KY   40523
6    Mr.  Timothy  Ford       4005 St. Ives Ct. Louisville     KY   40204
7    Ms.  Renee    Marie      4305 Winchester Dr. Clarksville  IN   47824
8    Ms.  Maureen  Pawley     301 Hurstbourne Ln. Louisville   KY   40205
9    Ms.  Ann      Rockers    1816 Norris Pl.   Sellersburg    IN   47364
10   Mrs. Elayne   Noltemeyer 1257 Cherokee Rd. Lexington      KY   40570
11
12
```

We'll print form letters like the one shown in Figure 19-16 for each record in this database that has the entry KY in its State field.

Figure 19-18

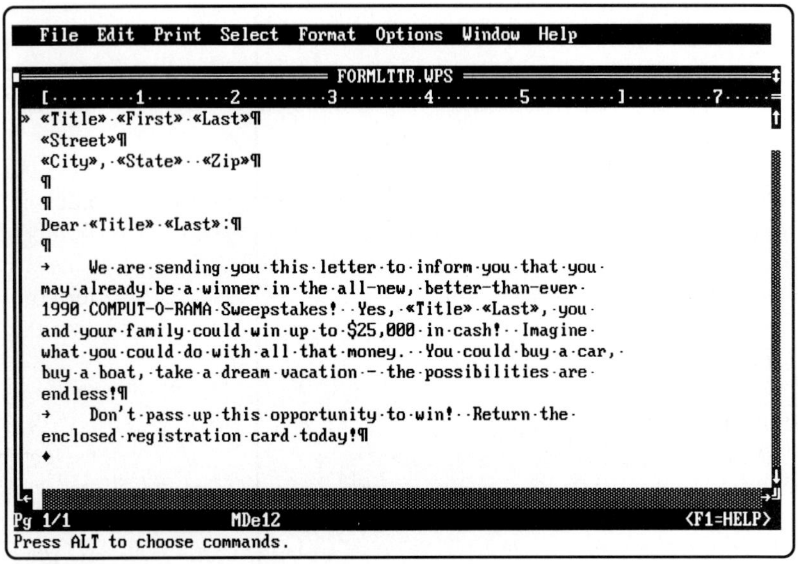

```
┌──────────────────────────────────────────────────────────────┐
│  File  Edit  Print  Select  Format  Options  Window  Help      │
│ ═══════════════════════ FORMLTTR.WPS ═══════════════════════   │
│ [········1········2········3········4········5········]·······7····│
│»«Title»·«First»·«Last»¶                                      ↑ │
│ «Street»¶                                                      │
│ «City»,·«State»···«Zip»¶                                       │
│ ¶                                                              │
│ ¶                                                              │
│ Dear·«Title»·«Last»:¶                                          │
│ ¶                                                              │
│ →    We·are·sending·you·this·letter·to·inform·you·that·you·    │
│ may·already·be·a·winner·in·the·all-new,·better-than-ever·      │
│ 1990·COMPUT-O-RAMA·Sweepstakes!··Yes,·«Title»·«Last»,·you·     │
│ and·your·family·could·win·up·to·$25,000·in·cash!··Imagine·     │
│ what·you·could·do·with·all·that·money.···You·could·buy·a·car,· │
│ buy·a·boat,·take·a·dream·vacation--·the·possibilities·are·     │
│ endless!¶                                                      │
│ →    Don't·pass·up·this·opportunity·to·win!··Return·the·       │
│ enclosed·registration·card·today!¶                            │
│ ◆                                                             │
│                                                               │
│ Pg 1/1              MDe12                         <F1=HELP>    │
│ Press ALT to choose commands.                                 │
└──────────────────────────────────────────────────────────────┘
```

To print form letters like the one shown in Figure 19-16, you must create a merge document like this one.

To insert a placeholder for the Title field at the upper-left corner of the document, pull down the Edit menu, select the Insert Field... command, highlight MAILLIST.WDB from the Databases list box, highlight the field name Title in the Fields list box, then choose <OK>. Press the [Spacebar] once to move the cursor one space to the right, and insert a placeholder for the First field by selecting the Insert Field... command again, highlighting the database name MAILLIST.WDB in the Databases list box, highlighting the field name *First* in the Fields list box, and choosing <OK>. Then, press the [Spacebar] one more time and place the Last field by selecting the Insert Field... command again, highlighting the database name MAILLIST.WDB in the Databases list box, highlighting the field name *Last* in the Fields list box, and choosing <OK> once again.

After completing the first line of the document, press [Enter] to move the cursor to the beginning of the second line, then use the Insert Field... command to insert a placeholder for the Street field at the beginning of that row. Next, press [Enter] once again to move the cursor to the beginning of the third line of the document, then insert placeholders for the City, State, and Zip fields on that line. Between the placeholders for the City and State fields, you should type a comma and a space; between the placeholders for the State and Zip fields, type two spaces.

After completing the inside address of the letter, you should press [Enter] three times to move the cursor to the beginning of the sixth line, then compose the greeting. First, type the word *Dear*, followed by a space. Next, use the Insert Field... command to insert a placeholder for the Title field, and type another space. Then, use the Insert Field... command to insert a placeholder for the Last field. Finally, type a colon.

After completing the greeting, you should type the body of the letter. As you can see, the body consists mostly of text, but it also contains placeholders for the Title and Last fields. To insert the text, simply type it. To insert the placeholders, use the Insert Field... command. You can insert these placeholders as you are typing the body of the letter, or you can go back and insert them after you have finished typing. When you are finished, your screen should look like the one shown in Figure 19-18.

Preparing the database.   Since you want to print letters for only the records in the MAILLIST database that have the entry *KY* in their State field, you must select those records before you print the letters. To do this, first activate the database document. Then, pull down the View menu and select the Query command. If the Query mode already contains entries, pull down the Edit menu, and select the Delete command to erase them. Then, move the highlight to the State field and type *KY*. Finally, press [F10]. When you do this, Works will bring the database back into view. Only the records with the entry *KY* in their State field will be visible within it.

Since you want to print the letters in ascending zip code order, you must sort the database before you print from it. To sort the visible records into ascending zip code order, pull down the Select menu, select the Sort Records... command, type the field name *State* into the 1st Field text box, and make sure that Ascend is selected. Type the field name *Zip* into the 2nd Field text box and make sure that Ascend is selected there also. If there is an entry in the 3rd Field box, delete it. When you choose <OK>, Works will sort the database and return you to it. At this point, your database will look like the one shown in Figure 19-19 on the following page.

Printing the letters.   Once you have created the merge document and queried and sorted the database, you can print the letters. To do this, make sure both the database document shown in Figure 19-19 and the word processor document shown in Figure 19-18 are open and the word processor document is the active document. Then, pull down the Print menu, select the Print Form Letters... command, select MAILLIST.WDB from the Print Form Letters dialog box, and choose <OK>. At this point, Works will present a regular Print dialog box.

Figure 19-19

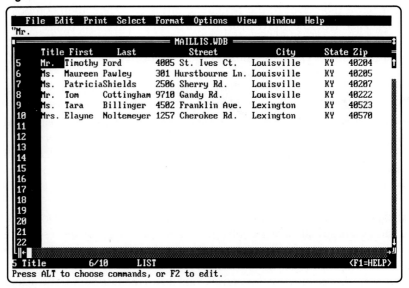

If you want to print letters for only certain records, you must query the database; if you want to print those records in a certain order, you must sort it.

When you choose <Print> from the Print dialog box, Works will begin to print the letters. Since six records are visible in the database, Works will print the form letter six times. When Works prints the first letter, it will replace the placeholders in the document with the entries from the fields of the first record, producing a letter like the one shown in Figure 19-16. When Works prints the remaining letters, it will replace those placeholders with the entries from the remaining records, producing letters like the one shown in Figure 19-20. Works will continue in this fashion, printing letters for the four remaining records in the database. As Works is printing, it keeps you informed of its progress by displaying a record counter on the status line. This counter tells you how many letters it has printed and how many letters it will print.

Mailing labels

Works also makes it easy to print information from a name and address database in the form of mailing labels. The process of composing and printing mailing labels is similar to that of composing and printing form letters. First, you must create a merge document that contains placeholders for the fields of the database from which you want to draw information, arranged in the form of a mailing label. Next, you may want to query and sort the database from which Works will be extracting information to limit the number of labels that Works prints, and specify the order in which it will print those labels. After doing these things, you can select the Print Labels... command from the Print menu to begin the process of printing the labels.

Figure 19-20

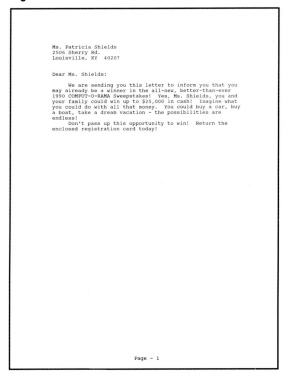

```
Ms. Patricia Shields
2506 Sherry Rd.
Louisville, KY  40207

Dear Ms. Shields:

     We are sending you this letter to inform you that you
may already be a winner in the all-new, better-than-ever
1990 COMPUT-O-RAMA Sweepstakes!  Yes, Ms. Shields, you and
your family could win up to $25,000 in cash!  Imagine what
you could do with all that money.  You could buy a car, buy
a boat, take a dream vacation - the possibilities are
endless!
     Don't pass up this opportunity to win!  Return the
enclosed registration card today!
```

```
Page - 1
```

Works will print this letter for the third record in the database.

Creating the merge document required to print mailing labels is similar to creating the merge document for form letters. Instead of having both field placeholders and text, however, the word processor merge document for mailing labels usually will have just field placeholders. You should insert the placeholders so that they are arranged in the form of a single mailing label. To insert these field placeholders into the document, you can either use the Insert Field... command on the Edit menu, or you can type them into the document yourself. For information on inserting field placeholders into a word processor document, see the section entitled "Creating a Form Letter" earlier in this chapter.

Creating the merge document

When Works prints mailing labels, it prints one for each visible record in the database, in the order that those records appear. If you want to print labels for only some of the records in the database, you should hide the records you don't

Preparing the database

want to print. If you want to print the labels in an order other than the one in which the records in the database are currently arranged, you should rearrange them. For information on querying and sorting a database, refer to the section called, "Preparing the Database" in the previous example about creating form letters.

Printing the labels

Once you've created the merge document and, optionally, queried and sorted the database, you can print the mailing labels. To do this, make sure that both the word processor merge document and the database document from which it will extract information are open. Then, make the word processor document the active document, pull down the Print menu, and select the Print Labels... command. When you do this, Works will present a dialog box like the one shown in Figure 19-21.

Figure 19-21

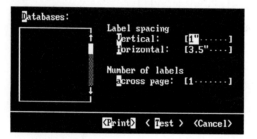

Works will present a dialog box like this one when you select the Print Labels... command from the Print menu of a word processor document.

Selecting the database. As you can see, the Print Labels dialog box contains a number of elements. In the Databases list box, Works will display the names of any database documents that are open at the time. In this box, you should highlight the name of the database whose records you want Works to print in the form of mailing labels. The database whose name is highlighted when you choose <Print> from the bottom of this dialog box is the one from which Works will extract information when it prints.

Setting the label dimensions. Within the Vertical and Horizontal text boxes, you should enter the dimensions of the labels on which you will be printing. Within the Vertical text box, you should enter the distance between the top of one label and the top of the next label. The default value in this box is 1". In the Horizontal text box, you should enter the distance between the left edge of one label on a row and the left edge of the next label on a row. The default value in this box is 3.5". If the label stock on which you are printing has only one label on each row, you should enter the width of that label into the Horizontal text box. If you plan to print three labels across the page, as we do in this example, enter the value 2.75 into the Horizontal text box.

Specifying the number of labels across each page. The Number of Labels across Page text box allows you to specify how many labels there are on each row of the label stock on which you are printing. For instance, if you are printing on label stock that has only three labels across each page (3-up labels), you should enter the value 3 into this box. The default value in this box is 1.

Printing test labels. After you've specified the appropriate settings in the Print Labels dialog box, you should choose either <Print> or <Test> from the bottom of that box. If you choose <Test>, Works will print a single test label instead of printing a label for every visible record in the database. You can use this test label to ensure that your label stock is aligned correctly in the printer. ▶Before Works 2 prints, it will display the Page Setup & Margins dialog box. (In earlier versions of Works, you adjust the Layout settings before you select the Print Labels… command.)◀ You will need to adjust a number of settings in this dialog box before you print the mailing labels. (A word of caution: These settings work on our printer. They may differ from the settings you need for your printer.) First, you should enter the value .7 into the Top Margin text box, .25 into the Left Margin text box, and 0 into the Bottom Margin, Right Margin, Header Margin, and Footer Margin text boxes. Second, you should enter into the Page Width text box a value that is greater than or equal to the width of the label sheet on which you will be printing, multiplied by the number of labels that appear across each page. For example, if you are printing on label stock that has three $3^1/_2$-inch-wide labels across each page, you should enter a value no less than 8.5" into the Page Width text box. Third, you should enter into the Page Length text box a value that is equal to the length of the label sheet. For example, if your label sheet has ten rows of labels, you should enter a value no less than 11" into the Page Length text box.

▶**WORKS 2**◀

When you are finished adjusting the Page Setup & Margins settings, choose <OK> to print. When you do this, Works will present the familiar Print dialog box. The elements in this dialog box allow you to specify how many copies of each label you want Works to print, whether you want it to print only certain pages, whether you want it to print to a file, and whether you want to include special styles in the print-out. For more on the effects of the elements in this box, see Chapters 3 and 4.

If you are printing to a laser printer, Works may display the alert box shown in Figure 19-22 on the next page when you choose <Print> in the Print Labels dialog box. This box tells you that if the text of your labels is cut off, you can adjust your Margins and Label Size settings and try to print the labels again.

Works will print a label from the first record in the database (if your label stock has more than one label across each page, Works will print the first row of labels), then display a dialog box like the one shown in Figure 19-23. If the printed information is aligned correctly on the label(s), you should choose <Print> from this box.

Figure 19-22

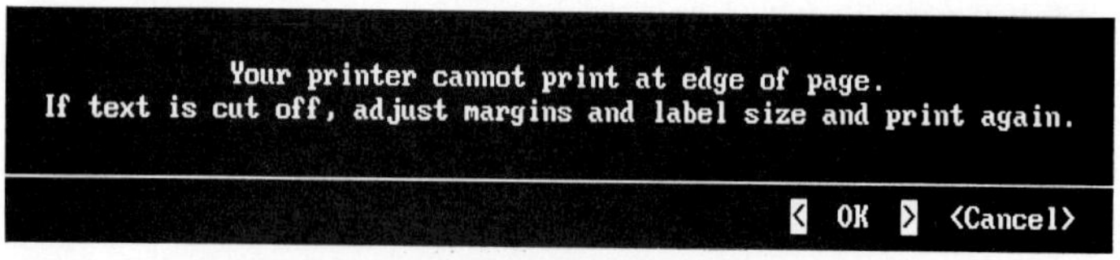

```
          Your printer cannot print at edge of page.
 If text is cut off, adjust margins and label size and print again.


                                        〈  OK  〉  〈Cancel〉
```

Works alerts you of a crucial laser printer limitation related to the printing of mailing labels.

Figure 19-23

```
 Print all labels or reprint test labels?

                  〈Print〉  〈 Test 〉  〈Cancel〉
```

Works will display this dialog box after it prints one or more test labels.

Printing the real labels.   If you chose <Print> instead of <Test> in the Print Labels dialog box, the procedure you follow to print the labels is the same as the one you follow to print a test label. The result, however, will be different. Instead of printing one label or row of labels, Works will print the entire set of mailing labels.

An example

As an example of printing mailing labels, suppose you wanted to print 3- by 1-inch mailing labels for the records in the database shown in Figure 19-17 that have the entry *KY* in their State field, in ascending zip code order. To do this, you would begin by creating the merge document shown in Figure 19-24 within a new word processor document.

Figure 19-24

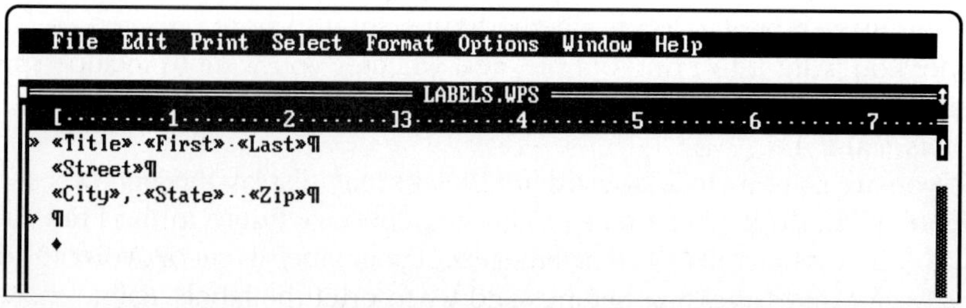

We'll use this merge document to print mailing labels from the database document shown in Figure 19-17.

To create a new word processor document, pull down the File menu, select the Create New File... command, choose the <New Word Processor> option in the Create New File dialog box, then choose <OK>. Once you've created this document, you should insert field placeholders in the arrangement shown in Figure 19-24. Specifically, you'll want to insert placeholders for the Title, First, and Last fields onto the first line of the document, with a single space between each placeholder. Onto the second line, you'll want to insert the Street field placeholder. Onto the third line, you'll want to insert placeholders for the City, State, and Zip fields. You should type a comma and a space between the placeholders for the City and State fields, and two spaces between the place holders for the State and Zip fields.

To insert these placeholders, you'll probably want to use the Insert Field... command. If you want to choose the field names from the Fields list box within the Insert Field dialog box, the database document whose records you want to print (in this case, MAILLIST.WDB) must be open. It doesn't need to be open if you type the field names into the Field Name text box, or if you type the field placeholders directly into the document. For information on inserting field placeholders into a word processor document, see the sections entitled "Creating a Form Letter" and "Creating the Merge Document" earlier in this chapter.

Once you've placed the field placeholders into the word processor document, you should arrange the information in your database. Since you want to print mailing labels in ascending zip code order for only the records in the MAILLIST database that have the entry *KY* in their State field, you must select and sort those records before you print the labels. For instructions on how to perform these manipulations, see the section entitled "Preparing the Database" earlier in this chapter during our discussion of form letters. After you query and sort the database, it should look like the one shown in Figure 19-19.

Now, you're ready to print the labels. First, make sure that the database named MAILLIST.WDB is open and that the word processor document shown in Figure 19-24 is the active document. Then, pull down the Print menu and select the Print Labels... command to reveal the Print Labels dialog box. Within the Databases text box, highlight the name MAILLIST.WDB. Since you'll be printing on 1- by $3\frac{1}{2}$-inch 3-up labels, make sure that the Vertical text box contains the entry 1", that the Horizontal text box contains the entry 2.75", and that the Number of Labels across Page text box contains the value 1.

After you have specified these settings in the Print Labels dialog box, turn on your printer, align the label stock in it, then choose <Test>. ▶When you do, Works will display the Page Setup & Margins dialog box, so you can alter the Page Setup & Margins settings of that document. In this dialog box, you should enter the value .7 into the Top Margin text box, .25 in the Left Margin text box, and 0 in the Bottom Margin, Right Margin, Header Margin, and Footer Margin text boxes, a value greater than or equal to 8.5" into the Page Width box, and a value of 11" into the Page Length text box. Once you have changed these settings, choose <OK>. Works will present the familiar Print dialog box. When you choose <Print> from

▶WORKS 2◀

the bottom of this box, Works may present the alert box in Figure 19-22 that warns of a possible printer limitation.◄ If your text is cut off from the edge of the sheet it's printed on, you should return to the Print Labels and Page Setup & Margins dialog boxes to readjust the Label Spacing and Margin settings.

Next, Works will print a single test label, then present the dialog box shown in Figure 19-23. If the information is not aligned correctly on that label, you should adjust the label stock within your printer, then choose <Test>. If the label is adjusted and aligned properly, you should choose <Print>. After you choose <Print> from this dialog box, Works will print the information from the Title, First, Last, Street, City, State, and Zip fields of each of the six records visible in the database shown in Figure 19-19 on their own 1- by $3^1/_2$-inch labels. Figure 19-25 shows this result.

Figure 19-25

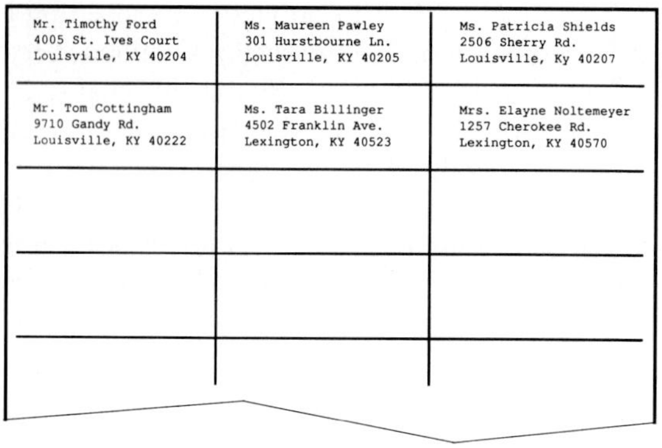

Mr. Timothy Ford 4005 St. Ives Court Louisville, KY 40204	Ms. Maureen Pawley 301 Hurstbourne Ln. Louisville, KY 40205	Ms. Patricia Shields 2506 Sherry Rd. Louisville, Ky 40207
Mr. Tom Cottingham 9710 Gandy Rd. Louisville, KY 40222	Ms. Tara Billinger 4502 Franklin Ave. Lexington, KY 40523	Mrs. Elayne Noltemeyer 1257 Cherokee Rd. Lexington, KY 40570

As you can see, Works has printed a 3-up set of 1- by $3^1/_2$-inch mailing labels for each of the six visible records in the database shown in Figure 19-19.

Notes

Unlike many mail-merge programs, Works does not allocate a constant amount of space for each field you merge into a document. Instead, it rejustifies the document after it makes each set of substitutions prior to printing each letter. Consequently, the printed form letters and mailing labels don't appear "gappy" when Works prints from a record that has a short entry in a particular field.

If you want, you can assign formats like boldfacing, underlining, italicizing, and even special fonts and sizes to the field placeholders in a merge document. To do this, simply extend the cursor to highlight one or more characters in the field placeholder (there's no need to highlight the entire placeholder), then assign the format, just as you would to any other block of characters in a word processor document. When you print the document, Works will print the entries it substitutes for that field according to the format(s) you assigned to that field. For more on formatting the characters in a word processor document, see Chapter 5.

Finally, although it is possible to insert placeholders for fields from more than one database document into a single word processor document, Works can merge information from only a single database document (the one you specified in the Print Form Letters dialog box) when it prints. If Works finds a placeholder for a field that is not in the database document you specify in the Print Form Letters dialog box, it will display a dialog box like the one shown in Figure 19-26. If you choose <OK>, Works will print the letters or labels, ignoring the placeholders for the fields that are not in the database you specified. If you choose <Cancel>, Works will cancel the Print Form Letters... command.

Figure 19-26

Works will display a dialog box like this one if it encounters a placeholder for a field that is not in the database you specified in the Print Merge dialog box.

CONCLUSION

In this chapter, we've demonstrated the variety of ways that Works lets you share information between various types of documents. We showed you how to copy information between different types of documents; how to merge charts into word processor documents; and how to merge information from a database document into a word processor document to create form letters and mailing labels. In the final chapter of this book, we'll explore Works macros.

Macros 20

*I*n the previous chapters, we've explained the great variety of things you can do in each type of Works document. As you've seen, everything you do in Works—such as entering information into a document, moving around within a document, and selecting commands from menus—involves typing or using your mouse. In the course of a typical Works session, you're likely to press thousands of keys. In many cases, you press the same keys over and over as you repeat a task in different parts of the same document or in different documents.

Macros allow you to automate repetitive series of keystrokes. A macro is a text file that contains representations of keys and combinations of keys that you can press from the keyboard of your computer. When you play a macro, Works automatically "presses" the keys that are represented in it, performing the tasks that those keystrokes command it to perform.

In this chapter, we'll show you how to create, play, and manage macros that automate the things you do in Works.

MACRO BASICS

A macro is a collection of keystroke representations linked to a single key or to a combination of a key and the [Shift], [Alt], or [Ctrl] key. You can create a macro by recording it or by writing it. Once you create a macro, you can play it simply by pressing the key or key combination to which it is linked. When Works plays a macro, it presses the keys whose representations are stored in the macro, in the order that they appear in that macro. As Works presses the keys stored in the macro, it responds in the same way it does when you press those keys yourself.

By programming a task within a macro, you can save time and effort. First, you won't have to press the keystrokes yourself each time you want to perform the same task. Second, Works doesn't make typing mistakes when it plays a macro—it always presses exactly the keys whose representations are stored in the macro. Third, Works can press those keys significantly faster than you can yourself, even if you are an exceptionally good typist.

►WORKS 2◄

►The ability to record and play macros is built into Works 2. (The macro capabilities of earlier versions of Works are contained in a separate utility called MS-Key.)◄ To access Works' macro options, you simply press [Alt]/. When you do this, Works will display the dialog box shown in Figure 20-1. As you can see, this dialog box includes six options: Record Macro, Play Macro, Skip Macro, Delete Macros, Change Key & Title, and Turn Macros Off. These options allow you to create, play, and manage your macros.

Figure 20-1

Work will display this dialog box when you press [Alt]/.

RECORDING MACROS

Recording is the easiest way to create a macro, no matter how experienced you are with Works. (Later in this chapter, we'll show you how to write macros.) When you command Works to do so, it will record representations of the keys you press from the keyboard. As you press those keys, Works will do what those keys command it to do; that is, Works will perform the task while it is recording representations of the keys you press to perform it. Because you are actually working in Works as it is recording, you don't have to remember what keys you need to press to select certain commands from certain menus or to access specific elements within specific dialog boxes; you can see those menus and dialog boxes on the screen.

Before you begin recording a macro, you should make certain that everything in your document is just as it will be when you later play the macro. If you play a macro when a document is in a different condition than it was when you recorded the macro, the macro probably will not produce the intended results.

The Record Macro command

To begin recording a macro, press [Alt]/ to display the dialog box shown in Figure 20-1, then select the Record Macro command. When you do this, Works will present a dialog box like the one shown in Figure 20-2. This dialog box allows you to define the playback key—the key you'll press to play the macro—and, if you want, to define a title for the macro.

Specifying a playback key

When the dialog box shown in Figure 20-2 appears, you should press the playback key—the key or key combination to which you want to link the macro you are about to record. This is the key you'll press to play the macro after you have recorded it.

Figure 20-2

Works will display this dialog box when you choose the Record Macro command.

You can link a macro to practically any key or key combination on the keyboard of your computer. For example, you can link a macro to the A key, the [F3] key, the [Alt]z key combination, the [Ctrl]q key combination, the [Ctrl][Shift]➡ key combination, and so forth. However, we recommend that you avoid assigning macros to keys and key combinations that you use for other things in Works. For example, you should avoid letter and number keys, since you use them to enter information into documents and text boxes. You also should avoid using the [Alt] key alone or in combination with other keys, since you use this key to access Works' menu bar, select commands from menus, and move within dialog boxes.

We find [Ctrl] key combinations to be most suitable for use as playback keys. Table 20-1 shows the [Ctrl] key combinations that Works doesn't use for any other purpose. Works uses the remaining [Ctrl] key combinations as shortcuts for selecting commands from menus.

Table 20-1

[Ctrl]0	[Ctrl]a	[Ctrl][F1]	[Ctrl]'
[Ctrl]3	[Ctrl]k	[Ctrl][F2]	[Ctrl]- (numeric keypad)
[Ctrl]4	[Ctrl]q	[Ctrl][F3]	[Ctrl]+ (numeric keypad)
[Ctrl]6	[Ctrl]v	[Ctrl][F4]	[Ctrl]5 (numeric keypad)
[Ctrl]7	[Ctrl]w	[Ctrl][F5]	[Ctrl][Ins]
[Ctrl]8	[Ctrl]y	[Ctrl][F6]	[Ctrl][Delete]
[Ctrl]9	[Ctrl]z	[Ctrl][F7]	
		[Ctrl][F9]	
		[Ctrl][F10]	

[Ctrl] key combinations are most suitable for use as playback keys.

When you press the key or key combination to which you want to link the macro, Works will enter the macro representation of that key or key combination into the Playback Key text box. For example, if you press [Alt]a, Works will enter *<alta>*; if you press [Ctrl]z, Works will enter *<ctrlz>*; and so forth. Table 20-2 shows the macro representation of every possible key and key combination. (The [Alt] key alone is represented as *<menu>*.)

Table 20-2a

Key	Alone	With [Shift]	With [Alt]	With [Ctrl]
a	a	A	<alta>	<ctrla>
b	b	B	<altb>	<ctrlb>
c	c	C	<altc>	<ctrlc>
d	d	D	<altd>	<ctrld>
e	e	E	<alte>	<ctrle>
f	f	F	<altf>	<ctrlf>
g	g	G	<altg>	<ctrlg>
h	h	H	<alth>	<ctrlh>
i	i	I	<alti>	<crtli>
j	j	J	<altj>	<ctrlj>
k	k	K	<altk>	<ctrlk>
l	l	L	<altl>	<ctrll>
m	m	M	<altm>	<ctrlm>
n	n	N	<altn>	<ctrln>
o	o	O	<alto>	<ctrlo>
p	p	P	<altp>	<ctrlp>
q	q	Q	<altq>	<ctrlq>
r	r	R	<altr>	<ctrlr>
s	s	S	<alts>	<ctrls>
t	t	T	<altt>	<ctrlt>
u	u	U	<altu>	<ctrlu>
v	v	V	<altv>	<ctrlv>
w	w	W	<altw>	<ctrlw>
x	x	X	<altx>	<ctrlx>
y	y	Y	<alty>	<ctrly>
z	z	Z	<altz>	<ctrlz>
1	1	!	<alt1>	<ctrl1>
2	2	@	<alt2>	<ctrl2>
3	3	#	<alt3>	<ctrl3>
4	4	$	<alt4>	<ctrl4>
5	5	%	<alt5>	<ctrl5>
6	6	^	<alt6>	<ctrl6>
7	7	&	<alt7>	<ctrl7>
8	8	*	<alt8>	<ctrl8>
9	9	(	<alt9>	<ctrl9>
0	0	)	<alt0>	<ctrl0>
[space]	<space>[1]	<shiftspace>[2]	<altspace>	<ctrlspace>
-	-	_	<alt->	<ctrl->
=	=	+	<alt=>	<ctrl=>
[	[	{	<alt[>	<ctrl[>
]	]	}	<alt]>	<ctrl]>
;	;	:	<alt;>	<ctrl;>
'	'	"	<alt'>	<ctrl'>
`	<skip>	~	<alt`>	
\	\	|	<alt\>	<ctrlenter>
,	,	<	<alt,>	<ctrl,>
.	.	>	<alt.>	<ctrl.>
/	/	?	<alt/>	
Esc	<esc>	<shift><esc>	<altesc>	<ctrlesc>
Tab	<tab>	<shifttab>	<alttab>	<ctrltab>
Backspace	<back>	<shiftback>	<altback>	<ctrlback>
Enter	<enter>	<shiftenter>	<altenter>	<ctrlenter>

[F1]	<f1>	<shiftf1>	<altf1>	<ctrlf1>
[F2]	<f2>	<shiftf2>	<altf2>	<ctrlf2>
[F3]	<f3>	<shiftf3>	<altf3>	<ctrlf3>
[F4]	<f4>	<shiftf4>	<altf4>	<ctrlf4>
[F5]	<f5>	<shiftf5>	<altf5>	<ctrlf5>
[F6]	<f6>	<shiftf6>	<altf6>	<ctrlf6>
[F7]	<f7>	<shiftf7>	<altf7>	<ctrlf7>
[F8]	<f8>	<shiftf8>	<altf8>	<ctrlf8>
[F9]	<f9>	<shiftf9>	<altf9>	<ctrlf9>
[F10]	<f10>	<shiftf10>	<altf10>	<ctrlf10>
[F11]	<f11>	<shiftf11>	<altf11>	<ctrlf11>
[F12]	<f12>	<shiftf12>	<altf12>	<ctrlf12>
↑	<xup>	<shiftxup>	<altxup>	<ctrlxup>
↓	<xdown>	<shiftxdown>	<altxdown>	<ctrlxdown>
→	<xright>	<shiftxright>	<altxright>	<ctrlxright>
←	<xleft>	<shiftxleft>	<altxleft>	<ctrlxleft>
Insert	<insert>	<shiftinsert>	<altinsert>	<ctrlinsert>
Home	<xhome>	<shiftxhome>	<altxhome>	<ctrlxhome>
Page Up	<pageup>	<shiftpageup>	<altpageup>	<ctrlpageup>
Delete	<delete>	<shiftdelete>	<altdelete>	<ctrldelete>
End	<xend>	<shiftxend>	<altxend>	<ctrlxend>
Page Down	<pagedown>	<shiftpagedown>	<altpagedown>	<ctrlpagedown>
1 (keypad)	<k1>[3]	<end>[4]		<ctrlend>
2 (keypad)	<k2>[5]	<down>[6]		<ctrldown>
3 (keypad)	<k3>[7]	<pgdn>[8]		<ctrlpgdn>
4 (keypad)	<k4>[9]	<left>[10]		<ctrlleft>
5 (keypad)	<k5>[11]	<clear>[12]		<ctrlclear>
6 (keypad)	<k6>[13]	<right>[14]		<ctrlright>
7 (keypad)	<k7>[15]	<home>[16]		<ctrlhome>
8 (keypad)	<k8>[17]	<up>[18]		<ctrlup>
9 (keypad)	<k9>[19]	<pgup>[20]		<ctrlpgup>
0 (keypad)	<k0>[21]	<ins>[22]		<ctrlins>
. (keypad)	<k.>[23]	<del>[24]		<ctrldel>
/ (keypad)	<k/>	<shiftk/>	<altk/>	<ctrlk/>
* (keypad)	<k*>	<shiftk*>	<altk*>	<ctrlprt>
- (keypad)	<k->	<shiftk->	<altk->	<ctrlk->
+ (keypad)	<k+>	<shiftk+>	<altk+>	<ctrlk+>
Enter (keypad)	<kenter>	<shiftkenter>	<altkenter>	<ctrlkenter>

Notes:

[1] The [space] key also can be represented by a literal space character

[2] The [Shift][space] combination also can be represented by a literal space character

[3] <end> if Num Lock is off

[4] <shiftend> if Num Lock is off

[5] <down> if Num Lock is off

[6] <shiftdown> if Num Lock is off

[7] <pgdn> if Num Lock is off

[8] <shiftpgdn> if Num Lock is off

[9] <left> if Num Lock is off

[10] <shiftleft> if Num Lock is off

[11] <clear> if Num Lock is off

[12] <shiftclear> if Num Lock is off

[13] <right> if Num Lock is off

[14] <shiftright> if Num Lock is off

[15] <home> if Num Lock is off

[16] <shifthome> if Num Lock is off

[17] <up> if Num Lock is off

[18] <shiftup> if Num Lock is off

[19] <pgup> if Num Lock is off

[20] <shiftpgup> if Num Lock is off

[21] <ins> if Num Lock is off

[22] <shiftins> if Num Lock is off

[23] <del> if Num Lock is off

[24] <shiftdel> if Num Lock is off

This table shows the macro representations of individual keys and combinations of those keys and the [Shift], [Ctrl], and [Alt] keys.

Table 20-2b

Key	With [Ctrl][Alt]	With [Ctrl][Shift]	With [Alt][Shift]	With [Ctrl][Alt][Shift]
a		<ctrlshifta>		
b		<ctrlshiftb>		
c		<ctrlshiftc>		
d		<ctrlshiftd>		
e		<ctrlshifte>		
f		<ctrlshiftf>		
g		<ctrlshiftg>		
h		<ctrlshifth>		
i		<ctrlshifti>		
j		<ctrlshiftj>		
k		<ctrlshiftk>		
l		<ctrlshiftl>		
m		<ctrlshiftm>		
n		<ctrlshiftn>		
o		<ctrlshifto>		
p		<ctrlshiftp>		
q		<ctrlshiftq>		
r		<ctrlshiftr>		
s		<ctrlshifts>		
t		<ctrlshiftt>		
u		<ctrlshiftu>		
v		<ctrlshiftv>		
w		<ctrlshiftw>		
x		<ctrlshiftx>		
y		<ctrlshifty>		
z		<ctrlshiftz>		
1	<altctrl1>	<ctrl!>	<altshift1>	<altctrlshift1>
2	<altctrl2>	<ctrl@>	<altshift2>	<altctrlshift2>
3	<altctrl3>	<ctrl#>	<altshift3>	<altctrlshift3>
4	<altctrl4>	<ctrl$>	<altshift4>	<altctrlshift4>
5	<altctrl5>	<ctrl %>	<altshift5>	<altctrlshift5>
6	<altctrl6>	<ctrl ^>	<alt^>	<altctrlshift6>
7	<altctrl7>	<ctrl &>	<alt&>	<altctrlshift7>
8	<altctrl8>	<ctrl*>	<altshift8>	<altctrlshift8>
9	<altctrl9>	<ctrl(>	<altshift9>	<altctrlshift9>
0	<altctrl0>	<ctrl)>	<altshift10>	<altctrlshift0>
[space]	<altctrlspace>	<ctrlshiftspace>	<altshiftspace>	<altctrlshiftspace>
-	<altctrl->	<ctrlshift_>		<altctrl_>
=	<altctrl=>	<ctrl+>	<alt+>	<altctrl=>
[		<ctrlshift[>		
]		<ctrlshift]>		
;		<ctrl:>	<alt:>	
'		<ctrl">		
`				
\		<ctrlshiftenter>		
,		<ctrl<>	<alt<>	
.		<ctrl>>	<alt>>	
/			<alt?>	
Esc	<altctrlesc>	<ctrlshiftesc>	<altshiftesc>	<altctrlshiftesc>
Tab	<altctrltab>	<ctrlshifttab>	<altshifttab>	<altctrlshifttab>
Backspace	<altctrlback>	<ctrlshiftback>	<altshiftback>	<altctrlshiftback>
Enter	<altctrlenter>	<ctrlshiftenter>	<altshiftenter>	<altctrlshiftenter>

[F1]	\<altctrlf1>	\<ctrlshiftf1>	\<altshiftf1>	\<altctrlshiftf1>
[F2]	\<altctrlf2>	\<ctrlshiftf2>	\<altshiftf2>	\<altctrlshiftf2>
[F3]	\<altctrlf3>	\<ctrlshiftf3>	\<altshiftf3>	\<altctrlshiftf3>
[F4]	\<altctrlf4>	\<ctrlshiftf4>	\<altshiftf4>	\<altctrlshiftf4>
[F5]	\<altctrlf5>	\<ctrlshiftf5>	\<altshiftf5>	\<altctrlshiftf5>
[F6]	\<altctrlf6>	\<ctrlshiftf6>	\<altshiftf6>	\<altctrlshiftf6>
[F7]	\<altctrlf7>	\<ctrlshiftf7>	\<altshiftf7>	\<altctrlshiftf7>
[F8]	\<altctrlf8>	\<ctrlshiftf8>	\<altshiftf8>	\<altctrlshiftf8>
[F9]	\<altctrlf9>	\<ctrlshiftf9>	\<altshiftf9>	\<altctrlshiftf9>
[F10]	\<altctrlf10>	\<ctrlshiftf10>	\<altshiftf10>	\<altctrlshiftf10>
[F11]	\<altctrlf11>	\<ctrlshiftf11>	\<altshiftf11>	\<altctrlshiftf11>
[F12]	\<altctrlf12>	\<ctrlshiftf12>	\<altshiftf12>	\<altctrlshiftf12>
↑	\<altctrlxup>	\<ctrlshiftxup>	\<altshiftxup>	\<altctrlshiftxup>
↓	\<altctrlxdown>	\<ctrlshiftxdown>	\<altshiftxdown>	\<altctrlshiftxdown>
→	\<altctrlxright>	\<ctrlshiftxright>	\<altshiftxright>	\<altctrlshiftxright>
←	\<altctrlxleft>	\<ctrlshiftxleft>	\<altshiftxleft>	\<altctrlshiftxleft>
Insert	\<altctrlinsert>	\<ctrlshiftinsert>	\<altshiftinsert>	\<altctrlshiftinsert>
Home	\<altctrlxhome>	\<ctrlshiftxhome>	\<altshiftxhome>	\<altctrlshiftxhome>
Page Up	\<altctrlpageup>	\<ctrlshiftpageup>	\<altshiftpageup>	\<altctrlshiftpageup>
Delete	\<altctrldelete>	\<ctrlshiftdelete>	\<altshiftdelete>	\<altctrlshiftdelete>
End	\<altctrlxend>	\<ctrlshiftxend>	\<altshiftxend>	\<altctrlshiftxend>
Page Down	\<altctrlpagedown>	\<ctrlshiftpagedown>	\<altshiftpagedown>	\<altctrlshiftpagedown>
1 (keypad)		\<ctrlshiftend>		
2 (keypad)		\<ctrlshiftdown>		
3 (keypad)		\<ctrlshiftpgdn>		
4 (keypad)		\<ctrlshiftleft>		
5 (keypad)		\<ctrlshiftclear>		
6 (keypad)		\<ctrlshiftright>		
7 (keypad)		\<ctrlshifthome>		
8 (keypad)		\<ctrlshiftup>		
9 (keypad)		\<ctrlshiftpgup>		
0 (keypad)		\<ctrlshiftins>		
. (keypad)		\<ctrlshiftdel>		
/ (keypad)	\<altctrlk/>	\<ctrlshiftk/>	\<altshiftk/>	\<altctrlshiftk/>
* (keypad)	\<altctrlk*>	\<ctrlshiftk*>	\<altshiftk*>	\<altctrlshiftk*>
- (keypad)		\<ctrlshiftk->	\<altshiftk->	
+ (keypad)	\<altctrlk+>	\<ctrlshiftk+>	\<altshiftk+>	\<altctrlshiftk+>
Enter (keypad)	\<altctrlkenter>	\<ctrlshiftkenter>	\<altshiftkenter>	\<altctrlshiftkenter>

This table contains the macro representations of all possible [Ctrl][Alt], [Ctrl][Shift], [Alt][Shift], and [Ctrl][Alt][Shift] combinations.

Every macro must be linked to a key or combination of keys. If you choose <OK> from the bottom of the dialog box shown in Figure 20-2 without making an entry into the Playback Key text box, Works will display an alert box that contains the message *No playback key* and a single button: <OK>. When you click this button, Works will clear the alert box from the screen, revealing the dialog box shown in Figure 20-2. At that point, you can specify a playback key.

Specifying a title

In addition to specifying a playback key for a macro, you can specify a title for it. To do this, simply type up to 255 characters into the Title text box. In most cases, you'll use a title that describes the action of the macro. For example, you might use the title *Transposes two letters* for a macro that switches two adjacent letters in a word processor document. That way, you'll have a reminder of what the macro does when you invoke it. However, you can omit the title, if you want.

Choosing OK

Once you have defined the playback key and the optional title, you should choose <OK> or press [Enter] to begin recording. (If you want to return to Works without recording the macro, you should choose <Cancel>.) If you specified a letter, number, or punctuation key (keys that are commonly used for other purposes) as the playback key, Works will display the dialog box shown in Figure 20-3, which asks you to confirm your choice. If you choose <OK>, Works will redefine the specified key. From that point on, when you press that key, Works will run a macro. If you choose <Cancel>, Works will let you supply a new playback key.

Figure 20-3

If you specify a letter, number, or punctuation key as the playback key, Works will ask you to confirm your choice by displaying this dialog box.

If the key you supply already serves as the playback key for another macro, Works will display the dialog box shown in Figure 20-4, which asks you to confirm your choice If you choose <OK>, Works will redefine the specified key so that it plays the new macro instead of the old one. The old macro will be erased. If you choose <Cancel>, Works will let you supply a new playback key.

Recording the macro

Once you've defined a playback key for the macro, Works will begin recording each key you press. As you press these keys, Works will perform the actions they command it to perform. While Works is recording, it will display the word *RECORD* at the right edge of the message line. While this word is visible, Works is in the Record mode.

Figure 20-4

*If the key you specify already serves
as the playback key for another macro,
Works will ask you to confirm your
choice by displaying this dialog box.*

Although Works will record the keystroke-equivalents of commands you select with your mouse, it will not record other mouse actions, like moving the cursor, extending the highlight, and so forth. Consequently, you should not use your mouse while you're recording a macro.

You inevitably will make mistakes as you are recording a macro. For example, you may pull down the wrong menu, overshoot the cell to which you are moving the highlight, misspell what you are typing into a text box, and so forth. When this happens, you can cancel the macro. Alternatively, you can continue recording, typing whatever keystrokes are necessary to "undo" what you did wrong. As you type these keys, Works will record them. After you correct the mistake, you should continue performing the task you wanted to record. When you play the macro, Works will repeat the mistake you made, then make the correction—just as you did. In most cases, you'll want to edit the mistake out of the macro once you have finished recording it. We'll show you how to do that later in this chapter.

Correcting mistakes

Figure 20-5

*Works displays this dialog box when you
press the [Alt]/ combination while you're
recording a macro.*

After you've performed the task you want to record, you should press [Alt]/ again. This time, Works will display the dialog box shown in Figure 20-5. To end the recording of the macro, choose the End Recording option, then choose <OK>.

Ending the recording

Selecting this option ends the recording session and saves your macro in RAM. You also can end the recording of a macro and save it by pressing [Alt]-.

If you want to cancel the recording session without saving the macro, just press [Alt]/ to display the dialog box shown in Figure 20-5, then choose the Cancel Recording option and choose <OK>. Selecting this option will cancel the recording of the macro and return you to your Works document.

An example

Suppose you want to create a macro that transposes two letters in a word processor document and link the macro to the [Ctrl]a key combination. We'll do this by recording the process of transposing the letters *r* and *c* in the misspelled word *marco* in the word processor document shown in Figure 20-6.

Figure 20-6

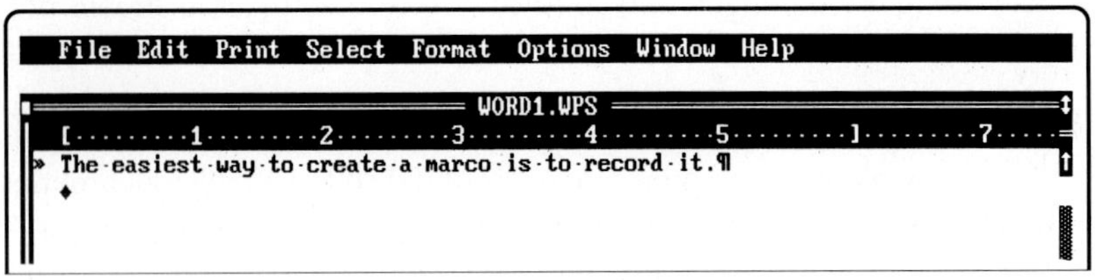

```
┌─────────────────────────────────────────────────────────────────┐
│   File  Edit  Print  Select  Format  Options  Window  Help       │
│ ┌═══════════════════════ WORD1.WPS ═══════════════════════════┐  │
│ [·········1·········2·········3·········4·········5·········]·········7·····│
│ » The·easiest·way·to·create·a·marco·is·to·record·it.¶          ↑  │
│   ♦                                                              │
│                                                               ▓  │
└─────────────────────────────────────────────────────────────────┘
```

We'll record the process of transposing the letters r *and* c *in the misspelled word* marco *in this word processor document.*

To record the process of transposing two letters, begin by positioning the cursor on the *r* in the word *marco*—the leftmost of the two characters you want to transpose. Next, press [Alt]/ to access the dialog box shown in Figure 20-1, choose the Record Macro command, and choose <OK> or press [Enter]. When the dialog box shown in Figure 20-2 appears, press [Ctrl]a to specify the playback key for the macro, type *Transposes two letters* into the Title text box, and choose <OK>.

At this point, Works will begin recording your keystrokes—in this case, the process of transposing the two letters *r* and *c*. To transpose these letters, hold down the [Shift] key and press → to highlight the letter *r*. Next, press [Alt]e to pull down the Edit menu then type *m* to select the Move command. Now, press → twice to move the cursor to the *o* at the end of the word. Finally, press [Enter] to complete the process. Figure 20-7 shows how your screen will look at this point. As you can see, Works has switched the letters *r* and *c*, transforming the word *marco* into the word *macro*.

Once you have performed the transposition, you should tell Works to stop recording. To do this, either press [Alt]- or press [Alt]/, choose the End Recording command, and choose <OK>. When you do this, Works will stop recording and save the recorded macro in RAM.

Figure 20-8 shows what Works recorded. When you pressed [Shift]→ to highlight the current character, Works recorded <shiftright>. When you pressed

[Alt]e to access the Edit menu, Works recorded *<alte>*. When you typed *m* to select
the Move command, Works recorded *m*. When you pressed the ➡ key twice to
move the cursor to the destination, Works recorded *<right><right>*. When you
pressed [Enter] to complete the move, Works recorded *<enter>*.

Figure 20-7

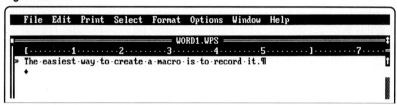

*This figure shows the word processor document shown in Figure 20-6
after we recorded the process of transposing the letters* r *and* c *in the
misspelled word* marco.

Figure 20-8

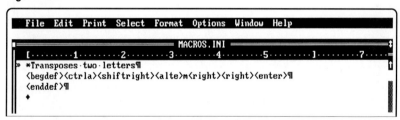

This figure shows what Works recorded when we transposed the letters
r *and* c *in the misspelled word* marco *in the word processor document
shown in Figure 20-6.*

We'll explain how you get Works to display a macro later in this chapter. For
now, simply understand that Works records special representations of the keys
you press while it is in the Record mode.

Another example

Let's record a macro linked to the [Ctrl]w combination that sets the width of
every column in a spreadsheet to 12 spaces. To do this, create a new spreadsheet
document or open or activate one that already exists. Then, press [Alt]/ to access
the dialog box shown in Figure 20-1, choose the Record Macro command, press
[Ctrl]w, press [Tab], type *Sets width of all columns to 12*, and choose <OK>.

To set the width of every column in the spreadsheet document to 12, press
[Alt]s to access the Select menu, then type *r* to select the Row command. This
selects every cell in the current row. Next, press [Alt]t to pull down the Format
menu, type *w* to select the Column Width... command, type 12 into the Width text

box, and press [Enter] or choose <OK>. Since one cell in every column of the spreadsheet is selected, these actions set the width of every column to 12.

Once you have performed these actions, you should end the recording of the macro. To do this, simply press [Alt]/ to access the dialog box shown in Figure 20-5, highlight the End Recording option, and choose <OK>.

Figure 20-9 shows what Works recorded. (Again, we'll show you how to view a macro later.) The keystroke *<alts>* pulls down the Select menu; the keystroke *r* issues the Row command; the keystroke *<altt>* pulls down the Format menu; the keystroke *w* issues the Width... command; the keystrokes *1* and *2* type the value 12; and the keystroke *<enter>* presses the [Enter] key.

Figure 20-9

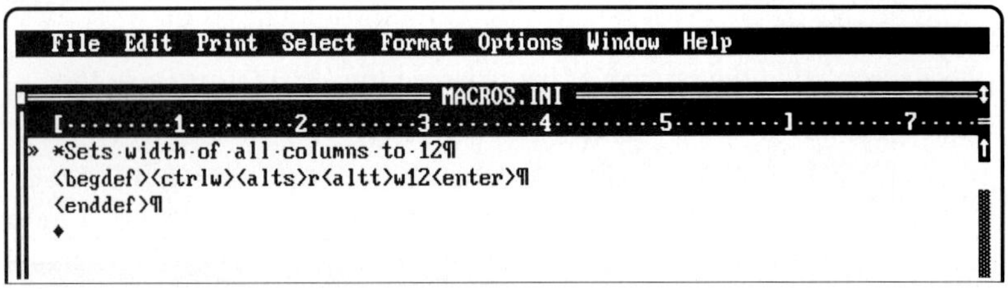

```
 File  Edit  Print  Select  Format  Options  Window  Help

══════════════════════════════ MACROS.INI ══════════════════════════
[..........1..........2..........3..........4..........5.........]........7.....
» *Sets·width·of·all·columns·to·12¶
  <begdef><ctrlw><alts>r<altt>w12<enter>¶
  <enddef>¶
  ♦
```

When played, this macro will set the width of all the columns in the active spreadsheet document to 12 spaces.

Using alternative keystrokes

Works records your keystrokes literally. Consequently, the way you perform a task while Works is recording determines which keystrokes it will record. For example, to record the letter-transposing macro shown in Figure 20-8, we pressed [Shift]➡, pressed [Alt]e, typed *m*, pressed ➡ twice, and then pressed [Enter]. We could have performed the same task by pressing and releasing the [Extend] key([F8]), pressing ➡ to highlight the character on which the cursor was positioned, pressing and releasing the [Alt] key to access Works' menu bar, pressing ➡ to move the highlight to the Edit menu, pressing ⬇ two times to open the Edit menu and to position the highlight on the Move command, pressing [Enter] to select that command, pressing ➡ twice to specify the destination of the move, then pressing [Enter] again.

Figure 20-10 shows what Works would have recorded if we had pressed this sequence of keys. This macro and the one shown in Figure 20-8 both use the Move command to transpose two characters. Because we used different keystrokes to execute this command, however, Works recorded different macros. Both macros will produce the same result when invoked—they transpose the character on which the cursor is positioned with the character to its right. However, they will achieve that result in different ways. Because the macro shown in Figure 20-10 contains more keystrokes than the one shown in Figure 20-8, it will take longer to run. To make your macros as short as possible, you need to perform the task you are recording in the most efficient way you can.

Figure 20-10

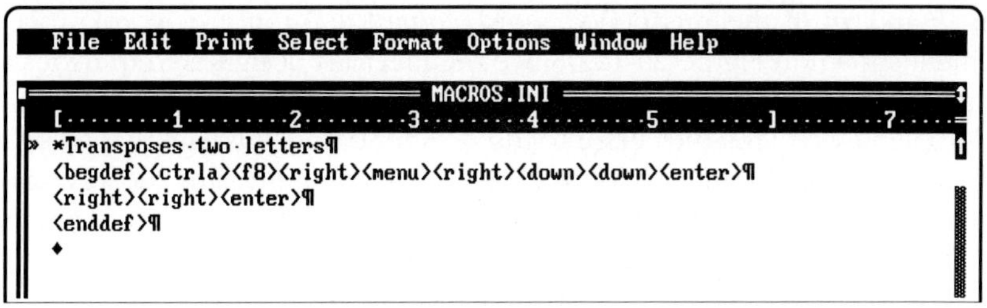

```
 File  Edit  Print  Select  Format  Options  Window  Help
══════════════════════════════ MACROS.INI ══════════════════
[········1·········2·········3·········4·········5·······]·······7····
» *Transposes·two·letters¶
  <begdef><ctrla><f8><right><menu><right><down><down><enter>¶
  <right><right><enter>¶
  <enddef>¶
  ♦
```

This macro uses different keystrokes to perform the same task as the one shown in Figure 20-8.

PLAYING MACROS

Once you have recorded a macro, you can play it in either of two ways. The easiest way is to press the key or key combination to which the macro is linked. When you do this, Works will press the keys that are represented in the macro in the order that they appear in the macro. When Works does this, it will perform whatever actions those keys command it to perform, exactly as it would if you pressed those keys yourself. You'll be able to see the results of each keystroke on the screen. Since Works presses keys rather quickly, however, the changes will happen fast.

The Play Macro command in the dialog box shown in Figure 20-1 provides the second way to play a macro. (To access this dialog box, you simply press [Alt]/ when Works is not recording a macro.) When you choose the Play Macro command, Works will display a dialog box like the one shown in Figure 20-11. Within this box, Works lists the representations of the keys to which all active macros are linked, as well as the first 33 characters of the titles you may have assigned to those macros. For example, Works displays the names and titles of both macros we've created so far in the dialog box shown in Figure 20-11. To play a macro, simply highlight its name and choose <Play>.

Figure 20-11

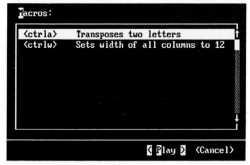

Works will display a dialog box like this one when you choose the Play Macro command from the dialog box shown in Figure 20-1.

An example

Suppose you want to use the macro shown in Figure 20-8 to transpose the letters *b* and *m* in the misspelled word *cobmination* in the word processor document shown in Figure 20-12. Since the macro is designed to transpose the character on which the cursor is positioned with the character to its right, you should begin by moving the cursor to the *b*. After doing, this, simply press [Ctrl]a to play the macro. When you do this, Works will begin pressing the keys whose representations are stored in the macro. First, it will press [Shift]➔, which highlights the *b*. Second, it will press [Alt]e, which pulls down the Edit menu. Third, it will press the m key, which selects the Move command. Fourth, it will press the ➔ key twice, which moves the cursor to the *i*. Finally, it will press the [Enter] key, which completes the move. These four steps relocate the *b* to the right of the *m*, transforming the word *cobmination* into the word *combination*, as shown in Figure 20-13.

Figure 20-12

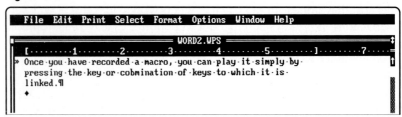

We'll use the macro shown in Figure 20-8 to transpose the letters b *and* m *in the misspelled word* cobmination *in this document.*

Figure 20-13

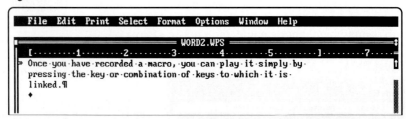

This shows the result of playing the macro shown in Figure 20-8 while the cursor was on the letter b *in the misspelled word* cobmination *in the document shown in Figure 20-12.*

Playing macros out of context

Most macros are "context sensitive"; that is, they are designed to be played within a certain type of document when the cursor or highlight is positioned in a certain place within the document. For example, the macros shown in Figures 20-8 and 20-10 are designed to be run in a word processor document when the cursor is on the leftmost of the two characters you want to transpose; the macro shown in Figure 20-9 is designed to be run within a spreadsheet document.

Playing a macro in a context other than the one for which it was designed will not produce the results you intended. If you played the macro shown in Figure 20-8 (the one designed to transpose two letters in a word processor document) while the highlight was marking cell A1 in a spreadsheet document, Works would expand the highlight to cover cells A1:B1, issue the Move command, move the highlight to cell C1, then press [Enter]. This sequence of steps would move the entries from cells A1:B1 into cells C1:D1.

As another example, suppose you played the macro shown in Figure 20-9 (the one designed to set the width of every column in a spreadsheet document to 12 spaces) while the cursor was on the letter *b* in the misspelled word *cobmination* in the word processor document shown in Figure 20-12. If you did this, Works would select the Replace... command from the Select menu to reveal the Replace dialog box, beep as the macro pressed [Alt]t, type *w12* into the Search For text box, then press [Enter]. This process would command Works to search for the first occurrence of the string *w12* in the document. To avoid problems like this, always play your macros in the context for which you design them.

Stopping macros

Normally, Works will execute all the keystrokes stored in a macro when you press the key or key combination to which that macro is linked. However, you can cancel the execution of a macro before Works has finished playing it by pressing the [Alt]/ key combination. When you do this, Works will stop pressing keys. Your screen will reflect the changes the macro made to it up to that point.

You'll want to cancel the execution of a macro for two principal reasons. First, you might have invoked the macro accidentally. Second, the macro might not be doing what you intended it to do. This will happen if you play a macro in the wrong context or if you didn't press the keys you intended when you recorded the macro. If the macro contains a major programming error, Works will stop the macro on its own before it finishes playing it. If the macro simply presses an inappropriate key, Works will beep (just as it would if you had pressed the key yourself), then continue playing the macro.

DEACTIVATING MACROS

In some cases, you may not want Works to play a macro when you press the key or key combination to which that macro is linked. Instead, you may want Works to do what it would do if that macro did not exist. You can make this happen in three ways. First, you can press the ' key or press [Alt]/ and select the Skip command before you press the key to which the macro is assigned. Pressing the ' key or selecting the Skip command instructs Works not to play the macro (if there is one) to which the next key you press is linked. You'll need to press this key or select this command each time you press a key or key combination to which a macro is linked.

The Turn Macros Off command (also in the dialog box that Works displays when you press [Alt]/ while Works is not in the Record mode) provides the second way to prevent Works from playing a macro when you press the key to which that macro is linked. When you issue this command, Works will deactivate all macros that are active at the time; that is, it won't run a macro when you press the key to which that macro is linked or when you choose the name of that macro from the list Works presents when you press [Alt]/ and choose the Play Macro command.

Turn Macros Off is a toggle command. When you issue this command, Works will change it to Turn Macros On. Choosing the Turn Macros On command reactivates all the macros that the Turn Macros Off command deactivated.

The third way to deactivate a macro is to remove it from your computer's memory. To do this, press [Alt]/ and select the Delete Macros command. When you do this, Works will present a dialog box like the one shown in Figure 20-14. This box will list the playback key for every macro that is currently in RAM. To delete a macro, simply select it from the list and choose <Delete> . When you do this, Works will remove the macro from RAM and return the key or key combination to which the macro is linked to its original function. At that point, you can delete another macro or choose <Done> to close the dialog box.

Figure 20-14

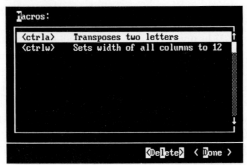

Works will display a dialog box like this one when you press [Alt]/ and select the Delete Macros command.

SAVING MACROS

When you record a macro, Works stores it in a portion of your computer's RAM. All the macros you record remain in RAM until you exit from Works, turn off or reboot your computer, or use the Delete Macros command.

Whenever you use the Exit Works command on the File menu to exit from Works, Works saves all the macros that are currently in RAM into a text file named MACROS.INI. Consequently, they can be used in a future Works session. (Works also will update the MACROS.INI file when you load it into a word processor document—a process we'll explain in the next section of this chapter.)

Whenever you load Works, it reads the MACROS.INI file and loads all the macros from it into RAM. Therefore, you can run those macros in the same way you did during the session in which you recorded them. The next time you exit from Works, it will overwrite the MACROS.INI file with a file that contains the macros that are in RAM at that time. This will include the macros that were in the WORKS.INI file at the beginning of the current session, plus any macros you recorded during the current session, minus any macros you deleted during the current session.

It is important to note that Works will not alter the MACROS.INI file if you exit from Works in any other way (for example, by turning off your computer or by rebooting it). In those cases, none of the macros you recorded during the current Works session will be added to the MACROS.INI file, and none of the macros you deleted from RAM during the current session will be deleted from that file.

EDITING MACROS

Once you've recorded or written a macro, you may want to revise it for one reason or another. For example, the macro may not have done what you wanted it to do when you played it. In other cases, you may want to streamline or add to a macro that already works correctly.

To edit a macro, you must load the contents of the MACROS.INI file into a word processor document. To do this, pull down the File menu, issue the Open Existing File... command, choose MACROS.INI from the Files list box, and choose <OK>. When you do this, Works will display the alert box shown in Figure 20-15, which warns you that you can't use any macros while the MACROS.INI file is open. When you choose <OK> to acknowledge this box, Works will read the contents of the MACROS.INI file into a word processor document.

Figure 20-15

Works will display this alert box before it opens the MACROS.INI file.

Figure 20-16 shows how the MACROS.INI file that contains the two macros we've recorded so far will look when opened into a word processor document. As you can see, the macros are arranged in the order they were created. The definition of each macro begins with a line that contains an asterisk, followed by the title of the macro. The second line of each definition begins with the key word <begdef>, which stands for "*beg*inning (of macro) *def*inition." This key word is followed by the macro representation of the key to which the macro is linked. Following the representation of that key are the macro representations of the keys that the macro commands Works to press. The definition of each macro ends with the key word <enddef>, which stands for "*end* (of macro) *def*inition."

Figure 20-16

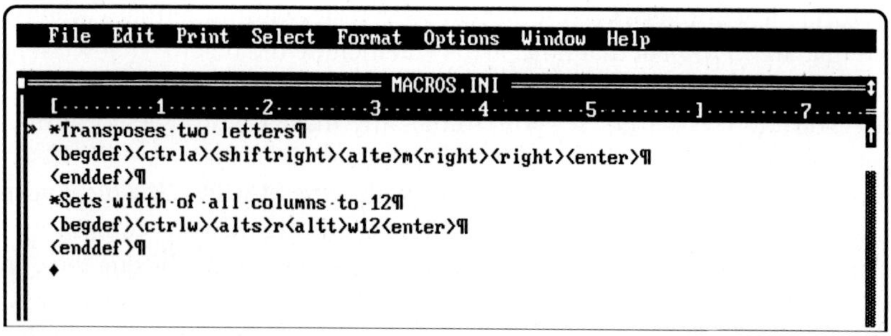

This is how the two macros we've recorded so far appear in a word processor document.

Once the contents of the MACROS.INI file are in a word processor document, you can use normal word-processing techniques to edit the macros. To delete a keystroke from a macro, simply highlight the representation of that keystroke and press [Delete]; to insert a keystroke, simply move the cursor to the rightmost character of the pair of characters between which you want to insert the keystroke, then type the representation of that keystroke; and to replace a keystroke, simply highlight the representation of the keystroke you want to replace, then type the representation of the new keystroke. Whenever you insert or replace a keystroke, be sure that you use the proper representation. If you're not sure how to represent a keystroke, see Table 20-2.

Once you've edited the macro (or macros) you want to change, you should resave MACROS.INI. To do this, simply pull down the File menu, select the Close command, and choose <Yes> in response to Works' *Save changes to: MACROS.INI?* prompt. Since MACROS.INI was a text file when you loaded it into Works, Works will resave it in that form. If you want, you can use the Save command (but not the Save As... command) to save the document before you use the Close command to close it.

When you resave the MACROS.INI file, Works doesn't just save the changes to disk; it also reads the revised file into RAM. Consequently, any changes you made to the macros in the file will be made to the macros in RAM. The changes you made will be in effect as soon as you resave MACROS.INI.

An example

To demonstrate the process of editing a macro, let's revise the macro linked to the [Ctrl]w key so that it changes the width of all the columns in the current spreadsheet document to 20 (rather than 12) spaces. To do this, use the Open Existing File... command to open MACROS.INI into a word processor document, as described above. Then, move the cursor to the 1 at the end of the fourth line of the document, press [Delete] twice, and type 20; repeat this process to replace the number 12 on the fifth line of the document with the number 20. Figure 20-17 shows how the document will look at this point.

Figure 20-17

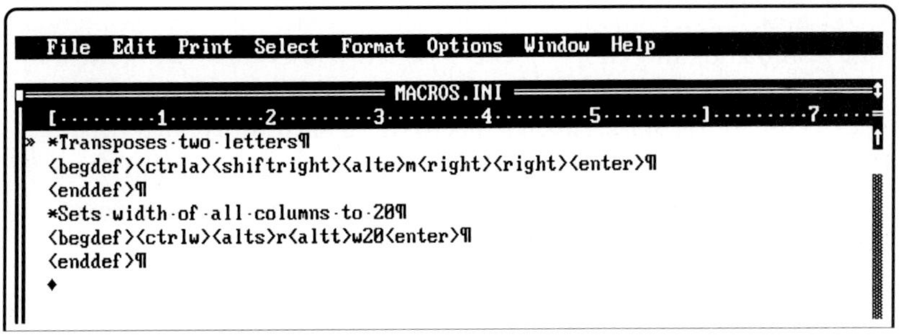

```
 File  Edit  Print  Select  Format  Options  Window  Help
========================== MACROS.INI ==========================
[·········1·········2·········3·········4·········5·········]·········7·····
» *Transposes·two·letters¶
  <begdef><ctrla><shiftright><alte>m<right><right><enter>¶
  <enddef>¶
  *Sets·width·of·all·columns·to·20¶
  <begdef><ctrlw><alts>r<altt>w20<enter>¶
  <enddef>¶
  ♦
```

This is how the document shown in Figure 20-16 looks after we modified the second macro so that it changes the width of all the columns in a spreadsheet to 20.

After making these changes, pull down the File menu, select the Close command, and choose <Yes>. From that point on, pressing [Ctrl]w will set the width of all the columns in the current spreadsheet document to 20, not 12, spaces.

Deleting macros

Although the Delete Macros option in the dialog box shown in Figure 20-1 provides the easiest way to delete a macro, there is another way: Open the MACROS.INI file into a word processor document, highlight the definition of the macro you want to delete, press the [Delete] key, and then resave the document. When Works rereads the MACROS.INI file, it won't find the macro you deleted. Consequently, it won't load that macro into RAM.

WRITING MACROS

In addition to editing existing macros, you can write new ones. To do this, begin by loading the contents of the MACROS.INI file into a word processor document. Then, instead of editing an existing macro, type the definition of a new macro. In most cases, you'll type the new macro after the final macro in the document. However, you can insert the new macro ahead of the first macro in the document or between any two macros.

When you type the definition of a new macro, you should use it the same structure Works uses. The first line of the definition should begin with an asterisk, followed by the title of the macro. (If you omit the title, the macro must begin with an asterisk on a line by itself.) The second line of the definition should begin with the key word <begdef> and the macro representation of the key to which you want to link the macro, and it should be followed by the macro representations of the keystrokes you want Works to execute. You can use the [Enter] key between (but not within) the macro representations of keys to divide the definition of the macro onto more than one line, or let Works wrap the definition for you. At the end of the macro, you should type the keyword <enddef>.

Once you added the macro to the word processor document, you should resave and close the document. To do this, simply pull down the File menu, select the Close command, and choose <OK>. When you do this, Works will replace the contents of the MACROS.INI file with the contents of the current document, close the document, clear the existing macros from RAM, and read the macros from the revised MACROS.INI file into RAM.

An example

For example, suppose you want to write a macro linked to the [Ctrl]z combination and entitled *Enters month labels* that enters the text values *January, February, March,* and so forth, into 12 consecutive cells of a single row of a Works spreadsheet document. To do this, you would use the Open Existing File... command to bring the MACROS.INI file shown in Figure 20-16 into a Works word processor document. Then, you would press the [Ctrl][End] combination to move the cursor to the end of the document and press [Enter] to move it to a new line. At that point, you would type **Enters month labels,* press [Enter], type *<begdef><ctrlz>,* type

"January<right>"February<right>"March<right>
"April<right>"May<right>"June<right>"July<right>
"August<right>"September<right>"October<right>
"November<right>"December<enter>

and then type *<enddef>.* Figure 20-18 shows the complete macro.

Once you have added this macro to the word processor document, you should use the Close command to resave the macros into the MACROS.INI file and close the document. From that point on, you can invoke the new macro by pressing [Ctrl]z.

Some advice

Writing a macro requires you to visualize the keystrokes necessary to perform the task you want to automate. Therefore, you should be fairly experienced with Works before you try to write a macro. In most cases, recording a macro is far easier than writing one, even for skilled Works users.

RENAMING MACROS

When you create a macro (either by recording it or writing it), you specify the key to which it will be linked and, optionally, give it a title. If you want, you can change the key to which a macro is linked and supply (or change) the title of that macro after you have created it. The easiest way to do this is to press [Alt]/ and choose the Change Key and Title option. When you issue this option, Works will display a dialog box like the one shown in Figure 20-19. In this box, Works will list the playback key and first 33 characters of the title for each macro that is currently in RAM. To change a macros key or title, simply highlight that macro and choose <Change>. When you do this, Works will overlay the dialog box shown in Figure 20-19 with a dialog box like the one shown in Figure 20-20 on the following page. To change the macro's playback key, simply move the cursor to the Playback Key text box and press the key or key combination to which you want to link the macro ; to change the title, simply type it into the Title box. Once you have made all the changes you want to make, choose <OK> . When you do this, Works will return you to the dialog box shown in Figure 20-19. At that point, you can repeat the process to change the playback key or title of another macro or choose <Done> to return to Works.

Figure 20-18

```
  File   Edit   Print   Select   Format   Options   Window   Help
======================================= MACROS.INI ========================
  [··········1·········2·········3·········4·········5·········]·········7····
» *Transposes·two·letters¶
  <begdef><ctrla><shiftright><alte>m<right><right><enter>¶
  <enddef>¶
  *Sets·width·of·all·columns·to·20¶
  <begdef><ctrlw><alts>r<altt>w20<enter>¶
  <enddef>¶
  *Enters·month·labels¶
  <begdef><ctrlz>"January<right>"February<right>"March<right>¶
  "April<right>"May<right>"June<right>"July<right>¶
  "August<right>"September<right>"October<right>¶
  "November<right>"December<enter><enddef>¶
  ♦
```

The final macro in this document will type month labels into 12 consecutive cells of a single row of a spreadsheet document.

Figure 20-19

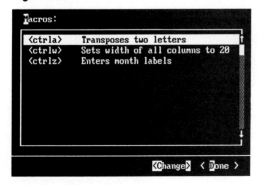

```
Macros:
  <ctrla>    Transposes two letters
  <ctrlw>    Sets width of all columns to 20
  <ctrlz>    Enters month labels




              <Change>   < Done >
```

Works will display a dialog box like this one when you press [Alt]/ and choose the Change Key and Title option.

Figure 20-20

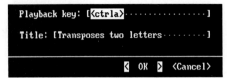

Works will display a dialog box like this one when you choose a macro from a dialog box like the one shown in Figure 20-19.

Alternatively, you can change a macro's playback key or title by loading the MACROS.INI file into a word processor document, editing the definition of the macro, and then resaving it. To learn how to do this, see the previous two sections of this chapter.

ADVANCED MACRO TECHNIQUES

So far, we've demonstrated the skills required to build macros that mimic keystrokes you can type from the keyboard yourself. Most of your macros will be of this type. However, you can include several advanced features in your Works macros. Specifically, you can program macros to loop, call subroutines, solicit input from a user, and pause. In this section, we'll explore these advanced macro techniques.

Looping

In most cases, Works will stop playing a macro after it presses the final keystroke in that macro. If you want, however, you can make Works replay a macro again and again automatically. To do this, you simply press the key or key combination to which the macro you are recording is linked, after Works has recorded the remainder of the macro. When you do this, Works will display the alert box shown in Figure 20-21. The message in this box indicates that you have created a looping macro. If you choose <OK>, Works will stop recording the macro and retain it in RAM. (Since the macro will end with the representation of the key to which it is linked, Works will replay the macro each time it reaches the end of that macro.) If you choose <Cancel> instead, Works will stop recording the macro but not retain it in RAM.

Figure 20-21

Works will display this dialog box when you press the key to which the macro you are recording is linked while you are recording that macro.

Figure 20-22 shows an example of a looping macro. This macro, which is linked to the [Ctrl]b key combination, assigns the Bold attribute to the words in a word processor document, one at a time, starting with the word on which the cursor is positioned. The first two keystrokes in this macro, *<f8><f8>*, extend the highlight to cover the word on which the cursor is positioned at the time. The next keystroke, *<altt>*, accesses Works' menu bar and pulls down the Format menu. The fourth keystroke, *b*, selects the Bold command, assigning the Bold attribute to the current word. The fifth keystroke, *<right>*, contracts the highlight back to a cursor and positions it on the first character of the next word.

Figure 20-22

This looping macro assigns the Bold attribute to the words in a word processor document, one at a time.

The final keystroke in this macro, *<ctrlb>*, commands Works to replay the macro. Since the cursor will be on the word to the right of the one Works just boldfaced, Works will boldface this new word when it replays the macro. Then it will move the highlight one more word to the right, and replay the macro again. Works will repeat this process until you press the [Ctrl][Esc] key combination to stop it.

Works stops recording when you press the key to which the macro is linked. Consequently, no keystrokes will follow the one that causes the macro to loop. When you create a looping macro by writing it or editing it, you can include keystrokes after the key representation that causes the macro to loop. However, Works will never execute those keystrokes.

Subroutines

You can also command Works to play one macro within another. A macro that is played within the context of another macro is known as a subroutine. To make Works play a subroutine, simply include the playback key for the macro you want to play within the other macro. When Works reads the representation of that key while playing the main macro, it will play the macro assigned to that key (the subroutine). When Works has finished playing the subroutine, it will return to the main macro and resume playing it with the keystroke that follows the one that "called" the subroutine.

An example

Figure 20-23 on the next page contains an example of a macro that calls a subroutine. The two macros shown in this figure print the spreadsheet shown in Figure 20-24 three times—once for an inflation rate of 3%, once for an inflation rate of 4%, and once for an inflation rate of 5%. Cells C5:D8 of the spreadsheet contain formulas that multiply the values in the cells to their left by the inflation factor in cell B1. For example, cell C5 contains the formula *=B5*(1+$B$1)*. These formulas will return different results as different values are plugged into cell B1.

Figure 20-23

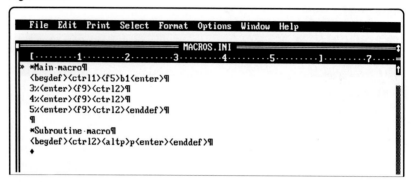

This first macro in this figure calls the second one three times.

Figure 20-24

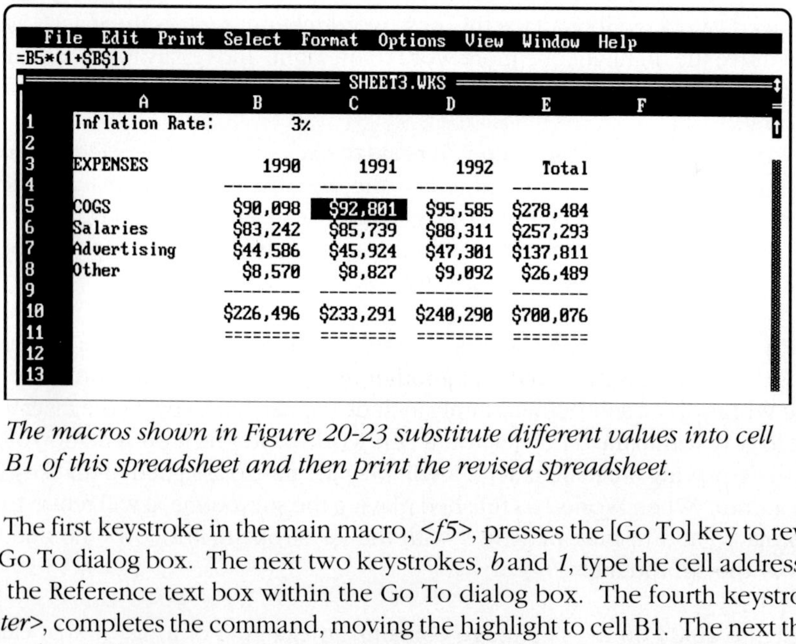

```
 File  Edit  Print  Select  Format  Options  View  Window  Help
=B5*(1+$B$1)
═══════════════════════════ SHEET3.WKS ═══════════════════════════
            A            B          C          D          E         F
 1   Inflation Rate:        3%
 2
 3   EXPENSES           1990       1991       1992       Total
 4                      ————————   ————————   ————————   ————————
 5   COGS               $90,098    $92,801    $95,585    $278,484
 6   Salaries           $83,242    $85,739    $88,311    $257,293
 7   Advertising        $44,586    $45,924    $47,301    $137,811
 8   Other               $8,570     $8,827     $9,092     $26,489
 9                      ————————   ————————   ————————   ————————
10                     $226,496   $233,291   $240,290   $700,076
11                      ════════   ════════   ════════   ════════
12
13
```

The macros shown in Figure 20-23 substitute different values into cell B1 of this spreadsheet and then print the revised spreadsheet.

The first keystroke in the main macro, *<f5>*, presses the [Go To] key to reveal the Go To dialog box. The next two keystrokes, *b* and *1*, type the cell address *b1* into the Reference text box within the Go To dialog box. The fourth keystroke, *<enter>*, completes the command, moving the highlight to cell B1. The next three keystrokes in the macro, *3*, *%*, and *<enter>*, enter the value .03 into cell B1. The next keystroke, *<f9>*, recalculates the spreadsheet.

The ninth keystroke in this macro, *<ctrl2>*, is the key to which the second macro shown in Figure 20-23 is linked. When Works encounters the representation of this key, it will play that macro. The first keystroke in the subroutine, *<altp>*, accesses Works' menu bar and pulls down the Print menu. The next keystroke, *p*, selects the Print... command. The final keystroke, *<enter>*, commands Works to print.

When Works has printed the spreadsheet for the first time, it will resume playing the main macro with the keystrokes that follow the first subroutine call. The next three keystrokes in this macro, *4,%*, and *<enter>*, replace the value .03 in cell B1 with the value .04. The next keystroke, *<f9>*, recalculates the spreadsheet. The keystroke that follows, *<ctrl2>*, calls the subroutine, which prints the revised spreadsheet.

When Works has printed the spreadsheet for the second time, it will resume playing the main macro with the keystrokes that follow the second subroutine call. The next three keystrokes in this macro, *5,%*, and *<enter>*, replace the value .04 in cell B1 with the value .05. The next keystroke, *<f9>*, recalculates the spreadsheet. The keystroke that follows, *<ctrl2>*, calls the subroutine, which prints the revised spreadsheet. Since the third call to the subroutine is the last keystroke in the main macro, Works will stop at that point.

Including subroutines in recorded macros

To include a subroutine call in a macro you are recording, you simply press the playback key for the macro you want to call. When you do this, Works will play that macro; that is, it will press the keys represented in that macro. Consequently, Works will perform whatever actions it would perform if you had typed those keystrokes yourself. However, Works won't record each of those keystrokes in the macro it is recording. Instead, it will record only the key that caused it to play the macro. For example, if a macro is linked to the [Ctrl]a key combination, Works will play that macro if you press [Ctrl]a while recording another macro. However, Works will enter <ctrla> (the representation of the [Ctrl]a key combination) into the macro it is recording.

Skipping subroutines

In some cases, you may not want Works to play the macro to which a key is assigned either when you press it while recording a macro or when you subsequently play it. To prevent this from happening, you can either type ' or press [Alt]/ and select the Skip Macro option before pressing the key to which a macro is linked. Doing either of these things inserts the marker *<skip>* into the macro you are recording and tells Works to ignore the macro (if there is one) that is linked to the next key you press. If you then press a key to which a macro is linked, Works will record the representation of that key in the macro but will not play the macro to which that key is linked. Instead, Works will do whatever that key instructs it to do normally. The *<skip>* marker in the recorded macro prevents Works from playing the macro to which that key is linked when you play the macro that contains the subroutine call.

Calling a non-existent macro

In order to be called as a subroutine, a macro must be in the memory of your computer. If it is not, Works will perform whatever non-macro action it normally would perform when it presses the key to which that macro is assigned. For example, if a macro contains the keystroke representation <ctrlb>, but the macro linked to that key is not in RAM, Works will select the Bold command from the Format menu (the non-macro function of the [Ctrl]b key combination). Before you play a macro that calls another macro as a subroutine, you should make sure that the subroutine macro exists in RAM.

Soliciting input

While Works plays any of the macros we've shown you so far, you simply sit back and watch them play. Works presses the keys that select commands, fill in dialog boxes, make entries into documents, and so forth. If you want, however, you can make Works pause while it is playing a macro to let you enter information. Three markers make this possible: <vfld>, <ffld>, and <nest>. In this section, we'll show you how to use these markers.

Variable-length fields

The <vfld> marker instructs Works to pause the execution of the macro until the user presses [Enter]. During the pause, the user can enter information from the keyboard. To insert a <vfld> marker into a macro that you are recording, simply press [Ctrl]-. (Alternatively, you can press [Alt]/, and select the Variable Input option.) When you do either of these things, Works will display the indicator *VARINPUT* at the right edge of the message line, which indicates that what you are typing is not being recorded. At that point, you should type a sample of what you would want the user to type when he or she plays the macro. When you press [Enter], Works will break from the VARINPUT mode, place the marker <vfld> in the macro, and resume recording your keystrokes. (Alternatively, you can exit from the VARINPUT mode by pressing [Alt]/ and choosing <OK> in response to the *End of input* message that Works displays at that point.) If you are writing or editing a macro, simply type a <vfld> marker at the appropriate place in that macro.

Figure 20-25 shows an example of a macro that uses a variable length field to solicit input from the user. This macro is actually a modification of the one shown in Figure 20-9, which sets the width of each column in a spreadsheet to 12. Unlike that macro, this one lets you specify how wide the columns will be.

The first keystroke in this macro, *<alts>*, pulls down the Select menu. The next keystroke, *r*, selects the Row command. These two keystrokes expand the highlight to cover at least one cell in every column of the spreadsheet. The next two keystrokes, *<altt>* and *w*, pull down the Format menu and select the Width… command, revealing the Width dialog box. At this point, Works will encounter the *<vfld>* marker in the macro. When it does, it will pause until you press [Enter]. During the pause, you should type into the Width text box the width to which you want to set all the columns in the spreadsheet. When you press [Enter], Works will end the pause and choose <OK> from the Width dialog box. This completes the command, expanding or contracting the columns in the spreadsheet to the width you specified.

Figure 20-25

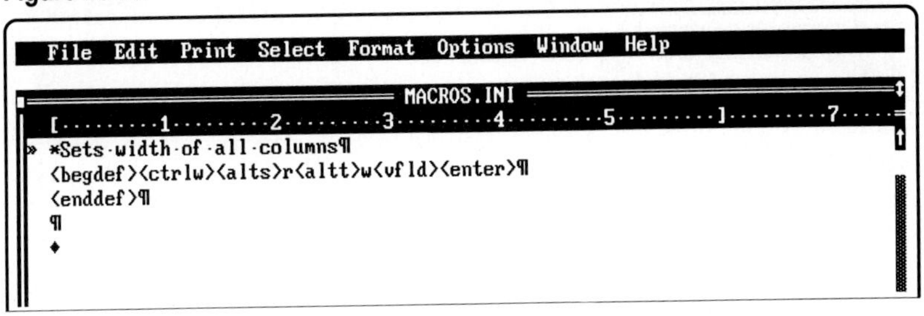

```
 File  Edit  Print  Select  Format  Options  Window  Help
 ═══════════════════════ MACROS.INI ═══════════════════
 [·········1·········2·········3·········4·········5·········]·········7·····
» *Sets·width·of·all·columns¶
  <begdef><ctrlw><alts>r<altt>w<vfld><enter>¶
  <enddef>¶
  ¶
  ◆
```

This macro uses a <vfld > marker to solicit input from a user.

The <ffld> marker instructs Works to pause the execution of the macro until the user presses the number of keys specified by that marker, at which point Works will resume playing the macro. To insert an <ffld> marker into a macro that you are recording, press [Ctrl]]. (Alternatively, you can press [Alt]/ and select the Fixed Input option.) When you do either of these things, Works will display the indicator *FIXINPUT* at the right edge of the message line and stop recording your keystrokes. At that point, you should type as many characters as you'll want the user to type when the macro reaches that point during playback. For example, if you'll want Works to pause while the user types five characters, you should type five characters at this point.

When you have typed the number of characters you'll want the user of the macro to type at that point, you should press [Alt]/ and choose <OK>. When you do that, Works will insert a marker in the form <ffld X> into the macro, where *X* is the number of characters you typed. For example, if you typed five characters, Works would enter the marker <ffld 5> into the macro. This marker instructs Works to pause until the user presses five keys. If you are writing or editing a macro, simply type a <ffld X> marker at the appropriate place in that macro.

Figure 20-26 shows a simple macro that uses an <ffld> marker to solicit input from a user. Specifically, it commands the macro to pause while the user types the key letter of the type of document he or she wants to create. The first keystroke in this macro, *<altf>*, accesses Works' menu bar and pulls down the File menu. The second keystroke, *n*, selects the Create New File... command. When Works presses this key combination, Works will reveal the Create New File... dialog box. At that point, Works will read the *<ffld 1>* marker, which causes it to pause until the user presses a single key. During this pause, the user should type the key character of the desired document type. Works will then create the type of document you specified.

Fixed-length fields

Figure 20-26

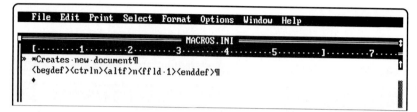

This macro uses the marker <ffld 1> to solicit a single keystroke from the user.

Nesting

The <nest> marker allows you to record one macro while you are playing another. This marker is useful for soliciting input you'll want to use later in the macro. When Works encounters a <nest> marker as it is playing a macro, it will pause until you press [Enter]. During the pause, you can type whatever you want. In addition to passing these keystrokes on to Works, Works records them in a macro linked to the key specified by the marker. If Works encounters the representation of that key later in the macro, it will replay what you typed.

To insert a <nest> marker into a macro you are recording, you must press [Alt]/ and select the Nested Input option. When you do this, Works will present a dialog box like the one shown in Figure 20-27. As you can see, this dialog box looks just like the one Works presents when you choose the Record Macro command.

Figure 20-27

Works will display a dialog box like this one when you command it to insert a nested macro while you are writing, editing, or recording a macro.

At this point, you should press the key or key combination to which you want to link the nested macro and, optionally, type a title into the Title text box. For example, if you want Works to link what the user types to the [Ctrl]z key combination, press *[Ctrl]z* and, if you want, type something like *Nested macro* into the Title box. When you choose <OK>, Works will insert a marker in the form <nest *keyname*> into the macro, where *keyname* is the representation of the key you specified. If you press [Ctrl]z in response to the dialog box shown in Figure

20-27, Works will enter the marker *<nest ctrlz>* into the macro. Then, Works will temporarily suspend recording and display the indicator *NSTINPUT* at the right edge of the message line. At that point, you should type a sample of what you would want the user to type when he or she plays the macro. When you press [Enter], Works will resume recording your keystrokes. (If you are writing or editing a macro, you should simply type a marker in the form <nest *keyname*> at the appropriate place in the macro.)

Figure 20-28 shows a macro that uses a <nest> marker to solicit input from a user. This macro is another modification of our "global column width" macro. Instead of soliciting the column width after it issues the Width... command, this macro solicits the width ahead of time and links it to the [Ctrl]z key combination.

Figure 20-28

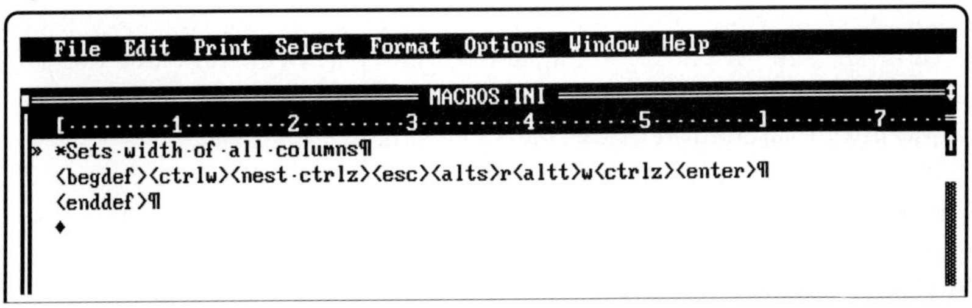

```
  File  Edit  Print  Select  Format  Options  Window  Help

========================== MACROS.INI ==========================
[........1.........2.........3.........4.........5.........].........7.....
» *Sets·width·of·all·columns¶
  <begdef><ctrlw><nest·ctrlz><esc><alts>r<altt>w<ctrlz><enter>¶
  <enddef>¶
  ◆
```

This macro uses a <nest> marker to solicit input from a user.

As you can see, this macro begins with the marker *<nest ctrlz>*. When Works reads this marker, it will pause the macro and begin recording whatever you type from the keyboard. During this pause, you should type the width that you want Works to assign to the columns in the spreadsheet. For example, if you wanted to set the width of all the columns in the spreadsheet to 25 spaces, you would type 25. As you type these characters, Works will record them and link them to the [ctrl]z key combination. The characters will also be passed on to Works. Consequently, they will appear on the formula line, as if you were typing them into the active cell.

When you press [Enter], Works will stop recording what you type, end the pause, then continue playing the macro. The first keystroke representation in this macro, *<esc>*, clears the input from the formula line. The next two keystrokes, *<alts>* and *r*, extend the highlight to cover at least one cell in every column of the spreadsheet. The next two keystrokes, *<altt>* and *w*, pull down the Format menu and select the Width... command, revealing the Width dialog box. The next keystroke, *<ctrlz>*, is the representation of the key combination to which Works linked what you typed at the beginning of the macro. When Works encounters this key representation, it will play the macro linked to that key, retyping what you typed earlier. For example, if you typed 25 earlier, Works will type a 2 and a 5 at this point. Since the Width dialog box will be open at the time, and the current entry in the Width text box will be highlighted, these characters will replace the current entry in that box. The final keystroke in the macro, *<enter>*, chooses the <OK> button, changing the width of all the columns to the width you specified.

Prompts

As you have seen, Works gives you three ways to solicit information from a user while it is playing a macro. In many cases, the user of the macro will be able to figure out what he or she is supposed to do during a pause. In other cases, however, he or she won't. For example, unless you created the macro shown in Figure 20-28, you probably wouldn't know you are supposed to enter a width when the macro pauses.

If you want, you can supply an informational prompt to the user by programming Works to type it into the current document, type it into another document, or activate a document that contains a prompt you have prepared ahead of time. After a pause of a specified duration, you can erase the prompt or reactivate the document in which you were working. We'll demonstrate this technique in our discussion of the Pause command.

Pausing a macro

The Pause option in the dialog box shown in Figure 20-5 allows you to command Works to pause the playing of a macro at any point within that macro for the amount of time you specify. When you press [Alt]/ and select this option, Works will present a dialog box like the one shown in Figure 20-29. In the Time (hh:mm:ss.t) text box, you should type in hh:mm:ss form the amount of time you want Works to pause when it plays the macro. For example, if you want Works to pause for five seconds, type 00:00:5 (or simply 5). When you press [Enter], Works will insert into the macro a marker in the form <pause *duration*>, where *duration* is the amount of time you specified. If you type 5 into the dialog box shown in Figure 20-29, Works will enter the marker *<pause 0:00:05.0>* into the macro you are recording. (If you are writing or editing a macro, you should simply type the <pause> marker at the appropriate place within the macro.)

Figure 20-29

Works will display this dialog box when you press [Alt]/ and select the Pause command.

Although the <pause> marker is useful in many situations, it is especially useful for pausing a macro while the user reads a prompt. The macro shown in Figure 20-30 uses a <pause> marker for this purpose. As you can see, this macro is a modification of the one shown in Figure 20-28, with the addition of an informational prompt before the <nest ctrlz> marker.

Figure 20-30

```
 File  Edit  Print  Select  Format  Options  Window  Help
══════════════════════════ MACROS.INI ══════════════════════════
[········1·········2·········3·········4·········5·········]·······7····
*Sets·width·of·all·columns¶
<begdef><ctrlw>As·soon·as·this·prompt·disappears,··type·the·
column·width·and·press·[Enter]¶
<pause·0:00:05.0><esc>¶
<nest·ctrlz><esc><alts>r<altt>w<ctrlz><enter>¶
<enddef>¶
◆
```

*This macro uses a <pause> marker to pause the macro while the user
reads an informational prompt.*

The first keystrokes in this macro, *As soon as this prompt disappears, type the
column width and press [Enter]*, create the informational prompt. When Works
presses these keys, this prompt will appear on the formula line of the spreadsheet
document, just as it would if you typed the characters yourself. Because these
characters are not followed by a representation of the [Enter] key, Works does not
lock this entry into the active cell of the spreadsheet. Instead, it reads the marker
<pause 0:00:05.0>, which pauses the execution of the macro for five seconds.
During this pause, the prompt will be visible on the formula line. When five
seconds have elapsed, Works will continue playing the macro. The next
keystroke, *<esc>*, clears the prompt from the formula line without entering it into
the spreadsheet.

From that point on, this macro is identical to the one shown in Figure 20-28.
First, Works pauses while you type the global width, which it stores in a macro
linked to the [ctrl]z key combination. When you press [Enter], Works will clear
your input from the formula line, extend the highlight to cover at least one cell
in each column, pull down the Format menu, and select the Width... command.
Then, Works will type the width you entered earlier into the Width text box and
press [Enter]. These keystrokes cause Works to set the width of all the columns
in the spreadsheet to the width you specified.

CONCLUSION

In this chapter, we've shown you how to use macros to automate tasks in
Works. Although we covered all of the features available in Works, we were able
to show only a few of the many situations in which macros are useful. We
encourage you to use the techniques presented in this chapter to develop your
own time-saving macros.

Importing and Exporting Information *A1*

*T*hroughout this book, we've shown you how to work in various types of Works documents. In most cases, you will create the information you use within Works yourself and use that information only in Works documents. However, you can import information into Works from other programs and export information from Works to other programs. You can also convert a file to Works from another program with most of its formatting intact. In this appendix, we'll show you how to import and export information.

You can import information into Works from a variety of programs. You can import information from Lotus 1-2-3 simply by opening a 1-2-3 file into Works. To import information from any other program, you must have saved that information in an ASCII text file. Although most programs don't store their information in ASCII form automatically, they provide an option that allows you to do so. Once you save the information in this form, you can open it into Works.

Lotus 1-2-3 saves files in the same form that Works uses to save its spreadsheets. Consequently, you can open a 1-2-3 spreadsheet into Works the same way you would open a Works spreadsheet document: by pulling down the File menu, selecting the Open Existing File... command, specifying the name and directory of the file you want to open, then choosing <OK>. Since 1-2-3 files have a .WKS or .WK1 extension, Works will list them along with Works spreadsheet files in the Files list box. Works will read files from Releases 1A, 2/2.01, and 2.2 of 1-2-3.

When you choose <OK> from the bottom of the Open Existing File dialog box, Works will open the 1-2-3 file into a Works spreadsheet document. For the most part, the spreadsheet will come into Works in complete working order. For example, all values, labels, dates, and times will appear as they did in 1-2-3, and all range names, chart definitions, and most formats will be maintained. Works will convert 1-2-3 functions into the Works equivalent of those functions; it will import the current value of 1-2-3 functions for which there is no Works equivalent. Formulas also will be imported intact, except for formulas that use the & operator; Works imports the results of those formulas.

Once you open a Lotus 1-2-3 file into Works, you can save it into a Works file simply by pulling down the File menu and selecting the Save command. When you do this, Works will save the document on top of the 1-2-3 file. If you want to preserve the 1-2-3 file, you should use the Save As... command to save the Works document under another name or in another directory.

Importing information from other programs

Although Works can read 1-2-3 files, it cannot read the binary files created by most other programs. To import information from those programs into Works, you must save that information in an ASCII text file. To learn how to do that, consult the manuals that come with those programs.

Once you have saved the information in an ASCII text file, you can open that file into Works. To do this, pull down the File menu, select the Open Existing File... command, specify the name of the file you want to open, then choose <OK>— just as you do when you open a Works file or a Lotus 1-2-3 file. Instead of opening the file immediately, however, Works will display a dialog box like the one shown in Figure A1-1.

Figure A1-1

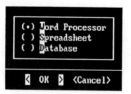

Works will display a dialog box like this when you command it to open a non-Works file.

As you can see, this dialog box contains a single box with three options: Word Processor, Spreadsheet, and Database. The option you choose determines the type of document into which Works will read the information from the non-Works file. Which option you should choose depends on how the information is stored and how you want to use it. If the file contains paragraphs of text, you should open it into a word processor document; if it contains columns of numbers that you'll want to manipulate mathematically, you should open it into a spreadsheet document; and if it contains a list of information that you'll want to query and sort, you should open it into a database document. In the following paragraphs, we'll explain what happens when you import a non-Works file into each of these types of documents.

If the information in the text file you are importing is arranged in sentences and paragraphs, you should open it into a word processor document. To do this, choose the Word Processor option from the dialog box shown in Figure A1-1, then choose <OK>. When you do this, Works will create a new word processor document, assign it the name of the file you are importing, and enter the information from that file into it.

Once you have imported the information from a text file into a word processor document, you'll probably need to do some editing to clean it up. In many cases, the file will contain a series of space characters where tabs should appear. To replace these series with tab markers, you can use the Replace... command on the Select menu, specifying ^w as the search string, and ^t as the replacement string. In other cases, there will be a carriage return at the end of each line, not just at the end of each paragraph. You can use the Replace... command to remove these extra carriage returns. To do that, specify ^p as the search string and leave the Replace With text box blank. Since this removes even the carriage returns that mark the end of each paragraph, you'll have to go back and replace them afterward. For more on searching and replacing in a word processor document, see Chapter 5.

You'll probably want to format the information once you have imported it. You can do this by using any of the techniques covered in Chapter 5.

Importing information into a word processor document

If you want, you can import information from a text file into a spreadsheet document. In order for Works to divide the information in the file into individual cells of a spreadsheet, that information must be arranged in a certain way. Specifically, the entries on each row must be separated from one another by either tabs or commas, and there must be a carriage return at the end of each row. Each tab or comma tells Works to skip to the next cell on the row; each carriage return tells Works to skip to the leftmost cell on the next row. If a string that contains a comma is enclosed in quotes, Works will treat the comma as a literal character instead of as a marker for the end of an entry.

As Works imports information into the cells of a spreadsheet document, it determines what type of entry it is entering into each cell. If the entry is in one of the forms in which Works allows you to enter a value, Works will enter it as a value. In many cases, Works will assign a format to the cell into which it enters a value. For example, if the entry begins with a $ sign, Works will assign the Currency format to that cell; if the entry ends with a % sign, Works will divide the value by 100 and assign the Percent format to its cell; and so forth. If the entry is one of the date or time formats that Works recognizes, Works will enter it as a serial value and assign the appropriate date or time format to its cell. Unless the entry is in a recognizable value, date, or time format, Works will enter it as a label. For more on these types of entries, see the section of Chapter 7 entitled "Making Entries into Cells."

Importing information into a spreadsheet document

As you can see, it's easy to import tab- or comma-delimited information into a spreadsheet document. Unfortunately, you may encounter information that is not delimited in either of these ways. For example, the entries on each row may be separated with semicolons, colons, a series of spaces, and so forth. If you import files of this sort directly into a spreadsheet document, Works will enter each line of the file as a single long label in the leftmost cell on each row, instead of dividing it into individual cells on those rows.

Fortunately, there's a way to import information from files of this sort into a spreadsheet document in a usable form. To do this, begin by importing the information into a word processor document, then use the Replace... command to replace the occurrences of the current delimiting character with either a tab or a comma. After doing this, you can resave the word processor document in the Text format, then import it into a spreadsheet document. Alternatively, you can create a new spreadsheet document, then use the Copy command to copy the information from the word processor document into it. (For this to work, you must have replaced the delimiting characters with tabs instead of commas.) For more on the Replace... command, see Chapter 5; for more on copying from a word processor document to a spreadsheet document, see Chapter 19.

Importing information into a database document

You also can import information from a text file into a database document. When you do this, Works will create a database to fit incoming information. Specifically, Works will create a field for each column of information in the text file, using default names like Field1, Field2, Field3, and so forth. Works will also create a default form for the database, arranging the fields down the left edge of the screen in the order of the columns in the text file. In order for Works to separate the information into individual fields, the entries in each field of a given record must be separated from one another with either tabs or commas, and each record must end with a carriage return.

Just as it does when it imports information into a spreadsheet document, Works tries to determine what type of entry it is entering into each cell of a database document. If the information you are importing is not delimited with tabs or commas, you must import it into a word processor document, replace the delimiting characters with tabs or commas, then either copy it into a database document or save it in the Text format and import it into a database. See the section of this appendix entitled "Importing Information into a Spreadsheet Document" for more on this process.

Saving imported information

Once you've opened a text file into a Works document, you'll probably want to save it in the Works format. To do this, you must use the Save As... command. When you issue this command, you'll see the familiar Save As dialog box. The current name of the document will be in the Save File As text box, and the Text option will be chosen in the Format option box. To save the document in the

Works format, you must choose the Works option from the Format box before you choose <OK>. In most cases, you'll want to specify a different drive and/or directory as well, so Works doesn't overwrite the original file.

In some cases, you may want to use the information from a Works document in another software program. Unfortunately, most programs cannot interpret Works files. However, many can read ASCII text files. To export information from your Works documents into those programs, you should save your documents in the Text or Printed Text formats. (The Printed Text format is available only for word processor documents.)

To save a document in one of these formats, pull down the File menu and select the Save As... command. Within the Save As dialog box, specify the name under which you want to save the file (this should be a different name from that of the file that contains the Works version of the document), choose either the Text or Printed Text option from the Format option box, then choose <OK>.

When Works saves a word processor document in the Text format, it strips all the formats and margin information from the file, so that each paragraph is a single long line of unformatted text. When it saves a word processor file in the Printed Text format, it strips all the formats from the document, replaces tabs with series of spaces, and places a carriage return at the end of each line. When you command Works to save a spreadsheet or database document in the Text format, it will save the information from the document in a comma-delimited text file. The entries on each row will be separated from one another with commas; label entries will be enclosed in double quotes; and formulas and functions will be transformed into their current values. For a general discussion of saving documents in alternative formats, see Chapter 2. For specifics on saving word processor documents, spreadsheet documents, and database documents in alternative formats, see Chapters 4, 7, and 15, respectively.

As we mentioned earlier, Works saves spreadsheet documents in the same format that 1-2-3 uses to save its files. Consequently, you can export Works spreadsheets saved in the Works format directly into 1-2-3; you don't need to save them in the Text format. When you export a Works spreadsheet document into 1-2-3, all entries, formulas, functions, formats, range names, graphs, and so forth, remain intact.

▶The Convert... command on the File menu lets you convert a file from another word processing program into a Works word processing file and lets you convert a Works word processing file into a file format that can be read by another word processing program.

The Convert... command can translate files in three formats—the Microsoft Word format, the Microsoft Interchange Rich Text Format (RTF), or the IBM

Document Content Architecture (DCA) format—into Works .WPS files. Likewise, it can convert a Works .WPS file into any of these formats.

Converting files into Works format

To convert a word processor file from another program as a Works word processor document with most of the original formatting intact, select the Convert… command. When you do, you'll see a dialog box like the one shown in Figure A1-2. You can type into the File to Convert text box the name of the file you want to convert or use the scroll bar to highlight its name in the Files list box. As you can see in Figure A1-2, Works arranges the file names according to the name of the program in which they were created. (The Convert dialog box resembles the Open Existing File dialog box. To find the file you want to convert in the Convert dialog box, use the Directories list box and the Files list box in the same way you use them in the Open Existing File dialog box.)

Figure A1-2

File to convert: [COLUMN.DOC · · · · · · · · ·]

Directory of A:\

Files: Directories:

▶ Microsoft Word ↑   BACKUP ↑
COLUMN.DOC   [-A-]
▶ Other Files   [-C-]
A1.WDB
ADDRESS.WDB
ADDRESS2.WDB
APPX.WKS
ASAMPLE.WDB
ATA1.WDB
CONSOL.WKS ↓

◀ OK ▶ <Cancel>

The Convert dialog box lets you convert a document to a Works format.

For example, if you want to convert a Microsoft Word file named COLUMN.DOC into a Works word processor file, select the Convert… command. When the Convert dialog box appears, type *COLUMN.DOC* into the File to Convert text box or scroll through the Files list box until you highlight the file name COLUMN.DOC. This name will be categorized by Works as a Microsoft Word file. When you highlight the file name, it will appear in the File to Convert text box. (If the file is in a different directory, highlight the directory name in the Directories list box, and choose <OK>.) When the file name appears in the File to Convert text box, choose <OK>.

Next, Works will display a New File Name dialog box like the one shown in Figure A1-3. The name of the file you want to convert will appear in the New File Name text box with the Works word processor file-name extension .WPS. Choose the Microsoft Works option, if necessary. It should be the default selection. When Works finishes the conversion, it will present an alert box that says *Conversion successful.* At that point, choose <OK> or press [Enter]. Works will then convert the file to a Works word processor format and save it in the directory you chose in the Convert dialog box. (If you want to save the file to a different directory, highlight the proper directory in the Directories list box, then choose <OK>.) Then, when you select the Open Existing File... command, you'll see the converted file COLUMN.WPS listed with the other Works word processor files.

Figure A1-3

The New File Name dialog box lets you rename the file you want to convert.

When you convert a Microsoft Word file, be sure to copy the accompanying style sheet file (*.STY). If you don't, when Works converts the Microsoft Word file, Works will display an alert box that says *Cannot find style sheet.* If you choose <OK>, Works will finish the conversion procedure. When you open the converted file, some formats, such as paragraph indents and spacing, will not transfer, but most, such as boldfacing, italics, underlines, margins, and so forth, will.

To convert a word processor file from Works to another program with most of the file's original formatting intact, select the Convert... command Then, type into the File to Convert text box the name of the Works file you want to convert or use the scroll bar to highlight its name in the Files list box. Next, choose <OK>. When the New File Name dialog box appears, that file's name will appear in the New File Name text box. By default, Works will add the extension .DOC (the Microsoft Word file-name extension) and, as you might guess, Works will activate the Microsoft Word option in the Format option box. If you want to convert your Works file to a Microsoft Word format, press <OK>. When Works finishes the conversion, it will present an alert box that says *Conversion successful.* At that point, choose <OK> or press [Enter].

Converting Works files into other formats

The remaining two Format options—Microsoft RTF and IBM DCA—allow you to convert files to and from these formats. When you do, you can use a file in different applications with most of that file's formatting intact. The Microsoft RTF format uses the file-name extension .RTF; the IBM DCA format uses .DCA. If a file you've created in another program isn't saved in one of the four formats listed in the Format option box, check to see if that word processor offers a way for you to save the file in IBM DCA format before you save it as a text file for use in Works. If so, save it in that IBM DCA format, then import the file into Works with its formatting intact.

The Works file conversion utility

In your Works 2 package, you'll find a Conversion Utility disk. This disk contains the WPTOWP.EXE file. This file lets Works convert the word processor files from other programs to the Works word processor format. If you don't copy this file to your Works directory, the Convert... command on the File menu will not be able to convert the file, and Works will display the alert boxes shown in Figure A1-4 and A1-5 after you choose <OK> in the Convert dialog box.◄

Figure A1-4

Works will display this alert box first if you have not copied the WPTOWP.EXE file to your Works directory.

Figure A1-5

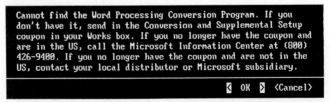

Works will display this alert box second if you have not copied the WPTOWP.EXE file to your Works directory.

CONCLUSION

You can share the work that you do in Works with other programs. In this appendix, we showed you how to import information into Works from other programs, how to export information from Works to other programs, and how to convert files from another word processor to Works' word processor without losing their formats.

Configuring Works A2

*I*n this book, we've talked about several settings that affect all Works documents. In Chapter 2, for example, we showed you how to control whether Works keeps a backup copy of your work when you resave a document. In Chapter 3, we showed you how you can change Works' default unit of measure. These two settings are controlled by elements in the Works Settings dialog box. Other settings are controlled by other commands and elements in other dialog boxes. For example, the printer you select in the Printer Setup dialog box determines what printer Works will use when you print a document.

No matter where these settings are located, they all share two features. First, they affect the way Works operates not only in the current document, but in all other documents. Additionally, they last longer than the current Works session. Each time you load Works, these settings will be the same as they were the last time you loaded it.

In this appendix, we'll cover these "configuration" settings. First, we'll take a look at the settings controlled by the Works Settings... command. Then, we'll review the configuration settings controlled by other commands.

The Works Settings... command allows you to specify how Works will display formatted values and dates, what the default unit of measure will be, what colors and screen resolution Works will use for the various structures on the screen, whether Works uses templates when you open your documents, what modem port Works will use, what dial type your phone has, and in what mode you want to display your screen. When you pull down the Window menu and select the Works Settings... command, Works will reveal a dialog box like the one shown in Figure A2-1.

THE WORKS SETTINGS... COMMAND

Figure A2-1

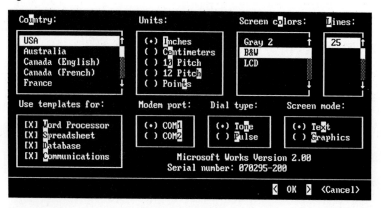

The elements in the Works Settings dialog box allow you to customize Works documents.

As you can see, the Works Settings dialog box contains eight items in addition to the <OK> and <Cancel> buttons: a Country option box, a Units option box, a Screen Colors option box, a Lines option box, a Use Templates For option box, a Modem Port option box, a Dial Type option box, and a Screen Mode option box. The Units, Use Templates For, and the Screen Mode option boxes should be familiar to you: They allow you to control Works' default unit of measure, templates, and screen display capability, respectively. The Country option box controls the way Works displays formatted dates and values; the Screen Colors option box allows you to control the colors that Works uses for different parts of the screen; the Lines option box controls the resolution of the image on the screen (how many lines per inch Works will display), the Modem option box controls the port to which your modem is connected, and the Dial Type option box sets Works to match the dial type of your telephone.

The Country setting
►WORKS 2◄

The Country list box allows you to control the way Works displays currency-formatted values and most formatted date entries in spreadsheet and database documents. ►(In Works 2, you'll see eight Country options. Works 1 offered three: US, Int'l A, and Int'l B.)◄ For example, Figure A2-2 shows an example spreadsheet document when USA is the Country setting. Figure A2-3 shows the same document after we changed the Country setting to France, and Figure A2-4 shows it after we changed the Country setting to UK.

Figure A2-2

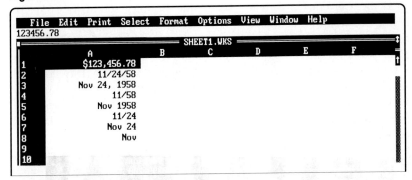

This figure shows a spreadsheet when the Country setting is USA.

Figure A2-3

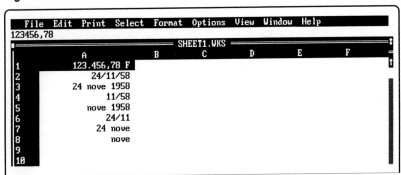

This figure shows the same spreadsheet when the Country setting is France.

Figure A2-4

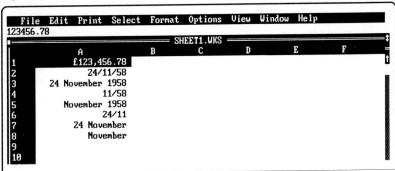

This figure shows the same spreadsheet when the Country setting is UK.

Cell A1 in each of these spreadsheets contains the value 123456.78 and is assigned the Currency 2 format. When the Country setting is USA, Canada (English), or Australia, Works displays this value as $123,456.78. When the Country setting is UK, however, Works displays that value as £123,456.78.

Cells A2:A8 in these spreadsheets contain the value 21513—the serial date value for November 24, 1958. Cell A2 is assigned the Month, Day, Year (Short) format. When USA is the Country option, Works displays the date in mm/dd/yy form: 11/24/58. Under the France and UK options shown in Figures A2-3 and A2-4, Works displays this date in dd/mm/yy form: 24/11/58. Other date formats show similar differences.

Since these Country options control the way that formatted values and dates are displayed, they also determine the form in which you can enter values and dates. For example, if you type $123 and press [Enter] while USA is the Country option, Works will enter the value 123 into the active cell and assign the Currency 0 format to that cell. If UK is the Country option, Works will enter the label "$123. Similarly, if you type 7/4/56 then press [Enter] when USA or Canada is the Country option, Works will enter the value 20640 (the serial date value for July 4, 1956) into the active cell. If Australia, France, Mexico, or UK are the Country options, Works will keep the value 20640, but display 4/7/56.

The Country option box also controls the form in which Works enters the current date in a document. If you press the [Ctrl]; key combination in a spreadsheet or database document when USA or Canada is the Country option, Works will enter the serial date value for the current date on the formula line and display it in mm/dd/yy form. Under the other Country options, Works will display that date in dd/mm/yy form. If you press the [Ctrl]; key combination or select Current Date from the Insert Special dialog box in a word processor document when USA is the Country option, Works will enter the date in mm/dd/yy form; under the other options, Works will enter the date in dd/mm/yy form.

The Country option also affects the form in which Works prints the current date in a document. If the USA or Canada option is the Country option, Works will replace the *&d* characters and **date** placeholder with the current date in mm/dd/yy form; if the other countries are the Country options, Works will print the current date in dd/mm/yy form.

The Units setting

The Units option box allows you to control Works' default unit of measure. You'll enter measurements in several places within Works, but most often into the Page Setup & Margins, Indents & Spacing, and Tabs dialog boxes. Unless you follow a measurement with a special suffix (", cm, p10, p12, or pt), Works will assume the default unit of measure. Originally, the default unit of measure is inches. However, you can change it to centimeters, 10-pitch units, 12-pitch units, or points, if you want. To do this, simply choose the appropriate option from the

Units option box. The unit that is selected when you choose <OK> from the bottom of the Works Settings dialog box will become the default unit of measure. For more on changing the default unit of measure, see the section of Chapter 3 entitled, "Using Alternative Units of Measure."

The Screen Colors option box allows you to alter the colors that Works uses for various structures on the screen. As you can see in Figure A2-1, this box contains three options based on the type of video card (monochrome Hercules) we are using in our computer: Gray 2, B&W, and LCD. (The Color choices in your computer may differ according to the video card your computer uses.) The choices that you make during the setup procedure determine which of these options will be selected initially.

The Screen Colors setting

In most cases, the option that Works selects for you will be the best one for your system. However, you can choose another color option if you want. To do this, simply move the dot to the color option you want. When you choose <OK> from the bottom of the Works Settings dialog box, Works will display the screen according to the color option you selected.

The color options cause different structures on the Works screen to appear in different colors. For example, if you have a VGA card and a color monitor, and have chosen the Color 2 option, the work area will be pale yellow, the key characters in menus and dialog boxes will be bright white, the shadow around dialog boxes and menus will be black, the message line and the active cell will be fuchsia, other highlighted cells will be black, the borders of a spreadsheet will be white, and the mouse pointer will be blue. If you chose the Gray 2 color option instead, the work area and the message line will be black, the key characters in menus and dialog boxes will be bright white, the shadow around dialog boxes and menus will be black, the mouse pointer will be white, the active cell will be a medium gray, and other highlighted cells will be even lighter, plus a spreadsheet's borders will be gray. Feel free to experiment with the different color options and choose the one that you like best.

▶The Lines setting allows you to display fewer or more lines of your document on the screen. For example, the default setting for a Works screen is 25 lines from the top to the bottom of the screen. If you choose a setting of 50 from the Lines list box, then choose <OK> in the Works Setting dialog box, Works will double the number of lines on your screen. The active document will appear compressed and will extend from the top of your screen halfway to the bottom. The window elements—message line, status line, menu bar, and so forth—will be reduced to half their default height. At this point, you can use the various sizing techniques we discussed in the Chapter 1 section "Sizing the Window" to expand your document to fill the work area.

The Lines setting
▶WORKS 2◀

The Use Templates For setting

The Use Templates For setting lets you turn off or on the template files for each Works document type. You should be familiar with this setting from reading Chapter 2. When you create a template file for a Works document, you must ensure that the corresponding Use Templates For setting is activated on the Works Settings dialog box. When a template setting is activated (its default state), Works will use the template file you created for that document type each time you select that document type from the Create New File dialog box.

The Modem Port setting

The Modem Port setting lets you select the port to which you attached your modem. You should match this setting to the modem port you're using or you won't be able to use your modem or the automatic telephone dialer we discuss in Appendix 3.

The Dial Type setting

The Dial Type setting lets you match Works to the dial type of the phone you've connected to Works through your modem: tone or pulse. You should match this setting to your phone's dial type. Otherwise, you won't be able to use your modem or the automatic telephone dialer we discuss in Appendix 3.

The Screen Mode setting

You should be familiar with this setting from reading Chapter 5, where we discuss Works' Text and Graphics modes. If you are using Works in the Text mode, what you see depends on whether you have a color or black and white display. If you have a color display, entries that have been assigned the Bold, Italic, and Underlined styles will be displayed in different colors (the exact color for each style depends on which of the color options you have selected in the Screen Colors list box). If you have a black and white display (or if you have a color display and you have selected either of the Gray options in the Screen Colors list box), entries that have been assigned the Bold, Italic, and Underlined styles will be displayed in bright characters. Additionally, the mouse pointer appears as a rectangle, one line high.

If you have a graphics card, you can display your Works document in Graphics mode. When you display your document in Graphics mode, you'll see the styles you applied to your text just as they will appear when you print them out. Finally, the mouse pointer will change shape to an arrow.◄

Saving these settings

The settings specified in the Works Settings dialog box go into effect as soon as you choose <OK> from the bottom of that box. These settings will remain in effect until you change them again. When you exit Works by pulling down the File menu and selecting the Exit Works command, Works will save these settings into a file named WORKS.INI. Works reads this file each time you load it into your computer. Consequently, the settings that were current at the end of the last Works session will be in effect the next time you load Works. Works won't update the

WORKS.INI file if you exit from Works any other way; for example, by rebooting your machine or turning it off. Consequently, any changes you made to these settings will not be saved.

Works features a number of other configuration settings in addition to the ones controlled by the Works Settings dialog box. When you pull down the File menu and select the Exit Works command, Works saves into the WORKS.INI file the Printers, Model, Graphics, Page Feed, and Connect To settings on the Printer Setup dialog box and the status of the Show Ruler, Show All Characters, and Typing Replaces Selection commands on the word processor document's Options menu. Consequently, the status of these settings at the beginning of each Works session will be the same as they were at the end of the previous session.

OTHER CONFIGURATION SETTINGS

In this appendix, we've explored Works' configuration settings—settings that affect more than a single document and last longer than the current Works session. Most of these settings are controlled by the Works Settings… command; others are controlled by other commands. When you exit Works, it saves these settings in a file named WORKS.INI. Whenever you load Works, it reads this file, activating the settings in the file.

CONCLUSION

Works 2 contains three new accessories: the alarm clock, the calculator, and the automatic phone dialer. The alarm clock lets you set alarms that will remind you of appointments. The calculator lets you perform mathematical functions and, if you want, insert a number into the document you're working in. If you have a Hayes-compatible modem, the automatic telephone dialer lets you dial your phone directly from a Works document.

As we said, Works' alarm clock lets you set alarms that will remind you of appointments. You can change, delete, and suspend these alarms at any time. To use the alarm clock, select the Alarm Clock... command from the Options menu. When you do this, Works will display the dialog box shown in Figure A3-1. The settings in this dialog box let you set, change, delete, and suspend alarms.

THE ALARM CLOCK

Figure A3-1

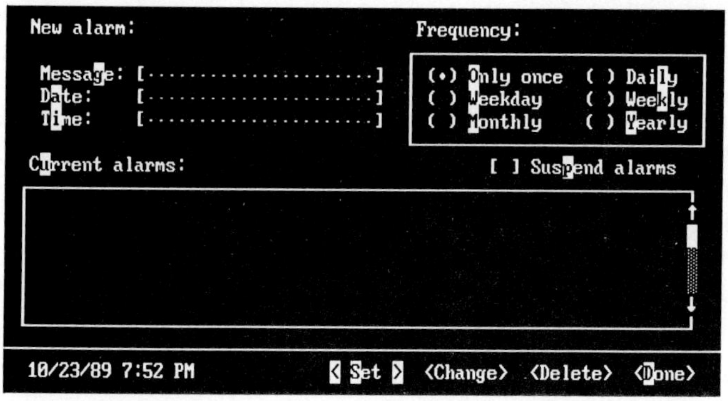

You set, change, delete, and suspend alarms in the Alarm Clock dialog box.

At the top of the Alarm Clock dialog box, you'll see three New Alarm text boxes: a Message box where you type the message (up to 60 characters) that Works will display when the alarm goes off, a Date box where you type the date when you want the message to appear, and a Time box where you type the time of day when you want the message to appear. To the right, you'll see a Frequency option box. The options in this box correspond to the frequency with which you want the message to appear: once, daily, on weekdays only, once a week, once a month, or once a year. Under the Frequency box, you'll see the Suspend Alarms check box. You'll use this option to prevent Works from displaying the alarms you've set. The greater part of the dialog box is filled with the Current Alarms list box. Every alarm you set will appear in this list box. At the bottom of the dialog box is the current date and time supplied by your computer's clock.

Setting the alarm

Suppose you want to remind yourself of your daughter's weekly flute lesson, but you find yourself incapable of wresting your attention from your computer. When you establish the time for her lesson, you can set an alarm. To set the alarm, select the Alarm Clock... command from the Options menu. When the Alarm Clock dialog box appears, type *Time for lesson* into the Message text box. Next, activate the Date text box and type the date of the lesson. For this example, type 10/23/89. Then, activate the Time text box and type the time you want to be reminded. (Let's say 8:00 PM to give you time to make her 8:30 lesson.) Next, choose the *Weekly* Frequency option so the alarm will appear every Monday at 8:00 PM. Finally, choose <Set>. When you do this, Works will enter the alarm instructions into the Current alarms list box, reactivate the default Frequency option (Only Once), then place the cursor in the Message text box. At this point, you can type another message or choose <Done> to close the dialog box.

The date and time you type into the Alarm Clock dialog box indicate the first time Works will ring the alarm. When an alarm rings and you respond to it, Works will advance the date of the next alarm according to the setting in the Frequency option box. For example, when the alarm in our example above rings and you respond to it, Works will advance the date in the alarm to read 10/30/89, exactly seven days later than 10/23/89. On 10/30/89 at 8:00 PM, the alarm will ring again.

Changing the alarm

To change an alarm, open the Alarm Clock dialog box, and highlight the alarm you want to change in the Current Alarms list box. Works will then place the alarm information in the three New Alarm text boxes as shown in Figure A3-2.

When the alarm information appears in the New Alarm text boxes, you can edit that information in the usual ways. For example, if your daughter's lesson has changed to 4:00 PM, then you can delete the 8:00 PM in the Time text box, replace it with 4:00 PM, then choose <Change> at the bottom of the dialog box. When you do this, Works will update the alarm information in the Current Alarms list box and reset the dialog box so you can type your next message or choose <Done> to close the dialog box.

Figure A3-2

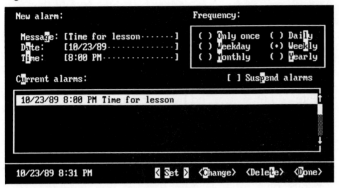

When you highlight an alarm in the Current alarms list box, the information pertaining to that alarm will appear in the New Alarm text boxes.

Deleting an alarm

To delete an alarm, open the Alarm Clock dialog box, and highlight the alarm you want to delete in the Current Alarms list box. When the alarm information appears in the three New Alarm text boxes, choose <Delete> at the bottom of the dialog box. After you do this, Works will delete the alarm information from both the New Alarm text boxes and the Current Alarms list box, then reset the dialog box so you can type your next message or choose <Done> to close the dialog box.

Suspending alarms

Works lets you turn off your alarms without erasing them. To suspend an alarm, simply activate the Suspend Alarms check box. Works will not sound any alarms until you deactivate this option.

When the alarm rings

When it's time for your alarm to sound, Works will beep and display the dialog box shown in Figure A3-3 on the following page. If you choose <Snooze>, Works will close the dialog box, then beep and display the dialog box again in ten minutes. If you choose <Reset>, Works will display the Alarm Clock dialog box, so you can change the alarm information. If you choose <OK>, Works will close the dialog box.

If your computer is not on when it comes time for Works to display an alarm, Works will display a dialog box for each past due alarm the next time that you load Works.

Figure A3-3

Works beeps and displays this dialog box when it's time for your alarm.

THE CALCULATOR

The Calculator... command on the Options menu lets you perform the arithmetical and mathematical functions you would perform on a standard calculator. In addition, you can insert the number displayed in the calculator into an active Works file. To use the calculator, select the Calculator... command to reveal the Calculator dialog box shown in Figure A3-4. When the dialog box appears, just use it like an ordinary calculator by typing numbers and pressing function keys (+,-,/,and *) into the dialog box from the corresponding keys on the numeric keypad (if the Num Lock key is on), from the regular keyboard with the digit keys and the minus, plus, multiplication, division, and equal keys, or from the calculator keys by clicking the mouse. To change the sign of the displayed number, type *S* or click <CHS> on the calculator with the mouse. To clear the calculator of all entries, type *C* or click <CL> on the calculator with the mouse. To clear the entry only, type *E* or click <CE> on the calculator with the mouse. When you finish working with the calculator, choose <Cancel> at the bottom of the dialog box.

Figure A3-4

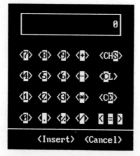

This is the Calculator dialog box.

To insert a number from the calculator into the active Works file, move the cursor to the place in the file where you want to insert the number. Then, open the Calculator dialog box and make the calculations you want to make. When the number you seek appears in the calculator's text box, choose <Insert> from the bottom of the dialog box. When you do, the number will appear in the file where you placed the cursor.

To copy a number from an active Works file to the calculator, highlight the number and select the Copy command from the Edit menu. When you open the Calculator dialog box, the number will appear in the calculator text box.

The automatic telephone dialer will dial your telephone for you only if you have connected your computer to a 1200-baud or higher modem. To use the automatic telephone dialer, highlight in a word processor, spreadsheet, or database file the telephone number you want to dial. Select the Dial This Number command from the Options menu. When you do, Works will dial the phone number and display the message *Pick up phone and press OK to answer.* Now, you can continue with the call as though you dialed it by hand. If no one answers or you want to cancel automatic dialing, press the [Esc] key.

AUTOMATIC TELEPHONE DIALING

To ensure that your modem works correctly, there are two options in the Works Settings dialog box that affect the automatic telephone dialer: the Modem Port and Dial Type settings. Make sure these settings correspond to the port you've connected your modem to and the dial type of your phone.

Two words of warning: If you plan to dial a long distance number or need to dial a code to reach an outside phone line, make sure that all the numbers you need to dial are included in the highlighted phone number. Finally, you cannot use the telephone dialer if you are connected to another computer.

In this appendix, we discussed the accessories that Works includes on the Options menu. We told you how to use the alarm clock, calculator, and automatic phone dialer features.

CONCLUSION

INDEX

| marker, 140

A

[Abs] key, 270
Accessing DOS from Works, 62-63
Accessing other programs from
   Works, 64-65
Accessories
   alarm clock, 715-718
   Alarm Clock... command, 715-718
   automatic telephone dialing, 719
   calculator, 718-719
   Calculator... command, 718-719
   Dial This Number command, 715-719
Activating documents, 22-23
Advanced macro techniques
   looping, 688-689
   pausing , 696-697
   soliciting input, 692-696
   subroutines, 688-697
Alarm Clock... command, 715-718
All command, 104
[Alt] key
   key characters, 24, 31-33, 37,
Apply Query command, 528
Area Line command, 398-407
Arrange All command, 21-22
Arranging documents, 21-22

B

100% Bar command, 398-402
[Backspace] key, 106
Bar charts
   100% bar, 402-404
   clustered bar, 399-400
   simple bar, 398-399, 444-445
   stacked bar, 398-404, 434
Bar command, 398-399
Bold command, 123
Bookmark Name... command, 189-193

Bookmarks
   Bookmark Name... command, 189-193
   creating, 189-191
   deleting, 193
   Go To... command, 188-193
Borders
   adding, 151-152
   border area, 152-153
   changing, 153
   charts, 440-441
   removing, 151-154
Borders... command, 151-154
Break command, 619
Buttons, 32, 36-37

C

Calculation
   circular references, 231-232
   manual, 230-232
Calculator... command, 718-719
Cancel button, 37
Capture Text... command, 632-634
Cell alignment
   changing , 254-255
   copying and moving, 254-255
Cell entries
   data, 209-210
   dates, 221-224
   editing entries, 227-229
   formulas, 216-221
   functions, 227, 297-336
   labels, 214-216
   times, 224-227
   values, 211-213, 208-227
Cell protection
   activating unlocked cells, 366-367
   Clear command, 365
   Column Width... command, 365
   Delete Page Break command, 365
   Delete Row/Column command, 365
   erasing unlocked cells, 366
   Fill Down command, 365
   Fill Right command, 365

D

T

Y